Comparative Reading and Learning Difficulties

Comparative Reading and Learning Difficulties

Edited by
Lester Tarnopol
Muriel Tarnopol

LexingtonBooks
D.C. Heath and Company
Lexington, Massachusetts
Toronto

Library of Congress Cataloging in Publication Data

Main entry under title:
   Comparative reading and learning difficulties.

   1. Learning disabilities. 2. Reading disability. 3. Comparative education.
I. Tarnopol, Lester. II. Tarnopol, Muriel.
LC4704.C65   371.9   80-8423
ISBN 0-669-04107-6   AACR2

Published simultaneously in Canada

Printed in the United States of America

International Standard Book Number: 0-669-04107-6

Library of Congress Catalog Card Number: 80-8423

To our parents,
Morris and Sadie and David and Leah,
who worked so hard and cared deeply for
their children, and to our sons,
Matthew and Daniel,
for whom we care so deeply

Contents

Preface

During the past seventeen years we have visited a number of countries, discussed learning disabilities with professionals and parents, and lectured on the subject at universities, hospitals, and other institutions. We visited both public and private schools and teacher-training institutions, and we informally interviewed many children, parents, teachers, and other professionals. The countries and territories visited included Australia, Austria, Canada, Czechoslovakia, Denmark, England, Finland, Fiji, France, Germany, Greece, Israel, Italy, Japan, Mexico, New Zealand, Norway, Puerto Rico, Republic of China, Sweden, Switzerland, Union of Soviet Socialist Republics, and Venezuela.

In 1973 we met with V.I. Lubovsky, head of the Laboratory of Higher Nervous Activity and Psychology of Abnormal Children (learning disabilities) at the Institute of Defectology in Moscow. We discussed the need for books summarizing the reading and learning problems of children in many countries. It was considered that such books would be useful in the developing countries by indicating the incidence of specific learning disabilities in intelligent children and the remedial methods used in the more advanced nations. These books could also help the advanced countries by describing the work done in many different places. This information could then be used to improve existing programs.

In 1976 the first book, under the title *Reading Disabilities: An International Perspective*, was published. In 1979 the World Association of Learning Disabilities and Dyslexic Organizations (WALDDO) was formed in San Francisco during the International Conference of the Association for Children and Adults with Learning Disabilities. Lord Renwick, chairman of the British Dyslexia Association, was elected chairman. He stated that the purpose of WALDDO was to collate and disseminate evidence of successful changes of attitude toward the problem of the learning-disabled in our respective countries. His primary concern was to get educators and others in Great Britain to accept the concept that specific learning disabilities exist. This indicated a major need for books describing the problem worldwide to assist those working in their countries to get learning disabilities recognized so that programs could be established for children and adults.

Another area of research and public education has come into focus recently with attempts to improve the education of bilingual children in the advanced nations. Multicultural and multiethnic studies have recently come into prominence, but current university reading courses tend to lack this comparative dimension, which could greatly enhance the value of such courses for reading teachers. By becoming aware of the different methods of solving problems related to teaching reading, writing, spelling, and

ix

arithmetic in different cultures and languages, teachers would find that many of their problems are international in scope and that there are many ways of approaching solution.

There has been a tremendous increase in the efforts of the United Nations Educational, Scientific and Cultural Organization (UNESCO), the International Reading Association, and others to expand and improve literacy worldwide. This book is part of that effort.

The contributors were asked to use the following general outline and to add any other important information about the development and progress of the treatment of specific learning disabilities in their countries:

1. Background of special education in the country.
2. Statement of the reading problem and the percentage of children involved.
3. Facilities and methods for testing and diagnosis.
4. Facilities and methods for remediation.
5. Results of remedial methods used.
6. Medication used, if any, and results.
7. Case histories of children.
8. Research.

Originally, we asked for a statement about the learning-disabilities problem in each country, but we soon found that most countries had advanced only to a consideration of reading and spelling problems, and in some of the developing nations the major problem was the educational and cultural deprivation of large sections of their depressed populations.

Added to the chapters from different countries is a chapter describing the learning, social, and vocational problems of a mature dyslexic. There are also two chapters on our research on the educational development of Chinese, Japanese, and Caucasian American children and a chapter based on our research on the basic-skills requirements of American teachers. In these chapters we have not carried the analyses of our data beyond correlation, because multiple regression or other analyses would not materially add anything beyond what was obtained from the correlational analyses.

Although it is customary to place a summary at the end of a book, we have chosen to begin with summaries of comparative reading and learning difficulties in many countries. Since chapters 1, 2, and 3 introduce the book with summaries of our worldwide findings, no further summation is necessary at the end of the book.

We hope that this volume will provide the intended salutary effects for the benefit of children and adults with reading and learning difficulties everywhere.

Acknowledgments

The editors gratefully acknowledge the assistance and encouragement received from everyone who contributed to this volume. We are also greatly indebted, for the help and hospitality so generously given to us by the professionals and parents in Taiwan, Japan, and South San Francisco who made it possible to obtain test data in the second and fifth grades, to observe classroom teaching in both public and private schools, to visit and observe in hospitals and clinics, and to interview parents. We are especially thankful to the principals, teachers, and children in the cooperating schools.

In Taiwan Dr. Wei-fan Kuo, president of the National Taiwan Normal University, appointed Dr. Wu-tien Wu and our interpreter, Mrs. Mei-chi Lai, to work with us. Professor Hung-hsiang Liu also worked with us and cooperated in the testing. Mrs. Mei-chi Lai translated our tests into Chinese and had them printed for us. She also procured a prepublication copy of the Chinese edition of the Wechsler Intelligence Scale for Children—Revised (WISC-R) norm data for us, and Dr. Wei-fan Kuo later sent us the published manual for this test, for which we are grateful. Professor Emily Miao extended warm hospitality to us and showed deep interest in this research. Rev. Brendan O'Connell, Rev. Wim Bollen, and Sr. Eugenio Chu arranged visits to their special-education centers and assisted us in every way possible and with much hospitality.

In Japan Professor Mohachi Motegi organized a meeting at Nihon Bunka Kagakusa, the publisher, in Tokyo, which was attended by many of that country's leading special educators, psychologists, physicians, speech and language therapists, and others interested in learning disabilities, at which Miss Moranaga translated. Professor Motegi and his wife helped us in countless ways and extended most generous hospitality to us. They conducted a trip for us to the Izu Teishin Hospital in Hirai Kannami to observe the program there and to confer with Dr. Kikuro Kamimura and Mrs. Ryoko Morinaga, who had attended the Tokyo meeting. We are indebted to them for their data on children with learning disabilities diagnosed by them at the hospital. In Tokyo Professor Motegi presented us with copies of the Japanese editions of the Wechsler Preschool and Primary Scale of Intelligence (WPPSI), WISC-R, and Draw-A-Person Test published by Nihon Bunka Kagakusha, for which we are most grateful. Mrs. Yoko Suzuki arranged a meeting with mothers of children with learning disabilities in Tokyo. She also took us to visit a private school that serves some of these children and offered us help with many other important needs. Dr. Kaoru Yamaguchi rendered help to us continually during our time in Tokyo, with extensive hospitality and cooperation. Special mention must be made of the encouragement, interest, warm hospitality, and professional cooperation extended to us by Dr. Yoshitatsu Nakano of Hiroshima University, who led our team there with the most able assistance of Professor Norioshi Taguchi, Dr. Sinagawa, and our interpreter, Mrs. Izumi Allen. Dr. Nakano took us to observe many special-education facilities for the hard-of-hearing, partially sighted, speech-handicapped, and mentally retarded. We are also greatly indebted to Professor and Mrs. Taguchi for arranging interviews with mothers at their home and for their gracious hospitality. Professor Taguchi also translated our tests into Japanese and duplicated them, arranged for the testing, and assisted us in the classes.

In the South San Francisco Unified School District, we wish to acknowledge the enthusiasm, support, and encouragement for this study from the Board of Education, which voted unanimously to permit us to test in their classes. We are indebted to Dr. Thomas Gaffney, Superintendent, Dr. Leonard Levine, Director of Pupil Personnel Services, Michael Y. Miyahira, principal, and the teachers, district psychologists, and speech and language therapists for their ongoing cooperation and encouragement.

We were pleased to receive permission to use the transparency material, "Due Process Procedures for Special Education," received from Vicki Brummel, Compliance Officer of the Consortium for the Master Plan for San Mateo County. Dr. Badrig Mélékian arranged for copies of *L'alouette* and *Jeannot et Georges* to be sent to us from France, and we are indebted to the publisher, Les Editions du Centre de Psychologie of Paris, for permission to use illustrations from each test. Permission was also granted for the WISC profiles of Chinese-Canadian children from the Board of Trustees, Vancouver, and for the material from *Focus on Learning Problems in Mathematics* from the publisher, M. Sharma. Dr. Marjorie Goody contributed data from the files of the Diagnostic Reading Clinic of the San Francisco Unified School District, on WISC profiles, Wide Range Achievement Test, and Bender scores, for which we are most grateful. In the Richmond School District we were assisted by Dr. Steven Cederborg, who gathered data on children in special-education classes and helped us in many ways.

It would have been impossible to complete our research without the cooperation and interest of Dr. Keith Beery, coauthor of the Developmental Test of Visual Motor Integration, and of Jastak Associates, who granted us permission to translate into Chinese and Japanese the arithmetic portion of the Wide Range Achievement Test for research purposes.

At San Francisco State University we were encouraged to gather data by the following professors, who arranged for us to test their classes: Dr. Merle A. Akeson, Dr. Robert H. Bradfield, and the late Dr. Robert Thrapp. We are also most appreciative of the vocabulary and reading-test data donated by Dr. James Duggins. Special mention should be made of the continuing assistance and encouragement from Professor Mary Grimm and Dr. William Evraiff, chairman of the Department of Counseling. We also wish to thank G.A. Collado for his consultation and help with our statistical analysis at the Computer Center of San Francisco State University.

A partial subsidy was received from the Pacific Cultural Foundation, Taipei, Republic of China. The cooperation, endorsement, and warm hospitality received from Dr. Jeanne Tchong Koei Li, president of the Foundation, are most warmly acknowledged.

The Charles Dorsey Armstrong Memorial Foundation of Menlo Park awarded a partial grant for our research. We are particularly grateful to Wilbur E. Mattison, Jr., M.D., and Edward A. Barthold, Jr., M.D., of the Armstrong Foundation for their interest and support in investigating learning problems among Chinese, Japanese, and American children.

We are greatly indebted to Mogens Jansen for translating chapter 13, Special Education in Greenland, from Danish into English.

1

Introduction to Reading and Learning Problems

Lester Tarnopol and
Muriel Tarnopol

The rapid advance of industrialization throughout the world has produced a need for greatly increased literacy. The ability to live and work in an industrialized society demands ever-increasing reading, writing, and mathematical skills. The attainment of these skills, in turn, depends upon a viable educational system. Therefore, to a great extent, the development of nations and the welfare of peoples depend on the adequacy and level of training for literacy.

The United Nations Educational, Scientific and Cultural Organization (UNESCO) is especially aware of the worldwide literacy problem. A number of surveys and studies have been conducted under its auspices to investigate various aspects of this problem. Several approaches have been used in attempts to find the most practical and efficient methods of achieving large-scale literacy. A major dichotomy exists in the approaches to finding the most effective methods of teaching beginning reading: methods used in general education for normal children and those used in special education for handicapped children. Many professionals believe that the most efficient methods devised for special education should be generally applicable to teaching all children, with modifications for the different languages, backgrounds, and skills with which children enter school and the types and degrees of handicap. However, it does not seem reasonable to expect the methods of general education, which were developed primarily for normal children, to be equally applicable to other categories of pupils. At the same time, it is recognized that the methods of education used in those countries that have few learning difficulties among their pupils and have achieved unusually high levels of literacy should be subjected to considerable scrutiny.

Our thesis is that cross-national studies of the preschool preparation of children, methods of teaching in regular classrooms, methods of assessment of reading and learning problems and their remediation, preservice and inservice training of teachers, and any other factors found to influence learning, as well as the results obtained under different conditions, should provide a better understanding of the variables that contribute to literacy. Therefore, we will consider the basic methods of teaching reading, in both general and special education, but we will investigate the failure-preventive

1

and remedial techniques in greater detail. Although writing, spelling, and arithmetic teaching will also be considered, they will not receive as much attention as reading, since most countries are involved only with examining the basics of reading or remedial reading, and only a few nations have been able to consider the broader aspects of learning.

In almost all industrialized nations, the professionals associated with the pedagogical system—educators, psychologists, speech and hearing therapists, physicians, and so on—are acutely aware of the difficulties that children may have attaining literacy and are actively engaged in the study and amelioration of these problems. In the emerging nations, however, more basic problems of education are so pressing that special education is often nonexistent. This situation is documented by the 1971 UNESCO study of special education. The secretariats of the national commissions of member states were sent questionnaires, to which many replied. The respondent from Dahomey stated that, in practice, handicapped children were excluded from ordinary education. In 1971 there was no compulsory education for either handicapped or nonhandicapped children in Ethopia. Syria replied that there were no special provisions for handicapped children. No special education was provided in Togo. Tanzania had no compulsory education for either normal or handicapped children. And so it continued. In these countries the most pressing problems involved building a total educational system. Therefore, information derived from cross-national studies could be used to advantage in the development of these emerging school systems.

It now appears that a great many nations recognize the difficulties inherent in learning to read and are actively investigating this area. The concept of dyslexia or specific reading difficulties in nonretarded children has been recognized, and special remedial programs are being funded by a number of governments, including Austria, Canada (some provinces), Czechoslovakia, Denmark, Finland, France, Germany, Israel, Luxembourg, Mexico, The Netherlands, Norway, Poland, Rumania, Sweden, Switzerland, Union of Soviet Socialist Republics, United States of America, and Yugoslavia. The degree of recognition of the problem and the amount of financial aid vary considerably among the countries named.

Prevalence of Handicaps

Silverman and Metz (1973) surveyed a sample of 2,000 local public schools that were representative of 81,000 schools in the United States enrolling 300 or more pupils. They asked the principal of each school for an estimate of the number of pupils with specific learning disabilities (SLD) being served by the school and an estimate of the number of SLD pupils who were not in special programs. It was estimated from this survey that of 24,985,000 children in grades 1 through 6, 1.9 percent were in SLD classes, with a total of 3.1 percent who were SLD.

The final report of the UNESCO Expert Meeting on Special Education, published in 1979, contained the following information: "At least 10 percent of all children are born with or acquire physical or mental impairments of sufficient degree to need special help in order to carry out the basic activities of daily living." The report also quoted the following from the Office of Education of the U.S. Department of Health, Education and Welfare: "In 1966, Dr. Romaine Mackie established 10 percent as an estimate of handicaps in the school age population. Learning disabled, however, was not one of the handicaps considered at that time. The prevalence of learning disabilities is generally considered to be about 2 percent, hence the total rate of 12 percent."

The semiannual report, Implementation of U.S. Public Law 94-142: The Education for All Handicapped Children Act, August 1979, states: "During the past year, the number of states serving more than 9 percent of their school enrollment as handicapped has increased from 15 to 26 percent."

Reading-Disabilities Survey

A questionnaire we sent out received replies from 26 countries: Argentina, Austria, Brazil, Canada, Chile, Republic of China, Czechoslovakia, Denmark, Finland, France, Greenland, Hungary, India, Japan, Malaysia, Mexico, The Netherlands, New Zealand, Norway, Poland, Rhodesia (now Zimbabwe), South Africa, Sweden, United States, Venezuela, and Yugoslavia. From this survey it was possible to make some generalizations about the prevalence and handling of reading problems in these countries.

It is not possible to estimate the relative extent of reading problems in different countries because there are no internationally standardized reading tests. The replies to the question, "In your country, approximately what percentage of nonretarded school children have reading disabilities?" ranged from the low in Japan and the Republic of China (1 percent) to the high in Venezuela (33 percent), with a median of 7 percent. Since there is no internationally accepted definition of *reading disability* the problem of finding its prevalence is compounded. Most of the respondents defined *reading disability* as a child reading significantly below either his age level or grade level.

The ratio of boys to girls having specific reading disabilities was estimated to be between three to one and four to one in all countries. The universal constancy of this ratio seems to implicate a genetic basis for the problem, especially since the ratio holds up even in the countries where boys equal or excel girls in reading under normal conditions in regular classrooms.

Most of the countries surveyed provide special part-time programs in regular schools for children with reading problems; and about half of them have full-time classes for such pupils. Programs of early case-finding and failure-prevention are relatively rare. However, it is generally recognized that this approach to the problem of reading and learning disabilities is most important.

Testing and Tests Used

Testing for reading and learning disabilities is usually done by an individual, but testing is also being done by multidisciplinary teams in a number of countries, and this technique is growing in use. Individual testing is done most often by psychologists, teachers, and speech therapists, in that order. Teams usually include these three professionals plus a physician and others as required. The tests used, in order of precedence, are reading, standardized reading, intelligence, visual perception, visual-motor coordination, auditory memory, auditory perception, visual memory, and equilibrium.

The reading tests are usually developed locally, although some countries have used tests developed in other countries that use the same language. The psychometric tests most often included are, in order of precedence, the Wechsler Intelligence Scales for Children (WISC), the Binet Intelligence Tests, modified in different countries, the Illinois Test of Psycholinguistic Abilities, the Bender Visual Motor Gestalt Test, the Marianne Frostig Developmental Test of Visual Perception, the Draw-A-Person Test, the Stambak Memory for Rythmic Sequences Test, and selected tests from Piaget.

Some of the Wechsler Intelligence Scales for children have been translated and normed in the following countries: Chile, Republic of China, Denmark, France, Germany, Israel, Italy, Japan, Poland, Spain, Sweden, and the United States. Other countries also use these tests but have not yet developed local norms. In general, the Wechsler tests are used because they provide a Verbal IQ, a Performance IQ, a Full Scale IQ, and up to twelve possible subscale scores, permitting considerable diagnostic information to be derived from the tests. The profile of the subscale scores is considered to be especially valuable for assessment of the child's strengths and weaknesses for purposes of preliminary diagnosis to be used in developing an individual remedial plan for the child.

Almost all countries have courses at their teacher-training institutions to prepare teachers in remedial-reading techniques. In some countries psychologists have special training to assess a child's reading problems and to plan a remedial program for the pupil, which is usually carried out by a special-education teacher.

Causes for Reading Disabilities

The survey respondents were asked to state the main causes of reading and learning disabilities in their countries. In almost all cases neurological dysfunction came first, followed by genetic causation, with emotional problems and teaching defects mentioned in a few instances. The respondent from Hungary stated, "disturbances of the underlying neurophysiological and psychological functions; especially speech disturbances, very mild manifestations of asphasia, disturbed feedback or motor processes in speech, and genetically based disturbances." "Heredity and minimal brain dysfunction," was the reply from Czechoslovakia. The Norwegian reply included, "In our country the population is highly homogeneous and the language is relatively regular. Therefore, the main causes of reading disabilities are assumed to be of genetic or psychoneurological origin." In Belgium, it was estimated that more than half of the learning problems (school maladjustment) stemmed from emotional factors, about one-fourth were considered to be neurogenic, and about 10 percent were mainly due to intellectual causes (Tarnopol and Tarnopol 1976).

The best methods of teaching remedial reading were said to be eclectic. Individual instruction, prescriptive teaching based on differential assessment, and the teaching of phonics were also mentioned. It was the consensus that direct teaching of the subject matter in a structured, well-organized environment was of paramount importance. For children with learning problems, immediate success in a psychologically supportive setting was stressed. Almost all respondents recognized that the behavior problems of these children tended to dissipate rapidly in such a supportive milieu as soon as the children found that they could learn and were, in fact, learning. Thus, the emotional factors were seen as secondary to the children's learning problems rather than as causative.

Teaching disabilities were seen as either producing or compounding the learning problems of the pupils. In Ethiopia, some of the primary teachers had only a fourth-grade education. The Indian educational system has grown at a tremendous rate since independence in 1947 and now has over 3.5 million teachers. In Brazil about 30 percent of the teachers have only a fourth-grade education. In Venezuela the problem is described as stemming from an inadequately organized school system. In France methods of teaching reading are not taught in the normal schools (teacher-training institutions). The Norwegian respondent stated, "Even though the teaching profession is held in high regard in Norway, the traditionally trained teachers are too poorly qualified to provide remedial instruction." In Sweden it was estimated that from 10 to 15 percent of the reading problems were due to inadequate teaching.

From Hungary the defects mentioned included, "The faults that can occur in teaching reading are: wrong sequence in teaching letters; faulty association between letters and pronunciation; and not giving the longer words gradually enough, so that the children soon become overloaded.'' In the United States, we have studied the types of teaching errors that occur and the literacy and arithmetic levels of teachers (Tarnopol and Tarnopol 1976, 1979). The results will be described in later chapters.

Terminology

The disparity in terminology concerning reading and learning difficulties creates a problem for everyone attempting to study these problems. Different terms for the same disorders exist both within and among countries. These differences in terminology also tend to be associated with different opinions concerning the etiology and correction of the problems. Moreover, the various professions prefer to use their own terms and definitions of reading and learning problems, further adding to the confusion. This continuing controversy has not helped the children.

At the same time, there is some order within the total field of learning disabilities. It is generally agreed that a significant number of children with adequate intelligence have great difficulty learning to read, write, spell, or do arithmetic. Almost all respondents agreed on the neurological or genetic causes of the problems, often compounded by poor school organization and inappropriate teaching. Only the French literature was cited as continuing to believe that these problems are primarily of emotional origin and to look at mother-child and teacher-child relationships for the causes. It is also generally recognized that there is another major group of children with learning problems related to primary emotional problems, cultural deprivation, lower socioeconomic status, or transient status. The backgrounds of these children confound the problem of determining to what extent specific learning disabilities exist in these populations.

It is generally agreed that reading disabilities in nonretarded children are one manifestation of the more general problem of specific learning disabilities. The terminology for children with learning difficulties includes dyslexia, specific language disabilities, perceptual disorders, minimal brain dysfunction, word blindness, minimal cerebral damage, instrumental disabilities, brain damage, educational handicap, learning difficulties, neurological handicap, learning disabilities, and more. The children referred to in each case tend to be in either the same or overlapping groups.

Terminology in Different Countries

In each country the terminology used to describe reading and learning disabilities tends to be related to the local development of the field. In 1887 Rudolf Berlin, of Stuttgart, first suggested the term *dyslexie* for the ''word-blindness" previously described by Kussmaul (Wagner 1973). The German-speaking countries use the terms *legasthenia* (specific weakness in learning to read and spell) and *Lese-Rechtschreibe Schwäche* (reading-writing weakness). In Czechoslovakia, Poland, Yugoslavia, and Hungary the terms *dyslexia, learning disabilities,* and *specific reading disability* are in use. Danish literature refers to *word-blindness, reading retardation, learning difficulties,* and *learning disabilities.*

In Canada *specific reading disabilities, educational disabilities, learning disorders,* and *learning disabilities* are all used. British literature refers to *dyslexia, specific reading difficulty,* and *learning disabilities,* the latter term often referring to mental retardation. Finnish children who are not retarded but have learning problems are termed *reading-writing disabled.* In Norway *dyslexia* is in use, and the children are grouped, according to the mode of their disability, as auditory, auditory-visual, emotional, or educational dyslexics. Rhodesians refer to *dyslexia.*

Learning disabilities are generally referred to in Ireland, The Netherlands, and the Republic of South Africa. *Specific learning difficulties* is the term in general use in Australia. The Belgians speak of *instrumental impairments* and *learning disabilities,* which are called *troubles spécifiques du développement.*

In America, thirty-eight different terms have been used to describe essentially the same condition (Clements 1966), many of which have been mentioned. Adoption of *specific learning disabilities* in federal legislation has failed to quell the controversy concerning both terminology and definitions in America. However, school districts will be obliged to use both the federal terminology and definitions in order to receive federal funding for their mandated programs, so there should be a tendency toward common usage in the future.

Sources of Reading and Learning Problems

The factors related to learning problems in children have been generally listed as exogenous, or environmental, and endogenous, or coming from within the person. Learning problems may be caused by any one or more of the following variables, based on Eisenberg (L. Tarnopol 1969):

1. Educationally deprived early environment.
2. Lack of environmental motivation.
3. Excessive absences.
4. Defects in teaching.
5. Lack of motivation due to emotional factors.
6. Chronic illness or malnourishment.

7. Severe hearing or vision losses.
8. Mental retardation.
9. Brain damage.
10. Genetic or congenital brain dysfunction.

Some Environmental Factors

Studies have indicated that relatively few children seem to overcome the effects of an educationally deprived early environment. However, the specifics of an appropriate early-life milieu for the future education of children still tend to be elusive. Attempts to determine the most important variables affecting the mental development of children have met with only partial success. However, enough is known about the qualities of an adequate early environment so that education for parenthood could significantly improve the linguistic, social, and intellectual development of many children. "People could grow up to be more able and more secure if their first teachers did not have to be 'self-taught' and unsupported," according to White, Kaban, and Attanucci (1979).

In a longitudinal study of early childhood, twenty families were observed raising children for two years from age one, and another twenty were followed for one year from the child's second birthday (White et al. 1973, 1978). Each home was visited every other week to gather data on child-rearing practices. The children were comprehensively tested at about their third and fifth birthdays. From these data it was possible to develop a series of preliminary hypotheses about the practices that distinguished the highest-achieving from the lowest-achieving children. A pilot study was then constructed, giving the parents of eleven infants training in what were considered to be the four foundations of education: the development of language, curiosity, social skills, and intelligence.

The pilot parent-training program covered the crucial period from about eight to twenty-four months of age. Testing performed at about one and two years of age determined that these children scored more like the advanced group than like the less well-developed group in the original study.

Based on the experiences of the pilot study, an experimental program was devised using an experimental group and three different control groups. Fourteen sets of parents, the experimental group (E-group), received special training. One control group had fifteen sets of parents, who received no training but whose children were tested on the same schedule as the E-group. A second control group consisted of fifteen sets of parents, who received no training but whose children were tested at the beginning of the study and at the end. The third control group was composed of fifteen sets of parents, who were selected and trained by a pediatrician and whose children were tested according to the E-group schedule (White, Kaban, and Attanucci 1979).

The most significant finding of this research was that the important area of language development in the child appears to be greatly enhanced by an adult speaking directly to the child about something of interest to him so that he listens attentively. For twenty-seven children in the E-group and two control groups (the third control group couldn't be used), the correlation between language development at three years of age and amount of live language directed to the child was 0.42, and the Stanford Binet Intelligence Scale score versus live language directed to the child correlated at 0.36.

Another finding of interest was that the twenty-three firstborn children in these three groups did significantly better than the twenty laterborns on the Stanford Binet at three years of age (118 IQ versus 103 IQ). The average IQ of the eight firstborn children in the first control group was 122, compared with 118 for the seven firstborns in the E-group. The thirteen laterborn children in the two control groups had an average IQ of about 106, compared with 98 for the seven laterborn children in the E-group. It was found that firstborn children were given twice as much attention by their mothers than were the laterborn children. Moreover, the effects of training the E-group mothers were said to be only moderately successful when compared with the child-rearing efforts of the control group mothers who received no training but whose children had the same testing program as the E-group.

It was also noted that children who ate a great deal between meals (generally as a way of keeping them quiet) tended to receive reduced stimulation from the mother and scored lower on the tests. Exploring and practicing fine motor skills were found to be positively related to language development in this research. The authors suggested that when children are spaced less than three years apart, the mothers tend to be under greater stress and are less able to attend to the young child's needs than when the children are further separated in years. Finally, it was found to be most important to detect hearing losses early in life, since children who are hard-of-hearing suffer poor language and social development and appear to be unresponsive and sometimes even defiant.

This study, using primarily middle-class families, and other studies, using lower socioeconomic-status (SES) parents, indicate that the development of language, socialization, and intelligence can be accelerated temporarily when the parents are given child-rearing training and the children are placed on an intensive program of stimulation. However, there are no longitudinal studies that demonstrate that the gains are retained after children enter school and that their academic and intellectual abilities continue at the high level achieved by the stimulation. Such further research is clearly essential if large-scale training of people for parenthood is to be considered.

Moreover, these research projects did not consider the large numbers of children with neurogenic learning disabilities and the larger number from lower SES minority families who appear to have multiple disabilities, that is, early educational deprivation and specific learning disabilities. We have found that educationally deprived minority children tend to have the same types of perceptual and small-motor deficits as children with learning disabilities (L. Tarnopol 1969, 1970; Tarnopol et al. 1977). With this combination of problems, it is often not possible to know if the motor and perceptual deficits are neurogenic or are the result of lack of practice. As an example, these children and adults typically are unable to copy geometrical designs that can be copied by much younger children with normal early educational backgrounds. In middle-class children, this deficit is highly correlated with learning disabilities, but its significance for lower SES minority children is unclear.

Enviromental Motivation

A major factor in children's progress in school is their desire to learn. This motivation comes from several sources, including parents, peers, teachers, and within the individual. In general, middle and upper SES children enter school with adequate motivation, but some may lose it if severe learning or emotional problems occur. Emotionally disturbed children may have no specific learning disabilities buy may fail to learn due to lack of motivation related to difficulty concentrating. Children with primary specific learning disabilities typically try very hard with little reward for their efforts. If appropriate assistance is not forthcoming, these children suffer great frustration, leading to secondary emotional disturbances and subsequent loss of effort.

It is stated that lower SES children also come to school with the desire to learn. However, some of the parents of these children do not believe that education is important, or they may feel that since they did not achieve in school, their children might not be expected to achieve. At the same time, the peer pressures against academic learning are very great in some cultures and tend to be the controlling factors in these children's education. It is also considered that some teachers with middle SES mannerisms and teaching methods may fail to reach certain minority and lower SES children. All of these hazards appear to face large numbers of children entering schools in many countries.

Excessive Absences

Children may be absent from school because of illness; however, only prolonged or chronic illnesses are sufficient to create major learning difficulties. In America the greatest causes of absences in elementary school are probably various types of transient status. The many children whose parents are farm laborers who follow the crops to be picked as they ripen may have no stable home base and so may change residence and schools often. Other children, whose parents' work causes them to move often, both within and between cities, tend to lose a great deal of continuity and time in school. In the developing nations excessive absences tend to be related to economic factors and a shortage of local schools. Children may fail to attend school because of lack of suitable clothes, the need to stay home and babysit other children, or the need to work and help support the family. If the school is too far away from home, absences may be related to transportation difficulties or economic problems.

Malnourishment

Protein deficiency during pregnancy and the infant years, when brain cells are forming, seems to have a deleterious effect on learning, probably due to inadequate central nervous system development. In America it was customary for children to be sent to school with an adequate breakfast; however, when the parents both work and in certain lower SES groups, children either get their own breakfasts or come to school with little or no breakfast (some buy a pickle and a Coke on the way to school). When children buy their own lunches, unsupervised, they may disregard the requirements of nutrition. Some of these children often are unable to pay attention or to stay awake in class. There is also a tendency to permit many of these children to stay up late at night watching television or playing in the streets, so they get insufficient rest. These problems tend to be related to inadequate parent training for raising children and are most often found among poorly educated parents.

Defects in Teaching

In the developing countries a major problem is the necessity to establish teacher-training institutions and to train enough teachers. In some countries pupils with a primary or elementary-school education are considered suitable to become teachers of the young. Higher minimum standards must be set. In the developed countries it is customary for teachers to have from two years of teacher training at the college level to, in some countries, a minimum of five years of university education, including one year of teacher training at the postgraduate level.

Although this latter requirement exists in California, we and others have found that more than 5 percent of the teachers there score below the ninth-grade level on various literacy tests, and very few achieve at their actual grade levels, grades 17 through 19 (first through third year of graduate school at the university). However, the most important problem facing the developed countries appears to be the need to determine the most effective methods of teaching both normal and handicapped children and to train the teachers in these methods (Tarnopol and Tarnopol, 1976, 1979, and chapter 6 herein).

Hearing and Vision Losses

Mild vision loss rarely causes learning problems once the appropriate lens correction is applied. Severe vision disturbances that cannot be corrected impair learning somewhat. However, deafness and other hearing defects cause much greater problems for the learner. As a rule deaf people do not go as far in school as the blind. Deafness and some hearing deficiencies make it extremely difficult for the person to acquire language and also limit the amount of language that is developed. Considerable work over many years has gone into the study of how to teach the blind, deaf, and severely hard-of-hearing, and great strides have been made in reducing the effects of these handicaps. Intensive work is now being carried on to develop effective methods of teaching the multiply-handicapped who may be blind or deaf and have other handicapping conditions.

Mental Retardation

When Alfred Binet developed the first viable intelligence test in 1904, his purpose was to be able to assess mentally retarded children before they entered first grade so that they could be placed in special-education classes. With the further development of intelligence tests, it was arbitrarily decided that children who scored less than two standard deviations below the mean (Binet IQ 68 or Wechsler IQ 70) were to be designated retarded. This constituted about 2 percent of the population. A child was considered retarded if he scored below the cut-off IQ when his teacher requested that he be tested because he was not functioning academically in the regular class.

The use of this rule led to a number of problems. About half of the general population tend to have fluctuating IQ scores, so it is possible for some children to score below and above the cut-off at different times. The intelligence tests tend to measure aptitude for academic achievement but not for social and many work aptitudes. Consequently, it was found that many "mental retardates" functioned quite adequately on the job and in society. Finally, since the tests had been developed and normed on the Caucasian population, they were found to be unsuitable for use with some of the minority groups. Improperly trained psychometrists were found to be using the tests with children for whom standard English was not the first language, thereby getting inappropriate results.

These deficiencies were partially corrected by adding a social-development test to the IQ tests and by resorting to other means of establishing retardation in certain minorities. At present the designation "educable mentally retarded" is being done away with in California by combining these children with the learning-disabilities group and renaming them "learning handicapped." This has created controversy, since the parents of learning disabilities children had fought for many years to establish a distinct category for their nonretarded children, the "educationally handicapped." The reason given for creating the learning-handicapped category was that some of the retarded children were found to be doing as well in regular classrooms as in special classes. Therefore, it was decided that they should either be placed back into regular classes (mainstreamed) or combined with the learning-disabilities children for special education, since this group was receiving appropriate academic training.

Gifted Underachievers

One way of resolving the problem of having children with such a wide diversity of IQ scores in the same special-education class was to create classes for gifted children with learning disabilities. The San Francisco Unified School District has two such classes, with a maximum of twelve children in each. These children score above either Stanford Binet or Wechsler IQ 130, which is about two standard deviations above the mean.

Whitemore (1980) described the special program for gifted underachieving children in the Cupertino Union Elementary School District in California. The district introduced an extended learning program (ELP) for gifted children in the early 1960s. Children were identified in kindergarten and first grade based on teacher evaluations and group tests, including assessments of readiness or achievement and intelligence. If this evaluation indicated that a child might be gifted, he was given an individual intelligence test, usually the Stanford Binet Intelligence Scale, and a score above 130 IQ was the criterion for entry into the ELP class.

As the result of systematic testing, some surprising discoveries were made: "there frequently were several children in a classroom who scored high on aptitude tests but who had not manifested signs of giftedness to the teacher" (Whitmore 1980). Most such children had been shy, doing only the expected work; some had been disruptive or were described as socially immature. Sometimes as many as one-fourth of the children who scored high on the group tests surprised their teacher, who had failed to see any signs of intellectual superiority in these children. Some had even been considered as failures and were to be refused promotion.

Whitmore (1980) described three behavioral syndromes of the gifted underachieving pupils that came to her attention: aggressive, withdrawn, and erratic. Her first group of sixteen underachieving gifted children included twelve boys and four girls, giving the characteristic ratio of three to one for boys and girls with specific learning disabilities. The children's IQs ranged from 130+ to 169+, with an average of 151 IQ, ignoring the pluses. Further testing indicated that most of the children were suffering from visual-motor deficits, with primarily weak fine-motor skills. The test battery employed did not appear to have an adequate assessment of auditory perceptual skills, so deficiencies in that area tended to be neglected. One child was found to have primary emotional problems, but the others appeared to have various types of specific learning disabilities of neurogenic origin. The children spent two years in the special class, and subsequent follow-up indicated that they tended to function at a very satisfactory level through higher education.

Brain Dysfunction

Cerebral dysfunction can derive from damage or from genetic or congenital brain differences. Early American studies of children with learning disabilities from 1920 to 1940 assumed that genetic differences were the primary causes of these problems, while another group of psychologists and educationalists were looking at psychogenic or emotional causation. In the 1940 to 1960 period it was found that children with learning disabilities had the same types of perceptual and motor deficits as brain-damaged children, so subtle forms of cerebral trauma were postulated to be the cause of the learning problems. From 1960 to 1980, it was accepted that both brain damage and brain differences were at the base of the learning difficulties. Research is now under way to attempt to determine by autopsies and electroencephalographic-evoked potentials the types of genetic or other brain differences responsible for dyslexia and learning disabilities.

Literacy

Literacy is a major concern throughout the world. But literacy means different things in different countries and is further redefined in various subcultures within nations. In the United States attempts are being made to increase the prevalence of "functional literacy," which may be defined as the ability to perform those literacy functions required to operate at the job-market entry level and to subsist in our industrial society. The requirements of functional literacy include certain minimum standards of reading, writing, and arithmetic skills. It has been estimated that from 10 to 25 percent of the population do not meet these standards.

Japan claims to be the most literate country worldwide, with a literacy rate of 99.7 percent. The definition of illiteracy in Japan is the inability to read or write *kanji, hiragana,* and *katakana* at all (see chapter 16 for details). It is stated that if a person can read these characters, he can read at the level of functional literacy.

In most developed countries attention is being given to the major problems of increasing the literacy of the lower socioeconomic classes and to reducing the extremely high percentages of children who fail and are retained in the elementary school grades. As an example, in France and Belgium about 50 percent of the pupils repeat one or more times in the elementary grades.

In the developing countries that have had school systems for many years, the problems are similar to those in the developed countries, except that they are far greater and include many children who never start school and large numbers of pupils who drop out in the primary grades. For example, in Argentina it was reported that 58 percent dropped out of elementary school before graduation. In Chile in 1976, almost 19 percent of the children repeated the first grade, and the percentage of repeaters continued above 11 percent through the seventh grade, when 16 percent repeated. In Brazil the drop-out rate at the end of the first grade was reported to be 54 percent. In Colombia a drop-out rate of 75 percent was reported in the first grade. In Mexico 16 percent of the pupils failed first grade and 7 percent left school, and by sixth grade 43 percent had left. In India it was said that about 60 percent of the pupils dropped out of school during the first five grades, and by the eighth grade 75 percent had gone. Moreover, although about 83 million children are enrolled in grades one through eight, it will be necessary to bring in an additional 52 million children to achieve full enrollment by 1985.

Finally, in the developing countries that are in the early phases of building school systems, the concept of literacy and the requirements of education are more basic. For example, in Ethiopia it is said that only about 10 percent of the school-age children attend school, and the literacy rate is also about 10 percent. In a survey by Waller (1974), an educator from Tanzania remarked, "As so many children never receive full-time education, those with any type of problem would drop out unnoticed."

Linguistic Problems

Linguistics may be defined as the scientific study of speech and language and the relationships between writing and language. Considerable research has been done correlating reading with linguistic and other variables.

Unfortunately, the results of these studies have often been contradictory. There appear to have been three basic difficulties with this research, which tend to plague all psychometric inquiries. First, some of the variables affecting the results are very difficult to recognize and therefore to control. Second, attempts to replicate the same research on different populations have at times been frustrated by uncontrolled variables, causing the results to vary in the different studies. Third, correlations between reading ability and other variables have sometimes been assumed to indicate a causal relationship even though there are numerous warnings against this interpretation.

An example of the latter problem is the movement in America to teach the alphabet before beginning reading because high correlations have been found between alphabet knowledge and primary-grade reading performance. Subsequent research found that, under controlled conditions using matched groups of children, those who were taught the alphabet did not become better readers than those who were not taught the alphabet (Downing 1973). The point is that, based on the correlation studies alone, teachers should not expect beginning pupils to learn to read better if they have learned the alphabet. However, there may still be other reasons, not related to this research, for teaching the alphabet to children.

As a rule, the methods of teaching reading and other subjects have been based on previous experience and pragmatic trial-and-error learning by the teacher. Educationalists have developed theories about how to teach, based primarily on logical extensions of their subjective experiences or on hypotheses posed by others. Although attempts have been made to test some of the hypotheses, contradictory results tend to be the rule when experiments are replicated, because important variables remain unrecognized and uncontrolled.

Orthography

In general, four types of written language may be postulated, namely, alphabetic, syllabic, pictographic, and logographic. In the alphabetic writing system the characters stand for the phonemes (smallest units of speech) of the language. In syllabic orthography syllables instead of phonemes are represented by the characters. Pictographs indicate their meanings in pictorial form, and logographic characters give the form and meaning of morphemes (meaningful linguistic units).

Alphabetic systems of writing are most commonly used today, probably based on the Semitic alphabet of the Phoenicians of about the thirteenth century before the Christian era (BCE), which was the basis for the early Greek alphabet (Mathews 1966). Although the Semitic alphabet did not use vowels (Hebrew is written with vowels only for beginning readers), the Greeks included the vowel sounds in their alphabet.

The Chinese developed the logographic writing system from their earlier pictographs. The Chinese characters are used in many Asian countries, but are pronounced in the language or dialect of the readers. Early pictographs date from the Shang dynasty (1766-1122 BCE), and major changes in these characters occurred during the Chin dynasty (221-207) BCE), the Han dynasty (207 BCE-220 ACE), and in modern times (Tarnopol and Tarnopol 1976).

In mainland Chinese schools, the children learn to read about 3,000 ideograms in five years, which is considered to be the literacy level required to read a newspaper in the People's Republic of China. In Hong Kong, on the other hand, about 3,500 characters are learned in the first five grades, and it is said that about 7,000 characters are required to "adequately" read the newspapers. However, scholars need to know about 50,000 ideograms, said to take about twenty years of study in Chinese.

In order to make reading easier for the population at large, Mao Zedong proposed some years ago to introduce the Latin alphabet to China so that words could be read phonetically. He believed that this reform would make advanced reading accessible to the masses. The Central Committee never accepted this reform because of tremendous opposition from the population of readers. However, some reforms were instituted, and a number of commonly used characters were simplified (see figure 1-1).

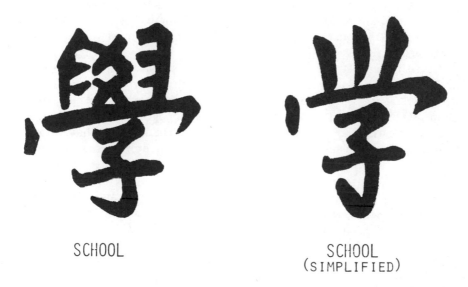

SCHOOL   SCHOOL
                                        (SIMPLIFIED)

Figure 1-1. Example of a Chinese Character Simplified

Although both Hong Kong and the People's Republic of China use the "whole-character" approach to teaching reading, the Republic of China uses a modified phonetic system to teach beginning reading. Symbols were invented representing all of the sounds of Mandarin plus four signs to indicate the voice inflections or pitch variations used in speaking. These signs and symbols are written to the right of the characters to be learned by the children and are used during the first three years of school (see figure 1-2).

The Japanese use a combination of the alphabetic and syllabic systems (*kana*), composed of five vowels and one consonant (alphabetic) and sixty-five syllabic characters in each of two sets of symbols, *hiragana* and *katakana* (see chapter 16 for details). Any word can be written in either of these "alphabets." They also use about 1,850 Chinese logographic characters (*kanji*) and both the Chinese and Arabic systems of numerals, as well as the Latin alphabet.

Structure of Language and Reading

The structures of languages, in terms of the relationships between the written and spoken forms, influence the degree of difficulty encountered by children learning to read. The pictographs are probably the least difficult to read because of the pictorial representation of objects. However, this may not necessarily be true in learning to decipher concepts. The next in order of difficulty may be the most phonetic languages, such as Japanese *kana,* Greek, and Spanish; followed by the modern Chinese characters; with the least phonetic languages, such as English, being the most difficult for beginners.

It has been noted that some dyslexic children seem to encounter greater obstacles with phonetic and syllabic orthography than with logographic characters. This problem appears to be related to the need to blend the phonemes or syllables to make words, whereas a logograph may be read as a complete word. Examples are bilingual dyslexic children who have more problems with English than with Chinese, and Japanese children with learning disabilities who have greater difficulty with *kana* than with *kanji.* Children who have deficits of visual perception may be frustrated by orthographies that have visually similar symbols, such as b and d, p and q, m and n. These pupils may continue to make reversals and inversions long after other children have stopped this process. Those with defective auditory perception also tend to have characteristic difficulties. For example, Keir (1977) found that six- and seven-year-old children who failed an auditory closure test (ability to repeat whole words when only parts of the words are heard) were unable to perform even the simplest blending or phonic syntheses of words. The dyslexic pupils who experience confusion

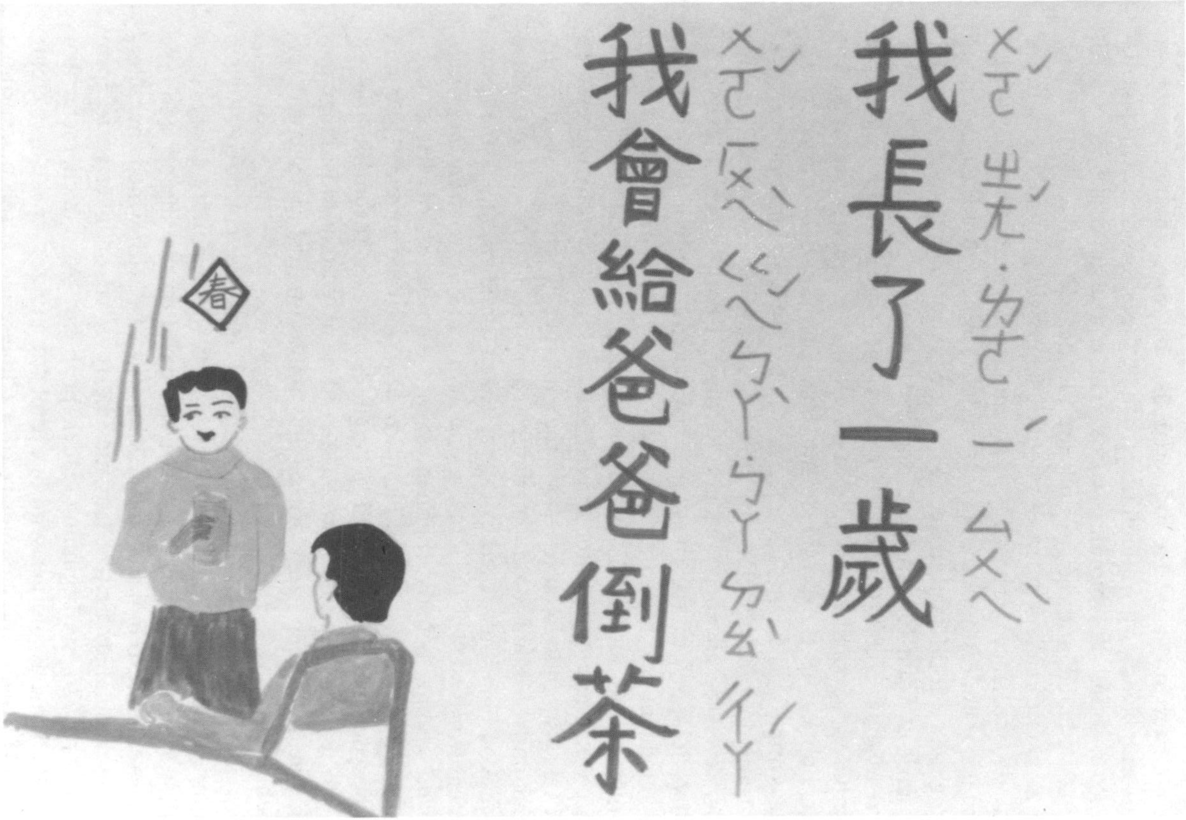

Figure 1-2. Mandarin as Taught in Taiwan

The large characters are the words. At the right of each character are phonic symbols and inflection markings, used for beginning readers. Reading from top to bottom and from right to left, it says, "I grow one year. I can pour father tea." The phonic symbols in the right-hand column are *oo wah*, *tch amg, le wah, ee su w ay*. The check marks indicate a falling inflection followed by a rising inflection. A line slanting up indicates rising inflection, and a line slanting down means falling inflection.

with *kana* (requiring blending) but not with *kanji* (whole words) probably have auditory perceptual deficits but not visual perceptual problems.

Elkonin (1973) believes that blending difficulties are caused by teaching the letter names too soon. He indicated that Russian children who have problems with blending are attempting to name the letters rather than utilizing the letter-sounds for building words. The confusion arises, he stated, because some letters and their sounds are identical.

For advanced readers the most phonetic languages probably remain the easiest to decode, since it is possible to pronounce any word correctly even if the word is not understood. Languages such as Chinese and English tend to be among the most difficult to decode. There is controversy over which, in fact, is more difficult for advanced readers. Although scholars need to be able to read about 50,000 Chinese characters, the more complex logographs are composed of smaller units in a systematic manner. Although the characters appear to those who do not read Chinese to be unsystematic, separate symbols, they are actually composed of combinations of previously learned radicals. In English, however, decoding new words remains a problem even for advanced readers. Because of both the complexity and the many violations of the rules of pronunciation, only a few rules are usually taught in school, so almost everyone tends to be at a loss when attempting to read new words that do not follow the simpler rules.

Moreover, the sounds of the English language are not fully represented in the twenty-six individual letters of the alphabet. There are about forty phonemic units in English to be made up from these letters. There are also numerous combinations of letters that are used to indicate the same sound in different words such as the long *i* sound in *my, eye, buy, guide, lie, thigh,* and *grind.* Some sounds (phonemes) are composed of letter pairs (digraphs), as *ch, ea, th, ck,* and *ph,* in *cheat, thick,* and *phone.* These and other idiosyncracies of the English language increase the difficulties of learning to read. At the same time, it should be noted that most languages have similar and other irregularities that impose hardships on primary-school children.

Two characteristics of written symbols may be considered when attempting to determine the relative ease with which children may learn them: first, the complexity of the character, based on the number and type of strokes required to make it; and second, the ease with which characters may be discriminated. Letters that may be reversed or inverted to form other letters tend to give beginning readers problems. Also, a character that is almost the same as another symbol except for a minor stroke may create confusion. However, the complexity of a Chinese ideograph or a printed alphabetic word does not determine its relative difficulty for the learner. It has been noted that relatively short English words tend to cause more reading problems than do longer words. In Chinese, Kawai (cited in Downing

1973) determined that subjects found it easier to learn verbal associations with more complex nonsense patterns than with the simpler ones.

Leong (1973) pointed out that reading does not rely as much on rote memory as has been assumed. Learning to read Chinese is not the same as memorizing thousands of arbitrary stroke sequences. The square-shaped characters have "symmetry and balance," and there is "orderliness and progression." In Chinese the characters are composed of a radical, from which the meaning is derived, and a phonetic or stem giving the sound. There is considerable redundancy, because new characters tend to be constructed from the radicals and stems that the reader already knows. In research with Hong Kong children, Leong determined that simple ideograms with fewer than about seven strokes may produce cognitive confusion by having too few contrasting elements. He found that, of 400 children, only 21 percent wrote a certain four-stroke character correctly, as compared with 73 percent for a more complex one.

Another source of confusion that perhaps exists in all languages is the use of a single sound or sequence of sounds to indicate different words, sometimes spelled the same way and sometimes differently, for example, the homonyms *read* and *red* in English. Also consider the meanings of "*read* the book," and "he *read* the book." The first is present tense and the second is past tense, pronounced differently but spelled the same. A difficult group of homonyms in English for many people are the variations of the morpheme *to, too,* and *two.*

In most languages sentences are written as a series of discreet words, with the words separated by spaces. However, spoken language does not usually contain spaces between the words. On the contrary, the words tend to be run together when speaking. This appears to be a source of confusion for some children who have difficulty separating the spoken words.

Elkonin (1973) discussed research on the relationship between sound analysis of words and learning reading and writing. In teaching kindergarten children how to analyze the sounds of words, the children were first given a picture of the word, with a form consisting of empty boxes drawn in a row. The boxes represented the number of sounds characterizing each word, and the consonants and vowels were the sounds to be analyzed. Thus, *pot* was considered to have three sounds. The child was required to say each sound as /p/ /o/ /t/ and to place a block on a box as he said the sound of each letter. It was found that the children learned sound analysis of words best if they were taught "stressed intonation of the separate sounds." This type of training for five-year-old children was said to improve subsequent learning of reading and writing.

A somewhat similar approach to developing reading and spelling skills was introduced in the form of the Lindamood Auditory Conceptualization (LAC) Test and a remedial program that may be used at all ages from kindergarten (Lindamood and Lindamood 1971). The test has two parts, with a gradual increase in the complexity of the sound patterns in each. In the first part of the test, the subject must discriminate each sound that he hears and must determine whether it is the same or different from the others. The subject places a block in a row for each sound heard, using the same color when the sounds are the same and different colors to indicate different sounds. A heard pattern might be *b b s*, which would call for two blocks of the same color followed by one of a different color.

In the second part of the test, the subject uses blocks in the same manner to represent sound patterns within syllables. For example, *pif* would call for three blocks of different colors. In the next test, the sound patterns are changed by omissions, substitutions, or additions. Thus, *pif* might be followed by *bif,* in which case the person would have to observe the change and replace the first block with one of a different color. The Lindamoods' research has determined that high correlations exist between LAC Test scores and Wide Range Achievement Test, Reading and Spelling subscale combined scores at each grade level from kindergarten through grade 12 ($r = 0.66$ to 0.81). They have also developed a remedial program to go with their test.

In some countries reading is considered to consist entirely of decoding or "word-calling." At the elementary level this tends to remain true, since the reader's spoken vocabulary and understanding are still well above his reading level. However, most children soon learn to decode more words than they know the meanings of, and, more importantly, they can "read" passages that are well beyond their level of understanding. Therefore, comprehension becomes an essential element in reading ability. From the point of view of linguistics, the question arises about how easily complex ideas may be expressed in different languages and whether all languages are capable of purveying all possible concepts. This remains a field to be explored more fully.

Reading Direction

It appears that, for mature readers, the direction of reading is not a problem. Gray (1956) performed eye-movement studies in fourteen languages and found that the reading direction did not appear to have an important influence. However, this may not be the case for immature children and dyslexics. Developmentally, children are able to draw a vertical line before they can draw a horizontal line. It is believed that this is due to crossing the midline of the body when executing a horizontal line. At any rate, in chapter 16 of this book, Nakano and Suzuki cite the case of a dyslexic boy whose reading in Japanese was better vertically than horizontally.

Harmon (1979) has been studying the direction of attack when reading words and the relative speeds of reading from right to left, left to right, and with the letters arranged upside down. He found that "American dyslexics have less difficulty, relatively, reading in a right to left direction than non-dyslexics, and have more difficulty reading in the left to right direction of English." In our own experience, a second-grade left-handed boy who had difficulty learning to read was being tested in visual perception, comparing a stimulus figure with a series of figures on the same horizontal line to find the ones that were the same as the stimulus. He was proceeding with great difficulty when he suddenly turned the page upside down and was able to continue both rapidly and accurately. When the next page was presented, he again turned it upside down and continued with alacrity. No attempt will be made to explain these phenomena at present. There seems to be a tendency for dyslexics to make reversals and inversions in all languages in which studies have been made. However, an acceptable explanation of this characteristic has not been forthcoming.

English and many other languages are not actually read consistently from left to right. In order to pronounce certain words it is necessary to inspect the final letter or letters first, as for example, *at* and *ate.* However when *saw* is pronounced as *was* and *on* is called *no,* it is probable that the child is reading the word backwards, scanning from right to left. Alternatively, he may not yet be sure of the perceptual difference between the word pairs, so that *no* and *on* are not clearly differentiated. Downing (1973) suggested that these reversals may also be due to confusion in the disabled reader over the "relationship between graphemes and phonemes." He noted that reversals seldom occur with words that have regular grapheme-phoneme relations, such as *pat* and *tap,* whereas all of the well-known examples are pairs of words with irregular relationships, such as *saw* and *was.*

Bilingual Environments

A great deal of attention is being given in the United States to the problems of teaching children whose first language is not English. First, classes were established in English as a second language (ESL). Then bilingual-education classes were developed for these children as the result of a Supreme Court decision based on the San Francisco case of *Lau* v. *Nichols.* In these classes bilingual teachers generally speak in the children's native language and then repeat each sentence in English. They also teach the pupils about their cultural heritage. Evaluation of this program by the California State Department of Education has determined that the children in the bilingual programs do not learn better than those who remain in the regular classes.

In the USSR each republic has its own language, such as Armenian, Lithuanian, or Uzbek. In these republics the children first learn to read and write in their native languages and then learn Russian as a second language. To attend higher institutions of learning, the students may go to Russian universities and therefore must be proficient in Russian. Similarly, in Greenland the children start school in the vernacular and learn Danish as a second language, often using it in commerce and in higher education when attending a university in Denmark.

Within a country with a single national language, there is little precedent for having children first learn to read and write in their own native languages or dialects before they are educated in the standard language of the country. Some research has been done along these lines, but not enough to establish the validity of this approach or lack thereof. Consequently, great controversy is raging based on subjective feelings about how to best help bilingual children learn. The resolution of this question is of great importance, because most countries seem to have one or more large groups of children who are either bilingual or who speak a dialect of the national tongue and may therefore be considered to have the same learning problems as the bilingual population. Moreover, these minority groups are often, but not always, significantly below the native majority in educational functioning (see chapter 4).

Comparative Learning Studies

The first major attempt to investigate reading problems internationally was the survey done for UNESCO by Gray (1956). He visited several countries and held informal conferences with individuals and small groups, sent out a questionnaire by mail, reviewed publications from many countries, and did an empirical study of eye movements made by readers in fourteen languages. From this material Gray attempted to make some useful generalizations about the relationships between learning to read and methods of teaching. Gray's work has received wide international recognition.

Foshay and his associates (1962) did a survey for UNESCO of the reading achievements of thirteen-year-old children in twelve countries. This study clarified some of the problems involved in attempting to test reading cross-nationally. Both the tests and the sampling techniques were subject to limitations that precluded making useful conclusions about the relationships between teaching methods and progress in reading and literacy (Downing 1973).

Husén (1967), Thorndike (1973), and Wolf (1977) have published the results of large-scale studies of mathematics, reading, and science in fifteen countries. The research group organized under the name International

Association for the Evaluation of Educational Achievement (IEA) aimed to test a number of hypotheses that they had developed. Essentially, they were attempting to determine the "causative factors behind the development and 'productivity' of educational systems" (Husén 1967).

The relationships to be examined were mentioned, and the questionnaires and test items used to check the hypotheses were published. The major differences considered important to study among the school systems in the different countries included the way in which students were selected for the different types of secondary-school programs; the content of the curricula in various nations and school systems; and the attitudinal value, financial support, and opportunities for the graduates that communities extended to the education of students. Some of the items in hypothesis-building included age of starting school, teacher competence, funding per pupil, number of years of schooling, amount of time devoted to each subject, and students' attitudes toward the subject and the teacher. A great deal of data was gathered, listed in tables, correlated, and subjected to regression analysis.

The authors were aware of the great difficulties inherent in attempting cross-national research of this type, but they claim to have overcome most of the obstacles. However, Freudenthal (1975), editor of the international journal *Educational Studies in Mathematics,* attempted to analyze the research in some detail and concluded that the main objective of the study was to compare national education systems and that not only had this not been attained but it had "hardly been attempted." He also stated that the descriptive statistics of these studies were unreliable; the regression analyses were "not founded in mathematical statistics"; the test instruments were not validly translated; the populations studied were not comparable; "the main variable, the curriculum, was obstinately ignored"; and the use of psychometry was inappropriate. Freudenthal's conclusions followed after more than fifty pages of analysis of the IEA studies.

Some examples of the items Freudenthal considered to be errors included the following. Rather than asking directly whether or not a test item was included in the contents of the curriculum, teachers were asked what percentage of their students "have had an opportunity to learn this type of problem." Freudenthal considered the question to be "incomprehensible" and consequently interpreted differently by the individual teachers. He then demonstrated from the data that the interpretations varied, destroying the validity of the results. A table of teachers' mathematics-training indicated that most French teachers had one year or less, while Dutch teachers had "training of 5 years or more, though no professional training," indicating misunderstanding in the survey item. A table in the IEA study indicates that 75 percent of the eighteen-year-olds were in school in the United States while only 9 percent of this age population were attending school in the

Federal Republic of Germany. Freudenthal questioned these data, stating that in the late 1950s 33 percent of this age group were in school in the Federal Republic of Germany.

One population was to be composed of "all pupils at the grade level where the majority of the pupils age 13:0-13:11 are found." The Netherlands selected the sixth-grade pupils and England the eighth-grade pupils for this population, indicating some of the confusion that existed in the selection of populations for study. In The Netherlands, normal schools are considered secondary education, and all primary-school teachers receive the same amount of education, which does not include postsecondary education. However, the number of years of postsecondary education for these teachers is recorded as from 18 percent with one year to 36 percent with five years or more.

Examples of paragraphs in English from the reading test are given with their back-translations from Dutch to English, with the comment that one is "entirely double-Dutch" and the others are imprecise. Also, only a few countries returned back-translations, so it is not known what happened in the others.

The purpose of reviewing some of the "errors" claimed by Freudenthal is not to censure the IEA studies but rather to indicate the inherent difficulties involved in attempting multinational cross-cultural research in education, even when performed by a very high-level team of educationalists. Also, we believe that, by careful selection of data from these studies, one may make some valid observations and draw some useful relationships.

It is much easier to review and criticize this kind of research than it is to organize, fund, and carry out studies of comparative education. Such efforts are essential for international progress. Gray, Foshay, Husén, Thorndike, Wolf, and the others were pioneers in attempting cross-national studies of educational systems. Such research needs to be continued and expanded without introducing contests among nations. International studies are stimulating to the flow of important knowledge. Every country in the world sees children as being a most precious commodity to be nurtured and educated. We can learn much from each other through continued efforts at cross-national research in education.

References

Clements, S.D. 1966. *Minimal Brain Dysfunction in Children,* NINDB Monograph No. 3. Washington, D.C.: U.S. Department of Health, Education and Welfare.

Downing, J. (ed.). 1973. *Comparative Reading*. New York: Macmillan.

Elkonin, D.B. 1973. USSR. In J. Downing (ed.), *Comparative Reading*. New York: Macmillan.

Foshay, A.W., et al. 1962. *Educational Achievements of Thirteen-Year-Olds in Twelve Countries*. Hamburg: UNESCO Institute for Education.

Freudenthal, H. 1975. Pupils' achievements internationally compared—the IEA. *Educational Studies in Mathematics* 6:2.

Gray, W.S. 1956. *The Teaching of Reading and Writing*. Paris: UNESCO.

Harmon, G. 1979. Personal communication.

Husén, T. (ed.). 1967. *International Studies of Achievement in Mathematics: A Comparison of Twelve Countries*. 2 vols. New York: Wiley.

Keir, E.H. 1977. Auditory information processing and learning disabilities. In L. Tarnopol and M. Tarnopol (eds.), *Brain Function and Reading Disabilities*. Baltimore: University Park Press.

Leong, C.K. 1973. Hong Kong. In J. Downing (ed.), *Comparative Reading*. New York: Macmillan.

Lindamood, C.H., and Lindamood, P.C. 1971. *Lindamood Auditory Conceptualization Test*. Boston: Teaching Resources.

Mathews, M. 1966. *Teaching to Read: Historically Considered*. Chicago: University of Chicago Press.

Silverman, L.J., and Metz, A.S. 1973. Numbers of pupils with specific learning disabilities in local public schools in the United States. In F.F. de la Cruz, B.H. Fox, and R.H. Roberts (eds.), *Minimal Brain Dysfunction*. New York: New York Academy of Sciences.

Tarnopol, L. (ed.). 1969. *Learning Disabilities: Introduction to Educational and Medical Management*. Springfield, Ill.: Thomas.

_____ . 1970. Delinquency and minimal brain dysfunction. *Journal of Learning Disabilities* 3:4.

Tarnopol, L., Breed, J.S., Tarnopol, M., and Ozaki, M. 1977. Learning disabilities in minority adolescents. *Bulletin Orton Society*.

Tarnopol, L., and Tarnopol, M. (eds.). 1976. *Reading Disabilities: An International Perspective*. Baltimore: University Park Press.

Tarnopol, L., and Tarnopol, M. 1979. Brain function and arithmetic disability. *Focus on Learning Problems in Mathematics* 1:3.

Thorndike, R.L. 1973. *Reading Comprehension Education in Fifteen Countries: An Empirical Study*. New York: Halsted Press.

Wagner, R.F. 1973. Rudolf Berlin: Originator of the term dyslexia. *Bulletin Orton Society* 23.

Waller, E. 1974. Provision for dyslexia overseas. *The Dyslexia Review*. North Surrey Dyslexia Society, England.

White, B.L., Kaban, B.T., and Attanucci, J.S. 1979. *The Origins of Human Competence: The Final Report of the Harvard Preschool Project*. Lexington, Mass.: Lexington Books, D.C. Heath.

White, B.L., Kaban, B.T., Attanucci, J.S., and Shapiro, B.B. 1978. *Experience and Environment: Major Influences on the Development of the Young Child, Vol. 2.* Englewood Cliffs, N.J.: Prentice-Hall.

White, B.L., Watts, J.C., Barnett, I., Kaban, B.T., Marmor, J.R., and Shapiro, B.B. 1973. *Experience and Environment: Major Influences on the Development of the Young Child, Vol. 1.* Englewood Cliffs, N.J.: Prentice-Hall.

Whitmore, J.R. 1980. *Giftedness, Conflict, and Underachievement.* Boston: Allyn and Bacon.

Wolf, R.M. 1977. *Achievement in America.* New York: Teachers College Press, Columbia University.

2

Summary of Comparative Reading and Learning Difficulties: North America and Europe

Lester Tarnopol and
Muriel Tarnopol

Reading and other learning difficulties in intelligent children have been found to exist in all countries and languages surveyed. However, the definitions, etiologies, and treatments of these problems remain controversial. It is generally recognized that large numbers of children from all socioeconomic levels, who test within the normal to superior range of IQs and have no readily visible deficits to account for their problems, may be found to have severe learning difficulties. This situation warrants serious attention.

Historical Development

Until recently, when American children who were not retarded and who had normal educational opportunities and no apparent physical defects had great reading or learning difficulties, several possible causes were considered. These included emotional disturbance, poor motivation, and nonstandard-English speaking homes. It was often assumed that these children could learn to read if they wanted to and were willing to try. Orton (1925, 1928) may have been the first American to postulate that many of these children were suffering from subtle neurological differences, which were causing their unusual learning problems.

The earliest contributions to the subject of neurogenic reading disabilities appear to have come from physicians who were interested in aphasia (loss of ability to use words as symbols of ideas, caused by a brain lesion). Strother (1973) stated that cases have appeared in medical literature dating back to 400 B.C. These aphasia cases in adults, resulting from central nervous system traumas, later became analogues of the speech and reading problems in children that are now considered to be symptoms of minimal cerebral dysfunction.

Reading problems based on neurological differences or abnormalities were reported by physicians at the end of the nineteenth century. These cases were at first considered to be medical anomalies of rare occurrence. It has been suggested by Critchley (1970) that Rudolph Berlin, a German ophthalmologist, first coined the term *Dyslexie* in 1887. Berlin stated that the condition was a type of aphasia and was closely related to Kussmaul's *Wortblindheit* (word-blindness), described in 1877 (Wagner 1973). This term is now in universal usage as *dyslexia,* following the English form of the word. Hungary, Austria, and Germany also use the term *legasthenia* (specific weakness in learning to read and spell), which was introduced by a Hungarian, Paul Ranschburg (1916).

British literature on learning disabilities may have begun with a Scottish opthalmologist's report of some cases of word-blindness (Hinshelwood 1895). This was followed shortly by reports from an English ophthalmologist (Morgan 1896) and a school physician (Kerr) on cases of reading disabilities among intelligent children. Critchley (1970) noted that James Kerr, medical officer of health to the city of Bradford (England) was awarded the Howard Medal by the Royal Statistical Society for his essay, "School hygiene, in its mental, moral and physical aspects," in 1896. Kerr stated that, besides the retarded students, there were the "mentally exceptional." They were often capable of ordinary school work, provided the teacher understood their peculiarities. Unique cases with bizarre deficits could be found. In one of Kerr's cases, for example, a boy who did arithmetic well, using Arabic numerals, wrote gibberish in a neat hand from dictation. His handwriting was unintelligible to the teacher. Kerr called this condition "word-blindness." As a school physician, Kerr may have been the first person to describe learning disabilities in the student population.

Once the condition of congenital word-blindness was recognized, many more cases were soon found and reported. Critchley (1970) noted that in 1902, after contributing a series of case reports, Hinshelwood stated that he had no doubt that congenital word-blindness was not so rare as the absence of recorded cases tended to indicate. Their rarity, he said, was accounted for by the fact that they were not recognized when they occurred. Moreover, it was most important to perceive the true nature and cause of children's reading difficulties, otherwise they might be considered to be incorrigibles or imbeciles, in which case they might be punished or receive no help for their congenital deficits.

Between 1900 and 1909 reports of cases of congenital word-blindness were made in numerous countries, including Argentina, France, Holland, Germany, Great Britain, and the United States. In 1917 Hinshelwood published his second monograph, *Congenital Word-Blindness,* which seemed to mark the close of this period of identification of the problem, probably partly related to the concentration of effort in other directions during World War I.

During the next period, beginning after the war, the bulk of the research on children's learning problems passed from Great Britain to the United States and the Scandinavian countries. In general American psychologists and educators concluded that children's reading and spelling problems were due either to low IQs or to environmental and emotional factors, while a few interested physicians continued to pursue the neurological hypothesis. Because of the relatively large numbers of immigrant children who spoke a language other than English at home while attending American schools, environmental factors tended to overshadow any specific learning disabilities that these children may have had. A second intruding factor was the fact that children of lower socioeconomic status tended to do less well in school than children from higher-status families. The effect of socioeconomic level also tended to cover up the effects of specific learning disabilities in this population. Therefore, the overpowering effects of visible environmental factors obscured any underlying subtle neurological dysfunctions. A third factor was the emergence of psychodynamic theory, taken up by psychiatrists, psychologists, educators, social workers and many others. Psychodynamic theorists were convinced that school failures were related to emotional problems stemming from inappropriate early child-rearing practices and were ascribable to inadequate mother-child relationships. An equally important fourth factor was the lack of an appropriate test battery that educational psychologists could use to parcel out the distinct effects of subtle neurological dysfunctions that might cause specific learning disabilities.

This combination of conditions fostered the development of the environmental and emotional disturbance hypotheses about reading and learning problems in children. Among the causative factors included were broken homes, drunken parents, nonstandard-English-speaking parents, overprotective parents, overly aggressive parents, pushy parents, passive parents, and teacher-pupil hostility. Finally, many professionals were skeptical about the existence of specific learning disabilities; many continue to deny their existence.

Klasen (1972) stated that the reading process is so complex that only multiple factors could possibly account for the different types of reading disabilities, not any single etiology. Recognition of all the factors that might influence learning to read is becoming an increasingly critical area. This has resulted in the emergence of multidisciplinary communication and cooperation.

American Developments

Jackson (1906) may have been the first American physician to describe congenital word-blindness in this century. However, in 1861 Dr. Little described learning problems associated with brain damage by discussing at a medical meeting some of the observed sequelae when asphyxiated or apoplectic children were saved:

> The proportion of entire recoveries from the effects of asphyxia neonatorum is smaller than has hitherto been supposed. . . . The muscles of speech are commonly involved, varying in degree. . . . The intellectual functions are sometimes quite unaffected, but in the majority of cases the intellect suffers. . . . The individual may acquire a fair knowledge of music. . . . A fair capacity for arithmetic and language may be displayed, but there commonly exists a great want of application, a slowness of intellect. . . . In other cases, where intellectual powers are good, a preternatural impulsive nervous condition of mind exists, combined with an agitated, eager, anxious mode of performing acts of volition (cited in Peters et al. 1967).

Samuel T. Orton (1925, 1928, 1937) is usually credited with being the first American both to recognize the learning disabilities problem and to take positive steps to develop a remedial program for these children. Working as director of the Greene County Medical Clinic in Iowa, Orton observed a number of cases of severely retarded readers and some nonreaders. These cases tended not to be confounded by the environmental factors previously mentioned. By studying the children's writing and spelling problems and observing associated phenomena, he noted a high degree of left-handedness, ambidexterity, and writing and reading reversals, as well as some mirror-reading and mirror-writing. He coined the term *strephosymbolia* (twisted symbols) to characterize this condition and postulated that lack of cerebral dominance may have caused these problems.

Orton made a major contribution to the remediation of children with reading problems by engaging a psychologist, Anna Gillingham, to organize a special curriculum for these children. Working at the Ethical Culture School in New York City, Gillingham and Bessie Stillman, a remedial-education teacher, developed a unique program. A manual was first published by Gillingham in 1934 and was later expanded in several editions by Gillingham and Stillman (1960). In the foreword to the manual, Gillingham described her relationships with Orton and Stillman. An outstanding experience for Gillingham was the two years spent as research associate to Samuel Orton, studying language and its relation to reading English. She was particularly impressed by their contact with neurology and the concept of scientific cautions. She was asked to develop remedial-reading techniques consistent with Orton's neurological hypotheses. Later she worked with Stillman, who made important contributions to the manual, so that by the 1946 edition, Stillman had contributed a large part of the text.

The Orton, Gillingham, Stillman remedial methods are still widely used and are considered to be among the best developments in remedial training for children with reading problems. The manual has also served to spawn other remedial programs of value, for example, Cox (1967), Hathaway (1970), Saunders, Gialas, and Hofler (1969), Slingerland (1971), Rome and Osman (1972), and Oliphant (1977).

In 1936 Mary Winne, head of the elementary section of the Punahoe Schools in Honolulu, instituted a Gillingham program in her school. Both Gillingham and Stillman came to the Punahoe Elementary School and spent two years working at the school and training Beth Slingerland, who then took over and continued the work. Slingerland adapted the Gillingham program of one-to-one or small-group training, to be used with an entire class. She also developed screening instruments and prereading-level, basic language-development programs.

Concurrently with Orton, Gillingham, and Stillman, a group in Los Angeles was working independently on the same problems. Fernald (1943) discussed her early work as a psychologist prior to 1920 in Los Angeles, testing children with learning problems. In 1921 a clinic school was established at the University of California at Los Angeles to handle "cases of normal or superior intelligence with extreme (learning) disabilities." During the five years before the publication of Fernald's book, the clinic school handled more than one hundred cases of total or partial reading disability. Fernald stated, "Our high schools are loaded with unhappy youngsters who are attempting to do some type of 'activity work' as a substitute [for courses requiring reading] in spite of the fact that they know, as we do, that they have little chance to obtain a job unless they can read."

This problem became severe in America when it became mandatory for children in most states to remain in school until the age of eighteen. Fernald stated that the children with severe learning problems tended to have primary neurological dysfunctions, and rarely primary emotional disorders, but that they usually developed secondary emotional problems.

Fernald developed a complete remedial curriculum for reading, writing, spelling, and arithmetic. She and the clinic school in Los Angeles began to work on the remediation of reading problems long before it became established as a national "epidemic." Since there have always been intelligent children with severe reading problems, many teachers throughout the nation were devoting themselves to remedial work, unheralded, struggling with the problem alone.

Minimal Brain Damage

The relationship between minimal brain damage and learning problems was established early. In 1908 Tregold stated, "In the milder cases (of injury during birth), the initial symptoms may rapidly pass off and it is only when the child begins his schooling that deficiency is noted" (Strother 1973). Goldstein (1939) made an important contribution to our understanding of the relationship between areas of brain injury and behavioral and learning disabilities by his studies of soldiers wounded in World War I. His clinical studies of brain-damaged soldiers led to the determination of several effects of such injuries, including figure-ground confusion, hyperactivity, forced responsiveness to irrelevant stimuli (distractibility), catastrophic reactions to probable misperceptions (temper tantrums), and organization of the environment to prevent environmental confusions.

The concept that nonbrain-injured retarded children sometimes displayed very similar learning disabilities to those of the minimally brain-injured children grew out of observations documented by Strauss and Werner (1938) in a series of publications. However, Strauss concluded that all these children must be brain-injured, including those in whom direct evidence of trauma cannot be established, since their perceptual and learning problems tend to be similar; and some professionals still adhere to this concept. Strauss and Lehtinen (1947) published a classic work on the psychopathology and education of brain-injured children in which the teaching of arithmetic and reading were detailed and the basis was laid for further developments in education. Methods of testing visual perception, visual-motor function, and tactile performance were also described in this book.

Cruickshank, Bice, and Wallen (1957) published an important text examining the perceptual characteristics of cerebral-palsied children. Many of the tests that they used were later incorporated into batteries for children without cerebral palsy who were suspected of having learning disabilities. Teaching techniques evolved, based on information gleaned from the diagnostic procedures. These techniques for brain-injured and cerebral-palsied children not only have been adopted into the teaching curriculum for learning-disabled children but have also greatly influenced preschool and early-childhood education in the United States.

The study of the educational problems of children with cerebral palsy made a definitive contribution to the field of learning disabilities. Denhoff and Robinault (1960) published the Meeting Street School Screening Test for early identification of children with learning disabilities. The team, which had been working in the field of cerebral palsy, started to build a bridge to transmit the information acquired from cerebral palsy to working with children with specific learning disabilities who were normal-appearing. They had found important clinical similarities in both learning-disability and cerebral-palsy cases.

Based on a thirty-six–item screening test, taken from the method of examining children with cerebral palsy used by this team, it was predicted with 89 percent accuracy that 19 percent of 355 normal first-grade children would fail either the first or second grades (Denhoff and Tarnopol 1971).

This may have been the first time that testing was used to predict which normal children would fail in school based on a test devised for brain-injured children. Since the test measured primarily visual and auditory perception and memory, visual-motor integration, balance, attention span, and hyperactivity, it tapped central nervous system functions that tended to be affected in cases of cerebral palsy but that also seemed to correlate with learning skills in young children. This appeared to indicate that lack of development of these skills in normal children was predictive of learning problems. Since the same tests predicted learning problems in both brain-injured and normal children, it appeared that some form of minimal brain dysfunction (implying either brain damage or genetic brain differences) underlay the learning disabilities in both populations. The controversy still continues over whether normal-appearing children actually have very minor brain damage, which is difficult to detect, or if their problem is caused by genetic brain differences or perhaps even by emotional disorders.

Pilot Programs

Cruikshank and associates (1961) published the results of a demonstration-pilot study based on extensive research, *A Teaching Method for Brain-injured and Hyperactive Children,* extending the work of Strauss, Werner, and Lehtinen. The pilot program was based on a study done in Montgomery County, Maryland, of forty children separated into four groups, two experimental and two control. In this controlled study, both the psychological testing and educational aspects of working with brain-injured children were scrutinized in some detail. The teaching methods and materials developed in this project have acted as catalysts to spawn many more along the same lines. A highly structured classroom was developed, permitting a minimum of distracting stimuli, and a curriculum characterized by very small, sequential steps, with overlearning emphasized. Most remedial programs, worldwide, seem to emphasize these same general principles, often independently determined.

In the late 1950s and early 1960s, pilot programs were conducted in several school districts in California to attempt to develop a remedial program for children with "neurological handicaps." After several years of such experiments, the program for "educationally handicapped" children was instituted in 1963 in California public schools (Tarnopol and Tarnopol 1976).

In this same period New York began to develop programs for "brain-injured" children, New Jersey for "neurologically impaired," and Michigan for "perceptually handicapped" students. Other states starting early programs used either these terms or others to designate this new category for special-education classes.

Speech and Language Therapists

Speech and language therapists became interested in the problems of children with learning difficulties and began to investigate the relationship of auditory perception and speech deficits to these problems. Eisenson (1946) had been studying the psychology of speech and stuttering for some years when he published a manual on examining for aphasia. Wepman (1958) developed a test for auditory discrimination, which was widely used, and in 1960 he published studies in aphasia. Kirk had been studying the problems of children with reading and learning disabilities for some time before McCarthy and Kirk (1961) published their test of psycholinguistic abilities, which broadened the scope of available testing in this area. Myklebust (1964) also was working in the field studying aphasia and loss of hearing. As a result of all this and other similar activity, the role of auditory perception in learning was subjected to intensive investigation.

Visual-Motor Skills

It was early found that children with learning problems tended to have motor, visual-motor, and visual-perceptual deficits. Tests of motor functions and a remedial program were developed by Kephart (1960), and visual-motor tests and a program of remediation were developed by Frostig (Frostig, Lefever, and Whittlesey 1964; Frostig and Horne 1964). Further work in developing programs for visual-motor training was done by Getman (1965) and Barsch (1967). Beery (1967) published a visual-motor test and a remedial program. Others who helped develop this field include Delacato (1959), Ayres (1965), and Cratty (1967). The visual-motor area of remediation has received intensive study over the years and remains a field of considerable controversy.

The Task Forces

In 1964 three task forces to investigate reading and learning problems in children were jointly sponsored by the National Institute of Neurological Diseases and Blindness, of the U.S. National Institutes of Health, and the National Society for Crippled Children and Adults; and Task Force II was also cosponsored by the U.S. Office of Education. Sam Clements was project director for Task Forces I and II. Task Force I considered the problems of terminology and identification (Clements 1966). The committee was composed of nine physicians, two psychologist-educators, and an agency executive. They managed to locate thirty-seven different terms being used to designate the learning disabilities resulting from possible neurological deficits in children of substantially normal intelligence. The terms were of two types: those designating organic aspects of the problem, such as "organic brain damage" and "minimal cerebral palsy"; and those that were related to a segment or consequence of the disorder, such as "hyperkinetic behavior syndrome," "dyslexia," and "learning disabilities." This primarily medical committee adopted the term *minimal brain dysfunction* as best representing the disorder. Task Force I based its terminology on the following premises:

1. Brain dysfunction can manifest itself in varying degrees of severity and can involve any or all of the more specific areas, e.g., motor, sensory, or intellectual. This dysfunctioning can compromise the affected child in learning and behavior.

2. The term minimal brain dysfunction will be reserved for the child whose symptomatology appears in one or more of the specific areas of brain function, but in mild, or subclinical form, without reducing overall intellectual functioning to the subnormal ranges (Note: The evaluation of the intellectual functioning of the 'culturally disadvantaged' child, though perhaps related, represents an equally complex, but different problem.)

The term *minimal brain dysfunction* (MBD) has been accepted primarily by physicians and is meant to be the counterpart of *specific learning disability*, which was adopted by many educators. In the medical term, *minimal* differentiates the condition from obvious brain damage, as in cerebral palsy, and *dysfunction* indicates the possibility of developmental, genetic, or other deviations as well as damage.

Task Force II reported on the extent of the need both for medical diagnosis and treatment and for identification of educational capabilities and methods of educating afflicted children (Haring et al. 1969). Task Force III reported on research aspects of the problem (Chalfant and Scheffelin 1969). The effect of these task forces was to summarize the state of the art and to give official government sanction to the concept of specific learning disabilities.

An important development has been the inclusion of specific learning disabilities as a diagnostic category taught in certain medical schools. For example, at the University of California Medical Center, children with reading problems are given a four-day evaluation in the Child Study Unit, including a "pediatric history, physical examination, psychological testing, parent or family interview, neurological examination, evaluation of hearing, speech and language, ophthalmological examination and educational evaluation. Following a team conference, the findings are summarized and beginning plans for management are discussed with the parent and child. This four-day study is provided by the Child Study Unit as a part of its training program for senior medical students and house staff in pediatrics and ophthalmology'' (Gofman 1969). Selected children may attend the Child Study Unit's remedial-reading program.

Research in the fields of delinquency and adult crime determined that an unusually large number of inmates were significantly deficient in literacy. Studies of the relationships between crime, delinquency, literacy, and learning disabilities established high correlations (L. Tarnopol 1969, 1970; Tarnopol et al. 1977).

Learning Disabilities Defined

In 1970 the U.S. Office of Education defined children with *specific learning disabilities* as

> those children who have a disorder in one or more of the basic psychological processes involved in understanding or in using language, spoken or written, which disorder may manifest itself in imperfect ability to listen, think, speak, read, write, spell, or do mathematical calculations. Such disorders include such conditions as perceptual handicaps, brain injury, minimal brain disfunction, dyslexia and developmental aphasia. Such term does not include children who have learning problems which are primarily the result of visual, hearing, or motor handicaps, of mental retardation, of emotional distrubance, or of environmental disadvantage.

The term *general learning disabilities* has been similarly defined, except that it refers to children who are mentally retarded. These definitions are similar to those proposed by the Council for Exceptional Children, the organization for professionals working in the field of exceptional children. The concept of exceptional children refers to all children outside the "normal" range and includes both the retarded and the gifted as well as all forms of handicapped children. Unfortunately, the definitions of learning disabilities remain in dispute, as some people have proposed different variations of the definitions.

Parents Take Action

In the United States it has been customary for parents to organize for political action in order to get desired programs for their children. In 1963 California parents of children with learning disabilties organized the

California Association for Neurologically Handicapped Children (CANHC) by combining local associations, which had begun to form some years earlier. Nationally, the Association for Children with Learning Disabilities (ACLD) was being formed. At this time there were parent and professional organizations, as well as special classes for the mentally retarded, the orthopedically handicapped, the emotionally disturbed, the blind, the deaf, and cerebral-palsied children; but there was very little special help for children of substantially normal intelligence with severe learning problems.

State Assemblyman Jerome Waldie sponsored CANHC's legislation to provide special educational programs in the California public schools for "educationally handicapped" children, which included both neurologically and emotionally handicapped children of substantially normal intelligence; and this law was passed in 1963. Robert O'Reilly (1965), who was president of CANHC, stated that a lawyer member of CANHC wrote this momentous legislation, which was guided through the state legislature by a salesman member of CANHC and was argued in the legislative hearings by a physician CANHC member. The bill provides for both neurologically handicapped and emotionally disturbed children because it is difficult to separate the two disorders, since emotional problems often occur as sequalae to a neurological handicap. Since this legislation was passed in California, other states have passed similar legislation.

In the late 1970s, a number of professional and parent organizations, including ACLD, worked for federal legislation to aid all handicapped children. Their efforts were crowned by the passage of Public Law 94-142, the Education for All Handicapped Children Act, and PL 93-112 (section 504), Nondiscrimination on the Basis of Handicap Act. The first law, mandated in 1978, assures "that all handicapped children have available to them a free appropriate public education." Section 504 states, "No otherwise qualified handicapped individual in the United States . . . shall, solely by reason of his handicap, be excluded from the participation in, be denied the benefits of, or be subjected to discrimination under any program or activity receiving Federal financial assistance." These civil-rights regulations have had profound effects on the development of all forms of equal rights for handicapped persons.

Canadian Developments

Knights, Kronick, and Cunningham (1976) summarized the situation with respect to learning disabilities in Canada. Legislation concerning special education is the responsibility of each province, since there is no federal office of education. Only two Canadian provinces require school districts to provide special education, and the other provinces operate through exclusion clauses, so that "it is even possible that a student can be prohibited from receiving a public education."

The development of facilities for aiding handicapped children was greatly helped by volunteer organizations. In 1964 the first such group was formed in Toronto to aid children with learning disabilities, and in 1969 the Canadian Association for Children with Learning Disabilities (CACLD) emerged. The Commission on Emotional and Learning Disorders in Children, sponsored by many agencies including CACLD, conducted a three-year study of handicapped children in Canada. Their 1970 report concluded that one million children in Canada required special educational assistance and that this number constituted a national emergency.

Perhaps the first clinic for children with learning disabilities was established at Montreal Children's Hospital in 1960, under the direction of M. Sam Rabinovitch. The Learning Centre is now jointly sponsored by Children's Hospital and McGill University and handles learning problems in both French and English, which are the official languages. The Centre has a complete multidisciplinary staff and administers an extensive assessment-test battery to the children. A decision is made concerning tutoring the child at the Centre or recommending services to be given at school. The Centre provides materials for classroom teachers, and staff personnel visit the teachers to ensure that recommended programs are implemented by the schools. The staff also work with and assist parents to participate actively in the rehabilitation of their children.

In 1965 a clinic was opened in Guelph, Ontario, by Denis H. Stott, with remediation based on the premise that most learning problems are the result of inadequate cognitive processes leading to inappropriate learning styles. Remediation is effected by correcting the child's learning style, based on the standard learning principles of psychology. The training attempts to develop attention, motivation toward competence and appropriate learning tasks, and the ability to restrain inappropriate impulsive acts. Games are used, which involve problem-solving and suitable learning styles that are rewarded for success. Other clinics for children with learning problems, emphasizing various remedial methods, have since been opened in different communities throughout Canada.

Private and governmental organizations have pressured the boards of education to develop special educational programs for learning-disabled children. As a result, most boards in the larger Canadian districts have introduced consultants and special programs to serve the children with various handicaps, including the learning disabled. Smaller school systems may not be able to provide services comparable to those available in cities, but they often have a consulting psychologist and a special-education teacher who do assessment and make suggestions to the regular classroom teachers concerning remedial measures.

In 1963 William Gaddes established the first neuropsychology laboratory in Canada at the University of Victoria. The research included comprehensive assessment of children with learning disorders or brain lesions. The test results were used to develop remedial-educational programs for these children. A test in which the child was asked to identify changes in a simple pattern of lights presented in sequence was found to reliably distinguish brain-damaged from normal children. The laboratory has added greatly to the literature on learning disabilities.

European Developments

A French neurologist, Dejerine (1892), may have published the first postmortem study of an alexic (inability to read following a stroke) patient. The postmortem examination of his brain revealed a lesion in the left angular gyrus, below the cortex. The angular gyrus is located in the lower parietal area adjacent to both the occipital and temporal lobes. It therefore is part of the system that carries messages from the visual-perceptual brain area (occipital) to the language brain area (usually left-temporal). It has subsequently been suggested that lesions in the left angular gyrus may create reading difficulties.

Czechoslovakia

In 1904 Heveroch, a professor of neurology at Prague University, published the first paper on alexia in Czechoslovakia. He described the case of an eleven-year-old girl who learned only the most basic elements of reading and writing, although her abilities in arithmetic and other school subjects were adequate for her age (Matějček 1976). From his detailed case history and analysis, Heveroch concluded that it was a case of alexia due to underdevelopment of areas of the brain required for reading in the absence of any trauma. Heveroch accurately predicted, "In my opinion, such cases are comparatively frequent in school practice; yet it is feared that they will not come to the attention of educators as much as to neurologists."

Matějček (1976) described the field of learning disabilities in Czechoslovakia, where systematic care for children with reading disabilities began to be instituted after World War II, due to the intervention of child psychiatrists. The main center for the diagnosis and treatment of reading disabilities (dyslexia) was the Child Psychiatric Clinic in Dolní Počernice, near Prague. Brno established the first special classes for retarded readers in

1962, and Prague followed in 1965. In 1972 the Ministry of Education issued a uniform statute for special classes for dyslexic children.

Czechoslovakian spelling was made phonetically consistent with the introduction of diacritical marks in the fifteenth century by Jan Hus, rector of Prague University. "As soon as a Czech child learns the letters of the Czech alphabet and acquires the basic ability to join them, he can read any word and almost any text" (Matějček 1976). By the end of the second or third grades, the children are reading at about sixty or seventy words per minute, which is relatively fluent and is satisfying to the child.

The estimate of the incidence of reading disabilities is based on the difference between the children's grades in arithmetic and reading. About 1.5 percent of the pupils were found to have achievement in reading at least two grades below their arithmetic levels. If those who did not receive low grades because of indulgent teachers and those whose poor reading has caused them to be sent to schools for the retarded are added, then 2 percent of the children may be considered to have reading deficits.

These figures indicate that "dyslexia occurs in the Czech language substantially less frequently than reported in the English language" (Matějček 1976). Between 1954 and 1960, eighty-one boys and ten girls were being treated for severe dyslexia at the Children's Psychiatric Hospital in Dolní Počernice; 37 percent were found to have hereditary causes.

In another research study, the types of reading errors made by dyslexics in Czech and English were compared. Basic agreement was found in the types of reading errors, indicating that the process of relating the visual perception of letters to the sound patterns is similar in both languages. Only the degree to which the languages are phonetic is different, so that spelling is much easier in Czech. With the highly phonetic character of spelling, auditory perception becomes important and deficits therein tend to cause spelling disorders.

The diagnosis of dyslexia is made at special centers by a team composed of psychologists, psychiatrists, pediatricians, speech therapists, and remedial teachers. The treatment of children with reading problems is carried out on four different levels. The mildest cases remain in their regular classrooms and receive remedial help from the teacher by being taught differently from the other pupils, based on their needs. Those children who cannot be remediated in the regular classroom attend special classes at psychiatric or psychopedagogic centers after school until they are able to cope with the normal school program. More severe cases attend special classes for dyslexics, usually in a different school. The most severe cases of dyslexia are subjected to concentrated therapeutic care in a special residential center. "After many years of experience, we have come to the conclusion that above all, the single most difficult task is to create a general psychotherapeutic atmosphere of understanding and acceptance for children who cannot readily cope with one of the main demands of modern society, reading and writing" (Matějček 1976).

Sweden

Hallgren (1950), working in Sweden, published a study of 276 cases of specific dyslexia, which concluded that dyslexia may be inherited through an autosomal dominant gene. He found that in a study of 112 families, 160 of 391 parents and siblings could be considered to have had reading problems. Malmquist (1958, 1977, and chapter 20 of this book) has done a great deal of research on the reading problems of Swedish children and has concluded that "it is extremely difficult to clearly differentiate a special group of poor readers, who can be classified as dyslexic . . . The simple explanation is that such a specific group of poor readers does not exist . . . a reading disability should be regarded as a phenomenon which falls within the framework of normal variation."

Malmquist (1973) asserted that Sweden has had special classes for children with reading disabilities in the regular schools since 1938. They were called "word blind classes," but are now termed "remedial reading classes." In 1947 there were no reading clinics in Stockholm, but there were 22 remedial-reading classes. By 1972 the remedial classes had increased to 159 and there were also 72 reading clinics in the first nine school grades. The less-severe cases receive several hours a week of individual or small-group tuition in these clinics. Similar developments have taken place throughout Sweden. Since 1964 primary teachers have two paid, regularly scheduled hours each week to help children individually with their reading problems. For very severe difficulties, special help is available.

Denmark

In Denmark Edith Norrie established the Word-Blind Institute about 1931. She had been unable to learn to read in school and subsequently taught herself to read. She therefore used her self-teaching methods as a basis for developing a program for teaching others who were similarly afflicted.

Knud Herman (1959) was chief of the neurological unit of the University Hospital in Copenhagen. He found that about 10 percent of the children seen in his clinic were severely retarded in reading, but that they appeared to be of normal intelligence. Herman noted from the literature that from 10 to 20 percent of hard-core-disabled readers were being reported in England, Germany, and Sweden. He concluded from his studies that the children with reading problems could be divided into two main groups: primary or congenital word-blindness and secondary word-blindness derived from trauma, disease, or contributing environmental factors. Jansen and colleagues (1976) have summarized the educational system in Denmark. Nine years of compulsory education begin for the child at 7 years of age, with school 5 days per week, forty weeks per year. About 5 percent of the school population attend private schools, and 1 percent are educated in twenty-four-hour institutions. In 1971-1972, almost 11 percent of the children in grades one to ten were receiving some form of special education.

The elementary school law of 1973 relates to the education of children with learning difficulties: "children whose development requires special consideration and support, should be rendered special instruction or some other kind of special pedagogical assistance." Even though there is no requirement for classification according to the type of learning problems, in practice, special education is based on a system of categories. The prevalence of reading retardation is estimated at about 5 percent, while the incidence (percentage who have received assistance at any time during the school year) is from 15 to 20 percent.

In elementary schools, supplementary instruction is given either in special classes or special schools. "Seventy-five percent of the children given special education remain in their regular classes while getting supplementary lessons for 2 to 5 hours per week in groups or in individual instruction in a clinic" (Jansen et al. 1976).

Studies of children with behavior disorders severe enough to require special education were done in 1969 and 1971. It was found that over 2 percent of the children were in this category, the ratio of boys to girls being three to one in 1969 and six to one in 1971. Special education for these children was decreed by the Ministry of Education in 1972.

In Denmark the elementary-school teachers usually remain with their classes for about five years. If a child has serious difficulties, the teacher refers the child to the school psychological office, which is staffed with three school psychologists, two clinical psychologists, a social worker, and advisers for each type of handicap. If necessary, assistance from experts in ancillary professions may be requested.

Since Danish society is considered to be relatively homogeneous, the school psychologist evaluates the pupil's reaction to the demands placed on him, that is, his relationships with his teacher, schoolmates, friends, and so on. The teacher and the psychologist cooperate in this diagnosis. For the children with reading difficulties, diagnostic instruction is developed. This consists of continuing analysis of the child's reaction to the instruction and corrections made in the teaching methods as required. Three-fourths of the learning-handicapped children remain in their regular classes and go to a separate room for supplementary instruction. The remaining one-fourth are in full-time special classes, with an average of nine children in each class.

Austria

In Austria a neurologist, Joseph Gerstmann, has been considered to be the first person to describe the syndrome of learning disorders derived from neurological dysfunctions (Herman 1959). The Gerstmann syndrome, described in 1924, includes left and right disorientation, finger agnosia (inability to tell which finger has been touched), loss of ability to write (agraphia), and loss of ability to do mathematics (acalculia). It has been suggested that the children with developmental Gerstmann syndrome, who generally have greater retardation in spelling than reading, might be reacting to difficulties of linear sequencing.

Kowarik (1976) stated that, after World War II, the Vienna Psychological Consulting Service to Public Schools, directed by Schenk-Danziger, started to develop special aid to dyslexic pupils. A few special classes were established for dyslexics in Vienna schools, and after a while it became apparent that these classes were creating many negative side effects. Therefore, in 1962 Viennese schools turned to having special groups instead of full-time classes for students with reading problems at both the primary and secondary levels in public schools. In 1956 Schenk-Danziger tested 1,402 Viennese second-graders, and the tests were evaluated. Excluding repeaters, it was found that 4 percent had severe reading problems and 18 percent were considered to be mild dyslexics. The ratio of boys to girls among the severe dyslexics was two to one. Subsequently, it was found that rural children had even higher rates of reading problems than these Viennese children.

Norway

In Norway Vik (1976) stated that approximately 11 percent of all first- and second-graders require some type of remedial reading instruction. Gjessing (1958) reported that 3 to 4 percent of schoolchildren will need assistance in clinics or special classes, while about 7 percent will require extra help in the regular classrooms. Hans-Jorgen Gjessing, a psychologist, is credited with doing the pioneer work on the study of children with learning disabilities in Norway. Based on his research, Gjessing grouped the disabled readers into five categories and developed remedial programs for each. His groupings were:

1. Auditory dyslexia.
2. Visual dyslexia.
3. Auditory-visual dyslexia.
4. Emotional dyslexia.
5. Educational dyslexia.

Gjessing defined dyslexia as synonymous with reading-writing difficulties. Most children with reading problems fell into the first three categories. Gjessing developed a complete treatment plan for each type of dyslexia, which is in common use throughout Norway. Auxiliary education had been provided for children with moderate reading problems for about 75 years when it became compulsory in the School Act of 1955. The Elementary and Secondary School Act of 1959 stated that special educational help was mandatory for children who had difficulty keeping up with their classmates, regardless of the reason, provided the problems were not severe enough to require a special class program or a special school (Vik 1976).

Germany

Klasen (1976) summarized the situation in Germany:

> In psychology the American influence is quite impressive. Behaviorism, learning theories, behavior modification, group dynamics, sensitivity training, nondirective psychotherapy as well as research on intelligence, and cognitive and early learning are on the Germany psychology market. In a 1971 catalogue of newly announced books 55 percent were of American origin.

> In education the picture is much the same. The controversial American authors . . . became widely known and quoted in Germany! . . . These theories are no longer accepted by most American psychologists. . . . Unfortunately, many an American project, innovation, or "scientific" finding is published and hailed in Germany without understanding how limited and insubstantial it is, or how seriously questioned it may be in America.

We quote this statement because we believe, from our observations, that other countries have had similar unfortunate experiences.

In the Federal Republic of Germany (West Germany) about 6.6 percent of the children are considered to be in the exceptional category, as compared with 10 to 12 percent in the United States. Nevertheless, the learning-disability group has been estimated to be between 2 and 20 percent. Since assistance to schoolchildren came primarily from church and humanitarian groups in Germany during the past century, the Federal Republic has not established a uniform law or system for the rehabilitation of handicapped children. "A group of German educators, after visiting special schools in other European countries in 1966, said that the special school system in the Federal Republic, with the exception of schools for the blind and the deaf, still requires considerable development" (Klasen 1976). In about 1950 awareness of the problem of children with reading and writing deficiencies began, and by about 1975 an awareness of the minimal-brain-injured category developed. The concept of dyscalculia (mathematics disability) tends to be relatively restricted. An investigation in 1970 determined that one-third of 295 slow learners could be classified as having *Leserechtschreibschwäche* (LRS), or reading-writing weakness. One of the first LRS remedial programs was begun in 1972 in a medium-sized city. Slow but steady progress is being made throughout the Federal Republic in developing special programs for the LRS pupils.

Belgium

Klees (1976) said: "A disturbing feature of school performance in Belgium is that 48 percent of the children find it difficult to reach the final year of primary school without repeating either one, two, or even three years. This percentage does not include children attending special classes." About 7 to 8 percent of the children attend special classes, which have been organized by the state, provinces, communes, or independent schools. Eight types of special education are provided:

1. Slightly mentally retarded.
2. Moderately and severely mentally retarded.
3. Behavioral problems.
4. Physically handicapped.
5. Children who are ill.
6. Visually impaired.
7. Hearing impaired.
8. Instrumentally impaired (learning disabilities).

Very few schools in Belgium provide special education for children with learning disabilities. The existence of learning disabilities per se tends to be disputed in the French psychoeducational literature, and children's difficulties in school are generally considered to be the result of emotional problems due to poor child-family or child-school relations. In order to study the problem of children with global learning disabilities, special classes were established at the Saint Pierre Hospital, associated with the University of Brussels, in 1970. The children attending the special research and educational program were diagnosed as having instrumental impairments (*troubles spécifiques du développement*). "Instrumental handicaps include perceptual, psychomotor, and linguistic impairments, that occur in the presence of normal visual and auditory acuity and include auditory, visual, kinesthetic, and tactile perceptual dysfunction as well as visual-motor, psychomotor, speech and language disabilities" (Klees 1976).

Hungary

Illés and Meixner (1976) have summarized the situation in Hungary. Only children with vision and hearing impairments have special nursery schools and different vocational training available. In general, special education is available to children from six to fourteen years of age. Children with learning disabilities are to be found in the regular schools and in schools for the educable mentally retarded. "Although the scientific notion of legasthenia was introduced by a Hungarian, Paul Ranschburg, in the first decade of the century, the educational care of learning disabled children is still relatively undeveloped in Hungary. There are no special classes or special schools for these children" (Illés and Meixner 1976).

Some assistance is afforded children with various types of handicaps by the compulsory school-maturity examinations, which were instituted in 1965, beginning with a medical diagnosis of physical maturity, and in 1966 were extended to include maturity of the psychological functions. Immature children who are classified as somatically retarded but not mentally retarded may remain in kindergarten for an extra year. Those classified as having abnormal ability profiles and developmental retardation, but who are not mentally retarded, may be placed in the experimental correctional-remedial classes in the regular schools, of which there were 115 in 1972-1973. The children who succeed in these remedial classes go to regular classes, and those who fail are sent to a school for educable mentally retarded (EMR) children.

Finland

Syvälahti (1976) reported that, in Finland, special instruction for children with reading and writing disabilities began in 1949 with two classes in Helsinki for Finnish-speaking elementary-school children. Both Finnish and Swedish are official languages in Finland, with about 7 percent of the population speaking Swedish. The special classes were converted to reading clinics in 1950. By 1965 there were seven reading-clinic teachers throughout Finland. In 1968 there were eighteen clinic teachers, and by 1973 there were nearly three hundred, some of whom were also speech therapists.

In 1968 it was estimated that between 9 and 22 percent of the children encountered reading and writing difficulties, depending on where they lived. In Espoo, 14.8 percent of the pupils in grades two through eight required extra help in reading and writing. It was estimated that about 10 percent of the children in regular elementary classes were in need of extra instruction.

Ireland

Kellaghan (1976) reported that, in Ireland, surveys made in 1962 and 1966 indicated that over one-third of the elementary-school pupils were one or more grades below the achievement levels their teachers expected for students of their age levels. Tests of attainment in English were carried out in 1964 and 1969, using English norms based on a mean of 100 and a standard deviation of 15. In Dublin the ten- and eleven-year-old children, on the average, scored thirteen points below the British mean. About 25 percent of Irish children were reported by their teachers as having difficulty in English, 48 percent as having difficulty with arithmetic, and 50 percent as having difficulty in Irish, which is a compulsory second language in all schools.

There are no services specifically for nonretarded children with learning disabilities, but these children do benefit from the services that are provided for other categories of children. Most of the help for children comes from clinics that provide services for schoolchildren. In 1975 there were fourteen clinics in the Dublin area and three for the rest of the country. These clinics are staffed by psychologists, psychiatrists, social workers, speech therapists, and diagnostic and remedial teachers. The number of cases seen per month averaged sixty-five for the Dublin clinics.

France

The French Revolution of 1789 gave birth to the ideal that every child had a right to an elementary education in the vernacular (Ruthman 1973). Ruthman further stated that the French system of education has been widely followed by many nations, including many of the developing countries, because "it does not require time-consuming democratic experimentation and it quickly produces, under strict government control, a professional elite." He pointed out that the curriculum in the French schools is precisely prescribed by the Ministry of Education in terms of the number of hours per day and week to be spent by the teacher on each subject, as well as the teaching materials to be used. For example, in the first grade the teacher must spend ten hours each week on reading, based on two hours each day of reading instruction, composed of two thirty-minute lessons in the morning and two thirty-minute lessons in the afternoon. It is prescribed that writing must take two fifteen-minute lessons daily, and these must be integrated with reading. Language consisting of "spelling, elocution, recitation and vocabulary" must also supplement the reading instruction for two and one-half hours each week. The most important teaching on school entry is reading. It is said that it is possible for someone at the

Ministry of Education to state precisely what all the teachers in the same grade are teaching throughout France at a given hour and day in certain subject areas.

Ruthman indicated that the four-year normal schools include courses in methods of teaching science, arithmetic, art, music, and physical education, but that there are no courses in methods of teaching language arts or reading. Yet, in primary school, "the basic criterion for promotion is fluency in oral reading." Moreover, in 1959 Rene Zazzo reported that 50 percent of eighth-grade children had repeated one or more grades and that 10 percent of first-grade children had not learned to read at all, while 30 percent could not read fluently. Mélékian (see chapter 12) states that about half of the fifth-graders have been repeaters, and that about 5 percent of the children in primary school are dyslexics. These figures tend to be similar to those reported from French-speaking Belgium earlier in this chapter.

In France the universities do not have education departments and consequently do not do research on such educational problems as reading. However, the Ministry of Education has a research section, and some educators, physicians, and psychologists have been engaged in educational research. The study of pupil nonpromotion and reading and spelling problems has been undertaken by several researchers. For some years Mira Stambak had been studying the problem of reading disabilities, but in 1976 she told us that her entire attention was shifted to the much greater problem of pupil nonpromotion in the public schools. Stambak was in charge of the Institut National de Recherche et de Documentation Pedagogiques under the Ministry of Education in Paris. At that time she had found that teachers rarely communicated with the pupils who were failing, but rather tended to call on those who knew the answers. Research was under way to correct this problem, with the hope that it might also positively affect the learning of the backward students.

Greenland

Bent Wenstrup (see chapter 13) reports that the official languages in Greenland are Danish and Greenlandic. For many years the children, who may speak Greenlandic at home, have been taught in Danish, to a great extent by Danish teachers who could not communicate in Greenlandic. After the compulsory nine years of schooling, many children attend boarding schools locally or in Denmark for further education.

Special education was instituted in Greenland in1967, and about 10 percent of the children in public schools are now receiving special eduational assistance. Special education is available to children with speech, visual, and auditory deficits; to mentally retarded children; to those with reading problems; and to children who for other reasons are unable to benefit from regular education. Since there are no special schools, the children are integrated in elementary school and are given extra help within the school. Assessment of a child's problems is made by a well-trained school psychologist, and a conference is held in which all of the teachers involved and, if possible, the parents participate. Most children remain in their regular classes and receive extra assistance, although about 10 percent of those receiving special education are in special classes. Consideration is given to a pupil's linguistic background and development when initiating a program of special education.

Great Britain

Although many of the original findings about dyslexia are attributable to British physicians, specific reading difficulties are not considered among the eleven handicapping conditions that require special educational treatment in Great Britain. In 1979 the World Association of Learning Disabilities and Dyslexic Organizations (WALDDO) was formed in San Francisco during the International Conference of the Association for Children and Adults with Learning Disabilities (ACLD). Lord Renwick, chairman of the British Dyslexia Association, was elected chairman of WALDDO. Lord Renwick said that the purpose of WALDDO was to collate and disseminate evidence of successful changes of attitude toward the problems of the learning-disabled in our respective countries and to ascertain and report on improving provisions for individuals so handicapped. His primary concern was to change the attitudes of educators and others toward the concept of specific learning disabilities and thereby to get programs for those afflicted, since Great Britain and most other nations did not appear to recognize the problem and very few countries had developed programs for dyslexics.

Critchley (1970) stated that the "detailed and erudite" British research by Burt, Schonell, Vernon, Monroe, and others rarely mentioned the organically determined defects in reading described by neurologists. He termed the educationalists "both muddled and opinionated" and said that they have also been wrong by addressing more attention to "etiology than cure."

In Great Britain, as elsewhere, there continues to be serious disagreement over incidence, etiology, and terminology. The Tizard report, cited by Gessert (1976), states that specific reading disabilities describe "the problems of the small group of children" with reading and perhaps writing, spelling, and arithmetic difficulties.

In Great Britain much of the literature on reading disabilities has been categorized under *dyslexia,* probably due to the influence of both the neurological literature and the British Dyslexia Association, which was formed in 1966. This group, which consists largely of the parents and teachers of children with reading problems, has worked strenuously to aid the dyslexics in the British population. However, since both parents and teachers tend to believe that education is best left to professionally qualified persons, parental pressure did not win programs for their children as it did in the United States (which may well be the only country where parental pressure can effect political and educational changes of such magnitude).

Gessert asserted that the large, well-established organizations tend to be most effective in supporting recognition of educational-handicapping conditions and research into these areas. The Invalid Children's Aid Association (ICAA) assisted in founding the Word Blind Centre, and along with the National Society for Mentally Handicapped Children has supported research on teaching children with reading difficulties.

Children start infant school in Great Britain at the early ages of four and five years, when reading, writing, and arithmetic are begun. They advance from infant school to the junior school at about seven or eight years of age, when they are expected to be able to use the skills previously acquired. Secondary school begins at age eleven, after leaving the junior school. These children enter schools from one to three years earlier than in most other countries, where children start school at age six, or at age seven or even eight, as in Greenland. Children who fail to learn to read in the infant schools are at risk if the teachers feel that they will grow out of their problems, and the junior-school teachers maintain that it is not their responsibility to teach basic reading skills. This same problem occurs in many countries and tends to be exacerbated by the fact that teachers above the primary level often have not been trained to teach basic reading skills.

In Scotland Clark (1970) made a survey of reading deficits in the primarily industrialized urban area of county Dunbarton. After two years of school it was found that 11 percent of the seven-year-old children with IQs at least in the normal range (above 90 on either the Wechsler Verbal or Performance scales) had reading quotients of 85 or less on the Schonell Graded Word Reading Test. Two years later 6.3 percent of the total population were reading one or more years below grade level, and 1.2 percent, primarily boys, were reading two or more years below expectation.

Rutter, Tizard, and Whitmore (1970) tested children on the Isle of Wight, about four miles off the south coast of England. Children "specifically retarded in reading" were defined as those who were twenty-eight months or more below their expected reading level based on mental age. Of the total nine- and ten-year-old group tested, about 5.7 percent proved to be specifically retarded in reading. After two years retesting indicated that these children were all still reading below their age levels.

In Great Britain children are examined by a physician at about six weeks, six months, and twelve months of age and yearly thereafter, and detailed records are kept, which are available to school psychologists and physicians. It is claimed that children who are at risk are noted and supervised most carefully. However, Gauntlett (see chaper 7) notes that dyslexics have not been diagnosed and appear to be falling through the open mesh of the medical sieve. This most likely occurs because there is no medical diagnostic category of dyslexia or specific learning disabilities that is generally recognized (especially in medical training), and if no category exists, the condition cannot be diagnosed by physicians (or psychologists or educators). This type of inflexibility tends to be a human condition found almost everywhere.

Psychological services are available for children with severe reading problems. However, the school psychologists each cover a fairly large number of schools, and they tend to miss the diagnosis of either dyslexia or specific reading disabilities, probably due to the nonexistence of these categories, with the untoward results so graphically described by Gauntlett. This is not to say that diagnostic category is of paramount importance: rather, it holds true that if adequate remedial measures are available for children with reading difficulties, the questions of etiology and diagnostic label become irrelevant. Nevertheless, correct understanding of the etiology of the condition might make preventive measures possible.

In the schools of Great Britain there are, of course, remedial programs for students with reading difficulties at both the primary and secondary levels. In 1975 there were about seventy special classes in London for children with severe reading problems at the elementary level. At the secondary level there are services within schools as well as mobile teachers. A major problem there, as everywhere, is the adequate training of the remedial-reading teachers, as well as special training for regular classroom teachers, since most children with reading problems tend to remain in regular classes because of the overwhelming numbers involved.

There are also several facilities for assessment of children with learning problems in hospital settings. For example, in 1964 the Newcomen Clinic was opened for diagnostic evaluations, and it has recently added a remedial-teaching unit. There are also a number of remedial-reading centers that have been opened in connection with the work of the British Dyslexia Association. Recently, this association has greatly expanded its influence and work. In 1978 the *Dyslexia Review* appeared, published jointly by the Dyslexia Institute at Staines and the Department of Applied Psychology at the University of Aston. The Symposium on Dyslexia held at Manchester University in 1978 included papers from a number of universities and dyslexia units, indicating considerable recognition of the problem and research on dyslexia. The indications are most encouraging.

Poland

Zakrzewska (see chapter 19) has summarized the developments in Poland. In the 1930s, research began on the problems of specific reading and writing disabilities. After World War II, in the late 1950s, the Department of Mental Hygiene and Child Psychiatry of the Polish Academy of Sciences undertook intensive research, along both theoretical and practical lines, into the problem of dyslexia. At the same time the University of Warsaw's Department of Psychology instituted a similar program of research. In the 1960s remedial-reading and writing programs were introduced based on these research efforts, "using both didactic and psychomotor aspects of education."

Remediation of children with reading and writing deficits is done in two programs: "compensatory groups within the elementary school" and, for more serious problems, "classes at educational vocational centers or mental health dispensaries." In chapter 19 Zakrzewska presents Poland's remedial programs in some detail, indicating the theoretical considerations as well as the diagnostic methods used and the practical educational techniques employed. These programs have been worked out in great detail for both the assessing psychologists and the remedial teachers.

Yugoslavia

Yugoslavia is composed of six republics and two autonomous provinces, each of which is responsible for its own educational system (see chapter 23). Since World War II elementary schooling has been compulsory from ages seven to fifteen years. Originally, "developmental" classes had been instituted for the children who were not able to keep up. These classes have been supplanted by specially organized supplementary schoolwork and special schools for those who cannot manage with this extra tutoring.

In 1960 regulations were issued establishing the conditions for enrolling in special schools children who had deficiencies in sight and speech or hearing, or who had physical disabilities or mental retardation. In 1973 the regulation was amended to include "children with behavioral disorders of organic ediology." Laws have been passed in some of the republics requiring special education to be available to all children who need such help.

A movement is in progress to reintegrate special-education children into the regular schools when possible. And "an education is to be available to every child, even those who have minimal subjective prerequisites." *Learning disabilities* is a new category and has been defined as "children who, in spite of average or above average intellectual abilities, are not successful in school." Learning disabilities are seen as stemming from minor disorders of the sensory apparatus, emotional disturbances, anemia, retarded maturation, and the like, and appear primarily to affect reading and arithmetic, but may also affect other functions in the entire range of learning abilities.

Several studies, published in 1973, showed from 8.7 to 16 percent of the pupils with reading and writing disorders, and a study in Zagreb found 9.7 percent of 421 pupils tested to have dyslexia. In 1974 data from a study of 10,000 school children indicated that 5.6 percent of the children had "minimal cerebral dysfunction" and large percentages had speech defects or were neurotic. A symposium was held in 1972 in Zagreb with the purpose of calling attention to the "existence of dyslexia . . . among children and adults, and stimulating work on diagnosis and systematic treatment of the disorders." It was also recommended that teachers receive refresher courses to acquaint them with methods of remediation. The assessment and remediation of children with reading and writing problems are discussed in detail in chapter 23.

Union of Soviet Socialist Republics

The Russian Federated Soviet Socialist Republic supports a center in Moscow called the Institute of Defectology. This institute does research on the diagnosis and correction of children's disorders and maintains pilot educational programs with small numbers of children to develop methods of teaching handicapped children. The results of these studies are then made available to educators throughout the Soviet Union. The institute concentrates on blindness, deafness, hard-of-hearing conditions, mental retardation, motor defects, speech and language deficits, reading deficiencies, and learning disabilities. This last area was added about 1969.

The research and correctional work are performed by teams of specialists, including physicians, psychologists, speech and language therapists, and educators. The approach to an individual child's problems includes establishing a definite diagnosis and finding means of compensating for the deficit, while attempting to correct it if at all possible.

An attempt is made to provide children in special schools with about the same education that they would receive in a regular school. The concept is that the handicapped child graduating from a special school should have an education equivalent to that of children from regular schools. The difficulties inherent in accomplishing this with handicapped children are readily admitted. Handicapped children may also receive vocational higher education so that they may become productive citizens.

The government has issued instructions to the effect that handicapped children are to be assisted by early special training and home upbringing methods based on the theory that prevention of difficulties and compensation for handicaps are easiest at preschool ages. At school age there is a mandatory eight-year program to correct or compensate for the handicap. This also includes a general educational curriculum similar to regular school.

The Soviet psychologists do a great deal of testing but do not rely on quantitative psychometric test scores. Rather, they use qualitative, clinical judgments to assess a child's problems and to develop a retraining or compensatory educational program. A.R. Luria told us that he saw this as a major difference between American and Soviet psychologists. Luria (1963, 1977) made important contributions internationally to the understanding of the relationships between different areas of the brain and their functions in learning. His studies stemmed from extensive work with brain-injured soldiers in World War II and his creative work at the Moscow Institute of Defectology.

The Netherlands

Special education in The Netherlands was discussed by Dumont (1976). About 5 percent of the schoolchildren in The Netherlands are in special education, more than 75,000 of almost 1.5 million attending regular schools. Education is free and equal for all children, and schools can be established by municipalities or by private organizations at government expense. Although the law permits special classes to be formed within the regular schools, this is seldom done. Rather, special schools have proliferated.

Dumont stated: "It is striking how rapidly schools for children with learning disabilities have increased in number. These schools (in Dutch, *school voor kinderen met leer-en opvoedingsmoeilijkheden,* or LOM school) are now the fastest growing type of special schools and much of the professional attention of administrators, researchers and educators is fixed on them." In 1972, the largest numbers of special schools (of a total of 819) were as follows: for the mentally retarded, 398; for children with learning disabilities, 175; for the emotionally disturbed, 40; for the deaf and hard of hearing, 36; for the physically handicapped, 35; for those with poor health, 21; and for the blind and visually impaired, 13.

The LOM schools do not take children with severe emotional problems, but they do accept those with behavioral problems in conjunction with learning disabilities, since most children with learning deficits also have emotional problems. "Hyperactivity, impulsive behavior, anxieties, aggressiveness, lack of self-confidence, and feelings of inadequacy appear with learning disabilities."

The definition of learning disabilities used for admission to the LOM schools seems to be similar to American definitions, stressing a discrepancy between intellectual potential and scholastic achievement when the IQ is at least 90 on either the Wechsler Verbal or Performance scales. This tends to leave the "slow learners" between 80 and 90 IQ in the regular schools without special help, since retardation is defined as below 80 IQ.

Referral to the LOM school is made by an assessment team composed of a principal, a psychologist or educator, and a psychiatrist, and is based on a standard battery of tests, including intelligence, visual-motor, projective, and achievement tests, plus an examination by the psychiatrist who may order an electroencephalogram (EEG).

Basic treatment includes a "therapeutic climate," which excludes permissiveness, since this tends to make children "insecure and confused," but rather is structured, as a proper climate for remediation. The curriculum is designed to support the needs of the child and includes the basics of reading, writing, spelling, and arithmetic plus a synthesis of geography, history, and biology, as well as music, crafts, expressive language, and rhythmic movement.

References

Ayres, A.J. 1965. Patterns of perceptual-motor dysfunction in children: a factor analytic study. *Perceptual and Motor Skills* 20.

Barsch, R.H. 1967. *Achieving Perceptual-Motor Efficiency*. Seattle: Special Child Publications.

Beery, K.E. 1967. *Developmental Test of Visual-Motor Integration*. Chicago: Follett.

Chalfant, J.C., and Scheffelin, M.A. 1969. *Central Processing Dysfunction in Children*. National Institute of Neurological Diseases and Stroke Monograph No. 9. Washington, D.C.: Superintendent of Documents.

Clark, M. 1970. *Reading Difficulties in Schools*. Harmandsworth, Great Britain: Penguin.

Clements, S.D. 1966. *Minimal Brain Dysfunction in Children: Terminology and Identification*. U.S. Department of Health, Education and Welfare, NINDB Monograph No. 3. Washington, D.C.: Superintendent of Documents.

Cox, A. 1967. *Structures and Techniques: Multisensory Teaching of Basic Language Skills*. Cambridge, Mass.: Educators Publishing Service.

Cratty, B.J. 1967. *Developmental Sequences of Developmental Tasks*. Freeport, Long Island: Educational Activities.

Critchley, M. 1970. *The Dyslexic Child*. London: William Heinemann.

Cruikshank, W.M., Bentzen, F.A., Ratzeburg, F.H. and Tannhauser,

M.T. 1961. *A Teaching Method for Brain-injured and Hyperactive Children: A Demonstration-pilot study*. Syracuse: Syracuse University Press.

Cruickshank, W.M., Bice, M., and Wallen, N. 1957. *Perception and Cerebral Palsy*. Syracuse: Syracuse University Press.

Dejerine, J. 1892. Contribution a l'étude anatamo-pathologique et clinique des differentes varietes de cecite berbale. *Memoirs de la Societé de Biologie* 4:61.

Delacato, C.H. 1959. *The Treatment and Prevention of Reading Problems: The Neurological Approach*. Springfield, Ill.: Thomas.

Denhoff, E., and Robinault, I.P. 1960. *Cerebral Palsy and Related Disorders*. New York: McGraw-Hill.

Denhoff, E., and Tarnopol, L. 1971. Medical responsibilities in learning disorders. In L. Tarnopol (ed.), *Learning Disorders in Children: Diagnosis, Medication, Education*. Boston: Little, Brown.

Dumont, J.J. 1976. Learning disabilities in the Netherlands. In L. Tarnopol and M. Tarnopol (eds.), *Reading Disabilities: An International Perspective*. Baltimore: University Park Press.

Eisenson, J. 1946. *Examining for Aphasia*. New York: Psychological Corporation.

Fernald, G.M. 1943. *Remedial Techniques in Basic School Subjects*. New York: McGraw-Hill.

Frostig, M., and Horne, D. 1964. *The Frostig Program for the Development of Visual Perception*. Chicago: Follett.

Frostig, M., Lefever, D., and Whittlesey, J. 1964. *The Marianne Frostig Developmental Test of Visual Perception*. Palo Alto: Consulting Psychologists.

Gessert, B. 1976. Specific reading difficulties in Great Britain. In L. Tarnopol and M. Tarnopol (eds.), *Reading Disabilities: An International Perspective*. Baltimore: University Park Press.

Getman, G.N. 1965. The visuomotor complex in the acquisition of learning. In J. Hellmuth (ed.), *Learning Disorders, Vol. 1*. Seattle: Special Child Publications.

Gillingham, A., and Stillman, B.W. 1960. *Remedial Training for Children with Specific Disability in Reading, Spelling, and Penmanship*. Cambridge, Mass.: Educators Publishing Service.

Gjessing, H. 1958. *En Studie av Lesemodenhet ved Skolegangens begynnelse*. Oslo: Cappelens.

Gofman, H. 1969. The physician's role in early diagnosis and management of learning disabilities. In L. Tarnopol (ed.), *Learning Disabilities: Introduction to Educational and Medical Management*. Springfield, Ill.: Thomas.

Goldstein, K. 1939. *The Organism*. New York: American Book.

Hallgren, B. 1950. Specific dyslexia: a clinical and genetic study. *Acta Psychiatrica et Neurologica,* Supplement 65. Copenhagen.

Haring, N.G., et. al. 1969. *Minimal Brain Dysfunction in Children: Educational, Medical and Health Related Services. Phase Two of a Three-Phase Project.* U.S. Department of Health, Education and Welfare, Public Health Service Publication No. 2015. Washington, D.C.: Superintendent of Documents.

Hathaway, E. 1970. *The Teaching Box.* Cambridge, Mass.: Educators Publishing Service.

Herman, K. 1959. *Reading Disability.* Springfield, Ill.: Thomas.

Hinshelwood, J. 1895. Word-blindness and visual memory. *Lancet* 2.

_____ . 1917. *Congenital Word Blindness.* London: H.K. Lewis.

Illés, S., and Meixner, I. 1976. Learning and reading disabilities in Hungary. In L. Tarnopol and M. Tarnopol (eds.), *Reading Disabilities: An International Perspective.* Baltimore: University Park Press.

Jackson, E. 1906. Developmental alexia (congenital word-blindness). *American Journal Medical Sciences* 131:843-849.

Jansen, M., Søegård, A., Hansen, M., and Glaesel, B. 1976. Special education in Denmark. In L. Tarnopol and M. Tarnopol (eds.), *Reading Disabilities: An International Perspective.* Baltimore: University Park Press.

Kellaghan, T. 1976. Learning disabilities in Ireland. In L. Tarnopol and M. Tarnopol (eds.), *Reading Disabilities: An International Perspective.* Baltimore: University Park Press.

Kephart, N.C. 1960. *The Slow Learner in the Classroom.* Columbus: Merrill.

Klasen, E. 1972. *The Syndrome of Specific Dyslexia.* Baltimore: University Park Press.

_____ . 1976. Learning disabilities: the German perspective. In L. Tarnopol and M. Tarnopol (eds.), *Reading Disabilities: An International Perspective.* Baltimore: University Park Press.

Klees, M. 1976. Learning disabilities in Belgium. In L. Tarnopol and M. Tarnopol (eds.), *Reading Disabilities: An International Perspective.* Baltimore: University Park Press.

Knights, R.M., Kronick, D., and Cunningham, J. 1976 Learning disabilities in Canada: a survey of educational and research programs. In L. Tarnopol and M. Tarnopol (eds.), *Reading Disabilities: an International Perspective.* Baltimore: University Park Press.

Kowarik, O. 1976. Reading-writing problems in Austria. In L. Tarnopol and M. Tarnopol (eds.), *Reading Disabilities: An International Perspective.* Baltimore: University Park Press.

Luria, A.R. 1963. *Restoration of Brain Functions after War Trauma.* Oxford: Pergamon Press.

———— . 1977. Cerebral organization of conscious acts: a frontal lobe function. In L. Tarnopol and M. Tarnopol (eds.), *Brain Function and Reading Disabilities*. Baltimore: University Park Press.

Malmquist, E. 1958. *Factors Related to Reading Disabilities in the First Grade of Elementary School*. Stockholm: Almqvist and Wiksell.

———— . 1973. Sweden. In J. Downing (ed.), *Comparative Reading*. New York: Macmillan.

———— . 1977. *Läs-och Skrivsvårigheter hos Barn*. Lund, Sweden: Liber Läromedel.

Matějček, Z. 1976. Dyslexia in Czechoslovakian children. In L. Tarnopol and M. Tarnopol (eds.), *Reading Disabilities: An International Perspective*. Baltimore: University Park Press.

McCarthy, J.J., and Kirk, S.A. 1961. *Illinois Test of Psycholinguistic Abilities*. Urbana: University of Illinois.

Morgan, W.P. 1896. A case of congenital word blindness. *British Medical Journal* 2:1378

Myklebust, H.R. 1964. *The Psychology of Deafness*. New York: Grune and Stratton.

Oliphant, G. 1977. *Sounds and Symbols*. Cambridge, Mass.: Educators Publishing Service.

O'Reilly, R. 1965. CANHC and the NH child. *California Parent-Teacher* (September).

Orton, S.T. 1925. "Word blindness" in school children. *Archives of Neurology and Psychiatry* 14:581-615.

———— . 1928. Specific reading disability—strephosymbolia. *Journal American Medical Association* 90:1095-1099.

———— . 1937. *Reading, Writing, and Speech Problems in Children*. New York: Norton.

Peters, J.E., Clements, S.D., Danford, B.H., Dykman, R.A., and Reese, W.G. 1967. A Special Neurological Examination for Children with Minimal Brain Dysfunctions (mimeographed). Little Rock: University of Arkansas Medical Center.

Ranschburg, P. 1916. Die Leseschwäche (Legasthenie) und Rechenschwäche (Arithemie), der Kinder im Lichte des Experiments. *Abh. aus. d. Grenzgeb. Paed. Med. (Berlin)*.

Rome, P., and Osman, J. 1972. *Language Tool Kit*. Cambridge, Mass.: Educators Publishing Service.

Ruthman, P. 1973. France. In J. Downing (ed.), *Comparative Reading*. New York: Macmillan.

Rutter, M., Tizard, J., and Whitmore, K. 1970. *Education, Health, and Behavior*. London: Longman.

Saunders, R., Gialas, A., and Hofler, D. 1969. *Links to Writing, Reading and Spelling*. Cambridge, Mass.: Educators Publishing Service.

Slingerland, B. 1971. *A Multi-Sensory Approach to Language Arts for Specific Language Disability Children: A Guide for Primary Teachers.* Cambridge, Mass.: Educators Publishing Service.

Strauss, A.A., and Lehtinen, L.E. 1947. *Psychopathology and Education of the Brain Injured Child.* New York: Grune and Stratton.

Strauss, A.A., and Werner, H. 1938. Deficiency in finger schema in relation to arithmetic ability. *American Jounral of Orthopsychiatry* 8:719-724.

Strother, C.R. 1973. Minimal cerebral dysfunction: a historical overview. In F.F. de la Cruz, B. Fox, and R.H. Roberts (eds.), *Minimal Brain Dysfunction.* New York: *Annals New York Academy of Sciences* 205.

Syvälahti, R. 1976. Reading-writing disabilities in Finland. In L. Tarnopol and M. Tarnopol (eds.), *Reading Disabilities: An International Perspective.* Baltimore: University Park Press.

Tarnopol, L. (ed.). 1969. *Learning Disabilities: Introduction to Educational and Medical Management.* Springfield, Ill.: Thomas.

———. 1970. Delinquency and minimal brain dysfunction. *Journal of Learning Disabilities* 3:4.

Tarnopol, L., Breed, J.S., Tarnopol, M., and Ozaki, M. 1977. Learning disabilities in minority adolescents. *Bulletin of the Orton Society* 27.

Tarnopol, L., and Tarnopol, M. (eds.). 1976. *Reading Disabilities: An International Perspective.* Baltimore: University Park Press.

Vik, G.H. 1976. Reading disabilities in Norwegian elementary grades. In L. Tarnopol and M. Tarnopol (eds.), *Reading Disabilites: An International Perspective.* Baltimore: University Park Press.

Wagner, R.F. 1973. Rudolf Berlin: originator of the term dyslexia. *Bulletin of the Orton Society* 23.

Wepman, J. 1958. *Wepman Auditory Discrimination Test.* Chicago: Chicago Language Research Associates.

3

Summary of Comparative Reading and Learning Difficulties: Australia, New Zealand, Central and South America, Africa, and Asia

Lester Tarnopol and
Muriel Tarnopol

Developments in Australia and New Zealand

Hagger and Stewart (1976) have summarized developments in Australia. The Commonwealth of Australia collects most of the taxes from the people and reimburses the states according to an agreed-upon formula. Education accounts for about 27 percent of the state budgets, the largest single slice. At the national level, Australia "spent only 4.3 percent of its gross national product on education in 1970—a lower proportion than in most industrialized nations." Twenty-two percent of Australian children were attending nongovernmental schools, mostly Catholic parish schools with low budgets and therefore unable to afford special education.

After the poliomyelitis epidemic of 1938, Dame Jean Macnamara, a Melbourne pediatrician, became interested in the education of spastic children and later, when working with the victims of cerebral palsy, "came to realize that there was a group of apparently intelligent children, some, but not all, of whom were spastic, whom she referred to as having the 'can't read, can't spell' syndrome." Dr. Macnamara communicated her information to Mona Tobias, a state education department teacher who had been doing successful home teaching as a volunteer with the poliomyelitis victims. In the late 1950s, Dr. Macnamara gave Miss Tobias a copy of the Gillingham reading program, which she had obtained from the United States, bringing to her attention the work of Orton, Gillingham, and Stillman.

In 1951 a remedial-reading center was established at the University of Queensland by Professor Fred Schonell. Later a course was given at the Fred and Eleanor Schonell Educational Research Center for a Certificate in Diagnostic Testing and Remedial Teaching. This was the only course given in Australia to train remedial teachers. In 1971 the course was absorbed into a three-year Bachelor of Education degree.

Under the medical direction of Corrie Reye, researchers at the Spastic

Centre of New South Wales organized a treatment plan for the development of basic abilities in "ordinary" children. They had studied and diagnosed specific defects in cerebral-palsied children, based on normal development. Their work with cerebral-palsied children was soon extended to children with learning disabilities. By learning how children obtain information from visual observation and manipulating things, they were able to teach children how to plan appropriate movements and to pay attention (Brereton and Sattler 1967). This work added significantly to the understanding of developmental sequences and to remedial work with children with both overt and hidden handicaps.

The Queensland Association for Children with Learning Problems was formed about 1966 by parents and professionals, and in 1968 the Specific Learning Difficulties Association (SPELD) was created in New South Wales to attempt to get special educational programs for children with learning problems who were not retarded. These organizations were formed in recognition of the plight of children with neurologically based learning deficits, since this was not generally regarded as a problem by school administrators or educational psychologists. The Australian College of Speech Therapists organized the first symposium on dyslexia in Melbourne in 1968, and in 1970 the Australian Council of SPELD Associations (AUSPELD) was formed.

Hagger stated: "Australians have always been more impressed by statements from a foreign visitor than from an indigene. Added to that is the undoubted quality of the visitors; there can be no doubt of the value to the SPELD movement of the visitors Australia has had in the past few years, particularly the Tarnopols, Marianne Frostig, Sam Clements, John McLeod, Macdonald Critchley, and Barbara Bateman" (Hagger and Stewart 1976). This same problem is well-known everywhere; it is said that "a prophet is not without honor, save in his own country."

Hagger pointed to a reading attainment survey of 31,000 students entering secondary schools in Victoria in 1968. It was found that 14.7 percent of the children were three or more years retarded in reading skill, while another 16 percent were from one and one-half to three years behind. In another study by Professor R.J. Walsh of the University of New South Wales, it was determined that 7.6 percent of the boys and 1.9 percent of the girls, in a suburban school population of 462 eight-year-old children, had specific dyslexia. Children with a history of possible brain damage were excluded from this diagnosis. With such large numbers of children requiring assistance, various remedial-educational programs and centers have sprung up. The public schools appear to be overwhelmed by the problem but have not received very much extra financial assistance to meet this emergency. Western Australia seems to have made the most progress in providing remedial teachers. It had Australia's highest ratio of remedial teachers and psychologists to children. Other remedial-teaching services are located in hospitals, universities, teachers' colleges, and private facilities.

New Zealand

Mitchell and Nicholson (see chapter 18) note: "In New Zealand very few special provisions have been made for children with reading difficulties." However, it is pointed out that, on the 1970 International Reading Survey, the New Zealand fourteen-year-old children scored highest among the fourteen nations participating in the reading tests.

Since there are no local education taxes, control of the New Zealand education system is lodged in the Central Department of Education and is financed by the House of Representatives for the nation. Policy dictates that "children with special needs should be educated in ordinary classes, with support for their teachers where needed." Those requiring further assistance are helped in clinics or special classes within the regular schools.

The New Zealand Council for Educational Research has a major project under way to determine the percentage of children with specific learning disabilities. An incidence study has been made of 2,000 eleven-year-old children representative of that population who have been tested in reading, mathematics, and spelling. Present indications are that about 10 percent of the population with IQs above 85 will be found to be two or more years retarded in reading or mathematics. This percentage is sufficiently like that found in European countries to indicate that New Zealand may not be immune to the educational problems found in other developed countries.

In order to assist the children whose parents feel they are not progressing adequately in school, SPELD has been training tutors in remedial methods gleaned from the literature, and both children and adults may be tutored privately for a fee.

In recognition of the importance of learning difficulties, the Dunedin Multidisciplinary Child Development Study was organized at the Medical School of the University of Otago in Dunedin (Silva 1979). The purpose of the study was to investigate the incidence, nature, etiology, correlates, and long-term significance of learning disorders in children. The population of Dunedin was considered to be particularly suited to epidemiological and developmental studies because the effects of socioeconomic status (SES) are especially weak there since there is no significant correlation between SES and birth weight, the correlation between SES and IQ for children in especially low (0.20 to 0.25), and the population lacks extremes of SES. Therefore, the socioeconomic effects on learning would not be likely to obscure the effects of biological, other environmental, and experimental factors.

Studies published in 1975 to 1978 reiterated the fact that low birth weight and preterm delivery tend to be associated with developmental deficits. Most recently, a five-year longitudinal study was completed on the 1,037 Dunedin children born at the obstetric hospital between 1 April 1972 and 31 March 1973. These children were studied as infants, at three years, and at five years of age. One of the major concerns of this study was developmental disorders in language, because language is a major factor of intelligence and language disorders are well known precursors of learning and behavior problems.

The children were divided into three experimental groups and a control group. The four groups were composed of the children who at age three were delayed by six months or more in either verbal comprehension or expression. Experimental group 1 was given a special intervention program from ages three to four years, with follow-up preschool. Experimental group 2 received only the special intervention program from ages four to five years. Experimental group 3 started preschool early. The control group had no special program and started preschool at the usual age.

Comparisons of all four groups at ages four and five years showed no statistical difference between any of the groups in their language development at either age. The five-year well-controlled study demonstrated what all previous research had shown, namely, that maturation is the strongest factor controlling language development in young children.

It should be noted that none of these children were educationally deprived at home in their early years. The experimental results warn that it is important to remain extremely cautious and to avoid labeling maturing children with developmental deficits. Even with brain damage, it is best to avoid a pessimistic prognosis, because the central nervous system of young children is extremely flexible in terms of intact brain areas being able to take over the functions of damaged neurons.

Central and South America

Argentina

Robles Gorriti and Rodriquez Muñiz (1976) have summarized developments in Argentina. Children start compulsory education at age six, when over 90 percent of the children register for school; however, "a staggering number of children, 58.3 percent, dropped out of elementary school before graduation." According to Perelstein de Braslavsky (1973), less than half of the children in the Pampas region and Buenos Aires fail to complete the seven grades of primary school, whereas in northern agricultural regions, about 72 percent of the children are drop-outs. The percentage of drop-outs is lower in the more prosperous regions and higher in the less prosperous, and literacy and schooling are inversely related to the degree of rural populalation. Another factor in the educational system is the very large number of children repeating grades (58.8 percent).

In 1972 the National Board of Education and UNESCO collaborated on a "Program for the Promotion of Health and Education" in Argentina. The purpose was to attempt to improve the educational yield by reducing the number of grade-repeaters and drop-outs from elementary schools. Preschool testing was done on 25,000 children in Buenos Aires who were entering the first grade in 1972. Nine hundred seventy-five teachers were trained to administer a battery of tests to these children, including the Metropolitan Readiness Test, the Perspective Organization Test (Santucci), the Bender Visual Motor Gestalt Test, and Piaget's operational tests. The children were also examined by a medical team.

Approximately 35 percent of the children exhibited significant delay in maturational readiness for first grade. Special classes for children with maturational lags were to be created to prepare these children for first grade. Robles Gorriti and Rodriquez Muñiz (1976) stated: "It is our feeling that this study is beginning to modernize the concept of school readiness and will influence the future of education in Argentina."

According to Perelstein de Braslavsky, the "alphabetic" or "letter" method of teaching reading was used in the colonial days and after independence, into the nineteenth century. Toward the end of the last century, the phonic method was introduced, apparently originating in Germany. Soon afterward the whole-word method arrived from the United States, brought by North American teachers who had been hired by the first normal school in Paraná.

Thereafter, opposing camps developed, following and promoting either the global, whole-word, "look and say" method or the phonic, analytic-synthetic method of teaching reading. Another group combined these methods. The denouement of this argument was reached when Carbonell de Grampone and associates (1967) tested the two methods in Uruguay on normal children. Results favored the analytic-synthetic method at the end of the first year, but after the second year both groups were performing equally well. However, an unexpected result proved to be the most important finding of this research. Very large numbers of children had not learned to read, including 31 percent who had been taught by the whole-word method and 22 percent of the analytic-synthetic experimental group. This research revealed the real problem.

Perelstein de Braslavsky stated that for about twenty years teachers have not been receiving training in how to teach reading. Moreover, there appear to be no provisions at the universities for specialization or research in reading. The training of teachers for the remediation of dyslexic pupils has begun, but the overall problem of reading deficiencies in larger numbers of children has not been attended to. Most facilities for remediation of reading problems are in the psychiatric departments of hospitals or audio-logical services. These neuropsychiatric departments are credited with leading the way in developing diagnostic methods for learning problems and promoting remedial education.

De Quirós (1964) has been studying dysphasia and dyslexia in children as a function of vestibular disorders for a number of years. He has found fairly substantial correlations between vestibular maladies of the inner ear and learning disabilities. Such disorders can be identified in newborn in-fants, thereby alerting physicians, parents, and educators to modify their learning environments as a preventive measure.

Brazil

Brazil's educational system and problems are described by Aratangy and his colleagues (see chapter 8). The school system in Brazil consists of three parts: the first level has eight grades, the second level has three grades, and college has from four to six years. Compulsory education is from ages seven to fourteen years.

The drop-out rate is extremely high, with 54 percent leaving school at the end of the first grade. Popovic's research showed that low SES six-year-old children were functioning at the level of four-year-old middle-class children and so were not ready for school. Moreover, about one-third of the primary-school teachers had not attended school beyond the fourth grade (Popovic 1968). Remediation for children with learning disabilities is scarce in public education.

In 1977 *programma alpha* was begun to attempt to overcome the effi-ciencies of both the pupils and the teachers. This program, for grades one through three, is detailed and structured, with all teaching materials plus daily teaching routines provided for the teachers. It appears that positive results are being obtained from this program.

For children with learning disabilities, private schools and clinics are available for those who can afford them. These facilities tend to be available only in the larger cities. In 1971 the Neurology Section of the Psychology Faculty at the Catholic University of São Paulo began research on learning disabilities. Later a multidisciplinary team organized a private clinic to assess children with specific learning disabilities. The team included a neurologist, two psychologists, and a speech therapist. The tests used, the results of their research, and remedial methods are detailed in chapter 8.

Chile

Bravo-Valdivieso (see chapter 9) describes the educational situation in Chile. Although eight years of school are compulsory and free, only about 50 percent of the children entering first grade reach the eighth grade, and, on the average, about 14 percent of the children in each grade fail to pass and are repeaters. The children enter school at six years of age and must remain until fourteen years of age. The curriculum and teaching methods are determined by the centralized Ministry of Education. Four years of secondary education are available to those who complete elementary school.

As in many other countries, the massive school failures primarily affect the lower SES rural and urban children, who, at age six, are often unready for academic curricula. At the same time, the inflexibile curricula and methods of teaching are frequently more suited to the middle and upper SES children, who tend to be better prepared for school. Individualization and consideration of the cultural differences of the children are not part of the centrally directed program of education. In recognition of the high failure rate, special education for learning disabilities was begun in 1968.

Bravo-Valdivieso considers the effects of both general learning problems and specific learning disabilities in Chile, and concludes that "it is probable that the percentage of children with specific learning disabilities is greater in the underdeveloped countries, owing to poor nutrition, unsanitary conditions, less intellectual stimulation, and the like.

Schools for the deaf, blind, and emotionally disturbed were started many years ago. In 1945 several schools for the mentally retarded were established, followed by psychodiagnostic clinics in the 1950s, and in the 1960s special schools for learning disabilities appeared at pediatric hospitals. In the past ten years, 197 special schools have been opened to help children with different types of developmental deficits, servicing about 20,000 children annually. This development was for the most part due to the efforts of child psychiatrists, pediatric neurologists, and the special-education faculties of the universities. Until 1975 the pediatric hospitals bore the complete burden of both diagnosis and rehabilitation of children with developmental disturbances.

Most special-education teachers had been self-taught. However, as a result of the case conferences on individual children at hospital clinics, the teachers began to individualize their instruction to suit the needs of the children. In 1968, the Universidad Católica de Santiago began a training program in learning disabilities in the graduate school. As the result of a conference on special education in 1974, a government commission was created to explore the special education needs of children and to make recommendations. In 1975 diagnostic centers and educational-support teams were created by law in regular schools. These developements and the functioning of this system are described in detail in chapter 9.

Mexico

Nieto Herrera discusses the development of education and special education in Mexico (see chapter 17). National schools for the deaf and blind were founded in the last century, and in 1914 a school for mentally retarded children was built. In 1942 the first class for handicapped children in regular schools with special teachers formed. In the 1940s normal schools were founded to prepare teachers for the education of blind, deaf, mentally retarded, speech-impaired, and delinquent children; and in 1955 the education of children with motor problems was included. In the 1970s the normal school curriculum was expanded to include specialization in teaching children with learning disabilities.

In 1972 16 percent of the children failed first grade and 7 percent dropped out of school. Among all elementary-school children, about 11 percent failed and 5 percent left school during the school year. In 1974 1,200 children entering the first grade in the Federal District (Mexico City) were administered a developmental profile and visual-motor tests. It was found that about 35 percent of the children lacked adequate readiness for the first grade. To aid in the preparation of these children for the primary-school program, the regular teachers were given training in motor development, perceptual training, and rhythm and music therapy to be used prior to beginning reading.

Africa

Ethiopia

In Ethiopia there are more than seventy tribal languages and only five written languages, according to Starr and Starr (see chapter 11). The literacy rate is said to be about 10 percent, with the same percentage of children enrolled in school. In grades one through six the national language, Amharic, is taught; beyond grade six, instruction is in English. One problem facing these children who speak different dialects is that the government schools generally require that children be able to read Amharic before they are admitted to school, so they must first attend a private school to learn basic Amharic.

Since many children attend church schools to get their initial education, they first learn to read Ge'ez, the language in which the church literature is written. However, it is not a spoken language, so they do not learn the meanings of words, only the pronunciations. Then the children are introduced to Amharic. The Muslim children generally go to Arabic schools, however, and in some Koran schools they may start both Amharic and Arabic in the first grade.

The Ethiopian Education Sector Review, adopted in 1973, stated: "We have no plans to educate the handicapped." This is usual in developing countries with very low literacy rates, since the main thrust must be to introduce mass education. Starr and Starr review the situation in Ethiopian education in excellent detail in chapter 11.

Republic of South Africa

Logue (1976) has described learning disabilities and special education in the Republic of South Africa. The Department of National Education, under the control of a cabinet minister, determines the principles and framework for education, including special education, in South Africa. "At the present time, four-fifths of the African children, and wherever practicable, all Asian and colored children are at school." There are also special classes for slow learners. There is compulsory education for white children as well as special education for epileptic, cerebral-palsied, and physically handicapped children.

In 1968 a committee was appointed by the Minister of National Education to report on the problems and education of children with minimal brain dysfunction. The report was issued in 1969 and was tabled by the government, probably because of the immense cost of carrying out the proposals. The committee had adopted the definition of the U.S. Task Force I, as follows: "The term 'minimal brain dysfunction syndrome' refers in this paper to children of near-average, average, or above-average general intelligence with certain learning or behavioral disabilities ranging from mild to severe, which are associated with deviations of function of the central nervous system. These deviations may manifest themselves by various combinations of impairment of perception, conceptualization, language, memory, and control of attention, impulse or motor function" (Clements 1966).

Based on American estimates the committee suggested that South Africa could expect that about 15 percent of the pupils with IQs above 89 would be found to have significant learning problems, and that almost half of this population would have minimal brain dysfunction. It was estimated that about 125,000 white pupils had learning problems. For the moderately involved children (estimated at about 28,000) 280 new clinic schools, with 3,500 specialist, remedial teachers, would be required. For about 94,435 students who could remain in their regular classes, considerable expansion of the number of remedial-reading and clinic classes would be required. Finally, such facilities must also be extended to the other groups in the republic as needed. The combination of cost and lack of trained administrators, psychologists, speech and language therapists, and remedial teachers, plus a number of other considerations, undoubtedly contributed to a reluctance on the part of the Minister of National Education to rush into this program. However, the report brought the plight of many children to the attention of educators, psychologists, and physicians.

During the 1960s three full-time schools for children with learning problems appeared and at least one remedial clinic was established. At the same time, three national organizations interested in the welfare of these children were organized. The diagnosis of learning disabilities and the remedial measures used appear to have followed developments in the United States, both in scope and in lack of uniformity.

Zimbabwe (Rhodesia)

Hall (1976) described the development of the educational system in Rhodesia. "As Europeans settled in Rhodesia, they set up schools for their own children and subsequently for the indigenous African children. Many of these schools were established by religious bodies." Teachers are prepared at the teacher-training colleges and, at the graduate level, at the multiracial University of Rhodesia. All children are taught in English.

There are thirteen grades prior to entering the university, and the primary schools have seven grades. Until recently, 50 percent of the African students who graduated from primary school went on to high school, and of these one-fourth continued on to academic, university training and three-fourths received vocational training. Under the new Ministry of Education, the education of the African students will be further expanded.

Special classes have existed for mentally retarded children for some time. In the 1960s remedial teaching of children with at least average intelligence but mild academic retardation was begun with very satisfactory results. Special tutors then were appointed to visit urban junior schools, each with a caseload of about one hundred pupils. The children were seen twice a week. Part-time ex-teachers were employed to work with rural children. Children who were diagnosed as having severe learning problems were referred for treatment to the more-established South African centers in Johannesburg and Durban.

Asia

China

Chinese pictograms were developed about 1700 BCE in the area of the Yellow River. Education and the art of calligraphy have been revered in China for a great many generations. In the 1860s Mark Twain visited the Chinese colony near Virginia City, Nevada, and was constrained to write that all of the Chinese men appeard to be able to read and write in their script. He noted that it seemed incongruous that these men who were literate could not vote in the Virginia City elections, while most of the white men who were voting were illiterate and could only make their "marks."

The same Chinese characters are used with essentially the same meanings in many Asian countries. Each group reads the characters in its own language or dialect, so they can often communicate by writing but not with speech. Before the revolution in China, it was estimated that about 20 percent of the population was literate.

Hong Kong. Che Kan Leong (1973) described education in Hong Kong, a British Crown Colony. Since the early 1950s schools have been built and teachers have been educated by the Hong Kong government, so that by 1971 there was a free primary-school place available for every child. With a population of about four million people, there are more than one million students in Hong Kong.

According to Butler (1976), at age three years Chinese children enter the two-year kindergarten, where they begin to read and write Chinese characters, pronounced in Cantonese, the local language. Although education is not compulsory, from age five years most children attend at least the six-year primary school, where they learn about 3,500 characters. At the end of primary school, extremely difficult, competitive examinations are given to determine who will continue on in either the government-controlled or government-subsidized schools and who will receive scholarships to private schools.

In Hong Kong the whole-character method of learning to read is used. Butler notes that the children learn the characters by copying them from the chalkboard in the proper stroke sequence, form, and orientation, on square-lined paper. "Subsequently, the children proceed to copy more stylish forms of characters by inserting a master sheet under a transparent piece of exercise paper." Later they copy the ideograms freehand onto square-lined sheets and ultimately onto plain paper. Using the "look and say" method, new characters are written on the chalkboard and pronounced by the teacher, who explains the important features of the radical and phonetic parts of each character. Chinese-language homework is given from first grade on.

Butler states that the Department of Education provides psychological, audiological, and speech assessments. It also follows up and offers some remedial services, including special classes for slow-learning children, the blind, the deaf, the physically handicapped, and the emotionally disturbed; and in-service training is provided for their teachers. Private diagnostic and remedial facilities are also available to assist underachieving children.

People's Republic of China. Educational developments in the People's Republic of China have been described by Butler (1974, 1976). Children start elementary school at six years of age and attend school Monday through Friday from approximately 8 A.M. to 5 P.M., with a half-day on Saturday. About 80 percent of the children complete the five years of primary education, and in the cities many continue for the two years of junior middle school. However, only a few complete the next two years of senior middle school to finish the nine-year course. It is roughly estimated that 95 percent of urban and 80 percent of rural children are enrolled in primary schools, totaling 127 million pupils. Approximately 37 million are said to attend middle schools, and about 250,000 students attend the universities.

The Cultural Revolution began in 1966, when the universities were closed and the professors and staff were sent to work on farms and in factories. Education was considered to be a means of mobilizing the masses to accomplish the goals of the revolution—to achieve a unified proletarian society based on selfless endeavor rather than individual interests. In 1970 some departments of the universities reopened; however, a severe shortage of trained teachers had developed, partly as the result of the hiatus.

Schools are run by revolutionary committees composed of teachers, soldiers, students, and workers in the cities, or peasants in the rural areas. The committee tends to be all-powerful, since its administration includes the determination of courses, teaching methods, and textbooks, and there is considerable local autonomy. During primary schooling two months are usually committed each year to labor in a factory or farm or in a military unit. The selection of children to continue to the middle schools is based on political views, health, and academic performance. At higher levels of education, selection rests heavily on recommendations by fellow workers.

The methods of teaching Chinese in the People's Republic are similar to those in Hong Kong. Butler (1976) states: "Like the golf grip, the brush grip is unnatural and needs practice. In the early stages of using the brush, the teacher holds the pupil's hand to guide him to achieve the correct grip. It is not unknown for the teacher to occasionally try, without warning, to knock the brush out of the child's hand to test the child's grip. The children receive intensive practice by tracing lightly printed sets of characters."

The children master about 3,000 characters in the five primary years. Chinese literature is introduced early, with stories of revolutionary heroes and how life is now greatly improved over prerevolutionary days.

At age three children are often sent to kindergartens, where they receive motor-skills training and learn the importance of community labor by being given little productive jobs to do, such as folding boxes for a factory. Misdemeanors are handled by the children rather than by adults. The children are taught to collectively address a child's errors and pursuade him to think about them and correct them himself. For those with learning problems, the approach is to assign children who excel to tutor those who need help. Teachers may also assist the backward children during the two self-study periods each day. Retired workers may be assigned to supervise homework, and they or other pupils also help children who have problems.

In-service training for teachers is used to teach general skills rather than those required for special education. Due to the shortage of trained teachers, some senior middle-school graduates (ninth-graders) begin teaching primary school after six to twelve months of training. In some rural areas, children with seven grades of education are given from one to twelve months of training and are then sent to primary schools to teach. Because of the massive problems of general education, special education has not yet been able to receive adequate attention.

Republic of China. From 1895 to 1945 Taiwan was occupied by the Japanese, who conducted the educational system in their language. In 1949 the Republic of China temporarily moved its government to Taiwan, and the official language is Mandarin. In 1968 the basic period of free education was increased from six to nine years, and by 1975 over 27 percent of the population were attending school. Less than 7 percent of the population were illiterate, and another 10 percent were semiliterate. Now, over 99.4 percent of the elementary-school-age children are in school, and 90 percent of these children go on to junior high school. About 300,000 students are enrolled in colleges and universities as undergraduates out of a total population of about 16.5 million people (Chung Hwa Information Service 1977).

Children start school at the age of six years and have six grades of elementary education followed by three grades of junior high school. In Taipei the largest public elementary school has about 12,000 pupils, with from 50 to 60 pupils in each classroom. Enrollment in the 2,395 primary schools in Taiwan was 2,341,413 in 1976-1977, and 1,530,745 students were in the secondary educational system.

Kuo (see chapter 10) has described special education in the Republic of China. Special-education programs were first initiated by religious and welfare agencies (Ministry of Education 1976). In 1880 a training program for the blind was begun in Tainan, and in 1886 a school for the deaf was established. The Nine-Year Fundamental Education Act of 1968 stated that the physically handicapped, the mentally deficient, and gifted and talented children should be provided with special education. However, "only a small percentage of the exceptional children are being accommodated in special education programs; curriculum guides for special education are still lacking and teacher training programs and diagnostic prescription procedures need to be systematized immediately to meet urgent demands" (Ministry of Education 1976).

In 1970 the Regulation of Special Education Development and Improvement Act stated that special education should be provided for children who are mentally retarded, visually impaired, hearing impaired, speech-handicapped, orthopedically handicapped, chronically ill, and socially maladjusted and emotionally disturbed. A 1977 amendment added the gifted and talented and the learning handicapped. In 1974 the Ministry of Education promulgated the Regulation of Exceptional Children Identification and Educational Placement Act, containing procedures and criteria for identifying exceptional children using clinical teams. In 1975 the Regulation of Teaching Certificates for Teachers of Exceptional Children Act stated that, in addition to a regular teaching certificate, a minimum of sixteen hours of special education were required for a special-education certificate. Kuo (chapter 10) discusses the problems associated with case-finding and remediation of learning-handicapped children in excellent detail.

India

India has about one-third of the area of the United States but over twice the population. It is said to have 179 languages and 544 spoken dialects, which have been classified into four family groups: Indo-Aryan, Dravidian, Austro-Asiatic, and Tibeto-Chinese (Oommen 1973). About 70 percent of the people speak Indo-Aryan languages (primarily Hindi, Guharati, Bengali, Assamese, Oriya, and Sanskrit) while about 25 percent speak Dravidian languages. Almost half of the population speak four languages, namely, Hindi, Urdu, Hindustani, and Punjabi, and another 10 percent speak Telegu. The constitution of India states that the official language is Hindi; however, for the first fifteen years after formation of the Union in 1947, English continued to be the official language. After 1965 Hindi became the official language, but English continued to be the subsidiary official language.

Muralidharan (see chapter 15) states that 60 percent of the population is illiterate. Free public education is provided by the states until fourteen years of age. The Union government retained responsibility for university education, for the promotion and coordination of research, and for education in the Union territories and for the children of government employees. Primary education is free in all states; in some states middle school is also free, and in a few states education is free up to the college level. Primary school generally begins at six years of age (as early as five years in some states), and has five grades followed by three grades in middle school.

In 1975-1976 there were 66.4 million children in primary school and 16 million in middle school; however, to reach universal enrollment by 1985, it will be necessary to add another 52 million children. The most formidable problems to be overcome are breaking through traditions and convincing the lower castes of the value of education and the need for girls to be educated and the extremely high drop-out rate of about 75 percent in the first eight grades. Children usually are removed from school for economic reasons, since at about nine years of age they can be of help to their families. For girls, there is also early betrothal and prejudice against allowing grown girls to attend mixed schools.

There is seldom a reading-readiness program in primary schools, so reading and writing instruction may begin immediately upon entering school. No kindergarten or nursery schools are provided for in the compulsory-education act; consequently, most preschool training is in private, tuition-charging schools, available only to the middle and upper classes. Studies of urban versus rural children indicated that the rural preschool children were severely retarded in language development as compared with urban children, while those from industrial areas were found to be intermediate in development.

In 1963 a battery of reading-readiness tests was given to 3,500 first-graders in Delhi (Rawat 1964). It was found that 40 percent of the children were unable to discriminate between various phonemes in Hindi. Directional confusions occurred in the copying test, and village children were unfamiliar with objects in pictures that were readily recognized by city children. As a result of this study, a reading-readiness kit was devised, with a manual for the teacher. The kit was distributed free to all Delhi schools, which then began to provide a four- to six-week readiness program (Oommen 1973).

Sachdev and Singh (1975) reported on the factors related to poor school performance in Delhi. Two experimental groups of children with poor school performance were made up of 46 children from upper- and middle-income families (group 1), and 28 children from poor and lower-middle-income families (group 2). A control group of 24 children with normal school performance (group C) was used for comparison. Prenatal and perinatal abnormalities were found to be three times more common in the poor-performance children than in the controls. Hyperactive or aggressive behavior characterized 50 percent of group 1 and 65 percent of group 2, with none in the control group. Abnormal Bender Visual Motor Gestalt Tests were found in 100 percent of group 2 cases, 73 percent of group 1 cases, and 25 percent of the controls. Mild to moderate mental retardation characterized 79 percent of group 2, 11 percent of group 1, and none of the controls. Soft neurological signs, including poor copying of finger designs, choreiform movements, excessive motor overflow, right-left discrimination deficits, and face-arm sensory extinction, in descending order of frequency, were found in 48 percent of group 2, 42 percent of group 1, and 16 percent of the controls.

Oommen stated that there were no special provisions for children who failed reading, primarily because reading disability had not yet been determined to be a school problem. Students who fail in reading must repeat the grade until they are able to pass. Many children are retained, and this is a serious problem in India. The census of 1961 found that only 24 percent of the population was literate at that time, 34.5 percent of males and 13 percent of females. Since then the literacy rate has increased to 40 percent. Muralidharan describes recent developments in Indian education in some detail in chapter 15.

Israel

A major dispersal of Jews from their homeland occurred in 70 ACE, after the destruction of the Second Temple in Jerusalem by the Romans. However, several ancient Jewish communities have continued to exist to the present time in the area where the State of Israel was established in 1948, at which time there were 650,000 Jews living on the land. Most immigrants had come from Europe before 1948; however, after statehood, the majority came from the Middle East and North Africa. By 1968 the population was 2.8 million, of whom 88 percent were Jews, 44 percent of whom had been born in Israel (Feitelson 1973).

The earlier European settlers had founded a complete system of education from nursery school through the university, with Hebrew as the language of instruction. With the founding of the state, nine years of free compulsory schooling for children from five through fourteen years of age were instituted. The compulsory-education law applies to all inhabitants regardless of religion and is administered by the Ministry of Education. However, the schools for minorities are operated in their own cultural traditions and languages, based on curricula developed in their own teacher-training institutions.

The educational system is centralized under the Ministry of Education in the manner of European systems. This includes formulation of all policy matters, curricula, number of hours for each subject, expected levels of achievement, and so forth. Children start free kindergarten at five years of age and enter the first grade at six years. Compulsory education has been extended two years to age sixteen, and the eight-year elementary school followed by four years of secondary school has been changed to the six-year elementary school, three-year middle school, and three-year high school.

Feitelson (1973) stated that by the end of the first grade it is necessary for the children to read well, since from second grade on Bible study is a major subject for all grades. Traditionally, children were first taught to memorize the names of the 36 Hebrew characters plus some rules, then they learned the names of the consonant-vowel combinations, and finally they learned how to pronounce them and how to decode words. This method required two or three years of practice in order to be able to read. The Europeans who started the educational system were influenced by Gestalt psychology in Europe and behaviorism in America to establish a modern way of teaching called "center-of-interest" (words of interest to the child), which was widely used by the 1940s. Reading was taught in phrases, with the expectation that the child would discover the meanings of single words himself. This method was found satisfactory until the 1950s, with most children learning to read during their first school year.

Feitelson indicated that, in the early 1950s, there was mass immigration from the Arab countries, and "failure to acquire reading in the first grade rose alarmingly." The problem was blamed on the poor living conditions of the immigrants, want of motivation, and uneducated parents. In 1952 Feitelson conducted a study to determine the causes of this high failure rate. It was found that failure was not evenly dispersed among the ten first-grade classes studied, rather, "the whole class" did either well or poorly. The traditional teachers (center-of-interest method) had the poorest results; those who had used supplementary methods fared better.

Since Hebrew words tend not to have distinctive patterns but rather require attention to small details, the whole-word and phrase method of learning to read was illogical. Moreover, since the written language has an almost perfect sound-symbol relationship, it is more suited to a phonics method of teaching. Therefore, the question arose of how the whole-word method could have been successful for so long.

Interviews with the parents in the control group of Feitelson's study supplied the answer. These educated middle-class parents followed the progress of their children carefully. When it was found that the child was not learning to read, or didn't understand something in any course, the parents usually taught the child themselves. Therefore, when the whole-word method failed, the parents taught their children to read, so that failure of the method didn't become evident until children whose parents couldn't help them came to the schools.

Israel has a well-developed system of special education, including assessment and remediation for specific learning disabilities. Parents early became interested in the problems of their learning-disabled children, and in 1965 they formed the Organization for Children with Developmental and Learning Difficulties (NITSAN). The organization was to help children who were not retarded but were either dyslexic, aphasic, autistic, or brain-damaged, and for whom no remedial facilities existed in the public-school system. Their normal intelligence precluded education in the existing settings for retarded children. In Tel Aviv-Jaffa the Department of Education opened a special school for children of normal intelligence with brain dysfunction for about eighty children in 1967. At this time there were also twenty classes of ten children each dispersed throughout Israel. Recent research indicates that the prevalence of specific learning disabilities is about 1.5 percent in Israel. At present, complete diagnostic facilities are available as well as remedial education.

Japan

Originally, the numerous *kanji* characters used in Japan were Chinese ideographs that came to Japan via Korea. However, only 1,850 *kanji* are now in daily use. During the ninth century, an "alphabet" of phonetic characters was developed (*kana*), which permitted the Japanese to easily write anything they wished, fostering the production of a great deal of poetry (Reischauer 1978).

Hiragana is the first form of *kana* that children learn. It consists of forty-six basic phonetic symbols now used, plus twenty-five more that are derived by adding diacritical marks to the basic characters to produce additional phonetic values. A second system of *kana*, *katakana*, is learned in the second grade; it duplicates all the *hiragana* symbols but is used only for foreign words. It is possible to communicate anything in writing using either system of *kana*, because all the necessary sounds are available in essentially a one-to-one relationship between the symbol and the sound. By the time children enter the first grade at the age of six years, almost all can read *hiragana*.

Vogel (1979) stated that American reporters in Tokyo often indicated that they wish the American reading public were as sophisticated as the Japanese. Tokyo readers of the major newspapers may be assumed by the reporters to be better informed about international affairs than an equivalent American group of readers. When discussing pollution or nuclear power, the television news commentators use chemical formulas, since it is taken for granted that viewers can understand them.

It is claimed that over 99.7 percent of the Japanese people are literate. An illiterate person is defined as one who cannot read *kanji*, *hiragana*, and *katakana* at all. By contrast, illiteracy in America is defined in "functional" terms, so that a person who cannot read and understand the daily newspaper might be considered illiterate. The Japanese do not believe that this type of problem exists in Japan.

Nine years of compulsory free education are available in Japan. However, very large numbers of children attend kindergartens from three years of age to get a good start before entering primary school. At the end of secondary school a great many students take the national college-entrance examinations, which determine the colleges and universities they may enter. These examinations are fiercely competitive, since only about half of the students taking them are able to matriculate each year because of the limited number of freshman places available and the intense desire of the students to enter the most prestigious universities, a major factor in determining their career possibilities. In order to prepare for these examinations, children are sent to the "best" nursery schools, and at about the sixth grade most children start attending *juku* (tutoring schools) for two hours after school several days a week.

One result of the intensive, structured teaching program in the schools, the competitive examinations, and the families' beliefs in the importance of education has been the excellent showing of Japanese children on the international achievement studies in mathematics and science. Israeli and Japanese thirteen-year-old children led in the twelve-nation international study of achievement in mathematics in 1964 (Husén 1967); and in the 1970 science tests Japanese fourteen-year-old children were first in physics and chemistry among nineteen countries (Vogel 1979).

Sakamoto and Makita (1973) indicated that "reading readiness is attained in Japan at about 4½ years of age." They point to a report to the effect that, in Tokyo, all the *hiragana* symbols could be read by 31 percent of the three-year-olds, 58 percent of the four-year-olds, and 83 percent of the five-year-old children. Makita (1968) sent questionnaires to teachers to determine how many children had difficulty learning to read. The incidence of poor readers was found to be 0.98 percent of 9,195 pupils, reported by 247 teachers. Sakamoto and Makita (1973) state that special education for children who have reading disabilities is almost nonexistent in Japan. Such cases are so rare that there is no need for remedial facilities. Makita also sent questionnaires to some child-guidance clinics and child-study institutions to determine their experience with reading problems. None admitted having children with reading difficulties, "except for a single case of congenital word blindness." Also, "Japanese child psychiatrists have never encountered a child with this circumscribed difficulty [dyslexia, or reading disability] in the reading area."

Sakamoto and Makita speak of "problem children in reading" to describe children with poor reading ability who are otherwise normal. "Defective readers" are described as those whose reading levels are significantly below what would be expected from their mental abilities and who may read only comic books or science fiction, for example. They cite research by Sakamoto and Takagi on 664 fourth-, fifth- and sixth-grade pupils who were given both reading and intelligence tests. It was found that more boys than girls were disabled readers. Compared with the able reader, the disabled readers were slower readers and did less well in sentence comprehension. Both groups did about equally well in reading *kanji*, where one or two characters may represent a whole word.

Nakano and Suzuki (see chapter 16) report on twenty-six boys and thirteen girls evaluated by Suzuki as dyslexics at the Tokyo University Hospital, Department of Pediatrics. Tarnopol and Tarnopol (see chapter 4) discuss the data collected on thirty-three boys and three girls with learning disabilities who were assessed by Kamimura and Morinaga at the Izu Teishin Hospital in Hirai Kannami. These cases, found since Sakamoto and Makita's report, probably indicate that renewed interest in children's reading problems, plus the use of more complete test batteries, have made it possible to find cases of learning disabilities that were previously undetected. It should be mentioned that American and European teachers, physicians, psychologists, and parents also tended to be unaware of the syndromes of dyslexia and learning disabilities until after widespread publicity had been given to these conditions. Consequently, questionnaires answered by teachers and others would not have been expected to reveal the extent of the problem until it became well known.

In Summary

In the newly emerging nations, where very few children attend school, there is little room for special education in the instructional systems. The major problems are building schools, training teachers, getting the majority of children to start school, overcoming the prejudice against educating girls, and keeping the children in school. Consequently, reading and learning problems, as such, tend to receive very little attention. Nevertheless, if teacher training were to be based on an adequate, workable foundation, it may be presumed that significantly fewer children would fail and be retained, thereby increasing substantially the numbers of children continuing their education. Therefore, any useful contribution to the theory and practice of teaching reading that can be derived from studies of comparative educational systems and methods could help to increase literacy through appropriate teacher training.

In the developing nations that have had educational systems for many years, the major problems appear to be building more schools, training more teachers, increasing the number of children starting school, significantly reducing the number of children failing and being retained, increasing the number of children who complete their education, and developing special educational methods for the large number of children who have difficulty learning to read. In some countries it is also necessary to overcome the prejudice against educating girls. Since a major problem exists in the adequate training of teachers to overcome early reading failures, which are causing retentions and drop-outs from the schools in very great numbers, any practical contribution from comparative studies will prove to be of great value.

In the developed nations, where well over 90 percent of the children attend school, the major problems appear to be significantly reducing the number of children failing in the elementary grades and being retained, reducing the drop-out rate, developing quality special education for intelligent children with reading and learning difficulties, and training the teachers in adequate methods to accomplish these objectives. Clearly, any contribution from comparative studies could assist in this endeavor.

With respect to the problems of children with specific learning disabilities, it is obviously impossible to determine the incidence of this subgroup so long as 50 percent or more elementary school children continue to fail, as seems to be the case in a great many countries. Moreover, the solution to the failure problem instituted in most American states is equally untenable. These states have been using social promotions based on age rather than on academic accomplishments to overcome the grade-retention problem. The results have been disastrous from the point of view of academic learning. Recently, a number of states have introduced "functional literacy tests" which must be passed in order to graduate from high school (twelfth grade). These tests, primarily in reading, seem to be passable at about the sixth- to eighth-grade level. In California each local school district makes up its own tests and determines the passing score. Consequently, there is no uniformity within the state about how well a student must be able to read in order to graduate from high school.

The most outstanding features of the approaches to remediating specific reading and learning disabilities internationally are as follows:

1. Diagnosis is usually made by a multidisciplinary team.

2. The team generally consists of a physician; a psychologist; a speech, hearing, and language therapist; a special-education teacher; and other professionals, including social workers, vocational therapists, physical therapists, and nurses.

3. A battery of tests tends to be used, including an intelligence test; reading, spelling, and arithmetic tests; gross- and fine-motor-coordination tests; visual-motor tests; visual-memory and perceptual tests; and auditory-memory and perceptual tests.

4. An attempt is made to prepare a remedial program based on the results of the tests and other information.

5. It is recognized that reading and learning disabilities are not a single problem but rather a group of syndromes stemming from different etiologies.

Another area requiring continued effort is the dissemination of information about specific learning disabilities based on continuing scientific research. It appears that a great many educationists and other professionals are not aware of the research literature in this field, and many doubt that neurologically based specific learning disabilities exist—or they believe that such disorders affect only a tiny percentage of the population. The controversies over etiology tend to do a disservice to the children around the world who are in dire need of immediate remedial assistance because they focus attention on disagreements rather than directing the much-needed energy into the constructive path of research on remediation.

There is a great deal of evidence to indicate that the early home environments of the children and the continuing assistance from parents during the school years play a vital role both in preparing children for school and in their continued functioning through the school years. In those families where the children are able to receive motivational support and added help with their basic skills and homework, the children tend to flourish in academic achievement. This indicates that parent training to motivate and assist their children through the school years will be of great importance in all lower socioeconomic communities. This type of help can also be derived through the use of parent surrogates, as in the People's Republic of China. The use of national reading and literacy campaigns, as in Japan, where "education mama" helps the children in many ways, can also be of great value.

Finally, the problem of teacher training is a crucial one worldwide. Primary-school teachers have been found to have from a fourth-grade education to several years of graduate university training. Moreover, it seems that the number of years of education does not necessarily determine either the literacy level of the teacher or the quantity and quality of his training in remedial reading. Our tests of teachers indicate that, with five or more years of university education, they range from functional illiteracy to superior literacy (see chapter 6). It is therefore suggested that minimum literacy requirements should be established for teachers (especially in the United States) and that all elementary- and middle-school teachers would profit from training in the most modern methods of prescriptive (individualized) teaching of reading, based on the ability to analyze the pupil's deficiencies from a battery of tests. If all teachers received this training, it would be possible for them to individualize instruction in practice—rather than in theory, as is now the case.

References

Brereton, B.L., and Sattler, J. 1967. *Cerebral Palsy: Basic Abilities.* Mosman, Australia: The Spastic Centre of New South Wales.
Butler, S.R. 1974. *Impressions of China Today.* Sidney: Paul Hamlyn.
———. 1976. Reading problems of Chinese children. In L. Tarnopol and M. Tarnopol (eds.), *Reading Disabilities: An International Perspective.* Baltimore: University Park Press.

Carbonell de Grampone, M.A., et al. 1967. *Comparative Study of the Analytic-synthetic and Global Methods of Teaching Reading.* Uruguayan Association for Dyslexia.

Chung Hwa Information Service. 1977. *141 Questions and Answers about the Republic of China.* Taipei: China Art Printing Works.

Clements, S.D. 1966. *Minimal Brain Dysfunction in Children: Terminology and Identification.* U.S. Department of Health, Education, and Welfare, NINDB Monograph No. 3. Washington, D.C.: Superintendent of Documents.

De Quirós, J.B. 1964. Dysphasia and dyslexia in school children. *Folia Phoniatrica.* (Basel) 16.

Feitelson, D. 1973. Israel. In J. Downing (ed.), *Comparative Reading.* New York: Macmillan.

Hagger, T.D., and Stewart, Y. 1976 Learning disabilities in Australia. In L. Tarnopol and M. Tarnopol (eds.), *Reading Disabilities: An International Perspective.* Baltimore: University Park Press.

Hall, H.H. 1976. Remedial education in Rhodesia. In L. Tarnopol and M. Tarnopol (eds.), *Reading Disabilities: An International Perspective.* Baltimore: University Park Press.

Husén, T. 1967. *International Studies of Achievement in Mathematics: A Comparison of Twelve Countries.* 2 vols. New York: Wiley.

Leong, C.K. 1973. Hong Kong. In J. Downing (ed.), *Comparative Reading.* New York: Macmillan.

Logue, G.D. 1976. Learning disabilities in the Republic of South Africa. In L. Tarnopol and M. Tarnopol (eds.), *Reading Disabilities: An International Perspective.* Baltimore: University Park Press.

Makita, K. 1968. The rarity of reading disability in Japanese children. *Journal of Orthopsychiatry* 38.

Ministry of Education. 1976. *Special Education in the Republic of China.* Taipei: Department of Special Education.

Oommen, C. 1973. India. In J. Downing (ed.), *Comparative Reading.* New York: Macmillan.

Perelstein de Braslavsky, B. 1973. Argentina. In J. Downing (ed.), *Comparative Reading.* New York: Macmillan.

Popovic, A.M. 1968. Alfabetização—Disfunções Psiconeurólogicas. São Paulo: Vetor.

Rawat, D.S. 1964. *A Battery of Reading Readiness Tests.* New Delhi: National Council of Educational Research and Training.

Reischauer, E.O. 1978. *The Japanese.* Cambridge, Mass.: Harvard University Press.

Robles Gorriti, C.J., and Rodriquez Mũniz, A.M. 1976. Learning problems in Argentina. In L. Tarnopol and M. Tarnopol (eds.), *Reading Disabilities: An International Perspective.* Baltimore: University Park Press.

Sachdev, K., and Singh, N., 1975. Etiology of poor school performance. In First International Congress of Child Neurology, Toronto.

Sakamoto, T., and Makita, K. 1973. Japan. In J. Downing (ed.), *Comparative Reading*. New York: Macmillan.

Silva, P.A. 1979. Learning Difficulties in the Preschooler (mimeographed). Dunedin, New Zealand: University of Otago.

Vogel, E.F. 1979 *Japan as No. 1: Lessons for America*. Cambridge, Mass.: Harvard University Press.

Arithmetic and Visual-Motor Abilities in Chinese, Japanese, and American Children: A Preliminary Study

Lester Tarnopol and
Muriel Tarnopol

The purpose of the preliminary study reported here was to find hypotheses to be tested in a subsequent research program and to learn how to do the follow-up study. It is possible to develop an adequate research design using experimental and control groups to test hypotheses; however, it is necessary to have one or more preliminary or pilot studies in order to develop tests and questionnaires that are standardized, reliable, and valid. The problems tend to be compounded when attempting cross-national research. Freudenthal's analysis of the IEA studies of reading, science, and mathematics in many countries (discussed in chapter 1) attests to the inherent difficulties. Some examples of problems to be solved in the preliminary studies include finding or developing tests and questionnaires that can be used in all the countries; translating and trying them out to learn how to give them in each country and retain standardized administration and scoring; revising tests and procedures as required; and performing the analysis and testing of questionnaires. These are some of the issues we addressed in this preliminary study (L. Tarnopol 1957*a*, 1957*b*, 1957*c*, 1961, 1963, 1967, 1969, 1971; M. Tarnopol 1977).

Comparison of Learning Disabilities in Asian and American Children

Makita (1968) sent questionnaires to 323 teachers requesting information about the number of children with learning problems in public and private schools in Japan. Replies were received from 247 teachers (73 percent) covering 9,195 children in grades one through six. The total number of children reported to have some degree of reading difficulty was 89, or 0.98 percent of the group. Also, the percentages of pupils with reading problems

Work for this chapter was subsidized in part by grants from the Pacific Cultural Foundation, Taipei, Taiwan, Republic of China, and the Charles Dorsey Armstrong Foundation, Palo Alto, California.

decreased with increasing grade level (1.2 percent in first grade to 0.4 percent in grades four and above). Since well over 99 percent of the children attend school in Japan, the figures are meaningful. However, since the selection of pupils with reading difficulties was made by the teachers' subjective estimates, an accurate determination of the prevalence of reading problems must await objective, standardized testing.

Kuo, Chen, and Liang (1976) published a survey of exceptional children in Taiwan, Republic of China, conducted by the Ministry of Education between December 1974 and June 1976. The prevalence of mental retardation was reported as significantly lower than that in Japan and the United States (0.43 percent compared with 2.07 percent and 2.3 percent, respectively). This report was based on questionnaire replies from all of Taiwan's teachers, and again, since well over 99 percent of the children attend school, the figures assume significance. However, since the data were based on the subjective replies of teachers, final determination awaits standardized, objective test results.

Kuo (see chapter 10) found that the ratio of boys to girls with reading retardation in Taiwan was three and a half to one, in agreement with our international findings (Tarnopol and Tarnopol 1976). He surveyed 250 teachers with 13,519 pupils in grades one through five, using a questionnaire, and found that 2.91 percent of the children were reported to have reading problems. It was also noted that the prevalence of difficulties with reading was greater in the rural than the urban areas sampled (3.7 percent versus 2.8 percent). Since 30 percent of the Taipei subsample were found to have IQs between 60 and 80, the percentage of pupils with IQs above 80 with reading deficits was 1.95 percent.

United States data tend to indicate that over 10 percent of the high school graduates have reading problems, based on tests of functional literacy requiring comprehension at about the sixth-grade level on standardized tests. However, the demands of functional literacy have increased and now include being able to read and understand the directions on the labels of canned goods and the manual required to pass the driver's license tests; to fill out applications for employment; to manage a checking account; and other such practical abilities.

It is estimated that between 2 and 5 percent of the population may have specific learning disabilities. In order to cope with what appears to be a growing rate of illiteracy, several states have introduced literacy tests that must be passed before high school graduation, except for students in special education (retarded, learning handicapped, and the like), for whom reduced standards may apply.

Both Chinese and Japanese researchers have attributed the lower rates of reading deficiencies in their languages, as compared with English, to the orthographic differences in the languages. Makita (1968) stated that the problems of reading English were attributable to the lack of one-to-one correspondence between the letters, digraphs, and so forth, and their pronunciations. However, this fails to account for the relatively high incidence of reading problems in Danish and Spanish, for example, which are more regular than English.

We agree that part of the difficulty confronting children who are learning to read English is the irregularity of the language. If this were the main problem, both Chinese-American and Japanese-American children would experience learning difficulties similar to other American children. We therefore tested the null hypothesis that Asian-American children and Caucasian-American children should not have significantly different percentages of reading disabilities and mental retardation.

Prevalence Data, California and Hawaii

In the San Francisco Unified School District (1976-1977), there were 65,177 pupils, including 11,797 Chinese-American and 1,003 Japanese-American children. The percentage of pupils in the programs for mental retardation or learning disabilities was found to be 3 percent for the total population, while the percentages for Chinese-Americans and Japanese-Americans were significantly lower (0.8 percent and 0.2 percent), as shown in table 4-1. In seventeen California regions with a total school population of 820,363 pupils, 5.6 percent were in these two programs, including 4.9 percent of the

Table 4-1
Prevalence Data, California and Hawaii

	Total Number of Pupils	Learning-Disabled and Retarded Pupils	
		Number	Percent
San Francisco Unified School District (1976-1977)			
Total population	65,177	1,949	3.0
Chinese-American	11,797	99	0.8
Japanese-American	1,003	2	0.2
California, 17 regions (1978-1979)			
Total population	820,363	45,879	5.6
Caucasians	540,513	26,222	4.9
Asians and Pacific Islanders	20,318	468	2.3
Hawaii (1979)			
Total population	169,575	7,752	4.6
Caucasians	49,191	2,616	5.3
Japanese-Americans	34,184	703	2.0
Chinese-Americans	7,000	230	3.3

Sources: Hawaiian data were adapted from table 14-9. California data were supplied by the State Department of Education. San Francisco data were supplied by the school district.

Caucasian population and 2.3 percent of the Asians or Pacific Islanders. In Hawaii the percentages of the Caucasians, Chinese-Americans, and Japanese-Americans in the learning-disabilities and retarded programs were 5.3, 3.3, and 2.0 percent, respectively, in 1979. In 1978 there were 32,949 pupils in the Richmond Unified School District in California, of whom 1,318 were Asian-Americans. Of the 261 children in special day classes for the learning-handicapped, none were Asian-American, and of the 94 pupils in the classes for the mentally retarded, only one was Asian-American (Cederborg 1979).

When testing a hypothesis, one often finds data that are contradictory, and it is most important to report all such information. In this case, we have found no data that uphold the null hypothesis.

From this and other similar evidence (Kline and Lee 1972), it was deduced that significantly fewer Asian-American than Caucasian-American pupils are found to be mentally retarded or learning-disabled in the English language. Since the nonspecificity of English orthography does not appear to affect Asian-American students as much as Caucasian-Americans, other causes of this phenomenon must be sought.

Some Causes of Learning Problems

Until recently, when American children who were not retarded, and who had normal educational opportunities and no apparent physical defects showed great reading or learning difficulties, several possible causes were considered. These included poor motivation, emotional disturbance, and nonstandard-English-speaking homes. It was often assumed that these children could learn to read if they wanted to and were willing to try. More recently some new factors have been added, including inadequate early-childhood educational opportunities in the home environment; genetic differences; allergies; chemical imbalances, especially hormonal and of the neurotransmitters; and brain damage. Because of the subtle nature of some of these factors, it is often not possible to clearly distinguish which, if any, are causing the observed behavioral or learning disturbances.

If a child does, in fact, have some form of brain damage, genetic difference, or chemical imbalance, it is important to recognize that the disturbed behavior is not a direct result of these factors but is rather the consequence of developed patterns of behavior resulting from atypical interactions with the environment. These underlying causes of learning disabilities are usually only indirectly observed through behavioral syndromes.

Birth Traumas

Birch (1964) stated: "It is probable . . . that increasing numbers of children with brain damage are to be found in the general population as one unintended consequence of medical progress." Some examples of this are children suffering from anoxia, jaundice, or prematurity at birth (Masland 1969).

Intelligence tests tend to show only a modest decrease when comparing groups of childen who have had insufficient oxygen, jaundice, or birth weights below five and a half pounds (2,500 grams) with those whose births were normal. However, follow-up studies of premature infants at age six demonstrate significant decrements in visual-motor skills (Bender Visual Motor Gestalt Test of copying geometrical designs) and in a composite index of neurological damage (see figure 4-1). These children tend to be "high risk" for learning disabilities.

Brackbill and Broman (1979) studied 3,528 full-term infants born to healthy mothers with normal pregnancies and deliveries to investigate the relationship between the medications and anesthesias used in obstetrics and subsequent neurobehavioral functioning through the first year of life. Pediatric examinations were conducted at four months of age; at eight months Bayley mental and motor scales were administered; and at 12 months the children received a pediatric-neurological examination. "Overall, there were highly significant associations between the infant's development through the first year and medication administered during labor and delivery." It was found that inhalant anesthetics had the most adverse outcomes. The following obstetrical medications were implicated, in order from most to least adverse effects: scopolamine, promazine, secobarbital, oxytocin, promethazine, and meperidine.

The functions that were most adversely affected were the gross-motor skills, including attempts to sit, stand, and locomote, as well as muscular strength and coordination. Lack of findings in fine-motor skills and other areas may be due to the fact that testing did not go beyond one year of age. The findings were also reported to be in agreement with those of previous studies. Since forceps are known to have been implicated in neurological damage, it remains to compare the effects of unmedicated, natural childbirth with other procedures.

Agents during Pregnancy

Several agents have been reported to have adverse effects on fetal and subsequent child development. Well-known among these agents are a number of viruses, bacteria, and chemicals. Previously, it was believed that chemicals breathed or injested by mothers were prevented from entering the fetal bloodstream by a filtering system. It has been found in recent studies that this is not entirely true. A number of chemicals, previously thought to be benign, have been implicated in producing malformed or malfunctioning infants. These include the smoke from cigarettes and marijuana, alcohol, caffeine, food additives that cause allergic reactions, and some prescription and over-the-counter drugs.

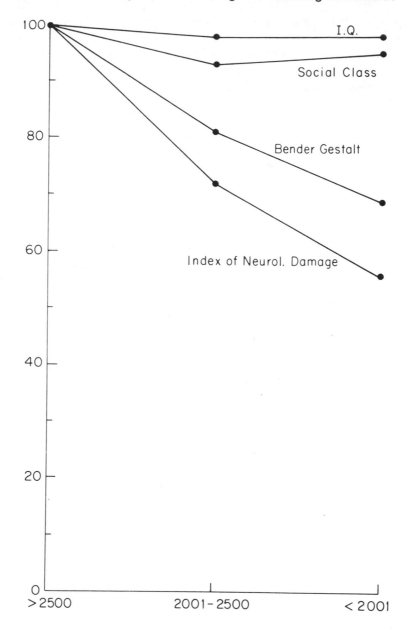

The scores have been converted to show relative impairment ratings on the vertical axis, with the score for the over-2500-gram group taken as 100.

Source: After G. Wiener, R.V. Rider, W.C. Oppel, L.K. Fischer, and P.A. Harper. Correlates of low birth weight: psychological status at six to seven years of age, *Pediatrics* 35 (Part 1):434-444, 1965.

Figure 4-1. Mean Scores on Measures of Child Development by Birth Weight for White Males

A recent pamphlet issued by the U.S. Department of Health and Human Services and the National Institute of Alcohol Abuse and Alcoholism states that the possible effects of alcohol during pregnancy on the offspring include mental retardation, shorter height, lighter weight, small head, face deformities, heart defects, joint and limb problems, and nervousness (*Should I Drink?* 1980).

Galton (1977) cited the National Child Development Study in England, where physicians had followed 1,500 children from birth through eleven years of age. It was found that mothers who had smoked ten or more cigarettes a day had children who were, on the average, slightly shorter and were three to five months behind the children of nonsmoking mothers in general ability, arithmetic, and reading. Another study of a random sample of 10 percent of the 1970 and 1971 births in Quebec was cited. In this research it was found that the offspring of smoking mothers had a much lower birth weight and a 24 percent greater mortality risk than the children of nonsmoking mothers.

Early Child Development

A number of well-known factors during childhood are associated with probable later learning disorders. These include high fevers, seizures, concussions, and bacterial, chemical, and viral attacks on the central nervous system.

For many years, it has been known that lead is toxic to the nerves. Recent research has demonstrated that relatively low lead dosages, below clinically observable symptom levels, were associated with various deficiencies that could impair academic performance (Needleman et al. 1979). Fifty-eight children with high-lead dentine levels were compared with 100 children with low-lead dentine levels. The lead concentrations in shed baby teeth were determined in a population of 2,146 children whose average age was about 7.4 years. Significant differences were found between the high-lead level and low-lead level pupils (favoring the latter) on the Wechsler Intelligence Scale for Children—Revised (WISC-R), especially the Verbal subscales; on three measures of auditory perception and speech processing; on an attention and reaction-time test; and on most items of the teachers' behavioral ratings. These effects of relatively low dosages of lead tend to implicate pollution from leaded (especially high-octane) gasolines plus possible ingestion of lead from paint.

Feingold (1975) hypothesized that certain food dyes may bring on allergic reactions in children and cause them to become hyperactive. Various studies have reported contradictory results when attempting to confirm this hypothesis. Swanson and Kinsbourne (1980) considered that the lack of positive results in some of the previous studies might have been due to an insufficient dosage of the dye, so they tested children with 100 and 150 mg of a food-dye blend. This dosage (150 mg) was considered by the Food and Drug Administration to be at the ninetieth percentile of daily intake for 5- to 12-year-old children. Forty children whose average age was ten years and who had symptoms suggesting hyperactivity were selected for study. Twenty children had evidenced favorable reactions to stimulant medication and were rated hyperactive on the Conners Rating Scale (Conners 1971); and another twenty children had responded adversely to the medication and were rated nonhyperactive. They were given a diet containing the food-dye blend for three days and a placebo for three days, with the order of administration counterbalanced. It was found that those classified as hyperactive made significantly more errors on a learning test under the dye condition than with the placebo, while there was no significant effect for those rated as nonhyperactive. Moreover, the time pattern of the response to the dye (started after one-half hour) reached maximum at one and a half hours and subsided after about three and a half hours, indicating that the mechanism was consistent with a toxic reaction to the dye rather than an allergic reaction.

Possible Male Risks

A new hypothesis concerning birth defects has been generated, based primarily on animal studies, indicating that fathers may be implicated (Medicine 1979). Soyka and Joffe, working at the Vermont College of Medicine, fed methadone to male rats which then mated with "clean" females. The results included an excessive number of neonatal deaths, low birth weights, and small litters. They then began to test the effects of morphine, caffeine, and propoxyphene hydrochloride (Darvon) when administered to the male laboratory animals, with similar results. Finally, a case was reported showing signs of fetal alcohol syndrome in a neonate when the father was a heavy consumer of alcohol but the mother was not (case by Dr. L. Bartoshesky of Tufts-New England Medical Center, cited in Medicine 1979). These reports indicate the possibility that fathers may produce defects in their offspring. Confirmation of this hypothesis awaits further research.

Effects of Dietary Deficiencies

It is well known that certain dietary deficiencies can affect neuronal development in the fetus and neonate. Birch and Gussow (1970) stated that a child born in poverty "is likely to be smaller at birth than his more fortunate contemporaries and is more likely to die at birth. . . . Throughout the preschool and school years . . . [they] are more likely to be more poorly fed . . . [and] overexposed to disease. . . . The failure of such children in school is not only not a mystery but is virtually foreordained."

A major dietary deficiency associated with various infant behavioral deficits was found to be protein intake. The level of protein in the maternal daily diet was found to be significantly correlated with the percentage of "excellent" babies born and was inversely related to the incidence of spontaneous abortions. Nutrients from natural sources—for example, diets containing adequate quantities of protein—are likely to be balanced in other requirements, whereas attempts to supplement with an "artifically isolated nutrient or combination of nutrients" can upset the nutritional balance, causing malnutrition. Early malnutrition has been found to depress the tested IQ scores of children at school age.

Birch and Gussow (1970) also reported on a study of 146 Guatemalan children, aged six to eleven years, from the same village. Differences in height were used as an indication of prior level of nourishment, the shortest being considered to have been malnourished. These children were tested in ability to make judgements concerning the similarity or difference of pairs of geometrical forms. The tests were performed in the visual, kinesthetic, and haptic sensory modalities and in the visual-kinesthetic, visual-haptic, and haptic-kinesthetic cross-modalities. The results indicated that differences in ability on all tests were in favor of the taller children. When the same tests were repeated on 120 short and tall children from an urban private-school population where no possible malnutrition had occurred, there was no difference in the performance of the two groups of pupils.

These studies demonstrated that, when short stature is due to malnutrition, there are accompanying unfavorable sequelae in the sensory-learning modalities. However, when no nutritional risk is present, height differences are not related to such sensory dysfunction. Other studies are cited indicating that, in rural Mexican populations having mild to moderate protein-calorie deficiencies, a positive correlation was found between IQ and height. In all, a great deal of research is cited to confirm the relationship between poverty, malnutrition, and reduced intellectual functioning.

Mayeske and Beaton (1975) have reported further analyses of the data from the Coleman report (Coleman et al. 1966), which included data on more than 600,000 pupils with about 60,000 teachers in some 4,000 schools. In previous analyses of this data, it had been found that "about 50 percent of the individual student achievement could be explained in terms of a linear relationship between achievement, family background, area of residence, and type of school attended." Sex had been found to be unimportant in the explanation of either achievement or motivation. School-related factors were found to play less of a role than family background. It was found that "for virtually all students, the role of family background factors in achievement exceeds that of school factors." These findings tend to verify the value of investigating the education-related environments of high-achieving populations.

The purpose of presenting this summary of the etiologies of learning disabilities has been to introduce a rationale for the types of questionnaire items devised to investigate the environments of children from conception through school entry. We will wish to compare the environmental factors that may have some bearing on academic progress in the different cultures studied.

Comparative Test Results: Asian and American Children

WPPSI Comparisons: United States and Japan

Comparison of the scores attained on the Wechsler Preschool and Primary Scale of Intelligence (WPPSI) by American and Japanese children aged four through six and a half years gives some indication of their levels of preparation for learning in school. (There are no Chinese WPPSI norms for comparison). The American and Japanese tests were published in 1967 and 1969, respectively.

Of the ten subscales on the WPPSI, the five Performance tests and the Arithmetic subscale among the Verbal tests are the same in the Japanese and American versions of the test. It is therefore possible to compare the achievements of Japanese and American children on these scales (see table 4-2). To make this comparison, the Japanese average raw scores taken from the published norms were converted to American scaled scores. The scaled scores were based on a mean of ten and a standard deviation of three points, and they range from one through nineteen. As an example, the Japanese mean raw score on the Arithmetic subscale at six and one-quarter years of age is 15 points. This is equivalent to a scaled score of 12 on the American norms for the six-and-one-quarter year-olds. The average American child at this age by comparison, earned a raw score of 13. Although IQs cannot be calculated from single tests, it may assist in understanding the meaning of a scaled score of 12 to indicate that it would be equivalent to 112 IQ on the Verbal scale (Tarnopol and Tarnopol 1980).

Since 200 American and 100 Japanese children were tested at each age level, a difference of one scaled point is significant at the 0.01 probability level, and 1.5 scale-points difference gives better than the 0.0001 level of probability. However, this is meaningful only to the extent that the groups on which the tests were normed were representative of the populations of

Table 4-2
**Japanese Mean Wechsler Preschool and Primary Scale of Intelligence
(WPPSI) Scaled Scores and IQs, Based on U.S. Norms**

Age (Years)	Arithmetic	Animal House	Picture Completion	Mazes	Geometric Design	Block Design	Performance IQ[a]
4	12.0	12.8	11.7	11.5	10.0	14.0	114
4¼	12.0	12.2	10.7	12.0	12.0	14.5	115
4½	12.0	11.5	10.5	12.0	12.7	14.0	115
4¾	12.0	11.8	10.5	12.5	12.0	14.0	115
5	12.0	11.5	11.0	13.0	12.5	14.3	116
5¼	12.0	11.5	11.5	12.5	13.0	14.0	117
5½	12.5	12.0	11.0	12.0	12.5	13.5	115
5¾	13.0	11.0	11.0	11.5	11.5	14.0	112
6	12.5	10.5	11.0	11.5	11.0	13.0	110
6¼	12.0	10.0	11.5	11.5	10.5	12.5	106
6½	11.0	9.7	10.5	11.5	11.0	12.5	107

Source: Adapted from N. Oda, M. Motegi, T. Yasutomi and T. Matsubara. 1969. *Wechsler Preschool and Primary Scale of Intelligence* (Japanese edition). Tokyo: Nihon Bunka Kagakusha. Reproduced with permission from L. Tarnopol and M. Tarnopol. 1980. Arithmetic ability in Chinese and Japanese children. *Focus of Learning Problems in Mathematics* 2:3.

Mean = 10; standard deviation = 3 for scaled scores.

[a]Performance IQ is based on the sum of the five performance test scores.

the respective nations. Although both the Japanese and Americans very carefully selected representative population samples for testing, it is not known how well they succeeded.

Japanese children aged four through six and a half years averaged 12.1 in Arithmetic based on American norms, which is significantly above the average of 10 for American children (see table 4-2). The Japanese children achieved their highest scores on the Block-Design test, averaging 13.7. The Block-Design scores are significantly related to both Verbal and Performance IQs. The mean Performance IQ of the Japanese children, based on U.S. norms, was 113, which would imply that they are very well prepared on these types of tasks before entering first grade. The combination of very high Arithmetic and Performance scores tends to indicate that Japanese pupils begin school with excellent readiness. It remains to determine the sources of their preschool educational capabilities.

WISC Comparison: Japan and United States

Lynn (1977) published the Japanese mean scaled scores and IQs based on U.S. norms for the Performance scales of the Wechsler Intelligence Scale for Children (WISC), normed in 1951. From these data the average Performance IQ of five- to fifteen-year-old Japanese children was 103, ranging from 110.5 at age five to a low of 100.5 at age fourteen. By 1969 the Japanese WPPSI data indicate significant increases in Performance scores based on a different set of subtests. Lynn argued that the increase in Japanese mean Performance IQ over the mean American IQ of 100 is primarily due to genetic factors. However, the proportion of genetic versus environmental influence over these scores remains to be determined.

WISC-R Comparisons: Japan, Taiwan, and United States

The Wechsler Intelligence Scale for Children—Revised (WISC-R) was published in 1974 in America, in 1978 in Japan, and in 1980 in Taiwan, Republic of China. The subscales that remained essentially unchanged were Arithmetic and Digit Span on the Verbal scale and Block-Design, Object Assembly, Coding, and Mazes on the Performance scale. In addition, the American and Japanese tests have Picture Arrangement in common.

In all cases our scaled scores and IQs for the Japanese and Taiwanese tests were derived by converting their mean raw scores to standard scaled scores using the tables of U.S. norms for each age (see tables 4-3 and 4-4). On the Taiwan-Chinese WISC-R, the average Performance IQ for children six through fifteen years of age, based on U.S. norms, is 98.4 (see table 4-3).

Table 4-3
Taiwan-Chinese Mean Wechsler Intelligence Scale for Children—Revised (WISC-R) Scaled Scores and IQs, Based on U.S. Norms

Age	Arithmetic	Digit Span	Block Design	Object Assembly	Coding	Mazes	Performance IQ[a]
6	9.2	11.7	10.2	8.8	9.8	10.3	98
7	8.3	12.5	10.3	8.0	10.0	11.0	99
8	8.8	12.8	10.6	7.2	12.2	10.3	100
9	9.5	12.8	10.5	7.8	11.5	10.2	100
10	9.3	13.0	10.0	7.5	11.7	10.3	99
11	9.7	13.0	10.3	7.2	11.5	9.7	97
12	9.0	13.0	10.4	7.2	11.5	10.3	99
13	10.0	13.3	9.8	7.3	11.3	10.0	97
14	11.0	13.2	10.5	7.0	10.5	10.0	97
15	11.3	13.0	11.1	7.3	10.8	10.0	98

Source: Adapted from Y. Chen et al. 1980. *Wechsler Intelligence Scale for Children—Revised* (Chinese edition.) Taipei: Psychological Corporation. Reproduced with permission from L. Tarnopol and M. Tarnopol. 1980. Arithmetic ability in Chinese and Japanese children. *Focus on Learning Problems in Mathematics* 2:3.
Mean = 10; standard deviation = 3. Mean IQ = 100; standard deviation = 15.
[a]Performance IQ is based on the sum of the 4 Performance test scores.

Table 4-4
Japanese Mean WISC-R Scaled Scores and IQs, Based on U.S. Norms

Age	Arithmetic	Digit Span	Picture Arrangment	Block Design	Object Assembly	Coding	Mazes	Performance IQ[a]
6	10.0	10.5	11.8	13.9	11.6	9.0	13.2	112
7	9.7	10.5	11.7	14.2	11.7	7.7	13.0	111
8	9.8	10.7	10.8	14.4	11.5	9.4	12.7	112
9	10.7	9.8	12.0	14.9	11.0	9.2	12.0	112
10	11.0	10.7	11.3	14.7	11.7	9.2	11.7	111
11	12.0	10.7	11.0	14.9	11.7	9.3	11.5	111
12	14.0	10.7	11.0	14.3	11.7	9.7	11.8	112
13	13.0	10.0	11.0	14.1	11.7	9.9	11.3	111
14	12.4	10.8	11.0	14.2	11.0	9.8	12.0	111
15	12.0	10.5	11.0	14.2	11.0	9.8	11.0	109
16	12.7	11.5	11.0	13.5	11.0	9.3	10.0	106

Source: Adapted from H. Kodama, F. Shinagawa and M. Motegi. 1978. *Wechsler Intelligence Scale for Children—Revised* (Japanese edition). Tokyo: Nihon Bunka Kagakusha. Reproduced with permission from L. Tarnopol and M. Tarnopol, 1980. Arithmetic ability in Chinese and Japanese children. *Focus on Learning Problems in Mathematics* 2:3.

Mean = 10; standard deviation = 3. Mean IQ = 100; standard deviation = 15.

[a]Performance IQ is based on the sum of the scores of 5 Performance tests.

The difference between the American mean of 100 and the Chinese mean of 98.4 is not significant. However, on Digit Span, the Chinese mean is significantly above both the American and Japanese means (12.8, 10, and 10.5, respectively) whereas Object Assembly is significantly below the American and Japanese means (7.5, 10, and 11.4, respectively). We have no explanation for these differences as yet.

The Japanese mean WISC-R scaled scores and IQs based on U.S. norms are given in table 4-4. All the tests are comparable, except that the Japanese Arithmetic test omits problem 7 and substitutes a difficult problem as number 18, the last item. Thus, the Japanese scale becomes a little more difficult than the American scale above about age ten. Also, the Japanese Block-Design test has a more troublesome problem substituted as the last item, making it more challenging at the upper age levels.

Chinese, Japanese, and American children all start school at age six years. Although the correlation between Verbal IQ and academic school grades is higher ($r = 0.5 +$ approximately), the correlation between Performance IQ and grades is still significant ($r = 0.3$ approximately). Thus, the IQ scores of children entering school may be considered to be an important determinant of how well prepared they are for the normal educational process.

On the 1953 WISC (Lynn 1977), the Japanese Performance IQ for children about to start school at ages five and six years, based on American norms, averaged 108.5; on the 1969 WPPSI it was about 111, and on the 1978 WISC-R it was 112 at age six (see tables 4-2 and 4-4). This indicates that the Performance abilities of these children have remained uniformly high over at least twenty-five years. On the other hand, the data on Arithmetic achievement for the same ages are unclear, since the WPPSI mean score is about 12 and the WISC-R mean is 10 for age six. At the same time, the average WPPSI Arithmetic score for ages four through six and a half is significantly above the American mean (12.1 versus 10), and the WISC-R Japanese mean for ages six through sixteen is also significantly higher than the American and Chinese scores (11.6, 10, and 9.6, respectively). If these normative data were gathered on representative populations, we should expect Japanese children to be significantly better prepared for academic education than either American or Chinese children, and it would be of immense value to determine the sources of this preparation. Another factor to be explored is the significant rise in the Japanese Performance IQ over a 25-year period from WISC Performance IQ 103 to WISC-R Performance IQ 110.7.

Chinese-Canadian Children

Kline and Lee (1972) tested 277 Chinese-Canadian pupils in the first three grades of Vancouver public schools who were also attending Chinese school in the late afternoon. Chinese was almost always spoken in their homes. All the pupils were tested with both English and Cantonese versions of the Iota Oral Reading Test. Those with reading problems in either language were administered the Ayers Spelling Test, Monroe Auditory Discrimination Test, Monroe Auditory-Visual Learning Test, Bender Visual Motor Gestalt Test, Draw-A-Person Test, and the Wechsler Intelligence Scale for Children.

It was found that prevalence of reading problems in each language decreased greatly during the three years of school. Eighteen children of the 277 (6.5%) were found to have reading difficulties in both English and Chinese. With increasing grade level, the percentage dropped precipitously (first grade, 17 percent; second grade, 5 percent; and third grade, 3.4 percent). The ratio of boys to girls with reading deficits in the total group of 277 pupils was three to one, which conforms with our international figures (Tarnopol and Tarnopol 1976). However, for children having difficulties in both languages, the ratio was ten boys to one girl.

Of the students with difficulty in both English and Chinese, 83 percent had abnormal Bender tests, compared with 21 percent for the controls; and 77 percent scored in the abnormal range for the Draw-A-Person Test, with 24 percent among the control group. It was also reported that only 30 percent of the pupils drew Oriental-appearing figures. All the children spoke both Chinese and English, and many were more fluent in Chinese; nevertheless, their prevalence of reading difficulty in English in grade three was well-below the national average. Moreover, there was no bilingual program in the Canadian schools.

Peters and Ellis (1970) analyzed the WISC data from this research. The students who had difficulty in English only were significantly below the controls on the subscales of Information Vocabulary, Digit Span and Verbal IQ. Those pupils who had reading deficits in both English and Chinese were lower on these subscales and on Arithmetic, Similarities, Picture Arrangement, and Full Scale IQ (see table 4-5). It is interesting that these pupils did not do less well than the controls on the Coding subscale. Many Caucasian-American children tend to do poorly on the classical triad—Arithmetic, Digit Span, and Coding, often including Information. It is also noted that the Chinese-Canadian children did unusually well in Block Design, and their Performance scores were relatively unaffected as compared with the controls.

Japanese Children with Learning Disabilities

Makita (1968) reported: "Not a single case [of dyslexia] has been brought into our children's psychiatric service since its opening in 1958." Only a few cases of word-blindness had been reported in the Japanese psychiatric literature. Also, no reports had been published on dyslexia in the broader sense of poor readers, as applied in Western literature. Sakamoto and

Table 4-5
WISC Scores in Grades One through Three in Vancouver

Scale	Mean Score, Dyslexics (N = 18)	Mean Score, Controls (N = 40)	t Value	p
Information	7.3	10.5	4.05	0.01
Comprehension	7.2	8.6	1.62	
Arithmetic	9.5	11.9	2.82	0.01
Similarities	7.8	10.2	2.32	0.05
Vocabulary	6.5	9.6	3.30	0.01
Digit Span	8.4	10.0	2.20	0.05
Picture Completion	9.7	10.3	0.57	
Picture Arrangement	9.6	11.5	2.36	0.05
Block Design	11.6	13.0	1.54	
Object Assembly	10.8	11.5	0.82	
Coding	11.9	12.6	0.70	
Verbal IQ	86.4	101.0	3.90	0.01
Performance IQ	105.1	112.9	1.91	
Full Scale IQ	94.8	107.3	3.11	0.01

Source: Reprinted with permission from L. Peters and E.N. Ellis, *An Analysis of WISC Profiles of Chinese-Canadian Children with Specific Reading Disabilities in Chinese, English or Both Languages* (Vancouver, B.C.: Board of School Trustees, 1970).
Sample consisted of eighteen Chinese-Canadian children with reading difficulties in both English and Chinese and forty controls without reading problems, from the same population.
p = probability level. Mean = 10; standard deviation = 3.

Makita (1973) reported that over 99 percent of the Japanese population are literate, with the major exception of the mentally retarded. "Japanese child psychiatrists have never encountered a child with this circumscribed difficulty in the reading area. Educational consultation services have never experienced such a case, at least to the knowledge of these writers."

Nakano and Susuki (see chapter 16) describe thirty-nine pupils who were diagnosed as having reading disabilities in the Department of Pediatrics at the Tokyo University Hospital. In January 1980, at the Izu Teishin Hospital in Hirai Kannami, we were given data on thirty-three children diagnosed for learning disabilities, including thirty boys and three girls, aged 6.7 to 13.7 years, with a mean of 9.7 years (see table 4-6 and Kamimura and Morinaga 1980; Tarnopol and Tarnopol 1980). Moreover, we interviewed parents of children with learning disabilities in Tokyo in 1980. It seems that, since Makita's search, the concept of dyslexia has become better understood in Japan and some cases have been uncovered. In December 1980 Dr. Kamimura told us that 80 cases of dyslexia had been diagnosed.

It should be noted that many American psychiatrists and educators also denied the existence of dyslexia and reading and learning disabilities until rather recently, and the existence of these conditions is still denied by some. However, the massive numbers of children with severe learning problems

Table 4-6

Japanese Mean WISC Scaled Scores and IQs for Children with Learning Disabilities Diagnosed at the Izu Teishin Hospital, Hirai Kannami, Japan

Scale	Group 1 (N = 20)	Group 2 (N = 9)	Group 3 (N = 4)
Information	11.5	13.8	6.8
Similarities	10.8	10.7	6.3
Arithmetic	10.9	12.9	7.5
Vocabulary	12.9	15.7	6.3
Comprehension	8.8	14.7	7.8
Digit Span	10.4	13.6	9.8
Picture Completion	9.9	9.4	9.8
Picture Arrangement	9.8	9.6	10.8
Block Design	11.5	10.8	10.5
Object Assembly	11.1	9.1	12.5
Coding	10.2	9.3	10.3
Mazes	10.4	9.9	11.5
Verbal IQ	106.0	122.0	79.0
Performance IQ	106.0	98.0	105.0

Source: Adapted from data supplied by the Learning Disabilities Clinic, Izu Teishin Hospital—Dr. K. Kamimura, pediatrician, and Mrs. R. Morinaga, psychologist, 1980.

Sample consisted of thirty-three children, including thirty boys and three girls, aged 6.7 to 13.7 years, mean 9.7 years. Group 1 included twenty children whose Verbal and Performance IQs were within 11 points. Group 2 included nine children whose Verbal IQs were from 16 to 39 points greater than their Performance IQs. Group 3 included four children whose Performance IQs were from 24 to 28 points greater than their Verbal IQs.

that are known to exist in America do not seem to be found in some other societies, among which appear to be Japan and China. It is therefore most important to study these cultures in some detail to ascertain some of the reasons for their better academic situations.

The thirty-three children analyzed in table 4-6 had been assessed with a battery of tests, including WISC, Bender Visual Motor Gestalt Test, Draw-A-Person Test, Letter Completion Test, standardized reading test, gross- and fine-motor tests, examination for "soft neurological signs," and electroencephalograms (EEGs). This battery is similar to those used in American and European practice, previously described (L. Tarnopol 1967, 1968, 1969, 1971).

Nineteen of thirty-one children tested (61 percent) had either borderline or abnormal EEGs. This is similar to American findings for children with specific learning disabilities (SLD), and the abnormalities reported appear to be the same as those found in the Caucasian SLD population. Of thirty-two children tested with the Bender Visual Motor Gestalt Test (copying geometrical designs), thirteen (41 percent) were borderline and eleven (34 percent) were abnormal. Only one child with a normal EEG also had a normal Bender test, and this nine-year-old boy had a 23-point discrepancy between his 136 Verbal IQ and his 113 Performance IQ. He scored highest in Comprehension (20), and his lowest score was in Coding (7). This enormous range of subscale scores indicates a probable substantial specific learning disability (relative to his Verbal IQ), based on a severe visual-motor deficit.

In general, Block-Design seems to be the subscale that gives the Japanese children least difficulty (see table 4-6). Even group 2, whose Performance IQ's were significantly below their Verbal IQ's, averaged above 10 on Block-Design, and none of the three groups averaged below 9 on any Performance subscale. It is also of interest to note that the triad, Arithmetic, Digit-Span, and Coding, does not appear to be low in any of the three groups. This seems to indicate that Japanese dyslexics may have different subscale deficits than American dyslexics.

Chinese-American Boys with Reading Problems

Sixty Chinese-American boys with reading problems were compared with sixty Caucasian-American children with similar problems in the public San Francisco Unified School District. Their ages ranged from 7.6 to 12.9 years, with a mean of 9.5 years. All the Chinese-Americans were living in the United States by two years of age and came from families in which Cantonese was spoken primarily at home. The children all had either a Verbal or Performance IQ above 90. The pupils were drawn from the files of the Reading Clinic, and it was necessary to cover about eight years in order to find thirty Chinese-American boys who had been administered an assessment battery including the WISC. A similar group of thirty boys were drawn who had taken the WISC-R. Girls were not included because it was not possible to find thirty Chinese-American girls with the qualifications for either the WISC or WISC-R studies.

From tables 4-5 and 4-7 it can be seen that the Chinese-Canadian and Chinese-American pupils with reading problems have much in common. On the average, the seventy-eight children are significantly higher in Performance IQ than in Verbal IQ. Their highest subscale scores are in Block Design and Coding, while their lowest scores are found in Vocabulary, Information, Comprehension, and Similiarities. On the Verbal scale, they performed best in Arithmetic. The WISC scores parallel their functioning on the Wide Range Achievement Test (WRAT)—highest in arithmetic, with reading and spelling much lower. Reading is slightly higher than spelling. These WRAT mean scores are typical of those found in the learning-disabilities population generally. However, since only the Canadian children were assessed in both Chinese and English, there is no way of ascertaining the effects of bilingualism on the San Francisco pupils other than to note that reading and learning problems are relatively rare in the quite large

Table 4-7
Scores for Chinese-American Children with Reading Disabilities in San Francisco

	WISC-Tested			WISC-R-Tested		
	N	Mean	S.D.	N	Mean	S.D.
Grade-level	30	4.9	1.4	30	3.7	1.4
Information	30	7.9	2.4	30	6.4	3.3
Comprehension	30	8.9	2.4	30	9.5	2.6
Arithmetic	30	9.2	3.0	30	9.0	2.6
Similarities	30	8.4	2.7	30	7.8	3.3
Vocabulary	30	8.5	3.1	30	7.9	2.2
Digit Span	28	9.0	2.2	14	7.6	2.1
Picture Completion	30	11.0	2.9	30	10.7	3.3
Picture Arrangement	30	10.8	2.1	30	11.5	3.3
Block Design	30	12.2	2.7	30	12.4	2.6
Object Assembly	30	10.9	3.2	30	11.2	3.5
Coding	30	11.9	2.9	30	10.5	3.1
Verbal IQ	30	91.9	12.4	30	88.5	14.1
Performance IQ	30	109.4	11.3	30	109.0	16.1
Full Scale IQ	30	100.2	10.5	30	97.7	14.3
Bender T-score	25	56.4	20.1			
Reading standard score	29	79.3	9.8			
Spelling standard score	28	77.6	10.8			
Arithmetic standard score	28	92.7	9.7			

Source: Calculated from data supplied by Marjorie Goody, Project Coordinator, Diagnostic Reading Clinic, San Francisco Unified School District.
Sample was thirty boys in each group; mean age 9.5 years, standard deviation 1.4 years. T-scores have a mean of 50 and a standard deviation of 10. Reading, spelling, and arithmetic scores are from the Wide Range Achievement Test, standard score mean = 100, standard deviation = 15.

population of Chinese-American students in San Francisco, as has been previously reported.

Whereas the Chinese-Canadian pupils who were deficient readers in both English and Chinese also tended to have difficulty with the Bender test (previously noted), most of the San Francisco children had normal Bender scores (T-score below 60, see table 4-7).

The scores of the Caucasian American boys from the same Reading Clinic who were matched with the Chinese-Americans are given in table 4-8. Their lowest mean subscale scores are in the well-known triad, Arithmetic, Digit Span, and Coding, plus Information. The Chinese-Americans and Canadians, on the other hand, have mean group scores that are generally average to high on Coding, and mean Arithmetic scores that tend to be above average on the Verbal scale. These data and the subscale pattern analyses of Goody (1980) confirm the observation that the WISC and WISC-R subscale patterns tend to be different for the Caucasian and Chinese pupils with reading disabilities in English.

It should also be cautioned that these mean group patterns often fail to be reflected in those of individuals. It is further noted that the majority of the Caucasian students had borderline or abnormal Bender scores (mean 64.9, see table 4-8). The relationships among the Caucasian children's WRAT scores are the same as those of the Chinese children (see tables 4-7 and 4-8)—arithmetic highest, with reading and spelling much lower and close together.

The low Verbal scores of the Chinese children may partly be accounted for by the fact that Cantonese was spoken at home and the children often spoke Chinese among themselves at play and school. The high Peformance scores and the relatively high Arithmetic and Coding subscale scores attest to their good intelligence. At the same time, this pattern of scores indicates that the Caucasian and Chinese pupils tend to have somewhat different skills and deficits. High Coding scores tend to indicate good visual-motor functioning, visual memory, and fluid analytical ability. These same skills and some other types of visual perception are measured by the other performance subscales.

Table 4-8
Scores for Caucasian-American children with Reading Disabilities in San Francisco

	WISC-Tested			WISC-R-Tested		
	N	Mean	S.D.	N	Mean	S.D.
Grade-level	30	3.9	1.3	30	3.4	1.2
Information	30	9.6	2.5	30	8.5	2.5
Comprehension	30	10.8	3.3	30	10.4	2.8
Arithmetic	30	9.9	2.7	30	9.1	2.5
Similarities	30	11.4	2.8	30	10.2	3.1
Vocabulary	30	10.9	2.7	30	10.5	2.8
Digit Span	22	9.0	2.7	15	8.1	1.8
Picture Completion	30	10.0	2.4	30	10.6	2.6
Picture Arrangement	30	10.7	2.7	30	11.4	2.6
Block Design	30	11.1	2.8	30	11.1	2.9
Object Assembly	30	11.7	2.9	30	11.7	2.8
Coding	30	10.2	2.7	29	8.6	2.9
Verbal IQ	30	103.3	12.8	30	97.8	13.0
Performance IQ	30	105.1	11.8	30	104.6	14.1
Full Scale IQ	30	104.4	11.4	30	100.9	13.0
Bender T-score	21	64.9	15.4	15	58.6	16.1
Reading standard score	30	73.7	8.6	30	75.1	10.6
Spelling standard score	30	72.7	7.9	30	73.9	10.0
Arithmetic standard score	30	88.1	11.3	29	87.2	11.7

Source: Calculated from data supplied by Marjorie Goody, Project Coordinator, Diagnostic Reading Clinic, San Francisco Unified School District.

Sample was thirty boys in each group; mean age 9.0 years, standard deviation 1.1 years. T-scores have a mean of 50 and a standard deviation of 10. Reading, spelling, and arithmetic scores are from the Wide Range Achievement Test; standard score mean = 100, standard deviation = 15.

The correlations between the WISC and WRAT scores for the Chinese-American pupils are given in table 4-9. WRAT Reading, Spelling, and Arithmetic scores correlate very well with WISC Verbal IQ (0.59-0.70), Arithmetic (0.62-0.72), and Vocabulary (0.42-0.54) scores. These high correlations attest to the validity of the WRAT tests for this population. Too few pupils were given both the WISC-R and WRAT to get correlations for this group.

The correlations for the Caucasian-American children are given in table 4-10. One set of correlations is for the thirty students who were given the WISC and another set is based on the scores of the thirty pupils who took the WISC-R. In general, the WRAT Reading, Spelling, and Arithmetic tests correlate well with both WISC and WISC-R Verbal IQ and adequately with the Arithmetic and Vocabulary subscales.

Bannatyne (1971) suggested a method of analyzing the WISC subscale scores of dyslexic children based on three groupings. He considered spatial ability to be found from the average of the scaled scores for Picture Completion, Block Design, and Object Assembly. In like manner, conceptualizing ability could be derived from averaging the scores of the Comprehension, Similarities, and Vocabulary tests; and sequencing ability would be found from Digit Span, Picture Completion, and Coding. Based on his experience, Bannatyne concluded that dyslexics tend to be highest in spatial ability, intermediate in conceptualizing ability, and poorest in sequencing ability. Children with minimal brain dysfunction (MBD), on the other hand, were found to do very poorly in the spatial category and to show no consistent patterns in the conceptualizing or sequencing categories.

Goody (1980) did pattern analyses on both the Chinese-American and Caucasian-American children, based on both the WISC and the WISC-R,

Table 4-9
Correlations between WISC and WRAT Scores of Chinese-American Children with Reading Disabilities in San Francisco

	WRAT Reading			WRAT Spelling			WRAT Arithmetic		
	r	N	p	r	N	p	r	N	p
WISC									
Verbal IQ	0.66	29	0.001	0.59	28	0.001	0.70	28	0.001
Arithmetic	0.72	29	0.001	0.60	28	0.001	0.63	28	0.001
Vocabulary	0.47	29	0.005	0.42	28	0.01	0.54	28	0.002
Picture Completion	0.59	29	0.001	0.52	28	0.002	0.17	28	0.2
WRAT									
Arithmetic	0.48	28	0.005	0.49	27	0.005			
Spelling	0.79	28	0.001						

Source: Calculated from data supplied by Marjorie Goody, Project Coordinator, Diagnostic Reading Clinic, San Francisco Unified School District.

r = coefficient of correlation, N = number of students, p = probability level.

Table 4-10

Caucasian-American Children with Reading Disabilities in San Francisco

	WRAT Reading			WRAT Spelling			WRAT Arithmetic		
	r	N	p	r	N	p	r	N	p
Group 1									
WISC									
Verbal IQ	0.52	30	0.001	0.41	30	0.01	0.41	30	0.01
Arithmetic	0.22	30	0.1	0.28	30	0.07	0.52	30	0.001
Vocabulary	0.42	30	0.01	0.38	30	0.02	0.24	30	0.1
WRAT									
Arithmetic	0.39	30	0.02	0.18	30	0.2			
Spelling	0.64	30	0.001						
Group 2									
WISC-R									
Verbal IQ	0.36	30	0.03	0.42	30	0.01	0.53	29	0.002
Arithmetic	0.35	30	0.03	0.48	30	0.004	0.58	29	0.001
Vocabulary	0.18	30	0.2	0.26	30	0.08	0.41	29	0.01
WRAT									
Arithmetic	0.78	29	0.001	0.63	29	0.001			
Spelling	0.70	30	0.001						

Source: Calculated from data supplied by Marjorie Goody, Project Coordinator, Diagnositc Reading Clinic, San Francisco Unified School District.

Correlations are based on standard scores. r = coefficient of correlation; N = number of students; p = probability level.

with 30 pupils in each group, totaling 120 children. Since Digit Span is an alternate test and was not always used, it was omitted from the analyses, leaving the sequencing category with only Arithmetic and Coding.

The genetic dyslexic pattern of spatial ability highest, conceptualizing next, and sequencing lowest occurred in fourteen cases out of sixty among the Caucasians (23 percent). The pattern most often found among the Chinese-Americans was spatial ability highest, sequencing intermediate, and conceptualizing lowest in twenty-six out of sixty (43 percent). The most often observed pattern among the Caucasians was conceptualizing highest, spatial ability intermediate, and sequencing lowest in seventeen cases out of sixty (28 percent). Although these relationships tend to occur, they may not be very meaningful, since the differences between the category means for individual pupils often are not significant. However, if the category differences are significant, they should be useful when developing an individual teaching prescription for a child.

Preliminary Study of American, Japanese, and Taiwanese Pupils

In January 1980 we did preliminary testing of 194 Taipei-Chinese and 89 Hiroshima-Japanese second- and fifth-grade pupils; and in June 1980 we

administered the same tests to 90 South San Francisco children. By coincidence, Harold Stevenson of the University of Michigan had also started a
study to test the same general hypotheses that we were examining, based on
his own preliminary findings in the literature, so that his group also tested
Taiwanese children in January, 1980. They tested in the first and sixth
grades in different schools from the ones we visited in Taipei.

For our preliminary investigation we used standardized American tests
that did not depend on reading vocabulary. This made it possible to derive
comparisons with a norm group, as had been done with the WPPSI, WISC,
and WISC-R. By eliminating reading from the testing, a variable that is
most difficult to control was fully controlled.

The battery used included the WRAT Arithmetic test (Jastak, Bijou,
and Jastak 1978), the Draw-A-Person or Human Figure Drawing Test
(Koppitz 1968), and the Developmental Test of Visual-Motor Integration
(Beery, Buktenica 1967). As part of the testing, the pupils were asked the
occupations of their fathers and mothers. In the second grade, birthdates
had to be confirmed from the teacher's files, and this was sometimes
necessary in the fifth grade. It was also often necessary to confirm the
fathers' and mothers' occupations. Right- and left-handedness were also
recorded.

The WRAT Arithmetic test contains sixty-three problems on level 1.
The first twenty problems are for preschool through grade one and are to be
individually administered. Since none of the children that we tested would
be required to take this part of the test, it was omitted. Problem 40, which is
about a fifth-grade item, had to be omitted because it could not be converted into a meaningful metric system equivalent (½ yd. = _____ in.).
This had a slight but tolerable effect on the norms for fifth-grade children,
since they could do other problems instead. Problem 60 (MCXLII =
_____) also had to be omitted because it could not be used in China and
Japan, but this had no effect since it is at the eleventh-grade level and none
of the children reached it. All other problems could readily be stated in
Chinese and Japanese. For the WRAT the 1978 norms were used.

On the WRAT the most useful score for comparing pupils in the same
grade is the grade-level score, not the standard score, which is based on age.
We appreciate that the standard scores give equal units of measure;
however, to be useful the standard scores would have to be based on grade-
level groupings rather than ages. This can readily be understood by considering an example. If two children are in the same classroom, they will
have had the same instruction. If these children are in the fifth grade and
earn the same raw score on the Arithmetic test, they will have the same
grade-level score, but if their ages vary so will their standard scores.

If these children both earn a raw score of 38, their grade-level scores will
be 5.5. However, the child who is ten years, eleven months old will get a
standard score of 106, and the child of eleven years will be placed at 96. This
discrepancy in the standard scores makes no sense and occurs only because

of the artifact of basing the scores on age rather than grade level. The student who is one month younger than the eleven-year-old, gets 10 points added to his standard score even though they are both in the same arithmetic class.

The Draw-A-Person Tests were group-administered and were scored by the Koppitz (1968) method, in which one point is given for items of anatomy and clothing present, to a maximum of 30 points. The raw scores were reported, as norms were not available. The emotional indicators were not used because of group testing and lack of adequate validity. All drawings were scored by Muriel Tarnopol to achieve maximum reliability.

The Developmental Test of Visual-Motor Integration (Beery, Buktenica 1967) involves copying geometrical designs, each of which is scored either *pass* or *fail* according to the criteria in the manual. There are twenty-four designs to be copied, and the age equivalent norms go from two years, ten months to fifteen years, eleven months.

Teaching methods were observed in the schools in which testing was done, and a number of other schools were also visited to observe teaching. Informal conferences were held with special educators, teachers, psychologists, physicians, and school administrators; some parents of school children were interviewed; and textbooks were examined.

All tests were administered by us, with the assistance of team members and translators in Taipei and Hiroshima. Each classroom teacher remained in the room during testing and gave complete cooperation. The principals accompanied us to the classes and at times were able to remain to assist and observe the testing.

In order to obtain maximum scorer reliability, all tests were very carefully hand-scored by ourselves. We could not select the schools in which testing was done; rather, we had to find administrators who were receptive to the research concept and would assist us in getting cooperating teachers. Abroad, we were dependent on the contacts of our cooperating teams at the National Taiwan Normal University and the University of Hiroshima.

Preliminary Study in South San Francisco

South San Francisco is a city of light industry, with a population of 49,290, adjacent to San Francisco. The school district has 10,614 students from kindergarten through twelfth grade.

Testing was done in two second-grade and two fifth-grade classes of an elementary school with an enrollment of 477 students in a lower-middle-class neighborhood. The average class size in this school is twenty-eight pupils from kindergarten through sixth grade. In addition to the regular classes, there are two special day classes for learning-handicapped children, each of which may enroll a maximum of twelve children and has a specially credentialed teacher plus a shared aide. The school is built in California ranch-style architecture and is a one-level complex with offices, library, classrooms, and a multipurpose auditorium and lunchroom. There is a large yard and playing space, and the school is clean and very well maintained, with no evidence of vandalism.

The ethnic composition of the school includes Filipinos (25 percent), Latin Americans (10 percent), Blacks (5 percent), Asian and Pacific Islanders (5 percent), and other Caucasians (55 percent). In the classes where testing was done, sixteen different languages were spoken in the homes, some of which were bilingual and others trilingual. The foreign language most often spoke was Tagalog (38 percent), followed by Spanish (15 percent), and Chinese (9 percent). Other foreign languages spoken included Arabic, German, Hindi, Hungarian, Ilocano, Italian, Japanese, Pampango, Portuguese, Samoan, Thai, and Slovenian. However, this school, with its own "United Nations," has no special programs in English as a second language or bilingual education. Nevertheless, these bilingual and trilingual children scored no differently from the monolingual English-speaking children on our tests, and the school as a whole had scored well above grade-level on all the state standardized tests at every grade. The scores on the California Test of Basic Skills for the second, fifth, and sixth grades are given in table 4-11. By the sixth grade the mean reading grade-level of the pupils was 9.0, with language at 10.5 and mathematics equal to 9.1. These results indicate what may be attained with an academically oriented curriculum. The very high reading and language levels are especially gratifying in view of the fact that so many of the children are not from primarily English-speaking families.

The effects of multilingualism on the performance of schoolchildren is an important subject at issue in the United States. We therefore collected data on all languages spoken in the homes of the pupils from the office files and used this information in our data analysis. A few cases are documented here to increase our understanding of this problem.

John's trilingual background includes German, Hungarian, and English, all three languages being spoken at home. At eleven years, five

Table 4-11
California Test of Basic Skills (CTBS) Grade-Level Scores for Pupils at the South San Francisco Elementary School, April 1980

Grade	N	Reading	Language	Mathematics
2.7	48	3.3	3.6	3.0
5.7	61	7.6	9.1	7.9
6.7	68	9.0	10.5	9.1

months of age, his scores on our test battery in the fifth grade (5.9) were: arithmetic grade-level, 6.3; spelling grade-level, 6.3; Beery VMI age-equivalent, 12.7 years; and Draw-A-Person, 26 (class average, 23.1). The multilingual home was not preventing John from functioning slightly above grade-level on these tests. We are aware that his reading and learning-expectancy levels are dependent upon his IQ, which was not available.

An interesting difficulty involving the usages of *wear*, *where*, and *ware* was found during this testing when students were asked to report if they did not have the glasses that they ordinarily wear. The problem seemed to be independent of language spoken at home. Nick, who comes from an English-speaking family, wrote, "Where's glasses but not today." His test scores in grade 5.9 were: Beery VMI age-equivalent, 11.8 years; Draw-A-Person, 27; arithmetic grade-level, 7.5; and spelling grade-level, 7.5.

Another fifth-grade pupil from an English-speaking home wrote, "Wares' glasses but not today." A student whose family spoke Tagalog wrote, "I were glasses when they are not broken." A fourth pupil, from a Tagalog-speaking background, wrote, "I don't like waring glasses and besides they are losted." These errors indicate some of the problems arising for all American children who are learning English. Problems exist with homonyms that have different meanings, with the use of the apostrophe, and with verb endings.

As in Hiroshima and Taipei, the teachers were very cooperative and were interested in the testing and research, and they remained in the classrooms during the testing to be of assistance. The principal also was most attentive and helpful, and he discussed the purpose of the research with the teachers and pupils and observed the classes during testing. We administered and scored all the South San Francisco tests ourselves.

In addition to the tests previously mentioned, the WRAT Spelling test and a measure of penmanship were added in South San Francisco. The forty-four second-grade pupils were in two classes at grade level 2.9 when tested (see table 4-12). Their mean grade-level scores in arithmetic and spelling were 3.4 and 4.2, respectively. The average age of the children was 8.2 years, and their mean age-equivalent score on the Beery test of copying geometrical designs was 7.4 years, indicating that, although they were above grade-level in arithmetic and spelling, their visual-small-motor skills were relatively underdeveloped.

When the data were broken down for boys and girls, no significant differences were found except that the girls were somewhat better in penmanship than the boys. The data were also analyzed for mother-at-home versus mother-works, socioeconomic status based on the father's occupation, and English spoken at home versus foreign language spoken at home. None of these pairs of variables produced significantly different means in arithmetic, spelling, Beery, Draw-A-Person, or penmanship. The correla-

Table 4-12
Test Scores of Second-Grade South San Francisco Children

	Total Group (N=44)		Boys (N=24)		Girls (N=20)	
	Mean	S.D.	Mean	S.D.	Mean	S.D.
Age (years)	8.2	0.6	8.2	0.7	8.1	0.5
Arithmetic grade-level	3.4	0.3	3.4	0.3	3.4	0.3
Arithmetic standard score	104.3	7.6	103.6	7.3	105.2	7.9
Spelling raw score	37.7	5.4	37.3	4.9	38.1	6.1
Spelling grade-level	4.2	0.6	4.2	0.6	4.3	0.5
Spelling standard score	113.8	13.1				
Beery raw score	14.3[a]	2.5	14.5	2.7	14.0	2.3
Draw-A-Person raw score	20.1	3.2	20.0	3.5	20.2	3.0
Penmanship raw score	2.1	0.8	2.4[b]	0.8	1.8[b]	0.8

Wide Range Achievement Test arithmetic and spelling scores, based on U.S. norms; Beery-Buktenica Developmental Test of Visual-Motor Integration, raw score; Draw-A-Person Test, Koppitz score; penmanship score, 1 = excellent, 2 = good, 3 = fair, 4 = poor. At testing, grade-level = 2.9.
S.D. = Standard deviation.
[a]Age-equivalent = 7.4 years.
[b]Difference of means is significant at $p = 0.02$

tion matrix for the forty-four second-grade pupils showed that only Beery and Draw-A-Person correlated at the 0.01 probability level or better ($r = 0.36$, $p = 0.01$).

In the fifth grade we tested two classes totaling forty-six pupils. However, there were sixty-one pupils in this grade, fifteen of whom were in a combined fifth- and sixth-grade class because they were the best academically of the fifth-graders, and these were not tested.

For the two fifth-grade classes tested, arithmetic was at grade-level (5.7) and spelling was above grade-level (6.7) (see table 4-13, which is similar to the data in table 4-11 showing language development to be above mathematics for the total fifth grade). As in the second grade, the mean Beery (copying geometrical designs) score is below the mean chronological age (10.3 versus 11.0).

Further analyses of the data by boys versus girls, mother-at-home versus mother-works, manuscript versus cursive writing, and father's occupation showed no significant differences in arithmetic, spelling, Beery, Draw-A-Person, or penmanship scores. Comparison of both the second- and fifth-grade pupils from English-speaking homes versus foreign-language-speaking homes is given in table 4-14. The only significant difference found was in Draw-A-Person at the fifth-grade level, which scored in favor of the foreign-language-speaking children.

A somewhat surprising result of the comparisons of children from English-speaking and foreign-language-speaking homes was that, at both the second- and fifth-grade levels, the bilingual pupils scored higher on the

Table 4-13
Test Scores of Fifth-Grade South San Francisco Children

	Mean	S.D.
Age (years)	11.0	0.4
Arithmetic grade-level	5.7	1.0
Arithmetic standard score	102.3	11.8
Spelling raw score	49.9	6.1
Spelling grade-level	6.7	0.8
Spelling standard score	112.3	15.2
Beery raw score	18.2[a]	3.3
Draw-A-Person raw score	23.1	3.3
Penmanship raw score	1.9	0.7

Wide Range Achievement Test arithmetic and spelling scores, based on U.S. norms; Beery-Buktenica Developmental Test of Visual-Motor Integration, raw score; Draw-A-Person Test, Koppitz score; penmanship score, 1 = excellent, 2 = good, 3 = fair, 4 = poor. At testing, grade-level = 5.9.
S.D. = standard deviation. N = 46.
[a]Age-equivalent = 10.3 years.

average than the other group in spelling. Even though the difference in the means did not reach significance, the finding is important because these children did not have any form of special help, such as bilingual or English as a second language programs. The bilingual children were also significantly better than those from English-speaking domiciles on the Draw-A-Person test in the fifth grade, and a low but significant correlation was found between Draw-A-Person and spelling (r = 0.27) as shown in table 4-15.

Analysis of the spelling errors made by the second- and fifth-grade students revealed that their mistakes were frequently sensible and appeared to reflect the strong phonics program that this school offers. One bilingual second-grade pupil, an eight-year-old girl, achieved a raw score of 49 on the spelling test, which is equivalent to grade 6.6, and a standard score of 138. All the spelling words that she missed were close phonic approximations of the stimulus words. For example, she wrote *resenable* for *reasonable*, *ocupied* for *occupied*, *caracter* for *character*, *recognise* for *recognize*, and so forth. The principal and teachers at this school expressed satisfaction with the program they had selected for the basic language arts curriculum, which places strong emphasis on applied phonics.

The correlation matrix for the fifth-grade pupils indicates that arithmetic and spelling correlate well (r = 0.49), arithmetic correlates with Draw-A-Person (0.33), Beery correlates with Draw-A-Person (0.36), and penmanship correlates with spelling and Draw-A-Person (0.42 and 0.44), as shown in table 4-15.

The good correlation between penmanship and spelling tends to further

Table 4-14

Comparison of Second- and Fifth-Grade South San Francisco Children from English-Speaking Families and Those from Foreign-Language-Speaking Families

	English-Speaking Families		Foreign-Language-Speaking Families	
	Mean	S.D.	Mean	S.D.
Second Grade				
Arithmetic R.S.	27.5	1.2	27.7	1.7
Beery VMI R.S.	14.1	2.0	14.3	2.7
Spelling R.S.	36.8	6.2	38.0	5.2
Draw-A-Person R.S.	19.7	3.2	20.2	3.3
Penmanship R.S.	1.9	0.8	2.2	0.9
Age (years)	8.1	0.4	8.2	0.7
Number of pupils	11		33	
Fifth Grade				
Arithmetic R.S.	39.0	3.8	37.9	4.3
Beery VMI R.S.	17.6	4.0	18.6	2.8
Spelling R.S.	48.9	5.5	50.5	6.4
Draw-A-Person R.S.	21.5	2.9	24.1	3.2
Penmanship R.S.	2.1	0.7	1.8	0.7
Age (years)	11.0	0.4	11.0	0.5
Number of pupils	17		29	

None of the differences of the means are significant, except the fifth-grade Draw-A-Person scores at $p = 0.01$. R.S. = raw score.

confirm the hypothesis proposed by Muriel Tarnopol and tested by one of her students, namely, that penmanship and spelling should be correlated for children and that if pupils with learning disabilities are taught to write rapidly in cursive, their spelling scores should improve significantly. These children usually print in a slow, labored manner and make reversals. It was hypothesized that some of their spelling difficulties were caused by an inability to think of two things simultaneously, that is, how to print the letters and how to spell. By eliminating interference from the printing problem, their spelling should improve spontaneously. Turnberg (1978) tested and confirmed this hypothesis with a junior high school class of learning-disabled students.

Preliminary Study in Hiroshima

In 1977 the population of Hiroshima was 842,095. In 1980 there were 91,584 pupils in 112 public elementary schools, 1,002 children in 3 elementary schools attached to a university, and 742 private-school pupils.

    Since the aftereffects of the nuclear explosion in 1945 were of concern in

Table 4-15
Correlation Matrices for Forty-four Second-Grade and Forty-six
Fifth-Grade South San Francisco Pupils

	Spelling		Draw-A-Person		Penmanship		Socioeconomic Status	
	r	p	r	p	r	p	r	p
Second Grade								
Arithmetic			0.30	0.03			0.31	0.02
Beery VMI			0.36	0.01				
Draw-A-Person							0.32	0.02
Fifth Grade								
Arithmetic	0.49	0.001	0.33	0.01				
Beery VMI	0.28	0.03	0.36	0.01	0.27	0.04	0.28	0.03
Spelling			0.27	0.03	0.42	0.002		
Draw-A-Person					0.44	0.001		

Only the significant correlation coefficients are given. r = coefficient of correlation; p = probability level.

connection with our research, we asked the school administrators what results had been observed on the schoolchildren over the years. If there were any untoward effects present in the generations of pupils after the explosion, the educators were not aware of them, they claimed, even though they had been looking for such problems.

Arrangements for testing had been organized by Professors Nakano and Taguchi of the University of Hiroshima. Professor and Mrs. Taguchi also very graciously arranged for us to interview in their home mothers of elementary-school children with the aid of our interpreter, Mrs. Izumi Allen. From these interviews and others in Tokyo, we were able to gain some preliminary information to be used in a survey questionnaire.

The Japanese mothers interviewed said that they had not smoked or used any nonprescription or prescription drugs, nor had they imbibed alcohol, tea, or coffee during their pregnancies. They also claimed to have had natural childbirth without the aid of anesthetics or forceps. In one case a mother reported that her legs had swelled during pregnancy and that the "water broke first." Labor was induced by medication and the baby was "blue" when born. However, this child seemed to have had no learning problems.

When asked who had told them what to avoid during pregnancy, they invariably indicated that their mothers had done so. The hospital personnel had given them lectures on diet and other things, advising them about the need for iron, calcium, and minerals to be derived from natural foods, and suggesting 2,200 calories per day for expectant mothers. These middle-class women had seen their obstetricians regularly during their pregnancies and had been given urinalyses and some blood tests but no x-rays. Pelvic measurements had been taken also.

The Japanese diet is very low in sugar compared with that in Western nations. It contains primarily vegetables, rice, and fish, with poultry and some meat added, especially in the higher income levels. Breast-feeding had usually been attempted but didn't seem to last very long in the mothers interviewed (two weeks to seven months). Girls were found to be easier to toilet train than boys and tended to be trained at an earlier age (about one and a half years for girls and two years for boys). The children entered kindergarten at about two to three years of age and remained until entering school at six years. The mothers said that they had been told to teach the children to count to twenty and to read and write their names before starting school.

Mothers in Japan are given a mother-child notebook in which entries are made by nurses and physicians each time the child is seen. All the mothers that we interviewed had their notebooks. A developmental history of the child is kept in this book so that precise information is always available concerning when any important event occurred and the types of immunizations, medications, and dosages given. These mothers considered their baby books to be most important documents. The advantages of having such correct information available, especially when families change residences, are apparent.

At school the children had been getting one or two hours of homework daily (including weekends), depending on their grade levels. The homework in Hiroshima was corrected by the mothers, who signed a receipt that was returned to the teacher each day with the corrected work. Some mothers have been urging the teachers to go faster and teach more so that their children will be well prepared for the highly competitive college-entrance examinations. The group that we interviewed in Hiroshima were of the opinion that too much homework was being given and that the children needed more time to play. The parents sometimes stated that "creativity was being beaten out of the children." Some educators and physicians expressed concern that Japanese nationals were not winning Nobel Prizes and they questioned the desirability of a continued "lock-step" curriculum.

Since the prestige of the university attended seems to determine the student's ability to get into a desirable business or industry after graduation, competition for matriculation to the best universities is keen. Consequently, the children tend to be sent to kindergartens that have the reputation for preparing them to get ahead in school. At about sixth grade many pupils begin to attend *juku* (tutoring school) for two hours an afternoon several days a week to help prepare for their college-entrance examinations. The mothers who push children are called "education mamas."

We got the impression that children with learning disabilities also attended *juku* as a way of getting extra coaching in areas of weakness. Between the added assistance rendered by their regular teachers, *juku,* and their mothers' tutoring at home, many of these children were being kept afloat in the curriculum. However, during interviews with some of their mothers, great feelings of despair were expressed at the time and energy necessarily devoted to these suffering children. These mothers felt harassed almost beyond endurance by their ordeals. One mother stated that she must devote "99 percent of her time" to the learning-disabled child at the expense of time available for her husband and family.

The Hiroshima School. The school is built around a large inner courtyard. A guard is usually posted outside the entrance to this yard, and visitors must stop to state their purposes before entering the school. The teachers' workday is from 8:25 A.M. to 5:10 P.M., but the principal said, "Of course, they usually work longer." They tend to use time before school, at lunch period, and after school to give extra help to pupils in need. The children attend school from 8:55 A.M. to 3:15 P.M. five and a half days a week.

Before class each morning the pupils line up in the courtyard to have physical exercises (like Swedish eurythmics) to music for about twenty minutes, along with the entire school staff. These eurythmics are used in all schools and appear to be well known to everyone. At their conclusion the children march to their classrooms, and when they get to class they are wide awake and ready for work.

It was January and there had been a little snow. The children were lightly dressed, usually uniformly, and the windows were open so that the room temperatures were never above 65°F, and no children wore hats or overcoats in the classrooms.

Both men and women taught in this elementary school, and our general impression was that they were well prepared academically. The children appeared alert and attentive, eager to answer questions, and they laughed readily. During our visits no children raised their hands to leave the room or to report that they had no book, paper, pencil, and so on. The teachers' chalkboard work was meticuluous, their writing of the ideographs was very rapid and precise, in straight vertical lines. Similarily, the children's blackboard work showed evidence of careful training in calligraphy and penmanship. The teachers were observed to be standing continuously and walking about the room to observe the pupils' work more closely, rarely sitting at a desk.

There appears to be a very active Parent-Teachers Association in this school, which meets once each month and sometimes sponsors a bazaar to raise money for the school. The slippers in the rack at the school entrance are marked PTA. Everyone changes from street shoes to slippers before entering the school. Parents are permitted to observe the classes in session at any time and to meet with the teachers afterwards. However, there is a day set aside each month for such observation and parent-teacher meetings, and 70 percent of the parents are said to attend (usually the mothers), and twice-yearly child-parent-teacher meetings are held.

The children entered into the spirit of our testing with enthusiasm and apparent motivation. Professor Taguchi and our interpreter, Mrs. Allen, helped us get the testing sessions under way. After the second-graders were finished, Muriel Tarnopol led them in singing songs in English that featured hand and body movements to accompany the words. The children entered into the singing with action and great zeal, including boys climbing onto their chairs and desks in some cases as they vied to be recognized to respond to questions and to suggest what to sing or whom they nominated to perform. They were serious when working and exuberant when playing.

When doing arithmetic problems, the pupils used their six-inch plastic rulers to line up the multiplication and division problems. As a result, they avoided errors due to misaligned work and demonstrated the effects of structured teaching both in their way of doing the problems and in their high scores. They also wanted to use the rulers to do the Beery test of copying geometrical designs. However, on this test they were not permitted to use rulers or erasers. When they were asked to draw a human figure, the students evidenced great enthusiasm and gleefully showed their work to others after finishing.

The second-grade class of forty-seven pupils had been augmented by several children from a class whose teacher was absent that day. Rather than using substitutes, the pupils are divided among other classes at the same level when a teacher is absent for only a short period of time.

Hiroshima Test Results. One class of forty-seven second-grade pupils was tested in Hiroshima. On the WRAT Arithmetic test, using 1978 U.S. norms, the pupils averaged almost one year (0.9 year) above grade-level, as shown in table 4-16. On the Beery test of copying geometrical designs their age equivalent was 9.8, compared with their chronological mean age of 8.3, and their mean Draw-A-Person score of 24.2 was significantly higher than the South San Francisco children's 20.1 (see table 4-12). In general, these second-graders appear to be functioning significantly above U.S. norms.

When the data for mother-at-home versus mother-works were compared, a significant difference was found in arithmetic in favor of the children whose mothers were at home. Comparisons between girls and boys and among socioeconomic levels (father's occupations) revealed no significant differences in arithmetic, Beery, or Draw-A-Person scores. In the second grade, arithmetic was found to have a modest but significant correlation with both Draw-A-Person and mother's occupation (0.32 and 0.34), as shown in table 4-17.

A class composed of forty-two fifth-grade pupils was also tested. In

Table 4-16
Test Scores of Second-Grade Hiroshima Children

	Total Group (N=47)		Mother at Home (N=23)		Mother Working[a] (N=17)	
	Mean	S.D.	Mean	S.D.	Mean	S.D.
Age (years)	8.3	0.3	8.3	0.3	8.3	0.3
Arithmetic grade level	3.7	0.3	3.8[b]	0.3	3.6[b]	0.2
Arithmetic standard score	105.0	5.1	106.9[b]	5.4	103.4[b]	3.9
Beery raw score	17.3[c]	3.2	17.8	2.7	17.1	3.1
Draw-A-Person raw score	24.2	1.6	24.3	1.4	23.8	2.0

Wide Range Achievement Test arithmetic grade-level and standard scores, based on U.S. norms; Beery-Buktenica Developmental Test of Visual-Motor Integration, raw score (maximum obtainable score = 24), Draw-A-Person test, Koppitz score (maximum obtainable score = 30). At testing, grade-level = 2.8
[a]Nonprofessional worker.
[b]The difference between the means is significant, p = 0.02.
[c]Age equivalent = 9.8 years.

arithmetic their mean score was 1.1 years above grade-level (6.9 versus 5.8), as shown in table 4-18. However, their grade-level scores ranged from 4.3 to 10.0, or from 1.5 years below to 4.2 years above grade level. The very high scores may possibly be attributable to the influence of *juku*.

When the data were analyzed for boys versus girls, mother's occupation, and father's occupation, no significant differences were found for arithmetic, Beery, or Draw-A-Person scores. The only significant correlation found was between arithmetic and Beery scores (r = 0.36), as shown in table 4-17.

Table 4-17
Correlations for Second and Fifth-Grade Hiroshima Pupils

	Arithmetic Scores		
	N	r	p
Second Grade			
Beery VMI	47	0.15	0.2
Draw-A-Person	47	0.32	0.01
Mother's occupation	46	0.34	0.01
Fifth Grade			
Beery VMI	42	0.36	0.01
Draw-A-Person	42	0.02	0.5
Mother's occupation	42	0.08	0.3

N = number of pupils; r = coefficient of correlation; p = probability. Mother's occupation is composed of three items: mother at home, mother works as a professional, and mother as a worker.

Table 4-18
Test Scores of Fifth-Grade Hiroshima Children

	Mean	S.D.	Range
Age (years)	11.3	0.3	10.8-11.9
Arithmetic grade-level	6.9	1.3	4.3 10.0
Arithmetic standard score	108.5	12.1	80-142
Beery VMI	21.3	2.0	17-24
Draw-A-Person	24.9	2.1	19-29

Wide Range Achievement Test Arithmetic grade-level and standard scores, based on U.S. norms; Beery-Buktenica Developmental Test of Visual-Motor Integration, raw score (maximum obtainable score = 24); Draw-A-Person Test, Koppitz score (maximum obtainable score = 30). At testing, grade-level = 5.8. N = 42.

Preliminary Study in Taipei

In 1976 the population of Taipei City, Taiwan, Republic of China, was 2,089,288. There were 115 primary schools, 101 secondary schools, and 20 colleges and universities in Taipei at the time (*Essentials of the Taiwan Provincial Administration* 1977). These schools included 274,540 primary pupils, 231,420 secondary students, and 93,969 college and university students. In these schools there were approximately 10,400 primary teachers, 10,000 secondary teachers and 2,400 college and university teachers. For Taiwan as a whole, the rate of enrollment in schools was 99.4 percent in primary schools and 91.7 perccent in public junior middle schools (grades seven through nine).

In addition to the schools in which we tested, a number of schools and classrooms at all levels were visited to gain a broad understanding of the school system. We also went to private and church schools and special-education facilities connected with hospitals.

Art, Music, and Physical Education. In accordance with the principles of education formulated by Sun Yat-sen, a primary task is to insure "the continued existence of the nation and its cultural heritage," which was partly accomplished through music, art, and physical education. The empasis on these curricula in all types of schools was impressive, including instruction in many art forms, vocal and instrumental music, and gymnastics. During recess in an elementary school of 7,000 pupils, the teachers each brought small portable pianolike instruments onto the playground for combined physical education and singing by their individual classes of fifty to sixty pupils.

In many classes we observed students learning to read music and playing instruments or singing with excellent quality. The curriculum for handicapped students also includes much musical education. Both retarded and physically handicapped (including blind) children performed for us, combining physical education or eurythmics to recorded music or singing. A high school girls' a cappella chorus presented a concert in three-part harmony. Later we learned that the students were retarded. A band made up of blind students also played an excellent concert for us. Music therapy was used in a hospital program for autistic and brain-injured students to teach body awareness, right and left, and social skills, indicating further creative uses of music.

Art is given a major position in education. In one second-grade classroom, the children's self-portraits (faces) were mounted at the rear of the room. The children responded with enthusiasm when given the tasks of copying geometrical designs or drawing human figures, and no stick figures were found among the drawings of the Taipei pupils. The children did a great deal of writing in notebooks in order to learn their many characters, and they often illustrated the notebooks with pictures in color, using crayons and felt-tipped pens. One primary school had a library housing a collection of special handwritten and illustrated books donated by each student as a gift before leaving the school.

Physical education receives a high priority in the Republic of China schools. Students were seen coming to school equipped with a large array of special sportswear carried in small hand-cases. During physical education, the teachers frequently participated with the pupils in games as team members, rather than standing on the sidelines shouting instructions. The eurhythmic exercises are also widely practiced outside of the schools by adults, who may decide to swing their arms and bodies for relaxation at any convenient time.

Students Cleaning Schools. The pupils in each class were responsible for sweeping and dusting their rooms, and each room contained the necessary implements for this work. The children also were responsible for cleaning the hallways, stairs, and yard. As a result, litter was rarely evident and the pupils seemed to take pride in their schools and enjoyed the housekeeping tasks, as indicated by their enthusiasm at work. There were no signs of vandalism, so maintenance and custodial costs appeared minimized.

Taipei Schools and Testing. The schools are built around the courtyards so that the rooms are entered from the yard, which has a single large entrance with a gatekeeper. Before school starts, the children, teachers, and staff line up in the yard for morning exercises. A loudspeaker plays music and everyone performs the gymnastics, led by a teacher or administrator on a podium. Thereafter, the pupils march by classes, each led by a student, to their rooms, where they arrive awake and ready for work. The students generally wear uniforms, and even though it was winter and the rooms were unheated, the windows were open and they did not wear their overcoats or hats in the classrooms.

Arrangements for testing were made under the direction of Wei-fan Kuo, president of the National Taiwan Normal University, who assigned Wu-tien Wu, director of the Special Education Center, and Mrs. Mei-chi Lai of the Center to assist us. Mrs. Lai acted as our interpreter, translated and printed the tests in Mandarin, and arranged for testing at two schools. During the testing we were assisted by Mrs. Lai and Professor Hung-hsiang Liu.

Following our testing procedure, Mrs. Lai explained the ten-minute Arithmetic Test to the students, after which they did the untimed Developmental Test of Visual-Motor Integration (VMI) and the Draw-A-Person Test. When they first saw the arithmetic test, which contains problems through first-year algebra, many gasped and then got right to work. The second-graders completed all they could do in about two or three minutes and then went back over their problems, and some tried some of the more difficult ones. The pupils appeared able to do mental arithmetic without effort and very little lip or finger counting was observed; and no child needed to make little lines to count sums or differences. Numbers were written fairly carefully about the same size as the spaces allotted and in the correct columns. There was very little erasing, and the paperwork was generally neat and clean.

During both the arithmetic and VMI tests, there was virtually no talking and considerable concentration. However, when doing the human-figure drawing, the children relaxed and expressed pleasure and excitement. Afterwards they were observed holding up their work for their friends to see. Sex differences were noticeable in these drawings. The boys often drew persons with guns, swords, military hardware, uniforms, and sports figures and equipment, as well as some action figures, sometimes adding cars, airplanes, tanks, and ships, including battle scenes. The girls, however, tended to draw brides, mothers, teachers, and figures adorned with necklaces, earrings, and bouffant hair arrangements (which no child wore). The clothing included details such as flowers, birds, intricate designs, and many tucks, pleats, and gathers. Added drawings, when time permitted, included houses, rooms with furniture, dolls, doll houses, and clothes.

Taipei Test Results. Two classes of second-grade pupils, totaling ninety-nine children, were tested in Taipei (see table 4-19). At the time of testing the pupils were at mid-year, or grade level 2.5. Their grade-level range in arithmetic, based on 1978 U.S. norms, was from 2.5 to 3.9, with a mean of 3.3. One school had an upper-middle-class (USES) clientele and the other was lower-middle-class (LSES). Nevertheless, no child tested below grade-level on U.S. norms, and the range was not great, indicating that the classes were kept pretty well together by the teachers.

On the Developmental Test of Visual-Motor Integration (copying geometrical designs), they averaged one year above the U.S. norms (8.9 versus 7.9), as shown in table 4-19. Their mean score of 22.5 on the Draw-A-

Table 4-19
Test Scores of Second-Grade Taipei Pupils

	Number	Range	Mean	S.D.	Age-Equivalent (years) Mean
Arithmetic grade-level	99	2.5-3.9	3.3	0.3	
Arithmetic standard score	99	88-124	106.0	7.9	
Beery VMI	99	9-22	15.4	2.9	8.9
Draw-A-Person	89	14-28	22.5	2.9	
Age (years)	99	7.3-8.8	7.9	3.7	

Wide Range Achievement Test arithmetic; Beery-Buktenica Developmental Test of Visual-Motor Integration and Draw-A-Person Test, raw scores. At testing, grade-level-2.5.

Person Test was intermediate between the scores of the Hiroshima and South San Francisco children. In general, these second-graders appeared to be functioning quite adequately.

Comparisons of the data from the USES and LSES schools are given in table 4-20. On the Arithmetic Test and the Developmental Test of Visual-Motor Integration, the USES school's children scored significantly above the LSES pupils, whereas their age and Draw-A-Person means were smaller.

Further analyses based on boys versus girls, mothers' occupations, and fathers' occupations are given in table 4-21. The girls were significantly better than the boys on the Draw-A-Person Test. On the Arithmetic Test and the Developmental Test of Visual-Motor Integration, for the total population of second-grade pupils, those whose fathers were white-collar employees or professionals performed significantly better, on the average, than those whose fathers were blue-collar workers. No significant differences were found to be related to mothers' occupations.

Table 4-20
Test Scores of Second-Grade Taipei Pupils

	Number	Range	Mean	S.D.	p
USES arithmetic grade-level	49	2.9-3.7	3.4	0.19	0.001
LSES arithmetic grade-level	50	2.5-3.9	3.2	0.36	
USES Beery VMI	49	13-22	16.1	2.8	0.02
LSES Beery VMI	50	9-21	14.7	2.9	
USES Draw-A-Person	41	14-28	22.2	3.1	NS
LSES Draw-A-Person	48	17-27	22.8	2.7	
USES age	49	7.3-8.8	7.9	3.6	NS
LSES age	50	7.3-8.3	7.9	3.8	

USES = upper-middle socioeconomic level school; LSES = lower-middle socioeconomic level school. At testing, grade-level = 2.5. NS = not significant. p = probability level for the significance of the difference of the means.

Table 4-21

Test Scores of Second-Grade Taipei Pupils, Compared by Sex and Socioeconomic Levels Based on Father's Work

	Number	Range	Mean	S.D.	p
Boys' Draw-A-Person	53	14-28	21.9	3.1	0.004
Girls' Draw-A-Person	36	17-27	23.5	2.3	
FBC arithmetic grade-level	37	2.6-3.7	3.2	0.32	0.007
FWC arithmetic grade-level	52	2.5-3.9	3.4	0.26	
FP arithmetic grade-level	5	3.3-3.5	3.4	0.11	
FBC Beery VMI	37	11-21	14.5	2.5	0.02
FWC Beery VMI	52	9-22	15.9	3.1	
FP Beery VMI	5	14-20	16.6	2.6	

Significant differences only are given. At testing, grade-level = 2.5. p = probability level for the significance of the difference of the means. FBC = father blue-collar worker; FWC = father white-collar employee; FP = father professional.

The correlation matrix of significant relationships only indicates that the arithmetic scores were positively correlated with visual-motor integration, Draw-A-Person, and the father's socioeconomic level (see table 4-22). Visual-motor functioning was also found to be related to human-figure drawing and SES of father.

Ninety-five fifth-grade pupils in two classes were tested (see table 4-23). Their grade-level range in arithmetic was from 4.5 to 7.8, with a mean of 6.3, based on 1978 U.S. norms. Thus, no pupil was more than one grade below grade-level, and the average was 0.8 years above. The mean age and the visual-motor integration age-equivalent were the same (10.8 and 10.6 years) for these pupils. As with the second-grade students, the mean Draw-A-Person score was about midway between those of the Hiroshima and South San Francisco children.

Comparisons of the data from the USES and LSES schools, and based on fathers' occupations, is given in table 4-24. Once again, the USES children did significantly better than the LSES pupils in arithmetic, both in the comparison between schools and when the socioeconomic levels were

Table 4-22

Correlation Matrix for Second-Grade Taipei Pupils

	Beery Visual-Motor Integration			Draw-A-Person			SES of Father		
	N	r	p	N	r	p	N	r	p
Arithmetic	99	0.40	0.001	89	0.26	0.008	94	0.27	0.004
Beery VMI				89	0.24	0.01	94	0.25	0.01

SES = socioeconomic level; N = number of pupils r = coefficient of correlation; p = probability level.

Table 4-23
Test Scores of Fifth-Grade Taipei Pupils

	Number	Range	Mean	S.D.	Age-Equivalent (years), Mean
Arithmetic grade-level	95	4.5-7.8	6.3	0.8	
Arithmetic standard score	95	89-136	112.0	9.8	
Beery VMI	95	10-24	19.6	2.9	10.6
Draw-A-Person	92	18-28	24.0	2.2	
Age (years)	95	10.2-12	10.8	3.7	

Wide Range Achievement Test, arithmetic; Beery Developmental Test of Visual-Motor Integration and Draw-A-Person Test, raw scores. At testing, grade-level = 5.5.

determined from their fathers' employment, regardless of which school they attended. From table 4-25 we see that arithmetic is solidly correlated with socioeconomic status ($r = 0.49$), and human-figure drawing correlates with visual-motor integration ($r = 0.27$).

South San Francisco, Hiroshima, and Taipei

The class sizes in the schools in which testing was performed tended to be quite different, which is indicative of the general situations in the United States, Japan, and Taiwan (see table 4-26). The smallest elementary schools (477 in the South San Francisco school) and class sizes are found in the United States, where classes tend to contain from twenty to thirty-five pupils on the average. Japanese elementary schools tend to be larger (the Hiroshima school had more than 2,000 pupils), and classes range from about thirty-five to forty-five in Japan. In Taipei we tested in elementary

Table 4-24
Test Scores of Fifth-Grade Taipei Pupils

	Number	Range	Mean	S.D.	p
USES arithmetic grade-level	45	5.1-7.8	6.8	0.67	0.001
LSES arithmetic grade-level	50	4.5-7.3	5.8	0.62	
FBC arithmetic grade-level	28	4.5-7.1	5.8	0.71	0.001
FWC arithmetic grade-level	39	5.1-7.8	6.4	0.72	0.02
FP arithmetic grade-level	23	5.3-7.8	6.8	0.67	

Signficant differences only are given. At testing, grade-level = 5.5. USES = upper-middle class school; LSES = lower-middle class school; p = probability level for the significance of the difference of the means. FBC = father blue-collar worker; FWC = father white-collar employee; FP = father professional.

Table 4-25
Significant Correlations of WRAT Arithmetic versus Socioeconomic Level (Father's Occupation) and Draw-A-Person versus Beery Developmental Test of Visual-Motor Integration for Fifth-Grade Taipei Pupils

	Number	r	p
Arithmetic vs. SES	90	0.49	0.001
Draw-A-Person vs. Beery VMI	92	0.27	0.004

schools with more than 2,000 pupils. The largest school has 12,000 children. Class size appears to range from about forty to sixty in Taipei. These data indicate that neither class size nor school size are primary determinants of how well the children learn. Similar conclusions were reached from the International Association for the Evaluation of Educational Achievement studies of reading in fifteen countries (Thorndike 1973); and studies of mathematics achievement in twelve countries, where children did better in larger elementary school classes than in the smaller ones (Husén 1967).

We are aware that our data do not permit cross-national comparisons because too many variables remain uncontrolled, including the children's IQs, total environments, teaching methods, and language differences. However, we compiled table 4-27 to indicate some likenesses and differences among the pupils for preliminary consideration.

In the second grade, the visual-motor integration and human-figure drawing mean scores were highest in Hiroshima, intermediate in Taipei, and

Table 4-26
Relative Class Sizes in South San Francisco, Hiroshima, and Taipei in Tested Classes

Location of Elementary School	Grade	Number of Pupils
South San Francisco	2	22
South San Francisco	2	22
South San Francisco	5	22
South San Francisco	5	24
Hiroshima	2	42 + 5[a]
Hiroshima	5	42
Taipei USES	2	41
Taipei LSES	2	49
Taipei USES	5	42
Taipei LSES	5	50

USES = upper-middle socioeconomic level.
LSES = lower-middle socioeconomic level.
[a]The class was augmented by five pupils because of a teacher's absence.

Table 4-27
WRAT arithmetic, Beery Developmental Test of Visual-Motor Integration, and Draw-A-Person Test raw scores for Second- and Fifth-Grade Children in Hiroshima, Taipei, and South San Francisco

	Grade	Number	Arithmetic grade-level Mean	S.D.	Beery VMI Mean	S.D.	Draw-A-Person Mean	S.D.
Hiroshima	2.8	47	3.7	0.3	17.3	3.2	24.2	1.6
Taipei	2.5	99	3.3	0.3	15.4	2.9	22.5	2.9
South San Francisco	2.9	44	3.4	0.3	14.3	2.5	20.1	3.2
Hiroshima	5.8	42	6.9	1.3	21.3	2.0	24.9	2.1
Taipei	5.5	95	6.3	0.8	19.6	2.9	24.0	2.2
South San Francisco	5.9	46	5.7	1.0	18.2	3.3	23.1	3.3

$N = 373$.

lowest in South San Francisco. Since these scores remained in the same order in the fifth grade, preliminary indications are that the order may be meaningful. Either by coincidence or for good reasons, the three second-grade children who achieved the highest score (25) on the Draw-A-Person Test in South San Francisco, as well as the child with the highest score in the fifth grade, are all Chinese-Americans. Moreover, only 5 percent of the pupils in that school are Asian-Americans.

In the second grade, the scores for arithmetic were fairly close together in the three cities, and they could be placed in the same order as the VMI and Draw-A-Person means if we correct the Taipei score for grade-level to bring it up to the others (see table 4-27). By fifth grade the arithmetic scores had separated and were in the same order as the VMI and Draw-A-Person scores. Since arithmetic, visual-motor integration, and human-figure drawing have been found to be positively correlated, it may be concluded that these functions tend to be moderated by similar underlying central nervous system faculties. Lynn (1977) has proposed that the high perceptual-motor skills of Asian children may be the result of genetic endowment. However, the relative contributions of the cultural environment and inheritance remain moot.

Summary and Conclusions

The conclusions drawn from a preliminary study are in the form of hypotheses to be tested by further research. Therefore, they should not be accepted as confirmed.

Japanese psychologists and educators claim that there are no significant differences in either IQ scores or achievement levels among their socioeconomic groups. They do admit to a small difference between urban and rural pupils, in favor of city children. We are planning a larger study to test these hypotheses, since no differences based on SES were found in the one school in which testing was done. Significant SES differences in arithmetic and visual motor integration were found in the Taipei schools, where we were able to test in both lower and upper-middle SES schools. No SES-related difference was found in the single South San Francisco school in which we tested, but the relationship between SES and achievement in American education is well documented.

It must be considered that a major difference between the American and Asian schools under study is that U.S. school populations tend to be heterogeneous (ethnically and in terms of percentages of minority groups represented), whereas Asian schools have relatively homogeneous populations.

Preliminary discussions with both Chinese and Japanese mothers indicated that there may be significant environmental differences between Asian and Caucasian families. The prenatal care of the fetus by mothers (diet and avoidance of harmful chemicals), natural childbirth, and early mother-child relationships may prove to be meaningfully different across cultures. Divorce and one-parent families are unusual among the Asians, but they are abundant in America. The drug culture and many teenage births in America are major problems. The Asians generally marry later and start their families at more mature ages than the American average. All these cultural and environmental factors need to be assessed to determine their relative influences on children.

The Japanese children appear to have an important head start in both arithmetic and visual-motor (Performance IQ) types of development upon entering school. A similar but less impressive ability was seen in the Wechsler scores of the Chinese-Canadian and Chinese-American pupils (Cantonese speaking, generally from Hong Kong).

Chinese and Japanese schools tend to have a relatively stable curriculum that stresses basics. Also, the teachers we observed appeared to be well trained, with a solid knowledge of their curricula and standardized methods of teaching. In California there has been a tendency in some school districts to introduce curriculum changes often, sometimes at random, and before adequate testing and teacher preparation, with disastrous results. The Asian children appear to benefit from their stable, well-organized curriculum, as seen in their mathematics, visual-motor, and human-figure drawing performances.

In the Chinese and Japanese schools, the children sit in straight rows, usually in twos. They have been taught to sit up (as opposed to slouching or sitting back attempting to balance the chair, as has been seen in some California schools); to write clearly, neatly, and rapidly; to stand correctly;

to hold their books properly when reading; and the like. Some of these factors and a structured curriculum are the things that are usually reintroduced in special-education classes in an attempt to remediate many American children. Often there is no desk at the front of the room, and the teacher remains standing, teaching continuously, using the blackboard, asking questions for children's replies, and walking about the room observing the children while teaching. The basic facts, such as the multiplication tables, are thoroughly overlearned, so the pupils have no need for crutches. Multisensory learning is often used, and the children shout aloud in unison, sometimes while writing in the air to impress basic facts on several sensory learning modalities simultaneously.

Specific Learning Disabilities

Although early reports denied that Chinese and Japanese children had specific learning disabilities in measurable numbers, recent work tends to confirm that SLD exists in these populations but may not be as prevalent as it is among Caucasians. Moreover, when the same battery of tests is used to assess SLD pupils, similar basic findings appear among Asian and Caucasian children. However, the WISC and WISC-R profiles of dyslexic Asian and Caucasian children tend to be different. There is some evidence that genetic dyslexia may be rarer among Asians than among Caucasians.

Our preliminary study seems to indicate the need for further cross-cultural research to determine the effects of the different curricula and teaching methods to which we alluded. A comprehensive survey of the prenatal through school-entry environments of children could also produce some valuable information about child-rearing practices that help to prepare children for the educational process.

We recognize that, even after the developmental environments of children have been improved, some children will still require individualized teaching. Consequently, both aspects of the preparation of learning-disabled children for life will require intensive consideration. Such studies should assist materially in the training of American children.

References

Bannatyne, A. 1971. *Language, Reading and Learning Disabilities.* Springfield, Ill.: Thomas.

Beery, K.E., and Buktenica, N. 1967. *Developmental Test of Visual-Motor Integration.* Chicago: Follett.

Birch, H.G. 1964. The problem of "brain damage" in children. In H.G. Birch (ed.), *Brain Damage in Children.* Baltimore: Williams and Wilkins.

Birch, H.G., and Gussow, J.D. 1970. *Disadvantaged Children: Health, Nutrition and School Failure.* New York: Grune and Stratton.

Brackbill, Y., and Broman, S.H. 1979. Obstetrical Medication and Development in the First Year of Life (mimeographed unpublished manuscript). Bethesda: National Institute of Neurological and Communicative Disorders and Stroke, U.S. Department of Health, Education and Welfare.

Cederborg, S. 1979. Personal communication.

Coleman, J.S., et al. 1966. Equality of Educational Opportunity. Washington, D.C.: U.S. Government Printing Office.

Conners, C.K. 1971. Drugs in the management of children with learning disabilities. In L. Tarnopol (ed.), *Learning Disorders in Children.* Boston: Little, Brown.

Essentials of the Taiwan Provincial Administration. 1977. Taiwan Provincial Government Printing Factory.

Feingold, B.F. 1975. *Why Your Child Is Hyperactive.* New York: Random House.

Galton, L. 1977. *Medical Advances.* New York: Crown. Studies are cited from *Canadian Medical Association Journal* 109:1104.

Goody, M. 1980. WISC and WISC-R Subscale Patterns of Caucasian-American, Chinese-American and Hispanic-American Boys with Reading Disabilities. Doctoral thesis, University of San Francisco.

Husén, T. (ed.). 1967. *International Study of Achievement in Mathematics.* New York: Wiley.

Jastak, J.F., Bijou, S., and Jastak, S. 1978. Wide Range Achievement Test. Wilmington, Del.: Jastak Associates.

Kline, C.L., and Lee, N. 1972. A transcultural study of dyslexia: analysis of language disabilities in 277 Chinese children simultaneously learning to read and write in English and Chinese. *Journal of Special Education* 6:1.

Koppitz, E.M. 1968. *Psychological Evaluation of Children's Human Figure Drawings.* New York: Grune and Stratton.

Kuo, W., Chen, Y., and Liang, C.N. 1976. *National Prevalance Study on Exceptional Children in the Republic of China.* Taipei: National Taiwan Normal University.

Lynn, R. 1977. The intelligence of the Japanese. *Bulletin of the British Psychological Society* 30.

Makita, K. 1968. The rarity of reading disability in Japanese children. *American Journal of Orthopsychiatry* 34:4.

Masland, R.L. 1969. Children with minimal brain dysfunction: a national problem. In L. Tarnopol (ed.), *Learning Disabilities: Introduction to Educational and Medical Management.* Springfield, Ill.: Thomas.

Mayeske, G.W., and Beaton, A.E., Jr. 1975. *Special Studies of Our Nation's Students.* Washington, D.C.: U.S. Government Printing Office.

Medicine. 1979. *Time,* July 2, p. 76.

Needleman, H.L., Gunnoe, C., Levitson, A., Reed, R., Peresie, H., Maher, C., and Barrett, P. 1979. Deficits in psychologic and classroom performance of children with elevated dentine lead levels. *New England Journal of Medicine* 300:698-695.

Peters, L., and Ellis, E.N. 1970. *An Analysis of WISC Profiles of Chinese-Canadian Children with Specific Reading Disabilities in Chinese, English or Both Languages.* Vancouver, B.C.: Board of School Trustees.

Sakamoto, T., and Makita, K. 1973. Japan. In J. Downing (ed.), *Comparative Reading.* New York: Macmillan.

Should I Drink? 1980. DHHS Publication No. (ADM) 80-919. Rockville, Maryland: National Clearing House for Alcohol Information.

Swanson, J.M., and Kinsbourne, M. 1980. Food dyes impair performance on a laboratory learning test. *Science* 207:1485.

Tarnopol, L. 1957*a*. Evaluate your training program—use of surveys, reliability and validity measures. *Journal American Society of Training Directors* (March).

_____ . 1957*b*. Training supervisors through feedback. *Personnel Journal* (July).

_____ . 1957*c*. How to evaluate your training program. *American Association of Industrial Nurses Journal* (July).

_____ . 1961. *Report of Employee Opinion Survey.* U.S. Army Transportation Terminal Command, Pacific (July).

_____ . 1963. Motivation in Human Relations. Madison: American Society of Training Directors.

_____ . 1967. Testing the educationally handicapped child. *Academic Therapy Quarterly.* 3:2.

_____ . 1968. Children with learning disorders. *The Pointer* 13:1.

_____ . 1969. Testing children with learning disabilities. In L. Tarnopol (ed.), *Learning Disabilities: Introduction to Educational and Medical Management.* Springfield, Ill. Thomas.

_____ . (ed.), 1971. *Learning Disorders in Children.* Boston: Little, Brown.

Tarnopol, L., and Tarnopol, M. 1976. *Reading Disabilities: An International Perspective.* Baltimore: University Park Press.

Tarnopol, L., and Tarnopol, M. 1980. Arithmetic ability in Chinese and Japanese children. *Focus on Learning Problems in Mathematics.* 2:3.

Tarnopol, M. 1977. Reading problems worldwide. *Bulletin of the Orton Society,* 270.

Thorndike, R.L. 1973. *Reading Comprehension Education in Fifteen Countries.* New York: Wiley.

Turnberg, R.W. 1978. The Effect of Handwriting Improvement upon the Spelling Achievement of Junior High Learning Disabled Students. Field study for M.A. in Education, San Francisco State University.

Human-Figure Drawings by Chinese, Japanese, and American Children

Muriel Tarnopol

Although all 373 children who were tested in Taipei, Hiroshima, and South San Francisco drew a human figure, a few could not be scored because the children inadvertently made their drawings too large for the paper and were unable to include the feet. Generally, these oversized figures were drawn by girls, who brought the long dress down to the bottom edge of the paper. As a result, only 360 figure drawings were scored.

The Draw-A-Person Tests (Human-Figure Drawing Tests) were scored by the Koppitz (1968) method, which gives points for anatomical parts and certain articles of clothing present, to a maximum of 30 points. When this method of scoring is used, no consideration is given to the overall elegance of a figure or to artistic or creative value. Since these aspects of the drawings are of great interest, we are presenting a series of figures done by the highest and lowest scoring boys and girls in each school for analysis. We will also report the pupils' scores on the Wide Range Achievement Test in arithmetic (Jastak, Bijou, and Jastak 1978), and the Developmental Test of Visual-Motor Integration (Beery and Buktenika 1967).

Perceptual and memory deficits in the various sensory channels, such as visual, auditory, kinesthetic, tactile, and the cross-modalities, are considered to be major symptoms of learning disabilties. These deficiences are believed capable of adversely influencing the learning of both visual-motor and academic functions. Therefore, tests of the basic sensory-learning modalities are usually included in assessment batteries for learning disorders. The human-figure drawing test is very widely used in many countries as one of these instruments. The drawing gives a quick evaluation of the child's level of cognitive development and maturity in terms of knowledge of body parts and proportions, sometimes referred to as "self-image." It also gives evidence of possible brain damage and is used as a projective test by many psychologists, although validity for this use has not been adequately established.

Clements (1969) recommended the following identification test battery for case-finding purposes:

Wechsler Intelligence Scale for Children
Bender Visual Motor Gestalt Test

Draw-A-Person Test

Wide Range Achievement Test

Gray Oral Reading Test

At present, the revised Wechsler is used, the Developmental Test of Visual Perception or the Developmental Test of Visual-Motor Integration may be substituted for the Bender, and any standardized reading test may be used.

Gofman (1969) included the Draw-A-Person Test in the identification battery being taught to senior medical students and house staff in pediatrics and ophthalmology at the University of California—San Francisco Medical Center. As part of the physical examination, the physician is to observe the child dressing and buttoning his clothes and his use of paper and pencil. A preliminary assessment of coordination can be made by asking the child to "draw the best man he can," and the like.

Conners (1971) suggested that a number of brief clinical tests could be used as objective measures for evaluating the effects of medication. These tests included Draw-A-Person and copying geometrical designs, among others, to determine the effects of the drugs on motor control, impulsivity, and cognitive abilities.

In Argentina Robles Gorriti and Rodriquez Muñiz (1976), conducted a learning-disabilities clinic at the Psychiatric Department of the Children's Hospital in Buenos Aires. Their test battery for assessment of learning problems in children included the WISC, Bender, and human-figure drawing, among other tests.

In Japan, Kamimura and Morinaga (1980) used the Draw-A-Person Test (D-A-P) along with the Bender, WISC, and other tests. Of the thirty-three children examined for specific learning disabilities, they gave the D-A-P to thirty and found that three scored above average (10 percent), fourteen scored in the average range (47 percent), and thirteen were below average (43 percent). The below-average group scored from 2.2 to 6.7 years below their chronological ages on the test.

Human-figure drawings are also used as part of many other widely used assessment instruments for children, including the Metropolitan Readiness Tests (Hildreth, Griffiths, and McGauvran 1965), and the Psychoeducational Inventory of Basic Learning Abilities (Valett 1968). In view of the widespread use of human-figure drawing tests by psychologists, educators, physicians, and others concerned with school achievement and behavior, it appeared practical to include such drawings in our study. The advantages of this test include low cost, relatively easy administration, and reliable standardized scoring procedures. Moreover, this test is generally seen as fun by the children and lightens the test atmosphere for them. The instructions for giving the Koppitz-Human-Figure Drawing Test are very brief and may be used in different countries. The examiner states: "On this piece of paper I would like you to draw a *WHOLE* person. It can be any kind of person you

Table 5-1
Human-Figure Drawings, Koppitz Scoring, Raw Scores for Second- and Fifth-Grade Hiroshima, Taipei, and South San Francisco Pupils

	Grade	Number	Range	Mean	S.D.
Hiroshima	2.8	47	21-27	24.2	1.6
Taipei	2.5	89	14-28	22.5	2.9
South San Francisco	2.9	44	13-25	20.1	3.2
Hiroshima	5.8	42	19-29	24.9	2.1
Taipei	5.5	92	18-28	24.0	2.2
South San Francisco	5.9	46	16-29	23.1	3.3

want to draw, just make sure that it is a whole person and not a stick figure or a cartoon figure'' (Kopptiz 1968).

From table 5-1 it can be seen that the mean scores of the Hiroshima pupils at both second- and fifth-grade levels on the Human-Figure Drawing Test (24.9 and 24.2) were above the mean scores of the children in all the other schools. Next, in order, were the fifth-grade Taipei pupils (24.0) and the fifth-grade South San Francisco children (23.1). The lowest means were attained by the second-graders in Taipei (22.5) and in South San Francisco (20.1).

Kline and Lee (1972) noted that only 30 percent of the Chinese-Canadian children whom they had tested drew Oriental persons. However, it is quite difficult to determine if a drawing of a human figure represents an Oriental or Occidental face in many cases. Table 5-2 gives the percentages of Taipei and Hiroshima pupils who drew "definitely Occidental" and "definitely Oriental" faces. In Taipei most of the faces were judged to be definitely Occidental, with about 10 percent of the boys and 3 percent of the

Table 5-2
Taipei and Hiroshima Pupils Who Drew Human Figures with Either Definitely Oriental or Definitely Occidental Faces
(Percentages)

	Definitely Occidental	Definitely Oriental
Taipei		
Grade-two girls	82	0
Grade-two boys	48	6
Grade-five girls	81	5
Grade-five boys	23	13
Hiroshima		
Grade-two girls	16	28
Grade-two boys	0	50
Grade-five girls	5	14
Grade-five boys	5	53

girls drawing Asian faces. In Hiroshima, however, the reverse was true; only a few were seen as definitely Occidental. Most of the Asian faces were drawn by boys (about 52 percent), and the Japanese girls also made more Asian faces (21 percent) than the pupils in Taipei. Some of the drawings seemed to be based on cartoons seen on television, and others may have been similar to those found in schoolbooks. However, a great many figures were definitely imaginative, or perhaps based on magazine or advertising models, since the children rarely looked like their drawings in features, hair-dress, or clothing. None of the Asian children drew stick figures.

At the fifth-grade level in South San Francisco, the Draw-A-Person Test correlated with all the other measures used, namely, arithmetic, VMI, spelling, and penmanship (see table 5-3). It also correlated well with VMI in South San Francisco and Taipei at both the second- and fifth-grade levels. Finally, the human-figure drawings correlated well with arithmetic in the second grades at Hiroshima and Taipei and in the fifth grade at South San Franciso.

The higher-scoring figures were also generally the best qualitatively within each school system. However, interesting differences were noted across cultures. These are best seen in the drawings themselves.

Comparisons of Drawings

Second Grade, Hiroshima

The highest-scoring and qualitatively best human figure drawn by a second-grade Hiroshima boy (grade 2.8) is shown in figure 5-1. The features noted on this drawing included good body proportions; firm, heavy pencil pressure; and the lids on both eyes, which are rarely drawn by a second-grader. He also paid close attention to clothing details, including cuffs,

Table 5-3
Significant Correlations, Human Figure Drawing Test Scores versus Wide Range Achievement Test Arithmetic and Spelling Scores and Beery Developmental Test of Visual-Motor Integration Scores versus Penmanship Scores

	South San Francisco				Hiroshima		Taipei			
	Grade Two (N = 44)		Grade Five (N = 46)		Grade Two (N = 47)		Grade Two (N = 89)		Grade Five (N = 92)	
	r	p	r	p	r	p	r	p	r	p
Arithmetic			0.33	0.01	0.32	0.01	0.26	0.008		
Beery VMI	0.36	0.01	0.36	0.01			0.24	0.01	0.27	0.004
Spelling[a]			0.27	0.03						
Penmanship[a]			0.44	0.001						

[a]Spelling and penmanship were tested only in South San Francisco.

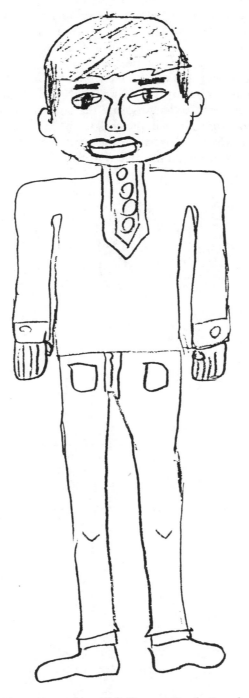

Figure 5-1. Hiroshima Boy: Age, 8.2 Years; Grade-Level, 2.8; Draw-A-
Person Test Score, 27

pockets, and zipper on the trousers, buttons and cuffs on the jacket, and a neckpiece. This 8.2-year-old boy's scores on the tests were: Draw-A-Person raw score, 27; Beery VMI age-equivalent, 9.3 years; arithmetic grade-level, 3.9; and arithmetic standard score, 105.

The lowest-scoring and qualitatively poorest figure drawn by a second-grade Hiroshima boy is shown in figure 5-2. Noted are the disproportionate sizes of the shoulders, leg lengths, and the body as compared to the legs. The facial features are minimal, the neck is small for the head, and there is a lack of detail in the clothing. Both the nose and mouth are indicated by straight lines, and one hand has five fingers while the other has only four.

Figure 5-2. Hiroshima Boy: Age, 8.0 Years; Grade-Level, 2.8; Draw-A-Person Test Score, 21

The scores earned by this 8.0-year-old boy were: Draw-A-Person raw score, 21; Beery VMI age-equivalent, 10.2 years; arithmetic grade-level, 3.3; and arithmetic standard score, 101.

The highest-scoring and qualitatively best human figure drawn by a second-grade Hiroshima girl is shown in figure 5-3. The figure is well proportioned and nicely dressed, with buttons and decorations on the blouse and skirt. The bangs are carefully drawn with gradations, and the eyes are very wide. The socks have ruffles and the shoes are styled. The over-all effect of this figure drawing is very mature for an 8.4-year-old girl. Her test scores were: Draw-A-Person raw score, 26; Beery VMI age-equivalent, 13.0 years; arithmetic grade level, 3.9; and arithmetic standard score, 110.

The lowest-scoring and qualitatively poorest human figure drawn by a second-grade Hiroshima girl is shown in figure 5-4. The eyes, nose, and mouth in this face are drawn somewhat like those seen in some of the illustrations found in Japanese primary books. The head is too large for the rest of the body, and the torso is too narrow. The blouse and skirt show attention to detail. This 8.1-year-old girl scored as follows: Draw-A-Person raw score, 22; Beery VMI age-equivalent, 9.5 years; arithmetic grade-level, 3.5; and arithmetic standard score, 104.

The drawings of the second-grade Hiroshima children are all unusually good, since the lowest score, 21, is above the lowest scores made in all other second- and fifth-grade classes (see table 5-1). Also, since the mean score of 24.2 is second only to the Hiroshima fifth-grade class, it appears that this particular class may be exceptional. Because of the solid correlations reported between human-figure drawing scores and intelligence test scores for this age group (0.5 to 0.6), we may assume that these children also have high IQs (Koppitz 1968). Since we do not have precise data on the IQs of the various groups of pupils under consideration, it is most important not to attempt comparisons that should be controlled for intelligence levels.

Since the scoring of the Draw-A-Person Test is based on the number of body parts and pieces of clothing drawn, a combination of training and practice would artificially inflate children's scores. In order to be able to make meaningful comparisons of the levels of development of different pupils, it is essential that they have been exposed to the same type and amount of education. Since these variables cannot be controlled in cross-cultural studies, any conclusions derived from the data must be tempered by both uncontrolled-environment and intelligence factors.

Second Grade, Taipei

The highest-scoring and qualitatively best human-figure drawing by a second-grade Taipei boy (grade 2.5) is shown in figure 5-5. Noteworthy are the firm, even pencil pressure; excellent proportions; partial profile on the face; stance; and the balance of the total figure. This 7.8-year-old boy's test

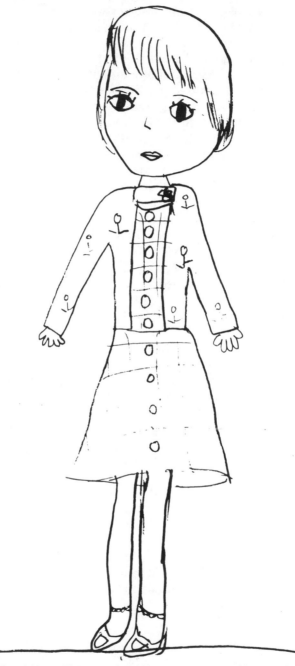

Figure 5-3. Hiroshima Girl: Age, 8.4 Years; Grade-Level, 2.8; Draw-A-
Person Test Score, 26

Figure 5-4. Hiroshima Girl: Age, 8.1 Years; Grade-Level, 2.8; Draw-A-Person Test Score, 22

scores were: Draw-A-Person raw score, 28; Beery VMI age-equivalent, 12.8 years; arithmetic grade-level, 3.3; and arithmetic standard score, 108.

The lowest-scoring and qualitatively poorest human-figure drawing by a second-grade Taipei boy is shown in figure 5-6. Although this figure is very small and appears immature, the pupil is clearly quite bright, as can be seen from his arithmetic and Beery scores. The proportions of the drawing are good except for the oversize cap visor. There are a number of anatomical parts missing, including the nose, ears, hands, and feet; and the eyes and mouth are indicated in a most elementary manner. Since he is one of the youngest childen in the second grade, his age may partly account for the immaturity of the drawing. This 7.4-year-old boy's test scores were: Draw-A-Person raw score, 14; Beery VMI age-equivalent, 10.9 years; arithmetic grade-level, 3.5; and arithmetic standard score, 121.

The highest-scoring and qualitatively best human-figure drawing by a second-grade Taipei girl is shown in figure 5-7. The figure drawn appears to be of a mature woman, with attention to intricate details on the skirt, cuffs, belt, and boots. A necklace and very long hair (much fuller and longer than any we can recall seeing in Taipei), with bows, frame a face dominated by

Figure 5-5. Taipei Boy: Age, 7.8 Years; Grade-Level, 2.5; Draw-A-Person
              Test Score, 28

enormous square eyes accentuated by eyelashes and eyebrows. The figure's
proprotions are quite mature for an eight-year-old child. This left-handed
8.3-year-old girl attained the following test scores: Draw-A-Person raw
score, 27; Beery VMI age-equivalent, 13 years; arithmetic grade-level, 3.5;
and arithmetic standard score, 104.

Figure 5-6. Taipei Boy: Age, 7.4 Years; Grade-Level, 2.5; Draw-A-Person
              Test Score, 14

Figure 5-7. Taipei Girl: Age, 8.3 Years; Grade-Level, 2.5; Draw-A-Person
Test Score, 27

The lowest-scoring and qualitatively poorest human-figure drawing by a
second-grade Taipei girl is shown in figure 5-8. This quite immature drawing has poor proportions and lacks ears and proper fingers. The arms are
emanating from the midbody and stick up like two pieces of wood, while
the hair is indicated in a most elementary fashion. This 8.3-year-old girl is

low on all of the tests, as follows: Draw-A-Person raw score, 17; Beery VMI age-equivalent, 5.8 years; arithmetic grade-level, 2.6; and arithmetic standard score, 88.

Second Grade, South San Francisco

The highest-scoring and qualitatively best human figure drawing by a second-grade South San Francisco boy (grade 2.9) is shown in figure 5-9.

Figure 5-8. Taipei Girl: Age, 8.3 Years; Grade-Level, 2.5; Draw-A-Person Test Score, 17

This student comes from a bilingual home, where Cantonese is the primary language, and both his parents are from Hong Kong. The drawing is of a boy and features interesting attention to small details, such as the decorations on the shoes, the baseball and "Giant's Base Ball" printed on the jacket, buttons on the cuffs, and a buckle on the belt. The body proportions are only fair, and the nose appears to be unusual. The test scores for this 8.1-year-old boy were: Draw-A-Person raw score, 25; Beery VMI age-equivalent, 10.2 years; arithmetic grade-level, 3.5; arithmetic standard score, 104; spelling grade-level, 5.7; and spelling standard score, 123.

The lowest-scoring and qualitatively poorest figure drawn by a second-grade South San Francisco boy is shown in figure 5-10. This pupil attained the lowest score in the total sample of 360 children. He is also the youngest child in the group (7.0 years). However, his academic work is quite ade-

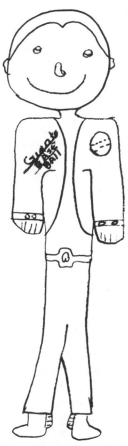

Figure 5-9. South San Francisco Boy: Age, 8.1 Years; Grade-Level, 2.9; Draw-A-Person Test Score, 25

quate. The figure drawn has details in the face only. Ears are missing, and everything below the head is poorly indicated. The arms extend from the neck, and no hands are shown. The body is immaturely drawn and has no clothing, and the legs are sticks without feet. The test scores for this left-handed 7.0-year-old pupil were: Draw-A-Person raw score, 13; Beery VMI age-equivalent, 6.4 years; arithmetic grade-level, 3.1; arithmetic standard score, 115; spelling grade-level, 4.1; and spelling standard score, 126.

The highest-scoring and qualitatively best figure drawing by a second-grade South San Francisco girl is shown in figure 5-11. This drawing has some interesting details and features a school cheerleader with pom-poms, tennis socks, and a block R (the student's first name begins with R) on the front of her sweater. The proportions are adequate for a child 7.8 years of age. This left-handed girl comes from a bilingual family, with Cantonese the primary language spoken at home. Her academic test scores were high, as follows: Draw-A-Person raw score, 25; Beery VMI age-equivalent, 7.9 years; arithmetic grade-level, 3.7; arithmetic standard score, 111; spelling grade-level, 5.9; and spelling standard score, 128.

The lowest-scoring and qualitatively poorest human figure drawn by a second-grade South San Francisco girl is shown in figure 5-12. This figure has a very large head with some features, while the remainder of the body lacks definition. There is no neck, the arms are indicated as tiny stumps with no hands or fingers, and they are placed at the side of the body with no indication of shoulders. Her low Beery score (copying geometrical designs) and immature figure drawing do not appear to have affected her academic work adversely, as seen from this 7.9-year-old girl's test scores: Draw-A-Person raw score, 16; Beery VMI age-equivalent, 5.8 years; arithmetic grade-level, 3.3; arithmetic standard score, 108; spelling grade-level, 5.4; and spelling standard score, 128.

Fifth Grade, Hiroshima

The highest-scoring and qualitatively best human-figure drawing by a fifth-grade Hiroshima boy (grade 5.8) is shown in figure 5-13. The figure features a very well-drawn body, with unusual details, such as the small dots and lines between the fingers and the double circles representing knees. The ears are also carefully executed, as are the eyes, eyebrows, creases between the eyes, and the nose with nostrils. The face may be a mask similar to those used in traditional Japanese theater. However, the clothing looks like that worn by present-day boys. This drawing features the most distinctly Asian face in the total sample and may be influenced by ancient Japanese art. The test scores for this 11.0-year-old boy were: Draw-A-Person raw score, 28; Beery VMI age-equivalent, 14.8 years; arithmetic grade-level, 7.3; and arithmetic standard score, 116.

Figure 5-10. South San Francisco Boy: Age, 7.0 Years; Grade-Level, 2.9;
Draw-A-Person Test Score, 13

Figure 5-11. South San Francisco Girl: Age, 7.8 Years; Grade-Level, 2.5; Draw-A-Person Test Score, 25

Figure 5-12. South San Francisco Girl: Age, 7.9 Years; Grade-Level, 2.9;
Draw-A-Person Test Score, 16

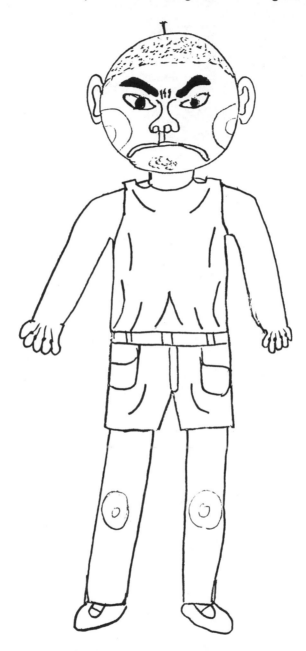

Figure 5-13. Hiroshima Boy: Age, 11.0 Years; Grade-Level, 5.8; Draw-A-Person Test Score, 28

The lowest-scoring and quantitatively poorest human-figure drawing by a fifth-grade Hiroshima boy is shown in figure 5-14. Although there is a general lack of detail in the clothing, the face features a nose with nostrils and well-drawn eyes. The body proportions would be adequate except that the arms and hands are underdeveloped and the arms are placed against the torso instead of coming out of the shoulders. An indicator of immaturity is the lack of detail outside the face and head. This left-handed 11.7-year-old boy's test scores were: Draw-A-Person raw score, 22; Beery VMI age-equivalent, 9.3 years; arithmetic grade-level, 6.0; and arithmetic standard score, 98.

The highest-scoring and qualitatively best human-figure drawing by a fifth-grade Hiroshima girl is shown in figure 5-15. This is the figure that is equal to the highest score in our total sample of 360 drawings. The face is executed partially in profile, and the hands have the thumbs in the right places on the inside. The proportions are good, and an ear is found under the hair line. There is very little decoration on the clothing, but much is suggested about the figure by just a few well-placed lines. This student is ambidextrous and was seen switching from her right to her left hand several times during the Draw-A-Person, Beery, and arithmetic testing. She is the only fifth-grade student that we observed doing this. The test scores for this 10.8-year-old girl were: Draw-A-Person raw score, 29 (30 is the maximum obtainable); Beery VMI age-equivalent, 11.1 years; arithmetic grade-level, 6.6; and arithmetic standard score, 116.

The lowest-scoring and quantitatively poorest human-figure drawing by a fifth-grade Hiroshima girl is shown in figure 5-16. This little figure is well drawn but was scored low because of some missing anatomical details. Since her arms are behind her back, the hands and fingers could not be scored. Also, the figure lacks pupils, nostrils, and two lips, and the head is disproprotionately large. The figure is artistically pleasing, but this cannot be reflected in the score. This bright 11.3-year-old girl achieved the following test scores: Draw-A-Person raw score, 19; Beery VMI age-equivalent, 14.9 years; arithmetic grade-level, 7.1; and arithmetic standard score, 113.

Fifth Grade, Taipei

The highest-scoring and qualitatively best human-figure drawing by a fifth-grade Taipei boy (grade 5.5) is shown in figure 5-17. The proportions are very good, and both anatomical features and clothing are well represented. The jacket features a zipper, breast pocket, collar, and ribbed waistline. A shirt or scarf appears under the jacket, and the socks have a design or may be wrinkled. The shoes have heels and tips, and the pants have pockets. The fingers are drawn with nails.

Figure 5-14.   Hiroshima Boy: Age, 11.7 Years; Grade-Level, 5.8; Draw-A-Person Test Score, 22

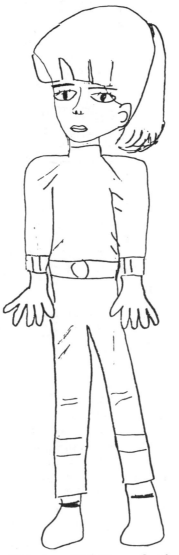

Figure 5-15. Hiroshima Girl: Age, 10.8 Years; Grade-Level, 5.8; Draw-A-Person Test Score, 29

Drawings that feature crossed eyes, as this one does, have been seen as clinical manifestations of hostility and "seem to be drawn only by children who are quite hostile towards others" (Koppitz 1968). To interpret crossed eyes as rebellion, anger, or inability to "see straight" would be inappropriate in a cross-cultural study without validating data. This student was

Figure 5-16.   Hiroshima Girl: Age, 11.3 Years; Grade-Level, 5.8; Draw-A-
                Person Test Score, 19

observed during testing and showed no evidence of esotropia (eye-muscle imbalance, where the eyes turn inward toward each other). His drawing may have been influenced by illustrations that appear in the school texts and other books or magazines. The test scores earned by this boy were: Draw-A-Person raw score, 27; Beery VMI age-equivalent, 13.8 years; arithmetic grade-level, 5.3; and arithmetic standard score, 104.

   The lowest-scoring and qualitatively poorest human figure drawn by a fifth-grade Taipei boy is shown in 5-18. The figure is among the smallest of those made by fifth-graders. The pencil lines were lightly drawn and had to be darkened for reproduction. The facial features are minimal, with no ears or nose and the eyes each represented by a single curve. Adequate hands and fingers are not represented, and the clothing is without decoration. The academic test scores achieved by this 10.9-year-old boy are adequate, as follows: Draw-A-Person raw score, 18; Beery VMI age-equivalent, 10.2 years; arithmetic grade-level, 7.8; and arithmetic standard score, 129.

   The highest-scoring and qualitatively best human figure drawn by a fifth-grade Taipei girl is shown in figure 5-19. This drawing contains a great

Figure 5-17. Taipei Boy: Age, 10.8 Years; Grade-Level, 5.5; Draw-A-Person Test Score, 27

Figure 5-18. Taipei Boy: Age, 10.9 Years; Grade-Level, 5.5; Draw-A-Person Test Score, 18

deal of detail. The pencil lines are firm, and the face features either cheeks or makeup on cheeks. The hair is bouffant and styled, which is interesting since almost all the schoolgirls wore the same short, straight hair style with bangs; yet they almost always depicted long hair styles on their drawings. The knees and elbows are shaded in this figure, and the dress has a pocket, buttons down the front, collars and cuffs, and gathers at the waist and on the sleeves. The girl has a belt and buckle and is carrying a purse. There are also flowers and other decorations on the dress and boots. This 11.3-year-old girl appears to have average academic ability in the presence of good visual-motor functioning, as seen in her test scores: Draw-A-Person raw score, 28; Beery VMI age-equivalent, 13.9 years; arithmetic grade-level, 6.0; and arithmetic standard score, 104.

The lowest-scoring and qualitatively poorest human-figure drawing by a fifth-grade Taipei girl is shown in figure 5-20. This picture of a young girl with long hair, bows, and long skirt is nicely drawn. It loses points because the hair hides any possible ears, the hands cannot be seen behind the back, and the long skirt hides the leg details. The face features wide, square eyes framed with long hair, and there is no decoration on the clothing other than an apron over the skirt and cuffs on the sleeves. The test scores for this 10.6-year-old girl were: Draw-A-Person raw score, 19; Beery VMI age-equivalent, 13.9 years; arithmetic grade-level, 6.6; and arithmetic standard score, 116.

Figure 5-19. Taipei Girl: Age, 11.3 Years; Grade-Level, 5.5; Draw-A-Person Test Score, 28

Figure 5-20. Taipei Girl: Age, 10.6 Years; Grade-Level, 5.5; Draw-A-Person Test Score, 19

Fifth Grade, South San Francisco

The highest-scoring and qualitatively best human-figure drawing by a fifth-grade South San Francisco boy (grade 5.9) is shown in figure 5-21. This student was born in San Francisco and comes from a Cantonese-speaking family. His D-A-P score is equal to the highest among the 360 pupils tested. The boy in the picture is showing the "V for victory" sign, and superman is flying above the lamppost. The high score was achieved by virtue of the many anatomical details present plus the items of clothing. The student appears to have observed many details of body parts and recorded them. The lamppost and bird, which are not scored, also have many details, including the inscription "I don't care." The other test scores for this 11.8-year-old boy were mediocre: Draw-A-Person raw score, 29; Beery VMI age-equivalent, 10.9 years; arithmetic grade level, 4.7; arithmetic standard score, 101; spelling grade-level, 6.3; and spelling standard score, 101.

    The lowest-scoring and qualitatively poorest human-figure drawing by a fifth-grade South San Francisco boy is shown in figure 5-22. This is one of

Figure 5-21. South San Francisco Boy: Age, 11.8 Years; Grade-Level, 5.9;
Draw-A-Person Test Score, 29

the smallest and least mature of all the drawings. The boy made several attempts to draw a figure and erased them. His first drawing featured an unusually large head, a round body, and stick legs. The anatomy in his figures is essentially the same, except for size. Since his test scores are also low, the child appears to have some type of learning handicap, which could be determined by a more complete test battery. The principal stated that the boy receives extra tutoring. This 11.9-year-old boy's test scores were: Draw-A-Person raw score, 16; Beery VMI age-equivalent, 6.8 years; arithmetic grade-level, 4.1; arithmetic standard score, 78; spelling grade-level, 4.3; and spelling standard score, 85.

The highest-scoring and qualitatively best human-figure drawing by a fifth-grade South San Francisco girl is shown in figure 5-23. This drawing scored lower than the other fifth-grade D-A-Ps that have been presented as top-level work. The face is formed as a circle, and the arms are too small. However, the figure has some details of both anatomy and clothing. The girls appears to be holding a bouquet of flowers and has a necklace plus a breast pocket and two skirt pockets with flaps, and the boots are laced. Other decorations include buttons on the pocket flaps and a ruffle on the skirt. The test scores for this 11.0-year-old girl were: Draw-A-Person raw score, 26; Beery VMI age-equivalent, 11.1 years; arithmetic grade-level, 5.5; arithmetic standard score, 99; spelling grade-level, 6.7; and spelling standard score, 112.

The lowest-scoring and qualitatively poorest human-figure drawing by a fifth-grade South San Francisco girl is shown in figure 5-24. This girl at-

Figure 5-22. South San Francisco Boy: Age, 11.9 Years; Grade-Level, 5.9; Draw-A-Person Test Score, 16

Figure 5-23. South San Francisco Girl: Age, 11.0 Years; Grade-Level, 5.9;
           Draw-A-Person Test Score, 26

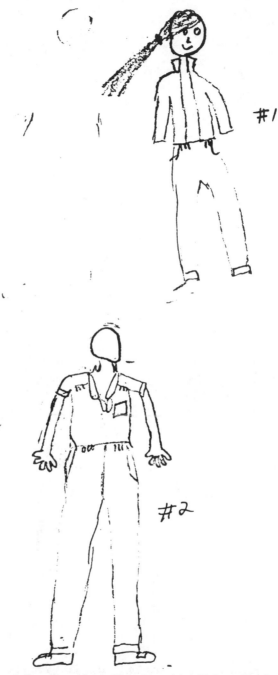

Figure 5-24. South San Francisco Girl: Age, 11.0 Years; Grade-Level, 5.9; Draw-A-Person Test Score, 16

tempted several drawings, erasing some and leaving two of them. Both were incomplete and scored 16 points. The completed face is immature and the other has no features. The clothing in both cases shows some attention to style and has gathers at the waist, a breast pocket, and pants pockets. The unfinished drawings indicate that the pupil was not satisfied with her work. She complained about having to draw a person and appeared to be under stress while doing her drawings. The test scores for this 11.0-year-old girl were: Draw-A-Person raw score, 16; Beery VMI age-equivalent, 11.1 years; arithmetic grade-level, 4.7; arithmetic standard score, 89; spelling grade-level, 6.8; and spelling standard score, 114.

Artistic Ability

Human-figure drawing from memory requires adequate maturity in visual perception, visual-motor coordination, memory, and discrimination. In addition, children need to possess sufficient maturation to recognize the whole or Gestalt of the body, to be aware of their own bodies, to have adequate fine-motor coordination, and to be able to implement cross-modality functioning in order to execute such figures.

It is difficult to assume that artistic ability can be divorced from visual-motor performance, memory, and discrimination. According to Koppitz (1968) it "might be assumed that a child with [artistic] ability would possess among other qualities good visual-motor perception and good fine motor coordination." There are many samples of human figures in this study that were not the highest scoring in each class but were nevertheless artistically pleasing.

For example, a fifth-grade Hiroshima boy drew the only figure that featured a shadow (see figure 5-25). The face was drawn partially in profile, with eyeglasses. Indications of strong visual-memory and visual-motor abilities were evidenced by the attention to details on clothing, such as the monograms on the pocket and shirt, the buckle design, and lacing on the boots. This left-handed student, aged 11.4 years, was the first in his class in mathematics, according to the teacher. His test scores were: Draw-A-Person raw score, 26; Beery VMI age-equivalent, 13.9 years; arithmetic grade-level, 10.0; and arithmetic standard score, 142.

Summary

The Human-Figure Drawing Test is used in a great many countries as a combination intelligence scale and measure of visual-motor integration. It is also used by clinical psychologists to assess brain damage and emotional lability. Since it is a nonverbal test with easily given directions, it is a prac-

Figure 5-25.   Hiroshima Boy: Age, 11.4 Years; Grade-Level, 5.8; Draw-A Person Test Score, 26

tical type of instrument to use for cross-cultural studies. When used in this manner, it must be considered that the ability to draw a human figure depends to a great extent on learned factors. For example, a child must first have experience holding and using a pencil or crayon. Then any practice or training that children have in drawing people will add to their scores.

The effect of previous experience may be seen in some human-figure drawings that were made by Indian children in Costa Rica who lived in a remote mountain village and had never attended school. These children were observed to be able to function adequately on many tasks in their society. However, they had to be taught how to hold and use a pencil, after which they were asked to draw a person. These children's drawings, which were sent to us, scored at about half their age levels, so that, for instance, a twelve-year-old boy's drawing was scored at the five-year-old level (Silesky 1979).

For this reason, it is possible to compare the drawings of children with the same backgrounds in the same school but, in general, not cross-nationally, except for certain circumspect purposes. The drawings tend to give some sense of the type of training children have had and their consequent developmental levels.

The Draw-A-Person Test scores correlated well with arithmetic, spelling, penmanship, and copying geometrical designs for many groups of children. The average scores for the drawings from Hiroshima, Taipei, and South San Francisco were relatively similar to the pupils' mean arithmetic and visual-motor integration scores.

In general the Draw-A-Person Test remains a satisfactory instrument for case-finding because it correlates well with other tests used to detect learning problems. Among the children tested, a few scored low on this test and also on the other tests, raising suspicion of possible learning disabilities.

References

Beery, K., and Buktenica, N. 1967. *Developmental Test of Visual-Motor Integration.* Chicago: Follett.

Clements, S. 1969. The psychologist and case finding. In L. Tarnopol (ed.), *Learning Disabilities: Introduction to Educational and Medical Management.* Springfield, Ill.: Thomas.

Conners, K. 1971. Drugs in the management of children with learning disabilities. In L. Tarnopol (ed.), *Learning Disorders in Children.* Boston: Little, Brown.

Gofman, H. 1969. The physician's role in early diagnosis and management of learning disabilities. In L. Tarnopol (ed.), *Learning Disabilities: Introduction to Educational and Medical Management.* Springfield, Ill.: Thomas.

Hildreth, G. H., Griffiths, N., and McGauvran, M. 1965. *Metropolitan Readiness Tests.* New York: Harcourt, Brace and World.

Jastak, J.F., Bijou, S., and Jastak, S. 1978. *Wide Range Achievement Test.* Wilmington, Del.: Jastak Associates.

Kamimura, K., and Morinaga, R. 1980. Mimeographed. Patients with learning problems at Izu Teisin Hospital.

Kline, C., and Lee, N. 1972. A transcultural study of dyslexia: analysis of language disabilities in 277 Chinese children simultaneously learning to read and write in English and Chinese. *Journal of Special Education* 6:1.

Koppitz, E.M. 1968. *Psychological Evaluation of Children's Human Figure Drawings.* New York: Grune and Stratton.

Robles Gorriti, C., and Rodriquez Muñiz, A. 1976. Learning problems in Argentina. In L. Tarnopol and M. Tarnopol (eds.), *Reading Disabilities: An International Perspective.* Baltimore: University Park Press.

Valett, R. 1968. *A Psychoeducational Inventory of Basic Learning Abilities.* Belmont, Calif.: Fearon Publishers.

Silesky, O. 1979. Personal communication.

6

Basic-Skills Requirements for Teachers

Muriel Tarnopol and
Lester Tarnopol

Some Literacy Problems

For a number of years it has been observed that many graduate students appeared to be deficient in the ability to express themselves in written English. In university department meetings complaints have been lodged about the deterioration of graduate students' written language. A few years ago individual departments within the graduate schools began to introduce writing-proficiency evaluations for their students. This was implemented in different ways in the various departments. For example, in one department a course taken by all students during their first semester was designated to be the one in which writing proficiency would be judged. The instructor provided a written assignment to be done in class, and the writing samples were then given to a committee for evaluation. The papers were graded for grammar, syntax, spelling, punctuation, logic, organization, and general legibility and style. The students who performed below the minimum standard were notified by their advisors of the remedial options available.

Although the literacy problem has existed for a great many years (it probably always existed), several converging influences have recently made it startlingly prominent. Among these factors are the rapid increase in the number of students entering the college and university streams; the general grade-inflation that began in the mid-sixties; the significant increase in students from minority populations electing to go into higher education; the attempts of colleges and universities to stem their declining enrollments, which are due to smaller high school graduating classes; and the deterioration of the college entrance examination scores.

In 1980 the College Entrance Examination Board announced that Scholastic Aptitude Test scores were continuing a decline that began seventeen years earlier in both the verbal and quantitative sections of the test. Prior to 1970 most of this decline in scores was said to be due to the increased number of minority, women, and low-income students taking the

This chapter is based in part on a paper given by Muriel Tarnopol at the International Seminar on Learning Problems in Children, Guadalajara, Mexico, 1978 (M. Tarnopol, 1979).

test; however, since 1970 the scores have been falling for all types of students. Among the possible reasons given for this deterioration are the effects of television, reduced school standards, and increasing family and national problems ("SAT Scores Continue Decline," 1980).

Graduate Record Examination Scores

Reports are available comparing students in different disciplines who have taken the Graduate Record Examinations (GRE) over many years. As a rule the students majoring in education have scored, on the average, at or near the bottom when compared with other groups. As an example, 309,757 examinees took the GRE Advanced Tests between 1 October 1974 and 30 September 1977, including 40,925 education majors (Graduate Record Examination 1979-1980). The data are given for students in twenty disciplines who participated in these examinations. The mean standard score of 454 for education majors is the lowest achieved by any of the twenty groups. On these tests the arbitrary mean is 500 and the standard deviation is 100.

The percentile ratings are also given for each discipline at different standard score levels. Percentiles range from 1 to 99, and a given percentile indicates the percentage of students who scored below the corresponding standard score. For example, the ninety-ninth percentile for education majors corresponds to a standard score of 660 (Graduate Record Examination 1979-1980, table 3A). This means that 99 percent of the education majors scored below 660 and 1 percent scored at or above this level. No other group attained this low a standard score corresponding to this same percentile. Mathematics, philosophy, and physics majors scored 980, which is the highest-scaled score in the table. At the lower end of the scale, both education and geography majors descended to a standard score of 240 at the first percentile, and this same percentile was reached by chemistry and philosophy majors at 440 and 420, respectively. Thus, the average education major scored at the second and fourth percentiles, respectively, for chemistry and philosophy majors. If education is to become a meaningful discipline, it must be able to compete with chemistry, philosophy, mathematics, and physics for competent students.

Although there is a fairly good correlation between GRE scores and academic achievement, the relationship of these test scores with clinical types of functions, such as ability to relate to children, parents, and other faculty members, or with student teaching is not very high. Therefore, some faculty members discount the value of GRE scores. If teachers were able to function generally with almost no academic knowledge or ability, GRE scores could be ignored. However, since this is certainly not the case, some graduate schools of education have been using a certain minimum competency score on the GRE for matriculation purposes.

Koerner's Report

Sterling M. McMurrin, former U.S. Commissioner of Education, commented on the factors in our culture that have contributed to the inadequacy of America's schools in the introduction to Koerner's *The Miseducation of American Teachers* (1963). He indicated that society as a whole is responsible for the concept of "doctrinaire egalitarianism" that has led to a "leveling process"; the "antiintellectualistic attitude" that tends to permeate society; and the concept that secondary and elementary teaching is a profession that does not require any special ability. The latter has led to providing teachers with "second- or third-rate educations and [to paying] them third- or fourth-rate salaries." He therefore suggested that raising both the pay of teachers and the professional standards for admission and retention in schools of education, as well as "scholarly demands," would attract more people from America's top talent pool into teaching. He further stated that this process would be "tragic" without a "corresponding upgrading of the educational program" for these students.

Koerner (1963) visited sixty-three accredited institutions with programs for teacher education, in all areas of the United States, to determine the status of teacher preparation and the suggested requirements to improve their training. He used several types of questionnaires to gather information about the feelings of students, teachers, faculty, and administrators concerning the educational process; and he examined the transcripts of graduates to determine the courses taken and the grades achieved by students in teacher-training institutions.

Koerner raised the issue of the academic caliber of the students who go into education as being most influential in determining the end product. By comparing the grade-point averages achieved by students in their liberal arts courses with those of their education courses, it became apparent that the students tended to get higher grades in the education curriculum. Moreover, the liberal arts instructors were inclined to state that the education majors were among their poorest students. Consequently, it was suggested that less-demanding courses were being offered in education than in the liberal arts curriculum, possibly in conjunction with grade-inflation. It was therefore recommended that serious consideration be given to upgrading the educational standards and curriculum.

From both his own questionnaires and those of others, Koerner concluded that the graduates of schools of education felt that student practice-teaching was the most helpful course, and that the other education courses were found to be relatively less useful. As an example, in 1969 1,391 high school teachers in California replied to a statewide survey asking the question, "How important do you believe the education courses were in making you an effecive teacher?" Only 6 percent replied "most important," 44.7

percent indicated "some importance," 42.2 percent checked "little importance," and 7.1 percent said "no importance." Thus, about half of these teachers had found their education courses of importance to them. Koerner posed the question of what would happen if this were determined to be the case in medicine or some other professional field, and then answered that the matter would probably get some "attention from the public and the profession."

Another major concern expressed by Koerner was that educationists appeared to be abandoning the English language, with most distressing results to the quality of education of both the teachers and their pupils.

Koerner noted that there had been some recent improvement in the efforts of institutions to raise their requirements for entrance and certification. Nevertheless, he stated that education, as a field, did not constitute a genuine discipline. In examining the course work in education, he concluded that intellectual impoverishment was evident and that the courses tended to be of the superficial, survey type, lacking depth. Moreover, a great many courses were found to repeat the same general principles, with considerable overlap and relatively little content. The curricula tended to be repetitive, with but minimal instruction in the liberal arts and with the English language mutilated in the form of a "patois" that he labeled "educanto." Finally, the graduate programs did not seem to overcome the difficulties found at the undergraduate level, but rather provided an even greater aggravation of the problems.

Conant's Report

Conant (1963), a former president of Harvard University, had been asked to assess the status of teacher-training and public education in the United States. He examined and reported on the certification policies of sixteen states and the teacher-training programs in seventy-seven institutions.

Conant indicated that the end product of a teacher-training institution depended heavily on the qualifications of the matriculating students. He therefore recommended that only the top one-third of high school graduates be permitted to enter teacher-training. He noted that the College Entrance Examination Board had for many years been defining the basic requirements in English and written composition necessary for a high school graduate to enter college as a qualified freshman. He stated that students should be able to pass this type of entrance examination in order to be prepared for college-level work. Those who failed to pass such a test were not yet ready and should be required to take remedial English at their own expense and without receiving college credits.

Although this suggestion is based on the way Harvard College and certain other top-level schools function, it is entirely foreign to the method of admission to the average college. Since most students entering the majority of American colleges probably are not prepared to pass the rigorous English and composition requirements of the College Board Examinations, it has been customary to attempt to adapt the curricula to the level of functioning of the students. Unfortunately, this has permitted students to graduate from college who still could not pass the freshman basic-writing test.

An important factor tending to promote illiteracy among college students is the multiple-choice examination. Since its widespread adoption, it is quite possible for a student to go through the four years of college rarely (or never) being required to write an essay in class. Moreover, papers written outside of class too often are returned to the students without any corrections marked on them, so the writers may never become aware of their spelling, grammatical, and other deficiencies.

University of California

The deplorable state of the basic-writing skills of the best (top 12.5 percent) of California's high school graduates was chronicled in a report to the Board of Regents of the prestigious University of California in 1975. Dr. Fretter, chairman of the University of California's statewide academic council, reported that 75 percent of the entering freshmen (on eight campuses) had failed the multiple-choice College Entrance Examination Board English Composition Test. However, 15 percent of the students who had failed the multiple-choice test passed the written composition test, which was compulsory for them. Those who had failed the written test were required to take a remedial English course with no credit. Since between 85 and 95 percent of these students passed the remedial course the first time they took it, the problem was attributed to inadequate previous training rather than to lack of ability. It was noted that California high school students are required to take only three years of English to graduate; and it was suggested that the university require four years of high school English for entrance.

Competency for Special-Education Teachers

Cruickshank (1966) reported on the results of a symposium that was held to determine the areas of competency required of teachers who would work as learning-disability specialists. Eighteen participants who were leaders in this field were called together, plus a number of observers representing national organizations that were interested in the education of exceptional children. The children under consideration were in the broad range of learning-disabled pupils, including the brain-damaged, perceptually handicapped, dyslexic, and so forth.

It was deemed essential that these specialized teachers receive advanced certification beyond the regular elementary and secondary credentials. The content areas in which they should be instructed and become proficient included remedial reading, spelling, writing, and arithmetic; communication and communicative disorders; cognitive, perceptual, and motor structures; and the neuropsychology, psychopharmacology, pediatrics, psychiatry, and psychodiagnosis of these neurologically handicapped children in sufficient depth to be able to communicate efficiently with the professionals on a multidisciplinary team.

Consideration of the scope, breadth, and depth of training required of teachers who are to become specialists in the remediation of children with learning diabilities clearly indicates that only persons with strong academic backgrounds would be capable of functioning adequately in this field. These teachers are required to perform the educational assessment of each pupil and to be able to meet with a multidisciplinary team to discuss the full psychoeducational diagnosis provided by the other members of the group. They must then be capable of developing an individual educational program for each of their pupils, based on this total evaluation process. Finally, they are expected to perform the remediation necessary to bring the child up to an adequate level of academic functioning, based on his expectancy levels in reading, writing, spelling, and arithmetic, or to higher cognitive achievement for an older child. Koerner (1963) and Conant (1963) proposed that only students possessing certain minimal academic skills be permitted to enter the teacher-training institutions and that the education curricula and courses be seriously upgraded to meet the needs of modern elementary and high school education. This would also provide more adequately prepared teachers for special education.

Lerner and List (1970) tested reading teachers on their knowledge of phonics and phonics generalizations. The results indicated that the teachers either had "not received phonics instruction in their previous teacher education" or they could not recall the phonic generalizations or facts from their own experiences when they were learning to read. We also administer the Lerner (1976) "Foniks Kwiz" to our graduate students in the reading-specialist or learning-handicapped credential programs, all of whom are credentialed teachers. The students are required to pass this multiple-choice test at the 84 percent level. In every class, a majority of the students has scored below 60 percent on this test. Most of the students must repeat the quiz several times before they pass. The fact that so many are unable to reply correctly to these test items seems to indicate that phonics is not considered to be an essential part of the reading teachers' armamentarium. This is unfortunate, since many excellent reading programs, both regular and remedial, are heavily phonics oriented.

In these courses, the students are also required to be able to pronounce the sounds of all of the letters of the alphabet, for example, "a apple /a/," and so on. In each graduate class of specialist and general-education teachers, a number of students cannot correctly reproduce the various sounds of the letters, especially vowels. Some also may have difficulty with digraphs and blends, and these students appear unable to "hear" the sounds they are attempting to use in a list of sound-symbols that they must reproduce. Some of these students never can learn to reproduce adequately all the required sound-symbol relationships, and they may have auditory-perceptual dysfunction. In the course of this research, a positive correlation was found between the scores on the Lerner "Foniks Kwiz" and the scores on the Wide Range Achievement Test in spelling. Also, a number of teachers with speech and hearing problems are uncovered each semester (and at times speech and hearing therapists). One might reasonably question how efficiently the teachers with deficits in auditory perception, who cannot reproduce the sounds of letters or digraphs and are unable to blend properly, can function as reading specialists. Would it not be more prudent to find these people before they have started in teacher-training or have started on a second or even third credential, so that they can be counseled into a more appropriate course of study?

The Coleman Report

If the selection of students for teacher-training and the professional level of the schools of education were substantially improved, what would be the effect on the education of America's children? This question cannot be answered with certainty because it is hypothetical and has not been tested experimentally. However, it may be considered, based on previous research in related areas. Logic suggests that the student body's academic functioning can be improved by an unknown quantity. However, there will probably always be some children whose ability to learn is so impaired that they will not be substantially remediated; and more importantly, the stratification of pupils' academic progress will probably continue to be highly correlated with socioeconomic status.

In 1964 a Civil Rights Act was passed by the U.S. Congress, requiring the Commissioner of Education to conduct a survey and report the results to Congress and the president within two years:

. . . concerning the lack of availability of equal opportunities for individuals by reason of race, color, religion, or national origin in public education institutions at all levels in the United States, its territories and possessions, and the District of Columbia (Mayeske and Beaton 1975).

The survey was conducted by Coleman and associates (1966) and included about 650,000 students, their teachers, principals, and superintendents, covering about 4,000 public schools. The survey used a stratified-cluster, 5-percent sample of schools. Its major findings included that the most important factors influencing student achievement at all levels were family background and general social context (home, neighborhood, and peer environment) and to a much lesser extent the teacher's characteristics (not facilities and curriculum).

Further analyses of the Coleman data were performed by Mayeske and colleagues (1973). Some of the major findings were as follows: In mathematics and reading comprehension, the average achievements of groups were, in order, whites and Oriental-Americans at the top, followed by Native Americans, blacks, Mexican-Americans, and Puerto Ricans, all four of which were closely clustered. The motivational aspects of family life were found to be more important than socioeconomic level or the presence or absence of key family members. Therefore, the "more immediate kinds of parent-child involvement, such as frequent discussions of school work, made a larger independent contribution than any long-range aspirations." Also, it appeared that when parents read to the child and talked with him about homework, the pupil's achievement was influenced more than it was by socioeconomic background.

Influence of Family on Achievement

The results of these research efforts indicate that family background has a greater influence on children's academic progress than does teacher characteristics. However, this relationship may not be applied to pupils with specific learning disabilities, since they were not parceled out of the data bank for analysis. Another important finding suggests that the greatest gains in student achievement might be made by intensive parent education along the lines suggested by White, Kaban, and Attanucci (1979), as discussed in chapter 1.

Research on normal children has demonstrated that, even if the teaching profession were significantly upgraded, many children might continue to lag seriously behind their expected levels of academic achievement until their home environments could be improved. The research on the environment and achievement of Oriental children, as described in chapter 4, may indicate some of the types of home life that promote pupil progress.

Further confirmation of the influence of family background on student attainment comes from the international reading study by the International Association for the Evaluation of Educational Achievement. Thorndike (1973) reported on the correlations of the countries' mean reading comprehension scores versus other national variables for the fifteen countries that participated in his study of fourteen-year-old children. Some selected correlations with reading comprehension were: number of books in home ($r = 0.85$), mother's education ($r = 0.73$), number of magazines ($r = 0.71$), father's education ($r = 0.60$), and parents' help with homework ($r = 0.53$). These correlations support the notion that help with homework by an educated parent is important to the academic progress of children.

We have long postulated this relationship from subjective experience, and the report of educational research in Israel by Feitelson (cited in chapter 3) tends to confirm it. It has been our hypothesis that a major reason middle-class children often progress better in school than lower-class children, if IQ is held constant, is related to tutoring of the pupils either by a family member or by an outside agency. Feitelson found that when the primary schools in Israel adopted the whole-phrase method of teaching reading, the children who received no tutoring at home often failed and those whose parents taught them to read carried on well, so the educators were unaware that it was the teaching method that had failed.

Since both the Mayeske report on the Coleman data and the Thorndike report indicate the strength of the influence of home tutoring on pupil achievement, it may be postulated that a significant factor in the failure of educational research on reading and other academics is the uncontrolled tutoring variable.

Some Basic-Skills Levels of Graduate Students

Teachers of learning-handicapped children are taught to assess the strengths and weaknesses of their pupils by administering a battery of standardized, normed tests and informal inventories. The test battery includes assessment of reading, writing, spelling, arithmetic, and handwriting skills, plus some visual-motor, auditory-perceptual, and memory testing. Based on the test results and the further assessment information supplied by a psychologist, a speech and language therapist, and others, the teachers are taught to develop individual educational plans for their students.

As an aid to learning how to use tests correctly, the students take many of the tests themselves and score and discuss them in class. This method tends to motivate the graduate students to do careful work and obtain the correct scores. The students are primarily credentialed teachers working on either the reading or learning-handicapped credentials, or both, plus a sprinkling of counseling, psychology, and speech, hearing, and language-therapy majors.

In 1975 Muriel Tarnopol began to collect and score the spelling tests before returning them to the students for rescoring. Gradually, tests and inventories on arithmetic, visual-motor integration, vocabulary, sex, handedness, cursive versus manuscript writing, penmanship, primary versus secondary teachers, undergraduate major, age, and years of teaching experience were included. Anonymity was preserved by having the students use fictitious names. At the same time, we began to collect data from undergraduates and high school and elementary school students, and also from students abroad.

A preliminary report on the arithmetic skills and visual-motor functioning of students at various levels has been published (Tarnopol and Tarnopol 1979). Of 152 California graduate students taking education courses, it was found that the Wide Range Achievement Test (Jastak, Bijou, and Jastak 1978) arithmetic grade-level scores ranged from 3.6 to 14.5 on the 1978 norms. Since there are only a few problems at each grade-level, these norms do not give the grade at which the person is actually functioning in arithmetic. However, they are useful for determining the approximate level at which to place a student who is being remediated, as the placement will be close enough for practical purposes. Nor do these scores indicate the student's potential ability in arithmetic. These achievement scores are indications of how far the person has studied in mathematics and how much arithmetic he has been using.

It was learned that many of the graduate education students had never had a mathematics course in college (although they may have had a course in how to teach arithmetic), and only a few students had taken more than one year of mathematics in high school (often the arithmetic-review course). As a rule the graduate students who had scored low on the arithmetic test had not taken a mathematics course since the ninth grade. Moreover, they generally claimed to have a "math block," or that they just "couldn't do math." We have found that this math anxiety is often unfounded. For students who are required to take statistics and who are weak in the necessary arithmetic and algebra backgrounds, we have recommended certain remedial arithmetic and algebra courses. So far these students have usually had no difficulty, and they are often surprised to discover that they perform at a good level in the subject that they so feared.

However, some students do have true dyscalculia. One 40-year-old female graduate student scored grade-level 3.6 on the arithmetic test; on the Developmental Test of Visual-Motor Integration (Beery and Buktenica 1967) her age-equivalent score was 8.8 years. Since she was right-handed and was able to produce only a two-dimensional square when copying the three-dimensional cube, we hypothesized that there was poor transmission through the corpus callosum (bundle of neurons connecting the left with the right brain hemispheres) and that she would be able to make a three-dimensional copy with her left hand (see figure 6-1).

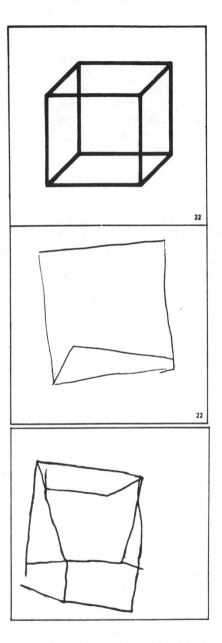

The center copy of the cube was done with the right hand and the lower copy was made some time later with the left hand. These copies are similar to those made by split-brain patients.

Figure 6-1. Copies of VMI Design Drawn by a Right-Handed Graduate Student Whose Arithmetic Score on the Wide Range Achievement Test was Grade 3.9.

If transmission via the corpus callosum is poor or missing, the person will function like a split-brain patient. Since spatial relations are usually mediated by the right hemisphere, the left hand, which is directly connected to the right brain, will be able to copy a three-dimensional figure. The right hand has difficulty with spatial relations because it is connected to the left hemisphere and must receive spatial information from the right brain via the dysfunctioning corpus callosum. This student's drawings are similar to those produced by split-brain patients (Gazzaniga 1970).

Tests Used with Teachers

Wide Range Achievement Tests (Jastak, Bijou, and Jastak 1978) have been widely used for many years in the United States because they give quick, easily administered and scored assessments of reading, spelling, and arithmetic. The tests are standardized for administration and scoring, have good reliability and validity, and are normed in terms of grade-levels, percentiles, and standard scores. The spelling and arithmetic tests may be administered to groups, so they could be used with an entire class simultaneously. However, the reading test must be individually given, which precluded use with the graduate students.

The arithmetic test covers from preschool to grade-level 17.5 and has standard scores from age five to sixty-four years. The spelling test includes grade-levels preschool to 13.1, and has the same range of standard scores as the arithmetic test. The level II arithmetic test has forty-three problems to be solved with pencil on a printed sheet. There are no "word problems"; all are computational. Therefore, the grade-level scores represent only the student's equivalent computational ability, not his actual grade-level functioning. The level II spelling test has forty-six words for the subject to write from dictation. There are either four or five words to represent each grade-level from grade 5 through 12.9. This test also permits the determination of manuscript versus cursive writing and penmanship scores. The major criticism of these tests is that there are too few items at each grade-level. However, the scores are reliable and valid, and the tests have not been lengthened because the time would be increased for administration without adding sufficiently to these properties.

It was found that the arithmetic test, which has a ten-minute time limit, did not give the graduate students sufficient time to complete as many problems as they could. Moreover, as people become older (the students ranged to sixty years of age), their speed decreases, but not necessarily their ability. Therefore, untimed tests were given after a two-week period following the timed samples of their work. In this manner, it was found that the poorer arithmetic students improved little, whereas the better ones usually could do many more problems. Since the other tests were untimed, no similar problems arose with their use.

The standard scores for the WRAT were based on ages, to conform with the scores derived from intelligence and other similar tests. We are reporting the raw scores, grade-level scores, and standard scores. Although the standard scores give equal units of measurement, which are most important for purposes of calculations, the grade-level scores are the most meaningful for our purposes because they are most readily understood by teachers. Also, the standard scores and percentiles are based on groups of subjects in the same age ranges from the total population, and we are only interested in the community of graduate students. Therefore, to be useful, the standard scores would have to be derived from representative samples of graduate students.

The Developmental Test of Visual-Motor Integration (Beery and Buktenica 1967) is composed of twenty-four geometrical designs to be copied by the subject, with no time limit. The raw score is equal to the number of drawings correctly executed within the limits permitted in the manual, and age-equivalent norms are available from two years, ten months through fifteen years, eleven months. Although none of the graduate students was less than twenty-one years of age, the test proved useful, since most students were unable to correctly copy all of the designs, and the scores correlated well with the arithmetic scores. Moreover, the students' copies gave some insights into the visual-motor problems that some of them had. Poor copying also tended to indicate both poor penmanship and inadequate chalkboard work, both of which create serious problems when teaching children.

The Wide Range Vocabulary Test (Atwell and Wells 1945) is an untimed multiple-choice test containing 100 items. Since none of the graduate students knew the meanings of all of the items, none scored above the test ceiling. The norms on the vocabulary test ranged from eight through twenty-one years of age, which was equivalent to a raw score of 89, or the fourth year of college. A few students scored above 89. The vocabulary scores correlated well with spelling and arithmetic, and are known to correlate very well with reading.

Penmanship was measured on a four-point scale, using the spelling tests. All scoring was done by Muriel Tarnopol to maintain consistency. The penmanship scores tended to correlate with all of the other tests.

Basic Skills of Graduate Students in Education

Although 313 California graduate students enrolled in education courses were tested, they did not all take the same group of tests, as seen in table

6-1. There were 85 males and 228 females, ranging in age from twenty-one to sixty years, with a mean of about thirty years. These students were in grades seventeen through twenty, where grade sixteen is the senior year of college, and they had an average of 4.2 years of teaching experience. About 12 percent of this group were left-handed. Approximately 35 percent usually printed and the same percentage preferred cursive writing, while 30 percent used both cursive and manuscript. As a group their penmanship was rated between fair and good (2.4), and their ability to copy geometrical designs (VMI mean score, 22.2) was at the fourteen-year-old level, which is adequate for an adult but may be inadequate for a teacher.

On the WRAT spelling test their mean grade-level score was 11.0; and on the WRAT arithmetic test their mean grade-level score was 9.3. Their mean raw score in arithmetic was 31.4 on the ten-minute timed test and increased to 35 with unlimited time, indicating that they were able to complete only 3.6 more problems, on the average. It was found that, in general, the students did not improve their arithmetic scores a great deal when there was no time limit. On the Wide Range Vocabulary Test (WRVT) (Atwell and Wells 1945), the mean score of these graduate students was at the nineteen-year-old level, or about that of college freshmen.

The correlation matrix indicates that spelling, arithmetic, and vocabulary are all correlated; that visual-motor integration (copying geometrical designs) is correlated with arithmetic, vocabulary, and penman-

Table 6-1

Scores of Graduate Students Enrolled in Education Courses, Tested from 1975 to 1980

		Raw Score		Grade-Level, Mean	Standard Score, Mean	Age Equivalent (years) Mean
	N	Mean	S.D.			
Age (years)	312	30.5	7.6			
Grade-level	312	17.5				
Years of teaching experience	160	4.2	5.7			
Spelling	311	41.4	5.4	11.0	116	
Arithmetic	281	31.4	6.6	9.3	114	
Arithmetic untimed	103	35.0	7.4			
Vocabulary	165	78.7	9.5			19
Beery VMI[a]	197	22.2	1.8			14
Penmanship	299	2.4	0.9			

The tests included Wide Range Achievement Test (WRAT) spelling and arithmetic, Wide Range Vocabulary Test (WVRT), Beery Developmental Test of Visual-Motor Integration, and penmanship ratings (excellent = 1, good = 2, fair = 3, poor = 4). The students included 85 males and 228 females.

[a]The maximum score obtainable on the VMI is 24, age-equivalent 15.9 years; the mean score of 22.2 is at the fourteen-year-old level.

ship; and that penmanship is correlated with spelling, arithmetic, vocabulary, and visual-motor integration (see table 6-2). The strongest relationships are found between spelling and vocabulary (0.61), spelling and penmanship (0.43), arithmetic and vocabulary (0.41), and arithmetic and spelling (0.39).

Since the correlation between spelling and penmanship was also significant for the fifth-grade South San Francisco pupils (0.42), it seems that the trend away from training small-motor coordination and writing skills in elementary education might profitably be reversed (see chapter 4, table 4-15).

The data were analyzed for the following groups of graduate students: right-handed, left-handed, cursive writers, printers (manuscript), and writers of both cursive and manuscript (see table 6-3). It was found that for these adults there were no significant differences of the means on the tests of spelling, arithmetic, vocabulary, visual-motor integration, and penmanship. Since mean scores may obscure relationships that exist at the upper and lower levels of accomplishment, it should not be inferred that these parameters have no influence whatever over academic variables.

Basic Skills of Elementary- and Secondary-School Teachers

In 1977 we began to collect more complete data and were able to differentiate the elementary-school from the secondary-school teachers. It was found that their mean ages were the same (about thirty-two years), as were their mean grade-levels (17.5) (see table 6-4). However, the elementary-school teachers averaged 5.9 years of teaching experience compared with

Table 6-2
Scores of Graduate Students Enrolled in Education Courses: Correlation Matrix

	Arithmetic		Arithmetic Untimed		Vocabulary		Beery VMI		Penmanship	
	N	r	N	r	N	r	N	r	N	r
Spelling	279	0.39	103	0.36	164	0.61	196	0.18	297	0.43
Arithmetic			101	0.83	162	0.41	195	0.37	269	0.25
Arithmetic untimed					103	0.35	102	0.32	93	0.06
Vocabulary							147	0.24	153	0.26
Beery VMI									184	0.25

WRAT spelling, arithmetic, and untimed arithmetic tests; WRVT; and Beery VMI.

N = number of students; r = coefficient of correlation. All correlations of 0.25 or greater are significant beyond the 0.001 level of probability.

Table 6-3
Scores of Graduate Students Enrolled in Education Courses.

	Right-Handed			Left-Handed			Cursive Writers			Printers			Crusive Writers and Printers		
	N	M	S.D.	N	M	S.D.	N	M	S.D.	N	M	S.D.	N	M	S.D.
Spelling	241	41.4	5.2	33	41.5	6.2	125	41.8	5.2	116	41.1	5.6	102	40.8	5.6
Arithmetic	239	30.8	6.4	32	30.6	7.3	111	30.7	5.8	101	32.0	6.9	101	30.8	6.7
Vocabulary	161	78.1	9.7	18	76.3	9.4	62	78.6	9.0	51	79.7	9.4	81	76.9	10.1
Beery VMI	177	22.2	1.8	19	22.4	2.2	59	22.0	2.1	52	22.3	1.9	88	22.4	1.6
Penmanship	226	2.4	0.9	33	2.5	0.9	120	2.3	0.8	112	2.5	0.9	97	2.5	0.9

WRAT spelling and arithmetic, Wide Range Vocabulary Test, Beery Developmental Test of Visual-Motor Integration, and penmanship raw scores. N = number of students; M = mean; $S.D.$ = standard deviation. Penmanship was rated excellent = 1, good = 2, fair = 3, poor = 4. None of the differences of the means is significant.

4.7 years for the secondary-school teachers; and the percentages of males in elementary and secondary education were 7 and 41 percent, respectively.

The range and mean scores of both the secondary-school and elementary-school teachers were essentially the same on the Developmental Test of Visual-Motor Integration, indicating that their ability to copy geometrical designs, based on the integration of visual perception and small-motor control, was similar, on the average (see table 6-5). However, there should be concern about those teachers who scored well below average, since raw scores of 16 to 20 are equivalent to ages 8.7 to 12 years, and approximately 15 percent were in this category. Although the meaning of this visual-motor ability in adults is not clear as yet, it is one of the predictors of learning disabilities in kindergarten children and correlates well with arithmetic scores at all levels, including graduate school (M. Tarnopol and L. Tarnopol 1979). It seems that some of the underlying brain functions that mediate visual-motor and several learning abilities are the same (Tarnopol and Tarnopol 1977, 1979b).

The elementary-school teachers scored somewhat better in penmanship, on the average, than the secondary-school teachers (2.3 versus 2.6), but the difference was not significant (see table 6-5). These scores are between good and fair on the scale used to obtain them. There are a number of important reasons why teachers should excel in penmanship, other than the fact that it correlates with spelling and other academic skills.

Teachers at all levels and in all subjects profit from good visual-motor abilities, which are reflected in their ability to write neatly and rapidly on the chalkboard and on paper. They are often required to draw diagrams, write arithmetic or science formulas, illustrate a passage in a text, and in other ways use visual aids to facilitate learning. Teachers who write poorly and who are unable to illustrate something they are trying to teach very often avoid using the blackboard for this purpose. They therefore spend a disproportionate amount of the teaching time in lecturing or talking. This

Table 6-4
Graduate Education Students Tested from 1977 to 1980

	Age (years)		Number			Grade-Level		Teaching Experience (years)	
	Range	Mean	Males	Females	Total	Range	Mean	Mean	S.D.
Elementary-school teachers	22-53	32.1	4	52	56	17-20	17.5	5.9	6.3
Secondary-school teachers	22-60	32.2	36	55	91	17-20	17.6	4.7	5.9

$N = 147$.

Table 6-5
Scores of Graduate Education Students Tested from 1977 to 1980

	Beery VMI[a]			Age-Equivalent (years)	Hand Preference (number)		Penmanship[b]	
	Range	Mean	S.D.	Range	Left	Right	Mean	S.D.
Elementary-school teachers	16-24	22.4	1.8	8.7-16+	8 (14%)	48	2.3	0.9
Secondary-school teachers	16-24	22	2.0	8.7-16+	8(8%)	83	2.6	0.8

[a]Beery-Buktenica Developmental Test of Visual-Motor Integration maximum score obtainable is 24.
[b]Penmanship was rated excellent = 1, good = 2, fair = 3, poor = 4.

can be a hindrance to students, who profit from visual as well as auditory presentations of material to be learned.

When a teacher's chalkboard writing is poor, children who have difficulty with visual closure are unable to decode what has been written; also, beginning learners have difficulties attempting to learn new letters and words because of the lack of visual constancy. Even secondary-school and college students have difficulty when their assignment has been poorly handwritten (or very badly typed) and duplicated. In such cases, few people seem to be able to decipher the writing to determine just what the assignment is supposed to be.

The average scores of the elementary-school and secondary-school teachers were not significantly different on the spelling, arithmetic, and vocabulary tests (see table 6-6). The mean standard scores, which range from 110 to 117, are deceptive because they are based on the total population of adults in each age range. Appropriate standard scores should be based on the population of university graduate students. In this case, it may be expected that the education students, as compared with the other graduate students, would be below the average range.

An approximation of the expected mean arithmetic standard score may be derived from the mean quantitative score on the Graduate Record Examination achieved by 16,677 students entering graduate school as education majors between 1 October 1977 and 30 June 1979 (Graduate Record Examination 1979-1980). The average standard score for these students was 468 on the quantitative test, for which the mean is 500 and the standard deviation is 100, giving 0.32 standard deviations below the mean. Converting this score to the type of standard score on the WRAT, for which the mean is 100 and the standard deviation is 15, gives a WRAT standard score of about 95. Therefore, if the teachers were compared with other graduate

Table 6-6
Scores on Wide Range Achievement Test (WRAT) and Wide Range Vocabulary Test (WRVT) of Graduate Education Students Tested from 1977 to 1980

	Number	Raw score Range	Raw score Mean	Grade-Level Range	Grade-Level Mean	Age-Equivalency (years) Mean	Standard Score Range	Standard Score Mean
Elementary-school Teachers								
Spelling	56	21-51	41	6.4-13.1	10.9		87-130	116
Arithmetic	56	14-51	30.4	3.6-15.8	9.0		78-154	112
Arithmetic untimed	56	17-52	36.1					
Vocabulary	56	46-95	77.8			18.8		
Secondary-school Teachers								
Spelling	91	21-51	41.6	6.4-13.1	11.1		87-130	117
Arithmetic	91	16-51	29.5	4.3-15.8	8.6		82-153	110
Arithmetic untimed	53	21-51	33					
Vocabulary	91	48-95	78.5			19		

$N = 147.$

students on the WRAT arithmetic test, their expected mean standard score would be approximately 95. This assumes that all the students are permitted to enter the fields of their choice, which is, of course, not the case, since most disciplines only admit those students who scored at or above an established minimum acceptable score. This would tend to lower the mean standard score of the education majors by an unknown amount. Since there is no spelling test in the Graduate Record Examination, the comparable expected standard score cannot be calculated. However, the mean verbal standard score of the education majors was 454.

Of greatest immediate concern are the teachers whose spelling, arithmetic, or vocabulary levels are near or below the grades in which they may be expected to teach. The minimum grade-level scores achieved by these teachers on the arithmetic and spelling tests were 3.6 and 6.4, and the lowest vocabulary score, 46, was equivalent to 12.8 years of age (see table 6-6).

From the correlation matrix for elementary-school teachers, it may be seen that spelling, arithmetic, vocabulary, and penmanship are all well-correlated (see table 6-7). Since the correlations between spelling and reading and between vocabulary and reading are known to be fairly high (see table 6-8), some of the graduate students' writing and other problems may be understood. The correlations also tend to hold up for the secondary-school teachers (see table 6-9), except for penmanship, which does not appear to correlate with arithmetic and vocabulary.

Table 6-7
Correlation Matrix for Elementary-School Teachers Enrolled in Graduate Education Courses

	Arithmetic			Vocabulary			Beery VMI			Penmanship		
	N	r	p	N	r	p	N	r	p	N	r	p
Spelling	56	0.48	0.001	33	0.40	0.01	52	0.16	0.1	56	0.51	0.001
Arithmetic				33	0.56	0.001	52	0.31	0.01	56	0.38	0.002
Vocabulary							33	0.1	0.3	33	0.52	0.001
Beery VMI										52	0.1	0.2.

WRAT spelling and arithmetic, Wide Range Vocabulary Test, and Beery Developmental Test of Visual-Motor Integration. N = number of teachers; r = coefficient of correlation; p = level of probability.

Reading Comprehension and Vocabulary Scores

Thirty-eight graduate secondary-education majors, mostly credentialed, took the Nelson-Denny Reading Comprehension and Vocabulary Tests (Nelson and Denny 1960). The students were given the adult, reduced-time form of the test by James Duggins of San Francisco State University, who kindly supplied us with the test scores. Since the test manual does not have norms for graduate students, the adult norms were recorded. This would tend to inflate the percentiles as compared with norms derived from the graduate population. The correlation between the vocabulary and reading-comprehension scores was determined to be 0.78 (see table 6-8). This corresponds well with other similar correlations, which are uniformly high because comprehension is clearly dependent on vocabulary.

The percentiles on the vocabulary test ranged from 6 through 90, with a median of 36 (see table 6-10). It is possible that the very low percentile

Table 6-8
Correlations between Wide Range Achievement Test Spelling and Reading Scores and between Nelson-Denny Reading Comprehension and Vocabulary Tests

	Number	Correlation Coefficient
WRAT spelling versus reading, age 20 years and up[a]	100	0.86
Nelson-Denny Reading versus Vocabulary[a]	38	0.78

[a]From the WRAT Manual.
[b]Calculated from data on two sections of graduate education students, supplied by J.H. Duggins 1980. Department of Secondary Education, San Francisco State University.

Table 6-9

Correlation Matrix for Secondary-School Teachers Enrolled in Graduate Education Courses

	Arithmetic			Vocabulary			Beery VMI			Penmanship		
	N	r	p	N	r	p	N	r	p	N	r	p
Spelling	91	0.32	0.001	71	0.70	0.001	89	0.28	0.004	91	0.25	0.008
Arithmetic				71	0.29	0.007	89	0.39	0.001	91	0.17	0.05
Vocabulary							71	0.27	0.01	71	0.1	0.1
Beery VMI										89	0.29	0.003

WRAT spelling and arithmetic, Wide Range Vocabulary Test, and Beery Developmental Test of Visual-Motor Integration. N = number of teachers; r = coefficient of correlation; p = level of probability.

scores achieved by most of the students were related to the fact that the test was timed, or the students may simply be deficient in vocabulary. Since the 91 graduate students with secondary credentials who were tested with the untimed Wide Range Vocabulary Test attained a mean score equivalent to the college freshman level, it may be assumed that the problem is inherent in this population of students (see table 6-6).

On the reading-comprehension test the percentiles ranged from 4 to 95, with a median of about 65. Dr. Duggins has suggested that the higher scores obtained in comprehension, as compared with vocabulary, may be due to the way the reduced-time test was given. The students were helped by being told to go on to the next paragraph after five minutes, even if they weren't finished with the first-paragraph multiple-choice items. It was thought that they probably earned more points by going to the next paragraph than they would have had they stayed on the first one. At any rate, a large number of graduate students scored below the fiftieth percentile for adults, which seems to be inappropriate for teachers whose job requires them to comprehend textbooks and explain the contents of these books to their students.

Table 6-10

Scores of Thirty-eight Secondary-Education Graduate Students Tested in 1980 with the Nelson-Denny Vocabulary and Reading Comprehension Tests (Nelson and Denny, 1960)

		Vocabulary				Reading-Comprehension			
		Raw Scores		Percentiles		Raw Scores		Percentiles	
	N	Range	Median	Range	Median	Range	Median	Range	Median
Males	21	34-67	43	17-90	37	32-64	46	29-90	73
Females	17	24-56	42	6-73	35	18-60	40	4-95	52

Age range, 20 to 50 years; median 27 years. The students took the adult reduced-time test.
Source: Adapted from data supplied by J.H. Duggins 1980. Department of Secondary Education, San Francisco State University.

Reactions of Graduate Students to Test Scores

In most of the special-education classes and all the remedial-reading classes, the students received their tests for class discussion and interpretation. The group range was put on the blackboard, and the median was located for each test. Students expressed intense interest in their own scores, the class scores, the range, and the median. Since, in other courses, the students had at times not had their written work consistently corrected for punctuation, grammar, spelling, and so forth, the low scores on standardized tests came as a shocking surprise to many of them. At first they were prone to question the reliability of the tests, and a debate ensued. Then they were encouraged to rescore their tests and look for scoring errors. Finally, a few of the teacher-students began to make such comments as, "I know I should not be teaching spelling, or arithmetic." In a number of classes for training remedial-reading specialists, the teacher-students suggested that, under the state guidelines for admission to their remedial classes, the entire graduate class qualified for remedial work because they were more than two years below their current grade-levels on several of the tests. Usually, the students who scored very low requested assistance, and they were advised to take certain available remedial courses or it was recommended that they tutor themselves, using appropriate remedial texts. A surprising number of the teacher-students enrolled in courses to remediate their deficiencies or used self-tutoring workbooks to bring up their skills. They appeared to recognize their needs and to be sufficiently dedicated professionals to want to improve their weak areas.

A requirement for being admitted to the reading-specialist (remedial-reading) program is that the candidate must have two or more years of "successful" regular classroom teaching experience at either the elementary or secondary level. These students generally appeared to be most capable of assessing the meaning of the scores attained on measures of reading, vocabulary, spelling, visual-motor skills, and arithmetic. Although many students were embarrassed by the scores achieved by their classmates, and perhaps themselves, they seemed to be able to handle what was, for them, an emotionally loaded experience.

They often expressed the concept of now knowing "what the remedial reader feels like," and often wished that they could have gone through this experience before beginning their teaching careers. At times graduates made remarks such as, "If I had only had this experience before I started to teach, I wouldn't have done the things I did." In general, they indicated that it was a humbling event, which contributed much to their understanding.

The attitudes expressed by remedial teachers with experience was often in direct contrast to those of inexperienced teachers. Preservice teachers or credentialed teachers who had not taught were sometimes hostile and dubious about the process, as opposed to the attitudes of experienced teachers. However, all groups that received their scores and participated in the subsequent class discussions about diagnostic testing testified to its value.

Arithmetic Errors

Tarnopol and Tarnopol (1979) have analyzed the arithmetic errors made by teachers who took the Wide Range Achievement Test in arithmetic. The errors made on the easier problems of addition, subtraction, multiplication, and division usually were the result of inattentiveness or impulsiveness. For example, signs were ignored, so addition might be performed when subtraction was called for, or multiplication was used instead of addition. Also, errors were made that indicated a lack of knowledge of the addition and multiplication tables. When similar errors were made on the untimed tests, carelessness or failure to proofread the work were indicated.

The very lowest scoring students were unable to perform division or any problems except the most elementary addition, subtraction, and multiplication. In general, a number of teachers had the same types of problems that were found in a class of eighth-grade pupils whose average grade-level score on the arithmetic test was 6.7. They had difficulty with decimals, percentages, fractions, and so forth. To score at the seventh-grade level on the test, it was necessary only to be able to perform computations in addition, subtraction, multiplication, and division, to be able to operate with simple fractions, and to handle the decimal point. Major obstacles for many teachers who went beyond these test problems included writing 52½ percent as a decimal, writing .075 as a common fraction in lowest terms, finding the complement of an angle of 30 degrees, finding ¼ percent of 60, and converting square feet to square yards.

In general, timed testing appeared to be inappropriate for graduate students, because they could almost always do more problems than they could on the ten-minute timed test. However, the correlation between the timed and untimed tests was very high (0.83; see table 6-2), indicating that the timed test could be used for relative placement of the students. If, however, it was desired to analyze the students' errors for remedial purposes, the untimed test was essential. It was also noted that those students who scored very low in arithmetic were usually poor in spelling, vocabulary, and copying geometrical designs, indicating that such deficits in arithmetic were not generally an isolated condition. It was found that about 16 percent of 281 graduate education students scored below grade-level 7.2 in arithmetic.

Spelling Errors

The lowest scores made by teacher-students in the graduate school of education on the Wide Range Achievement Test for spelling were in the fifth-grade-level range. In order to clarify the meaning of low-level spelling ability, the errors made by an experienced teacher whose spelling grade-level score was 6.0 are presented in table 6-11. Since this student was attending graduate school in grade 18, her spelling ability clearly leaves very much to be desired. In arithmetic she scored at the 6.6 grade-level, and her Wide Range Vocabulary Test age-equivalent score was 17 years, or about twelfth-grade level. The types of spelling errors made by this teacher seem to indicate a possible hearing problem, either acuity or perception, but we were unable to do that type of follow-up testing and so could not analyze the underlying difficulty.

As a rule, the poor spellers failed the same words on this test, but their misspellings were not always the same. These teacher-students had difficulty with multisyllabic words, often omitting a syllable. Most of the spelling errors were found to be in the use of vowels, consonants, roots, and affixes, with the highest frequency in suffixes but rarely in prefixes.

Table 6-11
Spelling Errors on the Wide Range Achievement Test Made by a Credentialed, Experienced Learning-Disabilities Teacher

Teacher's Spelling	Required Word	Teacher's Spelling	Required Word
fashions	fashion	lucity	lucidity
revarens	reverence	loquatious	loquacious
musium	museum	medievil	medieval
presious	precious	afemnine	effeminate
ilogical	illogical	recelious	resilient
decsion	decision	soverignity	sovereignty
quanity	quantity	accigious	assiduous
excutive	executive	acquiest	acquiesce
concouse	conscience	Sharleton	charlatan
phyican	physician	pusalanimius	pusillanimous
coutious	courteous	irredesen	iridescence

Age 36. Grade-Equivalent scores were 6.0 in spelling and 6.6 in arithmetic, and Wide Range Vocabulary Test age-equivalent score was 17 years. She was in the second year of graduate school, or grade eighteen.

About 16 percent of the 311 graduate education students tested were functioning at grade-level 9.7 or below in spelling. Generally, the teachers appeared to be dismayed by their low scores in spelling and asked for suggestions about how to remediate this deficiency.

When teachers write reports, their literacy skills become public. As an example, a teacher whose spelling score was grade-level 11.3 filed the following report in a student's folder (spelling errors italicized by editors):

> Sam can be *disrubtive*, *stuborn*, and have tantrums. He has poor motor skills such as poor *handwritting* and signing of name. He has good *menory* of life events His *nuerlogical* problems are big.

The teacher's penmanship was atrocious and the sentence structure was inadequate. What kind of model will this teacher be for the students who are being remediated, and how will he communicate with other professionals and parents?

Another example is a report sent to an English instructor at a college by the learning-disabilities specialist, who had recently received the master's degree in special education. The report, which we were asked by the instructor to interpret, follows (editor's italics):

> R is a very quiet 21 year old white man. He *doesntt* know what his learning disability is. He was *reefered* to us by Mrs. H and Mr. P because of reversals. in reading work. The testing results on the WRAT showed a 30 in spelling, 39 in reading and a 49 in arithmetic. R scored average intelligence on the Peabody. On the Beery Visual Motor he scored 102. He does have difficulty with reversals which showed up on his life story. I feel R could *benifit* from attending the Learning Disability Center.
> Recommendation:
> Fernald of VAKT
> tracking
> value clarification
> fusion
> visual perception skills
> Dear Mr. P.
> Sorry to have missed you before. *Lets* try to get *togeather* again.

If the reader can't make much sense out of this report, neither can anyone else, for the following reasons. Aside from the sloppy English, the raw scores on the spelling, reading, and arithmetic tests are meaningless without the test manual to assist in their interpretation. Moreover, the English instructor had no idea what WRAT or VAKT signified. The Beery-Buktenica Developmental Test of Visual Motor Integration raw scores range from 0 to 24, and the age-equivalent scores range from two years, ten months to fifteen years, eleven months, so a score of 102 is meaningless. How reversals showed up in R's life story is most fascinating to consider. As for the recommendations, they, too, had no meaning to the instructor, nor did they appear to have much meaning to the learning-disabilities teacher, who, it was reported, seemed to make the same list of recommendations for all students sent to this learning-disabilities specialist.

In-service training courses are given in most California school districts. As a rule, teachers take these courses for salary-increment credits, but they may also take them for credit toward another credential. These courses are usually paid for by the districts, and often the instructors are told that no homework or examinations are to be given and that attendance is not to be taken. However, when teachers take such a course for university credit, we require them to do the same work as students attending lectures at the university, and the teacher-students go along with these requirements because they say that they acquire a great deal of usable knowledge. At the end, the students are asked to evaluate the course. Figure 6-2 shows the written comment on the back of the sheet containing the multiple-choice evaluation of the course. This eleven-word statement contains three very interesting spelling errors: *finging, weeknesses,* and *sucess,* for *finding, weaknesses,* and *success.* The lack of organization of the thought into a sentence is another example of sloppy work.

Vocabulary Errors

On the Wide Range Vocabulary Test, 165 graduate education students' average age-equivalent score was 19 years (see table 6-1). Sixteen percent of the students scored at or below 17.2 years, equivalent to about twelfth

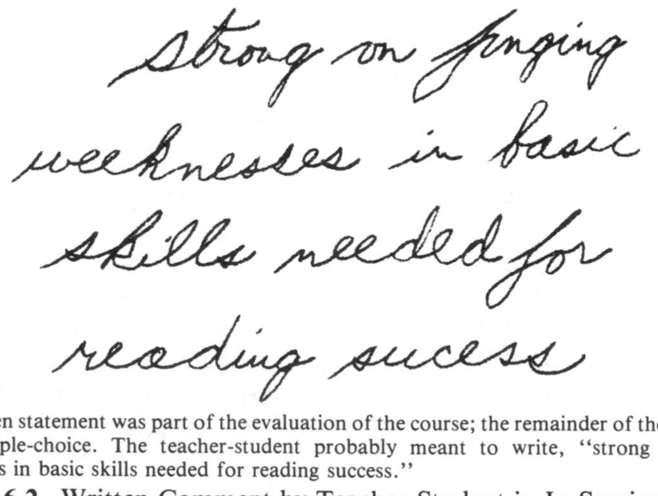

This written statement was part of the evaluation of the course; the remainder of the evaluation was multiple-choice. The teacher-student probably meant to write, "strong on finding weaknesses in basic skills needed for reading success."

Figure 6-2. Written Comment by Teacher-Student in In-Service Course

grade. The WRVT is a multiple-choice test, with five choices for each vocabulary item. Some examples of the errors made by two students on the easier items of this test are given in table 6-12. These students scored about one standard deviation below the mean of those tested. For the most part, these students missed different items, with *couch*, *bilge*, *flagstone*, *shroud*, *zigzag*, and *harum-scarum* in common. It is very puzzling to find 16 percent of these teachers with vocabularies in the high school range; it seems to indicate that they probably are not fluent readers.

Summary

We are well aware of the attitude of many colleagues toward these findings that a certain percentage of the graduate students in education show evidence of semiliteracy. In department meetings, there have been continuing complaints about the very poor quality of some of the term papers received from graduate students. Finally, a writing-proficiency test was instituted to attempt to reduce this problem.

However, some faculty members do not consider it important for a teacher to be able to spell. This implies, in turn, that it is not necessary for

Table 6-12
Words Incorrectly Defined by Two Graduate Education Students on the Easier Words of Wide Range Vocabulary Test

Student A	Student B
achieve	couch
rickets	seafarer
couch	whir
ladle	rations
straddle	ruthless
relapse	kingdom
leer	pun
rejuvenate	bilge
clubfoot	flagstone
bilge	shroud
flagstone	assent
shroud	dilemma
lenient	zigzag
rile	harum-scarum
assent	manifold
zigzag	sot
harum-scarum	indict
incur	
exemplify	

On this multiple-choice test each vocabulary item has five choices from which to select. Student A was twenty-two years old, in grade seventeen, spelling grade-level score 7.8, and vocabulary age-equivalent 16 years. Student B was thirty-six years old, in grade eighteen, spelling grade-level score 6.0, and vocabulary age-equivalent 17 years.

them to teach spelling or to correct their pupils' spelling, since they couldn't reasonably be expected to perform this function. Many colleagues have stated, "I don't think spelling is important." Another comment heard from professors, when they learn that the graduate students' mean spelling grade-level is about 11.0, is, "If you tested me, I wouldn't do that well." Although we have been assured by educationists that spelling is not a real concern, the English department faculty have lodged the complaint that faculty members in other departments were not correcting the students' spelling errors and were accepting any type of punctuation and grammar.

Since spelling, vocabulary, and reading are all highly correlated (see tables 6-8 and 6-9), it is evident that most of the poor spellers do not have an isolated deficiency. Moreover, the most basic tool of the teaching profession, obviously, is literacy. It is equally clear that a teacher cannot give what he does not possess. Moreover, those who disagree with the concept that teachers should be proficient in the basic skills that they are required to teach would very likely be upset if they found that the auto mechanics who were working on their cars lacked the basic skills required for their trade. The argument that literacy alone does not make a good teacher in no way invalidates the fact that a semiliterate person cannot be expected to teach literacy skills adequately.

Underlying this discussion is the concept that quality education is desirable and that basic skills are the necessary foundation for higher levels of education. In recognition of the poor quality of education, which leaves large numbers of high school graduates either illiterate or semiliterate, some states have passed legislation introducing basic literacy tests that students must pass in order to receive a high school diploma. A major argument against the introduction of minimum competency standards is that it permits legislators to dictate to educators standards of quality and what should be taught. However, such laws came about only after the educators had failed to reverse the two-decade decline in Scholastic Aptitude Test and other test scores, plus the growing complaints from business, industry, and universities about the decline in literacy of graduates. We have indicated that the problem appears to be greater than one involving the schools alone and also includes other environmental influences, especially home motivation and tutoring assistance to many students. However, this should not be used as an excuse for educators to evade their responsibilities with respect to quality education.

Some Special Considerations

Just as Thomas Edison became the acknowledged leading American inventor despite his handicaps of poor visual-motor coordination and unusual spelling and Nelson Rockefeller attained political distinction despite his acknowledged dyslexia, some learning-disabled students have become very good teachers, particularly in special education. These people all had compensating skills. Edison, for example, was a prodigious reader, had an unusually good memory, was replete with new creative ideas, and was doggedly able to work hard and continuously.

One of the best high school learning-disability teachers in a local school district is asked to address special-education classes at San Francisco State University on occasion. He discusses his own learning problems as a pupil and the puzzlement expressed by his parents at his strange difficulties as a student. However, they gave him considerable tutoring support and he finally received the master's degree. To illustrate his teaching methods, he brings some of his students to the graduate school and demonstrates applicable testing and teaching procedures. These practical demonstrations help the teachers-in-training develop a realistic understanding of the meaning of learning disabilities to both the students and their parents, and they indicate effective methods of dealing with the problems of individualized teaching, ego support, and vocational development for learning-handicapped students.

Classroom-Teaching Deficits

Most teachers are dedicated, hard-working people who derive great pleasure from seeing their pupils learn and mature. Nevertheless, there are always some teachers whose performance could be improved. Defects in teaching may come from a number of factors, including lack of academic ability; inadequate academic training; deficient preparation for teaching; inability to handle children; inappropriate relations with peers or supervisors; lack of practical supervision; insufficient maturity; and inability to organize time and the environment wisely. Tests can evaluate only the academic functions. Although there are personality tests, their validity is generally too low for safe use. Consequently, these factors must be evaluated by clinical means during student teaching. In many cases, a poor student-teaching demonstration may be greatly improved by proper supervision if the student makes an effort to learn and change. However, when all the student-teachers receive an automatic passing grade, or all As, the students have not really been helped. The desire on the part of instructors or supervisors to be "humane" may save either a student or a teacher from academic failure, but it places in jeopardy a very large number of pupils who will be taught by this inadequate person over many years.

Teacher deficiencies appear to be an international problem, greater in some countries than in others, occurring for different reasons, but universally acknowledged. One reported source of children's learning problems internationally has been defective teaching (Tarnopol and Tarnopol 1976), as shown by the following examples. A Norwegian educator stated, "Even though the teaching profession is held in high regard in Norway (it might be easier to enter a university than to gain admission to a teacher's college), the traditionally trained teachers are too poorly qualified to provide remedial instruction and, therefore, learning disabilities may arise, and be sustained, due to teacher incapability." In Sweden the extent of the reading problems arising from inadequate teaching was estimated at 10 to 15 percent. From Hungary an indication of flaws in teaching was seen in the statement, "The faults that can occur in teaching reading are: wrong sequence in teaching letters; faulty associations between letters and pronunciation; and not giving the longer words gradually enough so that the children are soon overloaded."

In the United States, Jansky and de Hirsch (1972) reported that they asked principals to rate the teachers in five public schools where children were "at risk." In the primary classes taught by the teachers rated as adequate, 23 percent of the children failed to learn to read by second grade. However, 49 percent of the pupils failed who were taught by teachers whom the principals had characterized as poor teachers. Finally, they stated, "It is well-known, moreover, that the reading curriculum in teacher-training institutions is poor." Jansky and de Hirsch saw the reading problems as arising, in part, from a combination of inadequate teacher-training and the inexperience of beginning teachers.

In another examination of the variables related to reading disorders in the United States, the Secretary's National Advisory Committee on Dyslexia and Related Reading Disorders (U.S. Department of Health, Education and Welfare 1969) reported that "a lack of consistency in the training of reading teachers, or more likely a lack of emphasis on reading and reading disorders within the curricula of the various teachers colleges and universities, is reflected by the inconsistency among school programs designed for children with reading disorders." This committee also observed that experienced teachers tended to gravitate to the upper grades, and the more difficult lower grades were often staffed by "new, young teachers, possibly on the assumption that enthusiasm and vitality may compensate for lack of experience."

Malmquist (chapter 20) discusses the factors in Sweden that might cause reading problems, such as the teacher's inability to adapt instruction for individual children so that their maturity and ability is taken into account. Stančić and his associates (chapter 23) cite a frequent lack of teachers' competence to individualize instruction in Yugoslavia, and they also identify "insufficient direction of teaching and school psychology aimed at qualifying teachers to handle individual differences" as factors.

In New Zealand Mitchell and Nicholson (chapter 18) conclude that educators realize that some children are not being supported as much as others during the process of learning to read and that, therefore, "more will need to be done to help teachers become better equipped to deal with failing students." A need is present, they state, for the Department of Education to begin a program aimed at improving the instructional abilities of reading teachers.

A major concern in Brazil, according to Aratangy and coauthors (chapter 8), is the drop-out rate of 54 percent at the end of first grade. Two main factors are cited, which "interact to determine the school failure of a great percentage of children; namely, the teachers and the pupils." Reasons given for teacher incapability are that about 30 percent of the teachers are not educated beyond fourth grade and that they have not been given any special training for their work. In Ethiopia the Starrs (chapter 11) state that many schools also employ teachers with little education beyond their teaching levels, and it would not be uncommon to have teachers of first-grade children who have themselves completed only third or fourth grade. This is also a major problem in India, according to Muralidharan (chapter 15), and in many other developing nations.

Bravo-Valdivieso (chapter 9) states that Chilean researchers are also concerned with teacher inflexibility, as demonstrated by programs and courses of study that are not geared to individual differences in children. In France Mélékian (chapter 12) notes that early detection of reading problems is hindered by many factors, including teacher inexperience, poor preparation of teachers, and too-frequent changes of teachers due to pregnancy or absences for other reasons.

Wenstrup (chapter 13) states that a major difficulty in Greenland is the number of teachers without college educations. Because teacher education is relatively new, not enough local teachers have been prepared, so teachers have to be imported from Denmark. They stay a relatively short time and "rarely master the Greenlandic language, and so they are unable to use it in teaching."

Problems Related to Inexperience in Learning-Disability Teachers

Some of the most common teaching defects observed in California, especially among inexperienced teachers (and sometimes experienced teachers who are having difficulty) are the following:

Problems in Instruction

1. Lesson plans not prepared each day for each student.
2. Lessons not building continuously on previous learning.

3. Learning increments too large or too small.
4. Lack of understanding of the linguistic forms of the English language and the application of phonics and other important techniques to teaching reading.
5. Lack of ability or interest in mathematics.
6. Difficulty understanding each child's instructional needs.
7. Inability to diagnose what is wrong with the teaching method when a child fails to learn.
8. Errors not anticipated or not immediately corrected.
9. Pupils permitted to continue to make the same mistakes, thus over-learning and "fixing" their errors.
10. Not enough structure in the teaching method.
11. Lack of teacher preparation so that students wait for materials, lessons, instruction, and so forth, resulting in disproportionate amount of time without meaningful work to do.
12. Poor choice of commercial programs and materials.

Problems in Behavior Management

1. Teacher sitting at the desk correcting papers, and the like, rather than moving among the students observing work, prompting, suggesting, helping, explaining.
2. Lack of understanding of individual differences in growth, development, and emotional-social needs of boys and girls.
3. Improper use of negative reinforcement (punishment) and positive reinforcement (reward).
4. Inability (afraid) to tell children exactly what to do.
5. Inability (afraid) to control children's behavior.
6. Inability to monitor his or her own behavior, mannerisms, voice, and attitude toward students, offering a poor model as a result.
7. Overpermissiveness or overrigidity.
8. Inconsistency in dealing with behavior and grades.
9. Insensitivity when discussing a pupil's behavior or work so that classmates or other adults hear the remarks.
10. Allowing students to spend time on nonlearning activities, such as eating, daydreaming, talking at random, combing hair, and other non-task-related behaviors, when they are supposed to be working on academic assignments.
11. Interrupting the lesson to call across the room to correct behavior, rather than using techniques to modify such activity that will not disrupt the flow of the lesson.

Personal Problems

1. Disorganization in the classroom.
2. Poor housekeeping in the classroom.
3. Uncomfortable and unrelaxed relationships with students, faculty, administrators, and parents.
4. Difficulty accepting and implementing insights and help from supervisor, administrator, consultant, psychologist, other teachers, and parents.
5. Rationalizing about problems that are evident to others, rather than trying to correct them through practical means.
6. Being sarcastic and verbally abusive.
7. Attempting to be a pal, friend, or peer to students, rather than maintaining the teacher-student relationship.
8. Causing students to distrust the teacher by revealing their confidences.
9. Unfair, biased treatment of students.
10. Frequent absences, arriving late to school, and unwillingness to stay after school if necessary.
11. Handling students in an overly authoritarian or permissive manner.
12. Overreacting to problems in the classroom, playground, cafeteria, and so forth.
13. Inconsistent behavior so that students, other faculty members, and parents are unsure of what to expect.
14. Impractical approach to problems, resulting in waste of time and resources.

It has been our experience that many of these problems can be significantly modified or overcome by adequate supervision in most cases. To accomplish this, it is necessary to have a competent, practical supervisor and a teacher who is interested in improving and is willing to try the methods proposed by the trainer. The time required for retraining varies from about six months to two years.

The Needs of Teachers

Inexperienced teachers usually have the most difficulty with teaching. Lack of experience can hamper even a person who is filled with good intentions, enthusiastic ideas, and youthful energy. It takes years to become armed with a repertoire of techniques for teaching different subjects, individualizing instruction, handling groups, attending to behavior problems, meeting the emotional needs of students, working with school administrators, and communicating with other personnel and parents.

Compounding the problem is the often-cited rapid turnover of new teachers, related to the fact that many who leave did not enjoy or could not cope with their situations. Among the 312 teacher-students tested, the mean age was 30.5 years, but their mean number of teaching years was only 4.2 (see table 6-1). Some of these students were women who had begun to teach in their early twenties, left to rear families, and were reentering the profession. However, it was found that a number of the graduate students had "floated" from one type of job to another, finally landing on a career of teaching for reasons other than a strong and lasting desire to work with pupils. When such people are faced with the intellectual, physical, and emotional drain of teaching in difficult situations, they tend to lack the ability, fortitude, and willingness to perform satisfactorily on the job.

Years of consulting with teachers in their classrooms have led to the observation of a number of the most common teaching defects, previously listed. Although these problems may be seen in some teachers of all ages and varying experience, they are particularly noticeable in inexperienced teachers. One of the most serious problems is disorganization in the classroom. This can occur when teachers are trying to do too much. For example, it is difficult to master a new reading method, introduce a textbook in mathematics, develop a social-studies program for the first time, teach health and science, and also be responsible for everything in the classroom. This is what elementary-school teachers are generally expected to do. If the teacher does not plan lessons carefully each day, and if the lessons do not build continuously on previous learning, chaos soon results. Teachers may find that they have not planned enough work to fill the time, and that some children finish in five minutes while others take thirty-five minutes to do the same work. It is important that the teacher plan more than enough meaningful activity to meet the individual needs of all the pupils (Jansen, Jacobson, and Jensen 1978).

Disorganization may sometimes cause the wrong worksheets to be stapled together, for example, or the incorrect assignment to be handed out. Students become restless and behavior problems are accelerated when they must wait because of inefficient use of their time. Beginning teachers may be assisted in getting organized if they have supervisory or peer guidance very early in the term, preferably commencing before school starts.

Experienced teachers may arrive at school several days or even a week before classes begin to organize their rooms, check supplies, review manuals, count the texts to be sure enough are available, begin to prepare lesson plans, and so forth. That is the time to find out if the typewriter is broken, the tape recorders need repair, the windows can't be opened, the thermostat isn't working, some light bulbs need replacing, and the chalkboards need to be cleaned, and so on.

Good classroom organization involves good housekeeping and attending to the total environment as well as to the curriculum requirements. If the teacher finds that the view through the lower windows may distract students (especially learning-handicapped pupils) or that too much sunlight causes glare or overheating, a semiopaque film may be sprayed on the bottom windows to forestall these problems. In the Japanese elementary schools visited, the lower windows were translucent, so that the children could not be distracted by outside activity or look outside and daydream, while light was permitted to enter the classrooms.

Although environmental control by the teacher appears to be a commonsense measure hardly worth stressing, lack of attention to these problems occurs often enough to warrant mention (Howell and Howell 1979). This includes manipulating the thermostat when necessary, opening and closing windows, shades, and doors when air, sound, or light require control, and taking command of the entire situation. Special-education teachers need to pay particular attention to distracting elements in the classroom, which must be minimized in order to help hyperactive, distractible, and impulsive students channel their efforts more directly into the work to be learned.

One of the major weaknesses observed in remedial-reading and learning-disability classes is lack of structure in both teaching method and classroom arrangement. Structure is one of the most effective supports that teachers can give to reading- and learning-handicapped students (Cruickshank 1977). Structure provides a controlled environment and teaching methods that students can depend on to take into account their individual learning and behavioral needs. A structured and well-organized curriculum is recognized as being important in every country that is attempting to provide remedial services for students.

Taking inventory of each child's individual methods of learning and being able to analyze what is wrong with the teaching methods, materials, or classroom is necessary. A teacher's inability to diagnose what is incorrect about a method when a child fails to learn may result in continuing a program that is inappropriate, making recommendations that result in misplacing a child, or mislabeling a student.

Inexperienced teachers sometimes have difficulty anticipating problems in the lessons and behavior problems. All teachers need to develop the art of constantly scanning with their eyes so that they are continuously seeing what is going on in their classes. Although remedial-reading and learning-disability classes tend to be smaller than regular classes, many reading- and learning-disabled students are distractible and hyperactive, and the resulting problems of inattention and lack of concentration make the teacher's role demanding. Scanning can forestall problems that might otherwise occur.

It is essential that special-education teachers understand the language they are teaching children to read and write. This means a thorough knowledge of the linguistic forms of English and the application of phonics to teaching reading. Teachers should have excellent enunciation, speech, and written language themselves, especially because they serve as models to their students. It is most important for teachers' writing to be both rapid and easy to read, especially blackboard work. Again, this serves as a positive model for the learner.

It is important to correct the work of students as quickly as possible—immediately in many cases. This eliminates the problem of pupils being permitted to make the same errors over and over again, in effect cementing the errors to the point that unlearning them may be almost impossible.

Understanding sex differences and the individual patterns of growth and development will aid all teachers and may prevent many problems. Boys have a greater need for motility, exhibit shorter attention spans, and are, in general, more difficult to manage than girls. Teachers who know that boys are "at risk" for reading, learning, and behavior problems will be able to anticipate and prevent them before they arise. Boys and girls also have different interests. Experienced teachers recognize this and capitalize on individual preferences when choosing texts and programs. Seating arrangements that take individual needs into account are also carefully thought out by effective teachers.

The appropriate uses of negative reinforcement (punishment) and positive reinforcement (reward) appear to be major dilemmas. This is an especially sensitive area in special education, where children have already experienced much failure and require continuous support to encourage them to try as long and as hard as will be necessary for them. Teachers with experience avoid sarcasm, loud voices, calling across the room, bringing attention to incorrect behavior or work, harsh and negative discussion, physical punishment, and embarrassing the children. Effective teachers know that they can control the behavior of children, and they are not afraid to tell children what to do; ineffective teachers may be unable to act to manage behavior.

Although these items that demand attention appear to be related to common sense, they only occur to people as the result of experience. Beginning teachers cannot be expected to anticipate the myriad of details that may need attention, so it is most important to have practical assistance available from the start of school, or before, if possible. Unfortunately, the tendency seems to be to leave the teacher alone to learn the hard way, too often with disastrous effects on both the teacher and the pupils.

Improving Instruction by Observing Pupils' Work

Children with learning disabilities have taught us more about learning and good teaching than all of the research with rats, or with college sophomores or nonsense syllables. Above average children seem to be capable of learning regardless of the methods used. On the other hand, children with learning disabilities will *not* learn as long as we continue to violate the principles of learning. Thus they represent our most valuable source of information about how children learn and how to teach (Bateman 1966).

Teachers may not be aware that something they are doing is confusing the pupils. However, once the problem is brought to their attention, it is often easily corrected. It has been our observation that a defect most commonly found in teaching elementary school pupils is permitting children to practice and overlearn their errors. Good pedagogy suggests that children learn best by practicing from a correct model, followed by overlearning. Teachers should be trained to observe their pupils' work carefully in order to be able to anticipate and prevent error-learning and to develop creative ways of teaching concepts that are misunderstood. A number of examples of how a teacher can do this are given in Tarnopol and Tarnopol (1976).

Observing Pupils' Work to Prevent Errors

Jane was a seven-year-old pupil in a primary special day class for children with learning disabilities. Among other things, she had visual-motor deficits and weak pencil control. She was very motivated to learn and tried hard to print the letters *p*, *j*, *g*, and *q* (see figure 6-3). However, she had only succeeded in practicing her errors. She was given the worksheet and told to copy the letters while the teacher went on to do something else.

When correctly used, this type of exercise can be helpful. After giving the pupil the worksheet, the teacher must explain its use. The student should be told that these are tail letters that occupy one space above and one space below the baseline, and that they are to be carefully placed as shown by the correct model. The child is to trace the dotted sample first, observing the directions indicated by the arrows, with the teacher watching her work. Then the pupil does the first copy of a letter, with the teacher still observing both the copy and the spacing to be certain that they are done correctly. If the pupil can master that much, she may be permitted to continue on her own, but the teacher should return intermittently to be sure that the copies continue to be correctly executed. This ensures that the pupil both copies and practices a correct model. It should be remembered that learning-

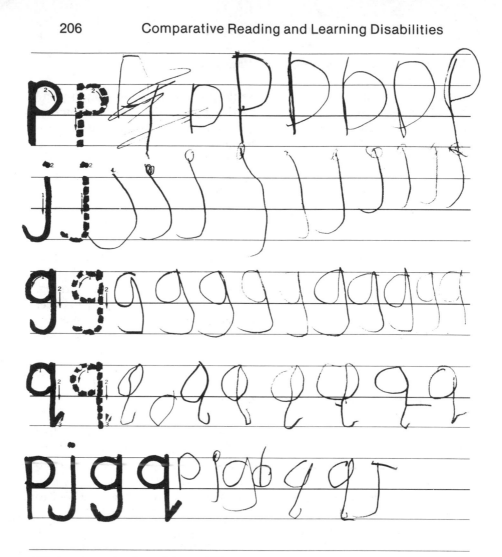

This is an example of permitting a child to practice her errors. This child appeared to need more practice tracing perfectly formed letters before going on to independent copying.

Figure 6-3. Practice Worksheet of Seven-Year-Old Pupil

disability teachers have small classes and sometimes have an aide, just so they are able to devote time to each pupil as needed.

A number of problems are evident when one examines the worksheet in figure 6-3. Jane's printing indicated that she might not have been ready for this level of work and that it might have been better to revert to prewriting exercises, such as large-motor work at the blackboard, in the air, with a stylus in clay, and on large-lined paper with a thick crayon or felt-tipped pen. When she appeared to be ready, the exercises could have been continued as previously, except that the dotted letters to be traced should be continued across most of the line, leaving two or three spaces for independent copying. Thereafter, if necessary, the next worksheet could contain a dotted letter followed by the stem only, to assist the pupil in both spacing and proper letter formation. Children with severe visual-motor deficits require a great many graduated exercises, in small steps. When this method is used, experience indicates that these pupils often develop excellent penmanship.

Learning-disabled students tend to be highly motivated to learn typing, and when they are taught with a good, liniguistically based program, they can usually learn linguistic patterns as well. Such a typing program embraces spelling and reading, is carefully sequenced, and is designed for the ages and reading levels of intermediate students (grades four through six). John was a sixth-grade reading-disabled boy who was waiting for his teacher to find such a typing book for him. Meanwhile, he placed a piece of lined paper in the typewriter and began to stab at the keys with a sharp pencil, producing the results shown in figure 6-4. By the time the typing book was recovered from under a pile of material strewn over the table, the typewriter had been "accidentally" rendered inoperable and the lesson had to be canceled. Although respect for the individual differences of teachers may permit some teachers to be disorganized, the consequences for many students may be detrimental.

Figure 6-5 shows the spelling test of a bright boy with learning disabilities who was well-motivated and worked hard. However, writing with a pen was very difficult for him because of a pronounced motor problem. He would have been able to perform more satisfactorily if wide-ruled paper were used and if he were given special training in penmanship to improve his letter formation and increase his speed.

j   jjjjjjjjjj nnnnnnnnUUUUUUUUUUU

Now is the time for ll jjdjfjfjdidujjjjj hhhhhhhhhhhhgggjjjjjjjjjjjj

jjjjjjjjjjjjjjjjjjjjjjjjjjjjjNow 1111234567890-=½poiu

poiuytrewqasdfghjkl;¢/.,mnbvcxz

&'()*+¼POIUYTREWQASDFGHJKL:@?.,MNBVCXZ

While the teacher was attempting to find the typing workbook under a pile of material on the table, this child punched the keys with a sharp pencil and broke the typewriter, ending the lesson.

Figure 6-4. Typing by Sixth-Grade Reading-Disabled Boy

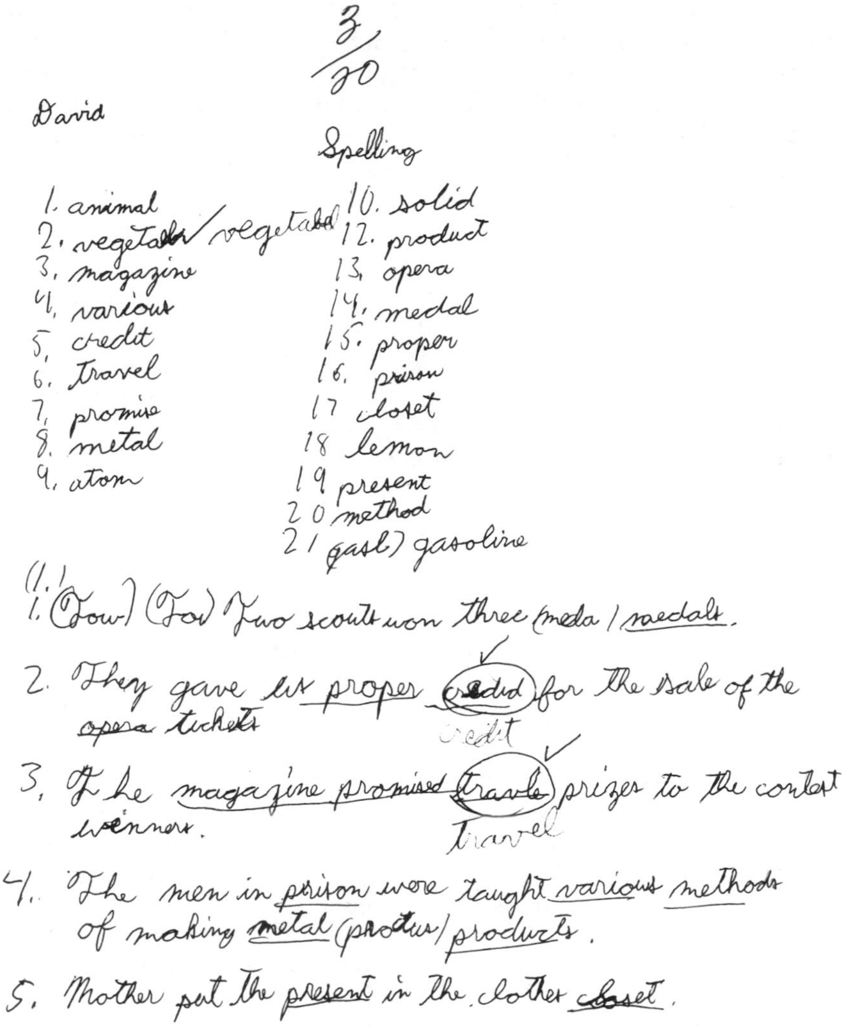

$\frac{3}{20}$

David

Spelling

1. animal
2. vegetab✓ vegetab 10. solid
3. magazine   12. product
4. various   13. opera
5. credit   14. medal
6. Travel   15. proper
7. promise   16. prison
8. metal   17. closet
9. atom   18. lemon
   19. present
   20. method
   21. (gasl) gasoline

1. (Tow) (Toa) Two scouts won three (meda / medals.

2. They gave us proper (redid) for the sale of the opera tickets.
     credit

3. The magazine promised (travle) prizes to the contest winners.
     Travel

4. The men in prison were taught various methods of making metal (protus / products.

5. Mother put the present in the clothes closet.

The teacher should have written the misspelled words correctly alongside the child's work. This would have avoided continued spelling errors, such as *vegetabel*, by the child. Scoring should have been positive, that is, 17/20, meaning 17 correct out of 20.

Figure 6-5. Spelling Test of a Bright Boy with Learning Disabilities

When a word—*vegetable*, for example—is misspelled, the teacher should write it correctly alongside. This would preclude having the pupil rewrite the word as *vegetabel*. The student was permitted to practice an error because it had not been properly corrected by the teacher.

The paper also illustrates negative grading, which may cause the student to think he has done poorly rather than indicating how well he has done. By the teacher's scoring the paper 3/20, meaning three wrong out of twenty items, the pupil may have seen himself as weak in spelling. A better method of scoring would be 17/20, indicating seventeen correct. There is a song that says, "Accentuate the positive, eliminate the negative," which is a most judicious axiom for teaching.

Case History: Consultation with an Inexperienced Learning-Disability Teacher

A teacher (T) requested consultation services for "the many perceptual problems that my students have which make it difficult for them to learn." Consultation included direct classroom observations, after-class conferences with the teacher, and visits with the teacher to observe well-managed programs in other schools.

Preliminary meetings revealed that T appeared, from conversation, to be a warm, interested professional, concerned about the varied educational, social, and emotional problems of the students. T spoke of the students in a pleasant manner and appeared genuinely concerned about their growth and development.

Observations in T's classroom over a two-year period revealed a number of problem areas in the first year, as follows:

1. The room was poorly organized. The students' work areas were not defined. There was an excessive amount of unused furniture, old books, art supplies, games, and miscellaneous materials in the room. The blackboards were covered with "pop" posters, leaving no space for the teacher or the students to write. On open bookshelves and on the teacher's desk were textbooks, with easily read titles, on brain damage, juvenile delinquency, birth defects, and various other handicapping conditions. These were readily seen by students, parents, and anyone who entered the room. Tables and desk tops were dirty, and the room was dusty and littered and had a bad odor.

2. A prevailing lack of structure allowed students to spend long periods of time in nonlearning activities, such as daydreaming, sleeping, nontask-related conversation, eating, and hair-combing.

3. There was no attempt to base the academic program of each student on current, pertinent diagnostic information provided by the psychologist or obtained from teacher testing. The teacher was not familiar with common tests used in special education, nor was T able to develop an academic program, individualized for each student, on the basis of psychoeducational testing.

4. A discrepancy existed between the teacher's goals and those of the administrators and parents. The teacher wanted a "relaxed" and "creative" curriculum. The parents and administrators desired teaching of basics and elimination of the overly permissive atmosphere.

5. Students had little opportunity to monitor their own academic or social progress. There was no system that enabled a student to know where he was and where he was going.

6. Lack of teacher preparation resulted in students waiting for materials and in a disproportionate amount of time without work to do.

7. Lack of positive reinforcement and an excessive amount of negative patterning on the part of the teacher was the basis for increasingly negative student responses, socially and academically, which escalated as the year progressed, resulting in the expulsion of several of the students by T. Other students requested to be assigned to another teacher.

8. The teacher was unable and unwilling to accept suggestions by the psychologist regarding behavior, curriculum, parent involvement, and the use of behavior modification.

9. The teacher took the students on numerous field trips without obtaining prior approval, which the principal stated he would not have given.

Some Classroom Observations

The students were working in books individually and in groups. Supplemental work was in the form of duplicated material that was single-spaced and extremely difficult to read because of small type. It was blurred and contained a large number of difficult-to-read words. Students called out to each other frequently, with much giggling, dropping of coins, searching in purses by the girls, and inattention by both girls and boys. The teacher remained seated, calling across the room to individual students about the bell schedule for the day and the next day's program, and answering questions about the work that students called out. At one point the teacher shouted, "Stop this yelling!" The students began to call out loudly with greater frequency.

It was noticed that students frequently helped each other. They told each other where to work on the page, how to spell a word, what the answer was, and what they thought something meant. The teacher did not discuss spelling or written grammar, nor were these corrected when the papers were checked, even though there were numerous errors.

Another Day

Students were taking turns reading an article. The girls did fairly acceptable oral reading, followed by class discussion. They began to giggle, pass gum, talk, and interrupt. They had difficulty continuing the discussion with seriousness. There was much talking and many inappropriate replies. One student sat back reading from a different textbook. Jane was reading aloud. The teacher interrupted in the middle of the paragraph being read with the question, "How much were the coats then and how much are they now?" She went to the blackboard and asked the class how much they would have to add or subtract to figure this out. The paragraph was not completed. Jane then opened to the second section of the paper and began a game. The boy in the rear continued in a completely different textbook. T got up and checked to see if students had the correct page. One student had appeared to be reading but actually was missing the page containing the article and so was unable to follow what the others were reading aloud. T asked Jane, "Do you think we need rules?" Jane replied, "Yes, we need rules. What grade do I get?" T replied, "B," and said, "everybody, page 1. OK, go ahead." Jane began to read with expression. T got up to see if the boys had the correct places. Carol called out inappropriately. Joe was seated at the rear of the room, both feet up on another chair. Discussion about the article followed. Students were asked, "What was the most important point of the article?" Joe answered with an immature and completely off-the-point discussion. Some students began to leave the room, although there were still five more minutes until the bell. The teacher made no effort to stop them.

The teacher said to Joe, "Do you know what I would like you to read? The one on the automobile. OK, Joe, go ahead." Joe became serious and started to read. In contrast to some of the girls, he read with the greatest difficulty. He hesitated frequently, and his reading rate was painfully slow, with no expression. Jane had great difficulty sustaining attention while Joe read. Dick smiled whenever Carol called out. He put his textbook away and put his head down on the desk. Carol called out, "What else are we going to do? It is almost time for the bell." Joe said, "I don't want to read." Kim was asked to continue the oral reading. The sentence was, "Last spring the farmer plowed his field early with his horse." The teacher had to supply *last*, *spring*, *farmer*, *plowed*, *field*, *early*, and *horse*. Kim said, "I can't read." Joe called out, "It is time to leave." The teacher replied, "Not yet." Frank said, "Yes, it is." He stood up and walked to a window. He said, "The others are outside." He and two others left the class.

And Another Day

The room had been rearranged; the teacher had seated the students in a circle and they had binders, which were open on each desk. T walked from student to student and frequently bent down to whisper something. Four students were working; others appeared sleepy, inattentive, and rebellious. Kim said, "I won't do it." She could not concentrate and called out frequently. The teacher went over to Kim and told her that if she did not do her work this period, she would have to go the office the following period. Kim began to pay attention. The others were restless. The circle arrangement appeared to facilitate much negative interaction, especially of a personal nature.

Sally wanted to show the consultant her binder. She exhibited much difficulty in penmanship. The consultant suggested to the teacher that all baselines be marked with a thick, black flow-pen and indicated with an X on the line so Sally would know on which line to place her letters. She had practiced many letters incorrectly over and over.

The Binders

The binders, which were instituted as a method to help the teacher and students keep work in categorical sections and in chronological order, were not up to date. It had been impressed upon the teacher that all student work was to be corrected as the students were working, if possible. If this was not possible, then all work was to be corrected during the preparation period. This was to ensure that students got immediate feedback. If this was not feasible, all work to be completed or to be redone, based on teacher corrections, was to be placed in the front of the binder. The students were told that their new, daily work and past work to be redone was to be found in the front of the binder. All work, completed and corrected to the satisfaction of the teacher, was to be dated and placed in the appropriate sections of the binder.

This procedure, in use in many special-education classes, works well when the teacher carefully corrects each paper daily and trains the students to organize their work. It had been a tremendous asset in other classes but appeared not to be effective in this class because of poor daily monitoring. It was observed by the consultant that many days would elapse between the start and finish of work, the work was frequently not corrected, and it was often carelessly done. This tended to confuse the students and reinforce incorrect learning patterns.

Discussion

The consultant spent many hours discussing curriculum, testing, and teaching strategies with the teacher, who was also taken to visit other special-education settings that were considered to be functioning well. The teacher frequently declined to meet or work after school. Moreover, T would not take papers home to be corrected or plan lessons after school. In the beginning of the semester, no lesson plans, either daily or weekly, had been in evidence. After discussions about the necessity for lesson planning, T continued to produce little daily preparation.

The following suggestions were made early in the term, and all the needed materials were provided for the class in order to carry out the program:

1. Student work was to be kept in binders.
2. Student work was to be corrected daily.
3. Student work was to be dated and kept in correct chronological order.
4. Student work was to reflect individualization based on diagnostic assessment of student ability.
5. Centers were to be organized for different subjects and activities.
6. The math center was to have suitable manipulative math aids.
7. The language center was to utilize cassette recorders, headphones, and training tapes for language development.
8. Each student was to have a daily, individualized lesson plan, which was to be prepared by the teacher at the end of each day and placed in the front of the binder.
9. All reading material was to be selected by the teacher to accurately reflect each student's instructional reading level.

The teacher tried to institute the highly structured remedial program suggested by the consultant. During the first year of consultation, T was not able to carry it out effectively because of poor preparation. The attitude of the students had become increasingly negative and they had become more difficult to handle.

An Administrative Decision

A meeting of involved personnel with school administrators was held to discuss ways of improving the physical situation in this classroom. It was decided to move the class to a more appropriate room with full carpeting, an acoustical ceiling, a telephone, adequate cabinets, file drawers, chairs, desks, and so forth.

Great Improvement during the Second Year

In the second year T was appropriately dressed and presented an excellent professional model for the students. This was in marked contrast to the previous school year. When the consultant entered the room, which had been moved from a classroom to a bungalow at the edge of the school grounds, the teacher was listening to oral reading with one student. This new classroom was carpeted, which effectively reduced the distracting noises of chairs scraping the floor and footsteps resounding, as had characterized the other classroom. Also, there was an improvement in the appearance of the room. Each student had a binder and used the binder to organize work. More-appropriate materials were evident, and students were using them with apparent enjoyment. A student was working in arithmetic using an up-to-date program, which was sequenced and well-monitored by the teacher. T came over frequently to check his progress. He had a tendency to arrange the worksheets out of sequence, and T would supervise this and the arithmetic entries he made. T effectively moved from student to student, all of whom appeared controlled and motivated. The class was attentive, and, for most of the time, students were engaged in learning activities.

Another Visit to the Class

All students were working with appropriate materials. They each had a binder, which they appeared to use effectively. T was first seated at a table with several students but during the period circulated from student to student. All students had some teacher contact during this observation. As students finished their pages or assignments, the teacher dated each sheet to indicate that it was completed. Students expressed satisfaction each time the teacher did this. There was frequent positive verbal reinforcement by the teacher, who appeared relaxed and more interested in the curriculum than in the past. The students were also more relaxed and interested in their work. In comparison to past visits, it was noticeable that students were kinder to each other. There was also a much healthier feeling between students and teacher.

In summary, there was marked improvement in the program. Some of the improvements, such as changing the location of the classroom, carpeting the floor, and so forth, were administrative decisions. The teacher, initially resistant to a more academic program, nevertheless made an effort to implement such a program. The students were better monitored and their work showed much improvement.

Conclusion

There is general agreement on one concept, namely, that the teacher is the most important single person, among the professional personnel working with pupils, affecting their moral, behavioral, and educational progress. Moreover, teachers may also have great influence in determining students' career aspirations. Consequently, it is imperative that teachers be adequately prepared for this demanding role.

In the field of special education, the teacher's job appears to be even more critical than it is in general education, because handicapped children are considerably more vulnerable than normal pupils. Since the children in special-education classes are usually much more difficult to manage, both behaviorally and academically, the requirements for teaching them are very much more demanding.

In the 1969 Symposium on Learning Disabilities held in San Francisco, Macdonald Critchley stated what he believed would be the ideal teacher in special education:

> I would like to see certain self-selected teachers who are particularly interested . . . choosing to specialize in remedial instruction. . . . I can imagine a band of crusading teachers undergoing courses of instruction. . . . When trained I can see them given a diploma, and accorded a special status as a *corps d'élite,* with special privileges and payment commensurate with their special skill (Tarnopol 1971).

References

Atwell, C.R., and Wells, F.L. 1945. *Wide Range Vocabulary Test.* New York: Psychological Corporation.

Bateman, B. 1966. New Approaches to Learning Disabilities. Presented at symposium, "Learning Disabilities," San Francisco: California Association for Neurologically Handicapped Children, October.

Beery, K., and Buktenica, N. 1967. *Developmental Test of Visual-Motor Integration.* Chicago: Follett.

Coleman, J.S., et al. 1966. *Equality of Educational Opportunity.* Washington, D.C.: U.S. Government Printing Office.

Conant, J.B. 1963. *The Education of American Teachers.* Toronto: Mc-Graw-Hill.

Cruickshank, W. 1966. *The Teacher of Brain-Injured Children.* Syracuse: Syracuse University Press.

———. 1977. *Learning Disabilities in Home, School and Community.* Syracuse: Syracuse University Press.

Gazzaniga, M. 1970. *The Bisected Brain.* New York: Appleton-Century-Crofts.

Graduate Record Examination. 1979-1980. *Guide to the Use of the Graduate Record Examinations.* Princeton, N.J.: Educational Testing Service.

Howell, R., and Howell, P. 1979. *Discipline in the Classroom.* Reston, Va.: Reston Publishing Company.

Jansen, M., Jacobson, B., and Jensen, P. 1978. *The Teaching of Reading Without Really Any Method.* Copenhagen: Munksgaard.

Jansky, J., and de Hirsch, K. 1972. *Preventing Reading Failure: Prediction, Diagnosis, Intervention*. New York: Harper and Row.

Jastak, J., Bijou, S., and Jastak, S. 1978. *Wide Range Achievement Test*. Wilmington, Del.: Jastak Associates.

Koerner, J. 1963. *The Miseducation of American Teachers*. Boston: Houghton Mifflin.

Lerner, J. 1976. *Children With Learning Disabilities*. 2nd ed. Boston: Houghton Mifflin.

Lerner, J., and List, L. 1970. The phonics knowledge of prospective teachers, experienced teachers and elementary pupils. *Illinois School Research* 7:39-42.

Mayeske, G., and Beaton, A., Jr., 1975. *Special Studies of Our Nation's Students*. Washington, D.C.: U.S. Government Printing Office.

Mayeske, G., et al. 1973. *A Study of the Achievement of our Nation's Students*. Washington, D.C.: U.S. Government Printing Office.

Nelson, M., and E. Denny, 1960. *The Nelson-Denny Reading Test*. Boston: Houghton Mifflin.

"SAT Scores Continue Decline." 1980. *San Francisco Examiner and Chronicle*, October 8.

Tarnopol, L. 1971. Introduction to neurogenic learning disorders. In L. Tarnopol (ed.), *Learning Disorders in Children: Diagnosis, Medication, Education*. Boston, Mass.: Little, Brown.

Tarnopol, L., and Tarnopol, M. 1976. Learning disabilities in the United States. In L. Tarnopol and M. Tarnopol (eds.), *Reading Disabilities: An International Perspective*. Baltimore: University Park Press.

Tarnopol, L., and Tarnopol, M. (eds.). 1977. *Brain Function and Reading Disabilities*. Baltimore: University Park Press.

Tarnopol, L., and Tarnopol, M. 1979*a*. Arithmetic disability in college students. *Academic Therapy* (January).

Tarnopol, L., and Tarnopol, M. 1979*b*. Motor deficits that may cause reading problems. *Journal of Learning Disabilities* 12:8.

Tarnopol, M. 1979. Quien debe enseñar a los niños con problemas de aprendizaje. In L. Garcia Jasso (ed.), *Problemas de Aprendizaje*. Guadalajara: EDI.

Tarnopol, M., and Tarnopol, L. 1979. Brain function and arithmetic disability. *Focus on Learning Problems in Mathematics* 1:3.

Thorndike, R.L. 1973. *Reading Comprehension Education in Fifteen Countries*. New York: Halstead.

U.S. Department of Health, Education and Welfare. 1969. *Reading Disorders in the United States*. Report of the (HEW) Secretary's National Advisory Committee on Dyslexia and Related Reading Disorders. Washington, D.C.: U.S. Government Printing Office.

White, B., Kaban, B., and Attanucci, J. 1979. *The Origins of Human Competence*. Lexington, Mass.: Lexington Books, D.C. Heath.

In Another's Shoes: A Case Study of a Mature Dyslexic

David A. Gauntlett

You can only hope to find a lasting solution to a conflict if you have learned to see the other objectively, but, at the same time, to experience his difficulties subjectively. —Dag Hammarskjöld, *Markings*

Introduction

The majority of erudite works written on the subject of specific language-learning disabilities or dyslexia refer to work done with children by researchers in the fields of neurology, psychology, and education. More recently this field has been attracting both multi- and interdisciplinary approaches, often related to socioeconomic environment and incidence of associated emotional and behavioral problems. Studies involving adult dyslexics remain comparatively few. Margaret Rawson's study (Rawson 1968) is one of the few longitudinal works available, and the British report *People with Dyslexia* (Kershaw 1974) deserves wider consideration.

Many of the accounts about adult dyslexics are of the "local boy makes good" type, written by a journalist, and more often than not they are relegated to the prosaic columns of the local press. To be newsworthy they need to be exceptional, and this by its very essence makes it hard for the dyslexic to relate to. The millionaire who had private tutors and is now supported by elaborate secretarial aid identifies poorly with the discouraged dyslexic who has a history of failure and often little financial or moral support.

Nor do the professional footballplayers, international scientists, or artists have more than a passing interest for the dyslexic person. The frequently cited examples of Einstein and Leonardo da Vinci provide little insight into the problems *he*, the dyslexic person, is experiencing. Many adults have reluctantly accepted such labels as "late developer" and "slow learner" in order to come to terms with the fact that in the eyes of others they lack ability. This is true for the countless thousands who passed through an educational system oblivious to their problems and needs in the days before the concept of dyslexia became known. The impact on their lives is a scar, which they continue to carry, often avoiding situations in which they might again fail, sometimes screened behind a wall of behavioral defense so elaborately constructed that, like some illiterate adults, even their marriage partners may be unaware of the nature of their problem.

I would emphasize that I see it as axiomatic that in the definition of dyslexia there is reference to the dyslexic person as being "of at least normal intelligence, if not indeed of high IQ" and that there is no evidence of primary disorders, emotional or perceptual, and no evidence of brain damage (Critchley 1964). The key is the discrepancy between his intellectual level and his actual performance in reading and spelling (Miles 1974). A definition acceptable for this chapter would be that of the World Federation of Neurology: "Specific Developmental Dyslexia: A disorder manifested by difficulty in learning to read [write and spell] despite conventional instruction, adequate intelligence and socio-cultural opportunity. It is dependent upon fundamental cognitive disabilities which are frequently of constitutional origin" (cited in Tarnopol 1971).

This case study was written in the hope that it may provide some insight into what it is like to be an adult dyslexic and into the effect that being labeled a "slow learner" rather than dyslexic has had on his life and behavior. What saves it from being mundane is the "sting in the tail," in that, for some reason, rather than accepting the pattern of expectations cast for him, he has persisted in his search for self-actualization in a fight to realize his own identity.

History

The subject of this case study is a male Caucasian, born in 1939 at Luton, England, of middle-class parents. His father was a professional engineer. Following a normal pregnancy and birth, he was a normal, healthy child. He was ambidextrous, with a tendency to write with his left hand. He had the usual childhood illnesses, and measles at the age of four affected his eyes.

Primary school from the age of five was followed by junior school. He learned to read between eight and nine years of age, after receiving help from parents and relations. He failed the "11-plus" examination twice, despite the "potential" teachers felt he possessed. The alternatives in British education then were either a secondary state-school education, for those without scholastic aspirations, or a private, fee-paying school with smaller classes and the goal of academic achievement. A private school was chosen. (Appendix 7A describes the British educational system at that time.)

Despite all the advantages this might have conferred, progress through the school was retrograde, in that from an "A" stream he went to a "B" stream and then was kept back to do a year again, in the hope of improvement. His school reports were poor, language being his worst subject and math only a little better. By spelling even the questions wrong, he succeeded in getting an overall minus mark in a French-language examination and seemed to merit the recurring comments: "must try harder," "could do better," and "should pay more attention to detail and written work." "Careless" was a commonly applied adjective to the lad, who, at 15, frequently misspelled his own name and address.

Arts and crafts were totally absent from the curriculum, and there was little cause for optimism, since he was also poor with figures. His spelling seemed to consist of letters in a random order, together with reversals (of both letters and numbers) and repetitions. So, without a testimony of scholastic achievement, he left school shortly before his sixteenth birthday to start work in the only field in which he had shown any interest—the antithesis of academic studies, farm laboring.

The story might well have ended there, for in the mid-fifties such a lad was at best labeled a "late developer" but more often "slow." His parents, however, persuaded him to attend a practical course at a farm school for two months; and a year later they talked him and the authorities into enrolling him in a practical and theoretical course at a farm college. Here the results were mixed; the theory was not easily evidenced in examinations, and, being left-handed, he used tools differently and sometimes awkwardly.

By misspelling or misreading the names of animals or the ingredients of food rations, his recorded details (such as milk yields or nutritional supplements) were often inaccurate, so, apart from success in college track events and in working with machinery, the results were mediocre. Nevertheless, much to his own surprise and the surprise of those around him, he gained a national college certificate and a pass in "O" level, General Certificate of Education (GCE), which was normally given to schoolboys four years younger than he. Then, nearly twenty, he was back as a farm laborer.

In those days national military service was easily avoided by those with academic careers, but those not so able were required to serve. For the next two years he was employed in Her Majesty's Military Service, too intelligent and well-spoken to be a private yet lacking the scholastic background necessary for an officer's commission. The Army Intelligence Test administered upon entry recorded an IQ of 120. This is the only IQ test known to have been given him of which a record was made. During service in Libya he passed the Army Certificate of Education at the level required to become a warrant officer (sergeant major). Toward the end of national service a commission as an officer was only available to graduates and those prepared to enlist for a short service commission.

After two years' service abroad, his background of farming skills and his athletic ability suited him poorly for returning to civilian life. However, with parental support and the remainder of his meager savings, he embarked upon a part-time course involving five GCE subjects at "O" level

(English literature, English language, geography, economics, and arithmetic). He showed educational films in schools during the day and attended night classes (see appendix 7A), and having passed the "O" levels, he went on, despite advice from lecturers that it was "beyond" him, to gain his first "A" level, in economics.

Again the story nearly ends, for in the next ten years there was little encouragement or success. Subdued by discouraging assessments of his ability, his slow reading and poor spelling and math, what little enthusiasm remained flickered more weakly following poor results in competitive professional examinations, for which he studied through correspondence courses. During this time he used his farming knowledge, first to obtain a post in a firm of agricultural estate agents (property valuators) and then to move to a similar post in a nationalized industry. But writing reports proved a stumbling block, virtually insurmountable in a period before the Kershaw report (1974) suggested alternatives, and before he learned that there was both a name and help for his predicament.

A growing realization that he could function effectively in other spheres came through sport. The competition and the related training had been a successful extension of a practical skill, but rewarding though it was, it had not served to restore his confidence in his academic ability. It was only through serving on committees in different posts and coaching, which provided the chance of extending himself into new spheres, that his confidence grew.

Regional and national posts in sport led to a further increase in confidence, mainly because he was treated as an equal (see appendix 7B) and was able to use the demands the posts made to extend himself into fields previously closed to him. During this period his initial interest in coaching developed further, leading first to teaching and then to education in general. In 1972 his involvement in judo led to him being head of the British judo delegation to the Munich Olympic Games. His work with young people had already led to his taking a training course as a part-time youth leader, but the influence of the more erudite writers on sport pointed him beyond sport itself to a wider perspective, then only dimly perceived. The main influence was that of G.R. Gleeson, then British national coach, who is possibly the world's foremost writer on judo, especially the analytical aspects. Within general sports literature, B. Knapp's and V. Thomas's works were of special interest to him and in turn led to an interest in sociology, psychology, and education via theories of motivation and learning.

Initially this led him to expand his reading laboriously via the college library, but without guidance this was a rather retroactive approach. The breakthrough came by his taking a teacher-training course for members of staff, which provided both direction and sequencing for his reading.

Dyslexia was initially self-diagnosed, stumbled on by chance while seeking to improve his learning efficiency in order to compensate for what he regarded as his "problem." As such it was a revelation; the fact that the problem was recognized and that it explained so many previously mystifying contradictions was of immediate help. This help took the form of recognizing the problem as being specific to a particular area, rather than as an implied (and secretly feared) manifestation of a general limitation in intellectual ability. Sometimes the degree of disability seemed to vary from day to day or in different (especially stressful) situations. One aspect in this particular case had been a recent diagnosis as visually handicapped due to poor binocular vision. Although he had worn glasses for nearly twenty-five years, the subject continued to experience headaches and migraines despite hospital treatment; but had never had an in-depth investigation of his vision, other than the normal monocular tests. There is insufficient data to make an assessment of what contribution this disability (if it were then present) may have made to his initial difficulty with language.

Even with the teacher's certificate completed there remained a "drive." Maslow (1943) hypothesized that there is a continuing drive toward "self-actualization," which might well account for the next step in this story.

Having heard of the Open University (see appendix 7C) and having met several of its students, our subject applied to become a registered student. After a cursory check to establish that his dyslexia would not prevent him from taking advantage of the courses, he was accepted and embarked upon a broadly based social-science course.

The courses proved to be demanding in terms of time and mental energy, but the feeling of achievement that success brought served to dispel many lingering doubts about his ability and reinforced his desire for knowledge. Yet, as "no man is an island," no body of knowledge exists independent of all others, so learning for learning's sake was not sufficient. If his own insight into learning problems could be linked with his interest in education and psychology, however, this would seem to be a suitable line to pursue.

In Britain an honors degree in psychology is a prerequisite for moving on to the necessary higher degree in educational psychology, so with the encouragement of his Open University tutor, and some trepidation, he resigned his employment to become a full-time student of psychology at a conventional university. Here history merges with the present. Our subject embarked on his full-time psychology course, teaching part-time to augment his student grant and working part-time in an educational guidance center as part of his goal of becoming an educational psychologist.

Discussion

If this case study is to have value, it is not as a sketch of an individual, for this merely serves as the backdrop against which the influences of development and socialization in the individual's life can be seen. The following discussion, returning to the use of first-person singular, is included not as a cathartic outpouring in an effort to purge the past but rather as an admittedly introspective assessment of what it is like to be an adult with dyslexia. It is hoped that this insight may have some more universal relevance in helping to develop an appreciation of what being dyslexic is really like. The discussion is part anecdotal evidence and part advice, aimed at those who have dyslexia and those involved with them, in the hope that they will find both the insight and exposure of my strategies of interest.

Strategies of Deception

Although I can now talk about my problem, what I still fear is being recognized as having a problem. Talking about it is a voluntary decision, which still involves some embarrassment, but being recognized is tantamount to an accusation of stupidity. Many dyslexic adults, like illiterate adults, will have developed—albeit unconsciously—elaborate defense mechanisms. These "strategies of deception" are initially defenses designed to prevent others from recognizing that the problem exists. However, in order to be effective they become a constant and integral part of the individual's behavior, and as such it becomes hard to differentiate cause from effect. Avoidance techniques are simply ways of avoiding embarrassment or having to admit to a problem. As such they are quite acceptable and even productive; they make it possible for me to function in spheres that initially seem to demand a high degree of obvious literacy, as in teaching, public speaking, committee work, or posts where written reports are required.

High on the list of avoidance techniques come those involved with avoiding reading or writing in public. For me this includes both reading aloud (which I avoid like the plague) and reading silently. Reading aloud can usually be avoided by preparing talks well in advance and rehearsing until they are nearly word-perfect. If necessary, I use notes, with single words printed in block capitals as a reminder or mental crutch. I never read long, involved passages in public, silently or aloud. If confronted with a situation where I am obviously expected to read—as when I am passed an academic paper to read or asked for comments on a press article—I resort to escape tactics. Flattery is my usual line: "Your work looks most interesting," I hear myself saying, or "may I have a copy to consider at home," or "would you send me a copy please?" Few can resist! In the case of a report suddenly produced in a committee meeting, more direct action is required. If the report is not circulated in advance, I find that few chairmen will resist a motion to defer discussion until the next meeting in order that the matter may be properly considered.

Concealment. My reference to reading in public is deliberately not restricted to reading aloud. Awareness that someone is or might be watching is enough to deter some dyslexics. I would rather not read at all than expose myself to even the casual observer on a crowded train, lest he realize how slowly I read. The fact that the observer might be one of the 10 percent of total illiterates helps very little! In academic situations I have been known to turn pages regularly in a vain attempt to give the impression of being "equal." By careful selection, through use of indexes, reading is reduced to a minimum.

As an alternative to reading I use tape-recorded readings of books where possible and listen to the radio news rather than trying to read newspapers. I am personally heavily dependent on an auditory basis for perception. I need to hear words to understand them, to the extent that I must mentally or vocally say the word before I can understand or remember it. Only by this means can I sort out words from nonwords or make correctly spelled words intelligible. (Even as I write this, I find I am unable to quote examples because of the restrictions that written language imposes upon me.) Few people are prepared (nor is it often convenient, in libraries, for example) to read aloud to you, but thanks to records and the radio, a new world of poetry and prose is open to me. Many dyslexic people are unable to enjoy poetry because their hesitant reading destroys the poem's meter. Live performances and records may be their only admission to this otherwise restricted art form.

Writing is potentially the more acute problem, as it involves spelling and an element of permanency not present in speech. When I am asked to write details—even my name and address—my first reaction is to freeze, but this very act of hesitation often makes the well-intentioned informant even keener on being helpful. He leans forward to add any lost syllable, an intentionally supporting action that is often seen as a threat by the dyslexic, as if there was an expectation that he will get it wrong—the only question is where! For this situation I use several strategies:

1. "Will you print it on this piece of paper for me, please, just so I get it clear" (tables turned).
2. "If you would repeat that, please, I will be able to remember it" (a lie). This is followed by a fast escape to privacy, where what can still be remembered is committed to paper.

3. The "doctor's scrawl," a defense that involves rejecting years of careful teaching aimed at written clarity and letter definition. In this case, where retreat is impossible, I bluff it out. I revert to a personalized form of shorthand in which the first letter of the word is clear and the following squiggle is only a guide to the meaning by its fluctuations and length. Alternatively, I use the first three letters of a known word and add what I think the remainder should be later. I use this only as a last resort when I am being watched, as I lose a high proportion of what I seek to record.

Writing for the public is far easier. Lessons or talks that can be prepared in advance can incorporate visual aids to alleviate the need to write on the board. Reports and articles can be drafted, and I then employ a typist to correct the spelling and retype them for me before circulation.

Typing, even with two fingers, can be an advantage. For me it has reduced reversals to a minimum, although it has also made clearer the spelling faults that remain, and mistakes in letter order seem to have become more prominent as a result. When I try to type fast, individual words tend to run into each other. This doesn't seem to be a breakdown of typing skill, but rather that I "hear" them in a form without pauses and reproduce them in that form. I must admit there are times when what I have typed seems to be a rival for the longest Welsh place name (llanfairpwllgwyngyllogogery-chwyrndrobwllllantysiliogogogoch - St. Mary's Church in a hollow by the white hazel close to the rapid whirlpool by the red cave of St. Tysilio.) and it makes no more sense to me than to the reader, especially when it is misspelled.

Phonetic Spelling. What I am left with, despite all my efforts, is a phonetic version of spelling, which is further complicated by my own auditory needs to "hear" the word. The context then further affects the spelling. Simple words are not excluded, although this seems to infuriate others more than misspelled complicated words. A two-letter word wrongly spelled incurs far more wrath and exasperation than a phonetic ten-letter word. An example to which my attention has been drawn is in the sentence in "Battle of Britain," where I misspelled the central word—ove—as it sounded totally different from the word in the sentence, "Moor the boat off the coast." More humorously, and to my embarrassment, I wrote to an eminent American professor before visiting him to explain that, although I was not well versed in his specialty, I was seeking information for use by a multidisciplinary team with which I was involved; at least that was what I meant to say. Unfortunately, by my misspelling a two-letter word (no), it became, "I have *now* deep experience in your field—a modest introduction!

Mental Flight. I am forced to admit to one bad psychological habit, unconsciously adopted many years ago. Although I am aware of it, I am still prompted to take refuge in what I call "mental flight." It is something I am painfully aware of in many children, and I sympathize with them. This technique was developed in answer to the persistent, albeit well-intentioned questioner, and as such it is not limited to the dyslexic child. It simply involves trying to detach one's thoughts from the immediate situation or making one's mind go blank, then outwaiting the questioner. In the face of this persistent lack of response in anything but monosyllables, the questioner usually retreats and draws an appropriate conclusion. This refined version of the sullen or bashful withdrawal of a younger child is little to be proud of. In many cases the unfavorable conclusions drawn about me were generous, considering the lack of response on my part.

Like the Grand Master who learned to "outwait" his opponents, I defeated well-intentioned questioning by others. Yet this is an aspect of behavior of which parents and teachers should be aware. Repeated questioning by a concerned mother about the day's school activities will often only cause further emotional stress to the child. There is no cure, just the need to appreciate how difficult it is to admit and discuss a language disability, especially when even that admission needs to be couched in language, the very sphere where the half-formed fears exist.

Dyslexia as a Limited Disability

Controversy rages in educational circles regarding the merits of applying a label to a child. I am unashamedly in favor of using the term *dyslexia* where applicable. Although the form assessment should take is outside the scope of this chapter, I would suggest using the World Federation of Neurology's definition, given earlier. In explanation, I suggest it is important to emphasize two aspects: first, that the term is used only in cases where there is evidence of intellectual potential in excess of performance, as recorded from tests involving language; second, that the problem is a constitutional one, or a syndrome consisting of a constellation of associated difficulties. Of these, the concept that dyslexia is a limited disability is the most important.

The labels "slow learner" or "language disability" can induce the fear that there is a limitation on the individual's intellectual capacity. Nor do they carry an implicit solution; at least the "late developer" can hope to grow out of the problem. This fear of limited intellect, if free to flourish, can result in the classic self-fulfilling prophecies (Rosenthal and Jacobson 1968), where the labeled person acts accordingly. "Eventually the patient himself accepts the diagnosis, with all of its surplus meaning and expectations, and behaves accordingly" (Rosenham 1973). If the previously cited definition of dyslexia were used and explained to the people concerned, this fear and misunderstanding would not arise. Nor do I accept that such a label would lead to the lethargy predicted by some critics.

Despite the act of labeling as dyslexic, the problem will remain, a fact of which the sufferer will be all too aware. But for me, at least, the knowledge that there was a recognized problem provided much-needed motivation. It provided a certain amount of reassurance, but, more importantly, I realized that it was a limited disability and could be circumvented. This allowed me to adopt positive strategies for learning, and, while still avoiding confronting the problem head-on, I can now pursue a "normal" academic life.

Reassurance is not limited to academic ability. Following my discovery of dyslexia and the Kershaw report (1974), I was able to discuss the matter with my superior, who had previously been critical of my "inability to comply with Board procedure." This bone of contention had been based on my inability to write reports of the standard he expected; the issue was simply resolved by allowing me to dictate reports, which a secretary typed with the correct spelling.

A Plea For Simplicity

I have mixed views about some of the approaches used in attempting to help dyslexic children. Although I favor a multisensory and phonetic teaching method, many others are dogmatic in their insistence that a mastery of linguistic structures is a prerequisite of, or the same as, the ability to read and spell adequately. By "adequately," I mean sufficiently well for the individual to operate competently in his chosen environment. I concur with the view that overlearning is a key approach to helping dyslexics, plus constant review and reinforcement. However, sometimes these are confused by the highly literate teacher with the need for an in-depth understanding of the linguistic theory upon which they base their teaching strategy. Personally, I find spelling rules and exceptions more confusing than the direct tasks of reading and spelling. They have no immediacy for me; rather, they put a functional (and sometimes conceptual) block between my vocabulary and my use of the words.

To avoid this confusion, I have issued receipts stating "Paid—with thanks," followed by my initials, rather than writing the word *received*, as I cannot remember whether it is the exception or the rule of "i before e except after c." Similarly, a problem with checks involving words such as fifteen (or is it fifeteen or perhaps, in view of the above rule, fieveteen?) can be overcome by using some excuse and asking the other person to make out the check. That only leaves you with your signature, which is accepted as being idiosyncratic, if only to prevent forgery; so the dyslexic person can make any consistent attempt without fear of correction. A problem occurs with hotel and motel registers, in which names are usually printed clearly. Recently I was suddenly faced with this formality, only to have my wife point out that I misspelled my own name! It may just be possible, that the couples signing in at motels under the name of Brown or Jones are dyslexics afraid of misspelling their own names! My plea is that teachers and those closely concerned with a dyslexic person treat him as just that—an individual person, with certain strengths and weaknesses.

Handwriting

Great emphasis is often placed on the child's ability to write clearly, but as Burt (1921) points out, the very formation of a long, rapid line drawn obliquely outward and upward (in normal script, from lowest left to upper right) is, with the left hand, the most difficult of all. Burt was writing in the days when (as in my own school days) nibbed pens were used, and this itself imposed an influence on my letter formation. I found that, by *printing* letters in script form, I was able to form the letters *l*, *t*, *f*, and *h* with a downward stroke and yet produce clear, acceptable writing.

Check marks were a problem that I solved by changing directions from right to left, a strategy adopted by many left-handed people. With the introduction of ballpoint and felt-tipped pens, the situation has improved, since these allow the left-handed person to make oblique strokes, still necessary for *e* and *b* without the nib cutting into the paper. At the same time, I found that turning the paper toward me enables me to see the letters being formed and reduces the problem of smudging. Today my recommendation would be to use felt-tipped pens, and if script is still a difficult form, the offending letters should be produced separately by drawing the pen down from the top. Where letter-direction reversal is a continuing problem, I would suggest typing as an alternative.

Lack of Understanding

Lay ignorance as to the nature of dyslexia and its implications still remains one of the main problems that the dyslexic person has to face. I often feel that, when dyslexia is diagnosed, the person should be given a supply of simple, printed handouts of the type used by many dyslexia organizations. These can be passed on to those who need to know something about the nature of the problem and its manifestations. This problem accompanies the dyslexic person throughout his life.

For the early part of my life I lacked an explanation of my language disability and was simply advised not to continue further studies. This advice was given at school, at agricultural college, after "O" level, and before entering the university. Although I had been assessed before entering the Open University, the bureaucratic system failed to make the problem known to my tutor, leading to his inevitable comments to "try harder" and his liberal use of red ink. I overcame this by writing "I am dyslexic" on my next paper, and then, to save us both embarrassment, I drafted my essays and paid a typist to retype them with corrected spellings. The result was all A grades.

Summer schools are an integral part of all Open University foundation courses (and some advanced courses, too). Here counseling advice is available when desired by the student or as a result of a report from his tutor. In my case the tutor's report led to an interview with the senior counselor, who advised that, in view of my problem with languages (slow reading and poor spelling), I should give up the course I was currently embarked upon and take at least a year off before re-registering, during which time I should seek help from an educational psychologist or psychiatrist. It was a frightening start to my academic career, which, even if unpalatable, demanded consideration. This attitude, which implies that the holder believes me to be intellectually inadequate, persists and has to be dealt with anew each time it is encountered.

It took me two soul-searching days to decide to ignore the advice. I felt that it was basically what I had heard for twenty-five years, it would result, at best, in renewed attempts at remedial language training; and it would probably deny me the chance to progress any further. So I paid to have essays retyped, summarized the course into brief notes, and, thanks to a good coursework mark and an extra hour in the examination, received a "Distinction" and have never regretted the decision to continue.

Techniques in Learning

The theme of my advice is, in the words of an old song, to "accentuate the positive, eliminate the negative" (see Haring and Bateman 1977). From my experience, the education of the older dyslexic child should have greater emphasis on learning strategies. I would stress efficient study techniques, especially for the creation and retention of concepts. My own approach is a modified version of the "thought plan" concept put forward by Buzan (1974) who used the term "brain patterns." Basically, this technique is to isolate the central theme and then link concepts to it by a system of tree-like branches, which bear succinct—preferably single word—"leaves." These thought plans are invaluable as a form of note-taking, providing a valuable structure for the retrieval of information and the creation of a framework that can serve as the basis of any written work or speech. This approach is wholly compatible with the dual needs of the advanced dyslexic student: to be clear and unambiguous. Detailed explanations often tend to confuse, because the dyslexic child may lack a language system as elaborate as the terms used in the explanation; partial understanding often only serves to confuse.

Simple presentation should be linked to different teaching aids, which, even when restricted to the blackboard, can be improved by the use of diagrammatic models and colors. For specific help with reading ability I recommend that students read Harris and Sipay (1977), but any good reference work on how to learn efficiently will help. Other examples are Rowntree (1970), Maddox (1963), and Robinson (1961). Their advantage is that they do not isolate the dyslexic as a person apart but rather concentrate on practical steps that can be valuable to anyone. Underlining words, writing in margins, writing key concepts on slips of paper to save re-reading, and speed-reading or skimming (a cultivated skill) can all help, and many people have benefited from the "SQ 3R" method, "Survey, Question, Read, Recall, Review" (Franklin and Naidoo 1970). Much advice can also be found in books about dyslexia.

Advice to Others with Dyslexia

1. Admit the problem to yourself and to others when necessary.

2. Stop worrying about it and concentrate on constructive action. Learn to laugh with others at your mistakes; then prevent them from happening again if possible.

3. Use a phonetic approach to language. Then try to improve on this base by techniques designed to improve reading speeds and by any spelling rules that help. (Parents of a schoolchild should seek sympathetic teaching along multisensory lines.)

4. Try typing all written work; letter reversals are reduced, at least in direction if not in order. Spelling out the word into keys that are then depressed aids clarity and develops an element of kinesthetic awareness, like touch-typing, which can aid spelling without conscious awareness.

5. Do not let a word throw you. When reading, try getting the meaning from the context or revert to deciphering it phonetically. (For those who find this obvious, try *sponged*.) Spell the word to the best of your ability, phonetically if in doubt, but do not allow yourself to be trapped into trying four or five alternative spellings and selecting the one that looks best. This is time consuming and destroys your confidence.

6. Seek educational help as soon as possible. Also seek out books on the subject to help you clarify your own weaknesses and possible remedial action.

7. Keep a list of difficult words, which you can try to memorize or refer to. Dictionaries are good, so long as you realize that you are misspelling the word (otherwise you won't need to look it up). If you don't know how to spell a word, and the difficulty is in the first few letters, then you may be unable to find it in a dictionary. You may find a bad speller's dictionary helpful (personally, I don't); but a thesaurus can be invaluable, for if you know roughly what the word means then you can look it up in the company of words of similar meaning that you can spell.

8. For those still struggling with examinations, I advise writing "I am dyslexic" at the top of the paper and then doing your best to answer the questions, relying on the examiner to mark for content rather than spelling accuracy. My first experience of using the "admit it and be damned" approach was in my first written teachers' examination, when, like most dyslexics, I found that my hard-won skills tended to break down under stress. I read the examination, composed my mind to make a positive bold start by heading the paper "I am dyslexic," then answered the examination to the best of my ability.

I boldly wrote:

> I am dislexik
> disclexic
> dysleksick
> disleyxic

I remembered it had an *i* and a *y*, so I crossed out the others and left the one I thought most likely to be correct!

9. Don't stop to wrestle with the idiosyncratic rules of English spelling; you will only impose a time restriction on the rest of your answers with usually fruitless speculation, which disillusions you and psychologically reduces your morale. Nor do I advocate re-reading your examination paper. If there are spelling errors, they are there because that is how you thought you should spell the word; they are not deliberately included (as some people seem to imply). Checking yourself is unlikely to reveal them but may prove a time- and morale-sapping exercise.

10. I support anything that will aid confidence. Even such superficial aids as a piece of candy in examination situations, just before and just after reading the paper, sometimes helps.

11. Informing the authorities of the problem is important. Try to secure extra time and, if not their sympathy, at least their understanding.

12. Examination proctors should be aware of the problem. An illustration of what can happen is drawn from my first university examination. When I was faced with a compulsory section of multiple-choice questions, which in itself meant protracted reading time, one word in particular remained a meaningless jumble of letters (similar to seeing a fish through

moving water), and I spent valuable minutes trying to decipher the segments or gain the meaning from the context. In desperation I called the proctor and asked what the word was, only to be told that it was printed clearly and spelled correctly and that proctors were not at liberty to discuss the paper in any way.

Summary

I have tried to describe my own background in the form of a case study in the hope that it will be of help both to other dyslexics and to those involved with them. I am unusual in that, despite my limitations, I have chosen to pursue an interest in people through academic subjects that demand a high standard of literacy. This involves frequently being reminded of my weakness, although for the most part I have been able to come to terms with it.

Some of the strategies I have used (strategies of deception, alternative approaches, and emphasis on using the most efficient learning techniques) were given in the hope that they may be of benefit to your understanding or may help when you advise others. My concluding plea holds good regardless of age. Dyslexia is a constantly open wound; despite the strategies of deception, one remains vulnerable. This does not decrease with age; being "hauled over the coals" for bad spelling when one is a mature, qualified teacher is an acute embarrassment. Such incidents might have been avoided had I accepted defeat and not persevered in a field demanding a high degree of literacy, or if the lecturers had had some understanding of what dyslexia is. My perseverance is a source of irritation to some people; yet a need for self-actualization, possibly mixed with naive idealism, seems to drive me on—down the road Robert Frost described as "the less traveled by." Perhaps that is what makes this case study unusual.

References

Burt, C. 1921. *Mental and Scholastic Tests*. London: Staples Press.
Buzan, T. 1974. *Use Your Head*. London: BBC Publications.
Critchley, M. 1964. *Developmental Dyslexia*. Springfield, Ill.: Thomas.
Franklin, A., and Naidoo, S. (eds.). 1970. *Assessment and Teaching of Dyslexic Children*. London: Invalid Children's Aid Association.
Hammarskjöld, D. 1977. *Markings*. New York: Knopf.
Haring, N.G., and Bateman, B. 1977. *Teaching the Learning Disabled Child*. Englewood Cliffs, N.J.: Prentice-Hall.
Harris, A.J., and Sipay, E.R. 1977. *How to Increase Reading Ability*. New York: David McKay.

Kershaw, J. 1974. *People with Dyslexia*. London: British Council for Re-
    habilitation of the Disabled.
Maslow, A.H. 1943. A theory of human motivation. *Psychological Review*
    50.
Miles, T.R. 1970. *On Helping the Dyslexic Child*. London: Methuen.
_____ . 1974. *The Dyslexic Child*. Hove, England: Priory Press.
Maddox, H. 1963. *How to Study*. London: Pan Books.
Rawson, M.B. 1968. *Developmental Language Disability*. Baltimore: Johns
    Hopkins University Press.
Robinson, F.P. 1961. *Effective Study*. New York: Harper.
Rosenham, D.L. 1973. On being sane in insane places. *Science* 179.
Rosenthal, R., and Jacobson, L. 1968. *Pygmalion in the Classroom*. New
    York: Holt, Reinhart and Winston.
Rowntree, D. 1970. *Learn How to Study*. London: Macdonald.
Tarnopol, L. (ed.). 1971. *Learning Disorders in Children: Diagnosis, Medi-
    cation, Education*. Boston, Mass.: Little, Brown.

Appendix 7A:
The British Educational
System

Compulsory education in Britain extended between five and fifteen years of age (recently the school-leaving age has been raised from fifteen to sixteen years). Primary school is followed by junior schooling until the age of eleven. The "11-plus" examination was introduced following the 1944 Education Act, aimed at directing children into one of two types of state schools. The grammar schools took the more academically capable students—those who passed—and provided a curriculum designed to provide a basis for university and higher education. The secondary modern school was for those who failed the examination. There the emphasis was on less-academic pursuits, such as crafts and practical activities thought to be best suited to students who were expected to leave and take jobs as soon as they reached the minimum school-leaving age.

Scholastic achievement was measured by reference to the ordinary ("O") level General Certificate of Education (GCE). This was normally taken at fifteen to sixteen years of age in a broad range of subjects, including English language and mathematics. For those with aspirations of going to the university, advanced-level GCE was usually taken in a minimum of three subjects, and Latin was normally required for medicine and language arts courses.

Selection was made on the arbitrary assessment of ability at age eleven. For those who failed the examination, the only alternative to a state secondary school was a private, fee-paying school. This choice was restricted to the wealthier families. But because they lacked the kudos of the elite British public schools, the private schools were often referred to in a derisory fashion as schools for the "stupid sons of wealthy fathers." Such schools tried to realize any hidden academic potential by concentrating on basic GCE subjects, such as English language, English literature, mathematics (arithmetic, algebra, and geometry), and perhaps a foreign language, history, geography, and a science subject, such as biology, physics, or chemistry. For the more successful student, there was an opportunity to stay on and attempt the advanced-level GCE.

For an adult in Britain many opportunities exist, through the Workers Educational Association and evening institutes associated with local educational bodies, to take courses in a wide range of subjects. It is possible to take both "O" and "A" level GCEs through these evening classes.

The British Open University is a unique educational institution created by Royal Charter in 1969 "to provide university and professional education to those with the keenness and ability to continue their education by study in their own time, particularly those who could not otherwise obtain education at University.'' There are no formal educational requirements, although students are normally over twenty-one years of age and in full-time employment. Studying is in their free time, with tuition on a correspondence-course basis combined with comprehensive tutorial and counseling support and augmented by regular radio and television programs. The degree status is equal to that of other British universities, with whom a credit-transfer system exists in many cases. All degrees awarded to undergraduates are that of Bachelor of Art, so it is the profile of courses taken that is the important factor. The Open University also awards further degrees, but due to pressure of demand and economic restrictions, the range of undergraduate course options, though broad enough for most students, in certain cases fails to permit sufficient specialization necessary to gain access to specialized courses of professional recognition.

Appendix 7B:
Sport

Sport is used in several ways in this chapter. Initially it referred to a participatory interest at school, club, and college level, covering a wide range of sports—swimming, team sports, and shooting. As my interests developed away from competitive sport into its administration, my involvement changed from a physical to an intellectual one.

In 1958 I took up judo, and, although my interest lay dormant during my military service, by 1964 I had obtained a black belt and won my first regional championships. While I was still active competitively I took an increasing interest in coaching and club administration. By 1969 I had held most positions at club level and, through being active at regional level, I represented the region at national level and then became a national officer. The national posts of public relations officer and grants officer within the British Judo Association made me responsible for communications and then for financial planning and negotiations with government officials on the subject of financial aid. In the region I continued to serve as an officer in several capacities, at the same time qualifying as a coach (later appointed regional coach), as a national referee (with experience including international matches abroad), and as a senior examiner of candidates for promotion to and within the black-belt grades. It was possibly my all-around ability and administrative experience that led to my appointment as head of the British Judo Delegation to the 1972 Munich Olympics, where I also represented Britain at the European and World Judo Conferences.

My interest in sport is not restricted exclusively to any one sport. I hold coaching qualifications in three very different sports, and I spend several weeks a year using my Mountain Leadership Certificate, taking groups walking in hill country. Since 1971, when I was a founder member of the Eastern Region Standing Conference on Sport and Recreation—comprised of the governing bodies of all sports—I have served on their executive board, first representing judo and now rambling. The Standing Conference has in turn elected me to serve on the full council and several subcommittees. Having been a delegate to the National Conference for the past three years, my experience of committee work is now wide and varied. Although the subject matter is still ''sport,'' the term is used in a general sense rather than being restricted to participation in competitive forms.

Appendix 7C:
Adult Dyslexics in the Open University: A Pilot Study

Little work has been done in the sphere of adults with specific language-learning difficulties, often referred to as dyslexia. Following the Chronically Sick and Disabled Persons Act of 1970, the Manpower Services Commission and the Employment Services Agency recognize dyslexia as a handicap. The Kershaw report, *People with Dyslexia* (1974), is possibly Britain's key reference work in this context.

Many medical sources prefer to use the term *syndrome* when referring to dyslexia (Zangwill 1974), while several authorities refer to *signs* that indicate aspects highly correlated with dyslexia (Miles 1970, 1974). In America, the President's Commission on Mental Health has recently received a report from their appropriately named Task Panel on Learning Failure and Unused Learning Potential. For adults, the central anomaly arising from the discrepancy between intellectual potential and intellectual achievement (measured in terms of Performance IQ and Verbal IQ scores) is the cause of both subconscious inferiority complexes and failure to realize potential. I believe this to be especially strongly felt by adult dyslexics who are "of at least normal intellectual level, if not indeed of high IQ" (Critchley 1964).

Although Rawson's (1968) longitudinal study follows the careers of children assessed as dyslexic into adult life, there is no major study of adults who were not aware of the concept of dyslexia when they were children and were consequently not diagnosed, often being labeled "slow," "lazy," or "careless" as a result. I am concerned here with adult dyslexics who have remained unrecognized, rather than with adults who have become dyslexic because of brain lesions after the age of maturity.

The work of the Adult Literacy Program embraces many adult dyslexics, but it is concerned with a wider range of etiological backgrounds and with providing an educational-assessment and remedial service. Dyslexia is more specific in nature and in its effect of limiting the individual's developmental potential. Since dyslexia was recognized by the Chronically Sick and Disabled Persons Act of 1970, the Manpower Services Commission, through the Employment Services Agency, is often able to offer help in practical ways, such as providing a tape recorder where it is necessary to enable an individual to do a particular job. However, such help and the availability of a "green card" is one extreme.

The individuals in this survey consisted of those who, despite earlier experience of educational failure, were seeking an opportunity to enter higher education. Motives were especially complex, since the drive for self-actualization was inextricably linked to the self-image influenced by earlier experiences and in some cases (certainly my own), the need for assurance that one is capable of functioning at university level. The two main advantages of the Open University seem to be the range of courses and the fact that no formal qualifications are needed for entry.

Following my own experience with the Open University and later discussions with David Gallon (deputy regional director, London), I decided to carry out this pilot study in the hope of (1) acquiring information regarding the experience of adult dyslexics in higher education and the strategies used by them; (2) relating these adult dyslexics to the Open University; and (3) investigating, as a result of these experiences, ways in which the university might consider helping such students.

Design of the Survey

Subjects were mature students (over twenty-five years of age) who were taking courses in the Open University. Only subjects who realized that they were dyslexic *after* leaving school were included. Both professionally assessed and self-assessed subjects were included, since intelligent subjects, once aware of the syndrome, can accurately assess if it is applicable to them. This is borne out by their questionnaire replies and also by the psychological reports of those who were assessed.

All subjects were those who voluntarily responded to a letter I published in the Open University newsletter, "Sesame," May/June 1978. A questionnaire was designed to seek information in the following general areas:

1. Personal details.
2. Age at which respondents became aware or were assessed.
3. Aspects of birth and childhood.
4. Aspects of hereditary and constitutional influences.
5. School experiences.
6. Effect of dyslexia on life and career.
7. Effect of diagnosis.
8. Attitude within the Open University.
9. Aspects for consideration by the Open University.

Subjects

This survey report relates to twelve of the sixteen subjects who replied. The response was better than expected, considering that it was an unofficial study, claiming neither recognition nor support. Furthermore, I was requesting that volunteers use the very medium of communication with which they had most trouble, and this in itself is known to discourage many dyslexic adults. The national population from which this sample was drawn is thought to include between 4 percent and 7 percent dyslexics. Whether the Open University attracts a higher or lower percentage remains to be investigated, but it seems possible that, as the discrepancy between potential and achievement is central to the concept of dyslexia, there may be a higher than national percentage of adult students entering the Open University without formal qualifications in order to overcome an unfavorable earlier educational experience. The geographical distribution of subjects covered much of England, but none from Scotland, Wales, or London.

Results

Six subjects were male and six were females. Eight of the twelve subjects were self-assessed, and four had been professionally assessed. The mean age at which the subjects became aware that they were dyslexic was thirty-five and a half years, with a range from twenty-nine to forty-five years. Four subjects indicated that there were circumstances related to birth or childhood that might have contributed to their learning problems, but eight could find no such contributing factors. One person stated that his father had similar learning problems. One reported total left-side dominance, and ten said they had mixed laterality.

All subjects had had school experiences that any dyslexic child might have, such as poor mathematics, poor spelling, slow reading, and dreading to read aloud. Eleven of this group reported some degree of unsatisfactory school experience, varying from being classified temporarily as educationally subnormal to being called "careless" or being told to "try harder." The effects on them as children ranged from hatred of school to feelings of inferiority.

Eleven subjects reported that their lives had been influenced in some manner by their dyslexia. They appear to have had no problems functioning orally. However, writing—spelling in particular—presented a serious problem. Several careers were turned to practical, scientific, or engineering areas in order to avoid writing. In some cases, when respondents were forced into situations where writing was the medium of expression—by promotion, for example—they not only were subjected to embarrassment, but their careers were adversely affected.

The effect of a positive diagnosis of dyslexia was generally reported to be great relief. This was because the concept of dyslexia carried with it the reassurance that the language difficulties were not due to lack of intelligence. In practical terms, assessment tended to be a psychological aid, sometimes inspiring respondents to take Open University courses in a quest for self-actualization. One subject, however, reported disappointment because the Open University course did not seem to help in overcoming the problem. Another evidenced concern about the possible inherited aspects of dyslexia and was worried that it might also affect his son.

The attitude of the Open University toward these dyslexic students is epitomized for most of them by the attitudes of their tutors toward them. This appears to be erratic, at best, often described as causing "great distress." One student questioned whether it was worth continuing in the face of caustic criticism. One student who had been professionally diagnosed as dyslexic, reported "no response" when he notified the Open University of his condition. Despite having submitted formal written notification and having informed his tutors of his condition for the past three years, he still has not had the courtesy of an acknowledgement or any offer of help.

Tutors involved in the same course vary in their approaches to dyslexics, so a sympathetic tutor during the spring term may be flatly contradicted by the tutor at summer school. The more "literary" the course, the less tolerant the tutor is likely to be. Some dyslexic students have been told that "someone who can't spell should not be awarded a degree." One student reported being advised to give up the Open University and seek psychiatric help before re-registering.

Two main suggestions were put forward by the students for the officials of the Open University to consider concerning the needs of dyslexic students in a university. First, tutors should know about dyslexia and the significance of specific language-learning difficulties in some detail. Second, term papers and examinations should be scored for content, and spelling errors should not be included in grading the papers of dyslexics. Those students who have been having their spouses check their spelling or who have employed a typist on term papers were especially worried about examinations. They claimed that they needed to know twice as much as other students to achieve the same examination grade. Some students requested oral examinations, especially in literary subjects, where it takes them longer to read the paper and compose the answers than it does other students. Another suggestion was to permit them more time on examinations; and giving them the option of typing their papers was also suggested.

To assist the slow-reading dyslexics with their coursework, taped materials were proposed. Since master tapes of course materials are being prepared for blind and visually handicapped students, this service could easily be extended to those with perceptual difficulties. Another suggestion was that the Open University should advise dyslexic students about courses that might not be suitable for them.

The Open University staff should develop a method of becoming aware of the needs of handicapped students and should have a way of registering such students so that this information is brought to the attention of personnel at the national, regional, and tutor levels. Although a plea is made for the recognition of dyslexia, it is also stressed that this problem should not become a bar to admission to the university. For many dyslexic students, the Open University represents a last chance to succeed in a sphere in which they have had to battle with a language problem subsumed in the very learning process. These students need every possible consideration if they are to achieve their full potential in spite of a severe handicap.

References

Critchley, M. 1964. *Developmental Dyslexia*. Springfield, Ill.: Thomas.

Kershaw, J. 1974. *People with Dyslexia*. London: British Council for Rehabilitation of the Disabled.

Miles, T.R. 1970. *On Helping the Dyslexic Child*. London: Methuen.

———. 1974. *The Dyslexic Child*. Hove, England: Priory Press.

Rawson, M.B. 1968. *Developmental Language Disability*. Baltimore: Johns Hopkins University Press.

Zangwill, O. 1974. Foreword. In T.R. Miles, *The Dyslexic Child*. Hove, England: Priory Press.

8 Learning Disabilities in Brazil

L.R. Aratangy, C. Bastos,
M. Goulart, B.R. Lerner,
M. Paulino, L. Rosenberg,
and *J.S. Schwartzman*

Brazil, with an area of approximately 3.3 million square miles, occupies almost half of the South American continent. The country is politically divided into twenty-three states and three territories, distributed into five regions. The population is more than 110 million, concentrated mainly in the southeastern region. According to 1976 figures, the per capita income is $1,450 per year. The language spoken is Portuguese.

Educational System

In Brazil the educational system is divided into first level (eight grades), second level (three grades), and college (four to six grades). The first level is relatively standardized in all schools, while the second level provides basic academic or technical subjects. School attendance is compulsory from seven to fourteen years of age.

The high drop-out rate at the end of the first grade of the first level (54 percent) sharpens the Brazilian educational pyramid and is a matter of concern to educational researchers and authorities. Research points to two factors that interact to determine the school failure of a great percentage of children; namely, the teachers and the pupils. About 30 percent of the active teachers in the country did not attend school beyond the fourth grade of the first level. They have received no special training and face many difficulties in carrying out their work.

Most of the children come from economically deprived homes. They have neither attended preschool nor received proper stimulation and nutrition at home to develop the basic abilities necessary for a successful first grade. They lack the training to ask questions in order to enlighten doubts; they are not able to clearly express their thoughts; their memories are not trained; they are not able to establish temporal sequences in their life histories; and they are not able to spend extra time studying in order to receive better rewards later. Instead, they have learned to suspect other people and to protect themselves from them, as well as to withdraw when faced with any unfamiliar stimulation, for example, the way the teacher speaks.

In 1974 Popovic and her associates carried out a research project in São Paulo with four-, five- and six-year-old children from homes of middle and low socioeconomic levels, to detect the causes of the massive school failure of these children. This research shov d that six-year-old children of low socioeconomic level scored the same as four-year-old children of the middle class. Thus, before entering school these children were already two years behind their contemporaries.

Free psychological treatment for children with learning disabilities is scarce; it is nonexistent in smaller cities. Another approach to the problem, in a national context, would be the development of a curriculum that would provide proper materials for these children and proper guidance for their teachers to help overcome their lack of preparation for school.

Programa Alfa (Popovic 1968) is a curriculum that covers all areas to be developed in the first three grades. It provides all the necessary materials and a detailed guide for the teacher, explaining how to teach, day by day, in each activity. This program is gradually being introduced in many cities and is supplied free to the school network under the supervision of a technical staff that is part of the board of education. In 1977 45,000 children used this material. In view of the results obtained, it was decided to increase the number of children that used this curriculum in 1978 to 100,000. In 1980 20,000 children will use the second part of the *Programa,* whose third and last part is now being developed.

The principles that underlie this program are as follows:

1. Take into account the environment and the psychological, social, and cultural features that shaped the student and his family, attempting to provide solutions that are suited to reality.
2. Emphasize the learning process more than the subject; that is, learning to learn is more important than learning specific subjects.
3. Stimulate as fully as possible the enrichment of the language, that is, the capacity to communicate. The ability to verbalize is essential for the development of the ability to think.
4. Develop positive self-esteem in the child, as this is the most efficient way to motivate him.

Brazilian Approach to Learning Disabilities

In the past few years an increasing number of children have appeared for clinical help because of learning disabilities. We believe that differential diagnosis, proper management, and medication, if necessary, should be coordinated by physicians. Thus, any multidisciplinary team dealing with the difficult task of determining the causes of academic failure should include a specialized physician, who would be responsible for the coordination of the team as well as for the promotion of conferences with the participation of all team members involved in each case.

In Brazil, although there is a general consensus about the role of the physician in the diagnosis and treatment of learning disabilities, there still persists a rather broad belief that this kind of problem does not belong to the medical field and therefore should be within the exclusive scope of psychologists, speech therapists, and educators.

A new kind of specialized physician is now emerging, dedicated specifically to the study and care of this condition. In São Paulo, neuropediatricians, child psychiatrists, speech therapists, and some pediatricians are now interested in the subject. Whatever the basic training of the physician, we consider it crucial that he have sufficient knowledge of pediatrics, neuropediatrics, child psychiatry, and related subjects to qualify in learning disabilities. He should also be familiar with the remedial techniques available, medications that may be prescribed, and community resources, such as special clinics and schools for the referral of the children.

When dealing with a child referred to the clinic because of academic failure, we must first check some basic data. We look at the mental level of the child, the educational level, and the potential abilities that may not be apparent at the moment. Perceptual (auditory and visual) deficits that could seriously affect the learning capacity of the child and the environmental situation, including emotional factors and the home level of stimulation, must be determined. It is also extremely important to get information about the kind of school the child is attending and the teaching methods that are used, since the learning problems may reflect a pedagogic environment unfavorable to the child's personality characteristics or to his particular strategies of learning.

After eliminating those with intellectual, educational, environmental, and other deficiencies, we still have some referred children who may be regarded as having "specific learning disability," "minimal brain dysfunction," "minimal brain damage," "hyperactive syndrome," "specific dyslexia," "developmental disorder," and so forth. These various designations refer to children of normal intelligence, without any important sensory deficiency, who do not present any classical neurological syndrome. They are exposed to an academically favorable environment but show academic achievement below that expected on the basis of their abilities.

There is great controversy regarding the main cause of this disorder. We believe that it could be explained by the presence of external determinants acting on individuals who have a neurological predisposition, generally of genetic origin. In our experience it is seldom possible to find a single cause in any particular case; in general, we find several overlapping factors.

However, contrary to the claims of many authors, we are not convinced that emotional problems, unless they were very severe, could promote this kind of disorder. We often think, when we examine a child who shows academic difficulties, that the apparent psychological problems reflect emotional aspects that are reactive and secondary to the primary academic difficulties. The most frequent problem is the hyperactive syndrome, which impairs the adjustment of the affected child to school, peers, and family.

Facilities and Methods for Testing
and Diagnosis

Although in recent years there has been increasing concern about learning disabilities, the official facilities for testing and diagnosis are rather scarce, mainly because we still face many problems in promoting education even for the normal population of children. The screening of children with learning disabilities is very difficult because we lack the economic and professional resources for the screening of children with mental retardation, perceptual deficiencies, or serious auditory or visual impairments. Thus, children with various disabilities are taught together, using teaching methods that are not specialized for each kind of disorder. However, there are private clinics and special schools for those who can afford the economic burden.

In São Paulo there are some clinics dedicated to the diagnosis and treatment of children with learning disabilities. In 1971, in the Section of Neurology of the Faculdade de Psicologia da Pontifícia Universidade Católica de São Paulo, a team was organized to carry out research on learning disorders. Later, some members of this group set up a private clinic for the differential diagnosis of learning disabilities in children and adolescents without mental deficiencies.

The scope of the clinic includes determining the primarily affected areas; referring patients to proper therapeutic management; and performing research in learning, including the development of neuropsychological tests. The team includes one neurologist, two psychologists, and one speech therapist; and it serves a population of upper-middle and high socioeconomic levels.

The testing covers the intellectual, motor, emotional, oral and written language, and educational areas. Each case is seen by all members of the staff, as follows:

1. Interview with parents or other person responsible for the child.
2. Battery of psychological tests.

3. Testing of oral and written language and educational testing.
4. Neurological examination and electroencephalogram (EEG).
5. Visits to school.
6. Contacts with other professional teams that have had any involvement with the case.
7. Case discussion by the staff.
8. Family guidance.
9. Referral for proper therapeutic management.
10. Follow-up and reevaluation.

Psychological Evaluation

The psychologists have a personal interview with the parents to investigate the symptoms shown by the child and to gather background and family data (according to a guide designed by the staff). Observation of play activities and free drawings is made. Standard intellectual, motor, and emotional tests are given.

For the play activities, a box is used containing structured toys (such as cars, furniture, dolls, and puppets) and unstructured materials (such as paper, pencils, paints and molding material). The observation of these activities allows not only rapport with the patient but also a diagnostic hypothesis.

For the assessment of intellectual, emotional, and motor functions, the most reliable standardized or adapted tests available in Brazil are as follows:

1. For testing intellectual function we use the Wechsler Intelligence Scale for Children (WISC), the Terman-Merril Intelligence Scale, and the Gesell Developmental Scale.

2. For assessing motor-function we evaluate visual-motor organization (Bender Test and Santucci Pre-Bender Test), body scheme and spatial orientation (Piaget-Head Tests), temporal structure (Stambak Rhythm Tests), and lateral dominance of upper and lower limbs.

3. Assessment of emotional function is approached through free drawings and a story about them (Walter Trinca's Clinical Investigation of Personality and the Rorschach Test) to eliminate the hypothesis of serious affective-emotional impairments affecting academic achievement.

Results of Psychological Assessment. In this population emotional disorders are rather frequent, but for the most part they are secondary to the difficulty of adjustment due to the primary learning disability. However, we have found some cases in which the affective-emotional impairments are serious enough to act as a real obstacle to the normal learning process (see case 4, later in this chapter).

Motor deficiencies in graphoperceptual organization have been found, as well as problems in spatial orientation and body scheme, motor coordination, and visual acuity. Evidence of latent intellectual capacity has generally been found, and it could be brought out with proper remedial management.

In a random sample of ten children (seven boys and three girls), with ages ranging from eight years to thirteen years, three months (average ten years, one month), tested with the WISC, the following results were found. In relation to total IQ there were one borderline score (79), two lower-than-average scores (80 and 84), six within the average range of 90 to 110, and one higher-than-average score (118). In five cases a significant difference (10 points or more) between Verbal IQ and Performance IQ was found, with higher Verbal IQ in three cases (two girls and one boy) and higher Performance IQ in two cases (two boys). On the Similarities subtest, six scores were higher (3 points or more) than the average (10), and no score was lower. On the Block Design subtest, four scores were higher and one was lower than the average. As these two subtests are heavily loaded with G factor (analytical ability), we assume that in this sample there was an intellectual potential higher than the total IQ would suggest. On the other subtests, we observed a tendency toward below-average scores in the Comprehension, Object Assembly, Digit Span, and Coding subscales. However, we believe that further research is needed before any reliable conclusions can be drawn.

Speech and Education Assessment

To evaluate oral and written speech, tests were used that were developed or standardized in Brazil for the assessment of oral reception and expression and auditory and visual processes. Educational assessment was obtained through tests of specific functions related to the learning of spelling, reading, and mathematics (Hildreth and Griffiths 1966).

Results of Speech and Educational Assessment. The highest incidence of learning disabilities is found among children in the first elementary grade, which is the beginning of regular school, and in the fifth elementary grade, when the school routine generally changes to a greater diversity of teachers and subjects. Most of the children who have been tested showed impairments in the auditory processes, mainly related to discrimination and auditory memory.

Another sample of ten children (six boys and four girls), with ages ranging from five years, nine months, to thirteen years, three months (average nine years, five months), was analyzed. These children were referred with learning difficulties in spelling and reading. Eight of them were reading, one was in the process of alphabetization, and one with learning disorders was in preschool. Two children had a history of otitis media, and another had a family history of congenital auditory disorder. The results of the tests were as follows:

1. Auditory discrimination (Wepman test) was checked by the identification of pairs of syllables and words as alike or different. All ten children made errors in the discrimination of pairs of words, the most frequent being *bode-pode* and *gato-cato*. Nine children made mistakes in the discrimination of pairs of phonemes, the most frequent being *p-b* and *k-g*. Nine made spelling mistakes, with letter substitutions that were mainly auditory—*g-q, c-g, t-d, d-t*.

2. Auditory memory was tested by repetition of digits, nonsense words, and words. Five scores below that expected for their chronological ages were found. Three of the children also showed impairment of visual memory.

A hypothesis can be postulated to explain these results. Most of the private schools attended by this population use a phonetic-alphabetization method of teaching reading. In preschool there is no real concern with readiness for alphabetization that includes the development of the auditory functions, since readiness-training is devoted to the improvement of visual abilities. Consequently, problems of auditory-perceptual dysfunction tend to show up when the children start to read.

Methods for Remediation

Our discussion of remediation techniques will be superficial, because our team is specialized in differential diagnosis and referral. When the impairment of learning is mostly educational and of simple resolution, a team consisting of an educator, a psychologist, and a speech therapist from the school takes charge of the case under our supervision for reeducation.

In Brazil few schools are specialized and structured to handle children with normal intelligence and learning disabilities. The treatment is to help these children for a limited period until they are able to attend a regular school. Most of the cases demand specific remediation. According to the primary area involved, referral is as follows:

1. Techniques for psychomotor reeducation, most often the methods of Boucher, Le Bouch, Vayer, Frostig, Ajuriaguerra, Raman, and Idla.

2. Psychomotor therapy, including a global therapeutic approach using psychomotor techniques but with broader goals than purely psychomotor reeducation.
3. Emotional therapy, when emotional problems seem to play a primary role in the origin or permanence of the learning disabilities.
4. Language and speech therapy, including special techniques designed according to individual assessment (oral language, speech, spelling, reading, and language development).
5. Educational therapy, dealing primarily with the underlying abilities necessary for academic work.

Medication

We assume that drug treatment of children with learning disabilities should be restricted to those who have serious deficiencies in the concentration-attention processes, as for example, patients with hyperactivity, or the few patients with all the clinical signs of hyperactivity but with manifest hypoactivity.

Amphetamines

Although amphetamine sulfate (Benzedrine) and dextroanphetamine sulfate (Dexedrine) are both broadly used, we prefer the latter because it has fewer side effects. The recommended doses are 5 to 40 mg daily, starting with low doses of 5 mg and gradually increasing until the greatest therapeutic effect is achieved. The most frequent side effects are sleeplessness and anorexia. These effects should not necessarily indicate withdrawal of the treatment. When amphetamines are used for a long period of time, we may note clinical aspects of exhaustion. It is believed that stimulant drugs may repress physical development in some children when used in high doses. In some hyperactive children, Dexedrine enhances hyperactivity, obviously indicating withdrawal of this drug from treatment. In Brazil, following restrictive measures adopted by the health authorities in an attempt to prevent the misuse of such drugs, the amphetamines were virtually withdrawn from the market, which forced the adoption of other drugs for the control of hyperactivity.

Methylphenidate

In Brazil, methylphenidate hydrochloride (Ritalin) is, at the moment, the first choice of medication being used on hyperactive children. Successful results have been reported in about 80 percent of the children studied. The prescribed dosage is between 5 and 200 mg daily, but, in our experience, a satisfactory behavioral control has been achieved with doses of 5 to 20 mg daily, in a single dose in the morning, or in two doses, the second one in the afternoon. As with amphetamines, this drug may induce hyperactivity and promote anorexia and sleep disturbance as side effects.

Antidepressants

Imipramine hydrochloride (Tofranil) and desipramine hydrochloride (Pertofrane), antidepressants of the tricyclic group, have been used in the control of the hyperactivity syndrome. Desipramine greatly enhances amphetamine action on motor performance and body temperature as well as methylphenidate action on conditioned reflexes. According to some reports, this drug has induced paroxysmal waves in the EEG, previously interpreted as normal.

We have been using imipramine (10 to 50 mg daily) as well as desipramine (12.5 to 50 mg daily) with hyperactive children, and the results have been satisfactory, sometimes achieving clinical results as good as those obtained with amphetamines and methylphenidate. We usually prescribe one single dose in the morning, or two doses, the second one around lunchtime. As with stimulants, some children under this treatment may become more hyperactive. Others may show side effects, such as anorexia, sleeplessness, or pallor, and may become tired. Only in a very small percentage of cases is it necessary to withdraw medication because of these symptoms.

As with other medications used with hyperactivity, we prescribe antidepressants in a continuous way and generally maintain the treatment for several months, even after achieving stable behavior. After this period, we discontinue medication during school vacations. If hyperactivity recurs, we decide about the advantage of returning to medication for one more school period.

This group of antidepressants should not be used in patients prone to convulsions or patients with paroxysmal anomalies in EEG patterns.

Anticonvulsants

Although the literature shows the value of anticonvulsants (for example, hydantoins, phenobarbital, and succinimides) in the treatment of hyperactivity, we think that these drugs are not usually indicated for these children. In our view, their use should not be considered as the first choice of treatment, even in hyperactive patients with altered EEGs (with obvious paroxysmal elements) but without obvious manifestations of epilepsy. In such cases, we may sometimes try to control hyperactivity with carbamazepine (Tegretol) or primidone.

When hyperactivity is associated with a clinical manifestation of epilepsy, the first choice should be primidone and, as an alternative, diphenyl-hydantoin. The use of phenobarbital should be avoided in these patients because it often enhances hyperactivity. This effect is quite well known and can be seen in children who receive this drug for convulsive problems and then begin to present behavioral alterations, sometimes quite serious, including hyperactivity. Withdrawal of medication alleviates the symptoms immediately.

Other Drugs

When a child does not respond to any of the aforementioned drugs or withdrawal of the medication is necessary because of serious side effects, we tend to use other groups of drugs, including those whose clinical effects are not yet well known, or drugs that will at least improve some "social" aspects of these patients, allowing the child to exhibit more adjusted behavior at home and school. In this group we include the derivatives of the benzodiazepines, diphenhydramine, and the phenothiazine neuroleptics.

Finally, we would like to mention some drugs that also act as central nervous system stimulants and are being used in Brazil, but with which we have no personal experience: phenozolone (Ordinator) and caffeine.

We believe that drug treatment of hyperactivity and hypoactivity is a very important feature of the therapeutic management of a child who shows learning difficulties. When effective, a medication will promote an improvement in the attention-concentration processes with resulting improvement in behavior, learning, and so forth, without significant side effects. A child under medication will be in better condition to benefit from the other prescribed treatments.

Case Histories

Case 1

In this case the learning disability was primarily based on audiological disorders. M.T., a boy aged nine years, seven months, was referred to our clinic because he had problems at school with Portuguese, presenting spelling errors both in reading and writing. He was attending the fourth grade of elementary school.

M.T. has an eleven-year-old sister; his father is an engineer and his mother a photographer, and the family has great expectations concerning his intellectual performance. In the interview with his parents, his motor, speech, and emotional development were described as normal, as well as his relationship with his sister and parents. The neurological assessment, including EEG, was normal.

Psychological Assessment. Intellectual level was above average: total IQ 118, Verbal IQ 110, Performance IQ 124, on the WISC.

Motor performance: Graphoperceptual organization on the Bender Test was beyond his age-level. He had established notions of left and right and good spatial orientation. Spontaneous rhythms were quite rapid, with slight difficulty in the reproduction of rhythm patterns.

Emotional investigation: M.T. presented a proper contact with reality and a high creative potential open to affective external stimulation, to which he reacted intellectually and sometimes impulsively. He felt his parents' expectations and criticized himself too much, although this did not impair his adjustment.

Speech and educational assessment: M.T. did not show oral-language errors. In written communication, he made spelling mistakes, primarily of auditory origin, during dictation and spontaneous writing. He also made mistakes in auditory discrimination of word pairs, and his auditory memory for nonsense words was below his chronological age-level. He showed no mistakes in discrimination, analysis, or synthesis and visual memory.

Recommendations: In view of the stated difficulties, we referred the child to a speech therapist.

Case 2

This case illustrates that, underlying learning disabilities, there may be multiple etiologies, which make it difficult to determine priorities in remedial therapy.

R.L., a girl aged nine years, six months, came to our clinic because she had failed in the first grade and presented general learning difficulties. She has a six-year-old sister and a two-year-old brother.

In the interview, the parents did not mention any problem related to pregnancy, birth, feeding, sleeping, sociability, or motor and speech development. The relationship between the parents was tense, and the girl was afraid of her father's reactions, although he regards her as his favorite child. R.L. gets along well with her sister and brother, protects them, and feels extremely sorry when something happens to them.

Her problems started in preschool, when she had difficulty in memorizing letters. She was not able to learn adequately in the first grade. She attended a rather large school with a great number of pupils in each classroom, so there is a lack of individual assistance. When she entered the first grade, she went through an ophthalmological examination that revealed farsightedness and a scar in the retina, but these findings did not explain the learning difficulties.

She was tutored for four months, was treated for "mental disorganization" for fifteen days in a neurological clinic, and had psychomotor training for two months. All these procedures were completely ineffective. In her neurological assessment, the EEG and neurological tests were normal.

Psychological Assessment. Intellectual level was borderline: total IQ 79, Verbal IQ 84, Performance IQ 74, on the WISC.

Motor performance: Bender Test scores were within the average range. The manual motoricity test showed right-hand dominance with slow production. Lateral dominance was right. Spatial orientation and Piaget-Head test body scheme (Zazzo 1963) were heavily impaired, with scores below chronological age-level. On the temporal orientation tests, rhythm was within the average for her age, but the reproduction of rhythmic patterns was heavily impaired, with failures in duration and number of beats.

Her readiness for alphabetization and reading were average, readiness for digits was high-average, and total readiness was above average.

Emotional assessment: R.L. is anxious and apprehensive and has difficulty in reacting objectively, logically, and clearly to stimulation. She tends to use the same frames of reference to explain events, thinking that reality evolves according to her wishes, and she generally comes to very improbable conclusions. She believes that she should repress her emotions in order to fulfill the expectations she feels others have about her. However, she is rather affectively responsive. She has no softening patterns for her aggressive drives, which may turn against herself, and she has no inner freedom to modulate her emotions, which hinders the establishment of significant and stable affective links.

Speech and educational assessment: R.L. shows impairment in elaborating oral language for reporting events away from an immediate context and also presents a disability in writing and spelling due to serious failures in discrimination, analysis-synthesis, and visual and auditory memory. In mathematics she maintains stereotyped thinking.

Recommendations: R.L. presents impairment in the motor (spatial and temporal orientation), emotional, speech, and educational areas. We recommend as a priority, an approach to the speech and educational areas through speech therapy and a change to a school that could provide more individual assistance.

Case 3

In this case we found that the learning disability was based primarily on organic deficiencies. M.M., a thirteen-year-old female, was referred for assessment because of academic difficulties. Her father, who died at forty-one years of age, was an industrialist, as is her mother, who is forty-seven years old. M.M. attends the fifth grade of elementary school and has an eight-year-old brother. The family history revealed that her father had died from Cursham-Steinert dystrophy.

Through the interviews we verified that M.M. did not show alterations in motor, speech, and emotional development until she was seven years old. When she was attending the first grade of elementary school, she began to show deficiencies in motor coordination and attention as well as emotional apathy. At that time she was given an EEG, which revealed diffuse paroxysmal abnormalities and was treated with phenobarbital. She was also given a psychomotor evaluation and was referred for psychomotor reeducation. In 1972 the EEG was repeated and presented normal results. The medication and psychomotor treatment were then discontinued.

Neurological assessment: The patient has subnormal growth of the facial muscles and underdevelopment of the whole muscle mass. M.M. presents difficulty in rapid and successive movements, with an obvious difficulty in muscle relaxation. She presents an evident myotonic (spasm) phenomenon under percussion of the palm muscles. Skeletal-tendinous reflexes, which are symmetrical and hypoactive, are also present.

Electromyogram: Electrophysiological findings were in accordance with typical myotonic dystrophy.

Psychological Assessment. Intellectual level was borderline: total IQ 77, Verbal IQ 89, Performance IQ 69, on the WISC.

Motor investigation revealed a marked deficit, mainly in visual-motor organization, on the Bender Test, and spatial orientation. Her performance on rhythm tests was adequate. Right-lateral dominance was harmonious for lower limbs and not harmonious for upper limbs. Her notion of body scheme was introjected. Her performance on the Piaget-Head Test was hesitant, getting worse as she progressed through the test.

Emotional assessment: M.M. is relatively well adjusted, although she sometimes loses self-control because she does not know how to handle her motor and intellectual difficulties. She shows a rather immature development for her age but has good contact with reality.

Speech and educational assessment: M.M. has hypotonic articulatory structures and nasal voice, with contaminations in the emission of consonant groups. Regarding written communication, she showed graphemic substitutions that were not systematic and were primarily visual. She has a disability in written language, with morphological, synthetic, and semantic alterations in spontaneous writing.

Recommendations: M.M. was referred to physical therapy because of her motor and organic problems.

Case 4

In this case a deep emotional disorder following neurological dysfunction may have precipitated school failure. F.N., a six-year-old boy attending a private preschool, was referred for diagnosis because he had difficulties in assimilation and needed personal attention in academic areas.

F.N. has a five-year-old sister, his father is thirty-two years old, and his mother is twenty-eight years old. He was born by cesarean section at eight months of pregnancy because of early rupture of the bursa. During infancy he had quiet sleep, but at present it is very disturbed. The child sits and swings, with closed eyes, and some time ago used to knock his head against the wall. His psychomotor development was apparently normal; he is right-handed but often uses his left hand. He is also awkward.

F.N. showed early difficulties in language development and always babbled. He was given speech therapy for six months (between two years, six months, and three years of age) and at present has great difficulty expressing himself, which increases when he is under stress.

His school complains about insubordination, inattention, and slowness in tasks. F.N. is an extremely excitable child, is fearful, tells lies, and makes up untrue events. He has poor relationships with children. Formerly, his peers rejected him because of his speech difficulties, and now he withdraws and feels frustrated. He is a very sensitive child and cries easily. In his relationship with his parents, he is very aggressive and blackmails his mother, always succeeding in overcoming her. He mostly obeys his father. The whole family environment is very confused. The mother feels unable to handle the house and looks for support to the father, who is unable to set the bounds he intends to impose.

Three years ago the boy had an EEG, after a sudden loss of consciousness that lasted five minutes, and the results pointed to a right-side brain lesion. He was not medicated on that occasion.

Neurological assessment: F.N. was not hyperactive during tests. He showed an evident language retardation, lameness of the left leg, and hyperflexion of the tendons, and an EEG and X ray of the skull were normal.

Psychological Assessment. Intellectual level was average: total IQ 101, Verbal IQ 96, Performance IQ 107.

Motor performance: Visual-motor organization was beyond his age-level. He showed right-hand dominance, with rapid and agitated production. Lateral dominance was right; spatial orientation and body scheme were below his age-level. He reproduced rhythm patterns at his age-level.

Emotional assessment. F.N. shows a great need to work and produce. He is able to grasp broad situations but also works on a concrete plan. However, when confronted with situations of affective interaction, he has a tendency to attach himself to small details. He is very sensitive to affective stimulation from the environment, and as he is not able to properly handle and manifest his feelings, he introjects his emotions. His inner life is very fanciful, tense, and anxious, and he feels unsafe, using manic defenses in an effort to adjust himself to the environment. His ego is weakened; he has difficulties in identification and in relationships with male and female figures. His perception of the world is fragmented, and he reacts to this in a manic way, which hinders him from using his intellectual and creative potential for more effective production.

Speech and educational assessment: F.N. showed alterations in the ability to decode oral messages that involved complex transformations, as well as semantic alterations and difficulties in the elaboration of oral language. Regarding specific functions for learning reading and spelling, he showed obvious deficits in the auditory and visual processes. His speech and educational levels are compatible with that of a child with serious psychiatric disorders.

Recommendations: F.N. was referred to a child-psychiatric therapeutic community and, for the time being, was removed from any school activity and family environment.

References

Hildreth, G.H., and Griffiths, N.L. 1966. *Teste Metropolitano de Prontidão.* Adapted and standardized for Brazil by A.M. Popovic. São Paulo: Vetor.

Popovic, A.M. 1968. *Alfabetização—Disfunções Psiconeuológicas.* São Paulo: Vetor.

Zazzó, R. 1963. *Manual para el Examen Psicologico del Nino.* Buenos Aires: Kapeluz.

Special Education and Learning Disabilities in Chile

Luis Bravo-Valdivieso

Primary Education in Chile

Primary education in Chile consists of eight years of schooling; it is compulsory and free of charge. It is estimated that in Chile there are a sufficient number of public schools and teachers to educate all children under the age of fourteen. The school system is centralized and directed by the Ministry of Education. The Ministry of Education specifies the academic curriculum and the teaching methods that should be used.

Chilean children must enter first grade at six years of age, and their advancement is determined by means of their teachers' subjective evaluations at the end of each grade. Each child is evaluated according to his mastery of the contents of the academic program. At the end of the eighth grade, the students may enter a new four-year cycle called secondary education (high school).

The greatest problem in primary education in Chile is the high percentage of children who repeat grades. Children are held back in a grade if they fail to pass the annual evaluation or if they fail to master the subject matter required by the official academic program. Table 9-1 presents the enrollment in each primary grade and the percentage of children repeating each

Table 9-1
Children Repeating Each Grade in 1976 and 1977

Grade	1976 Enrollment	1976 Percentage of Holdovers	1977 Percentage of Holdovers
1	354,745	18.8	18.3
2	325,917	15.7	14.3
3	319,136	13.1	12.1
4	302,601	12.7	11.7
5	287,022	14.0	13.4
6	258,321	11.5	10.7
7	220,539	16.0	15.0
8	176,839	9.0	8.3

Less than 50 percent complete eight grades.

257

grade for the academic years 1976 and 1977. This scholastic failure has spurred the growth of a national special-education program.

Among the causes that have contributed to this failure are the verbal and cognitive immaturity of the children from low socioeconomic groups entering first grade of primary school, who cannot assimilate into the regular school program because they have not had any preschool education; the large number of working-class and rural children, who manifest an intelligence that is primarily nonverbal and that will be of little help to them in the first grades in an academic learning situation; the presence of specific learning disabilities, especially dyslexia and dyscalculia; and, to a lesser extent, mental retardation (Bravo-Valdivieso 1980a, 1980b).

From the viewpoint of the schools, among the causes of this massive holdover rate are the use of inflexible plans and programs of study designed to be used by all and not adapted to the cultural differences among the children; the use of verbal teaching methodologies without the aid of audiovisual techniques; and a highly subjective system of annual evaluation. Since 1968 the educational authorities have encouraged the development of special education for learning disabilities as a partial solution to this problem.

Learning Problems and Cultural Differences

We have differentiated the origins of two types of academic difficulties, general learning problems and specific learning disabilities. The specific learning disabilities have their origin in the biological alterations and dangers of infantile development, and they are not solved by using the ordinary pedagogic methods (Bravo-Valdivieso 1973). This is true, for example, of specific dyslexia and the dyscalculias. Specific learning disabilities are associated closely with high-risk children. The incidence of high-risk children is generally greater in the poverty sectors, according to Birch and Gussow (1970).

It is probable that the percentage of children with specific learning disabilities is greater in the underdeveloped countries because of poor nutrition, unsanitary conditions, less intellectual stimulation, and so forth. We would also expect to find a high percentage of mentally retarded children in these countries (Bravo-Valdivieso 1975).

All the children with specific learning disabilities need special education in order to overcome their academic difficulties. However, general learning problems could be solved within the regular school curriculum, because they are not caused by a psychoneurological dysfunction or damage that alters the learning abilities of the child. These problems arise principally from the child's psychological and social immaturity and consequent inability to follow the programs of study brought about by insufficient cultural stimulation and insufficient motivation for academic activities, or by the use of inadequate academic programs and methods.

In the United States and other developed countries, when culturally deprived children are discussed, they are defined in terms of "subcultural minorities," in comparison to the great majority of children, who have had sufficient stimulation and who have been well motivated toward academic learning. In those developed countries the problem of poverty affects a minority of children, who must receive special help in order to compensate their cultural deficiencies. This minority of children must adapt themselves to the cultural and academic level of the majority of the students in order to succeed in school.

This is not the case in the underdeveloped countries. In these countries the poor children constitute the majority, and they must follow the program of studies for the minority, the middle-class children. The children who belong to the poverty majority show retardation in their cognitive and linguistic maturation that affects their academic performance and produces general learning problems.

Chilean research has shown that the academic maturity in children who are entering public schools is very different from that of children entering private schools (Bravo-Valdivieso, Moya, and Salas 1975). Children from the culturally deprived sectors of society will generally not finish the eight years of primary education, probably because of a lesser cognitive and linguistic maturation. This disadvantage in the psychological maturation of the basic functions could be one of the principal causes of the high number of children with general learning problems who are left back or who drop out of school in the underdeveloped countries that do not offer differentiated programs.

All the children who have learning problems need not be taught in special schools, nor do all of them have specific learning disabilities. Frequently the scarcity of diagnostic services and the rigidity of the traditional academic system keep the children from the poverty subculture from receiving an adequate education in their own schools. They must be held over in their grade or their parents request their admission to special schools.

The same phenomenon can be seen when we try to measure IQ with tests that have been validated using the criteria of academic performance. Children from working-class families who have difficulty in learning to read also do poorly on traditional tests because of their linguistic differences from middle-class children. This factor undoubtedly adds to the percentage of children with apparent mental retardation, because the traditional tests have been designed to measure academic intelligence, which is culturally determined.

As many of these tests have been validated with an external criterion of academic performance, it is natural that the children who have culturally caused learning problems will also receive low scores on these tests. Then it may be mistakenly assumed that the cause of the reading problem is low intelligence. This is why for a long time the major focus of special education was on the problems of mental retardation and not on sociocultural differences and learning disabilities that make school programs designed for middle-class children useless for children from different subcultures.

Historical Antecedents

Special education began in Chile in 1852 with the creation of a school for deaf-mutes, which subsequently added a class for blind children. In 1928 and 1929 three schools for children with behavior disorders and another school for the blind were opened. In 1945 several schools for mentally retarded children were established, along with a few special classes for retarded children within the regular schools. The first psychological diagnostic center, the Psychopedagogic Clinic, was created in 1955. Finally the 1960s saw the opening of various types of special schools annexed to pediatric hospitals. These schools served as both diagnostic centers and rehabilitation centers for specific learning disabilities.

A review of the creation of special schools in Chile would show that, between 1852 and 1951, there were six special schools; between 1953 and 1958, five more schools were opened. In the decade between 1960 and 1970, thirty-seven new special schools were opened. Finally, in the present decade, 113 special schools have been created that work with different types of developmental deficits (mental retardation, sensory and motor deficits, special learning disabilities, and so forth).

The number of children serviced by these schools annually is approximately 20,000. Since 1975 planning in the field of special education has been oriented toward the creation of diagnostic centers, psychopedagogic support teams for the regular schools, special classes within the regular schools, and vocational-training centers for handicapped children.

**Development of Special Education for
Learning Disabilities**

In describing the growth and development of special education for learning-disabled children in Chile, it is necessary to emphasize two essential elements: the contribution of the child-psychiatry and pediatric-neurology departments of the hospitals, and the contribution of the universities in the training of specialists.

In the absence of pediatric diagnostic centers, the requests for help for children with learning problems were principally directed to the hospitals that had children's psychiatric and neurological services. Until 1975 the pediatric hospitals bore the complete burden of both diagnosis and rehabilitation of children with developmental disturbances.

In a mental-health report in 1971 it was stated that, of the children diagnosed by these hospitals, 50 percent presented intellectual retardation, 30 percent were dyslexic, and 10 percent showed low scholastic achievement due to emotional problems.

The contribution of the child-psychiatry and pediatric-neurology services to special education was not limited to the diagnostic and treatment aspects but also included clinical investigation of specific learning disabilities, offering teachers a clinical picture of such disabilities as minimal brain dysfunction, specific dyslexia, epilepsy, and mental retardation. This work by the hospital services was strengthened enormously by the work done in the annexed special schools by clinical psychologists, who helped the teachers understand the psychopathological aspects of learning disabilities.

Until the 1960s most of the teachers who worked in special schools were self-taught and had never received any systematic training. It is interesting to consider that one of the most valuable things that education received from the clinicians was a change in the pedagogic orientation. The teacher almost always thought in terms of the problems of his class or group, rather than using an individualized or clinical approach adapted to each particular child. This change in perspective came about through the participation of the special-education teachers in the clinical meetings of their affiliated hospitals, where each child was discussed and an individualized treatment plan was developed.

The second fundamental support was given by the universities in creating postgraduate courses for training teachers of special education. Students in these programs were experienced primary-school teachers.

In 1968 the Universidad Católica de Santiago began a postgraduate special-education program in learning disabilities. The program lasts three years and includes courses in developmental psychology, learning psychology, child psychopathology, neurology, speech and language, diagnosis, education of children with reading and arithmetic disabilities, and family counseling. The program ends with practice-teaching with learning-disabled children in a public special-education school.

The Catholic University of Chile was the first Chilean university to begin teacher-training and research in the area of learning disabilities. Historically, this action was important, as it contributed to changing the emphasis of special education in Chile.

Until that time the principal preoccupation in this educational area was centered on mentally retarded children and those with sensory or motor handicaps. Thereafter, the focus began to shift toward learning problems in children without mental retardation or sensory deficits. This new outlook indirectly pointed to the necessity of evaluating the entire system of primary education and its plans and programs and the need to know the incidence and degree of learning problems presented by children in primary school, especially children coming from the subculture of poverty.

In 1970 the Catholic University alerted the Ministry of Education to the "urgent necessity" of establishing a national policy regarding the training of teachers specializing in the rehabilitation of nonmentally retarded, learning-disabled children. Until 1974 the Ministry of Education, the universities, and the National Health and Educational Services had acted independently. There were sporadic meetings, which produced no operational results. This lack of coordination hindered the establishment of a joint program in the area of learning disabilities.

In March 1974 a national Conference on Special Education was held. This seminar was organized jointly by the Ministry of Education, the Universidad Católica, and the Universidad de Chile. This conference, which was attended by more than 300 specialists, had the following objectives: to assess the current status of special education in Chile and to formulate a basis for a national policy toward public special education. It was believed that the training of specialists should be primarily the responsibility of the universities. Also, every teacher should be trained to work within the regular schools with children with minor learning disabilities, and the curriculum for training all preschool and primary-school teachers should include sufficient training in learning disabilities to permit early detection of learning problems. Furthermore, it was considered urgent to establish many diagnostic centers, to be affiliated with both hospitals and rehabilitation centers, where multidisciplinary diagnosis could be done. Agreements for exchanges of professionals between the areas of education and health were sought for these centers. Finally, this conference noted the necessity for a nationwide reform of primary education, proposing the use of a very flexible system of academic advancement by levels of education rather than by courses, according to the level of psychopedagogic maturation of the children.

The results of this conference were twofold. It was the first nationwide meeting in Chile of all the specialists from all the institutions that worked in any way with special education, with the goal of planning a national policy and making a public evaluation of the system; and it was the first time that the educational authorities publicly accepted the challenge presented by this problem and tried to confront the problem in a global manner.

Diagnosis and remediation of learning disabilities and mental retardation was no longer centered in the children's psychiatric and neurological services of the hospitals but became a responsibility of the educational sector. This policy increased the urgency for the creation of diagnostic centers.

In April 1974, as a result of this conference, the government created a commission on special education in order to implement these policies. This commission consisted of eleven specialists representing all the universities in Chile with special-education programs, representatives of the Ministry of Education, and representatives from private educational facilities.

In December 1975 this commission delivered its report. Special education was defined as "a differentiated and interdisciplinary specialization of regular education addressed to those children who, whether due to transitory or permanent causes, are prevented from following the regular educational program." Special education must not constitute a segregated or independent entity apart from the general educational system but must make its principal objective incorporating the child as quickly as possible into the mainstream of education. "Children with physical or psychic deficiencies cannot be maintained indefinitely in a segregated educational structure, however perfect that structure might be in itself, because at the end of his school years the student's integration into the social and economic communities will be even harder."

It was clearly expressed that special education does not constitute a different educational system; rather, it is an interdisciplinary differentiation of regular education, applicable to individual cases as needed. "The effectiveness of special education can be seriously compromised if it must receive an overpopulation of children due to inadequacies in the regular education system. Chilean primary education does not have sufficient flexibility and differentiation in its programs and methodologies to permit the schools to adapt to the characteristics of the children. The rigidity of the traditional programs stops children with minor difficulties from receiving individualized instruction, and this in turn contributes to the high number of students annually who fail academically without having specific disabilities."

Consequently, the commission felt that the plans for special education must be complemented by a plan for regular education that could be adapted to the psychological differences of the children in order to avoid the unnecessary proliferation of learning problems. The report concluded by stating that the work of special education as an interdisciplinary process must be complemented by preventive preschool education.

The National Commission on Special Education performed a survey of existing special-education resources, which indicated that there were 92 special schools serving 10,000 children, distributed among various types of mental retardation and defects in speech and hearing, vision, and motoric processes, as well as behavior disorders and multiple handicaps. There were only four diagnostic centers in all of Chile. Upon completion of the survey of special education, the commission recommended that several new diagnostic centers be created, to be located in different regions of the country.

The commission suggested a new solution for the cities that still would not be able to maintain a diagnostic center. It was suggested that they create psychopedagogic support teams that would diagnose the children who presented problems and would guide their regular teachers in the remediation of the learning problems. These teams were to consist of a psychologist and two special teachers, to be mobile within a province or region and to serve as a base for a future diagnostic center.

Both the diagnostic centers and the psychopedagogic support teams were created by a law passed in May 1975. For children with mild learning disabilities and mild mental retardation, special small groups (*grupos diferenciales*) were started in the regular schools. In 1980, in addition to the hospital centers, there were 113 public special schools and private facilities, 4,200 special groups in regular schools, with 24,600 children, 16 psychopedagogic support teams, and 15 diagnostic centers.

In summation, the structure of special education in Chile has changed over the past few years, now focusing greater interest on learning problems than on mental retardation. The special-education commission used the concerns of the teachers and specialists as a basis for formulating a special-education plan that was both operational and applicable to the reality of the educational system.

The results of this commission's work are emerging slowly because of the administrative and economic obstacles that required a change in a subsystem within a more complex educational system that did not develop from the same philosophical framework.

The principal changes that have been observed since 1975 are as follows:

1. An increase in the amount of treatment given (nearly 25,000 children in 1980).
2. A change in the focus of special education—away from mental retardation and toward the problems presented by learning disabilities and their relationship to the primary-education curriculum.
3. A change in the policy of creating special schools, which dated back to the last century, to a policy of creating special groups in the regular schools, diagnostic centers, and psychopedagogic support teams.
4. Transfer of the principal responsibility for diagnosis of students with learning difficulties from National Health Centers to centers supervised by the Ministry of Education.
5. The extension of special education as rehabilitation on the primary level to special education as a preventive or compensatory measure in the nursery schools and kindergartens.

Functioning of the Special-Education System

Diagnosis and Rehabilitation of Learning Problems

As we have seen, the Chilean special-education system consists of the psychoeducational diagnostic centers, the special schools, the special groups in the regular schools, and the psychopedagogic support teams that function in the cities where there is no diagnostic center.

There also are private rehabilitation centers, such as the Institute of Applied Psychology, and other cooperative centers, financed by the parents of children with problems. These centers primarily work with children referred by private schools.

Case Study of a Child with Reading Problems

Juan, a seven-year-old boy from a working-class family, was in the second grade and had not learned to read. He read only syllables, presenting inversions (*al-la*) and confusion of letters (*m-n*) and had a low level of reading comprehension.

His teacher had made him repeat a school year, but repeating the grade had not helped his reading. Rather, being left back produced emotional problems (depression) and behavioral problems (irritability and reluctance to attend classes).

His teacher referred him to a diagnostic center, where a team composed of a psychologist, a special-education teacher, and a speech and hearing therapist established that he had a normal IQ (WISC: Verbal IQ 102; Performance IQ 91) and a graphomotor retardation (Bender Test developmental age, 6 years). He showed no language retardation. However, he had left-right confusion, mixed dominance (left-eye and right-hand dominance) and problems in perceiving rhythm. Otherwise his auditory perception was normal. The child was sent for a neurological examination, in which his EEG showed mild diffuse alterations indicative of cortical bilateral immaturity, involuntary kinesthetic movements, and motor torpidity. His sight and hearing acuity were normal. The final diagnosis was specific dyslexia secondary to minimal brain dysfunction in the perceptual-motor areas, with normal intelligence.

The diagnostic center referred the child to a rehabilitation center for treatment. There he was taught to read, using a method to be described later. After a year, the child could read fluently. During the interviews with his parents, methods for handling the child's emotional problems were discussed and explained.

This case demonstrates how the special-education system functions. The child with learning problems is sent to a diagnostic center, which is staffed by psychologists, special-education teachers, and speech and hearing therapists. They do psychological and educational evaluations and then send the child to a hospital, where medical examinations (principally neurological and sensory) are given, if required. Then a formal diagnosis is made and the child is sent for individual or group treatment (six children), according to the problems presented, in classes of two hours each, two or three times a week. The child continues to attend his regular school, but with less-demanding evaluations, until his reading difficulties have been remediated. In the cities where there are no diagnostic centers, the child is examined by a psychopedagogic support team (a psychologist and one or two special-education teachers).

The remediation method employed in such cases is the following:

Development of a sight vocabulary: The child is first taught a group of words that, in general, do not have concrete meanings and are used very frequently, such as *these, with, will be, some, all, also,* and *when.* The child must be able to recognize these words automatically when they are printed in large letters.

Phonetic analysis: At the same time, the child must learn that the combinations of letters correspond to specific sounds. He is shown a letter and associates it with its corresponding sound. Following this, the auditory discrimination of the beginnings and endings of words is worked on, along with the visual perception of the same beginnings and endings. (The teacher shows the word and pronounces it; then the child does the same.)

Multisensory learning: Letters are taught by associating the corresponding sound and forms with a motor activity or gesture. This is taught as a progression, using combinations in which only letters previously studied by the child appear. As the child acquires the mechanisms of reading, the dependence on gestures is gradually eliminated. Along with the teaching of letters there is a gradual introduction of different combinations of letters used to form words. The degree of difficulty is controlled; the child begins with direct syllables (*la*), then proceeds to the inverse (*al*), and finally to complex syllables (*alas*). It is important to note that, in the Spanish language, the letters always have the same pronunciation, with few exceptions, which facilitates the learning of letter-sound associations.

Phonograms: When the child is taught the consonant groups, or phonograms (*pl, br,* and the like), the same method is used as was used for the simple syllables. The exercises for prevention of specific errors are based principally on the phonograms and complex syllables most frequently confused (*palta-plata*).

Writing: Writing is taught through copying and the dictation of phrases and sentences.

Once the child has mastered this stage, he begins to read brief stories in books with large type and drawings related to the text. This method of teaching reading is individualized and is useful for teaching the reading of Spanish to high-risk children with specific learning disabilities, or to children who are experiencing difficulties in the first stages of learning to read.

Methods of Diagnosis and Evaluation

The diagnostic methods used in the diagnostic centers in Chile by the psychologists and learning-disability specialists have two origins. First, there are the traditional tests, which are used internationally: WISC, WPPSI, Bender, Frostig, and Binet-Terman; Zazzo's battery of psychopedagogic tests; Piagetian tests; the Metropolitan Readiness Test; and so forth. Second, there are the tests that were designed and standardized in Chile.

The test for specific errors and reading level, by Condemarín, is designed to evaluate specific errors in reading and the reading-level of children who are beginning to learn to read. The test can be used for the diagnosis of reading retardation and specific dyslexias in children between six and ten years of age. This test is individually administered. The child responds orally, reading the syllables and words or pointing to the syllables read by the examiner. The test has been standardized in Chile for children from first to fifth grade (Berdicewski, Milicic, and Orellana 1977).

Another test is the reading-writing test of Olea. This test is composed of two subtests: a reading-writing subtest, for the diagnosis of errors in reading and writing, from the recognition of letters through the level of comprehension of passages; and a subtest of basic psychological functions, designed to evaluate visual perception, auditory perception, spatial orientation, laterality, and eye-hand coordination. These tests are administered individually, and from them we derive a percentage score that determines the degree of reading retardation of the child and the amount of retardation in the maturation of the basic function. Olea has not yet issued a definitive publication of the test, and the final standardization has not yet been completed, but several research studies have shown the test to have a high level of validity (Olea 1977).

The test of basic psychological functions by Milicic and Berdicewski (1976) was designed and standardized for use with preschool children. The test is used to determine the level of development of vocabulary, auditory discrimination, and visual-motor coordination in children entering the first grade. This test is administered collectively and has been validated using the reading-level attained in the second grade. It is a good test of the academic maturity required for the prevention of reading disabilities.

Currently being standardized are a reading-comprehension test and a battery of verbal tests, designed to diagnose the different language functions in children with reading difficulties.

The diagnostic tests designed in Chile in Spanish complement the international battery of tests used for diagnosing learning problems and constitute a valid instrument for special education in the Spanish language.

Research in Learning Disabilities

Methods of Teaching Reading

In Chile the analytic (letter-by-letter) method of teaching reading was traditionally used. In the 1960s the global (whole-word) method, derived principally from North American methods, began to be used. Experience has shown that in the Spanish language the whole-word method is inadequate, because in Spanish each letter is always read in the same way, and the syllables are read as the sum of their letters. In English, however, the letters are pronounced differently according to their context (for example, the letter *a* in *say, author, least, rat, rate*). Thus, the global method of teaching reading may be better for teaching children to read English but it is not better for teaching Spanish (or Italian).

An interesting new method of teaching reading in Spanish has been developed through research. This experimental method consists of teaching letters together with associated gestures that the child makes with his hands (see figures 9-1, 9-2, 9-3). Each time the child reads a particular letter he must make its associated gesture with his hands. This method uses as its point of departure the movements and rhythm that the child is able to execute in his spatial and temporal relations.

Once the child has learned to recognize and differentiate the letters, the gestures are abandoned, and the child is then taught some key words in the Spanish language (high-frequency words). The key words give the child visual-perceptual recognition and generalization of the written structure, which facilitates the recognition of new words.

This new method is recommended for children who have had difficulty learning to read because of improper teaching methods. It is both a normal and a remedial method of teaching reading. It is original to and designed for use in the Spanish language. Currently the authors are working on the validation of this method (Alliende, Condemarín, and Chadwick 1977).

Group-Teaching Method

In another investigation, Barriga and associates (1975) experimented with a group-teaching method for stimulating children with learning problems. In

Figure 9-1. Associated Gesture for the Letter *a*

this method, therapeutic pedagogic techniques are combined with the application of operant-conditioning techniques. This method also is still being investigated. It appears that it can be used by a regular teacher when there are no specialists in the school, and for children with minimal learning problems.

Figure 9-2. Associated Gesture for the Letter *d*

Figure 9-3. Associated Gesture for the Letter *u*

Prevalence of Disturbances

The figures for the number of children repeating courses in the first few primary grades, and some partial investigations, permit us to estimate that between 12 and 15 percent of the students in Chile's primary schools experience difficulties in learning to read. Represented within these percentages are children with simple reading retardation, specific dyslexia, and other disturbances, such as speech and language retardation, sociocultural retardation, and sensory-motor problems (Gazmuri, Milicic, and Schmidt 1978).

Clinical Research

Among the clinical investigations, Bravo-Valdivieso (1980a) discovered a wide overlap between the terms *minimal cerebral dysfunction* and *specific learning disabilities* and found that children with this diagnosis presented characterological and emotional alterations in addition to their learning problems. It appears that the term *minimal cerebral dysfunction* has surged into a vacuum in the diagnostic nomenclature for various psychological, neurological, and educational disturbances that affect the learning abilities and conduct of students. The use of the term *minimal brain dysfunction*

(MBD) by three different types of specialists has produced confusion, because each specialist principally observes the symptoms and alterations of most interest to his particular specialty. These distinct points of view serve to hinder any agreement among neurologists, psychologists, and educators about this syndrome.

One of the important characteristics of children with brain dysfunction is the alteration in the development of personality, which many times is a factor in character disorders in adolescence. Minimal brain dysfunction might also be the origin of many character disorders in adult life.

Condemarín and Salas (1975) studied a sample of dyslexic children with normal intelligence ten years after the initial diagnosis was made. The study of these children revealed the persistence of errors in reading and writing as well as a lack of interest in reading. In addition, the young people were observed to lack initiative, to be dependent, and to show signs of frustration because of their inability to live up to academic expectations. This investigation showed both the importance of social and familial attitudes toward the dyslexic child and the persistence of reading difficulties ten years later. We can assume that dyslexia will not resolve itself solely through maturation and that even after treatment the disability persists.

Another study of dyslexic children investigated the variables that influence the rehabilitative prognosis in dyslexia (Bravo-Valdivieso, Alvarez, and Haeussler 1979). After one year of treatment it was determined that the principal factors in rehabilitation were verbal factors, mainly the immediate assimilation of verbal information and the verbal abstraction of similarities. Second in importance was the WISC IQ (Full Scale). The third factor was the Frostig Developmental Test of Visual Perception. Correlations were made between the test scores before treatment and the reading-levels after a year of treatment.

Some Chilean researchers have shown interest in studying learning problems from the point of view of the Piagetian theory of development. One publication showed the relationship between functions basic to reading and the development of thought in Piaget's theories (Alvarez and Orellana 1979).

Clarke and Chadwick (1979) studied the differences in the concrete and operational aspects of thought in children with reading and math disabilities. They found that the children with reading disabilities had less-developed thought processes, according to the stages indicated by Piaget, in comparison with a control group.

Publications

Between 1970 and 1980 a number of publications that contain the results of research in the diagnosis and treatment of children with reading disabilities have been issued in Chile (Condemarín and Blomquist 1970; Bravo-Valdivieso 1972, 1974, 1980b). These reveal a growing interest both in research into the dyslexic disabilities using better empirical criteria and in the development of diagnostic and rehabilitative techniques. The principal limitation to this type of publication and investigation is the scarcity of original tests and teaching methods in the Spanish language, which in turn is due to the limited research funds and grants available.

Reading comprehension is a major problem in Chilean high schools. Condemarín (1980) proposed several strategies to improve the teaching of reading in order to increase comprehension. Bralic and colleagues (1978) have discussed early-childhood stimulation as a way of preventing learning disabilities in high-risk infants and young children with psychological or sociocultural forms of deprivation. Bravo-Valdivieso (1980a) examined the hypothesis that dyslexia is not a homogeneous syndrome but has several psychological concomitants. His results support this hypothesis, indicating that the dyslexias are a mixture of several types of reading disabilities. Another research team reported the same conclusions at the symposium on learning disabilities in Chile (Araya et al 1980).

In 1979 *Revista Latinoamericana de Psicología* published a special issue on educational psychology, containing several papers from Chile on learning disabilities. A symposium, "The Child with Learning Disabilities," was held in 1979 under the auspices of the Universidad Católica de Chile and UNICEF, and the papers were published by UNICEF in 1980. The symposium considered learning disabilities from sociocultural, psychological, and clinical viewpoints (Bravo-Valdivieso 1980b).

Conclusions

The psychological and educational problems of the children in the poverty subculture constitute the principal cause of general learning problems in an underdeveloped country such as Chile. In addition, specific learning disabilities are increased by the inadequate nutritional and health conditions of the majority of students, which adds to the risks of cerebral dysfunction and language and cognitive problems.

Since 1968 there has been a growing interest in diagnosis, treatment, and research in reading problems. One of the reasons for this interest is the high percentage of students who fail in the first few grades. Another cause of this interest is the small number of studies in learning disabilities and the scarcity of teaching methods for learning-disabled students in the Spanish language. The simple adaptation of tests and methods from English into Spanish has not been satisfactory, and original Chilean research has been required.

The work of the special-education program of the Universidad Católica of Santiago has had special relevance in the establishment of a national policy for special education. This policy has been principally directed toward the creation of diagnostic and rehabilitation centers for children with learning disabilities, as well as special groups within the regular schools and psychopedagogical support teams to assist teachers who have no specialized training.

References

Alvarez, A., and Orellana, E. 1979. Desarrollo de funciones básicas según la teoría de Jean Piaget. II parte. *Revista Latinoamericana Psicología.*

Alliende, F., Condemarín, M., and Chadwick, M. 1977. Dame la mano. Santiago: Editorial Magisterio Americano.

Araya, C., Lecaros, S., Sepúlveda, G. and Jofré, A. 1980. Enfloque Clínico y Psicopatología de la dislexia. In L. Bravo-Valdivieso (ed.), *El Niño con Dificultades para Aprender*. Santiago: UNICEF and Universidad Católica.

Barriga, E., et al. 1975. Diseño y aplicación experimental de un método de rehabilitación. Presented at "Symposium el Niño Limitado en Chile," Universidad Católica, Santiago, July.

Berdicewski, O., Milicic, N., and Orellana, E. 1977. Elaboración de normas para la prueba de Dislexia Específica de Condemarín-Blomquist. Escuela de Educación, Documento Estudio No. 41. Santiago: Universidad Católica.

Birch, H., and Gussow, J.B. 1973. *Niños en Desvetaja*. Buenos Aires: Eudeba.

Bralic S. and col. 1978. *Estimulación Temprana*. Santiago: UNICEF.

Bravo-Valdivieso, L. (ed.). 1972. Investigaciones sobre psicopedagogía y psicopathología infantil. *Anales Escuela de Educación*. Santiago: Universidad Católica.

———. (ed.). 1973. *Trastornos de Aprendizaje y de la Conducta Escolar* (3rd ed., 1980). Santiago: Nueva Universidad.

———. (ed.). 1974. Educación especial y psicopedagogía. *Anales Escuela de Educación*. Santiago: Universidad Católica.

———. 1975. Los niños limitados y nuestro sistema escolar. Presented at "Symposium el Niño Limitado en Chile," Universidad Católica, Santiago, July.

———. 1980a. Aportes a la psicopatología del fenómeno disléxico, *Revista Chilena de Psicología* 3:27-35.

———. (ed.) 1980b. *El Niño con Dificultades para Aprender* (papers from symposium, "The Child with Learning Disabilities," March 1979). Santiago: UNICEF and Universidad Católica.

Bravo-Valdivieso, L., Alvarez, A., and Haeussler, I. 1979. Factores Psicológicos que inciden en el pronóstico de la rehabilitación de los dislexios. *Revista Latinoamericana Psicología.*

Bravo-Valdivieso, L., Moya, J., and Salas, S. 1975. La madurez para iniciar los estudios básicos en dos grupos socioculturales. Presented at "Symposium el Niño Limitado en Chile," Santiago, Universidad Católica, July.

Clarke, N., and Chadwick, M. 1979. Análisis de algunos aspectos operativos y figurativos del pensamiento en niños con trastornos del aprendizaje escolar. *Revista Latinoamericana Psicología.*

Condemarín, M. 1980. Estrategias para el desarrollo de la comprensión lectora. In L. Bravo-Valdivieso (ed.), El Niño con Dificultades para Aprender. Santiago: UNICEF and Universidad Católica.

Condemarín, M., and Blomquist, 1970. *La Dislexia.* Santiago: Editorial Universitaria.

Condemarín, M., and Salas, S. 1975. Seguimiento de niños con trastornos de aprendizaje. Presented at "Symposium Psiquiatrie Infantil," Santiago: Colegio Médico, August.

Gazmuri, V., Milicic, N., and Schmidt, S. 1978. Prevalencia de retardo mental y evolución de rendimiento escolar en una muestro de 918 escolares del Gran Santiago. *Revista Chilena de Psicología* 1:57-64.

Milicic, N., and Berdicewski, O. 1976. Manual de Prueba de Funciones básicas para predecir rendimiento en lectura y escritura. Escuela Psicología. Santiago: Universidad Católica.

Olea, R. 1977. Batería de pueba de integración funcional cerebral básica. *Revista el Niño Limitado* (suplemento especial).

10 Preliminary Study of Reading Disability in the Republic of China

Wei-fan Kuo

Although the education of learning-disabled children has become a field within special education that has experienced the fastest growth and expansion in the English-speaking world during the last decade, most Chinese teachers are still unaware of the existence of such a problem. Only a few of them admit that they are troubled by the reading problems of their students. The terms *specific learning disabilties, minimal brain dysfunction,* and *reading disability* were introduced into the Republic of China (Taiwan) in the early 1970s and began to appear in local special-education literature. The arguments did not draw much attention from teachers, however, and consequently the discussion did not result in any investigation or in the establishment of any programs.

Ever since free basic education was extended from six to nine years in 1968, homogeneous-ability grouping has been widely practiced in Taiwan. Many efforts were made to develop diagnostic procedures and remedial programs for the lowest stream of junior high school students. Educational psychologists finally found that many students' academic failures could not be explained by either mental subnormality or sensory deficiency. Educators came to realize that learning handicaps were a nationwide problem that did not seem to fit into any of the existing categories of exceptional children.

The "Regulation Concerning the Expansion and Improvement of Special Education," issued in 1970, enumerates seven categories of exceptional children: the mentally retarded, the visually impaired, the hearing-impaired, the speech-disordered, the orthopedically handicapped, those with chronic diseases and delicate health, and the emotionally disturbed and behavior-disordered. An amendment in early 1977 added two new categories: the gifted and talented and the learning-handicapped. It appears that the term *learning-handicapped* does not correspond completely to the concept of learning disabilities in the English language. However, it designates a segment of the school-age population that is in obvious need of special education but with learning handicaps not included in the categories enumerated in the 1970 regulation.

Although no specific program has yet been designed for children with learning handicaps, school counselors with training in educational psychology are getting more and more involved in coping with the problem.

275

Also, the resource room was introduced in the junior high schools with a view to coping with the mild handicaps or learning problems of students. In teachers' colleges, educational diagnosis, learning disorders, and remedial teaching have become courses of study among the training programs for special-education teachers. Reading disability is discussed in the theoretical context, derived mostly from American reference sources. Professors as well as student-teachers raise such questions as, "Can we find dyslexic children in this country?" "Is reading disability a nationwide problem?" "What is the incidence of learning-disabled children and reading-disabled children in this country?"

In discussing "the rarity of reading disability in Japanese children," Kiyoshi Makita concluded that reading disability is more of a philological than a neuropsychiatric problem (Makita 1968). Makita assumed that the process of reading *kanji* script (Chinese characters) differs from reading a word in an alphabetical language because a symbol is grasped with the total perception of its figure at one sight, the perception being directly linked to the meaning represented by that symbol and the pronunciation being deduced from the comprehension of its meaning. In other words, Chinese characters are graphic, mostly derived from hieroglyphs. In reading Chinese characters, a total visual perception of the symbol is primarily connected with its meaning, and how it is pronounced becomes secondary.

Figure 10-1. Teacher and Student Working on Mouth Position, Using Illustrated Chart Made by Teacher

The study conducted by Kline and Lee (1972) with 277 Chinese children in Vancouver also demonstrated a low incidence of reading disability among Chinese children attributed to the multisensory training received in Chinese-language schools (see figures 10-1, 10-2, 10-3). The investigation found that surprisingly few Chinese children had difficulty with auditory-visual tests. The children doing well in Chinese were successful in rote memorization of the Chinese characters through the process of auditory-visual association, with multisensory reinforcement. Good eye-hand coordination is also required in forming Chinese characters. The research of Kline and Lee was in accord with the findings of Makita in the supposition that the problem of reading disabilities among Chinese children may be rare. This was an assumption worth investigating.

Method of Investigation

A questionnaire entitled "Inventory of Reading Disabilities in Primary School Students" was distributed to 209 teachers of third-, fourth-, and fifth grade classes from ten municipal schools in the Taipei area and 41

The teacher is giving individualized reading instruction, pointing to the phonic equivalent of each ideograph. Students at the tables are working on different aspects of the reading and writing lesson.

Figure 10-2. Teacher and Small Group

Note the carefully made materials.
Figure 10-3. Individual Lessons in Counting

teachers of the same grades from four public schools in the rural Hua-lien and I-lan areas. The investigation required the teachers to identify all the suspected reading-disabled pupils in their class according to twelve symptomatic traits, as enumerated in the inventory. For each of the suspected reading-disabled pupils, a referral form had to be filled out. In order to inform the teachers how to identify a reading-disabled pupil, teachers in each school were assembled for a discussion session, at which the background of the problem, the criteria of identification, and the behavioral characteristics of a reading-disabled pupil was explained. Questions raised by the teachers were answered after the presentation. The sessions generally lasted one hour.

Subjects

The target population of this study was 11,557 pupils in the Taipei area. Among them 5,909 were boys (51.1 percent) and 5,648 were girls (48.91 percent). In the rural areas of Hua-lien and I-lan, the target population was 1,962 pupils, of which 1,013 were boys (51.6 percent) and 949 were girls (48.4 percent). The distribution of these children, by region and grade-level is given in table 10-1.

Table 10-1
Target Population Distributed by Grade and Region

Grade	Taipei	Hua-lien & I-lan	Total
Third grade	3,600	577	4,177
Fourth grade	3,980	676	4,656
Fifth grade	3,977	709	4,686
Total	11,557	1,962	13,519

Criteria for Identifying Suspected Cases

In the instruction accompanying the inventory questionnaire, reading disability was defined as "concerned primarily with pupils of average or above average general intelligence, who do not show any sensory deficiency, but who are fairly retarded in reading and writing, and whose achievement in language studies is far behind their general academic achievement level." Based on the reference materials in which characteristics of specific learning disabilities and reading disabilities were reviewed, traits were enumerated as criteria and were explained as follows:

1. Confusion in writing: confusing the characters that look similar to one another and having difficulty in the task of visual discrimination.
2. Hesitation in reading: reading a text, word by word, and having difficulty in recognizing the characters, without any marked visual impairment.
3. Confusion in reading: substituting words frequently in oral reading and becoming confused when reading words that look similar to one another.
4. Poor visual memory: in copying a text, having to go back to the text and take a look every few seconds, and failing to remember a whole sentence.
5. Failure in dictation: being unable to take dictation and not succeeding in writing down a correct sentence.
6. Mirror writing: frequent occurrence of mirror writing, reversing either parts of the character or the entire character.
7. Awkwardness in motor activities: having jerky movements, poor balance, slow movements, general coordination deficits, difficulty with manipulation, and problems with finger dexterity.
8. Poor right-left orientation: becoming confused in distinguishing the right side from the left side, and having difficulties with spatial orientation.

9. Difficulty in rhythmic movements: being unable to keep pace with his group in rhythmic activity and appearing insensitive to auditory sequencing and temporal orientation.

10. Mistakes in oral input: being often confused by oral instructions of teachers, looking bewildered, and failing to comprehend the meanings of other people.

11. Disorders in attention: being distracted in the classroom and unable to concentrate on one thing.

12. Hyperactivity and irritability: being restless in the classroom setting and unable to sit still or to stand without wiggling or squirming, showing excessive reaction to stimuli.

Besides the basic information—the name of the teacher, the grade, the number of students in the class, and so forth—the teachers were asked the following in the questionnaire.

1. From your teaching experience, what do you think about the prevalence of reading-disabled children?

2. How many of your pupils write so poorly as to have difficulty in recognizing their characters and cannot make marked progress even with the diligent guidance and correction of their teacher?

3. How many of your students are left-handed?

4. Do you find any other reading problems that perplex you very much?

The following items were included in the referral form: date, school attended, grade, class, teacher's name, student's name, sex, date of birth, address, condition of health, intellectual status, academic achievement, general behavior, and finally the symptoms that might indicate a suspected case of reading disability.

Results

From the target population of 13,519 pupils from thirteen primary schools, 394 cases were referred by their teachers as suspected reading-disabled children. Since 250 teachers responded, fewer than two cases were found in each class, with a prevalence rate of 2.91 percent. It was surprising to find that many more boys than girls were referred. The prevalence rate was 4.44 percent for boys and 1.32 percent for girls. This was true in the Taipei sample as well as in the Hua-lien and I-lan samples (see table 10-2).

It was also remarkable that the incidence of suspected cases was higher in the rural areas than in the city (3.70 percent in Hua-lien and I-lan, 2.79 percent in Taipei). In both areas the incidence among girls was lower. We

Table 10-2
Number of Cases Identified and Prevalence

	Boys		Girls		Total	
Grade	Number of Cases Identified	Prevalence (%)	Number of Cases Identified	Prevalence (%)	Number of Cases Identified	Prevalence (%)
Third grade	126 (2,101)	6.00	40 (2,076)	1.93	166 (4,177)	3.97
Fourth grade	99 (2,441)	4.06	27 (2,215)	1.22	126 (4,656)	2.71
Fifth grade	82 (2,380)	3.45	20 (2,306)	0.87	102 (4,686)	2.18
Total	307 (6,922)	4.44	87 (6,597)	1.32	394 (13,519)	2.91

Numbers in parentheses are total populations.

also found that the incidence decreased in the higher grades. In Taipei, for example, the prevalence fell from 3.97 percent in the third grade to 2.64 percent in the fourth grade and 1.86 percent in the fifth grade. This tendency was true for both sexes (see table 10-3).

The distribution of the symptoms most frequently mentioned, in order of their frequency, was as follows: hesitation in reading, 237 cases; failure in dictation, 228 cases; disorders in attention, 224 cases; confusion in writing, 194 cases; confusion in reading, 130 cases; and poor visual memory, 119 cases.

The frequencies of the other six symptomatic traits were all less than 100. Half of the cases referred had two or three behavioral symptoms. A large number of pupils had three to five symptoms, and very few of the pupils had more than seven symptoms simultaneously (see table 10-4).

Concerning left-handedness, of the 206 teachers answering this question 155 (75.2 percent) mentioned that there were no left-handed writers in their

Table 10-3
Suspected Cases Distributed by Sex and Region

	Boys		Girls		Total	
Region	Number of Cases Identified	Prevalence (%)	Number of Cases Identified	Prevalence (%)	Number of Cases Identified	Prevalence (%)
Taipei	247 (5,909)	4.18	75 (5,648)	1.33	322 (11,557)	2.79
Hua-lien and I-lan	60 (1,013)	5.92	12 (949)	1.26	72 (1,962)	3.70

Numbers in parentheses are total populations.

Table 10-4
Number of Symptomatic Traits Appearing Simultaneously in Each Case

Number of Traits	Number of Cases
1	35
2	90
3	84
4	60
5	50
6	33
7	22
8	10
9	9
10	2

class. Forty teachers (19.4 percent) said that only one left-handed writer was found among their students (0.3 percent of pupils).

It is interesting to examine the impression of the primary teachers in regard to the severity of the reading-disability problems. More than two-thirds of the teachers estimated that the prevalence rate would be between 1 and 2 percent. Many even said that they were not conscious of the existence of any such problem.

Diagnosis of Suspected Cases

To verify the validity of the teachers' identification, twenty-seven cases that had been referred as highly suspected of having reading disabilties were selected from four schools in the Taipei area. These cases were examined by graduate students of special education who had some training in educational diagnosis and psychological measurement. Five subtests of the Wechsler Intelligence Scale for Children (WISC) and three other tests were administered to these suspected cases. The WISC subscales included Vocabulary, Digit-Span, Block-Design, Picture-Completion, and Coding. The other tests were the Bender Visual Motor Gestalt Test, the Zazzó Test des Deux Barrages (attention, visual perception, speed), and a Visual Perception Test (figure-ground discrimination and spatial relations).

The students who were assigned to examine the suspected cases were asked to judge both from their observations and from the results of testing. They also discussed their subjects with the teachers and consulted with the teaching staff for their opinions. Among the twenty-seven cases examined, twenty were boys. The distribution by sex was nearly proportional to that of the suspected cases identified by the teachers from the total target population. These children came mostly from families of lower socioeconomic status and had generally been deprived of adequate reading facilities at home. They had fewer contacts with their parents, who maintained long working hours outside of the home. Some of the students mentioned that they had to prepare dinner for the whole family and had to take care of their younger brothers and sisters after school.

It seems that the identification by the teachers was highly influenced by the interpersonal behaviors of the students in the classroom. Almost all these students were described by their teachers as distractible, hyperactive, or fatigued and some were labeled emotionally unstable. However, psychological measurements demonstrated that only three of them manifested symptoms of emotional disturbance. They also showed that the intellectual level of eight cases (30 percent) was below normal, with IQs approximately between 60 and 80.

Only eight of the twenty-seven students diagnosed, aged ten to thirteen years, could be confirmed as having a reading disability. All eight were boys. These reading-disabled children did very poorly on the Bender Visual Motor Gestalt Test (more than 3 points on the Koppitz scoring system), the Visual Perception Test, Zazzó's Test des Duex Barrages, and the Coding Subtest of the WISC. Their writing of Chinese characters was difficult to recognize. Also, three of them were highly suspected of having brain damage.

Discussion

When the term *learning-handicapped* was officially introduced into the Republic of China in 1977, it was supposed to designate a segment of the school-age population that had some specific learning difficulties but did not fit into any of the existing categories of exceptional children in need of special education. The reading-disabled children were usually referred to as one of the most important categories of the learning-handicapped by the professionals, although the problem of reading disability has not drawn adequate attention from teachers or the lay public.

This study was concerned primarily with those children who did not have marked general intellectual deficits but who were incompetent in their language studies and manifested certain associated characteristics of reading disability, as revealed by the American professional literature. Since terminological and semantic confusion still surrounds the term *reading disabilities* in the Western world, a vast number and variety of characteristics have been attributed to children labeled with this term. This study was obliged to assume arbitrarily a criterion scheme that consisted of twelve symptomatic traits most frequently cited by Western professionals. These traits may be divided into three types: (1) perceptual-motor deficits as revealed in writing and reading; (2) soft neurological signs, such as hyperactivity, distractibility, impulsivity, confusion in spatial orientation, and mirror writing; and (3) deficits in short-term memory.

The identification was made by teachers for whom some basic information about reading disabilities was provided. Although no reading tests had been taken to assess the reading-achievement level of the population, it was assumed that the teachers, most of whom had taught the pupils to be identified for more than two years, would be competent to evaluate the intellectual and reading levels of their students. The psychoeducational diagnosis of a small sample identified as highly suspected cases was helpful to verify the validity of the teachers' identifying procedure.

The results of this investigation demonstrate that reading disabilities are not a unitary phenomenon but rather include a heterogeneous group of children, with different categories of reading difficulties resulting from deficiencies in various psychological processes. It was also found that the linguistic factors involved in human information processing may contribute to the problem.

It has been emphasized ever since the term came to be used that learning disabilities are caused by organic factors, such as brain damage or minimal brain dysfunction, which may not specify actual tissue damage in the central nervous system. Although *dysfunction* does not refer to an irreversibility of the condition as *brain damage* might and thus reflects a softening of the neurological position, it still implies that the neuropsychological factor is the primary causative agent in reading disabilities. The author observes that constitutional and even hereditary factors may be involved in many cases of reading disabilities. The same soft neurological signs may also appear in normal children who do not show any difficulty in reading. This study tries to call attention to the fact that reading disability is not a unitary category. A number of environmental and cultural factors also play an etiological role in the problem. Among these factors, linguistic coding is particularly postulated as a contributing factor.

It is remarkable that the incidence of suspected cases decreases as the students' grade levels increase. This may imply that the reading-disabled can grow out of their symptoms. If reading disabilities were caused solely by a neuropsychological agent, it would not be possible to find such a distribution. The higher incidence in the rural areas also suggests that the problem may be relevant to socioeconomic status or to environmental deprivation as well as poor reading instruction in early school years.

The low incidence of suspected cases revealed by this study may be attributed to the educational level of the target population, which began in the third grade and had more than two years of reading experience. The statistics might be different if the investigated population ranged from the first to the third grade. Since many Chinese children start to learn to read as early as age four or five, it is reasonable to suppose that previous learning experiences in kindergarten and in the first two years of primary school help to alleviate the problem

If reading disabilities can be remedied through educational experiences, it is of doubtful value to advocate early identification. To identify a child with a potential learning problem before he is exposed to reading experiences could mean that the child might be negatively labeled, thus reducing teacher expectation and his chance for academic success before he can grow out of the problem.

The different rates of incidence between the two sexes seems to contradict the assumption made previously. A higher incidence among boys was found in this study and in many other surveys elsewhere. It was conventional to attribute this difference to genetic factors. However, the sexual difference may also be due to temperamental disposition and differential social expectations for academic achievement rather than hereditary attributes. Boys tend to be more responsive to physical activities and thus are more vulnerable to inattention. In some countries, such as in Taiwan, many parents and teachers are more tolerant toward scholastic failures of girls than of boys.

Philological differences could be interpreted as a contributing factor in reading disabilities. The process of reading Chinese characters differs from that of reading words in alphabetical languages such as English. A Chinese character is totally perceived as a figure, with its meaning being grasped at once and its pronunciation deduced from the comprehension of the symbol. In reading an English word, the visual perception of a symbol is primarily connected with its pronunciation, and its meaning is derived from auditory decoding.

Considerable evidence indicates that, when an English-speaking subject is presented with visual stimuli, he codes them auditorily and not in a visual form. This is not the case for a Chinese-speaking or Japanese-speaking subject, who usually codes visually. A Chinese reader understands many more characters than he can pronounce. In many cases words and phrases can be easily read and comprehended without bothering to think about how to pronounce them. It is also observed that Chinese words are encoded visually, while in English reading the items in immediate memory are related to the spoken representation. It often happens that the sounds *v, z,* and *b,* which are easily confused auditorily, are also confusing in visual presentation such as writing. One tends to claim that the errors made in short-term memory of verbal items are usually concerned with auditory confusion, when letters sound alike but do not look alike. Thus acoustic similarity of items is more likely to produce interference in short-term tasks, whereas semantic similarity leads to marked interference in long-term tasks.

Turnage and McGinnies (1973) remarked that immediate serial recall for verbal items varying in meaning was facilitated with visual input for Chinese subjects but with auditory input for their American counterparts. Because the linguistic background of the subject may influence coding, it can be expected that the corresponding coding patterns affect the reading task.

A comprehensive look at the Chinese language will indicate that each Chinese character constitutes an integrated unit. Each character is composed of two or three pictorial segments that represent a semantic meaning. Visually, each word also represents a gestalt and can be recognized as a whole even if its physical details may not be discriminated. Each Chinese character is by itself a phonological unit, since each character has one syllable. With such distinctive features, Chinese words are high in discriminatory power. It is also suggested that Chinese characters, being based on hieroglyphics, have a high image-arousing value. That is why Chinese characters, so complicated to those who cannot read them, are easy for a native speaker to decode.

Conclusion

The investigation reported here indicates that Chinese children seldom have problems of reading disabilities. It was also found that primary-school teachers in Taiwan are unaware of the existence of such an issue. When the characteristics of reading disabilties were explained to them, they remarked that only a very limited number of their students fell into such a category of exceptionality.

Three hundred ninety-four children from the third to the fifth grades were referred by their teachers as suspected cases, with a prevalence rate of 2.91 percent. Three times more boys than girls were referred. The incidence of suspected cases was remarkably higher in schools in rural areas than in municipal schools. It was also found that the incidence decreased inversely with grade-level.

Rather than considering reading disability a category of exceptionality, this study tends to consider it as a behavioral concept that relates to information processing. Reading disabilities may or may not be caused by some kind of damage or dysfunction in the central nervous system, but they can also result from deficiencies in encoding and retrieving processes, environmental deprivation, and emotional handicaps.

The author supports the philological assumption derived from the similar investigation carried out in Japan by Makita (1968) as well as from the research conducted by Kline and Lee (1972) with Chinese children in Vancouver. It is supposed that reading disability is also a philological problem in the sense that the linguistic background of children may influence the coding process in reading and thus contribute to the problem. The rarity of

the problem of reading disabilities among Chinese children may be explained by the fact that Chinese students are more familiar with visual-coding
processes and image-arousing tasks than their American counterparts
because of previous multisensory training, received in Chinese-language
school.

Of great significance are the physical attributes of Chinese characters.
Each word is a distinctive unit semantically, phonologically, and visually.
Each character becomes a perceptual gestalt ready for dual coding; that is,
the semantic component is registered simultaneously with the iconic component, while acoustic information is left behind. Considerable evidence indicates that for an English-speaking reader to whom visual information is
presented, coding is auditory and the semantic meaning is derived from
echoic storage.

The different coding mechanisms of the English and Chinese languages
still remain at the level of assumptions. However, it is worthwhile to con-
ceive of reading disabilities as a philological problem from the aspect of
human information-processing.

References

Kline, C.L., and Lee, N. 1972. A transcultural study of dyslexia: analysis of
    language disabilities in 277 Chinese children simultaneously learn-
    ing to read and write in English and Chinese. *Journal of Special
    Education* 6:1.

Makita, K. 1968. The rarity of reading disability in Japanese children. *Jour-
    nal of Orthopsychiatry* 38:4.

Turnage, T.W., and McGinnies, E. 1973. A cross-cultural comparison of
    the effects of presentation mode and meaningfulness in short-term
    recall. *Journal of Psychology* 86.

Education and Learning to Read in Ethiopia

Dartha F. Starr and
Fay H. Starr

Background Information

This chapter discusses Ethiopian culture and those variables that appear to have had a profound effect upon the emerging educational system. More specifically, it deals with the interaction of psycho-social-political-religious variables as they apply to learning to read and to other aspects of the educational processes in Ethiopia. The discussion is based on first-hand experiences in Ethiopia (1973-1975), observations and writings of others, and follow-up information covering the period 1975-1978.

Geographical Information

Ethiopia lies on the horn of East Africa and is bordered by the Red Sea on the northeast, by the Afars Territory and Somalia on the southeast, by Kenya on the south, and by Sudan on the west. Ethiopia is about the size of Arkansas, Louisiana, Oklahoma, and Texas combined. The land formation varies from below sea level to high plateaus and formidable mountain ranges. Agricultural experts have identified more than 100 microagricultural climates in the country. The proximity to the equator plus the high plateau results in a delightful springlike climate the year round for much of the country. Addis Ababa, the capital, varies in altitude from 7,200 to 8,500 feet from one side of the city to the other.

A number of variables are known to have contributed to Ethiopia's more than 4,000 years of independence, including (1) the unique land formation, which discouraged invaders and at the same time encouraged isolationism, tribalism, and a proliferation of languages; (2) an apparent lack of abundant natural resources, which also helped keep out the exploiting foreigners; (3) an intriguing intermix of tribalism and nationalism, fostered in the past by a feudal system in which tribal lords paid obeisance to the recognized king; and (4) a very strong religious force manifested in the Ethiopian Orthodox Church, which for centuries has maintained a reciprocal agreement of mutual support with various rulers.

There are more than seventy tribal languages in Ethiopia of Hamitic and Semitic origin. The variables already mentioned appear to have contributed to tribal isolationism and the proliferation of languages. (To illustrate the remoteness of rural Ethiopia, consider the plight of an American Peace Corps volunteer assigned to a remote post in southwestern Ethiopia. To reach his post, the volunteer rode a bus for eighteen hours and then walked or rode a mule for nine more days.)

The Preponderance of Oral Languages

The many languages of Ethiopia are oral, with the exception of five: the ancient church language Ge'ez (now confined to the church liturgy and used in the church schools), Arabic, Tigrinia, Galligna, and the national language, Amharic. The oral languages are of limited vocabulary, which directly affects the style and flexibility of thought and expression. The Amharic language was first declared to be the language of the court in 1270 A.D. and subsequently was chosen as the national language. Amharic is the language of the Amhara tribe, which ruled the nation for centuries until the cultural revolution that began in 1974. The Amhara tribe numbers about 2.7 million in a nation of 27 million people. The Galla tribe is much more numerous (about 16 million).

The literacy rate in Ethiopia is about 10 percent, but the literate are not necessarily from the Amhara tribe. The literacy rate is more nearly related to the 10 percent urban population, although this too could be misleading.

The Ministry of Education

The Ministry of Education was established in 1927, but its powers were virtually limited to the capital (Addis Ababa) until 1943, at which time the power of regional lords had been greatly diminished as a result of the Italian occupation (1935-1943) and the effects of World War II. With the resumption of power by Emperor Haile Selassie I, English was selected as the language of business and communication with the outside world. Thus Amharic, as the national language, is the language of instruction for grades one through six and English is the language of instruction beyond grade six.

Enrollment of Pupils in School

By U.S. standards only about 10 percent of school-age children are enrolled in schools of any kind. Thousands never enter school at all, as relatively few girls are encouraged or permitted to attend school, children are needed at home to help eke out a meager living, or there are no schools available where they live.

Of those who begin school in Ethiopia, thousands are eliminated from the system because parents cannot afford the monthly tuition or because of their failure to pass the national examinations at grades six (Amharic), eight (English), or twelve (English). Educational resources have been limited largely to urban areas, hence the government schools are too few and are unequally distributed throughout the country. Even in the cities, thousands of children are turned away because of limited space.

Educational Paradox

The selection criteria for admission to a government school presents an educational paradox. Ordinarily, we consider school as the place where one goes to learn to read and write, but in Ethiopia those likely to be selected to attend the government schools must first demonstrate their ability to read Amharic. This seems less strange when we realize that a similar procedure has been used by schools operated by foreigners in Ethiopia. For example, the American Community School was given property with the proviso that tuition-free scholarships be offered to Ethiopian children. Similar agreements have been made with operators of English, French, German, and other schools. The Ethiopian children who have received the scholarships invariably already speak the language that is used in the particular school. Thus the directors of all schools, including the government schools, have applied a criterion that is likely to assure success in school.

Sources of Initial Instruction in Reading

Since the child must know how to read Amharic before entering the government school, we must look elsewhere for the initial acquisition of reading and writing skills. A variety of schools in Ethiopia provide opportunity for learning to read and write, including the church schools operated by the Ethiopian Orthodox Church, Koran schools operated by Ethiopian Muslims, foreign private schools (for example, American, English, French, German), missionary schools operated by various foreign religious organizations, and Ethiopian private schools. For learning the Amharic alphabet, the church schools and the Ethiopian private schools are the most important.

Church Schools. The church school may have begun as early as the fifth century A.D. With territorial expansion and the growth of the church toward the south and southwest, churches and monasteries became important learning centers, each with a school. In their present form, the schools date from the golden era of the church (thirteenth to sixteenth century). The main goal of the church school has been to glorify the church through the ancient literature of the church and the bible. The literature and portions of scripture are written in Ge'ez, which is no longer spoken outside of the church liturgy. The church considers Ge'ez to be God's own language; thus the worshipper is expected to utter prayers and to speak to God in His language. Reading for personal understanding is of little importance, since to read God's language or to utter prayers in Ge'ez is to be in communication with Him. Therefore, it is essential that the church teach the Ge'ez language to its adherents. The primary level of the church school is called the House of Reading and the process by which Ge'ez is taught is analogous to an American "reading" a French newspaper with no formal instruction in the French language.

Historically, the curriculum of the House of Reading has been limited to the teaching of Ge'ez. Fortunately, most of the Ge'ez syllabary is also found in the Amharic script. In recent years some of the church schools have followed their teaching of Ge'ez (with little or no meaning to the child) with the Amharic language (with meaning and understanding). In many cases the learner's first language is likely to be something other than Amharic, which further complicates the process of learning to read and write.

Theoretically, children from any ethnic group may attend the church schools, but until recently nonmembers have been reluctant to send their children to the Ethiopian Orthodox Church schools because of the religious doctrine. Now the church school is viewed by many as the best way to secure admission into the government schools, and even Muslims now send their children to the House of Reading for the purpose of learning the Amharic syllabary. In so doing, their children first learn the Ge'ez syllabary along with all the others.

Ge'ez is thus the first language of instruction in initiating the reading process in the church schools. Children used to carry a rolled parchment containing the many syllables, each with its seven orders. The parchment was unrolled to the section to be memorized. The seven orders correspond to the vowel sounds, which are indicated by marks added to the base symbol in various ways and positions. The base syllable is a consonant accompanied by a schwa (a) sound except for the four *h* base syllables, which are followed by an *aw*. Using Latin letters, the first three syllables with their sets of orders would be pronounced as follows:

haw hoo hee haw hā   hŏe hō
la   loo lee lah lā   lŏe lō
haw hoo hee hah hā   hŏe hō

The church school is usually a one-teacher school taught by a priest or a church-educated layman. Most teachers use either a large printed chart or a chalkboard. The teacher points to a symbol and voices the sound. The children quickly join in. At first, each syllable is pronounced with its seven variations, then the next, and so on. The sequence is used to establish a left-to-right, top-to-bottom eye-movement pattern.

Some children memorize the entire sound sequence without being able to visually discriminate among the various syllables. In order to firmly establish the sound-symbol relationship, the teacher then begins to randomly select symbols for the children to vocalize. Individualized instruction consists of having each child point to symbols on his own practice sheet and vocalize each one in a loud voice. After weeks or months have passed and the child has mastered the entire system, a Ge'ez text is provided. The most commonly used initial text is the First Epistle of John.

Reading begins by having the child sound each syllable of the first word, pointing at each syllable symbol with a finger or straw. The pronunciation exercise is repeated until the teacher decides that the child has mastered the syllables in the word. After sounding out the remainder of the test for several days, the child is taught to read in phrases, pauses, intonation, and with proper pronunciation, all without understanding. No writing of Ge'ez is practiced, because the language is no longer used outside of prayers and the church liturgy. Children are expected to read well orally, especially the boys, since many of them will later become readers, deacons, or priests in the church. The natural outcome of the process is a lack of motivation and curiosity about the teachings of the church.

The transition from Ge'ez to Amharic symbols is relatively easy, since most of the syllables are common to both languages. In fact, Amharic is written with the Ge'ez syllabary, augmented by a few symbols for syllables that occur in Amharic but not in Ge'ez (characters for š, c, ñ, z, v, and so on). Two of the characters represent vowel sounds; otherwise all characters represent a syllable (a consonant plus a specific vowel). The order is left to right, top to bottom. Each syllable character has seven forms, traditionally called orders, to correspond with the vowels. The Amharic syllabary is presented in figure 11-1.

By the time children have mastered visual and auditory discrimination of the complete Ge'ez syllabary, they can be introduced to Amharic and are able immediately to sound out most words. Word meanings are then

	I /gı'ız/	II /kə ıb/	III /salıs/	IV /rabı/	V /hamıs/	VI /sadıs/	VII /sabı/
1.	ሀ ha	ሁ hu	ሂ hi	ሃ ha	ሄ he	ህ hı	ሆ ho
2.	ለ lə	ሉ lu	ሊ li	ላ la	ሌ le	ል lı	ሎ lo
3.	ሐ ha	ሑ hu	ሒ hi	ሓ ha	ሔ he	ሕ hı	ሖ ho
4.	መ mə	ሙ mu	ሚ mi	ማ ma	ሜ me	ም mı	ሞ mo
5.	ሠ sə	ሡ su	ሢ si	ሣ sa	ሤ se	ሥ sı	ሦ so
6.	ረ rə	ሩ ru	ሪ ri	ራ ra	ሬ re	ር rı	ሮ ro
7.	ሰ sə	ሱ su	ሲ si	ሳ sa	ሴ se	ስ sı	ሶ so
8.	ሸ šə	ሹ šu	ሺ ši	ሻ ša	ሼ še	ሽ šı	ሾ šo
9.	ቀ Kə	ቁ Ku	ቂ Ki	ቃ Ka	ቄ Ke	ቅ Kı	ቆ Ko
10.	በ bə	ቡ bu	ቢ bi	ባ ba	ቤ be	ብ bı	ቦ bo
11.	ተ tə	ቱ tu	ቲ ti	ታ ta	ቴ te	ት tı	ቶ to
12.	ቸ čə	ቹ ču	ቺ či	ቻ ča	ቼ če	ች čı	ቾ čo
13.	ኀ ha	ኁ hu	ኂ hi	ኃ ha	ኄ he	ኅ hı	ኆ ho
14.	ነ nə	ኑ nu	ኒ ni	ና na	ኔ ne	ን nı	ኖ no
15.	ኘ ñə	ኙ ñu	ኚ ñi	ኛ ña	ኜ ñe	ኝ ñı	ኞ ño
16.	አ a	ኡ u	ኢ i	ኣ a	ኤ e	እ ı	ኦ o
17.	ከ kə	ኩ ku	ኪ ki	ካ ka	ኬ ke	ክ kı	ኮ ko
18.	ኸ hə	ኹ hu	ኺ hi	ኻ ha	ኼ he	ኽ hı	ኾ ho
19.	ወ wə	ዉ wu	ዊ wi	ዋ wa	ዌ we	ው wı	ዎ wo
20.	ዐ a	ዑ u	ዒ i	ዓ a	ዔ e	ዕ ı	ዖ o
21.	ዘ zə	ዙ zu	ዚ zi	ዛ za	ዜ ze	ዝ zı	ዞ zo
22.	ዠ žə	ዡ žu	ዢ ži	ዣ ža	ዤ že	ዥ žı	ዦ žo
23.	የ yə	ዩ yu	ዪ yi	ያ ya	ዬ ye	ይ yı	ዮ yo
24.	ደ də	ዱ du	ዲ di	ዳ da	ዴ de	ድ dı	ዶ do
25.	ጀ jə	ጁ ju	ጂ ji	ጃ ja	ጄ je	ጅ jı	ጆ jo
26.	ገ gə	ጉ gu	ጊ gi	ጋ ga	ጌ ge	ግ gı	ጎ go
27.	ጠ Tə	ጡ Tu	ጢ Ti	ጣ Ta	ጤ Te	ጥ Tı	ጦ To
28.	ጨ Cə	ጩ Cu	ጪ Ci	ጫ Ca	ጬ Ce	ጭ Cı	ጮ Co
29.	ጰ Pə	ጱ Pu	ጲ Pi	ጳ Pa	ጴ Pe	ጵ Pı	ጶ Po
30.	ጸ Sə	ጹ Su	ጺ Si	ጻ Sa	ጼ Se	ጽ Sı	ጾ So
31.	ፀ Sə	ፁ Su	ፂ Si	ፃ Sa	ፄ Se	ፅ Sı	ፆ Sə
32.	ፈ fə	ፉ fu	ፊ fi	ፋ fa	ፌ fe	ፍ fı	ፎ fo
33.	ፐ pə	ፑ pu	ፒ pi	ፓ pa	ፔ pe	ፕ pı	ፖ po

The pronunciation aids are for the benefit of the English reader.

Figure 11-1. The Amharic Syllabary

given to the children in their own language, although this can occur only if the teacher speaks the tribal language of the children being taught. The writing of the Amharic syllabary is introduced simultaneously with the beginning of reading and understanding of the Amharic language.

Ethiopian linguists have proposed reducing the more than 231 syllable symbols (33 × 7 orders), since there are some that are rarely used or are considered to be duplications of others. Ge'ez and Amharic are both phonetic, thus to name the syllable symbol is to utter its sound. Today, the complete Amharic syllabary is printed on a single sheet of paper, which the children purchase.

As the central government has applied increasing pressure for Ethiopians to learn Amharic, and as government schools have become more numerous, the church-school curriculum has begun to change. In the more progressive church schools there is greater emphasis on learning Amharic. As a result, catechisms and religious texts are presented in Amharic rather than in Ge'ez. In addition, well-educated members of the Ethiopian Orthodox Church have greatly influenced the religious leaders in urban areas to experiment with a new curriculum. In 1975, for instance, 150 church schools were following the curriculum of the government schools but were also providing initial instruction in learning to read and write. These schools also provided some religious instruction, but the Ge'ez language was de-emphasized. At long last, the church schools are in transition, with an emerging dual role of providing secular as well as religious education.

The Koran Schools. About 35 percent of the Ethiopian population is Muslim, and for Muslims Arabic is the holy language of Allah. According to the Muslim view, Allah dictated the Koran in Arabic before the creation to be delivered to Mohammed in due time. With few exceptions, however, Arabic is a foreign language for Ethiopians. In several areas of Ethiopia, Arabic has continued to be the language of commerce, as it has been for centuries. In the Muslim urban areas, Arabic is used for bookkeeping and contracts. All Muslim worshippers are expected to learn to read Arabic in order to read the Koran. The Koran schools are operated by Muslims at primary, elementary, and secondary-school levels. The primary Koran school is similar to the House of Reading operated by the Ethiopian Orthodox Church, and instructional methods are very similar. Teachers in the Koran schools are either Arabs or Arab-educated Ethiopians (Dagne 1970).

The twenty-eight Arabic symbols are printed on a chalkboard or on a large chart. Each child has a copybook into which the alphabet symbols are to be copied. The teacher points to a symbol and calls out its name, and the children repeat the name. Each child points to a symbol copied into an exercise books, vocalizes the sound, and repeats the process until the entire alphabet has been memorized. Again, the child may memorize the complete sound sequence without being able to visually discriminate between one symbol and another.

Fifteen Arabic symbols have dots. Children learn the placement and sounds for the dots in a sequence spoken in their native language. The sequence may go like this: "Alif has none; ba has one below; ta has two above; tha has three above," and so on. Thus alif, ba, ta, and tha are written as ﺍ , ﺑ , ﺗ , and ﺛ , respectively. The letters and their sounds are practiced until they are memorized.

Four vowel marks and three symbols indicating elongated sounds are needed in order to read classical Arabic. Thus the consonants have seven variations. The long $\bar{a}$ sound is indicated by a slanted bar above the symbol. The child pronounces the name of each symbol, identifies the vowel sign, then pronounces the sound produced by the combination. The procedure is chanted in the native language of the child as follows, where ´ is pronounced long $\bar{a}$.

ﺑ	If ba has $\bar{a}$, I call it b$\bar{a}$
ﺗ	If ta has $\bar{a}$, I call it t$\bar{a}$
ﺛ	If tha has $\bar{a}$, I call it th$\bar{a}$

The long $\bar{e}$ sound is indicated by a slash mark below the symbol, and so on. When all the consonant and vowel sounds have been mastered and the child has demonstrated some skill in sound-symbol recognition, a beginning text is presented. Then, as in learning to read the Ge'ez symbols, the child vocalizes words with little or no understanding. Each symbol in a word is pronounced individually and then all together. Most teachers require the child to name the base symbol, identify the vowel mark, and then sound the combination for each symbol in the word. The teacher and pupil repeat the sounds until all symbols of the word have been pronounced.

Once the child has mastered all symbol variations, he begins copying the first chapter of the Koran into the exercise book and is expected to memorize it. Muslims are expected to read and memorize the entire Koran. Most children who attend the Koran schools memorize a few chapters and drop out of school. They sometimes quote memorized texts at funerals, but very few understand the message. Apparently, most Ethiopian children forget the Arabic alphabet after a few years.

A few of the Koran schools have begun following the government-school curriculum and now offer Arabic as a foreign language. Thus the children are introduced to both Amharic and Arabic as foreign languages in the first grade. English is usually introduced to children in the third or fourth grade in the government-school curriculum.

Private Schools. The typical Ethiopian private school is a primary school operated and taught by Ethiopians who have not finished high school. As

the desire for formal education has been fostered in the population, enter-
prising Ethiopians looking for a livelihood have partly filled the need for
teaching children the Amharic symbols so that they can be admitted into the
government school. The Ethiopian private schools flourished from World
War II until their nationalization in 1975, at which time the Ministry of
Education began to supervise their operation. In many instances teachers
with a fourth- or fifth-grade education were employed to teach the primary
grades. Private schools were financed by tuition at the rate of fifty cents per
month per child for grade one, one dollar per month for the second grade,
and so on. During the drought of 1974, few parents could pay tuition,
school directors could not pay teachers, and, in many instances, the schools
closed and the directors disappeared.

Some Ethiopian private schools operated with very high standards and
with well-trained teachers. In most instances, however, the methods
employed for teaching children were those mentioned in this report. At the
time of their nationalization in 1975, there were more than 200 private
schools in Addis Ababa alone, with hundreds more operating without any
charter from the Ministry of Education.

Other Schools. The mission schools are operated by foreign religious
groups granted permission to operate schools that follow the government
curriculum. In addition, the religious doctrine of the organization is taught
in areas designated as "open," where the Ethiopian Orthodox Church is
not numerically strong. Thousands of Ethiopians are grateful to the various
missions for their early education. Since few missionaries have mastered the
Amharic language, most mission schools employ as teachers those Ethiopians who have embraced the doctrine of the religious organization.
Amharic is taught in the mission schools in much the same manner as in the
church schools. Most of the missions supply Amharic Bibles, and the
Amharic language is taught, with emphasis on a personal understanding of
what is read. The foreign missionaries customarily teach their own languages in the schools as a foreign language, beginning with the first grade.

Adult Education. Everything that has been mentioned thus far about learning to read and write Amharic applies to adults as well as children. There is
always the possibility that adults of a particular tribe may know a few Amharic words or phrases, but the contracted form of Amharic street language
differs significantly from the formal Amharic of the printed page. Whether
it be with children or adults, where reading is taught without understanding,
as is typical for Ethiopians learning to read Ge'ez or Arabic, few learners
are likely to continue in school beyond a few weeks or months at best.

The educational system in Ethiopia is in a developmental stage, and
some necessary socioeconomic elements are lacking to give it vitality and

meaning. The presence of private and mission schools in rural Ethiopia since World War II has contributed to some of the current social problems. Teachers and missionaries portray literacy and education as a means to the good life—how else could such educational institutions flourish? The missionaries give emphasis to the good life through the acceptance of their religious doctrine and the customs of their own homelands. Few missionaries seem to realize the extent to which they inculcate the social values of their own countries and impose them upon their pupils. Inadvertently, many of the religious groups are giving credence to a popular attitude toward work in Ethiopia, which is set forth in the following Amharic proverb:

Work with hands—be a slave.

Work with mind—be a master. (Wagaw 1969)

Education and Social Problems

Thousands of young Ethiopians aged eight through eighteen roam the city streets with no place to sleep, without jobs, begging and seeking financial assistance by every conceivable means, including stealing. Most of these youths have had a few years of formal education and have run away from home, seeking a free education and a good-paying job. When asked about work, many of these youngsters respond, "I am a student." Their response is intended to convey the message, "I plan to work with my mind, not my hands." Some young men wear one extremely long fingernail, usually on the pinkie, to convey the same message.

Tourist organizations and foreign diplomats have complained to the Ethiopian government about the social blight caused by the thousands of street children. Most of the girls are not readily observable on the streets, since they wind up as prostitutes in the hundreds of "tea rooms" in the city. A 1974 study (Kebede, Starr, and Starr 1974) reported on interviews with more than 9,000 street children of Addis Ababa, but only 45 girls were included in that number because of the specific definition of *street children*. Although the girls are not readily visible, their plight is no less important. Most of these children of the streets had attended school for one or more years and had run away from home to avoid working in the fields or minding cattle and to seek the "good life" in the cities, which had been portrayed to them by their teachers. They were beggars or thieves; they sold candy, gum, or novelties on the streets; and they ran errands, or shined shoes. To further complicate matters, they had experienced the handling of money, and when asked if they would attend school if such could be arranged, most of them responded that they would do so but only if the government provided a cash allowance to be spent as they chose.

The presentation here is not intended to convey the thought that literacy and education are undesirable in a developing nation such as Ethiopia, but rather to give emphasis to the fact that literacy and education efforts will be less than successful unless certain socio-economic-political-religious elements keep pace. The work ethic, often mentioned as an important variable in the United States, is largely lacking in Ethiopia.

Special Education

The general attitude observed in Ethiopia toward those in need of special education is reminiscent of attitudes found in the United States thirty to forty years ago, which seemed to suggest that such children could not learn and that resources should be allocated toward the education of the able. The Ethiopian Education Sector Review adopted in 1973 was intended to outline the educational program for the balance of this century. We found only one sentence in that document pertaining to special education: "We have no plans to educate the handicapped." Taken at face value, the statement would suggest a lack of concern for the handicapped, but such is not the case. First, the government of Emperor Haile Selassie I had created the Rehabilitation Agency for the Disabled and had placed full responsibility for the training of the handicapped within that agency. Plans were being developed within that agency to train the handicapped for work in sheltered workshops. Second, it is our opinion that those who were responsible for preparing the Education Sector Review held the position reflected in a statement made by an Ethiopian university professor: "I appreciate your interest in the handicapped, but we do not have enough resources for the able. Therefore, the handicapped must wait."

Fortunately for the handicapped, at least, the new provisional government set aside the Education Sector Review and, after lengthy discussions, directed the Ministry of Education to set up a Department of Special Education. In making this decision, the government recognized the distinction to be made between education and rehabilitation. At approximately the same time, the provisional government approved the five-year plan of the Rehabilitation Agency for the Disabled, which included our recommendations for a number of diagnostic centers. The following is quoted from the five-year plan:

> Thus, unless the disabled are properly screened, and unless the type of rehabilitative service required for each individual is properly recognized, the chance for operating an effective program would be almost nil considering the following:
>
> a. The success of the Agency's fourth Five Year Plan will be contingent in part, upon the inclusion of a comprehensive diagnostic program which is broad enough to assess the skills and deficits that will be encountered in the 'intake' population. The diagnostic/prescriptive/treatment/education and training services planned for the Centers is nonexistent in Ethiopia at the present time. Therefore it is im-

perative that the Agency either develop and incorporate these services into the Centers or assist agencies such as the Ethiopian National Association for the Deaf in making such services available. Services are particularly needed for the mentally retarded, emotionally disturbed, and those who have hearing impairment.

b.   The success of future Five Year Plans of the Agency will be contingent in part, upon the early diagnosis, treatment, education and training of the handicapped. Within the Center, priority will be given to the urban beggars with various handicaps, but the diagnostic services will be available to other handicapped people. It is anticipated that the comprehensive diagnostic services will lead to new and improved educational and training programs, especially for the mentally handicapped, the emotionally disturbed, the hearing impaired, and those with impaired vision. For example, research studies indicate that about 80 percent of hearing impairment in school age children is of the type called "conductive loss." A high percentage of those with this type of loss can be helped by bone conduction hearing aids. The very early diagnosis (as early as 18 months of age), treatment, and fitting of a hearing aid (where applicable), followed by special auditory and speech training, will permit most of these impaired children to function as normal persons, thus eliminating the tremendous cost of rehabilitation if their needs are ignored until a later age. Also, the educable mentally handicapped, if diagnosed early, and if provided with appropriate educational opportunities, can achieve fourth or fifth grade schoolwork, and can perform a wide variety of meaningful and useful vocational skills (Kebede, Starr, and Starr 1973).

In conjunction with the fourth five-year plan of the Rehabilitation Agency, plans were formulated for the development of diagnostic and screening tests by psychologists at the National University. Such plans undoubtedly have been delayed. However, audiometric examinations are now offered in Addis Ababa, and the Ministry of Health, the Ministry of Education, and the Rehabilitation Agency announced the scheduled opening of a diagnostic center for the hearing impaired in September 1978.

Two schools for the visually impaired were operated for a number of years by the then-existing Haile Selassie I Foundation, with funds supplied by the emperor. At the present time, these schools are under the jurisdiction of the Ministry of Education. Also, three religious groups operated schools for the deaf, one in Kerens in the province of Eritrea and two in Addis Ababa. None of the religious groups provided professionally trained educators of the deaf, and until late 1974 the children were taught to read and write English or Swedish, whichever was the missionary's language. Sign language was taught with the Latin fingerspelling symbols. As a result, the children were not taught to read and write Amharic and there was no way that they could pass the national examination for the sixth grade. Since 1974, however, the Ministry of Education has taken a more active role, and Amharic is now being taught in these mission schools. The Ministry of

Education has announced plans for opening a government school for the hearing impaired in the near future.

Visits to Ethiopian Schools, 1973-1975

If you think learning to read English is difficult for children whose native language is English, consider the case of the Ethiopian student. The authors, while living in Ethiopia in 1973-1975, made a number of visits to elementary, junior high, secondary, and college classrooms in three different provinces of Ethiopia. These visits revealed the plight of the Ethiopian student who is seeking an education conducted in a language other than his mother tongue. In fact, English is often a third or fourth language for the Ethiopian student who lives in that nation of more than seventy different languages.

Background of Ethiopian Teachers of English

Most teachers who instruct the multilingual students of Ethiopia are handicapped by having a limited educational background for teaching subjects in the English language. As a result, secondary and college students plead for the teacher to provide mimeographed lecture notes or paraphrased passages from the textbooks. Since notetaking is very poorly executed by students, they rely heavily on visual learning and memorization.

Teachers who are unskilled in oral English are quite willing to accommodate the students' desires by providing simplified material. A common occurrence is for a teacher to fill the chalkboard with written notes while the students copy every word to take home for memorization. We observed classes even at the university level where there was very little oral communication between teacher and students or among students.

Textbooks

Until the change of government in 1974, textbooks for the seventh grade and beyond were published in the United States or England. The new government has issued directives to develop local textbooks, but the process of change is expected to be rather slow. Meanwhile, the texbooks depict cultures and subject matter with which the Ethiopian student is totally unfamiliar. The illustrations, subject matter, pictures, and examples are usually inappropriate for the Ethiopian context. For example, one young Ethiopian homemaking teacher was observed teaching a lesson on the sectioning of grapefruit. There it was in the textbook. But alas, neither the teacher nor the students had ever seen or heard of a grapefruit.

Reading-Levels of College Students

Reading-comprehension tests administered to students at the National University indicate a fifth-grade reading-level in English, based on U.S. norms. Using the same norms for interpreting the results of a similar test presented in Amharic, the same reading-level was obtained. When the time element is dropped from these tests, there is a marked improvement in grade-level equivalency. The university students are drawn from all fourteen provinces, which means that most of the seventy-plus oral languages of Ethiopia are represented in the university enrollment. Teshome Wagaw (1977), now at the University of Michigan, has stated that the limited vocabulary of the oral languages so consticts the flow of ideas that the transition to English by way of Amharic is difficult indeed.

Initial Steps in Learning to Read English

The school visits provided additional information concerning the initial steps used in learning to read English. Rote-memorization methods observed at upper grade-levels were also present at the third and fourth grades, when the English language is first introduced into the curriculum of the government schools. These methods include using alphabet charts, sounding the letters, writing words on the chalkboard, and then copying paragraphs from the chalkboard and writing from memory.

Educational Changes Introduced by the New Government in 1974

With the change of government in 1974 came intensified efforts aimed at encouraging the population to learn the national language, Amharic. The announced purpose of the attention given to Amharic was to reduce illiteracy and to unify the nation. However, the new government also reaffirmed the policy of retaining English as the language of business. Therefore, the educational system continues as a bilingual system of Amharic and English.

In order to prepare students for this language dichotomy, instruction begins with Amharic in grade one, and English is introduced as a foreign language in grade three or four. At grade seven, all instruction is in English, except for the continued study of Amharic. All sixth-grade students must take the national examination in the Amharic language. No further schooling is permitted in the government schools until the student has passed this examination.

The positions of the two languages are reversed beginning with the seventh grade. At the end of the eighth grade, a national examination is given in English, except for that part of the test covering the Amharic language. Again, no further education is permitted without the successful completion of the eighth-grade examination. Finally, to gain admittance to the university, students must successfully pass the school-leaving examination given at the close of the twelfth grade.

Updated Information on Learning to Read

In order to update information on learning to read English, seventy questionnaires were mailed to Addis Ababa in January 1977. By April 1977 fifty-four completed questionnaires had been returned. The respondents included 21 females and thirty-three males, ranging in age from thirteen to fifty years. Twenty-nine percent of the respondents were aged twenty or older. Five provinces were represented in the returned questionnaires. Respondents included students who had attended church schools, private schools, and mission schools.

Age-Range for First Instruction in English

The age-range for first instruction in English was from six to sixteen years for the total sample. Most students started English in grades two, three, or seven. Seventeen of the total sample attended government schools, twenty attended private schools, and ten attended mission schools. (It should also be reported that although the government curriculum provides for English instruction at the elementary-school level, this may or may not be the case in the nongovernment schools. In fact, in many nongovernment schools, no English instruction is provided. Even when English is taught, the quality of instruction is often substandard.)

Sequences of Reading Skills

The questionnaire provided a list of eight skills. Thirty-two of the respondents indicated that several of the skills were practiced and learned concurrently. According to the respondents, English instruction is likely to begin with the following sequence:

1. Memorize the twenty-six alphabet letters.
2. Memorize the sounds of the twenty-six letters.
3. Practice oral sounding of alphabet letters from a chart as the teacher points to the chart.

That list resembles mainstream American reading instruction prior to the advent of the sight-word method in the 1920s. The sounding of alphabet letters was typically followed by:

4. Memorize the whole word from lists of words copied from the chalkboard.
5. Memorize complete sentences copied from the chalkboard.

Thirty-eight respondents reported that they memorized mimeographed paragraphs and were trained to repeat the paragraphs orally and to write them from memory. A total of twenty-three respondents mentioned that conversational English was an important part of their instructional program. All but one respondent remembered the first reading book in English, and forty-seven liked the first book very much but complained about having to share the few copies with other students. There were few, if any, differences reported for the method of instruction, regardless of the age of the respondents (ages ranged rom 13 to 50 years).

The affective aspects of learning to read English were interesting. Most respondents indicated that they looked forward to English instruction and that learning English made them very happy. Some considered English difficult to learn and some found the study of English to be easy, reporting that they wanted more English books to read and wished that the teacher would move faster with the instruction.

Topics of Interest to Twelve-Year-Old Students

In answer to the question, "What was your main interest when you were twelve years of age?" there was no significant difference between the responses of females and males. Forty-one of the total sample indicated age-twelve interests to be science, sports, and medicine. Personal observations and numerous conversations with Ethiopians confirmed this. Visits to classrooms also indicated that students considered science classes to be exciting.

Any visitor to Ethiopia would soon observe the tremendous interest in sports. Even the poorest street boys band together, approach a foreigner, and offer ingenious reasons why he should become the "sponsor" of their sport club and purchase bright-colored shirts for their team. In exchange for sponsorship, the team will carry the donor's name to glory on the sports field. One such American, knowing full well the cost, said that he simply had to reward such ingenuity, and he bought shirts for fifteen boys.

Additional twelve-year-old interests included becoming musicians, engineers, teachers, traders, soldiers, and pilots. Two females indicated a desire to become nurses. A comparison of age-twelve interests and present accomplishments indicates that many have achieved their goals. Respondents included students, preachers, teachers, tradesmen, housewives and mothers, a nurse, and a college professor.

Respondents' Suggestions for Improving
Instruction in Reading English

Harris and Sipay (1975) and others have suggested that much insight can be gained into the teaching of reading to discouraged learners by simply asking the student what *he* thinks would help him to learn to read better. Toward this end, the following question was included in the questionnaire: "In your opinion, what changes do you think would improve instruction in the English language?" The respondents' suggestions could be derived from a modern textbook on how to teach reading. The responses mentioned most frequently were as follows

Learn the abc's.

Read posters, signs, names on buildings.

More oral language.

More listening skills.

More writing.

Many easy-reading books.

Read magazines and newspapers.

Less memorization.

Better teachers.

Best teachers at lower grades.

An explanation might be helpful in regard to the two items concerning teachers. Since much beginning instruction occurs in small, unaccredited private schools in Ethiopia, it is common for many such schools to employ teachers with only one or two years of education beyond the level at which they are assigned to teach. Hence, some teachers with a third- or fourth-grade education may be assigned by the school director to teach the first-grade children. One reason for such assignments is economic. The school director of the private school typically charges about fifty cents per month tuition for each first-grade child, one dollar per month for the second grade, and so on. Teachers are paid according to the level of instruction.

Conclusion

Suggestions from Ethiopian respondents indicate keen insight into some of the specifics that could improve the teaching of the English language in Ethiopia. It is hoped that some of these suggestions will be incorporated into the Ethiopian educational system. Anyone who plans to teach in Ethiopia, or in a country with a similar culture, might take note of the respondents' suggestions.

References

Dagne, H.G. 1970. Language Survey of Ethiopia: Part III, Language and Education in Ethiopia (mimeographed). Addis Ababa: Haile Selassie I University.

Harris, A.J., and Sipay, E.R. 1975. *How to Increase Reading Ability*. New York: McKay.

Kebede, K., Starr, F.H. and Starr, D.F. 1973. *Proposals for the Fouth Five Year Plan*. Addis Ababa: Ethiopian Government Rehabilitation Agency for the Disabled.

Kebede, K., Starr, F.H. and Starr, D.F. 1974. *Survey of Street Children in Addis Ababa*. Addis Ababa: Ethiopian Government Rehabilitation Agency for the Disabled.

Wagaw, T.W. 1969. Some Notes for the World of Work in Ethiopian Tradition (Mimeographed). Addis Ababa: Haile Selassie I University.

_____ . 1977. Personal communication.

12

Reading Disabilities in France

Badrig Mélékian

In France up to 15 percent of first-grade pupils repeat the grade, and at least 50 percent of fifth-graders have been repeaters. A good many repeat because they failed to master reading and spelling skills. Among 378 double-repeaters with a Wechsler Intelligence Scale for Children (WISC) IQ of 90 or higher, Debray and associates (1972) found that 70 percent were underachievers in reading (15 percent severe dyslexics).

There is general agreement that children with reading retardation form a heterogeneous group. A large proportion suffer from such adverse conditions as dullness, minor neurological or sensory deficiencies, emotional disturbances, and mild maturational lag. All these pupils might be classified in the category of simple, transient reading retardation, as opposed to the hard core of what is usually termed *specific dyslexia, developmental dyslexia,* or *true dyslexia.*

True dyslexics are a minority. Although they are like their nondyslexic classmates in other aspects, they display perennial inability to learn to read and spell. They appear to represent approximately 5 percent of the primary-school population in France, although there are no nationwide statistics on the subject. Those afflicted with the severest forms of dyslexia constitute a challenge to school and society. They are condemned to school failure and phobia, and ultimately to second-class professional and socioeconomic status, in spite of normal intelligence and extra-academic abilities.

As in other countries, the causes of true dyslexia are still the object of much controversy in France. Because of the multiplicity of possible underlying factors and their uncertain correlations with dyslexia, a wide variety of opinions obscure the issue (Colloque 1970). Most pediatricians and neurologists favor genetic or developmental theories, whereas educators, sociologists, psychologists, and psychiatrists usually emphasize environmental factors.

Linguistic Background

By tradition, reading and spelling have a prominent place in French primary and secondary curricula. In adult life one is often judged by his ability to spell correctly. Five to six years are supposed to be necessary for primary-school pupils to master written language. However, as mentioned previously, a good many pupils lag behind from the start and have to repeat, even if they are good at nonlinguistic subjects.

Written French, though phonetically less irrational than English, exhibits many pitfalls. According to Galifret-Granjon (1970), the difficulties stem from two main origins: grammar and homophony. French grammar is rather complicated, full of concordance rules and a wide variety of exceptions; verbs have at least five endings for each tense (as compared with two in English), most of them mute. Homophony is observed in many words and morphemes with a high frequency of occurrence, requiring separate spellings to avoid ambiguity. The following are examples of syllables that are pronounced in approximately the same way: *et* (and); *es, est* (thou art, he or she is); *ai, aie, aies, ait* (parts of the verb, "to have"); *hé!, eh!* (exclamations) *hais, hait* (I or thou hate, he or she hates); *haie* (hedge).

Educational Background

A high proportion of three- through six-year-old children attend kindergartens and nursery schools. During the last year of nursery school, many teachers manage to introduce elements of reading and writing. Compulsory education extends from six to sixteen years of age. Most children attend free schools (86 percent). Together, primary and secondary education span twelve years. The first grade is called *lleme,* and the two highest grades *premiere* (equivalent to the American twelveth grade) and *terminale* (first-year college).

Unfortunately, no systematic effort is made for early detection and remediation of reading disabilities. In theory, it behooves teachers to discover children with reading difficulties and bring them to the school doctor's or psychologist's attention. Actually, efficient early detection is hindered by many factors: overcrowded classes (thirty to thirty-five pupils); inexperienced teachers, ill prepared to understand learning and behavioral problems; frequent teacher changes because of illness or pregnancy; and too few and overworked school physicians and psychologists. When underachievers are at last recognized three to four years after beginning school, it is often too late; irreversible damage has been caused.

Some improvement has resulted from the creation, in recent years, of a corps of school psychologists and special educators. Their aim is the early detection of learning disabilities and behavioral problems and remediation whenever possible within the framework of the school. For the size of this task, this corps is still undermanned and of limited efficiency.

Once a pupil has proved unable to keep pace with his grade-level, three main solutions may be adopted. The first, to repeat the grade, is the simplest and hitherto most usual solution. The second solution is to be moved up in spite of the lag. This is often the case when the learning difficulties seem rather slight, in the hope that they will eventually smooth out with extra tuition. The third option is to go into a special class. These classes receive up to 8 percent of the school population. They must contain fewer than fifteen pupils, and they are the responsibility of experienced specialized teachers. Simultaneously, the pupils may get individual remediation, either at school or privately. These special classes were primarily intended for dull pupils (IQ less than 90). Actually, they have become a dumping-room for all kinds of backward pupils, such as children with emotional disturbances or with undiagnosed severe dyslexia. Prolonged failure, in spite of repeating or attending special classes, eventually leads to a fuller evaluation, which may uncover, among other disabilities, undiagnosed severe dyslexia.

Those children who are ultimately recognized as unable to pursue traditional curricula are shifted toward specialized institutions. New adjustment difficulties arise during the teens. In the past, when compulsory education extended only to twelve years of age, these children were not a lasting problem, since early apprenticeship or other training would quickly put them into the social stream, avoiding the frustration of prolonged school failure and the temptation of delinquency. Therefore, no real effort was made to analyze the causes of their difficulties. Nowadays, no teenager is allowed by law to get a job or have job-training before fifteen or sixteen years of age. In consequence, the cohort of retarded pupils has become a real challenge to all those concerned with their educational and behavioral problems. Special classes have been created for teenagers, as for younger pupils. Unfortunately, these classes have been created for moderate mental-deficients and have ultimately become an inadequate refuse dump for all kinds of backward pupils. A legal amendment lowering the age of entering job-training or half-time apprenticeship is much needed. It would certainly improve the fate of a great number of children with severe dyslexia who are unable to carry on secondary education and are at high risk of becoming juvenile delinquents.

Diagnosis

Learning disabilities reported by teachers can seldom be fully investigated within the framework of the school system. They are sent to pediatricians or psychiatrists in private practice, or to dispensaries or outpatient departments. The cost of these consultations is taken over by Social Security.

Besides a full medical, neurological, psychiatric, and genetic record, routine evaluation of reading problems includes IQ tests (usually WISC), reading and spelling tests, laterality-dominance tests, and spatial-orientation tests. If required, or in special research programs, a fuller evaluation would include audiometry, ophthalmological examination, electroencophalogram, projective tests (Children's Apperception Test, Rorschach), and so forth.

Half a dozen reading tests are available. Among them, two are well standardized: *L'alouette* (Lefavrais, 1967) and *Jeannot et Georges* (Hermabessiére and Sax 1972) (see figures 12-1 and 12-2). *L'alouette* evaluates the mastery of reading technique. Comprehension is not assessed. The score is based on a balanced combination of reading speed and number of errors. The yield is reading-level expressed in terms of a grade and age. Reading retardation is reckoned by substracting reading age from chronological age. This retardation is then interpreted in relation to the child's age; for example, a two-year retardation in an eight-year-old pupil means complete analphabetism and is much more serious than a similar two-year retardation in a twelve-year-old child. After the age of ten, the following criteria are accepted: a two-year retardation is labeled minor dyslexia, a three-year retardation is considered an average dyslexia, and four or more year's retardation is called major or severe dyslexia. The use of L'alouette has uncovered the existence of a wide range of reading ability (or disability) among French schoolchildren, ranging from super readers to the severest and most disabling forms of dyslexia. No significant correlation was found between the severity of dyslexia and IQ.

The *Jeannot et Georges* test is a newcomer. It evaluates both word-reading and comprehension. The results are given in quartiles of school grades. Unfortunately, the test has not been standardized for first-grade children. This is an important handicap in the assessment of children with severe dyslexia, since they are often unable to pass beyond the first-grade reading-level.

Spelling tests are not fully standardized. The most popular is Borel-Maisonny's dictations (Borel-Maisonny 1973). They give an approximate spelling-level and provide a basis for the qualitative study of the so-called typical dyslexic errors (inversions, confusions, additions, omissions). Spontaneous writing *(texte libre)* currently completes the assessment of dyslexics' spelling and may favorably replace it. Spontaneous writing provides useful material for the appreciation of the spontaneous language of these children and interesting clues to the dyslexic errors.

I have tried to find a simple quantitative method to assess spontaneous writings. From a preliminary study of various psycholinguistic variables, the orthographic quotient (OQ) has emerged as the most reliable and the easiest characteristic to compute (Mélékian 1977). Orthographic quotient is defined as the percentage of correctly spelled words in a spontaneous writing.

The child is asked to write freely about any subject he is interested in. Fifty to 150 words per text are deemed necessary. Some severely dyslexic children are unable to write more than 15 to 20 words per session without

L'alouette.

Sous la mousse ou sur le toit,
dans les haies vives ou le chêne fourchu,
le printemps a mis ses nids.
Le printemps a nids au bois.

Annie amie, du renouveau, c'est le doux temps.
Amie Annie, au bois joli gamine le pinson.
Dans les buis, gîte une biche, au bois chantant.
Annie, Annie! au doigt joli, une églantine laisse du sang :
au bout du temps des féeries viendra l'ennui.

L'alouette fait ses jeux; alouette fait un nœud avec un rien de paille.
L'hirondeau piaille sous la pente des bardeaux et, vif et gai, le geai
sur l'écaille argentée du bouleau, promène un brin d'osier.
Au verger, dans le soleil matinal, goutte une pompe dégelée.
On voit un bec luisant qui trille éperdument des notes claires
et, dans les pampres d'or que suspend la grille antique,
on surprend des rixes de moineaux.
Au potager s'alignent les cordeaux; l'if est triste à l'horizon
et lourd et lent l'envol des corbeaux.

Un lac étire ses calmes rives et, quand le soir descend,
le miroir de ses eaux reflète les poisons des brignoles perfides.
Et, quand descend le soir, quand joue la pourpre du couchant,
le ciel rougit ses eaux.
Dans la moire de l'eau danse l'ombre d'un écueil.
Tout est cris! Tout est bruits!

Une amarre est décochée... une barque est arrimée... des matelots
jettent leurs cassettes sur le rivage...
Tout est cris! Tout est bruits!
Au clair de la lune mon ami Pierrot...
Au clair de lune mon amie annie...
Au clair de la lune mon ami Pierrot, prête-moi la plume pour écrire un mot.

o u e i a

le la les un dans des do ti pu mi

The score is based on the number of errors made and the speed of reading. Norms convert the raw scores to age and grade-level scores. Reproduced with permission of Les Editions du Centre de Psychologie Appliquée.

Figure 12-1. *L'alouette*, a Standardized Oral Reading Test

undue fatigue. In that case, several written samples may be added together. Some writing is illegible, in which case the child is asked to read aloud what he has just written.

To compute the OQ the total number of words *(N)* is counted. Crossed-out words and the elements of compound words are counted as independent

This test evaluates both word knowledge and comprehension. Reproduced with permission of Les Editions du Centre de Psychologie Appliquée.

Figure 12-2. Illustration from *Jeannot et Georges*, a Standardized Reading Test

words (for example, doesn't = does not = two words, grandfather = two words). Then, in a similar fashion, the number of correctly spelled words *(n)* is counted. OQ = n/N x 100. Figure 12-3 provides an example of the computation.

The study of OQ was based on the spontaneous writings of thirty-one severely dyslexic children of normal intelligence (WISC Verbal or Performance IQ 90 or higher) aged 10 to 15.5 years. These children displayed three- to eight-year retardation in reading-age. Each child provided two to four writing samples. The statistical treatment of the data yielded two main conclusions:

1. The OQs of the individual samples were constant for each child within the limits of intraindividual random variability (*t*-test applied to the difference between proportions). This important finding allows several contemporary samples to be combined into a weighted OQ, a more accurate estimate than the OQ of individual tests. In the dyslexic group, the mean OQ was 49, ranging from 16 to 83, whereas normal schoolchildren in the same age-group scored between 90 and 100.

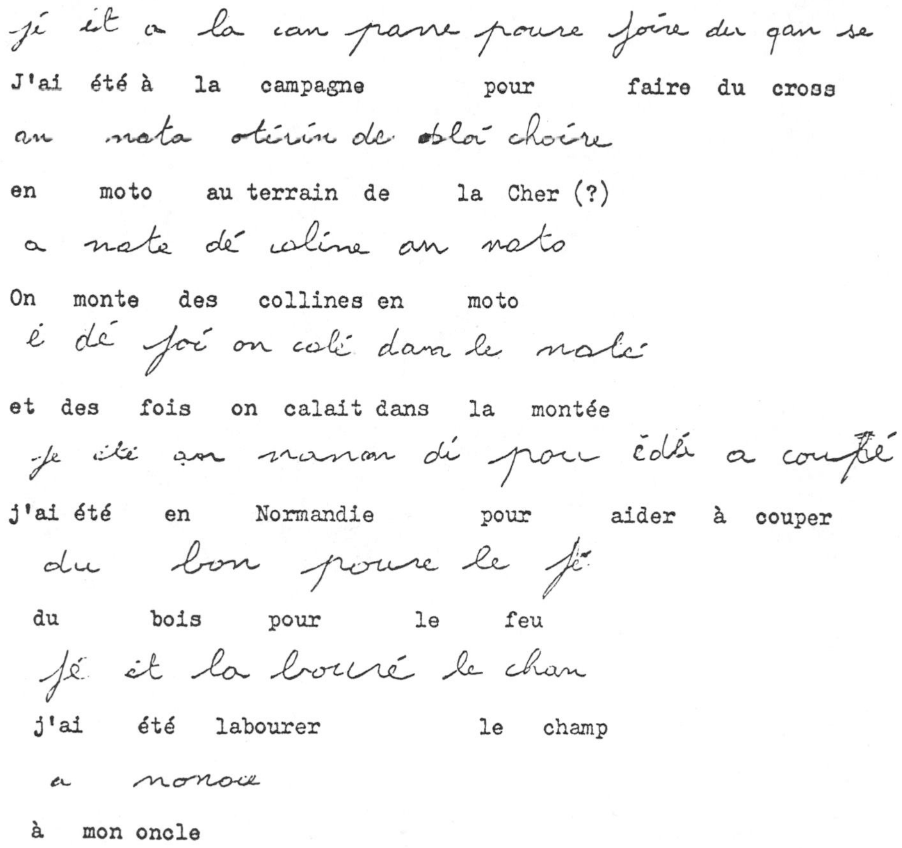

jé it a la can pame poure joie du gan se

J'ai été à la campagne pour faire du cross

an mota otirin de blai choire

en moto au terrain de la Cher (?)

a nate dé coline an moto

On monte des collines en moto

é dé joi on coli dam le male

et des fois on calait dans la montée

je ite an manan di pou édé a coupé

j'ai été en Normandie pour aider à couper

du bon poure le fé

du bois pour le feu

jé it la bouré le chan

j'ai été labourer le champ

a monoce

à mon oncle

$OQ = n/N \times 100$, where n is the number of correctly spelled words and N is the total number of words in a sample of spontaneous writing. This is a sample of writing from a fourteen-year-old dyslexic boy: WISC Verbal IQ 76, Performance IQ 91, Full-Scale IQ 82; reading-level (*l'alouette*) first grade (six years, nine months); OQ level, beginning first grade, in agreement with his reading-level ($OQ = 8/54 \times 100 = 15\%$).

Figure 12-3. Example of Orthographic Quotient (OQ) Computation

2. OQ correlates with reading-level as assessed by the *L'allouette* test. As shown in figure 12-4, there is a highly significant positive correlation between reading and spelling scores. ($r = .589$, P less than .001).

Thus OQ may be regarded as a measure of spelling skills, comparable to the reading-age provided by oral reading tests. Contrary to the reading test, however, OQ does not require any standardized material and may be repeated at will, the only limitation being the child's cooperation. I currently apply OQ to the diagnosis of dyslexia and the assessment of progress during remedial tuition.

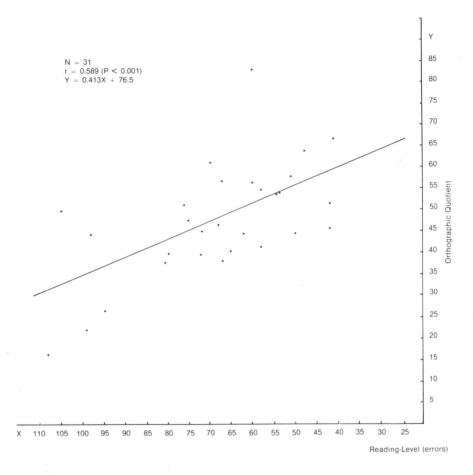

The reading-levels were assessed by the *L'allouette* test. The scores are expressed in terms of errors, that is, the more severe the dyslexia, the higher the score.

Figure 12-4. Correlation between Orthographic Quotient (OQ) and Reading-Level.

A further step in the study of OQ would be its assessment in normal school children. This would provide criteria allowing the use of OQ as an easy, quick, and inexpensive test for the early detection of reading and spelling disabilities in primary schools. A preliminary inquiry was conducted in two French primary schools in a residential middle-class area. The inquiry aimed at obtaining a rough estimate of normal criteria, without any claim to full standardization (author's unpublished data). The following approximate OQs (mean $\pm$ 1 standard deviation) may be helpful:

Second grade	60 ± 12
Third grade	70 ± 10
Fourth grade	80 ± 9
Fifth grade	90 ± 6

Reading and spelling evaluations are currently completed by the assessment of oral language (pronunciation, syntax, vocabulary) and other linguistic characteristics. To my knowledge, there does not exist, in France, fully standardized predictive batteries similar to those of de Hirsh and Jansky and others. Inizan's predictive battery (Inizan 1968) is actually intended for the early detection of reading difficulties during the first and the second grades in children who have already learned to read. A widely held opinion is that the prediction of reading disabilities is neither effective nor accurate before the children have actually been confronted with the task of learning to read and spell. Similarly, a firm diagnosis of developmental dyslexia is thought hazardous before the ages of seven to eight years. This belief is probably the most important factor, together with the nonavailability of reliable, predictive batteries, hampering early recognition and remediation of reading disabilities. To obviate this difficulty, some private schools returned to traditional alphabetic and phonetic reading methods and even made use of the remedial method by Borel-Maisonny (1973) routinely during the first grade.

Remediation

Specialized individual tuition is the main remedial method used widely throughout the country. Medications are scarcely used, unless it is necessary to alleviate associated troubles, such as behavior disorders or hyperactivity.

Individual tuition is given by language therapists with various backgrounds. Some are specialized teachers, psychologists, or physicians. The majority, however, have chosen language therapy as a profession and graduate after two to three years of theoretical education and practical work in outpatient clinics.

Private or public facilities are available in most urban areas. Some large school-groups have their own language therapists, who give remedial tuition in the school during school hours. Most dyslexics, however, have to go either to outpatient clinics or dispensaries or to language therapists in private practice. In all cases, the expenses are partly paid by social security. At least two sessions per week are deemed necessary, each tutorial session lasting from one-half to three-quarters of an hour. Fifty to one hundred sessions are a minimum requirement.

Methods of Remediation

Some psychiatrists use psychotherapy of Freudian inspiration as the sole remediation, under the pretense that most dyslexics exhibit emotional disorders. In my experience psychotherapy is very inefficient if it is not associated with specific language remediation.

The methods of language therapy used in France are various. They stem from two main approaches: Borel-Maisonny's (1973) phonetic and gestural method and Chassagny's (1962) method. Behind all these methods stand a few basic principles derived from the work of Samuel Orton (1937): (1) individual tuition should be adjusted to each case; (2) multisensory techniques are employed, aiming at the creation of strong associations between written symbols and spoken language; and (3) simplified teaching is used, in which each difficulty is treated until it is completely mastered. Borel-Maisonny's phonetic and gestural method is an analytical method (alphabetic and phonetic), as opposed to the whole-word methods widely used in primary schools. The association between written signs and spoken sounds is created with the aid of gestural (or kinesthetic) symbols. The method is best illustrated in Silvestre de Sacy's *Bien lire et aimer lire* (1965). Borel-Maisonny's method is rather rigid and technical, and it is well adapted to the initial steps of remediation in young children.

Chassagny's method is less rigid and is best adapted to children who have already acquired the rudiments of reading and have reached the stage when automatization becomes an essential prerequisite to the achievement of further progress. The method aims primarily at creating a good relationship between the teacher and the pupils. Through this relationship, the child is encouraged to communicate and gradually improve his own language. The two main principles of the method are learning word series and self-correction. Most speech therapists use both of these methods, alternately or in combination, usually supplementing them with a great deal of empiricism, know-how, and personal qualities.

Results of Remediation

Individual remediation restores moderate dyslexics to normal school life within one to several years, although they scarcely achieve good fluent reading and usually remain poor spellers. Remedial tuition fails conspicuously in children with severe dyslexia. These children set the most arduous and challenging problems for teachers, language therapists, psychologists, social workers, and psychiatrists. They are practically refractory to all available methods of language therapy and are unable to pursue ordinary school curricula. In the course of time they become increasingly frustrated by lasting academic failure and may develop school phobia, and they are at risk of becoming juvenile delinquents.

Nowadays in France very few special schools are available for major dyslexics. With Debray-Ritzen (Debray-Ritzen and Mélékian 1974), we had reached the conclusion that these unfortunate children are definitely maladapted to the ordinary school system and have to be freed from the imperialism of written language. This idea has been put into practice in an experimental center attended full-time by severely dyslexic children who failed in school in spite of remedial instruction or psychotherapy. The basic principle in this center is dual teaching, aiming to separate linguistic and nonlinguistic subjects completely. The latter are taught by specialized educators with the aid of audiovisual methods, thus avoiding the learning difficulties inherent in written language. In addition, language therapists give daily remedial tuition, individually and in small groups.

A follow-up study was made of thirty-seven children who attended this center between 1970 and 1975 (Mélékian and Lubet 1977). At admission these dyslexics were aged nine to fifteen years and had a mean reading retardation of 4.4 years. Half of them displayed behavioral disorders. Clearly these children were at great risk of becoming illiterates and juvenile delinquents, unable to acquire any work qualifications. After a mean attendance of 3.4 years, the outcome was very favorable. In spite of slow progress in reading and spelling skills, the general instructional level in nonlinguistic subjects reached or exceeded that of fifth grade, enabling 80 percent of the dyslexics to be accepted in vocational schools. At the same time, a very favorable improvement had taken place in their behavior ($p < .001$). This behavioral improvement is probably the most important single factor in the prevention of juvenile delinquency and the harmonious integration into social and vocational life. Comparison with the scanty, available data in the literature on the results of remediation tends to emphasize the importance of this dual teaching experience and the part audiovisual instruction should play in severe dyslexia.

Research

To my knowledge, there is no organized theoretical and experimental research on reading disabilities in France. Financial facilities and multidisciplinary cooperation, especially with teachers, are badly needed. Hitherto most work has aimed at the solution of practical problems: diagnostic tests, specialized tuition methods, and taking over of the finan cial burden of remediation by social security.

Isolated persons or organizations in France are striving, for the next stage, to promote theoretical research on such crucial aspects as memory, genetic and environmental factors, visual- and auditory-evoked potentials, hemispheric specialization, and predictive batteries.

References:

Borel-Maisonny, S. 1973. *Langage Oral et Écrit.* Neuchatel: Delachaux et Niestlé.
Chassagny, C. 1962. *Manuel pour Rééducation de la Lecture et de l'Orthographe.* Paris: Néret.
Colloque. 1970. *La Dyslexie en Question.* Paris: Armand Colin.
Debray, P., Viterbo, E., Bidault, H., Gensbittle, M., and Treca, M. 1972. Recherche par leximétrie de l'inaptitude à la lecture (dyslexie) chez 500 enfants double redoublants dy cycle élémentaire. In Entretiens de Bichat, *Chirurgie et Spécialités.* Paris: L'Expansion Scientifique.
Debray-Ritzen, P., and Mélékian, B., 1974. *La Dyslexie de l'Efant.* Paris: Casterman.
Galifret-Granjon, N. 1970. La langue écrite, objet de l'apprentissage. In Colloque, *La Dyslexie en Question.* Paris: Armand Colin.
Hermabessière, G., and Sax, H. 1972. *Epreuve de Lecture "Jeannot et Georges."* Paris: Centre de Psychologie Appliquée.
Inizan, A. 1968. *Le Temps d'Apprendre à Lire.* 5th ed. Paris: Armand Colin.
Lefavrais, P. 1967. *Le Test de L'Alouette.* Paris: Centre de Psychologie Appliquée.
Mélékian, B. 1977. Le Quotient Orthographique. Etude quantitative du texte libre des dyslexiques. *Archives Françaises de Pédiatrie* 33:263-276.
Mélékian, B., and Lubet, C. 1977. Le devénir des dyslexiques majeurs. *Archives, Françaises de Pédiatrie* 34:973-981.
Orton, S.T. 1937. *Reading, Writing and Speech Problems in Children.* New York: Norton.
Silvestre de Sacy, C. 1965. *Bien Lire et Aimer Lire. Vol. I: Méthode Phonétique et Gestuelle.* Paris: Editions Sociales Françaises.

13 Special Education in Greenland

Bent Wenstrup

Geography and Administration

Greenland is an island in the Arctic with a total area of 2,176,000 km² (840,000 mi²), of which 1,834,000 km² are covered by the ice cap. Thus, the ice-free part, consisting of the coastal area and the islands, contains 342,000 km², with a population of about 50,000 people. Greenland's dimensions are 2,670 km (1,670 miles) from north to south and 1,050 km (656 miles) from east to west, slightly larger in area than Alaska and Texas combined.

Geographically Greenland belongs to North America, but constitutionally it is a part of the Kingdom of Denmark. The Greenlandic population has a unique identity, which has its background partly in the Eskimo culture and an attachment to the Eskimo populations of Siberia, Alaska, and Canada and partly in several hundreds of years of contact with Europeans, especially Danes.

Administratively Greenland is split into three parts: Western Greenland (1977 population, 44,388), Eastern Greenland (3,086) and Northern Greenland (746). The East Greenlanders and the Polar Eskimos in the north are minority groups with their own distinctive cultures. Colonization in Western Greenland started in 1721. A mission and trading station were first founded in Eastern Greenland in 1894 and with the Polar Eskimos in 1909.

In 1953 Greenland's status as a colony was abolished, and the country became part of Denmark, with equal rights. Greenland has two representatives in the Danish parliament (Folketinget). The Greenlandic provincial council (landsrådet), the highest popularly elected assembly in Greenland, and the elected local councils have acquired further influence since 1953 and are responsible for a series of social and technical matters. A greater degree of political independence in the form of home rule is being planned.

Background of Education in Greenland

There is a long tradition for the education of teachers in Greenland. The teachers' college in Nuuk (Godthåb) was founded in 1845, and for many years the educational language was primarily Greenlandic. Today it is Danish, and Greenlandic is included as a subject. The education of teachers takes five years. In order to relieve the great lack of Greenlandic-speaking teachers in the past, a two-year program to teach a limited group of subjects

This chapter was translated by Mogens Jansen.

319

was established from 1973 to 1978. A few Greenlandic teachers are also educated in Denmark.

The first missionaries developed a method of writing based on the Eskimo dialect spoken around the middle of the west coast, where the Europeans first settled. Since then a single orthography has been developed for use in Greenland, without consideration of differences in dialect. Although this has created certain difficulties, especially in Eastern Greenland, where the language is most aberrant, it has been a great advantage to have a mutual orthography for the entire population in Greenland. However, for the time being, two orthographic systems are used in Greenland. The older generation uses a system created in the middle of the last century, whereas the children and the young people use a new and simpler system, which was introduced in the schools during the last few years.

Danish was made a compulsory subject in school in 1925, but as a rule the students had poor results because of a lack of teachers qualified in Danish and a lack of motivation. At the start of the reform period in 1950, Greenlandic politicians demanded that Danish be granted a more dominant position in school, to extend the students' horizons and to enable Greenlandic students to go through more advanced education in order to enable them to take positions occupied by Danes. With rising motivation among the pupils and an increased number of Danish teachers, the students' knowledge of Danish has improved considerably.

The situation is still far from satisfactory. The Danish teachers have been taught some Greenlandic, but only to a very limited extent, and few are able to carry on a simple conversation in Greenlandic. During the last few years there have not been sufficient educationally qualified people to occupy the vacant teaching positions, and one-third of the teachers have no real education. In 1977-1978, 531 of 1,021 educators in Greenlandic schools were estimated to be able to teach in Greenlandic.

In the school year 1977-1978, 13,700 Greenlanders attended school, 775 of these in Denmark. Some of the students in the voluntary classes after the seven compulsory years of school go to school in Denmark, mainly because there is a lack of teachers and school buildings in Greenland. Many Greenlandic schoolchildren spend some weeks or months in Denmark for combined vacation and schooling.

Many children of school-age from small places in Greenland attend boarding schools in towns. The attitude of Greenlandic politicians now is that, wherever possible, grades eight, nine, and ten should also be established in the hamlets in order to avoid alienating the older students from life in a hamlet. Experience shows that, after completing their education, many young people do not want to return to the hamlets. In those areas where seal-hunting plays an important role, the students are taught the technique of hunting, but otherwise education in school is not occupational.

At the start of the reform period in 1950 only a very small number of Greenlanders spoke enough Danish to be called bilingual. Today the young people know considerably more Danish than the older people, and Danish is generally spoken more frequently in towns than in hamlets. These differences are partly due to the educational system and partly to the fact that most of the Danes live in the towns, so the possibility of contacts with Danish-speaking people are better there.

The only institution in Greenland in which the Greenlandic language is clearly predominant is the church. Church in Greenland is part of the Danish Lutheran State Church and is served almost entirely by Greenlandic ministers and catechists. The church has taken the lead in recognizing the fact that Greenlandic needs can be complied with by means of a different sort of education than the one demanded in Denmark. To most Greenlanders, church, language, and ethnic identity are closely connected. This is reflected in the fact that the Greenlandic church employs a Greenlandic minister, who travels in Denmark to render services to about 3,000 to 4,000 Greenlanders.

There is an independent Greenlandic literature and a Greenlandic publishing firm. The Greenlandic authors—practically all of whom must also have other professions—are united in a Greenlandic authors' society. A selection of classics and modern literature has been translated into Greenlandic. In all towns and larger hamlets there are free libraries. However, an overwhelming proportion of the books in libraries are written in Danish.

Compared with other Eskimo peoples and other small language groups, the amount printed in Greenlandic may seem impressive. However, only a rather limited selection of reading material, especially professional literature, is accessible to those reading only Greenlandic.

Home Rule in Greenland

In 1978 a commission composed of Danish and Greenlandic politicians made a report proposing home rule in Greenland from 1 May 1979. The home-rule commission proposed that Greenlandic be the main language, because it is considered of vital importance in order to preserve and strengthen ethnic identity and to maintain the Greenlandic population's idea of itself as a nation. At the same time, it was proposed that education in Danish still be very thorough. Part of advanced education must still be expected to take place in Denmark. In official affairs an equality of languages was proposed so that, when contacting officials, every Greenlandic citizen could demand that communication take place in the language he wishes to use.

It is thus intended that Danish have a clear status as the first foreign language in Greenland's schools. The second foreign language will be English, which will be offered as a voluntary subject from grade six. This will make it easier to establish contact with the Eskimo minorities in Alaska and Canada.

During the last few years representatives of the Eskimo peoples have contacted each other on several occasions, and they have met at several seminars on education in the far north. They have expressed feelings of solidarity based on mutual backgrounds and the wish to cooperate in solving some of the problems the Eskimos have in common regarding education, political integrity, rights to resources of the sea and underground, protection of ecological values, language, and so forth.

Greenlanders form the largest group in the total of about 93,000 Eskimos living in the traditional Eskimo areas (Greenland, about 40,000; Canada, about 22,700; Alaska, about 28,000; Siberia, about 1,400). They also seem to find themselves in the strongest position regarding most of their mutual problems.

Special Education in Greenland

All children in Greenland are subject to compulsory education and are thus entitled to education in the *folkeskolen* (elementary school) from the start of the school year in which they reach the age of eight. In most schools they may start in kindergarten during the year in which they reach the age of seven. Seven years of schooling are compulsory; however, nine years of compulsory schooling are being planned. Students are offered education until grade twelve.

The Elementary School Act of 1967 states that children who, because of difficulties of speech, weakness of sight, weakness of hearing, low intelligence, or reading difficulties, cannot benefit sufficiently from the ordinary education be given special education. Also, the school authorities may authorize the establishment of special education for children who for other reasons lack the ability to profit from ordinary education either temporarily or permanently. Thus there exists the legal possibility of giving children a specially prepared education whenever they fail in school.

There are no special schools in Greenland. This means that, in principle, all handicapped children should be integrated in elementary school and given special support and education according to their needs. In a few cases children with especially difficult handicaps are sent for observation to special schools in Denmark for as much as one year, with the aim of planning for their future schooling in Greenland.

Compulsory Education

Compulsory education in Greenland is carried out in state schools under the Danish Ministry for Greenland. Schools are run by the School Management for Greenland, and their daily affairs are taken care of by a school director. All expenses are paid by the state.

Preparations have been made to transfer the school system to the Greenlandic home rule, initiated in 1979-1980. A new Greenlandic school act will extend compulsory schooling to nine years but will not change the principle that all children with learning problems shall be offered special education or other kinds of special educational support. In the draft of the act it states that "education of handicapped students shall be carried through for all groups of handicaps within the elementary schools. Education should be planned so that physically and psychologically handicapped students can be taught in the ordinary school to the greatest extent possible. In cases where placement in institutions is necessary due to family reasons or the kind of handicap, the elementary school will arrange for the necessary student housing." However, this education has been an obligation of the school for the past ten years, and special education has been developed so that it is possible to offer various kinds of special education in all town schools and in many village schools.

The Greenlandic school system is divided into eighteen school districts, of which one is School District Denmark, which includes four Greenlandic boarding schools where students can attend grades ten and eleven (1978-1979) if these grades are not available in their home districts. In a society such as Greenland, with approximately 50,000 inhabitants, of which about 10,000 live in very small villages, there will always be students who cannot be offered schooling above the compulsory school-age in their home areas. In 1977-1978 there were approximately 13,000 students in twenty-three elementary schools in towns and seventy-three schools in the very small villages. Of these 13,000 students, 9,300 were within the compulsory school-age.

Number of Children

The system of special education has been very much enlarged during the years since the 1967 act was passed, so that in 1976-1977 approximately 1,000 children received some kind of special education, ranging from lessons in single subjects to full-scale special education. It is intended that the content of education be planned according to the needs of each child. Ten percent of the students of compulsory school-age have received special education to some extent during a school year. Special education has mainly been used in teaching Greenlandic, Danish, and mathematics.

Teachers

The educational personnel at the Greenlandic schools consist partly of Danish teachers with a teachers' college education, partly of Greenlandic teachers with a teachers' college education, and partly of temporarily engaged teachers with little or no teacher education. These facts should be seen in the background of the development that has taken place in society and the school system during the last thirty years. The first independent school act for Greenland was passed in 1950. The teachers' college at Godthåb (the only one in Greenland) has not yet had time to educate sufficient Greenlandic teachers to cover the needs of the schools, so it has been necessary to employ many Danish teachers and a number of Greenlandic teachers without college educations. The majority of Danish teachers stay in Greenland only for two or three years. They rarely master the Greenlandic language and so are unable to use it in teaching.

While schooling was increased according to the model of the Danish school, the number of students has doubled from 1960 to 1970 because of an increased birthrate and greater effectiveness of the efforts of the health service, causing the infant mortality rate to drop.

Language and Education

Because of the large number of Danish-speaking teachers and the aim of making it possible for young people in Greenland to choose further education according to their abilities and interests without linguistic considerations impeding this choice, education in Danish was used in elementary school, for many years from the first grade on. In a society counting 50,000 members, of which approximately 40,000 are born here, there is no possibility of establishing a fully developed higher-educational system for young people. Therefore, those who want further education often have to seek it in Denmark.

During the last few years, Greenland has aimed at making kindergarten compulsory and at the same time making kindergarten, grade one, and grade two into a preschool. Here Greenlandic would be the educational language and Danish would be the first foreign language. Learning to read would be introduced in grade three. Thus a development aiming at strengthening the position of the Greenlandic language is being sought. Such a development does not mean that the students' possibilities of acquiring a knowledge of the Danish language would be diminished. On the contrary, present-day experience shows that a strengthening of the development of the language and concepts of the mother tongue creates better conditions for the students' later mastery of the Danish language.

Greenland has been considering offering a course comprising grades eleven and twelve for those students who after grade ten have not achieved sufficient academic competence to pass the examinations for higher education. This should enable them to pass the final tests in those subjects they may need to be able to continue in higher education.

Special Education and School
Psychological Guidance

Students with reading difficulties and students in special education for many years have had the extra handicap that a great part of their education was in Danish. Moreover, this education was at a level where the vocabulary and concepts of their Greenlandic mother tongue were still quite weak. Not only was the educational language Danish, except for the lessons in religion and Greenlandic, but learning to read in Danish was often started at an early stage.

The first step in the direction of establishing special education was taken in 1952, when a reading-class was established in Egedesminde. From the mid-sixties educational-psychological tests were used to evaluate the children's learning potentials. In 1970 the position of school psychologist was established in connection with the school director's office at Godthåb, as well as the position of consultant for special education. In 1978 the guidance and special-education administrations had four school psychologists, one consultant, and twenty-two counselors.

The School Psychologist and Counselor

In order to be a school psychologist in Greenland, it is necessary to have a degree in teaching and a university degree in psychology or the equivalent from the Royal Danish Teachers' College. The school psychologists have a professional background in modern Danish methods for school psychological work. Generally, they make two assessments. First, a thorough diagnostic examination is made, leading to an accurate description of the dysfunctions influencing the child's possibilities of learning. Second, the child's home environment and its socioeconomic and sociocultural factors are evaluated in order to determine the background of the sociopsychological problems in the school situation that may influence the child's possibilities of learning.

In a sparsely populated area such as Greenland, where each school psychologist must serve areas with as many as 4,500 children in the schools, his work will often turn out to be consultative, consisting of guidance more often than treatment. This is the background in which the school psychologist functions as a coordinating factor between normal education and the various forms of special education and among the health, social, and school-service systems.

Within the school and to a great extent on the outside, this consultative and coordinating work is taken care of in daily practice by a counselor for special education who has been appointed to all town schools. It is intended that the counselors should be teachers who have had postgraduate courses and work in the field of special education, plus experience in teaching children with learning difficulties.

During the visits of the school psychologist, the teaching and treatment of each student is discussed, and, in cases where the counselor needs further guidance regarding a student, the school psychologist will perform an examination of the child and his background. The results of the examination will be presented at a conference in which all the teachers involved and, if possible, the child's parents also participate. Based on this conference, suggestions regarding teaching and treatment are brought forward. If these suggestions include special education, the question is put before the teachers' council, which will take care of the referral. In practice, the principal of the school, assisted by the counselor, handles these referrals to and transfers back from special education.

All special education that is not considered merely routine is initiated in a background of discussion, which takes into consideration a wide circle of persons, including the student, parents, teachers, psychologist, doctor, health visitor, and social adviser.

A medical examination is performed before or parallel to the school psychological examination. Also, the social adviser is involved in the discussion whenever the child's family is already in contact with social service or it is determined that there is a need for such contact.

Therefore, diagnosis and suggestions for teaching should rest on an evaluation of the child's strong and weak points and his interaction with the environment both in and outside of school. The process is carried out and extended by the special-education teacher's observations of the student during special education and during ordinary lessons, whenever this is considered necessary. In this way, the experts' decisions and work recede into the background as teamwork develops, which is most essential in this work.

In order to coordinate the special educational work in schools, especially guidance of severely handicapped students, a consultant for special education has been attached to the school director's office. Rather heavy demands are made on this consultant. Since all children attend the elementary schools, this consultant must be acquainted with the problems of mentally retarded children of various kinds, children with difficulties in speech and hearing, children with motor handicaps, and the large group of reading-retarded pupils.

Special Classes

Although special education includes children with all types of handicaps, only eleven special classes with sixty-four students were established by the school-year 1977-1978. This means that more than 90 percent of the children in special education maintain their attachment to their regular classes, and less than 1 percent of the schoolchildren receive all their education in special classes. For special education, assessment starts with the teacher's description of the student's difficulties. The counselor or the school psychologist expands the evaluation by tests, observations, and relatively informal conversations.

Very little test material has been developed in Greenlandic or has been translated into Greenlandic. The evaluation of a student's reading-level must be based on an estimation, taking into consideration the level of his class, the education to which he has been exposed, and other environmental factors, plus types of errors made in reading aloud and in spelling tests.

If necessary, assessment is performed by means of tests that do not require spoken language. For instance, the Performance Scale of the Wechsler Intelligence Scales (WISC and WPPSI), Leiter International Performance Scale, subtests from the Illinois Test of Psycholinguistic Abilities (ITPA), The Bender Visual Motor Gestalt Test, and the Benton Visual Retention Test, when used with experience and suitable caution, may give valuable results.

An evaluation of the child's linguistic development is based on interviews with teachers, parents, and others. In this connection it should be mentioned that, at present, no fully Greenlandic-speaking school psychologists have been appointed, because of the lack of education of Greenlandic teachers in this field. Nor are there any Greenlandic special-education teachers with extra education in speech and hearing.

Socially, culturally, and economically the Greenlandic society is very heterogeneous. Therefore, it is absolutely necessary to evaluate the student's functioning not only from the viewpoint of the demands made on him or her in school but also in consideration of the society in which he lives. To the school psychologist, this means that he cannot use the child's reactions in school as a shortcut to a diagnosis. He has to include behavior and habits from life outside school in his considerations to a higher degree than is the case, for instance, in Denmark.

The Organization of Special Education

Special education is organized as follows:

1. A special-education teacher may enter the ordinary class and support those students who have difficulties in the subject being taught.

2. The children may join a reading team for two to four hours per week within normal school hours.

3. The children may attend the reading clinic during a certain period to receive all their education in the subject in which they have difficulties.

4. Children may receive private lessons outside of class.

5. The children may be transferred to a special class during all lessons. This is rarely used, except for severely handicapped students.

The objective of special education is to create the best possible conditions for the students to be able to participate in ordinary education again. In order to obtain this, the teachers are allowed a wide latitude in choosing their own methods and varying these according to the students' needs and the materials available. A few principal considerations, which are generally assumed, should be mentioned. One should teach to the student's strong points and should look at the entire situation and set up programs for each child, creating an atmosphere around the child that is as quiet and pleasant as possible.

Consideration of the student's linguistic background and development is strongly emphasized. the cause of many learning difficulties may be sought in the great difference in the children's language development within each grade. In relation to school functioning, many children must be considered to be linguistically handicapped. For this reason, a determined effort toward language-training during the first years in school is absolutely necessary in order to avoid learning difficulties later.

Case Study 1

Lars was a twelve-year-old boy who showed learning problems in reading when first seen. He is the youngest of four brothers and sisters, but since age three years he has lived with his mother only. His father was a seal-hunter. His mother had no education and works as a charwomen. Lars and his mother moved around a great deal, so Lars had no proper schooling until about third grade.

He received some special education at certain times, probably from second grade. There is no certain information available on Lars's early development, except that he suffered from fever and convulsions when he was two years old.

When he was referred for psychological testing, by agreement with his mother Lars was moved to a home for children. He attended fifth grade at this time. He was referred for special education because of a very low reading-level and speech difficulties. Lars would like to learn Danish, but in this language his reading-level is so low compared to that of his fellow students that he is totally blocked from learning Danish.

In psychological testing, which consisted of performance tasks, he obtained results corresponding with the average performance for his age. On the Wechsler Intelligence Scale for Children (WISC), he was given the performance tests only. His standard scores were: Picture Completion, 10; Picture Arrangement, 9; Block Design, 9; Object Assembly, 8; and Coding, 6. On the Bender Visual Motor Gestalt Test he made two errors, substituting circles for dots.

Therefore, the evaluation report of Lars's school situation concluded that he should be considered a child of average intelligence without any specific organically conditioned learning difficulties but with delayed language development. This was caused by lack of stimulation during his early childhood and by his ever-changing and uncertain schooling.

Lars's adaptation to school and to fellow students was poor. This might have been caused by the large difference between his potential and his performance in school, which made his situation in the class difficult. As a result of these considerations, it was decided that Lars should start with a special-education team, where he would be taught together with two or three other children with whom he was known to have good relationships.

Reading training in Danish should stop, and reading in Greenlandic should be carried on very cautiously. However, emphasis should be placed on arithmetic, in which he has shown much interest lately and is likely to obtain some success. Through conversations about arithmetic, his Greenlandic language should be systematically developed. Also, he should be offered tape recordings in Greenlandic from books in which he has shown some curiosity. If he is still interested in learning Danish, this teaching should be concentrated around the spoken language. It was agreed that the greatest importance be attached to attempting, at first, to make Lars feel considerably more secure in Greenlandic.

Lars is now in the eighth grade. He has finished special education and is doing well. In the seventh grade he changed special-education groups to join a friend who was two years older than he was, and Lars worked very well in the new group. Starting in January of that year he did practical, paid work in the afternoons. He is still on this part-time work program in the eighth grade.

Case Study 2

Jan was a nine-and-a-half-year-old boy with learning difficulties when first seen. He attended third grade. He has a sister three years older than he is. Both live with their parents in a small house. The father works as an unskilled laborer in a trade much dependent on weather conditions. He also receives support from social service. The mother does not work outside the home. The parents are positive and kind in their relationship with the children, but they render them no support in their schoolwork and speak very little to the children.

In school Jan is described as very quiet and reserved but very kind and almost always happy. His benefit from his first years of schooling has been very meager. He has difficulty in concentrating on learning reading and arithmetic. However, he is able to work very concentratedly on puzzles, drawings, and other manual tasks. Based on these facts, the school wanted a psychological examination in order to discover his strong points, which had not been found in his daily work.

Jan had not suffered from any diseases during his early childhood, and his birth was uncomplicated and not premature. He was tested with a series of performance tests, and in all tests he had a normal level of functioning and showed very well-developed powers of observation. His drawing of a man contained many fine details, normally seen from children about three to four years older. Thus everything in these tests indicated average or better intelligence. On the WISC performance scales, his standard scores were: Picture Completion, 16; Picture Arrangement, 7; Block Design, 10; Object Assembly, 10; and Coding, 8. On the Bender Visual Motor Gestalt Test he made two errors, substituting circles for dots. On the Draw-A-Man Test he scored the age equivalent of 13 years.

During further discussions of the causes of Jan's lack of progress in school, his home background had to be considered once more. His parents were rather old when Jan was born. They had grown up and gone to school in a society in which Danish had not yet become as predominant as it was in Jan's daily life. The parents had followed a life-style according to their own needs without adopting the new cultural patterns and the linguistic concepts that were necessary for Jan to have at his start in school in order to make it a success.

It was decided to give Jan special education in Greenlandic and arithmetic with a team outside of class. As for Danish, it should be limited to the speech taking place in the ordinary Danish lessons of the class. In arithmetic he should concentrate on conversations about the concepts, which are taught to the children in kindergarten classes through structured play situations. When Jan understands these basic concepts, he should proceed to real training in arithmetic. In Greenlandic, his comprehension and production of words and concepts should be trained through spoken language. His Greenlandic should be developed so that it can be a help to him in his further schooling and in the society in which he will have to function after leaving school.

At present Jan is in the sixth grade. His schoolwork is weak but he has had no problems adjusting to the other children and there are no signs of maladjusted behavior. He is being continued in special education to give him both educational and general-adjustment support.

Research Efforts

Experimental and developmental work are continuing, directed by a consultant at the school director's office who is specialized in this area. Within special education, a project that has lasted for several years, concerning the integration of emotionally handicapped children, has been brought to a conclusion. Now these children (according to a circular letter of 1977) are taught in the regular elementary schools. As mentioned earlier, this mainstreaming arrangement has been included in the coming Greenlandic School Act.

Summary

In summary it might be said that according to the coming development of the school system, the first three years of school (kindergarten and grades one and two) will be considered a phase of adaptation to school life. In this phase the development of the children's language will be emphasized in order to give them the best possible background for learning reading and arithmetic. At this level teaching should be planned so that it meets with the needs of all students.

Not until third grade will children with reading and arithmetic difficulties be referred to special education. Attempts will be made to keep children with severe handicaps in the regular classes to the greatest extent possible. However, out of consideration for these children, arrangements will be made as early as kindergarten to have a supporting teacher.

With regard to the students in higher elementary school grades, it will be possible to establish reading teams for them as needed. These teams will be an optional choice according to the student's wishes. A similar option will be available to the students in the special youth-education and evening schools.

It is the desire of the schools—through the daily contacts of all students—to create the greatest tolerance and acceptance of all kinds of handicaps among the children and, consequently, in society in general.

14

A View from the Bridge: Reading Problems in Hawaii

George Fargo and
Janice E. Laine

Hawaii as a Bridge: Background

If Hawaii may be said to form a cultural bridge between the mainland of the United States and the continent of Asia, the makeup of its population reflects both ends of that bridge. This fact is of particular significance because, in proportion to the other forty-nine state populations, Hawaii ranks first in immigrant settlement.

Although children with reading problems in Hawaii probably have much in common with their mainland peers, the critical differences between Hawaiian and mainland U.S. reading problems may be said to be a function of the state's unique cultural and ethnic composition.

Multiethnic Reading Problems

No certain estimate is available of the number of children in Hawaii who have or have had reading problems. Incidence is always a reflection of definition, and definition all too frequently is constructed for administrative purposes. In terms of schools, one may include in the scope of the definition the extent of the resources one is willing to commit to the solution of the problem.

If reading is a process of making meaningful discriminations, then numbers may not reveal the dimensions of what constitutes a problem in Hawaii. The child's perception of the problem may not be congruent with the teacher's. And because *meaning* is a term defined by the user, discriminating situations might well include the following: If the materials of reading, that is, words and concepts, present meaningful discriminations for the teacher, are they also meaningful to the learner? Does the teacher's understanding of *meaning* discriminate against the child?

Reading problems as currently designated in Hawaii are generally established as a result of grade-level achievement and reading-test scores. There are other ways to look at the problems. Although the measured representations of sublevel reading performance are likely to be accurate, defining some of the reasons for their existence requires moving from these available quantitative data to an exploration of qualitative considerations.

Some Population Estimates

Estimates by the Hawaii State Department of Planning and Economic Development (Hawaii 1977) indicate a population of 886,000 in 1976. This total includes approximately 56,000 members of the armed forces and 67,000 of their dependents stationed in Hawaii. The state's population rose rapidly from 154,000 in 1900 to 423,000 in 1940. Approximately 81 percent of the 1976 total lived on Oahu, giving that island a density in excess of 1,280 persons per square mile. The population of Hawaii is young (50 percent were under twenty-five years of age in 1970) and racially diversified, over one-fourth the product of mixed marriages. Immigration has been a major factor in the growth of the population. Between 1970 and 1976 approximately 177,700 persons moved to the state, while 119,200 moved away. The immigrants included 133,100 persons from the mainland United States and 44,600 from foreign countries, chiefly the Philippines and Korea.

The Texture of the People

Lena Younger admonished her daughter, in Lorraine Hansberry's "Raisin in the Sun":

> When you start measuring somebody, measure him right, child, measure him right. Make sure you done taken into account what hills and valleys he come through before he got wherever he is.

Gallimore and Howard (1968) have expressed some particularly astute observations about the native-born Hawaiians. After thirty months of participation and field research in Hawaii, the anthropologists concluded that values and rewards in the dominant ethnic group (white middle class) are slanted toward those whose life-style is achievement-oriented rather than affiliation-motivated. They stated that Hawaiians, contrary to the state's other ethnic groups, will "choose to honor a commitment to a friend, provide aid to another, and seek out situations of good fellowship before they will choose personal or economic gain." Also, they said that Hawaiians are popularly held to be lazy or unproductive, but they suggested that this perception ignores the importance the Hawaiian attaches to human relationships rather than to economic or individual achievement. Life in Hawaii, they reported, appears almost totally centered around those activities that either reaffirm or deepen affiliative bonds. The evident pleasure Hawaiians experience in "congenial interaction, helping others, and working together toward some common goal, i.e., preparing a luau, helping a friend repair his home or his car," effectively refutes the myth of indifference and lack of motivation. The authors cite the instance of Hawaiians working as a team on construction crews who, under the right conditions, have demonstrated their productivity. Thus, Gallimore and Howard effectively placed the often-heard derogatory epithets addressed to or about Hawaiians in the context of the state's achievement-oriented ethnic groups, whose life-style and social patterns paralleled those of the mainland in social and economic terms.

A look at some of the statistics relevent to education suggests that the Hawaiian school system needs to make a considerably greater effort to provide a better match between the school and home experiences of the affiliation-oriented children. It is a problem readily recognized among educated Hawaiians. Dr. E. Aluli, a Molokai physician, explained the alienation Hawaiians feel in school:

> I don't know if you realize it, but most of us felt and feel that the schools are very cold, that it was very competitive and it was pretty irrelevant in the kinds of things that we wanted to be doing at that time (Hawaiian culture 1977).

Relevance would require that schools become more responsive to differences among the various ethnic groups, and particularly that they accept that for the Hawaiian child affiliation orientation takes precedence over achievement orientation.

Some Geographical Facts

The state of Hawaii consists of eight major islands. They range from Hawaii, the largest (4,038 square miles), to Maui (1,858), Oahu (1,574), Kauai (1,433), Molokai (676), Lanai (361), Niihau (189), and tiny Kahoolawe (177). In addition, there are 124 minor islands. Together, the major and minor islands have a total land area of 6,425 square miles and a general coastline extending 750 miles.

Of the major cities, Honolulu, on the island of Oahu, is the largest. Honolulu is 214 miles from Hilo, on the island of Hawaii, which is 2,397 miles from San Francisco.

Hawaii's geological uniqueness is all the more striking when it is remembered that, although the state comprises these tropical islands located in the mid-Pacific, Hawaiians can ski any time of the year on the permafrost ice and snow of Mauna Kea. Indeed, Hawaii possesses a sense of extremes. In terms of rainfall, it is probably one of the driest spots on earth as well as one of the wettest. There is rich agricultural soil, and there are sandy and rocky beaches, forests of Ohia and bamboo, and moon-like fields of a'a and pahoehoe. Measured from the sea floor, Hawaii boasts the tallest mountain in the world, as well as one of the most active volcanoes. It is a land of sharp, natural contrasts that mark its people well.

Do Problems Begin at Home?

A Babel of Home Languages. The East-West Center Population Institute (1970) compiled a tabulation of languages spoken in Hawaiian homes. The question asked to collect these data was, "What language, other than English, was spoken in this person's home when he was a child?" The tabulation was made from a 1 percent population sample, and the results are therefore subject to considerable sample variation. Table 14-1 indicates that three out of four people in Hawaii spoke languages other than English in their homes as children.

The state has made extensive programmatic efforts to teach English as a second language. However, the many mother tongues do cause interference in learning to read.

Multiethnicity. Dramatic changes occurred in the composition of the state's ethnic stock from 1853 to 1970. As shown in table 14-2 in 1853 native-born Hawaiians constituted 70,000 (95.8 percent) of the state's 73,000 population, whereas in 1970 the 71,000 native-born Hawaiians represented only 9.3 percent of the state's population of 768,000. By contrast, the number of Caucasians rose from 1,687 in 1853 to 301,429 (39.2 percent) in 1970. The Japanese, not represented until 1900 in the population figures, began with a population of 61,111 in 1900 and increased to 217,669

Table 14-1
Mother Tongues Spoken in Hawaii, 1970

Mother Tongue	Number of People[a]
English	447,200
German	5,700
Portuguese	9,300
Spanish	13,300
Other European languages	10,400
Chinese, Cantonese, or Taiwanese	26,900
Korean	6,200
Japanese	116,900
Ilocano, Tagalog, or other Filipino tongues	50,200
Hawaiian	18,700
Other Polynesian, Melanesian, or Micronesian	4,200
Other languages	13,200
Not reported	46,100

Source: East-West Center Population Institute, *Special Tabulation of 1970 Census of the Population, Public Use Sample for Hawaii* (Honolulu: East-West Center, 1970).

[a]Total population = 768,300

in 1970, representing 28.3 percent of the state's population. Based upon the work of Andrew Lind (1967) and the compilations in the State of Hawaii *Data Book 1977* by Robert Schmitt (1977), a picture of these ethnic changes emerges in the latest current percentages: Caucasian, 39.2 percent; Japanese, 28.3 percent; Filipino, 12.4 percent; Hawaiian and part-Hawaiian, 9.3 percent; Chinese, 6.8 percent; Korean, 1.3 percent; black 1.0 percent; Indian, 0.2 percent; and others, 1.6 percent (see table 14.2).

It may be argued that the impact of cultural and ethnic divergences in the population and languages in Hawaii tends to produce a complex context for the recognition and resolution of reading problems. Still, Ernest Cassirer (1944) defined man as an "animal symbolicism." He suggested that man uses many symbol systems, of which language is the most powerful and universal. Cassirer believed that language is the means for learning, just as it is learned. And language use, of which reading ability is a basic part, constitutes the fundamental link to communication between people. Further, Lenneberg (1967) reported that all children, everywhere, seem to acquire their native language in similar chronological steps. He concluded that it may be that language is rooted in our biological makeup. By contrast, social influences such as the ones discussed here are acknowledged by almost all linguists to affect language development. It is the combination of these forces, then, that makes Hawaiian children's reading performances of special interest.

Table 14-2
Ethnic Distribution in Hawaii, 1853-1970

Ethnic Group	1853	1900	1940	1970	1970 Percent
All Groups	73,137	154,001	423,330	768,559	100.0
Hawaiian	70,036	29,799	14,375	71,274	9.3
Part-Hawaiian	983	9,857	49,935	—	—
Caucasian	1,687	26,819	112,087	301,429	39.2
Chinese	364	25,767	28,774	52,375	6.8
Filipino	5	—	52,569	95,354	12.4
Indian	—	—	—	1,216	0.2
Japanese	—	61,111	157,905	217,669	28.3
Korean	—	—	6,851	9,625	1.3
Negro	—	233	255	7,517	1.0
Other groups	62	415	579	12,100	1.6

Source: Data are derived from W. Lind, Hawaii's people, 3rd ed (1967), p. 28; and Robert C. Schmitt, Demographic Statistics of Hawaii, 1778-1965 (1968), pp. 74 and 120. In State of Hawaii, *Data Book 1977*. Honolulu: Department of Planning and Economic Development. U.S. Census of Population, 1960, Final Report PC (1) 13B, table 15, and Final Report PC (2)-1C, table 61; U.S. Census of Population, 1970, Final Report PC (1)-D13, tables 138 and 139. Washington, D.C.: U.S. Gov't. Printing Office.

The Schools

Hawaii presents some startling discrepancies between the percentage of each ethnic group in the population and their representations in the ranks of teachers and students. Perhaps most striking is the high percentage of teachers of Japanese heritage (57.9 percent) compared to their proportion in the population (28.3 percent). Filipinos represent 12.4 percent of the state's population, 16.8 percent of the public-school students, and only 2.1 percent of the public-school teachers (see table 14-3). It would appear that many children are mismatched culturally and ethnically with their teachers.

The relationship over the past several years between public-school and private-school enrollment is also significant. In 1976, of the state's 207,433 students, 84 percent (174,795) were enrolled in the 200 public-school programs from kindergarten through twelfth grade, while 16 percent (33,038) attended private schools (see table 14-4). More revealing is the fact that, for the sixth straight year, there has been a dramatic increase in private-school attendance, while public-school attendance has gone down. It is possible to suggest that "something is not happening" in Hawaii's public schools.

Fuchs (1961) went one step further. He wrote, some seventeen years ago, that "unless care is taken, Hawaii's public schools may one day serve mostly children of the poor, while parents of means send their children to private schools." A cursory examination of current socioeconomic figures clearly illustrates that "haves" and "have-nots" in Hawaii appear to fall into different ethnic groups. If Fuch's portent should occur, the situation would become a nightmare. Because Haole (mainland-born) families and those of Japanese and Chinese ancestry tend to be far better off economically than other ethnic groups, such segregation would not only

Table 14-3
Ethnic Representation in Hawaii's Public Schools
(Percentages)

	State Population[a]	Teachers[b]	Students[c]
Caucasian	39.2	18.7	30.4
Japanese	28.3	57.9	22.8
Filipino	12.4	2.1	16.8
Hawaiian and part-Hawaiian	9.3	6.9	17.4
Chinese	6.8	8.8	4.8
Korean	1.3	1.3	1.4
Black	1.0	.3	1.3
Other	1.8	3.6	5.1

[a]From 1970 Census data
[b]As of June 1974; includes teachers, counselors, registrars, and school librarians.
[c]As of June 1975.

cause the deterioration of the quality of Hawaii's public-school system, it would also certainly serve to exacerbate ethnic tensions. Youths of Haole, Japanese, and Chinese heritage would then be concentrated in private schools, and most of those attending the public schools would be Hawaiians, Filipinos, and Samoans (see table 14-5). If this were to occur, Hawaii would in effect be reverting to its two-class educational system of the early 1900s, when no Haole sent his children to public school.

Considerable discrepancies are shown between low public-school reading-achievement scores and the higher reading scores of the private schools. The same "have" and "have-not" profile that exists in the private- and public-school populations now aligns certain ethnic groups with school and reading achievement.

Secondary and Higher Education

A brief look at high-school-completion and university-attendance figures tells a similar story.

High-School Completion. A supplementary report on the census data (Schmitt 1977) indicates that in 1970 only 39.4 percent of the Filipinos in Hawaii who were sixteen years old and over completed high school. Comparable figures are 65.1 percent for children of Chinese heritage and 61.3 percent for the Japanese. Also, 49.7 percent of the Hawaiians twenty-five years old and over completed high school. These findings show that only slightly more than one-third of the students of Filipino cultural heritage and one-half of the Hawaiians old enough to have graduated from college completed high school—a dismal showing, indeed, when compared to the approximate two-thirds completion rate of the children of Chinese and Japanese heritage. Another comparative figure of interest is provided by Kahn (1973). He found that in 1971 79.5 percent of mainland Americans between twenty and twenty-nine years of age had completed high school.

Table 14-4
Comparison between Public- and Private-School Enrollments in Hawaii

Year	Enrollment K-12	
	Public School	*Private School*
1968	172,544	28,605
1970	180,209	27,382
1972	180,944	29,719
1974	176,381	31,452
1976	174,395	33,038

Table 14-5
Ethnic Representation in Hawaii's Private Schools

Group	Percentage of State Population	Percentage of Private School Enrollment	Percentage of Children in Private Schools
Caucasian	39.2	44	16
Japanese	28.3	21	11
Filipino	12.4	8	8
Hawaiian and part-Hawiian	9.3	11	13
Chinese	6.8	13	25
Other	2.8	3	13

Source: Compiled from *Honolulu Advertiser,* December 31, 1975, page A-3.

University Attendance. Because individuals who attend college generally have the greatest access to well-paying professional jobs, it is enlightening to look at those who "made it" in the educational system in Hawaii. From 1967 to 1977, 49,964 students attended colleges and universities in Hawaii. The figures are as follows:

University of Hawaii at Manoa	21,356
University of Hawaii at West Oahu	139
University of Hawaii at Hilo	1,037
Seven community colleges	21,380
Four private four-year colleges	5,252

An examination of the ethnic composition of the students enrolled at the University of Hawaii at Manoa, relative to overall percentages in the state's population, gives some indication of the distribution of educationally successful ethnic groups (see table 14-6). Once again, these data are glaring in the underrepresentation of students of Filipino and Hawaiian heritage. Of equal significance is the overrepresentation of students of Japanese and Chinese background at the universities in proportion to these groups' percentages in the state's population.

Ethnicity and Achievement

The facts and figures presented enable us, with a reasonable degree of accuracy, to discuss the relationship in the state of Hawaii between ethnicity and scholastic achievement. Haas and Resurrection (1976) pointed out that "as the ethnic balance of the schools has shifted over the years, the heavily

Table 14-6
Ethnic Distribution at University of Hawaii at Manoa

	Percentage of of University Population	State Percentage of Ethnic Distribution
Caucasian	26.6	39.2
Hawaiian and part-Hawaiian	4.4	9.3
Chinese	12.8	6.8
Filipino	2.0	12.4
Japanese	42.6	28.3
Korean	1.3	1.3
Black	0.2	1.0
Mixed and other[a]	10.0	1.7

Source: Data compiled by the University of Hawaii Survey Research Office, with a sample size of 1,432.

[a]Includes mixed Chinese-Japanese but not part-Hawaiian.

Japanese-American staff in the public schools is increasingly called upon to teach larger percentages of Filipinos, Hawaiians, Samoans, and students of other ethnic backgrounds with which they may be culturally unfamiliar.'' The result, as substantiated by Norton, Stout, and Fischer (1976), is that performance levels of students of Filipino and Hawaiian background fall below those of Caucasian, Chinese, and Japanese heritage. As can be expected in this context, children of Filipino and Hawaiian heritage decline in their relative levels of performance in each succeeding grade of their academic careers.

The literature presents a substantial basis for relating ethnicity and scholastic achievement in Hawaii. However, the quality of available data is somewhat in question. The achievement scores shown for each school are average scores for all sixth-graders who took the reading, mathematics, and language subtests of the Sequential Tests of Education Progress (STEP) (Department of Education 1973, 1975, 1976). There is room for argument about the effectiveness of STEP as an assessment tool of student achievement; however, STEP remains the only basis from which comparisons can be made among Hawaii's students and schools. Thus schools have been designated high-achievement schools when their STEP scores are equal to or higher than the composite STEP score for the state. Similarly, a low-achievement school has a STEP score lower than the composite STEP score of the state.

The Distribution of Achievement in Ethnic Groups. Using the STEP as a comparative device, high-achievement elementary schools in Hawaii number 85; low-achievement elementary schools, 76. The median proportions of students of Filipino and Hawaiian or part-Hawaiian background in the high-achievement schools' total enrollment are 9.1 percent and 7.2 percent, respectively. However, the median proportions of these groups in low-achievement schools are 20.7 percent and 16.2 percent, respectively. When these figures are compared to the proportions of these groups in the total public-school population (16.8 percent and 17.4 percent, respectively), it may be noted that disproportionately fewer children of Hawaiian and Filipino heritage are enrolled in high-achievement schools. Of the schools with 20 percent or more students of Filipino or part-Hawaiian heritage in their enrollment, eighteen (90 percent) are low-achievement schools. Similarly, of the forty-eight schools with 20 percent or more Filipinos, forty (83 percent) are low-achievement schools.

This form of ethnic isolation cuts across geographic boundaries. Regardless of district or island location, there are a significant number of low-achievement schools among those that have 20 percent or more Filipinos in attendance. If the results of the analysis of the sixth-grade data may be used to reflect the relationship between ethnicity and achievement in other grades, it is likely that children of Filipino and Hawaiian or part-Hawaiian background are not only isolated *in* low-achievement schools, they are isolated *from* high-achievement schools.

Reading Scores and Socioeconomic Status

If we now examine reading scores in elementary schools and look at their relationship to socioeconomic status (SES), we find that Haas and Resurrection's (1976) conclusion, "poor kids become poor readers," is particularly significant for Hawaiian children. A verification of the relationship between SES and reading achievement reported by these researchers is contained in a study by Lei (1975). Lei did a regression analysis of the relationship between socioeconomic variables and the Stanford Achievement Test (SAT) and the Otis-Lennon Test, administered to Honolulu-district fourth-graders in the fall of 1975.

Lei collected data from thirty-nine elementary schools concerning each school's percentage of foreign-born students, median family income, education of parents, percentage on welfare or unemployed, and transiency rate. He used these independent variables in several analyses with eleven dependent variables. Only results for vocabulary and reading comprehension from the SAT are reported here.

The correlations between the SES variables and vocabulary and reading comprehension ranged between 0.60 and 0.85. When the SES variables were combined in a step-wise regression, with the independent variables entered in the order of their contribution to the percentage of explained variance, 86 percent of the variance in SAT vocabulary scores was explained by variables unrelated to program or instruction. For the reading-comprehension

Table 14-7
Relationship between Parents' Education and Children's Stanford
Achievement Test Scores for Grade Four, Honolulu District

Number of Schools	Vocabulary Mean Stanine	Comprehension Mean Stanine	Parents' Education Median (years)
9	7.1	7.3	12.9-14.3
10	5.3	6.0	12.5-12.8
10	3.6	4.5	11.6-12.4
10	2.0	2.1	9.3-11.3

The correlation between parents' education and vocabulary scores is 0.66 and the correlation between parents' education and comprehension scores is 0.63.

analysis, SES explained 82 percent of the variance. Thus, only 14 to 18 percent of the variance remained to be explained by program or instruction. These figures represent the maximum possible percentage for which instructional or program variables could account.

Further documentation of the relationship between SES and reading achievement is reported in table 14-7. The table presents the mean of parents' education and its relationship to SAT scores for Honolulu-district children in grade four in the fall of 1975.

Table 14-8
Rank Order of Relationships between Parents' Education and Children's Stanford Achievement Test Scores for Grade Four of Selected Schools in Honolulu

Honolulu District	Vocabulary Stanine	Comprehension Stanine	Parents' Education Median (years)	Rank
Kahala	9	9	14.3	1
Aina Haina	9	8	13.5	3.5
Lincoln	4	5	13.3	5
Hahaione	6	6	13.0	7
Waikiki	5	6	12.9	9
Hokulani	7	8	12.8	10.5
Wailupe	6	6	12.7	12
Ala Wai	4	4	12.6	14
Kaahumanu	4	5	12.5	17.5
Maemae	6	8	12.4	20
Aliiolani	4	6	12.2	22.5
Anuenue	2	2	11.9	26.5
Kalihi	2	3	11.6	29
Kaewai	1	1	11.1	31
Fern	2	2	10.8	33
Kalihi Kai	2	2	10.6	35
Likelike	2	1	9.9	37
Kaiulani	2	1	9.3	39

Honolulu has 39 schools.

Table 14-9
Incidence Levels and Ethnicity Percentages for Hawaiian Special-Education Pupils in Specific Special-Education Categories

Catagories	Native American	Hawaiian	Part-Hawaiian	Chinese	Japanese
SLD					
Incidence Level	8	142	1,671	176	536
Percentage	.13	2.4	28.2	3	9
EMR					
Incidence level	3	74	376	39	88
Percentage	.21	5.3	27	3	6.3
TMR					
Incidence level	1	8	78	15	79
Percentage	.23	1.9	18.3	3.5	18.6
SED					
Incidence level	0	3	41	7	28
Percentage	0	1.3	18.2	3.1	12.4
Speech Impaired					
Incidence level	0	6	60	6	51
Percentage	0	2.1	21.2	2.1	23
Total Percentage of Population	.23	2.3	18	4.2	21

Additional data that firmly establish this relationship are found in table 14-8. This table illustrates, school by school, the rank-order relationship between the SES and education level of Honolulu parents and the vocabulary and comprehension SAT scores of their children. Briefly, well-to-do Kahala, with a 14.3 median grade-level for parents, shows the ninth stanine in vocabulary and the ninth stanine in reading comprehension for fourth-grade children. At the other extreme, Kaiulani, with parents' education at a ninth-grade level, shows a dismally low second stanine in vocabulary and a first stanine in reading comprehension for children at the same grade-level.

Ethnicity and Placement in Special Education

The statistics on ethnicity presented are rather dramatic, suggesting that ethnic factors are strongly related to reading achievement. Another set of data perhaps more emphatically reveals the impact of ethnicity on educational problems.

As shown in table 14-9, pupils with specific learning disabilities constituted 72 percent of the total number of children in special education (5,932 of a total 8,260); this group was made up of 4,363 males and 1,672 females. The ethnic distribution of these children with specific learning disabilities is

Table 14-9
Part II

Korean	Filipino	Samoan	Black	White	Total	Male	Female
43	939	224	83	2,110	5,932	4,363	1,672
.7	15.8	3.8	1.4	35.6		72.3	27.7
14	306	121	13	361	1,395	837	616
1	22	8.7	.93	26		57.6	42.4
4	83	11	1	145	425	270	165
.94	19.5	2.6	.23	34.1		62	38
5	23	5	9	104	225	192	44
2.2	10.2	2.2	4	46.2		81.3	18.7
2	69	6	2	81	283	187	109
.7	24.4	2.1	.7	28.6		63.2	36.8
2	18.3	3	1.5	29.7			

Source: OS/CR 102 Elementary and Secondary School Civil Rights Survey, Fall 1978. These data were consolidated by Michael Welch.

SLD = specific learning disabilities; EMR = educable mentally retarded; TMR = trainable mentally retarded; SED = seriously emotionally disturbed.

skewed, as 20.3 percent of the total school population is made up of Hawaiians and part-Hawaiians whereas 30.6 percent of the pupils with learning disabilities are from this ethnic group. A contrasting under-representation is shown by the Japanese subgroup, with 21 percent of the school population and only 9 percent of the pupils with learning disabilities.

A study of table 14-9 will show interesting underrepresentation and overrepresentation of ethnic groups in various categories of special educational placement. However, what makes the data most fascinating is that in the category of trainable mentally retarded, the percentage of pupils very closely parallels the ethnic balance of the state: 20.2 percent of the trainable retarded are Hawaiians and part-Hawaiians, who make up 20.3 percent of the total population, and 18.6 percent of the trainable retarded are Japanese, who make up 21 percent of the total population. How is it that the percentages of children who are severely and profoundly retarded closely parallel their distribution in ethnicity whereas every other special-education category is dramatically overrepresented by the Hawaiians and Filipinos and Samoans and underrepresented by Japanese and Chinese pupils? It may be due to prejudicial referral or the use of tests that are discriminatory.

Remediation and Intervention

The remediation of reading problems can be instituted only when a determination has been made of what constitutes a reading problem and how a child with a reading problem is to be differentiated from a child who does not have such a problem. In addition, each case must be examined in the context of its milieu: what kinds (and extent) of services are both required and available and how quality control of plans for manpower, materials, and organization can be ensured.

In Hawaii a number of remedial-reading projects have been initiated over the years for children who were recognized as having reading problems. Among these projects were several that seem pertinent here. No attempt will be made to rank, evaluate, or otherwise assess the success or failure of these programs. Rather, three major approaches will be discussed in terms of their particular responsiveness to reading problems in the state of Hawaii. The three are (1) compensatory-education programs; (2) the Hawaii English Program (HEP), specifically designed to adapt materials to address the local language patterns in order to improve English-language skills; and (3) the Kamehameha Early Education Program (KEEP), a model research and development program aimed at kindergarten through third-grade children who are of Hawaiian or part-Hawaiian background.

Compensatory-Education Programs

In fiscal 1976 the U.S. Congress appropriated $2 billion for compensatory education under Public Law 89-10, Title I. Hawaii's share of this money, which was earmarked for educationally disadvantaged children to receive supplementary educational services, was over $5.5 million. During 1975-1976, some 10,000 students participated in the various compensatory-education programs. Many areas of school and school-related problems were included, such as programs aimed at decreasing school alienation, teaching English and cultural orientation to foreign students, parent-child assistance, and many others. In Hawaii, as indeed elsewhere, many problems that are manifested in classroom performance may be seen in the framework of a child's background, attitude, behavior, parental SES, and a host of other factors. Some of these areas were assessed by seven of the state's school districts and rank-ordered to determine priorities for assistance with these problems. Table 14-10 illustrates these priorities for each district for the academic yar 1976-1977.

Title I allowed for the development of 122 individual projects, using differing techniques. The approaches used in the area of reading and language arts also varied widely. Four of these approaches are explained here.

Table 14-10
Summary of Individual and Total Assessments of Ranked Needs, Academic Year 1975-1976

Priority	Educational Needs
Individual district, Honolulu	
1	Poor performance on standardized test
2	Classroom performance significantly below grade-level in reading
3	Negative attitude toward school and education
4	High absentee rate
5	High drop-out rate
Totals of all 7 school districts	
1	Poor performance on standardized tests
2	Classroom performance significantly below grade-level in reading
3	High absentee rate
4	Negative attitude toward school
5	Low level of verbal function

1. *Diagnostic-prescriptive team*. This technique served the greatest number of students. The objectives were to provide a positive learning environment and to assist the individual classroom teacher in managing her classroom.

Through a diagnostic-prescriptive technique, the individual problems in reading and language-arts abilities of each student were to be defined. The descriptions of the learning problems or disabilities were forwarded to a team of special-services personnel for analysis and individual prescription. These prescriptions were carried out either by the classroom teacher or by special-services personnel brought into the classroom for the purpose of remediation.

The diagnostic team was composed of a school psychologist, a reading teacher, a speech and hearing therapist, and a social worker. The makeup of the teams allowed each child to be treated either individually or in a group. The learning environment could be adjusted within the regular Title I classroom to provide optimum reading instruction. Although the composition of the diagnostic-prescriptive team might vary from project to project, the concept of the program remained the same. It involved both state and federally funded personnel working closely with Title I teachers.

2.*Peer-tutoring*. Another approach under compensatory education was the peer-tutoring program. Instituted in several districts, these programs were designed to provide an educational structure in which students would help each other learn. The objective was to have both tutors and tutees improve their academic performance through interaction. There is some evidence that in this tutoring dyad the tutor gained as much as or more than the tutee.

3.*Centralized reading clinic.* One district developed a reading clinic that was available to a complex of schools for both teachers and students. Housed in adequate quarters, the reading clinic was able to serve most students and could be staffed by district teachers. Centralization of place and reading materials, both regular and remedial, allowed for ease of accessibility to schools, teachers, and students.

4.*Modified curriculum.* A few districts instituted a modified curriculum for students in intermediate and high schools. The objective was to create a more flexible schedule for students who were unable to cope with the constraints of the traditional block-period program. The curriculum in participating schools was self-paced, with time frames established by the judgment of the teacher and the needs of the student. Remedial reading and math were given priority. Educational assistants were used, and one district made a definite effort to recruit volunteer aides. In view of Hawaii's societal stratification, one of the prime benefits of this effort was that it brought together persons of varying socioeconomic levels.

All reading projects used standardized norm-referenced tests. Most widely used were the Wide Range Achievement Test (WRAT), the Peabody Individual Achievement Test (PIAT), the Gates-MacGinitie Reading Test, the California Achievement Test (CAT), the Woodcock Reading Mastery Tests, and the Gray Oral Reading Test. In each project the scores were converted to grade-equivalents and were used to calculate the growth in achievement made by the students, to be compared with the objectives.

Each project used the gain scores thus derived in a different type of analysis. Some evaluated them as a percentage achieving a certain growth level; others measured the significance of differences between results of pretests and posttests. Each district reported its individual scores for a statewide summary. The format established for this purpose asked the district to divide the individual scores into those achieving less than an eight-months' gain; those between a nine-months' and a one-year, six-months' gain; and those over a one-year, six-months' gain. The seven-month cut-off was selected because national research on underachieving disadvantaged children seems to indicate that such children generally achieve at about seven months per year (Department of Education 1975-1976). This formula yielded the information that, by grade four, an average underachieving disadvantaged child was approximately one and one-third grade-levels below his average-achieving peer. Table 14-11 reports the gain in reading achievement by grade-level. The data are categorized by number of months gained.

Table 14-11
Months Gained in Reading Achievement, by School District, 1975-1976

District	Percentage of Pupils Making Gains			Number of Children in District
	0-7 Months	8-18 Months	19+ Months	
Honolulu	43	40	17	2,447
Central	36	33	31	638
Leeward	64	26	10	1,797
Windward	43	30	27	867
Hawaii	38	39	23	761
Maui	43	36	21	332
Kauai	46	35	19	170

Although these data tend to indicate reading-achievement gains, they do not reveal long-term improvement. It is not possible to generalize the relative efficacy of techniques, strategies, or approaches used in more than 100 separate projects. But whatever these efforts and many others contribute to improving the situation in Hawaii, they also indicate that the correct balance of programmatic effort has not yet been achieved. Statewide reading-achievement scores may show some increase, but the number of children who need help also continues to increase.

The Hawaii English Program

The Hawaii English Program (HEP) was initiated in May 1966 as a federally funded joint activity of Hawaii's Department of Education and the University of Hawaii. HEP was designed as a kindergarten through sixth-grade language-arts curriculum in the areas of literature, language skills, and language systems. The goals may be described as follows:

1. The literature subprogram was to enable students to enjoy and understand literature, defined for the program as "an art which uses language to communicate ideas, experience, and feeling through symbolic forms."

2. The language-skills subprogram was to help students progress toward synthesized language control for the purpose of communicating and learning.

3. The language-systems subprogram was to have students learn about the nature and structure of their language.

In 1970-1971 HEP language-skills and literature subprograms for kindergarten and grade one were formally installed in at least one classroom in every school in the state; thus approximately 14 percent of the elementary-school children received some instruction in this program. In 1971-1972 six of fifteen language-systems units were installed. By the

1973-1974 school year approximately 57 percent of all kindergarten through sixth-grade students were in HEP classes.

Several evaluation studies of HEP were conducted. The studies varied in scope and sophistication. The results, in summary, favored HEP when compared to the non-HEP classes. HEP has received recognition and has won several awards, nationally and locally. In addition, HEP has been accepted and installed in several school systems outside the state of Hawaii. California, Wasington, Texas, Guam, and American Samoa and Trust Territory all have HEP programs.

A Recent Evaluation Study of HEP. The most recent evaluation of HEP was conducted by the Nomos Institute (Lai and Post 1976). The primary purpose of the Nomos evaluation was to compare the performances in English of pupils in fifth-grade HEP and non-HEP classes. The attitudes of pupils, teachers, and parents were also investigated. The study used a stratified, modified single-stage cluster sample of thirty-two HEP and non-HEP classes on Oahu. The selection of schools and classes within schools was carefully randomized to guard against bias in the sampling procedures.

The performance-levels of pupils were assessed by test results in such areas as language skills (reading comprehension, writing, punctuation, and capitalization), literature, functional literacy, speaking and listening (maps, questions and negatives, phrases, multiple meanings, directions, communication), spelling, oral sentence and paragraph reading, and language systems. Some tests were group-administered, some were individually administered. Interviews and questionnaires were used as attitude-measuring instruments with pupils, teachers, and parents. Classroom procedures were observed in HEP classes to assess "degree of implementation." Table 14-12 reports the test results comparing HEP and non-HEP performances on this series of tests, which may be summarized as follows:

Language-skills total scores. The language-skills total score reflects the sum of three subtests: reading comprehension, purposeful writing, and punctuation and capitalization. In reading comprehension the HEP students demonstrated a higher degree of proficiency than non-HEP students. The covariance-adjusted means in reading comprehension showed an educationally significant difference (not associated with any particular probability level) in student performance in favor of HEP.

In purposeful writing the difference in the means was generally small and may be of limited educational significance. In punctuation and capitalization student performance was generally low. The difference between the HEP and non-HEP students was small. Since the performance was so low, no educationally significant difference was apparent.

Total average scores showed that HEP students attained a higher degree of proficiency in language skills than did non-HEP students. Although the

Table 14-12
Summary of Test Results Comparing Hawaii English Program (HEP) and non-HEP Groups

Test and Subtests	Adjusted Group Means		Group with Larger Mean[a]
	HEP	Non-HEP	
Language skills	24.49	23.36	HEP
Reading comprehension	17.94	17.01	HEP
Purposeful writing	4.53	4.37	HEP
Punctuation and capitalization	2.03	1.98	HEP
Literature	13.76	13.39	HEP
Functional literacy	14.05	13.56	HEP
Speaking and listening	38.67	37.46	HEP
Maps	1.41	1.29	HEP
Questions and negatives	11.49	11.48	HEP
Phrases	2.89	2.84	HEP
Multiple meanings	13.26	12.78	HEP
Directions	4.68	4.18	HEP
Communication	4.94	4.88	HEP
Spelling	3.44	3.02	HEP
Oral sentence and paragaph reading	13.17	13.14	HEP
Language systems	24.64	25.65	Non-HEP

[a]Adjusted for differences in SES

difference in the language-skills total average scores may not seem dramatic, it was large enough to be educationally significant. Briefly, then, the HEP curriculum appeared consistently to have exerted a more favorable impact than the non-HEP curriculum on language-skills achievement.

Literature. The covariance-adjusted means in literature showed differences in student performance in favor of HEP. Analysis by SES levels revealed no apparent educationally significant differences between HEP and non-HEP students at the low and high SES levels. However, at the middle SES level the HEP students appeared to outperform the non-HEP students.

Functional literacy. The covariance-adjusted means in functional literacy showed that the HEP students seemed to perform slightly better than non-HEP students. Analysis by SES levels revealed that the difference was more pronounced at the middle SES level.

Speaking and listening total scores. The speaking and listening total scores reflected the sum of six subjects: maps, questions and negatives, phrases, multiple meanings, directions, and communications. On the maps subtest, HEP students generally performed better than non-HEP students. On the questions and negatives subtest no educationally significant differences in performance between HEP and non-HEP students were found. The covariance-adjusted means were virtually identical. On the phrases subtest, there were no significant differences in performance between HEP and non-HEP students. On the multiple-meanings subtest HEP students appeared to perform better than non-HEP students. The differences appeared consistent across socioeconomic levels. On the directions subtests a moderate trend emerged for HEP students to achieve higher scores than non-HEP students. The trend seemed strongest at the middle SES level. The communications subtest was so easy for all students (98 percent correct responses) that its value for program evaluation is doubtful.

Thus, on the battery of speaking and listening tests, the covariance-adjusted means showed an educationally significant difference in student performance in favor of HEP.

Spelling. HEP students achieved higher spelling scores than non-HEP students. This difference appeared large enough to be of educational significance.

Oral sentence and paragraph reading. No substantive difference was found between HEP and non-HEP students on this test.

Language systems. The results from the language-systems test appeared to be the sole exception to the trend in the other tests favoring the performance of HEP students. On language systems non-HEP students attained a higher mean score than HEP students.

With the exception of language systems, it seems evident that pupils in HEP classes performed at a higher level than those in non-HEP classes. These results may be attributable to the HEP curriculum.

Interviews and Questionnaires. The results from the student activities questionnaire, like the reading-achievement scores, may be interpreted to be related to socioeconomic status. In the low SES category no apparent difference appeared in attitude toward language arts. In the middle SES category, non-HEP students demonstrated a more favorable attitude toward language arts than did HEP students. In the high SES category there was a slight difference in favor of HEP.

In general, teachers and parents were more positive in their attitudes toward the HEP than toward the non-HEP curriculum. It would seem that a program that has affected thousands of students and on which an expenditure of millions of dollars has been made cannot be dismissed lightly. But however effective the HEP program may appear, it surely has not yet eliminated the major source of reading problems.

Interpreting Results for Hawaii

Once again we must pause to consider the particular problems that define education in Hawaii. Indeed, interpretation of test data in Hawaii cannot mean anything unless the multicultural makeup of its population is taken into account. For example, some test questions may be biased against one group but not another. Mainland-developed tests can be (and often are) biased against islanders (Dykstra et al. 1975). With a population that is approximately 8 percent immigrant (the national figure is 2 percent), it is virtually impossible to make valid, controlled comparisons on standard achievement tests with the rest of the United States. Yet such comparisons are constantly being made by many educators, legislators, and evaluators.

Similar problems undoubtedly exist elsewhere. It is not a new argument, nor does it apply only to the state of Hawaii. Norm-referenced, standardized achievement tests have been recognized as generally inappropriate. Possibly the least controversial reasons for invalidity are overgenerality, nonoverlapping of objectives, cultural bias, low reliability for individual scores, questionable norms, confusing directions, and poor selection of items (Dykstra et al. 1975).

A study of the Stanford Achievement Test results described earlier showed that the usual demographic variables that determine SES, such as family income or parents' education, accounted for as much as 86 percent of the variance in the test scores (Lei 1975). This finding obviously left very little that could be accounted for by the program being evaluated. Therefore, anyone who would like to find out how Hawaiian children compare with the rest of the United States is asking for a comparison that is basically impossible. If standardized achievement tests are used to compare achievement of Hawaiian fourth-graders with mainland fourth-graders, the results will be invalid unless at least four criteria can be met: (1) the Hawaiian children's socioeconomic status is similar to that of the mainland children; (2) the test measures only objectives that are considered significant by the group that constitutes an important part of those evaluated; (3) test administration is of the same caliber as that used when the norming was carried out; and (4) the norms are up to date as well as generally valid.

For Hawaii these assumptions cannot be made because (1) substantial evidence exists that the pattern of socioeconomic levels is not similar in Hawaii and the mainland; (2) subtest scores do not adequately differentiate functioning, since one or two items on a subtest may constitute as much as a year's difference in grade-equivalents; (3) the caliber of test administration is rarely equal to that used for the norming process; and (4) validity and appropriateness of the norms cannot be taken for granted when dealing with Hawaii.

Kamehameha Early Education Program (KEEP)

KEEP is an educational research and development center operated by the Kamehameha Schools, Bishop Estate. It was initiated in 1971 as a model research and development program to research learning problems of children of Hawaiian and part-Hawaiian background and to find a program that would be effective in teaching these children to read. Although some research was done in public-school classrooms, KEEP's major work is and was conducted at the four-classroom Ka Na'i Pono Research and Development School, serving approximately 110 kindergarten through third-grade children in Honolulu. The program includes disseminating the research findings to teachers in the public schools.

The school population for which KEEP has been designed consists of the 35,000 Hawaiian and part-Hawaiian children presently in the public schools. The major focus of the program is directed toward an urban area of Honolulu characterized by high population density, low SES, and low school achievement. Tharp and Gallimore (1976) reported on the common belief that the children's bidialect, with Hawaiian Creole English (pidgin) the preferred code, was the major cause of the children's reading underachievement. Previously, we saw that Hawaiian schools serving predominantly pidgin-speaking students registering the lowest achievement scores in the state. But these psychologists refute the position that bidialect is the problem; and indeed, they suggest that KEEP research revealed not only that pidgin was not the root of the problem but that the children were actually competent to learn to read, even if they did not. They found that, even though most of these children live in an urban environment, they are brought up with many features of traditional socialization practices.

KEEP is continuing its research in the areas it has found to be important to Hawaiian education: curriculum, linguistics, ethnicity, and psychology. Reading specialists are interested in KEEP because the program is based on reading lessons that take Hawaiian cultural events, such as "talking story" or story-telling, into consideration. Many observers charge that educational programs are often incongruent with the culture of many students. However, KEEP's acknowledgement of a Hawaiian child's patterns and behaviors tends to produce some positive results.

The scope of KEEP is broad. It has so far produced some seventy-seven technical reports in the areas of cultural considerations, reading, industriousness, language cognition, training and consultation, and curriculum. Tharp and Gallimore (1976) report that KEEP's reading program is based on the Flowing Wells Public School Reading Support Systems (Smith et al. 1976). The program provides specific objectives in decoding, encoding, vocabulary, comprehension, test-awareness, and reference skills and can be used with any basal reading series. Evaluation of the program is conducted with the Woodcock Reading Mastery Tests, Gates-MacGinitie Reading Test, and the Metropolitan Achievement Test, following each child through three criterion-referenced externally administered standardized measures at the middle and the end of the school year.

The results of the KEEP program indicate that grade two scores are slighly below grade-level and grade three is even further behind; however, there is substantial improvement over previous years. The ability to know and track areas or subareas of improvement directs the KEEP efforts toward the next programmatic steps. The use of an objective system, such as the Reading Support Systems, has helped to pinpoint the directions of efforts and has indicated the need for a greater emphasis on the development of comprehension skills.

A Hawaiian Case Study

Background

Larry was a sixteen-year-old Hawaiian student with a learning disability. His family background and early life history revealed extreme dislocation, neglect, and abuse, as documented by the family court. After Larry had spent a number of years in a series of foster homes, the family court judge helped the youngster be "hanaied" by his paternal grandmother, aunt, and uncle. (Hanai is an informal adoption procedure where a child, usually the first-born, is given to the grandmother—usually the maternal grandmother—who assumes all responsibilities.) This parental triumvirate raised eighteen children. The family operational language was Hawaiian-pidgin-English. The family modeled a Hawaiian life-style, with strong emphasis on nonverbal communication and action.

Although Larry's reading problems reflect a unique constellation of personal characteristics, his attitude toward learning, school, and teachers may be considered typical of a large number of Hawaiian, Samoan, Tongan, and Filipino students, who are mismatched to the dominant standard educational system. Larry was moved from a culture where nonverbal modeling was the predominant teaching modality to a school where verbal explanation constituted the prime teaching tool.

At sixteen, Larry was a tall, handsome high-school junior of normal intelligence, with leadership ability that was recognized by students and teachers alike. He was an outstanding football player and was captain of the team. With academic improvement he was considered a highly eligible prospect for a football athletic scholarship. Larry also presented himself as a "helper," for he had been a camp counselor for young children and very much enjoyed this activity.

An assault case brought Larry once again to the attention of the court, and subsequent psychological and academic workup resulted in a service mandate. He was diagnosed as learning-disabled by Children's Hospital Child Development Center, with specific difficulties in auditory memory and sequencing and visual memory and sequencing.

Larry's reading was at the first-grade level, with a lack of phonic knowledge, minimal sound-symbol linkages, and a meager sight vocabulary. Even the newspaper sports page presented a torturous reading trial to this student. His math functioning was at the low third-grade level, and his writing skills were in minimal form, with restricted context. Larry had not been reached by his previous teachers.

Larry's learning disability was sufficiently disturbing to be highly upsetting to an intelligent student. He presented a problem of disruption in school, precipitated by lack of attention to learning and resultant lack of self-esteem. No special educational services had been provided for this student until he was sixteen years of age and was referred by the court. In cooperation with the Hawaii State Department of Education, Carol Wood of the Learning Development Center provided the supportive tutoring service made available to Larry.

A sample of a story dictated to his tutor follows. It is reproduced in the best rendition possible of Larry's grammar and pronunciation when he tried to operate in standard English rather than in pidgin.

> I TINK [think] HAWAII WAS AND IS NICE. BUT THE HAOLE USE THIS HAWAIIAN ISLANDS FOR VACATION. BUT I TINK THAT THE HAOLE PEOPLES DID RIPOFF THE ISLANDS FROM THE HAWAIIAN. THE HAWAIIAN HAD NO PEOPLE TO HELP THEM.

Behaviorally, Larry exhibited an intense fear of failure, with a short attention span and motor overflow. He was low in verbal ability, unwilling to settle any dispute verbally, and unwilling to maintain eye contact with the tutor. Larry considered himself intellectually limited and totally lacking in academic potential. Prior school learning experiences had been unsuccessful. He considered an athletic scholarship out of reach because of his poor academic performance. Larry's self-image constituted the principal barrier to remediation, and behavioral change was expected to be slow and difficult.

The test scores shown in table 14-13 reflect Larry's school performance from age eight to age eleven. The decrement between language and nonlanguage measures manifest at age eight continued to be reflected throughout Larry's school years. This is clearly indicated by his age-eleven scores: verbal at the second percentile on the School and College Aptitude Test; reading at the tenth percentile; and writing at the fourth percentile on the Sequential Test of Educational Progress.

The tutorial objectives were academic-skill development, motivation and attitudinal change, increase in communication and problem-solving skills, and provision of increased life options. The focus was dual: to provide insight into the causes of Larry's academic-skill development and to remediate his specific learning disabilities. First, Larry was given an explanation of his test scores to enhance his self-image and to provide him with information about his intelligence and potential. As Larry progressed in the tutorial program, evidence of some resolution of his specific learning disabilities appeared. Also, different ways of handling academic situations were presented to Larry, since the general faculty opinion had been that Larry was "stupid" and a menace to faculty and student body alike.

Table 14-13

Test Scores for Case Study Subject at Ages Eight through Eleven

California Test of Mental Maturity, Age 8

	Raw Score	IQ	Percentile
Language	20	69	2
Nonlanguage	33	93	34
Total	53	77	7

California Achievement Test, Age 8

	Raw Score	Grade	Percentile
Vocabulary	12	1.5	10
Comprehension	6	1.7	14
Total	18	1.6	12

School and College Aptitude Test, Age 9

	Raw Score	Percentile
Verbal	230	20
Quantitative	242	40
Total	423	20

Sequential Test for Educational Progress, Age 9

	Score	Percentile
Reading	226	06
Math	230	17
Writing	223	10

School and College Aptitude Test, Age 10.3

	Score	Percentile
Science	242	19
Social Studies	238	17
Listening	253	17

School and College Aptitude Test, Age 11

	Percentile
Verbal	2
Quantitative	25

Sequential Test of Education Progress, Age 11

	Percentile
Reading	10
Math	14
Writing	04

Larry's reading program was based on instruction in systematic decoding. Workbooks were totally eliminated, to erase Larry's image of his academic materials as "baby-like." Newspapers, creative writing, novels, letters, telegrams, comics, games, and short stories to provide adult reading material became the content of the decoding program. When materials were too difficult, the tutor read or broke down the difficult words, and Larry read those within his competency level. The sessions were in dialogue, with positive reinforcement and direct confrontation at all times.

After six months of tutoring, two to three hours per week, Larry made very rapid progress in both silent and oral reading. He had progressed from the sports page (in Hawaii this is difficult, because the players' names are multiethnic, which posed his biggest reading obstacle) to other sections of the paper with good comprehension and minimal decoding problems. He was able to read simple novels such as *The Sting* and *Jonathan Livingston Seagull* with only one or two pronunciation errors per page.

Behaviorally, there had been rapid development of a close rapport in the tutorial relationship and an openness to instruction. Larry's self-image had significantly improved, as he believed himself to be intelligent and capable of learning. He considered academic skills to be a vehicle to increase his life options. His verbal ability had greatly increased, with much greater distance between impulse and action. Eye contact was achieved and maintained. Larry's problem-solving ability expanded; he was able to initiate verbal problem-solving discussions with adults, and his general demeanor was more calm, open, and accepting.

At the midpoint of tutorial instruction, Larry had to go through the reopening of a prior case for assault. He again became highly disruptive in school and with his family. His academic progress rate began to decline. Motor overflow increased, as did his apparent tension level.

At the culmination of the first year of tutoring, academic tests showed gains in all areas, particularly in math. Testing was accompanied by a high anxiety level, and his test performance was lower than his daily functioning level. His daily academic work improved in quality and quantity, and he read novels outside of class. Assignments were completed outside of tutorial sessions. There was a change from printing to cursive writing, and math proceeded from fractions to simple algebraic concepts.

Behaviorally, Larry solved a series of personal problems with his girl friend and his family in a mature and acceptable manner. There were significant positive changes for Larry in his relationships to staff, teachers, and fellow students.

Funding problems and, perhaps, a measure of success brought Larry's tutorial program to an end. Some of his progress is demonstrated by the following written passage, far different in quantity and quality from previous samples, for at the initiation of the program Larry could only dictate a story that was brief and meager in language expression. At age seventeen Larry wrote:

I WORKED WITH THE LITTLE KIDS—THE YOUNGEST GROUP [7 years and under] WITH THE PARKS AND RECREATION. WE WENT

CAMPING DOWN EWA [east end of island] FOR THREE DAYS. WE WENT SWIMMING THE FIRST DAY AND WE CAUGHT CRABS. WE HAD SNACKS, PLAY BINGO AND SPIN THE BOTTLE AND WE WENT TO SLEEP.

WE GOT UP, ATE BREAKFAST WE PLAYED FOOTBALL. WE GOT TOGETHER AND WENT SWIMMING IN THE OCEAN. WE CAME BACK, TOOK A SHOWER AND ATE LUNCH. THEN WE WENT HIKING UP IN THE MOUNTAINS. THEN WE CAME BACK, TOOK A SHOWER, ATE DINNER, PLAYED A FEW GAMES—THE KIDS PLAYED RECORDS AND HAD A DANCE CONTEST.

THE OLD FOLKS WENT DRINKING AND CRASHED [went to sleep] IN MY TENT. CURFEW IS 10 O'CLOCK, AND EVERYONE WENT SLEEP.

This essay demonstrates some of the benefits of the assistance Larry received and used. He continues to demonstrate the dual language system and the life-style that differentiates him from his peers who succeed in school.

It should be noted that the main artery of the instructional strategy used to increase Larry's competence in reading was the acceptance of his bidialect language and his cultural heritage. This was underscored by conducting the tutoring program in dialogue fashion. He was involved in making choices in what to write about, what he wanted to read, and what he wanted to know. These choices became the basis of his dialogue with the tutor. At the same time, the tutor learned a great deal about the Hawaiian life-style and the dimensions of Larry's life space. In the process, the tutor and her children were guaranteed safety in Larry's neighborhood by his family.

Skills were attended to in a tactical sense based upon the authors' dictum, "What do you need to know to do what you need to do?" The match between the tutor and the tutee was based upon mutual respect. It also involved a recognition of the adaptive skills Larry desired to develop in order to cope with the expectations of the school system that would allow him to pursue his personal goals. Unfortunately, funding was discontinued before Larry's remediation program was considered complete. Still, significant academic progress and behavioral change were made. After a two-year drop-out period, Larry went to the mainland and resumed his education in a junior college.

Summary

This chapter has been concerned with a context for viewing the major reading problems in the state of Hawaii. A brief description has been given of three large-scale programs that address reading-instruction strategies.

The case study of Larry was presented to provide insights into reading-program management for an individual with significant reading and learning disabilities. But Larry represents only one of some 3,648 children identified in Hawaii as having specific learning disabilities.

The state of Hawaii Special Education Advisory Council (1977) has released estimates about its future clientele. By 1980, 6,033 children will have been identified as having specific learning disabilities. Services will be provided for all. Programs for such children include self-contained classrooms, resource rooms, and diagnostic-prescriptive services. The services of ancillary professionals (that is, speech and language therapists, occupational therapists, and social workers) will also be provided. By 1980 the state of Hawaii anticipated that a total of 16,744 children would be served in special education programs.

> All children need the experience of knowing the excitement of cultural difference in the context of human needs. All children need the experience of knowing "their" difference is a plus rather than a minus in the context of common human learning. All children need to be able to "read" as much as they can, whether it be a contract with fine print, a repair manual, or an intimate letter. For that we are accountable and our accountability must emerge from a system founded on regard for the child, for every child is a possibility (Fargo 1973).

References

Cassirer, E. 1944. *An Essay on Man: An Introduction to a Philosophy of Human Culture*. London: Oxford.

Department of Education. 1973, 1975, 1976. Sequential Tests of Educational Progress Scores of Schools (unpublished computer printout). Honolulu: Department of Education, Office of Instructional Services.

———. 1975-1976. *Compensatory Education Report, 1975-1976*. Honolulu: Department of Education, Office of Instructional Services.

———. 1977. Hawaii Special Education Advisory Council (unpublished report). Honolulu: Department of Education.

Dykstra, G., Kohi, S., Lai, M., Look, M., Nunes, S., and Port, R., 1975. *Report of the C, D, and T Ad Hoc Committee on the State's Minimum Testing Program*. Honolulu: Department of Education.

East-West Center Population Institute. 1970. *Special Tabulation of 1970 Census of the Population*. Honolulu: East-West Center.

Fargo, G. 1973. It's a possibility. Talk at Claremont Reading Conference.

Fuchs, L. 1961. *Hawaii Pono*. New York: Harcourt, Brace and World.

Gallimore, R., and Howard, A. 1968. *Studies in Hawaiian Community: Na Mahamaha o Nanakuli*. Pacific Anthropological Records No. 1. Honolulu: B.P. Bishop Museum.

Haas, M., and Resurrection, P. (eds.). 1976. *Politics and Prejudice in Contemporary Hawaii*. Honolulu: Coventy Press.

Hawaii, State of. 1977. *Data Book 1977*. Honolulu: Department of Planning and Economic Development.

Hawaiian culture. 1977. *Hawaii Tribune-Herald*. November 9.

Kahn, E. 1973. In J. Dannemiller (ed.), *Ethnicity at the University of Hawaii*. Honolulu: Survey Research Office.

Lai, M., and Post, R., 1976. *Evaluation Report: Hawaii English Program*. Honolulu: Department of Education.

Lei, M. 1975. *Regression Analyses of the Relationship between Socioeconomic Variables and the SAT and the Otis-Lennon Test*. Honolulu: Department of Education.

Lenneberg, E. 1967. *Biological Foundation of Language*. New York: Wiley.

Lind, A.W. 1967. Hawaii's people. In State of Hawaii, *Data Book 1977*. Honolulu: Department of Planning and Economic Development.

Norton, N.E., Stout, W.T., and Fischer, C. 1976. Academic performance in Hawaii. In M. Haas and P. Resurrection (eds.), *Politics and Prejudice in Contemporary Hawaii*. Honolulu: Coventy Press.

Schmitt, R. 1977. Demographic statistics of Hawaii: 1778-1965, 1968, 1970. In State of Hawaii, *Data Book 1977*. Honolulu: Department of Planning and Economic Development.

Smith, H., et al., 1976. Flowing Wells Public Schools. In R.G. Tharp and R. Gallimore (eds.), The Mutual Problems of Hawaiian-American Students in Public Schools (Technical report). Honolulu: Kamehameha Schools.

Tharp, R.G. and Gallimore, R. (eds.). 1976. The Mutual Problems of Hawaiian-American Students in Public Schools (Technical report). Honolulu: Kamehameha Schools.

15

Learning Problems of Indian Children

Rajalakshmi Muralidharan

Background of the Indian Educational System

The extent and type of learning problems of Indian children can be better understood against the backdrop of the Indian educational system. The traditional system of education in India in the beginning of the nineteenth century was such that only a privileged few (the higher castes) were entitled to the highest education. Even formal primary education was available only to the boys of the higher castes. Girls and the lower-caste boys were not given the opportunity to learn. After the British invasion, the British administration introduced a system of education in India that prepared a class of people to work as intermediaries between the government and the masses. This privileged group had access to Western knowledge, knew English, and enjoyed the comforts of the colonial society almost as much as the British themselves. This led to the widening of the gap between the poor and the rich.

India became independent in 1947. Article 45 of the new constitution stated that by 1960 the state would strive to provide compulsory and free education for all children until they reach the age of fourteen years. But even thirty years after independence it had not been possible for the state to implement this, although a good distance has been covered, considering where the country was in 1947. The enrollments in 1975-1976 in grades one to five officially stood at 66.4 million and those in grades six to eight at 16.2 million. A primary school has been provided within walking distance of the homes of most children in the age group six to eleven years and for almost 60 percent of the children in the age group eleven to fourteen years. Yet if universal enrollment in the age group six to fourteen is to be reached by 1985-1986, it will be necessary to bring into the school stream an additional 52 million children (Naik 1977). This obviously is a difficult task.

Apart from the difficulty of bringing in such a large number of children, there are certain other repercussions. The nonattenders come from the most vulnerable sections of society. They are primarily girls or children of the lower castes. It is not easy to break through traditional beliefs to convince them of the need for education.

Universal enrollment is indeed a formidable task but even more so is universal retention. The drop-out rate in Indian primary schools is alarmingly high. The proportion is as high as 60 percent between grades one and five and 75 percent between grades one and eight. That is, for every hundred children entering grade one, only twenty-five go beyond grade eight. This has remained almost unchanged during the last thirty years.

The Indian educational system has assumed gigantic proportions. It has about 700,000 educational institutions, enrolls 100 million students at all stages, has more than 3.5 million teachers, and involves an expenditure of 25 billion rupees (about $3.3 billion). Yet it benefits only the children of the upper and middle classes. The disadvantaged children have very little chance of success in the present structure. Sixty percent of the people have remained illiterate and are in no position to profit from this vast educational endeavor. The majority of children who are enrolled in school today are first-generation learners. The stimulation and support that they receive from home are minimal. Neither the parents nor the children find much meaning or relevance in the present system of education so far as their day-to-day living is concerned.

Most of the schools have few teaching aids or educational equipment. A very large number of primary schools are single-teacher schools, particularly in the rural areas. By and large, teaching is very formal and rigid. Efforts are being made to revise the curriculum and make it more meaningful and realistic. The main catalytic agents for educational reforms are the National Council of Educational Research and Training at the central level and the State Institutes of Education at the state levels. The highest priority during the sixth five-year-plan period is being given to adult education and the universalization of primary education.

In this context one can very well imagine the extent and plight of children with learning disabilities. There are a limited number of special schools for the physically handicapped and the mentally retarded. But the majority of children with learning problems are in the regular schools and receive no help except that which can be given by the class teacher. However, it is also true that, in the metropolitan cities and big towns, child-guidance clinics are set up to help children, but these services are available only to a small minority.

Since children with learning disabilities are generally found in ordinary schools in India and since no special help is available to more than 95 percent of these children, some studies of children attending these schools are cited here to show the extent of existing learning problems.

Research Evidence

Developmental Studies of Indian Children Aged Two and One-Half to Five Years

A study of adaptive, language, personal-social, and motor development of children in the age group of two and one-half to five years was conducted in urban, rural, and industrial areas. Seven different centers in various parts of the country participated (Muralidharan 1970-1972). Only the urban samples were drawn from nursery schools. The study was done both longitudinally and cross-sectionally, and the sample comprised more than 7,000 children. The results demonstrated that rural children showed late development by one to one and one-half years in almost all tasks of language development as compared to urban children. Children from the industrial areas were found to be faster than rural children but slower than their urban counterparts. The language tests included naming and identifying pictures; use of objects; comprehension; concepts of time and right and left; ability to give one's own name, age and address; action-agent test; humor; following directions; following prepositions; naming parts of the body; and responding to picture cards and to picture books.

In adaptive development the nursery-school urban sample was found to be faster than the rural children or the children from the industrial areas. The tests included block-play, form-adaptation, drawing, form-discrimination, number-concept, color-identification, immediate memory, comparative judgment, and problem-solving. The differences were striking in all the drawing tasks, in number-concept, and in color-identification. In these tests rural children were far behind urban children.

In motor development, too, the urban children were found to be faster than the children from the other two areas. The tests included ball-play, standing, walking and running, ascending and descending steps, skipping, hopping, jumping, and handskills such as threading beads and cutting.

Personal-social development was studied by using interview schedules with mothers. The schedules covered the behaviors of eating, sleeping, elimination, dressing, personal hygiene, communication, play, and developmental detachment. The trend was the same as that seen in the other aspects of development in that, in the majority of tasks, the urban children were faster.

The implication of these results is serious. In almost all tasks the urban nursery-school children were found to do better than the rural children or children from the industrial areas. The differences are particularly striking in all tests connected with school, such as paper-and-pencil tests, number tests, and picture-vocabulary tests. Rural children were found to be having trouble in all these tests. This implies that the rural children, who form the majority in India, enter school without any kind of preparation for schooling. The primary school, on the other hand, is formal and rigid and does not give much scope to helping children adjust to the demands of school. The process of schooling therefore becomes too difficult for them, and many pupils either have to repeat the grade or leave school. This is partly the reason for the high figure of wastage and stagnation in the early primary classes.

Developmental Studies of Children Aged
Five and One-Half to Eleven Years

This study focused on the relationship between environmental variables and school achievement (Muralidharan, et al., in preparation). Seven different centers in various parts of the country participated in the study. Each center dealt with certain specific inconstancies, such as home or school variables and their relationship with school achievement. A core study at Delhi took into account many of the variables that were studied at the regional centers and their relationships with school achievement. The sample consisted of children in grades one, two, and five, including ages five and one-half to six and one-half, six and one-half to seven and one-half, and nine and one-half to eleven, respectively. The measures of school achievement were reading and arithmetic. The reading and arithmetic tests were first developed in Delhi, in Hindi, for grades one, two, and five. They were then adapted for use in the other regional languages. Thus, the tests administered at the different regional centers were not the same, but they were similar in content and type. Although these tests took into account the syllabi prescribed for grades one, two, and five, they were not based on any single textbook but were more general in nature.

The language-achievement tests for grade one were word-recognition, sentence-comprehension, and matching pictures with sentences. For grade two they were matching pictures with sentences (a common test for both grades one and two), sentence-completion, and read-and-do tests. In grade five the tests were finding synonyms, finding opposites, and reading-comprehension. The arithmetic tests, like the language tests, were founded on the syllabi for each class but were not based on any single textbook. They measured the extent of knowledge, skill, application, and logical reasoning that the children had acquired during the course of their study of arithmetic.

Tables 15-1 and 15-2 give the percentages of poor achievers in language and arithmetic, respectively, in the different centers. For convenience, the poor achiever was defined as one who scored 25 percent or below in the achievement tests. In the metropolitan cities of Delhi and Bombay, the sample of children studied did not include a rural sample. The Delhi sample was purely urban. Bombay had two types, one from urban industrial colonies and the other from the nonindustrial areas. In both Hyderabad and Varanasi urban and rural children were studied, but in Hyderabad no significant differences were found between urban and rural children or between boys and girls and therefore no attempt was made to report the data separately for the two groups.

The result given in table 15-1 show that language-learning difficulties are acute in the Hindi-speaking areas of Delhi and Varanasi. In grade one in Delhi as many as 75 percent of the boys scored below 25 percent on language-

Table 15-1
Distribution of Poor Achievers on Language-Achievement Tests
(Percentages)

	First Grade		Second Grade		Fifth Grade	
	Boys	*Girls*	*Boys*	*Girls*	*Boys*	*Girls*
Delhi urban	75	60	51	28	22	10
Bombay non-industrial	16	18	10	0	10	11
Bombay industrial	26	25	6	0	20	16
Hyderabad urban and rural	0	0	0	0	15	
Varanasi urban	64	40	42	23	20	21
Varanasi rural	52	58	32	32	24	45

Poor achievers are those who scored 25 percent or below.

achievement tests. Difficulties were found to persist in grade two also. However, in grade five the number of poor achievers goes down (comparatively), except in the case of rural girls of Varanasi, of whom 45 percent fall into the poor-achievers category. Results are not so bleak in the other states. In Telugu (Hyderabad-speaking) we found poor achievers only at grade-five level. In Bombay, which is in the west of India, the number of poor achievers is much less than in the Hindi-speaking areas.

Table 15-2 shows more or less the same trends in arithmetic achievement. However, there are some differences in that, in Hyderabad, the number of poor achievers seems to be increasing from class to class, while in Varanasi the number remains more or less the same.

As with language achievement, in arithmetic achievement children from Hindi-speaking areas show more problems than those from the other areas. This may be expected, as the Hindi-speaking belt is considered educationally backward from the point of view of enrollment ratio in schools and adult literacy. Consequently the learning problems of these children are also likely be be greater than those of the other children, who may be receiving more support from their families or communities.

Table 15-2
Distribution of Poor Achievers on Arithmetic-Achievement Tests
(Percentages)

	First Grade		Second Grade		Fifth Grade	
	Boys	*Girls*	*Boys*	*Girls*	*Boys*	*Girls*
Delhi urban	55	35	48	28	18	13
Bombay non-industrial	23	30	18	21	8	12
Bombay industrial	30	25	23	33	13	18
Hyderabad urban and rural	13		16		25	
Varanasi urban	48	32	38	29	43	34
Varanasi rural	48	60	38	34	43	58

Poor achievers are those who scored 25 percent or below.

The data indicate that learning problems, particularly in the first two years of primary school, are widespread and are not restricted to a small percentage of children. Therefore, what is required is a general toning-up of the total school system, including more realistic curricula, changes in the teaching-learning strategies, and support facilities such as provision of books and play materials to children.

High Intelligence and Poor Achievement

How many of these poor achievers were high in intelligence? For convenience, children having an IQ of 120 or above were considered the high-intelligence group. The poor achievers, as defined earlier, were those scoring 25 percent or below in achievement tests. Table 15-3 gives the percentage of children with high IQs who were poor achievers in language or arithmetic and in both. The results show intercenter variations, but by and large children in Varanasi appear to be having the most problems. The table also shows, however, the extent of the wastage of the talented children. Provision is scarce and facilities to diagnose the specific learning difficulties of these children or to organize remedial programs are limited.

International Studies of Educational Achievement

India as one of the fourteen countries that participated in the studies conducted by the International Association for the Evaluation of Educational

Table 15-3
Distribution of Poor Achievers on Language and Arithmetic Test with IQs of 120 or Above
(Percentages)

	Delhi	Varanasi	Bombay	Hyderabad
Language				
First grade	0	25	4	0
Second grade	22	0	1	0
Fifth grade	2	14	2	4
Arithmetic				
First grade	11	15	4	0
Second grade	22	24	11	8
Fifth grade	12	34	7	26
Language and Arithmetic				
First grade	0	10	2	0
Second grade	13	5	0	0
Fifth grade	2	9	2	5

Poor achievers are those who scored 25 percent or below.

Achievement (IEA). This study assessed the achievement of Indian children in their mother tongue (Hindi) and in science at ages ten plus and fourteen plus and in the last grade of secondary school. The study was done on children in the Hindi-speaking areas. The results showed that the achievement of Indian children was very poor when compared to children from the developed countries in Europe or from the United States (Thorndike 1973).

The samples for the IEA study and the study cited on children from five and one-half to eleven years were drawn primarily from among schools where the language of instruction is Hindi. However, the trend among the elite is to send their children to high-fee-charging English medium schools. Thus, the high-achieving students, by and large, must have been left out of both studies. To check this further, Shukla (1974) administered the IEA tests to a select sample of children drawn from three high-fee-charging English-medium private schools in Delhi. Table 15-4 shows the achievements of three groups: the sample from the developed countries, the Indian IEA sample, and the Indian select sample.

The results in table 15-4 indicate that the achievement level of the Indian select sample is far superior to that of the Indian IEA sample and compares favorably with the sample from the developed countries. Their achievement in language is not as good as that in science, but this is because these children have had all their education in English; despite the fact that Hindi is their mother tongue, their grasp of the language is limited. Had these children been tested in achievement in English rather than in Hindi, perhaps they might have scored as well as those in the developed countries. Patel's (1967) findings were that the Indian students in grade ten who learned English as the first language obtained scores comparable to grade-ten students in the United States.

Yet the fact remains that the majority of children in the Hindi-speaking areas (represented by the IEA sample) are having tremendous learning difficulties. Possible measures that may be tried to strengthen the achievement of children include improved facilities for language development outside the school, such as village libraries and reading rooms; better access to com-

Table 15-4
Mean Scores for Private-School and State-School Hindi-Speaking Children versus those of Developed Countries on the International Association for Evaluation of Educational Achievement (IEA) Reading and Science Tests

| | Age 10+ | | Age 14+ | | High-School Senior | |
	Science	Reading	Science	Reading	Science	Reading
Developed countries	16.7	17.6	22.3	25.5	21.9	25.2
Indian private schools	14.2	15.5	26.8	18.4	27.4	14.1
Indian state school	8.5	8.5	7.6	5.2	6.2	3.5

munications media, such as community television or radio sets; and refined teaching-learning stratagies.

Intervention Programs

Keeping the generally low level of development and achievement of children in mind, some attempts have been made to introduce intervention programs that would help to improve that general level of development and achievement.

Programs for Preschoolers

There is a growing awareness of the crucial significance of the early years for the ultimate development of the child. Preschool education is not a part of the school system in India, but in many areas of the country pilot projects and programs are being tried to provide children with a better start in life. Many of them are carried out by voluntary agencies, but some are also provided by the state governments. Coverage of this age group is very limited, but these attempts may be looked at as a beginning. Approximately one million children are covered under various programs.

Through its state boads the Central Social Welfare Board operates a grant-in-aid scheme for nursery schools (Balwadis) that run a composite program of education, health, and nutrition for young children. The Gram Bal Shikshan Kendra of Kosbad hills, founded by veteran educator Tarabai Modak, has been successfully experimenting with evolving suitable types of preprimary and primary schools for the children of the tribal community. Schools were initially set up in the meadows for those children who were busy grazing cattle. These were later termed "meadow schools." The institute works as a center for the health and development of the family as a whole through a variety of programs.

Village preschools of Tamil Nadu in the south of India are under the control of the State Social Welfare Board and the Department of Women's Welfare of the government of Tamil Nadu. This scheme is unique in that it trains local women with minimum educational qualifications for a short period, and then they are appointed preschool teachers at a very nominal honorarium. This has enabled the state to provide preschool education on a large scale.

The use of "mobile creches" is another scheme that is in operation for the disadvantaged children. Under this scheme children are provided with health, nutrition, and education while their mothers are at work. This project is for children of the construction workers at sites where huge building constructions are in progress. The term *mobile creches* is derived from the fact that these institutions are in temporary sheds on the construction sites; as the construction work at one site is completed, they move to the next site. Mobile creches function in the cities of Delhi and Bombay and are managed by a voluntary agency.

The Integrated Child Development Service Project is another scheme that is sponsored by the Department of Social Welfare of the government of India for children from birth to six years. This project aims to serve the children from the most vulnerable areas, such as the tribal pockets, the urban slums, and remote rural areas. It provides health care, supplementary nutrition, and education to young children up to six years of age and to pregnant and lactating mothers.

The municipal corporations in big cities also run preschool centers. The Municipal Corporation of Delhi, for example, runs about 500 nursery schools. A study was done on children who attended these nursery schools to find the effect of preschool education on the school-readiness of children (Muralidharan and Banerji 1975). A sample of children was drawn from grade one of twenty-seven primary schools of the Municipal Corporation of Delhi. The experimental (E) group had had preschool education, while the control (C) group came into grade one straight from homes, without preschooling. All the children tested belonged to the low-income group, the average income being around 200 rupees (less than $25) per month. The nursery schools that the E group had attended were not ideal; they were badly lacking in space and equipment but had trained teachers. Testing was done when both groups were newly admitted to grade one. The tests consisted of a reading-readiness test and a number-readiness test. The results showed that in both reading and number readiness the E group scored significantly higher than the C group (see table 15-5).

The findings imply that, although environmental deprivation has an adverse effect on child development, compensatory-education programs help to a

Table 15-5
Mean Scores of Children with and without Preschool Education in Reading- and Number-Readiness

	With Preschool Education		Without Preschool Education		
	Mean	S.D.	Mean	S.D.	Critical Ratio
Reading-readiness	14.26	3.45	10.39	3.45	8.80[a]
Number-readiness	14.77	3.15	12.07	3.90	5.68[a]

Number of boys: with preschool, 49; without preschool, 48. Number of girls: with preschool 60; without preschool, 95. Mean age: with preschool, 5 years, 3 months; without preschool, 5 years, 9 months.

[a]Significant at the 0.01 level.

large extent to prevent or ameliorate many conditions that affect development. This fact is of particular significance in the context of Indian conditions, wherein the majority of parents are economically or educationally disadvantaged and are in no position to give the required experiences to children for success in school.

Intervention through Television

Educational television is in its infancy in India. During 1975-1976 the Indian government launched a major experiment in education for the adults and children in far-flung remote rural areas through its Satellite Instructional Television Experiment (SITE). Children studying in approximately 2,400 schools in remote rural areas of six states were exposed to enrichment programs on television through a communications satellite. The programs were aimed at improving children's understanding of their environment, thus affecting their day-to-day living and their achievement in school.

A study was undertaken to evaluate the impact of these programs on children (Shukla and Kumar 1977). A sample of 100 third- and fifth-grade children who were exposed to television formed the experimental (E) group from each state, and a comparable sample of another 100 children who were not exposed to television formed the control (C) group. These children were given achievement tests in their mother tongue, in social studies, and in general science. They were also given a battery of language-development tests, including listening-comprehension, word-meaning, verbal analogy, and verbal fluency. Tests were given both before and after the television experiment. The findings showed that exposure to television did not make any appreciable difference in children's achievement in school subjects. However, that was not the case with the language-development tests. In all six states children showed a gain in mean score on language-development tests after they were exposed to the television experiment. This was perhaps because the programs were not syllabus-oriented but provided general enrichment. Or perhaps the intervention time was too short to make a real dent in the school subjects but was sufficient to make an impact on the child's language development. The findings implied that well-planned programs on television are likely to lift the general level of language development of the child.

Home Intervention

Some efforts have also been made to work with mothers at home, through home visits, in order to help children learn language and scholastic tasks better. This is particularly relevant in the present context, when preschool-education facilities are available to only a small minority of children. The studies are primarily experimental in nature and are being done on small samples by university students and staff.

One such study investigated whether specific learning experiences offered to the mothers for a short period of time helped the children to perform better in learning language and scholastic tasks (Parekh 1977). The mothers were drawn from the low-income group, the experimental group was given six weeks of training in the areas of story-telling, songs and rhymes, visual and auditory discrimination, concept-development, prearithmetic experiences, and understanding of cause-and-effect relationships. The control group did not receive any training. The children of both groups of mothers were given pretests and posttests in language and scholastic tasks. The mean age of the children under study was 62.8 months. The findings were that the experimental-group children showed a higher mean gain in both language and school-readiness tasks.

Such home intervention has a great deal of relevance in the present Indian situation. Programs directed at child-rearing can be built around adult education for young parents. Creating an interest in education and making the parents aware of their role and responsibility in the education of their children are of primary importance if we are to achieve the target of universalization of education.

Provisions for Children with
Learning Disabilities

Provisions for children with learning disabilities are very limited in India. Some help is available to them in the cities and big towns through the child-guidance clinics and speech clinics usually attached to big hospitals. There are also some private clinics that cater to the high-income group. Some municipal corporations, such as the New Delhi Municipal Committee, have also set up child-guidance clinics. Some schools have school counselors who help children with learning problems. A few private facilities have remedial classes attached to the schools, while some others have resorted to streaming by ability level and using different techniques of teaching for different ability groups. However, it should be made clear that all these facilities are primarily available only to the urban children.

Some facilities exist for the education of the severely handicapped. For example, there are about 100 institutions for the mentally retarded, about 150 schools for the blind, about 120 for the deaf, and about 12 for orthopedically handicapped children. The National Institute of Mental Health and the National Institute of Speech and Hearing are the leading institutes that train workers in psychological medicine, medical psychology, and speech and hearing. Some voluntary organizations, such as the Federation for the Welfare of the Mentally Retarded, have been active in projecting the needs of the mentally retarded and in activating programs and provisions for them.

Thus, although facilities and expertise are available, they are like drops in the ocean when one takes into account the size of the country and the number of children who need help. At present, the only possibility appears to be to concentrate on the training of teachers and the child-welfare workers who work directly with children. They should be acquainted with some of the common learning problems of children and methods for teachers to cope with such problems. With understanding, sympathy, and tolerance from the teachers, many of the children who drop out of school today should be able to face the demands of the school more adequately and competently.

References

Muralidharan, R. 1970-1972. Developmental Studies of Indian Children Age 2½ to 5 Years (mimeographed reports). New Delhi: National Council of Educational Research and Training.

Muralidharan, R., et al. A Study of Children, Ages 5½ to 11 Years: Relationship between Environmental Process Variables and School Achievement (in preparation). Development of Educational Psychology and Foundations of Education. New Delhi: National Council of Educational Research and Training.

Muralidharan, R., and Banerji, U. 1975. Effect of preschool education on the school readiness of underprivileged children of Delhi. *International Journal of Early Childhood* 7:2.

Naik, J. 1977. *Education for Our People.* New Delhi: Indian Council of Social Science Research.

Parekh, K. 1977. An experimental study determining the effects of learning experiences offered to the mothers on learning abilities of preschool children. In *Synopses Series No. 11* (March), University of Baroda Child Development Department.

Patel, K. 1967. Survey of language achievement, reasoning ability and memory in relation to academic achievement among high school pupils attending English medium schools in and around Calcutta. In M. Buch (ed.), *A Survey of Research in Education.* Baroda: Centre for Advanced Study in Education.

Shukla, S. 1974. Achievements of Indian children in mother tongue (Hindi) and science. *Comparative Education Review* 18:2.

Shukla, S., and Kumar, K. 1977 *SITE Impact Study on Children.* NCERT-ISRO Project, Space Application Center. Ahmedabad: Indian Space Research Organization.

Thornkide, R. 1973. *Reading Comprehension Education in Fifteen Countries. International Studies in Evaluation Vol. III.* International Association for the Evaluation of Educational Achievement. Stockholm: Almqvist and Wiskell.

16 Reading and Learning Disabilities in Japan

Yoshitatsu Nakano and
Masaki Suzuki

Background of Education in Japan

After World War II the organization of the various Japanese public institutions shifted to a democratic basis. The educational system was also reformed; the multitrack method of education was changed to a single-track system, and equal educational opportunity was provided for all people in keeping with their abilities.

Formerly, Imperial ordinances established basic principles and prescribed the forms and procedures of education in Japan. Since the end of the war, however, education has been governed by constitutional and statutory laws as implemented by cabinet orders.

The constitution sets forth the basic national educational policy as follows: "All people shall have the right to receive an equal education correspondent with their abilities, as provided by law. The people shall be obligated to have all boys and girls under their protection receive ordinary education as provided for by law. Such compulsory education shall be free" (Article 26). The Fundamental Law of Education sets forth in more detail the aims and principles of education in accordance with the spirit of the constitution as follows:

> Article 1. Aim of Education.
> Education shall aim at the full development of personality, striving for the rearing of the people, sound in mind and body, who shall love truth and justice, esteem individual value, respect labor, have a deep sense of responsibility, and be imbued with an independent spirit, as builders of the peaceful state and society.
>
> Article 4. Compulsory Education.
> The people shall be obligated to have boys and girls under their protection receive nine years of general education. No tuition fee shall be charged for compulsory education in schools established by the state and public bodies.

Furthermore, the School Education Law of 1947 specifies that school administration is to be under the jurisdiction of the Ministry of Education. Administration is centralized, with few, if any, local differentials. The content of school education is set forth on the basis of the course of study defined by the Ministry of Education. Since 1947 six years of elementary school plus three years of middle school, totaling nine years, have been made compulsory. Parents are obliged to place their children in school at the age of six. As a result, the school attendance rate is over 99 percent. Preschool education is not compulsory but is prevalent, and almost all children attend kindergarten.

Literacy

According to the results of comparative research reported in 1964 by the United Nations Educational, Scientific and Cultural Organization (UNESCO), the Ministry of Education of Japan reported that the problem of illiteracy has been completely solved. By definition, an illiterate person in Japan is one who cannot read or write *kanji, hiragana,* and *katakana* at all. Accordingly, 2.1 percent of the entire population was judged illiterate in 1948; in 1955 the rate of illiteracy was less than 0.8 percent.

Japanese students must learn four different reading and writing systems: two types of *kana* (*hiragana* series and *katakana* series) plus *kanji* and *romaji* (see detailed discussion in next section of this chapter). Moreover, they have to learn at least 1,850 kanji characters for daily use. Nevertheless, over 99.7 percent of the total population is literate; the remainder are considered mentally retarded.

This very high rate of literacy in Japan may be attributed to the following:

1. Phonetic symbols (*kana*), which are easy to learn, are used initially.
2. Education is compulsory from the first through the ninth grade. Over a period of 100 years a very strictly organized system of compulsory education has been developed.
3. Japanese parents have great respect for education and are very eager for their children to learn. Making sacrifices for a child's education is a common part of Japanese parenthood.
4. Publishing companies have made available many good reading materials at low prices.
5. Movements to stimulate reading have been very successful, including, for example, National Reading Week, the reading movement for mothers, the mother-child twenty-minute reading program, reading groups, and book-report contests (Sakamoto and Makita 1973).

Characteristics of Japanese Written Language

Japanese writing includes two different series of scripts: *kana* (phonograms) and *kanji* (ideograms). *Kana* appears in two versions, *hiragana* and *katakana.* Newspapers, magazines, and books use both *kana* and *kanji,* in mixed arrangement. *Hiragana* is most frequently used, and Japanese children must learn all *hiragana* letters in their first year of elementary school. Katakana is generally used for words originating in foreign languages, although the pronunciation of these words may be quite different from the original.

Each *kana* consists of seventy-one phonetic letters; as a rule, one letter represents one syllable. In Japanese there are only five vowels, *a, i, u, e,* and *o.* Syllables consist of a vowel only or a combination of a consonant and a vowel, such as *ka, ki, ku, ke,* and *ko.* There is only one case of a syllable that consists of a consonant only, that is, *n.* (See figure 16-1 for *hiragana* and *katakana* alphabets.)

There are some special cases of orthographic peculiarities in Japanese *kanas.* One example is *yoon,* which are contracted sounds, and another is *sokuon,* which is used as a sign for doubling the following consonant (see

HIRAGANA AND KATAKANA
ひらがな　と　カタカナ

pa	ba	da	za	ga	n	wa	ra	ya	ma	ha	na	ta	sa	ka	a
pi	bi	ji	ji	gi		i	ri	i	mi	hi	ni	chi	shi	ki	i
pu	bu	zu	zu	gu		u	ru	yu	mu	fu	nu	tsu	su	ku	u
pe	be	de	ze	ge		e	re	e	me	he	ne	te	se	ke	e
po	bo	do	zo	go		o	ro	yo	mo	ho	no	to	so	ko	o

ぱ	ば	だ	ざ	が	ん	わ	ら	や	ま	は	な	た	さ	か	あ	hiragana
ぴ	び	ぢ	じ	ぎ		い	り	い	み	ひ	に	ち	し	き	い	
ぷ	ぶ	づ	ず	ぐ		う	る	ゆ	む	ふ	ぬ	つ	す	く	う	
ぺ	べ	で	ぜ	げ		え	れ	え	め	へ	ね	て	せ	け	え	
ぽ	ぼ	ど	ぞ	ご		を	ろ	よ	も	ほ	の	と	そ	こ	お	

パ	バ	ダ	ザ	ガ	ン	ワ	ラ	ヤ	マ	ハ	ナ	タ	サ	カ	ア	katakana
ピ	ビ	ヂ	ジ	ギ		イ	リ	イ	ミ	ヒ	ニ	チ	シ	キ	イ	
プ	ブ	ヅ	ズ	グ		ウ	ル	ユ	ム	フ	ヌ	ツ	ス	ク	ウ	
ペ	ベ	デ	ゼ	ゲ		エ	レ	エ	メ	ヘ	ネ	テ	セ	ケ	エ	
ポ	ボ	ド	ゾ	ゴ		ヲ	ロ	ヨ	モ	ホ	ノ	ト	ソ	コ	オ	

Figure 16-1. Japanese Phonetic Alphabets, *Hiragana* and Katakana

figure 16-2). Also, there are some other instances in which letters are not read phonetically.

Another characteristic of the Japanese language is that most of the basic words, which children must learn in the first or second year of elementary school, are relatively short. Nevertheless, instances of confusion because of the order of letters, such as *was* and *saw* in English, are less frequent in Japanese because there are more *kana* letters than alphabetical letters. (Longer words may usually be represented with only a few *kanjis* (see figure 16-3).

Kanjis were originally borrowed from classical Chinese characters; they have the same meanings but are spoken differently. There are numerous *kanji* characters, and, at present, Japanese children must learn 1,850 *kanjis* during their nine years of compulsory education. Even during their first year of school they must learn about 46 *kanjis,* with all of the *hiraganas.*

Although each *kanji* possesses specific meaning, there are two reading procedures: *kun* (Japanese reading procedure) and *on* (Chinese reading procedure). When *kanji* is read by *kun,* the characters represent specific meanings. The *on* reading procedure may be partly phonetic, and one pronunciation may be represented by many characters. In addition, in the *on* reading procedure a word is usually formed with a sequence of *kanjis,* while one character represents one word in the *kun* reading procedure (see figure 16-4).

Most Japanese books, magazines, and newspapers are written vertically from top to bottom, while publications of mathematics and natural science are written horizontally from left to right, as in Western languages.

Special Education

The school education law provides for nine years of compulsory special education. However, only schools for the blind and the deaf have been placed under the compulsory system since 1948. A compulsory system of education for the mentally retarded, the crippled, and children with special health problems was scheduled to be enforced beginning in 1979.

Preschool education for handicapped children is most popular for the hearing-handicapped. It is normal to commence education for them at age three. In some schools education is started soon after birth. However, preschool education for other types of handicapped children is at the beginning state, with further development soon likely.

The present status of special education is shown in table 16-1. Reading or learning disabilities are not given consideration, and no special schools or classes are available for these handicaps.

拗音（ようおん）YŌON : contracted sound

pya	bya	j a	gya	r ya	mya	nya	cha	sha	kya
pyu	byu	j u	gyu	r yu	myu	nyu	chu	shu	kyu
pyo	byo	j o	gyo	r yo	myo	nyo	cho|	sho	kyo
pyū	byū	j ū	gyū	r yū	myū	nyū	chū	shū	kyū
pyō	byō	j ō	gyō	r yō	myō	nyō	chō	shō	kyō
びゃ	びゃ	じゃ	ぎゃ	りゃ	みゃ	にゃ	ちゃ	しゃ	きゃ
びゅ	びゅ	じゅ	ぎゅ	りゅ	みゅ	にゅ	ちゅ	しゅ	きゅ
びょ	びょ	じょ	ぎょ	りょ	みょ	にょ	ちょ	しょ	きょ
びゅう	びゅう	じゅう	ぎゅう	りゅう	みゅう	にゅう	ちゅう	しゅう	きゅう
びょう	びょう	じょう	ぎょう	りょう	みょう	にょう	ちょう	しょう	きょう

促音（そくおん）SOKUON : used as a sign for doubling a consonant

つ　cf。　らっぱ　rappa　(trumpet)
　　　　　いっしょ　issho　(together)
　　　　　きっと　kitto　(certainly)

う　used for lengthening a syllable with o ending.

　　　cf。　いこう　ikō　(Let us go)

は‥wa　when they are used as particles

へ‥e

Figure 16-2. *Yōon* and *Sokuon*, Orthographic Irregularities in Japanese *Kana*

EXAMPLES OF JAPANESE WORDS

kana	kanji (-kana)		
やま	山	yama	(mountain)
あるく	歩く	aruku	(walk)
あつい	暑い	atsui	(hot)
ぞう	象	zō	(elephant)
ちょうちょう	蝶々	chōchō	(butterfly)
びょういん	病院	byōin	(hospital)
しょうにしんけいがく	小児神経学	shōnishinkeigaku (pediatric neurology)	

Most basic words are shorter than English. *Kanji* shortens the words further.

Figure 16-3. Examples of Japanese Words

Reading and Learning Disabilities

In Japan the problem of learning disabilities, focused on reading and writing, has drawn almost no attention. Only a few pediatricians, child psychiatrists, neurologists, psychologists, and educators have been tackling the problem, because children with reading and writing disabilities have been deemed extremely few in number. Recently, influenced by American literature, reading disabilities due to minimal brain dysfunction (MBD) derived from abnormal prenatal or perinatal conditions have begun to attract attention.

   Although the problem of reading disability, or dyslexia, is very impor-

TWO DIFFERENT READING PROCEDURES OF KANJI

KUN (Japanese Reading procedure)

ON   (Chinese Reading procedure)

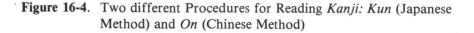

Figure 16-4. Two different Procedures for Reading *Kanji: Kun* (Japanese Method) and *On* (Chinese Method)

tant in American and European countries, it has been of little interest in Japan except for reports of sporadic cases. The study by Makita (1968), a Japanese child psychiatrist, indicated that the prevalence of reading problems in Japan was 1 percent, about one-tenth of that in English-speaking countries. It was proposed that the irregularity of the script-phonetic relationship in a language was the most potent contributing factor in the formation of reading disabilities.

However, the possibility exists that more dyslexic children might be detected if a more complete survey were performed in Japan. Suzuki (1976) found some dyslexic children in the Department of Pediatrics at Tokyo University Hospital and Tokyo University Branch Hospital. At present, thirty-nine children with dyslexia have been evaluated, twenty-six males and thirteen females.

Table 16-1
Esimated Number of Children, Number in School, and Attendance Rate, 1977

Division	Handicapped Children		Attendance in Special Schools or Classes		Number of Special Schools or Classes
	Appearance Rate (%)	Estimated Number	Number	Attendance Rate	
Visually handicapped	0.080	12,403	3,931 School for the Blind, 3,608; Special class, 323	31.7	77 schools 73 classes
Hearing-handicapped	0.110	17,053	9,573 School for the Deaf, 7,503; special class, 2,065	56.1	107 schools 396 classes
Mentally retarded	2.070	320,910	127,139 School for mentally retarded, 16,857; special class, 110,282	39.6	222 schools 17,562 classes
Crippled	0.180	27,905	16,093 School for crippled, 13,313; special class, 2,780	57.7	126 schools 523 classes
Special health problems	0.490	75,964	9,998 Special school, 4,683; special class, 5,315	13.2	73 schools 708 classes
Subtotal	2.930	454,235	166,734 Various special schools, 45,969; special class, 120,765	36.7	605 schools 19,262 classes
Speech disorders	0.330	51,160	6,063 Special class, 6,063	11.9	947 classes
Emotionally disturbed	0.430	66,662	4,108 Special class, 4,108	6.2	791 classes
Total	3.690	572,067	176,905 Various special schools, 45,969; special class, 130,936	30.9	605 schools 21,000 classes

Source: Ministry of Education

Testing and Diagnosis

Differential diagnosis of learning disabilities is performed by means of a battery of tests in which several examination methods are combined. In the neurological phase there are examinations covering soft neurological signs in motor function, cognitive ability, speech and language ability, arithmetic, laterality (evaluating hand, eye, and foot dominance), behavior evaluation, and electroencephalograms.

In addition, there are many psychological tests as well as behavior observations. Typical of these tests are the Wechsler Intelligence Scale for Children (WISC), Bender Visual Motor Gestalt Test, Frostig Developmental Test of Visual Perception, Illinois Test of Psycholinguistic Abilities (ITPA), Lincoln-Oseretsky Motor Development Scale, Benton Visual Retention Test, and the Draw-A-Man Test (Suzuki and Ohmi 1975). There are Japanese versions of all of these tests. In addition, the Standardized Reading Test and the Reading Readiness Test are used.

Some specialists put more importance on observations made by parents and teachers than on those made by psychologists. Also, there are differences in the tests used because of the different needs of medical treatment and remedial teaching. At present, diagnostic methods are still in the trial-and-error phase.

Clinical Observations

The clinical pictures of the thirty-nine schoolchildren who were diagnosed as having reading disability (dyslexia) in the Department of Pediatrics at Tokyo University Hospital and Tokyo University Branch Hospital are summarized in table 16-2. There was a high incidence of children with histories

Table 16-2
Clinical Observations of Dyslexic Children

Clinical Observation	Percentage
History of perinatal accident	41
History of delayed speech	59
Clumsiness, soft neurological signs	64
Hyperkinesia, short attention span	38
Dyscalculia	31
Spike discharges in EEG[a]	19

Source: Data collected by M. Suzuki in his clinical practice at the Tokyo University Branch Hospital.

Number observed: 26 males, 13 females.

[a]Number tested, 36.

of perinatal accidents and delayed speech development. Clumsiness and soft neurological signs were often observed. Some children showed hyperkinetic behavior, short attention span, and distractibility. Electroencephalographic examination revealed spike discharges in seven of thirty-six children. Therefore, most of these children might be diagnosed as having minimal brain dysfunction.

The characteristics of dyslexia in these children may be described as follows. Although most of the Japanese dyslexic children read one letter after another slowly and repeatedly, they often can read relatively well and can comprehend the meanings of words and short sentences. This is because each *kana* represents one syllable as a rule. In severe cases there are errors in speech sounds, and the comprehension of written language may be more difficult for them. Confusion of the order of letters in reading is sometimes observed, as in Western languages. Generally, it is difficult for them to comprehend longer sentences; when they take examinations, the results are poor (Suzuki and Miyashita 1968).

It is especially difficult for most of them to learn the orthographic pecularities, such as *sokuon* and *yōon*. They often read *sokuon* and *yōon* phonetically or with omissions. Reading *kanji* tends to be rather easy for Japanese dyslexic children, because each character has one meaning. However, when *kanji* is read using the Chinese reading procedure *(on),* in which the character is partly phonetic, it becomes more difficult for them.

Therefore, dyslexia in Japanese children results in milder difficulties than in Western children because of the specificity of the Japanese language. A boy who exemplifies how the differences in languages affects the severity of reading difficulty is described in case study 1.

Case Study 1

K.T. was a boy aged eight years, two months. He was of mixed heritage: his father was Japanese and his mother was American. He was born at thirty-six weeks gestation, and his birth weight was 2,043 grams (4.5 pounds). He sat at seven months of age and walked at fifteen months. There was a history of febrile convulsions. K.T. had lived in Japan continuously. He generally used English at home and Japanese when he played with his friends. He sometimes had hyperkinetic and impulsive behavior. Soft neurological signs, such as visuomotor incoordination, adiadochokinesis (inability to perform rapidly alternating movements), choreiform movements, and motor discoordination, were observed.

K.T. attended an American school in Japan, where most of the work was performed in English and only a few lessons were in Japanese. He could speak both English and Japanese, but in written language he learned

Japanese better, although he read one letter after another and made mistakes involving *sokuon* and *yōon,* which tends to be characteristic of Japanese dyslexic children. However, it was difficult for him to read and spell even basic English words, as shown in figure 16-5.

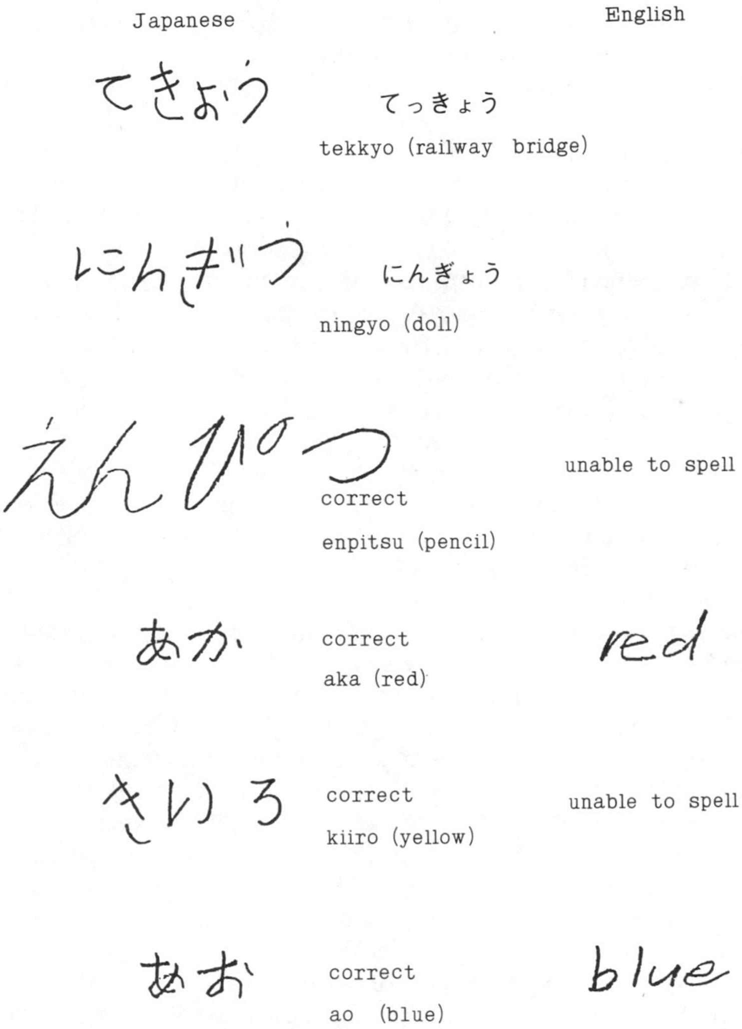

Japanese   English

てきょう   てっきょう
                tekkyo (railway bridge)

にんぎゔ   にんぎょう
                ningyo (doll)

えんぴつ   unable to spell
                correct
                enpitsu (pencil)

あか   correct   red
            aka (red)

きいろ   correct   unable to spell
            kiiro (yellow)

あお   correct   blue
            ao (blue)

In Japanese he made erors in *sokuon* and *yōon*. In English he was unable to spell many simple words.

Figure 16-5. Case Study 1: K.T., a Male Aged Eight Years, Two Months

**Comparison between Two Subtypes of
Japanese Dyslexic Children**

Recently the presence of subgroups of dyslexic children has been proposed
in some literature, including auditory dyslexia and visual dyslexia (Johnson
and Myklebust 1967); language retardation and the Gerstmann syndrome
(Kinsbourne and Warrington 1966); audiophonetic and visuospatial types
(Ingram, Mason, and Blackburn 1970); dysphonic dylsexia (Boder 1973);
and language-disorder syndrome, articulatory and graphomotor syndrome,
and visuospatial perceptual-disorder syndrome (Mattis, French, and Rapin
1975).

In our series of dyslexic children there was a high incidence of delayed
speech development but some of the children did not have histories of
delayed speech development. Our series of dyslexic children was classified
into two groups: audiophonetic types and visuospatial types.

The audiophonetic childen read words and sentences as a whole,
without correct phonetic analysis of speech sounds. They sometimes
substitute words and sentences for those of similar meaning. There are
often errors in speech sounds and omissions. Even when they read aloud, it
may be difficult for them to understand the meaning. *Kanji* may be easier
for them to read than *kana*, and the Chinese reading procedure (*on*) is
generally difficult for them. They are usually found to have more difficulty
in writing and taking dictation than in reading. There are often errors and
omissions, especially with *yōon* and *sokuon*. Even with known words there
are some mistakes in taking dictation. It is also very difficult for them to
write proper sentences.

The dyslexic children of the visuospatial type read analytically, one
phoneme after another. In Japanese, if they read slowly and repeatedly,
they may be able to understand the meaning to some extent, because
Japanese *kanas* are phonetic letters. If they read aloud, it becomes easier for
them to read and understand the meaning. However, they usually get poor
results on examinations, as the time is restricted. They usually write well but
sometimes phonetically, and they make mistakes with *yōon* and *sokuon* at
first. In most cases, errors due to orthographic peculiarities may be gradually improved, for there are only a few such peculiarities in Japanese.
Although rotations, mirror-writing, and confusion in the order of letters
may sometimes be detected, the incidence is seemingly lower than in
Western dyslexic children because of the characteristics of the Japanese
language. It must be emphasized that Japanese dyslexic children may even
read or write unfamiliar words using *kana*. They can read and write *kanji*
more easily than *kana* in the first or second year of elementary schools, but
it usually becomes more difficult for them later on, especially when the

Chinese reading procedure *(on)* is used. In junior high school they must learn English, which usually proves to be difficult for them.

Generally speaking, the dyslexic children of the audiophonetic groups have severe difficulties, while those of the visuospatial group have milder difficulties because of the characteristics of the Japanese language. Our comparison of the two types is summarized in table 16-3. Twenty-nine children were evaluated as audiophonetic. However, some children in the audiophonetic group showed abnormal results on the Bender Visual Motor Gestalt Test or the Frostig Developmental Test of Visual Perception (Japanese edition). Therefore, visuospatial disorders may also play an important role in the development of dyslexia in some of them.

The ratio of males to females was higher in the visuospatial group than in the audiophonetic group. The incidence of delayed speech development, soft neurological signs, behavior problems, dyscalculia, and electroencephalographic abnormalities was higher in the audiophonetic group.

Rabinovitch (1968) classified reading retardations into three groups: primary reading retardation (developmental dyslexia), reading retardation secondary to brain injury, and reading retardation secondary to exogenous factors. In our observations, most dyslexia in the audiophonetic group may be due to brain injury or minimal brain dysfunction. However, primary reading retardation, or developmental dyslexia, may be detected more in the visuospatial group. Dyslexic children in the visuospatial group generally show normal or above-normal intelligence. In Japan more dyslexic children of the visuospatial type may remain undiscovered, since they often have milder difficulties.

Examples of children with visuospatial dyslexia are described in the following case histories.

Table 16-3
Comparison of Clinical Observations of Audiophonetic Dyslexic Children and Visuospatial Dyslexic Children by Clinical History

Clinical Observation	Audiophonetic	Visuospatial
Perinatal accidents	13	3
Delayed speech	20	3
Clumsiness, soft neurological signs	22	3
Hyperkinesia, short attention span	12	3
Dyscalculia	10	2
Spike discharges in EEG	6	1

Source: Data collected by M. Suzuki in his clinical practice at the Tokyo University Branch Hospital.

Number of children observed: total audiophonetic, 29 (18 male, 11 female); total visuospatial, 10 (8 male, 2 female).

Case Study 2

S.U. was a boy aged nine years, five months. He had a normal birth history, and his physical, mental and speech development were normal in his preschool period. He had been referred to the Department of Pediatrics at Toyko University Hospital because of reading difficulty, at the age of nine years, five months. His parents found that he read words and sentences one letter after another and that it was difficult for him to comprehend longer sentences. When a sentence started on a new line, his reading was usually disturbed. Therefore, his schoolwork was very poor, but he could answer problems of natural science and civics orally if they were read to him. He had normal ability to calculate and was a sociable and cheerful boy.

His WISC revealed a Verbal IQ of 125, a Performance IQ of 93, and a Full Scale IQ of 111 (see table 16-4). His results on the Bender Visual Motor Gestalt Test were within the normal range. Electroencephalographic examination revealed 6 and 14 cycles-per-second positive spikes. This spike activity may partly account for the unusually low scores in Object Assembly (4) and Digit Span (5). The normal Bender test and Block Design subtest scores indicate adequte visual-motor functioning. Therefore, the low Picture Completion (7) and Object Assembly scores appear to indicate a possible figure-ground problem or inability to visualize the whole from the parts of an object.

S.U. was able to read all the *hiragana* and *katakana* letters, and, if he read one letter after another slowly and repeatedly, he could comprehend the meaning of longer sentences. He had fair ability in reading *kanji*,

Table 16-4
Scores on the Wechsler Intelligence Scale for Children for Subject of Case Study 2

Tests	Scaled Score	Age-Equivalent (years, months)
Verbal		
Information	13	11, 4
Comprehension	12	11, 4
Arithmetic	14	12, 6
Similarities	18	15, 10+
Vocabulary	19	15, 10+
Digit-span	5	6, 2
Performance		
Picture Completion	7	6, 10
Picture Arrangement	10	9, 6
Block Design	12	11, 6
Object Assembly	4	5, 0
Coding	11	10, 0
Mazes	10	9, 6

IQ = verbal, 125; performance, 93; full-scale, 111.

although it was more difficult for him to read using the *on* method. By reading aloud, his comprehension of long sentences was much improved. His reading of sentences written horizontally from left to right was poorer than for those written vertically.

In writing and dictation he was generally good, but he sometimes wrote phonetically. There were sometimes mirror-writing and rotations in his use of *katakana* (see figure 16-6).

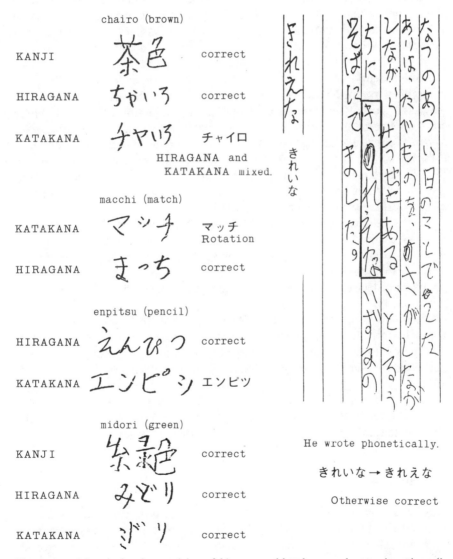

There are rotations in *katakana*, mixing of *hiragana* and katakana, and some phonetic spellings.

Figure 16-6. Case Study 2: S.U., a Male Aged Nine Years, Five Months

Case Study 3

A.K. was a girl aged nine years, nine months. Her father was also dyslexic when he was in the lower grades of elementary school. Although his reading and writing improved when he was in middle school, it was difficult for him to learn English. However, as an adult he was engaged in normal work in business.

A.K. was born at full term by cesarean section and had no accidents during her infancy. Motor, mental, and speech development were entirely normal during her preschool period. When she was in the second year of elementary school, her father observed that she had difficulty in reading. She read words and sentences one letter at a time, and it was difficult for her to comprehend long sentences. When a sentence started on a new line, she sometimes skipped the line. Confusions in the order of letters, such as mistaking *roku* "six" for *kuro* "black", were sometimes observed. There were no errors due to orthographic peculiarities such as *sokuon* and *yōon*. When she read aloud, her comprehension improved. It seemed to be more difficult for her to read books written horizontally than those written vertically. She could write sentences but sometimes wrote phonetically. There were some rotations in writing *katakana* letters. She did well in dictation, although there were some errors in writing.

Her school records were passable, except for Japanese in her first school year. She could calculate normally, but there were sometimes errors in number order, such as confusing 23 for 32. Neurological examinations were normal, including soft neurological signs. She had no particular behavior problems. Electroencephalographic examination showed no abnormal findings.

Her WISC revealed a Verbal IQ of 132 and a Performance IQ of 126. Her score on Block Design was poor (8). The Bender Visual Motor Gestalt Test was within the normal range by Koppitz scoring, although there was one rotation. Ophthalmological examinations showed no abnormal findings.

In Japan there have been no reports of hereditary dyslexia, except a case reported by Kuromaru and colleagues (1962). In our series of children, this girl was the only one who had a family history of dyslexia.

Case Study 4

M.S. was a twelve-year-old boy. There were no abnormalities connected with his perinatal period, and his physical, mental, and speech development were entirely normal during his preschool years. When he entered elementary school, it was noticed that he read one letter after another slowly, and that he had difficulty comprehending longer sentences. However, his ability within written language gradually improved, and his school record was average during his later years of elementary school. When he entered junior high school it was found that he had difficulty in learning English. He had neither soft neurological signs nor behavior problems. He was right-handed, right-footed, and left-eyed.

He could read, write, and comprehend long sentences that used Japanese phonetic letters (*hiragana* and *katakana*), and made no errors with *sokuon* and *yōon,* the orthographic peculiarities of Japanese phonetic letters. Reading *kanji,* he had some difficulty with compound words when using the Chinese reading procedure (*on*). Sometimes he made mistakes with letters of similar shape, and he had confusions in the order of letters in *kanji* writing (see figure 16-7).

難因   konnan na shigoto   試   shiken o ukeru
因難   験
因   (difficult task)   を   (take an examination)
左仕   授受
事。   け
                                        る

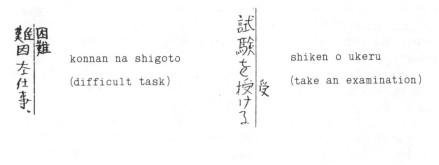

He made some errors because of confusion of the order of characters and of similar-shaped characters in *kanji*. He found spelling in English very difficult.

Figure 16-7. Case Study 4: M.S., a Twelve-Year-Old Male

In English he could read correctly such simple known words as *that, the, box, boy, book,* and *talk,* although he sometimes read in the Japanese phonetic manner, such as *kom* for *come* and *kould* for *could.* It was difficult for him to write or to take dictation in English. He sometimes wrote phonetically, such as *leter* for *letter, lan* for *learn, littl* for *little,* and *hed* for *head.* Confusions in the order of letters was also observed, as, for example, *hores* for *horse* and *houes* for *house* (see figure 16-7).

Educational Therapy

In Japan there are no special classes or schools for children with reading and learning disabilities, so most of these children attended ordinary schools. Some of the children in our study visited national or regional centers for handicapped children periodically and received educational therapy.

Some children who had milder difficulties showed adequate progress in Japanese written language, although they sometimes had difficulty in learning English, as in case study 4. Others had continuing difficulty for a long time, especially the severely dyslexic children of the audiophonetic type. They often had histories of delayed speech development, and some of them continued to have disorders in spoken language, such as poor speech-sound discrimination or shortness of auditory-memory span, even when they were elementary school children. Adequate speech therapy might prevent the appearance of severe dyslexia in some of them.

For three who had hyperkinetic behavior, short attention span, or distractibility, methylphenidate hydrochloride (Ritalin) was administered. The improvement of behavior and concentration resulting from the use of Ritalin might be a help to educational therapy.

Trends in Japan

A few specialists in the fields of pediatrics and psychiatry in Japan have been practicing diagnosis and medical treatment on children with reading and writing disabilities by handling them as children with a specific learning disability. However, because of the nature of the Japanese language, the type of reading disability frequently observed in Europe and America is quite rare. Therefore, research and treatment efforts have been modest. Reading and learning disabilities have come to the attention of psychologists and educational specialists only recently. There is still confusion of concept, and no real concensus about definitions exists.

Recently, Japanese versions of the ITPA and the Frostig Test have been made. Also, books by Johnson and Myklebust (1967), Tarnopol (1969), and Cruickshank (1977) have been translated into Japanese. The concern given to this field is on the rise. Case studies on reading and learning disabilities are reported in medicine, psychology, and special education, and the people at large have become interested. However, more research and practical efforts in this area will have to wait until some time in the future.

References

Boder, E. 1973. Developmental dyslexia: a diagnostic approach based on three atypical reading-spelling patterns. *Developmental Medicine and Child Neurology* 15:663.

Cruickshank, W. 1977 *Learning Disabilities in Home, School and Community.* Syracuse: Syracuse University Press. (Translated into Japanese by R. Itoh and Y. Nakano.)

Ingram, T., Mason, A., and Blackburn, I. 1970. A retrospective study of 82 children with reading disability. *Developmental Medicine and Child Neurology* 12:271.

Johnson, D., and Myklebust, H. 1967. *Learning Disabilities, Educational Principles and Practices.* New York: Grune and Stratton. (Translated into Japanese by R. Morinaga and K. Kamimura.)

Kinsbourne, M., and Warrington, E. 1966. Developmental factors in reading and writing backwardness. In J. Money (ed.), *The Disabled Reader: Education of the Dyslexic Child.* Baltimore: Johns Hopkins University Press.

Kuromaru, S., Okada, S., et al. 1962. On developmental alexia and agraphia. *Journal of Pediatric Practice* 25:853. (In Japanese.)

Makita, K. 1968. The rarity of reading disability in Japanese children. *American Journal of Orthopsychiatry* 38:599.

Mattis, S., French, J., and Rapin, I. 1975. Dyslexia in children and young adults: three independent neuropsychological syndromes. *Developmental Medicine and Child Neurology* 17:150.

Rabinovitch, R. 1968. Reading problems in children: definitions and classifications. In A. Keeney and V. Keeney (eds.), *Dyslexia, Diagnosis and Treatment of Reading Disorders.* Saint Louis: C.V. Mosby.

Sakamoto, T., and Makita, K. 1973. Japan. In J. Downing (ed.), *Comparative Reading.* New York: Macmillan.

Suzuki, M. 1976. Current problems on dyslexia with special reference to the Japanese language. *Pediatric Review* 9:238. (In Japanese.)

Suzuki, M., and Miyashita, H. 1968. Language disorders and minimal brain damage. *Journal of Pediatric Practice* 31:1220. (In Japanese.)

Suzuki, M., and Ohmi, K. 1975. Significance of ITPA for dyslexic children. *Journal of Pediatric Practice* 38:263. (In Japanese.)

Tarnopol, L. (ed.), 1969. *Learning Disabilities: Introduction to Educational and Medical Management.* Springfield, Ill.: Thomas. (Translated into Japanese by Y. Nakano, S. Kiode, and A. Katada.)

17

Learning and Reading Problems in Mexico

Margarita E. Nieto Herrera

Historical Development

Mexico is the third largest republic of Latin America, with an area of 760,000 square miles. Two mountain ranges parallel the west and east coasts, with the highest peak, Orizba, reaching above 18,500 feet. Between these mountain ranges lies the country's vast central plateau, which contains the area for growing Mexico's chief agricultural exports. A low desert plain rises from about 3,600 feet above sea level near the border of the United States to reach a plateau on which Mexico City is situated at an altitude of about 8,000 feet. This is Mexico's capital and largest city, with a population of approximately 8.9 million (Department of Programming and Budget of Mexico 1976).

The principal language of Mexico is Spanish. However, the Mexican people are mostly *mestizo,* mixed Indian and Spanish, and their culture derives from a combination of many groups of ancient Indian civilizations and the more recent arrival of the Spaniards (Dozer 1962). The Indian inheritance includes the great cultural developments of their Mayan, Toltec, and Aztec forebears, which occurred over many centuries before the arrival of the Spaniards.

These civilizations, which many historians claim surpassed all other American Indian peoples in written language, arithmetic, and calendar calculations, had a long history of education. Children were sent to schools that educated them according to their future roles, based on traditional social classes. There were different schools for training priests and warriors. The schools for training priests from the children of the ruling class instructed their students in reading, writing, and calculation, while other schools taught vocal and instrumental music and dancing. Sports were also important in the education of children.

The different written languages were based on hieroglyphs, which were meant to be representations of the objects being documented (pictographs) or which gave information about the objects. A transition from the pictographs occurred, and a system of phonic syllables (ideographs) slowly appeared. These ideographs were gradually embellished in great and varied detail, without concern for the other changes that were occurring. In this respect, their writings were similar to the calligraphic art form developed by the Chinese.

School Attendance
At present, children in Mexico start elementary school at six years of age, although they may attend preschool or kindergarten at earlier ages. School is compulsory to the age of fourteen. In the 1970-1971 school year, the number of school-aged children was 13,260,762, of whom 9,248,190 were attending school. The proportion of children attending school (70 percent) increased to almost 76 percent by the 1976-1977 school year. Of the children who entered school in 1970-1971, 57 percent were still enrolled (43 percent had dropped out) by the sixth grade in 1975-1976 (Department of Programming and Budget of Mexico 1976).

Historical Antecedents of Special Education

The development of special education in Mexico reflects the parallel social and historical movements. A synopsis of this development is given in appendix 17A. Briefly, special schools for the deaf and the blind were first founded when Benito Juarez was president, in 1866 and 1870, respectively. During the administration of Porfirio Díaz, correctional schools were founded for boys in 1905 and for girls in 1907. After the revolution, the first school for the mentally retarded was established in 1914.

Thereafter, individuals worked for the different types of handicapped people through the Ministry of Public Education, the Ministry of Public Health, and the services of social welfare. In recent years the presidents' wives generally have been active in helping children. Private initiative has also helped by promoting the institutions for special education and by preparing personnel. The most sophisticated educational, cultural, and economic resources of the country are located in Mexico City, along with the best educational institutions. Outside of Mexico City there are only a few such institutions.

Special-Education Facilities

Mexico has thirty-two states with a total population of about 64 million people. Of 549 special-education and rehabilitation centers, 273 are in the Federal District (population 8.9 million); 59 are in the state of Coahuila (population 1.3 million); 40 are in the state of Nuevo Leon (population 2.3 million); and the remainder are in the other states.

There are 126 learning-disability groups in regular schools concentrated in six states, with 69 in the Federal District and 46 in Coahuila. The 121 centers for mentally retarded children are found in twenty-one states. There are 22 psychological clinics and 44 speech-therapy clinics, all in the Federal District. There are 40 clinics for auditory and language problems in fourteen states and 8 centers for children with learning disabilities in four states.

Reading Problems

According to the 1972 statistics of the Ministry of Public Education on the average, 11 percent of the children failed in each elementary year and 5 percent left before finishing the school year. The problem was most acute in the first grade, where 16 percent failed and 7 percent left early, indicating that about 23 percent of the first-grade children probably had learning problems. In general, too many Mexican children have reading problems, and there are a great many children with learning disabilities who are not receiving any aid.

Diagnostic Methods

In clinics where diagnostic work is done, the full range of tests may be available. These include intelligence testing; sensory-learning modalities testing; speech, hearing, and language testing; and pediatric-neurological testing. Each clinic uses its own battery of tests, some being more extensive than others. As examples, in intelligence testing one may find the following being used: the Wechsler Intelligence Scales for Children; Terman-Merrill Intelligence Scales, Raven's Progressive Matrices, Porteus Mazes, and the Kohs Block Design Test.

Many other well-known tests, scales, and inventories are also in use, including the Frostig Developmental Test of Visual Perception, the Bender Visual Motor Gestalt Test, the Illinois Test of Psycholinguistic Abilities, the Draw-A-Person Test and other drawing tests, the Lincoln-Oseretsky Motor Development Scale, the Oseretsky Test of Motor Proficiency, the Peabody Picture Vocabulary Test, the Peabody Individual Achievement Test, the Battery of Psychomotricity by Picq and Vayer, the Valett Psychoeducational Inventory of Basic Learning Abilities, the Boder Diagnostic Screening Procedure, the Hilda Santucci tests, Ajuriaguerra tests, Piaget tests, and many others.

In additon to these, there are some instruments that have been developed in Mexico. The VISAM Test, developed at the National Institute of Pedagogy, measures verbal, intellectual, social, affective, and motor functioning. The Clinical Examination and Developmental Profile (see appendix 17B), by Nieto Herrera (1978a, 1978b), explores visual gnosis, visual-motor coordination, auditory gnosis, body notions, spatial relations, laterality, equilibrium, rhythms, finger and hand gnosis, understanding time, tactile functions, diadochokinesis, muscular energy and synergy, and language and speech development.

To prepare for the clinical examination, the teacher must gather stimulus cards for testing figure-ground, memory of forms, and visual analysis for primary, elementary, and secondary students. For color knowledge, two boxes with nine colors in each box, or a total of eighteen colors, will be needed. Color recognition is evaluated based on the stan-

The vertical-horizontal cross and the circle are at the three-year-old level; the oblique cross and the square are at the four-year-old level; the triangle is at the five-year-old level; and the vertical diamond is at the six- to seven-year-old level.

Figure 17-1. Designs Used in Test for Visual-Motor Coordination

dards adapted from Descoeudress (1943). To examine kindergarten children for visual-motor coordination, students are asked to copy designs, some of which are shown in figure 17-1.

A simple percussion instrument and a tape recorder and tapes of various kinds of music are needed to check diadochokinesia and synergy. Muscle tone is observed while relaxing music is played and the child moves to the rhythm. A mirror is needed to observe praxis of the mouth and tongue, and a small flashlight can be used to check ocular function. For spatial ability, designs of a house, cubes viewed from both the right and the left, and a circle are used.

The teacher will need twelve different surfaces for tactile discrimination and twelve different objects, such as a coin, a key, a ring, a pencil, a teaspoon, scissors, and so forth. Three boxes exactly the same size but of different weights are also used. To check laterality, a paper and pencil, a ball, a telescope, and a telephone are needed. For rhythm a metronome is helpful. By gathering all these materials before beginning the examination, testing can proceed rapidly and smoothly.

This examination can be adapted to different academic levels by varying the materials and questions according to the student's age and grade. When evaluating the response of the student, the examiner should compare findings on this clinical examination with age-related data from authorities in the field, such as Gesell, Piaget, Luria, Lezine, and Rossel. A developmental profile of the student will emerge, with each skill checked as either low, normal, or superior.

Methods of Remediation

Most of the remedial methods generally in use in Europe and North and South America are also used in Mexico. Various specialists incorporate the Frostig perceptual motor program, which offers experience in eye-hand coordination, figure-ground identification, form perception, and spatial relationships, into their rehabilitation. For training in body awareness, equilibrium, laterality, basic body movements, eye-hand and eye-foot coordination and rhythm, and other essential aspects of uneven or poorly developed motor functions, the Dubnoff, Kephart, and other motor or visual-motor sequences are practiced.

The psychomotor educational method of Picq and Vayer may be used to improve children's behavior and develop learning abilities. Psychomotor training with music, by Ercilia de Calvo's method, is used to improve body awareness, spatial relations, eye-hand coordination, and rhythm. Body awareness and expression may be developed by the techniques of Vayer, La Pierre, Nielssen, and others. These techniques use imitation of movements and actions, mime drama, and free body expression with music, using materials such as cloth, paper, ribbons, and balloons. Also used are the rhythm and music education methods of Orff, Kodály, Dalcroze, Yamaha, Von Hawer, and Tort, who adapted the Orff and Kodály methods to use in Mexican education. Ordinarily, these methods have been used with normal children; however, we have found them to be most efficacious in helping handicapped children.

Methods of Teaching Reading and Writing

In teaching remedial writing and reading, most of the well-known methods available in Europe and South and North America are also used in Mexico. Three general methods of teaching reading are in use. In the *método onomatopéyico* by Quintero, the phonetic system is used, proceeding from analysis to synthesis. The phonetic sounds of letters are associated with the names of animals, home, street, and so forth, by onomatopoeia. In the *métodos globales,* reading is taught in the opposite manner, from synthesis to analysis, learning whole words first, followed by phonics. The third way of teaching is called *métodos eclecticos.* The eclectic methods use whole words and phonics together.

When teaching children with learning disabilities, some teachers apply Boder's (1971) theory, as follows: If the child has better visual perception than auditory perception, proceed from reading whole words (visual) to phonetic analysis (auditory). If the pupil's auditory perception is superior to his visual perception, start with phonics and synthesis, followed by whole words. Often, we tend to be eclectic, using analysis (phonics) and synthesis (whole words) concurrently.

The McGinnis (1963) method was developed for aphasic children. However, some aspects of this method have been found useful for learning-disabled children, including auditory identification of letter sounds without seeing the teacher's lips; the lip lecture, where the children learn to recognize letters by watching the teacher's lips without sounds; recognition of letters by touch; and oral reading. McGinnis's method also uses large letters for the primary consonant sounds and smaller letters for the secondary consonant sounds, according to their common usage. The vowels are taught first and then the different syllabic combinations. Exercises are given in reading the syllables both horizontally and vertically. Frequent practice is important. Finally, a graphic calendar is used to help the children develop the concepts of time, involving days of the week and months as well as the year.

Methods of Teaching Mathematics

As with reading, most of the methods of teaching arithmetic used in Europe and North and South America are also used in Mexico. For children with learning disabilities, we instruct with multisensory methods as well as with some direct methods, such as Diennes games based on Piaget's theories, Cousinet, and others.

Emotional Problems, Neurological Problems, and Medication

From the early observations of organic signs accompanying mental illness in children, many studies have been made of the neurological basis of emotional problems. In the last decade, researchers have studied the three main classical bases of minimal neurological dysfunction that frequently accompany and complicate the learning problems, namely, hyperactivity, distractibility, and impulsiveness.

The causes of neurological dysfunction are not always clear, but some etiological elements have been discerned. Genetic influences have been found to be important, as learning problems often run in families. Prenatal, perinatal, and postnatal injuries are known to be among the causes of minimal brain damage or dysfunction leading to learning disabilities.

Some children with hyperkinetic syndrome exhibit spectacular improvement when they receive the proper medication in the right dosages. This is particularly impressive when the medication permits the children to suppress unwanted multiple stimuli so that they can attend to the single stimulus desired. Sometimes the appropriate medication is a stimulant such as amphetamine or methylphenidate hydrochloride (Ritalin), taken in dosages adjusted to the child's individual requirements.

A humane and sensitive approach includes taking into account the importance of the family environment in the development of the child's emotional health. We have found that, in some cases of behavioral disturbances, a change in the child's environment causes an impressive improvement in the child's behavior. But in other cases medication appears necessary to enable a hyperkinetic child to be more relaxed, less demanding, and less explosive. This positive behavioral change appears to be profitable from the viewpoints of the family, teacher, physician, psychologist, and social worker.

Other medications that are used as required include major and minor tranquilizers, stimulants, antidepressants, and anticonvulsants. In some cases tranquilizers may be combined with antidepressants, and other combinations may also prove useful.

Research

In 1949 Ortega and Bienvenú Herrera organized a research project to diagnose and analyze the reading errors of elementary-school children. As a result of their research, they constructed a test to measure the reading-levels of children.

In 1959 Berruecos examined a stratified sample of the population attending morning classes in the Federal District for language problems and reading comprehension. He then studied the relationship between these two variables.

In 1973-1974 Ezcurra and Konstant conducted two standardizations of Boder's test, based on three reading-spelling patterns.

In 1974 Nieto Herrera, Peña Torres, and Gallardo studied the relationships between reading and writing problems and sensory-learning modalities. They found a close relationship between reading and writing problems and diadochokinesia and muscular-synergy dysfunctions. They attributed this correlation to the relationship among such variables as motor discoordination, the disorders of rhythm, spatial relations, eye-hand coordination, time notions, and phonic-auditory functions.

In 1975-1976 Ruiz de Chavez performed an experiment to demonstrate the benefits of a program of psychomotor and music-education therapy. She used children with behavioral problems, brain injuries, and hyperkinesias. The evaluations included tests of their levels of psychomotor development, their behavioral problems, and their reading and writing abilities.

In 1974 we examined 1,200 children entering the first grade of elementary school in the Federal District. This examination included the Frostig Developmental Test of Visual Perception, the Bender Visual Motor Gestalt Test, the Goodenough-Harris Draw-A-Man Test, and the Nieto Herrera Profile of Development. Also included was an interview with each child's mother or someone else familiar with the child. The results indicated that 35 percent of these children had some learning disabilities. Since the percentage of children with probable learning problems was very high, there were not enough special teachers to take care of all of these children. Consequently, it was decided that the only possible approach to this overwhelming problem would be to give the regular classroom teachers special training. It was decided to orient these teachers to the more usual symptoms of these children and the main methods of handling their special needs. These methods included a motor program, perceptual training, and rhythm and music education and therapy.

Physical Education and Music Education in Japan

The motor program and rhythm and music therapy were partly the result of experiences in Japan in 1974 and 1975. My trip to Japan was primarily motivated by a desire to find out why Japanese elementary-school children do not seem to have learning disabilities, even though they must learn about 2,000 characters in elementary school. In Japanese there are three systems of codification for reading and writing: *hirakana, katakana,* and *kanji.* Both *hirakana* and *katakana* use a phonetic system, while *kanji* is pictorial and ideographic. Thus, what the children have to learn appears to be much more complicated than our alphabetic phonetic code. In Japanese, one character may represent a syllable, a word, or even a phrase, depending on its position in the paragraph.

After visiting several nursery schools, kindergartens, elementary schools, and high schools, it was concluded that the secret of their success lay in the factor of an integrated curriculum. This means that they give the same importance to physical education and music classes as they do to reading, writing, and arithmetic classes. The rhythm training, physical education (motor coordination), and extensive experiences in music must be of great assistance to the children when learning to read, write, and do arithmetic. This is because of the exercises in reading musical symbols and counting the values of the musical notes and the complexities of meter learned in music. This type of preparation for learning to read decreases the learning difficulties of these children when compared to Occidental children. Although the curriculum in physical education and music is extensive, the children are not being pushed to become either great athletes or polished musicians; rather, they are learning these subjects as a normal part of the total curriculum.

Even with this fine preparation for learning academic subjects, some children still require extra support with their studies. There were several clinics available to help these children. In some high schools, small groups of six or seven children were being given special assistance. Considering the complexities of the Japanese written language, the percentage of children with learning problems is very small compared to Western countries such as Mexico.

Based on the hypothesis that early and extensive training in motor coordination, balance, and rhythm and music education greatly improve the preparation of children for learning reading, writing, and arithmetic, an experimental study was launched in Mexico City. Twelve children with learning disabilities were selected. They were given three classes a week of one hour each, combining motor exercises, rhythm training, and musical education using percussion instruments. After three months the children were able to be promoted to the next grade. They were able to overcome their learning difficulties.

Musical Education in Hungary

In Hungary Kodály has promoted musical education. In elementary school, all children attend music classes two or three times a week. Kodály proposed a research project to demonstrate the efficacy of music education for promoting academic learning. In this project the experimental group was the students of one school, in which all children attended music classes every day. At the same time, the total number of hours of academic instruction was reduced accordingly. The control group consisted of the other schools, where the curriculum remained unchanged. At the end of the school year it was found that the children in the experimental school did better than the others in all academic subjects (reading, writing, mathematics, and so forth).

Conclusions

We understand the attitudes of the teachers who do not appreciate the advantages of motor-coordination exercises and music therapy. They believe that they do not have enough time to teach what they consider basic and that time spent on motor coordination and music constitute time taken away from their subjects. For this reason, it is suggested that these areas of teaching become part of the teacher-training curricula in normal schools, where elementary-school teachers receive their preservice preparation. The following curriculum is recommended in addition to that presently taught:

1. How to obtain a developmental profile of each child.
2. How to organize a motor-coordination program adapted to the characteristics of each child.
3. How to organize a music-education program, including rhythm training, body coordination, language rhythms, reading music, writing and taking dictation, improvisation, use of orchestration, canons, choral groups, and so forth.

If all children could receive this kind of instruction, we feel certain that the proportion of children with learning disabilities would be greatly reduced. Then the children who present severe dyslexic problems could be treated by special teachers. In that case, the special teachers who are now available would be sufficient to attend to all the severe cases of learning disabilities.

References

Boder, E. 1971. Developmental dyslexia: prevailing diagnostic concepts and a new diagnostic approach. In H. Myklebust (ed.), *Progress in Learning Disabilities. Vol. II.* New York: Grune and Stratton.

Department of Programming and Budget of Mexico. 1976. La Población de México. Su Ocupación Y sus Niveles de Bienstar. México, D.F.

Descoeudress, A. 1943. *Tests Parciales de Lenguaje.* Adaptados a México por la Profra. L. Alva. Mexico City: SEP.

Dozer, D. 1962. *Latin America: An Interpretive History.* New York: McGraw-Hill.

McGinnis, M. 1963. *Aphasic Children.* Washington, D.C.: Volta Bureau.

Nieto Herrera, M. 1978a. *El Niño Dislexico.* 2nd ed. Mexico City: La Prensa Médica Mexicana.

———— . 1978b. *Evolucion del Lenguaje en el Niño.* Mexico City: Editorial Porrúa.

Appendix 17A:
Synopsis of the History
of Special Education in
Mexico

1866	Founding of the National School for Deaf and Dumb (Don Ignacio de Trigueros and Eduardo Huet)
1870	Founding of the National School for the Blind (Don Ignacio de Trigueros)
1904	Founding of the first kindergartens (Prof. Justo Sierra, Profa. Estefanía Castañeda, and Rosaura Zapata)
1905	Founding of an orphanage (Lic. Justo Benitez)
1907	Founding of the correctional house for boys and another house for girls (Lic. Justo Benitez)
1914	Founding of the first school for mentally retarded children in Leon, Guanajuato (Dr. José de Jesús González)
1921-26	First convention concerning children held in Mexico
	Organization of the Department of Psychopedagogy and Student Health (Dr. Rafael Santamarina)
	Standardization of tests of mental ability for children (Prof. Salvador Lima and Roberto Solis Quiroga)
1935	Founding of the first institution for the education of mentally retarded children in Mexico City (Dr. Roberto Solis Quiroga)
1936	Founding of the National Institute of Psychopedagogy (Dr. Lauro Ortega)
1937	Founding of the Clinic for Children with Behavioral Problems (Dr. Rafael Santamarina)
1941	Founding of the Mexican Institute of Social Welfare (President Avila Camacho)
1942	Organization of the first groups of handicapped children in regular schools with special teachers (Dr. Roberto Solis Quiroga)
1943	Founding of the Normal School of Specialization to prepare special teachers for mentally retarded children and young delinquents (Dr. Roberto Solis Quiroga)

1945   Organization of career training for special teachers of the blind, deaf, and speech-disordered (Dr. Roberto Solis Quiroga)

1946   Founding of the first clinic for speech therapy in the Children's Hospital (Profa. Ma. Cristina Bienvenú Herrera)

1952   Organization of the General Department of Rehabilitation in the Ministry of Public Health and founding of the National Institute of Audiology (now National Institute of Human Communication) (Dr. Andres Bustamante Gurría)

1955   Organization to train teachers in education of motor-handicapped children in the Normal School of Specialization (Dr. Roberto Solis Quiroga)

1960   Organization of several new schools for mentally retarded children in Mexico City and in the country (Profa. Odalmira Mayagoitia de Toulet)

1964   Organization in the Normal School of Specialization for special teachers for young delinquents (Dr. Hector Solis Quiroga)

            Foundation of the Institution for the Protection of Children (President Lopez Mateos)

1964-70   Organization of clinics for children with behavioral problems in kindergarten

            Organization of speech therapy (Profa. Beatriz Ordoñez)

1970   Organization of the General Department of Special Education (Profa. Odalmira Mayagoitia de Toulet)

            Founding of the Mexican Institute for Children's Care (Sra. Luis Echeverria)

1971   Founding of the first Institution for Children with Learning Disabilities (Profa. Margarita Nieto Herrera)

1972-73   Organization in the Normal School of Specialization for specialist teachers for the learning-disabled (Prof. Salvador Valdes Cardenas)

1972-77   Organization of the Institutions for Special Education and Rehabilitation with the participation of Public Education and Public Health, respectively (Profa. Odalmira Mayagoitia de Toulet, special education; Dr. Guillermo Ibarra, rehabilitation and public health)

1977-78   Organization for the Development of the Infant and the Family (Sra. José Lopez Portillo)

1978   Organization of the International Seminar on Learning Problems in Guadalajara (Dr. Alfonso Peña Torres and Ps. Luis García Jasso)

Appendix 17B: Clinical Examination and Developmental Profile

Margarita Nieto Herrera

Date: Date of Birth: Age:

Name: Address:

Current grade in school:

What grade or grades has child repeated and why:

Gnosis

I. Visual Gnosis
   A. Figure-ground
   B. Memory for forms
   C. Visual analysis
   D. Knowledge of colors
   E. Identification of colors
   F. Finding similar colors
II. Visual-Motor Coordination
   A. Copy designs placed in front of child (preschool)
   B. Copy letters (if the child attends school)
   C. Copy words
   D. Copy sentences
   E. Copy paragraphs
III. Auditory Gnosis
   A. Simple exploration without equipment
      1. Ability to repeat words and phrases
      2. Oral synthesis of words divided into syllables
      3. Oral synthesis of words divided into letters
      4. Auditory figure-ground, with words divided into syllables or into letters
      5. Repeating the alphabet from memory
      6. Dictation of similar-sounding words to observe if the child changes similar sounds, the order of the letters, or the meaning of the words; for example, table, cable, fox, box

B. Exploration with equipment
   1. Test of repeating phrases
   2. Test of repeating sentences in order
   3. Association of words with designs
   4. Repetition of words of one or two syllables

IV. Body Awareness
   A. Parts that the child can name spontaneously and parts that the child can identify only
   B. Details that the child can say spontaneously
   C. Point out several parts of the body on a doll, or on his own body
   D. Imitation of movement
   E. Human-figure drawing

V. Spatial Relations
   A. Look to your right, left, up, down, behind, front
   B. Point to your front and jump three times forward, point behind you and jump three times backward, point to your right and turn to your right, point to your left and turn to your left
   C. From the place where you are, point out the wall nearest you, the wall farthest from you, the chair nearest you, the chair farthest from you (continue the exploration, changing the child's place)
   D. Stand to the right of the table, behind the chair, under the table, inside the circle, between the table and the chair, between John and Charles
   E. Imitate arm movements at different levels, and draw circles in space
   F. Copy a house (kindergarten children)
   G. Copy a cube (second grade or higher)
   H. Clock test (for third grade or higher, draw a circle and explain that they are to fill in the numbers)

VI. Understanding Left and Right
   A. Simple orders (for children aged six years or older: raise your right hand, raise your left foot, point to your right eye, touch your left ear
   B. Complex orders for children aged seven years or older: with your right hand touch your left eye, with your left hand touch your left foot, with your left hand touch your right ear, and so forth
   C. Questions for children aged eight years or older, which teacher asks when standing in front of the child: Which is my right hand? Touch it. Which is my left leg? Point to it.

    D. Imitation of movements of arms and legs with teacher standing in front of the child and child imitating: teacher swings right arm rapidly, teacher swings left arm rapidly, teacher kicks with left foot, teacher kicks with right foot, teacher rapidly twists body to right, teacher rapidly twists body to left

VII.   Gnosis of the Fingers
    A. Finger sensibility with children aged five years or older: teacher touches child's fingers when he has his eyes closed and then asks him which finger or fingers were touched

VIII. Temporal Understanding
    A. What day is today?
    B. What day was yesterday?
    C. What day is tomorrow?
    D. Tell me the days of the week in order
    E. Name the months of the year
    F. When is your birthday? When is Mother's Day? When does Santa Claus come?
    G. Find these dates on the calendar and tell me what day of the week they were: the tenth of May; the first of January; the twenty-fourth of December; and so forth

IX.   Tactile Discrimination
The child with his eyes closed must distinguish
    A. Different surfaces
    B. Different forms
    C. Different sizes
    D. Different weights
    E. Different surroundings
    F. Different parts of the body the teacher has touched
    G. How many times the teacher has touched some part of the child's body

Praxis

X.   Laterality
    A. The child uses his _____ hand for writing
    B. The child uses his _____ foot for kicking a ball
    C. The child places a telescope to his _____ eye
    D. The child places a telephone to his _____ ear
    E. Ask the mother which hand the child uses for painting, drawing, cutting, pasting, throwing a ball, and so forth
    F. Observe latent laterality when the child crosses his arms, his legs, places one hand over the other, and so forth

XI.   Rhythm
    A. Mark the rhythm of the metronome with the hand, foot, or movements of the head
    B. Teacher claps different rhythmic patterns and child repeats after each pattern
    C. Mark with hand on table the syllable or syllables in the following words: table, school, mother, father, notebook, Washington, civilization
    D. Mark with your hand on the table each syllable in each word of this rhyme:

> Mary had a little lamb,
> little lamb, little lamb.
> Mary had a little lamb.
> Its fleece was white as snow.

    E. With children of third grade or higher ask: How many syllables in each word? pencil, culture, apple, school, authority, power, flower, handkerchief, sculpture, movies, quickly, anniversary, geography, comfortable

XII. Equilibrium
    A. Tell the child to stand on one foot. Note which foot is preferred. How long can he remain standing on this foot? Have him stand on the other foot. How long for this foot?
    B. Have the child stand on tiptoe. How long can he stand like this?
    C. Have the child walk on one board. Can he keep his balance?
    D. Have the child jump with one foot if he is aged six years or older. What foot is preferred? How long can he jump on one foot? On the other foot?

XIII. Diadochokinesia and Synergy Examination
    A. Twist both wrists together
    B. Twist both wrists alternately
    C. Elevate the shoulders alternately
    D. Twist both heels alternately
    E. Tap the rhythm of a song with the right, then left heel
    F. Open the right hand at the same time you close the left; continue this rhythmically and alternately
    G. Twist your hands and feet at the same time, then alternately
    H. Lift your shoulders and knees one by one, using the same side (right knee and shoulder, left knee and shoulder)
    I. Lift your knees and shoulders crossing the opposite side (right knee and left shoulder; left knee and right shoulder)

        J. Open and close eyes and hands together

        K. Open your hands with your eyes closed. Close your hands with your eyes open. Do both rhythmically.

        L. Open and close mouth and eyes together

        M. Open your mouth with your eyes closed and close your mouth with your eyes open. Do both rhythmically.

XIV.   Observe Main Reflexes

XV.   Observe Synkinesia

XVI.   Observe Muscular Tone

XVII.   Observe Praxis of the Mouth and Tongue, Ocular-Motor Function, and Finger Manipulation

XVIII.   Language Development Observations

        A. Articulation

        B. Speech

        C. Vocabulary

        D. Syntax

        E. Level of the language

        F. History of the language-development of the child

        G. Information about the child's family

XIX.   Observations of the Child's Behavior During Testing

XX.   Summary and Recommendations

18

Reading Problems in New Zealand

David R. Mitchell and
Thomas W. Nicholson

In New Zealand very few special provisions have been made for children with reading difficulties. The emphasis is on prevention and on classroom teachers taking responsibility for assisting children with reading problems. Although this policy has led to generally high standards of reading among New Zealand schoolchildren and to some sound and even innovative reading programs, there is a growing awareness that a number of children are slipping through the net and that more systematic provisions will have to be made for them in the future.

New Zealand: The Society

Because the way in which an education system responds to any particular problem reflects the complex interaction of many factors—social, economic, and political—it might be helpful to provide a brief description of the New Zealand society and its education system.

New Zealand comprises two main and several small islands, stretching over 1,700 kilometers from the subtropical north to the temperate south and encompassing landscapes as diverse as fiords, high mountains, subtropical beaches, rain forests, grassy plains, and thermal areas. With an area of 269,000 square kilometers, it is similar in size to the British Isles and slightly larger than West Germany; but with only 3 million people, it is relatively sparsely populated. Almost 92 percent of its people are of European origin (mainly British), although the great majority were born in New Zealand. Of the remainder, the bulk of the people are Maoris (270,000 in 1976)—descendants of the pre-European settlers—and there is a significant group of immigrants from the South Pacific (61,000 in 1976).

New Zealand's economy is based largely on the marketing of primary products (meat, wool, and dairy products), which in 1974 comprised 85 percent of the value of its exports. However, with the rapid development of its manufacturing sector—especially rapid over the past decade—New Zealand is becoming increasingly industrialized and urbanized. Although difficulties in marketing primary products during the past decade have led to some deterioration in standards of living, New Zealand is nevertheless a technologically advanced society that enjoys a high standard of living and comprehensive social welfare and educational services.

417

A former colony of Great Britain, New Zealand is now a fully independent member of the British Commonwealth and has a stable democratic political system. Although there is some regional and local government, legislative powers are vested primarily in a central House of Representatives, located in Wellington. The main source of finance for education is money appropriated by the House of Representatives, there being no local education taxes. In view of this fact, it is not surprising to find that the real control and direction of the New Zealand education system is exercised by the central Department of Education (McLaren 1974), though with increasing attention to local decision-making.

The one feature that characterizes New Zealand society is its strong and long-standing aspirations to egalitarianism. As applied to education, this social philosophy was most clearly expressed in 1939 by Peter Fraser, then Minister of Education, when he asserted that "every person, whatever his level of academic ability, whether he be rich or poor, whether he live in town or country, has a right, as a citizen, to a free education of the kind for which he is best fitted and to the fullest extent of his powers." This desire to provide equal educational opportunity for all children has been reflected in a national, centralized system of education, which has done much in its first 100 years of existence to ensure that educational provisions are determined on the basis of needs of children, rather than on the availability of local finances. Above all, perhaps, the notion of equality of educational opportunity has found expression in the rapid expansion of special educational provisions in recent years. In the decade to 1976, for example, the number of children receiving special education of some kind increased from 8,690 in 1966 to 14,203 in 1976, an increase of 63 percent. By contrast, the total number of children enrolled in primary and secondary schools increased by only 15 percent in the same period.

The egalitarian tradition is also reflected in the policy of the Department of Education that, whenever possible, children with special needs should be educated in ordinary classes, with support for their teachers where needed. When this is not sufficient, they should be placed in special clinics or classes within the regular school system, rather than segregating them into residential institutions or special schools. Certainly, this policy has been followed for children with reading difficulties; very few have received special education beyond that offered by their regular teachers, with some support from "reading advisers" and reading-resource teachers.

Reading Problems—Their Nature and Incidence

One of the difficulties facing educational policymakers in New Zealand has been the lack of meaningful data on reading-attainment in schools. In the last few years, in the face of a growing insistence by parents and employers that schools are not adequately teaching the "basic skills," including reading, the need for carefully monitored national reading assessment has become even more apparent. To date, New Zealand has avoided committing itself to the kinds of criterion-referenced testing that has recently been carried out in both the United States (National Assessment of Educational Progress 1972) and Australia (Bourke and Keeves 1977). The Department of Education has, however, participated in and initiated several recent surveys of reading achievement in schools.

International Reading Survey (IEA)

In 1970, New Zealand participated in an international reading survey by the International Association for the Evaluation of Educational Achievement (IEA), which involved fifteen different countries (Thorndike 1973). The reading-comprehension results for New Zealand were slightly higher than all other countries among the fourteen-year-old sample and considerably higher for the sample group of children in their final year of school. The latter results, however, reflect the fact that only 13 percent of children reach the final year of high school in New Zealand, compared with 20 percent for Scotland and 75 percent for the United States.

The data for the fourteen-year-olds are more comparable. The New Zealand results for this group are highest, followed by Italy, Scotland, and the United States. Yet, as Thorndike, the IEA project director, pointed out, the differences among these countries are small compared to the reading scores of such countries as Iran, India, and Chile, where the general level of reading attainment is much lower.

Perhaps the fairest conclusion that can be drawn from the IEA data is that New Zealand reading achievement ranks high among the developed countries included in the survey. Whether this is cause for complacency or concern depends on how we view the reading-levels of the comparison countries. On the one hand, it is comforting to know that New Zealand is doing as well as if not better than all other countries surveyed. On the other hand, some of these countries, particularly the United States, are not at all satisfied with their general level of reading attainment (Why Johnny can't write 1975; The blight of illiteracy 1978), so perhaps there is no cause for complacency in New Zealand either.

Project CHILD

A research project concerned with investigating the problem of specific learning disabilities in New Zealand has been under way since 1976. This project, with the acronym CHILD (Children Having Individual Learning Difficulties), is sponsored and directed by the New Zealand Council for Educational Research (NZCER) in cooperation with the state Department of Education. A committee of specialists meets regularly to advise on the design and management of this investigation. The project has the following aims: to establish the incidence of children with specific learning difficulties in primary schools; to assess the children's achievements in as many of the basic skills of communication and mathematics as possible; to ascertain the extent to which certain variables play a causal role in learning difficulties in children; to devise and evaluate techniques that will make earlier and more accurate identification of such children possible; to plan and evaluate teaching programs designed to reduce the learning difficulties; and to provide the basis for the preparation of materials, aids, and teaching guides.

In order to establish the extent of the problem of serious learning difficulties that appear to be residual rather than transitory, an incidence study of 2,000 children aged between eleven years, three months, and eleven years, six months has been carried out. Care was taken to ensure that this sample was as representative as possible of the New Zealand population of 14,000 children of that age, taking into account such demographic considerations as ethnic status, family income, and rural-urban distribution. The aim of the first phase of this survey was to establish the incidence of children whose achievement in any or all of the skills of reading, spelling, and mathematics was two years or more below the levels achieved by most children in the age cohort. The tests used were three scales of a recently developed battery known as the Progressive Achievement Tests (reading-comprehension, reading vocabulary, and mathematics) and a group spelling test with New Zealand norms (N.S.W. E1 Spelling Test).

In the second phase of this incidence study, a 50 percent randomized sample of all the childen so identified will be tested individually with the Wechsler Intelligence Scale for Children—Revised (WISC-R) in order to establish the proportion of children whose two-year-plus achievement discrepancy is not associated with general learning difficulties (that is, an IQ of 85 or less on any of the three WISC scales). Data will also be obtained from the schools on the children's hearing, vision, and school-attendance so that these factors may be taken into account in ascertaining the incidence of children with specific learning disabilities.

At the time of this writing, the second aspect of this project has not been completed. What can be reported, however, are some of the data on the first phase of the survey. Table 18-1 summarizes the data on reading and mathematics that were obtained from the approximately 2,000 eleven-year-old children. Just how many of these children will turn out to be learning-disabled when intelligence levels and other factors are taken into account remains to be seen. Given that approximately 15 to 17 percent of this sample

Table 18-1
Eleven-Year-Old Children Found to Be Two or More Years Retarded in Reading, Spelling, and Mathematics

	Number Tested	Number Two Years Retarded	Percentage Two Years Retarded
Reading-comprehension	1,970	273	13.9
Reading vocabulary	1,967	348	17.7
Mathematics	1,962	383	19.9
All three	1,970	105	5.3
One or more	1,970	596	30.3

might be expected to have an IQ of 85 or below, it is likely that the number of children whose retardation is associated with low general ability will dramatically reduce the incidence rate. But one cannot assume that each of the percentages in the bottom row of the table can be reduced in that proportion, because, as can be seen, approximately 30 percent of the children were retarded in at least one area. Of 273 children who were retarded in reading comprehension, fifty-six were also retarded in reading vocabulary, sixty-five were also retarded in mathematics, and 105 were also retarded in both reading vocabulary and mathematics.

At this stage, a "best guess" might be that the proportion of eleven-year-old children whose two-plus years of retardation in one or more of these areas cannot be readily explained by a low level of general intelligence, sensory impairment, or poor school-attendance, will approximate 10 percent. The final results of the CHILD incidence study are awaited with interest.

Survey of Reading Standards

In October 1977 regional teams of inspectors from the Department of Education collected data on reading-attainment and observed the teaching of reading in schools throughout the country. Primary schools received most attention, as only a small number of secondary schools were visited.

The results of the survey were optimistic, though difficult to interpret, because no reading-attainment data from the survey were included in the report (Department of Education 1978). In essence, the report was a summary of the general impressions of inspectors regarding teaching standards in schools.

In regard to reading, the report concluded that "standards in reading are at least as good as they ever were. In most schools, average and above-average students are progressing well, and generally are achieving higher standards than their counterparts did in the past." In regard to children who were having difficulties with reading, however, the report stated that "too many students are still not making satisfactory progress."

In its discussion of differences among ethnic groups in reading skills, the report took the view that the causes of these differences were language-related: "a high proportion of the students in standard [grade] 4 and form 2 [grade 6] who were reading at or below the average eight-year-old level were non-Europeans, almost half of whom were having difficulties with the English language generally." Unfortunately, no data were presented to clarify what was meant by "language difficulties." Moreover, by using the term *non-European*, it seems that no distinction was made between the language difficulties of the established ethnic group (the Maoris) and those of the more recent Polynesian immigrants.

It is tempting to dismiss the standards report as a political document, produced in an election year as a defensive response by the Minister of Education to the vociferous demands of some sectors in the community for a return to the basics. Certainly, the report lacks the usual criteria applied to surveys of this type: stratified random-sampling was not carried out; only a few of the secondary schools were visited; different teams of inspectors with different views were used; and observations were informal rather than systematic.

Yet the conclusions of the report are in many ways consistent with the available data from the IEA survey and Project CHILD. The report is in agreement that "standards in the basics should, if at all possible, improve." In all, the flavor of the document is one of praise, with faint damns. While emphasizing the good work being done for the average and above-average student, the report insists that "more will need to be done to help teachers become better equipped to deal with failing students." Indeed, the director-general of education has interpreted these and other data as meaning that the progress of unskilled readers has not improved as much as that of the skilled readers (Renwick 1978), implying a certain lack of balance in our teaching of reading.

The Teaching of Reading in Schools

The New Zealand "Style"

In general, the style of teaching recommended for the classroom teacher is one in which reading is integrated with all aspects of the curriculum and is based as much as possible on the children's own language. In the junior school this means using language-experience stories, caption-books, and the shared-book technique, in which teacher and children read an enlarged book together. In the senior school, this often means class discussion of issues, listening to prerecorded stories of related interest, conducting research in the library, going on field trips, writing about their experiences, and then reading their work to each other.

Materials

Teachers also make use of graded readers issued by the Department of Education (the "Ready to Read Series"), which include "little" books and "big" books written especially for New Zealand children. (This series is about to be revised and supplemented.) The department, in addition, issues multiple copies of "school journals" to schools. These journals are published five times a year and range from about thirty-two to sixty pages in length. They contain a variety of narrative and expository stories and represent one of the few outlets for children's stories written by New Zealanders. The department puts out a special issue of the journal once a year, written especially for unskilled readers in both primary and secondary schools.

Parent Education

The need to involve parents in reinforcing what children learn at school resulted in a new radio series in 1978 called "On the Way to Reading," a series of twelve programs each about fifteen minutes in length. The program was targeted at parents of children in the five- to seven-year-old age-range. Many schools throughout the country formed listening groups of parents and a resource person (such as a teacher) to listen to the programs and discuss issues and problems raised throughout the radio series. A national evaluation of this method of getting through to parents has been carried out. The results, when available, may show that this series had a beneficial effect on parent's attitudes and knowledge about reading.

Teaching Children with Reading Difficulties

In general, the recommended approach to the teaching of reading is based on contextual analysis, by which the child is encouraged to predict what words will be and to check the initial letters of words in order to confirm the prediction. This is sometimes called the "search and check" method (Clay 1972). Another technique used in teaching word recognition is for the child to read to the end of the line and then go back to the troublesome word and try again to guess its meaning. If the child still does not guess the word, he is encouraged to look at the initial letters. If the child still has trouble, the teacher will then say the word and, if necessary, explain what it means. There is a general aversion to the use of phonics, which is often seen as a process in which reading becomes divorced from meaning because children learn words in isolation and useless rules to help them sound out words. Although there is very little research to support this view, the phonics approach has a poor reputation. Instead it is expected that, by showing children how to make use of context and initial-letter clues, they will be able to read for meaning, and phonics skills will develop naturally.

Special Facilities for Diagnosis and Prevention

Although schools in New Zealand try very hard to handle their reading problems within the school and even within the classroom, there are nevertheless certain specialist teachers and services available to assist them and to help children who have what seem to be intractable difficulties in reading.

Psychological Service

One of the most important agencies in providing for the needs of children with reading problems is the Psychological Service of the Department of Education, which in 1977 had 125 personnel distributed around the country. About 25 percent of their work involves helping children with reading problems. In the main, this service comprises experienced teachers who have obtained postgraduate qualifications in the field of educational psychology. Psychologists have three roles appropriate to children with reading problems. First, children can only be admitted to special facilities such as reading clinics, remedial classes, and assessment classes on the recommendation of a psychologist. Second, there is the traditional consultative and advisory role, in which psychologists carry out detailed assessments of children who have been referred to them from a variety of sources and advise teachers, parents, and others with an interest in the child's welfare. And third, psychologists are increasingly involving themselves in direct work with children and in preventive work in the schools and in the community.

Remedial Classes

A recent development in providing for reading-disabled children has been the establishment of two full-time remedial classes for children with severe reading problems. These classes—one in Hamilton and one in Well-ington—have been set up on a pilot basis, and they may well provide the pattern for future classes around the country. In each of these classes, small groups of children with a history of prolonged reading failure but with average or above-average intelligence are given intensive individualized assistance until they are deemed ready to return to their home schools.

Assessment Classes

Some children who show early signs of reading problems are cared for in the assessment classes around the country. These classes cater to new school en-trants who cannot cope with a regular school program and whose dif-ficulties are not severe enough or sufficiently obvious to warrant their being placed in existing special educational facilities. Assessment classes provide opportunities for teachers and specialists to undertake careful evaluation of these children and to provide intensive work for them in order to prevent subsequent failure in the school system. At least, that is the ideal; assess-ment classes share with most other sectors of special education in New Zealand the problems that arise from the lack of adequate training for the teachers. Although the vast majority of teachers working in special educa-tion have had general teacher training and experience in teaching normal children, only a small proportion of them has received anything more than short-term training or correspondence courses to prepare them for work in special education.

Itinerant Reading Teachers

Itinerant teachers are formally attached to one school but actually visit a number of schools to help teachers develop their skills in teaching children with reading difficulties. These itinerant teachers usually deal with children having severe difficulties. They provide detailed diagnostic help and teach-ing procedures suited to these children.

Reading Clinics

There are about twelve reading clinics throughout the country. Clinic work involves careful diagnosis of difficulties, one-to-one teaching, and a variety of methods adapted to children's needs. Children are usually sent to the clinics from nearby schools once or twice a week for specialized help. The clinics are usually only able to deal with three or four children at a time and only take children referred to them by the Psychological Services of the Education Department.

**Advisory Service and Special Staffing
Provision for Teachers**

As noted earlier, classroom teachers are chiefly responsible for providing appropriate programs for children with reading problems, but there are a number of special advisory services that both general and specialist teachers can call upon to help them with classroom teaching.

National Education Officer

There is one national education officer with special responsibility for reading. The role of this officer is, broadly, to provide leadership in the development of reading curriculum and research throughout the country, to initiate and coordinate in-service programs in reading, and to provide liaison with advisory staff and other departmental officers in matters concerning the teaching of reading.

Reading Advisers

Some thirty regional reading advisers throughout the country are responsible for improving the teaching of reading in schools. Advisers are expected to keep abreast of new developments in the teaching of reading, to conduct in-service courses for teachers, and to help schools with their reading programs. They also assist teachers and help provide liaison among the psychological services, teacher-training colleges, and curriculum officers in Wellington.

Advisers to Junior Classes

Throughout the country, approximately twenty advisers to junior classes visit schools and work with classes in the five- to seven-year-old age-range. A great deal of their work involves helping with the teaching of reading.

Advisers to Rural Schools

There are about thirty advisers to rural schools. Their role is to provide information on current trends in reading to teachers in rural schools, to help these teachers with children having reading difficulties, and to keep them up to date with current ideas on the teaching of reading.

Inspectors

There is at least one inspector in each district with special responsibility for the teaching of reading.

Senior Teachers

More than 4,000 teachers have been appointed in the last five years to positions of responsibility within schools. Among other duties, these senior teachers are expected to provide leadership and assistance to other teachers in the teaching of reading.

Staffing

On the average, there is one teacher to twenty children. In many cases an attempt has been made to appoint additional staff in the junior school to reduce teacher-pupil ratios among new entrant classes. It is hoped that this special staffing provision will enable teachers to provide more individualized teaching of reading to children.

Training of Personnel

Preservice Training

Teacher-training colleges in New Zealand vary considerably in course offerings. Compulsory coursework (lectures and tutorials) in the teaching of reading ranges from about 30 to 100 contact hours for primary-school trainee teachers and from 6 to 20 for secondary-school teachers. Training in teaching reading for preschool teachers is restricted to informal methods such as techniques for reading stories to children and studies of children's picture books. Preschool teachers receive approximately the same number of hours of training in this field as primary teachers.

The content of compulsory coursework usually focuses on developmental teaching of reading rather than on reading difficulties; coursework on the latter is usually offered as an option. The number of students taking these options in the various teachers' colleges ranges from 2 to 60 percent.

In-Service Training

A wide range of in-service coursework for teachers is offered by the Department of Education. Most courses are short-term—from a half-day to two or three days in length. These courses are usually provided at the request of schools, although for some courses teachers are released to attend in-service centers.

The short-term objective of the department is to reach as many teachers as possible. In order to achieve this goal, a series of tape-slide lectures, aimed at the five- to eight-year-old age-range, has been prepared and distributed to all districts. This course, called ERIC (Early Reading Inservice Course), consists of twelve one-hour units with accompanying booklets. Teachers are released from school duties to attend the course at in-service centers. In some areas each unit is followed with staff discussions. Since 1976, when ERIC was completed, more than 2,000 teachers have taken the course. This new emphasis on tape-slide in-service courses is currently being evaluated. In addition, a new course called LARIC (Later Reading Inservice Course) is now being developed for the nine- to twelve-year-old age-range. Finally, the department offers correspondence courses on reading for teachers. At present three courses are available to them.

The use of tape-slide courses to reach a wide range of teachers seems a realistic way to proceed, given that the ratio of reading advisers to teachers in the country is about 1:1,000. This concept also enables the department to focus on long-term objectives, which are to provide in-depth studies in reading for all teachers and to provide at least one specialist teacher in every school. As mentioned, there has already been an attempt to train specialists (reading-resource teachers). Such training is very expensive, however, and the trained teachers have not always been used to best advantage in schools, mainly because of staff shortages. The department now appears to be looking more closely at the provision of advanced courses and specialist training jointly with teacher-training colleges and universities.

In some universities courses are now available at the undergraduate level. Contact hours range from 0 to 170. The provision for specialist training is poor, however, with only one graduate course in the whole country. The need to establish a postgraduate degree, as is provided for the Psychological Service, is clearly apparent.

Parent and Professional Organizations

International Reading Association

The first council of the International Reading Association was established in 1968. There are now fourteen councils throughout the country, with a national coordinating committee to provide liaison among councils and to organize conferences. The ninth national conference, held in 1978 in Dunedin, drew about 600 participants. There are about 3,000 members of local councils throughout the country and about 500 members of the international body. The local councils organize regular meetings for members on topics of interest and even provide short courses. The Waikato Council, for example, offered courses for parents as well as courses in remedial reading for practicing teachers.

Specific Learning Difficulties
Association (SPELD)

In 1974 a nonprofit organization of parents, professionals, and others was formed with the objective of advancing the education and general well-being of children with specific learning difficulties—mainly in the area of reading. This organization, the Specific Learning Difficulties Association (SPELD), has recently started offering diagnostic and remedial services directly to children referred to them by their parents, as well as to adults who cannot read. These services are provided by nonpracticing certified teachers who have also attended a brief training course offered by SPELD. They are paid by the parents to do this work on an hourly basis. In carrying out this work, SPELD expects the tutors to cooperate with the child's classroom teachers and with the Psychological Service. In some places and at some times, however, this has not always been a smooth arrangement. On SPELD's part, this situation probably reflects the occasional lapses on the part of individuals in observing the guidelines laid down by the organization. As for the school system, communication breakdowns can often be explained in terms of the suspicion that some teachers and others have of the methods employed by SPELD in their work with children—and indeed of the existence of a group that by its very nature implies a criticism of the school system.

Adult Reading Association

In the last five years a number of adult-literacy schemes have been set up, staffed by volunteer tutors, with no funding except that which has been raised by members themselves. In 1977 a national reading coordinator was appointed by the National Council for Adult Education. The coordinator has been involved mainly in organizing and teaching short courses on reading methods for volunteer tutors. There has been rapid growth in the number of schemes operating, so that there are now more than thirty working in different areas throughout the country. It has been variously estimated that there are about 50,000 functionally illiterate adults in New Zealand, so there is still much room for expansion of service. Unfortunately, these schemes are working on shoestring budgets and are in desperate need of funds for materials. Many of the schemes are unable to accept new students because of the work involved. It is hoped that district coordinators will soon be appointed to provide continuity as well as proper administrative assistance.

Research

The major funding source for reading-curriculum development and research is the Department of Education in Wellington. Research is usually curriculum-oriented and is often conducted jointly with other agencies such as the New Zealand Council for Educational Research (NZCER). However, NZCER has mainly been concerned with test development in the field of reading rather than with basic research into the reading process. The department has recently initiated Project CHILD, a survey of children having unexplained learning difficulties, with a follow-up intervention program in the planning stage. The department has also funded the Reading Recovery Project, directed by Professor Marie Clay of Auckland University, which aims to analyze differences in children failing to read at six years and is designed to provide in-service materials to assist teachers. Nonfunded research is usually done in the universities, depending on the research interests of students and staff.

There is, however, no overall plan of attack on basic research needs in the area of reading difficulties. A national seminar on reading research needs is soon to be held in Auckland, and it is hoped that the participants will decide on a detailed statement of research priorities as a guide for future work in this area.

Conclusion

There is a growing realization among New Zealand educators that some children are not being helped as much as others in learning to read. Our most recent report on reading standards concluded that "more will need to be done to help teachers become better equipped to deal with failing students."

The exact nature of what needs to be done is more difficult to determine. Perhaps the New Zealand style of teaching, with its emphasis on language experience and the integration of reading with all aspects of the curriculum, needs to be supplemented by more direct teaching of reading skills to those children who are only slowly responding to conventional methods.

In addition, it seems that the Department of Education may need to expand and diversify its present attempts to improve the instructional skills of all teachers of reading. The trend has been to work on a broad front of providing in-service training for all teachers yet supplementing this with back-up advisory services and the provision of specialist resource teachers within the school. Special courses have also been developed for parents in order to keep them informed about the teaching of reading and to capitalize on the help that can be given to children at home. In the light of overseas experience (Mosley 1975; Collins 1961), this may well be the most appropriate way to proceed: to emphasize help within the school and the home environment rather than to create special classes and clinics.

What is lacking within the broad framework of in-service and specialist provisions, however, is field research and evaluation. Schools need to investigate ways in which specialist help can be best utilized. Research is also needed to determine the most effective means of translating in-service coursework into classroom realities. Finally, in a country such as New Zealand, where resources are limited, there needs to be a systematic approach to reading research, training programs, and curriculum development generally. Otherwise, we are in danger of repeating our own mistakes as well as those of others.

References

The blight of illiteracy. 1978. *Newsweek*, September 6.

Bourke, S., and Keeves, J. (eds.). 1977. *The Mastery of Literacy and Numeracy: Final Report*. Australian Studies in School Performance, Vol. 3. Hawthorn: Australian Council for Educational Research.

Clay, M. 1972. *Reading: The Patterning of Complex Behavior*. Auckland: Heineman.

Collins, J.E. 1961. *The Effects of Remedial Education*. London: Olive and Boyd.

Department of Education. 1978. *Educational Standards in State Schools: A Report to the Minister*. Wellington: Government Printer.

McLaren, I. 1974. *Education in a Small Democracy: New Zealand*. London: Routledge and Kegan Paul.

Mosley, P. 1975. *Special Provision for Learning: When Will They Ever Learn?* Windsor: New Zealand Council for Educational Research.

National Assessment of Educational Progress. 1972. *Preliminary Report: Reading Summary*. Denver: Educational Commission of the States.

Renwick, W. 1978. The Way Ahead in Reading. An address to the New Zealand International Reading Association Conference, Dunedin, August.

Thorndike, R. 1973. *Reading Comprehension in Fifteen Countries*. New York: Halsted Press.
Why Johnny can't write. 1975. *Newsweek*, December 8.

19 Children with Reading and Writing Disabilities in Poland

Barbara Zakrzewska

The ability to read and write is inseparable from the concept of a modern person. Developments in science are so rapid that much information becomes outdated almost overnight and therefore must be constantly verified. Although various means of transmitting information, such as radio, television, and movies, are very popular, reading skill is still of paramount importance. Reading remains an individual function leading directly to new intellectual, emotional, and moral horizons in the life of every human being.

Not all children, however, are fully capable of mastering reading and writing skills during the period of schooling. In cases of mentally handicapped children, special schools may solve the problem in the best possible way.

However, children who have no mental defects or disturbed functions of sight and hearing and who are sometimes overdeveloped in other respects, but who have reading disability, must be dealt with along different lines. Extra lessons based on traditional didactic methods do not prove very effective in these instances. Schoolteachers sometimes express the opinion that these pupils are capable but are lazy or mentally retarded. The social disapproval and school failures that children with reading and writing disabilities often encounter result in symptoms of neurosis and personality disorders. In extreme cases, the children may become lawbreakers.

Early recognition of difficulties during the first two years of elementary school, with corrective compensatory activities and other prophylactic procedures undertaken during the kindergarten period (in those instances when disturbed functions essential for the development of reading and writing skills have been observed), may help guarantee satisfactory psychomotor development in children and their full access to social functioning in the future.

The first experimental and research studies on the problem of specific reading and writing disabilities were initiated in Poland in the 1930s (S. Baley, S. Bychowski, and R. Zdanska). By the end of the 1950s, intensive studies were undertaken in the Department of Mental Hygiene and Child Psychiatry of the Polish Academy of Sciences. The research was carried out along two basic lines: diagnostic-theoretical and therapeutic-practical. In the 1960s the department, at the suggestion of J. Markiewicz, introduced

433

a method of reeducation of children with reading and writing disabilities, using both didactic and psychomotor aspects of education. A second scientific center active in the same period was the University of Warsaw, which concentrated mostly on the theoretical side of the problem. The results of research studies carried on for several years by the Department of Psychology (Scientific Research Group) of Warsaw University, about children with school failures, have been published in several books (Spionek 1965, 1973).

Both the research studies in the field of theory and the practical application resulted in a number of therapeutic methods applied to children with reading and writing disabilities (J. Magnuska, T. Danielewicz, B. Zakrzewska, J. Markiewicz, T. Gasowska, and Z. Stepkowska). These methods follow two lines: children with lesser degrees of reading and writing disabilities attend classes in "compensatory groups" within the elementary school. The classes are taught by qualified teachers, who keep in close contact with a psychologist in a nearby dispensary. Children with serious reading problems attend classes at educational-vocational centers or mental-health dispensaries.

Spionek (1973) characterized dyslexia and dysgraphia as "only those reading/writing disabilities that are caused by deficits of perceptual motor function development, estimated in relation to the child's age and evaluated in relation to the child's mental development." If the definition of dyslexia is accepted as such, many discrepancies connected with other developmental disorders that coexist with dyslexia (speech and lateralization dysfunctions), as reported in research studies, can be easily explained. Spionek worked out an indicator of fragmentary developmental deficit as a means of measuring the degree of defect in aural, visual, and kinesthetic-motor perception enabling a specialist to determine how far the retardation has gone. This information is important in the therapeutic treatment of dyslexia in children if the right methods are to be selected and put to use. The formula is

$$\text{fragmentary developmental deficit} = \frac{\text{fragmentary retardation (years)}}{\text{age}}$$

Thus, if the fragmentary retardation in visual perception of a child is three years and the child's age is ten years, the fragmentary developmental deficit is 3/10, or 0.3.

Spionek maintains that children whose developmental retardation amounts to more than 0.3 (even those with a high IQ) are not likely to overcome reading and writing problems without reeducation procedures. This is also true of children whose developmental retardation, though not very deep, affects some perceptual-motor spheres.

Visual Perception

Visual perception, one of the basic functions in the development of reading and writing skills, usually develops harmoniously and corresponds to the general degree of mental development in a child. However, children with reading and writing disabilities display retarded and disturbed visual analysis and synthesis. Disorders in visual analysis and synthesis cannot be reduced, however, to mere developmental retardation. In cases of total disorders, children usually confuse the letters bearing structural resemblances, such as *a-o, m-n, l-t, k-h*. To differentiate among forms that look very much alike is an exacting problem for the central nervous system.

In some complex instances, however, visual perception is not totally affected, showing traces of dysfunction only in some aspects of perception. The directional aspect of visual perception determines the characteristics of one's handwriting. This aspect of the visual perception of forms is connected with the total development of visual perception and with the development of spatial orientation. In cases of directional disorders, children persistently confuse the letters *p-g, d-b, m-w, n-u*, and the like.

Visual analysis and synthesis is essential not only in the process of differentiation among graphic forms in letters but also in memorizing and reproducing forms in relation to a model. Thus children affected with visual dysfunctions find it difficult to master both reading and writing skills. Apart from confusing and exchanging letters that are similar in form, children with disturbed visual perception encounter other problems, such as dropping small graphic details and punctuation marks. In higher grades students with disturbed visual perception often make spelling mistakes. Because visual memory does not function properly, the graphic forms of words do not become fixed in the memory, and spelling becomes a serious problem.

Remedial Reading

In the course of corrective-compensatory activities a number of diversified techniques and forms of reading exercises are used. We use manifold operations dealing with visual, aural, and motor functions starting with the smallest units (letters, syllables) in order to achieve the final effect of automatic, fluent reading. This course of action, apart from its educational purpose, has important psychotherapeutic effects. Success achieved through these exercises encourages a child to further efforts and strengthens the conviction that the skill of reading is not entirely beyond reach.

Reading texts comprise short, illustrated, easy stories to which a child responds emotionally. Schoolbooks are not recommended for use except when reading in the school manual has been given to a child as a homework assignment. The methods and techniques presented here should be applied individually with regard to reading difficulties and the general level of the child's advancement. For children with serious fragmentary deficiencies, a complete set of exercises should be applied. As the child progresses, the number of exercises dealing with syllables may be gradually reduced while more word-reading material is introduced.

Reading Exercises

1. While listening to a short, easy fragment (story, poem, puzzle) with all syllables strongly accented, a child simultaneously marks the syllables he hears with colored lines in his own copy of the text. For example:

Jo-la ma ma-le-go kot-ka.
Ko-tek ma na i-mie Mu-rek.
Mu-rek ra-no pi-je mle-ko.

In another variant of this exercise, a child reads the text, marking the syllables while pronouncing them.

2. At this stage one may proceed as follows: (a) Read syllables alternately with a child. While reading the syllables, the child hits a drum, stopping after each complete word. (b) Read one- and two-syllable words alternately with a child. (c) Work on longer units of the selected pieces and read alternately with a child the parts of the text between adjacent punctuation marks. Through this, the child learns to punctuate correctly while reading-comprehension is being developed. (d) Read complete sentences alternately. (e) Finally, the child reads the text unaided.

3. Individual reading as well as group reading, silent and aloud, should be diversified and individualized. The child reads the text that has been selected by the reeducator: (a) only one, two, three letters, and so on, in a word; (b) only one syllable, two, three, and so on; (c) words containing *ba*, *da*, *ab*, *ad*, and the like; (d) one *a* words, two *a* words, *oa* words, and so on; (e) one-syllable words, two-syllable words, and so on.

A selection consists of carefully prepared lists of words and reading pieces made up by the reeducator or picked up from the children's books.

4. The selective reading might be carried on with groups of children reading aloud. The participants, taking turns, find in the text a certain element of a word or a whole word, following the teacher's instructions. Similar methods may be applied to silent group-reading, using short contests. For this purpose, a single reading piece is read by all members of the group. In a limited period of time, the children pick out the right words, marking them in the text with colored pencils.

5. Reading in chorus provides an opportunity to check both individual participation and advancement in the reading process, while at the same time giving each child an encouraging feeling of anonymity and safety if he

does not consider himself equal to the task. The reeducator may give directions as to reading speed or, if he thinks it appropriate, may tone up the reading quality.

6. One could also use timed practice-reading of short pieces, for example, the number of words read in one minute. A child may wish to read the piece in a shorter time, setting the time limit himself. The indicated time limit should be reasonable and within the child's reach at the moment. The number of repetitions should be carefully noted until the child manages to go through the text in the selected time. Each reading speed is measured and the child is notified of the result.

Writing

Difficulties in writing should be treated with the utmost care from the very beginning, because errors in writing that are strengthened by everyday school practice cannot easily be eliminated. From the earliest stage of corrective-compensatory activities, when the child's knowledge of letter and syllable elements is very scanty, an integral relationship between a graphic representation of each word and its sound counterpart should be strongly emphasized, along with corresponding operations dealing with aural memory and perception, temporal-spatial orientation, and visual-motor coordination.

Similar to methods for teaching reading, various techniques of selective writing proved effective, both when a child copied what he wrote and when he was writing from memory. In carefully selected sets of words and sentences, the child comes across letters and sounds that he uses interchangeably. As a rule, difficulties should be carefully graded, starting with one-syllable words and proceeding to longer compound words.

Each of the exercises presented here may have two variants. With Variant I, a child looks into the text and concentrates his attention on the requirements set up by the reeducator. With Variant II, the reeducator dictates the words. The child makes an aural analysis of what he hears, getting the temporal succession of letters and writing them down in the right place in each word. If necessary, he may also classify the word in relation to a given group of words.

Variant I is applied mostly to children with defective visual perception, Variant II to those with defective aural perception. Using these exercises a child may write, for example (a) only the simplest elements of a word (vowels or consonants); (b) only the first letter or any other in succession as the reeducator requires, making the remaining ones by dashes as required; (c) only a letter preceding another letter; (d) only the first, second, or third syllable in a word, marking the remaining syllables with a long dash; (e) words with certain groups of letters, as *ao, ae, oa*.

In each of those exercises, the child uses a colored pencil to mark one element of a word or the word itself, or to better differentiate the elements that bear visual or phonetic resemblance.

In cases of serious spelling disturbances, Fernald's method should be used. It consists of a number of stages: (a) the teacher writes a word on a piece of paper and reads it aloud; (b) the child outlines each letter in the word, reading them aloud (this may be repeated several times); (c) with his eyes closed, the child outlines all the letters, naming them aloud; (d) with his eyes closed, he "draws" the word in space; and (e) he writes the word on the blackboard or in his notebook when he is able to do it without difficulty.

Exercises in Visual Perception

Exercises are used to develop visual perception, total and directional, and visual memory for dealing with nonliteral and literal material. The exercises presented here hint at the methods and means of stimulation and the development of visual functions at various stages of reeducation of dyslexic children. The exercises illustrate different stages of reeducation and may be subject to alteration as the situation requires. New exercises dealing with other parts of language material may be based on the same techniques. Exercises dealing with nonliteral elements are used at the initial stage of reeducation; those dealing with literal material are used at a later stage.

Identifying Figures in Relation to a Model

On a sheet of paper, twenty-five figures, each consisting of two or three perpendicular lines, are arranged into five rows (see figure 19-1). At the top of the sheet, four different figures are shown, each has a short slanting line drawn across one of the sides. The position of the lines varies, as does the coloring—red, blue, green, and orange, respectively.

The child examines the figures and finds the one corresponding to the first figure at the top. Having done so, he draws a slanting line across one of its sides, following the indicated coloring. The same operation is repeated with the remaining three figures. The position of the slanting lines should be carefully noted. While examining the figures, the child also states which lines are missing to form a complete square.

Differentiating among Circular Figures

The figures in this exercise look very much alike except for the "hands" pointing in different directions (see figure 19-2). At the top of the sheet, three circles, varying both in color and in the position of the hands, are in a frame. Looking at the model, the child determines the position of the hands

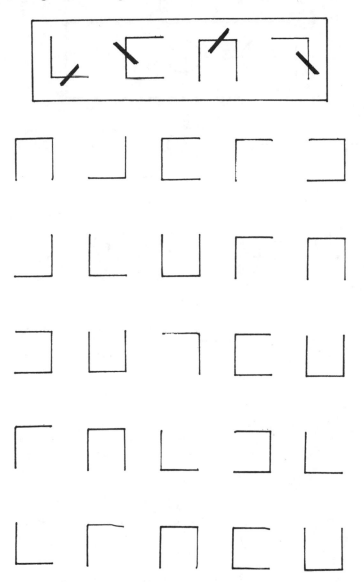

Figure 19-1. Identifying Figures in Relation to a Model

in each figure, stating whether they are pointing to the left, to the right, up, or down. He indicates all the circles with downward hands, all the circles with upward hands, and so forth. He determines the position of hands in the first framed circle. Then, looking at the model figure, the child finds the circle with the corresponding hand position and outlines the hand, using the red marker. He works similarly with the second and third framed circles.

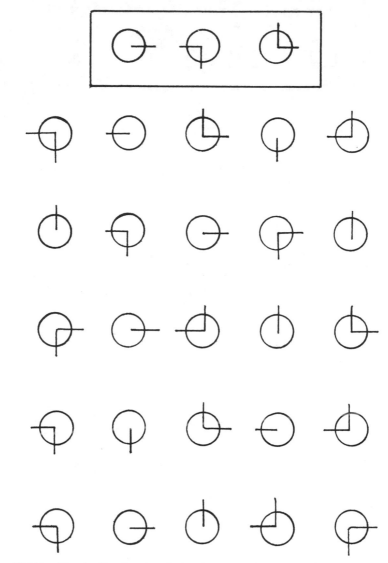

The child identifies the direction that the hands are pointing in each figure.

Figure 19-2. Differentiating among Circular Figures

Completing Figures with Missing Elements

A child completes the graphic figures, putting in the missing elements so that the final result in every instance looks like the model (see figure 19-3). The child observes a selected figure for awhile. After the model has been taken away, the child reconstructs the figure from memory. The test is repeated several times with different figures.

Figure 19-3. Completing Figures with Missing Elements

Coloring Circles Adjoining Vertical Lines

Looking at the model (see figure 19-4), the child draws black circles adjoining each vertical line. While doing this, the child specifies the position of each circle in relation to each line—on the right, on the left, at the top, or at the bottom. The circles should be drawn freehand. Having completed this, the child similarly draws red circles, then orange circles, specifying their position in reference to the lines.

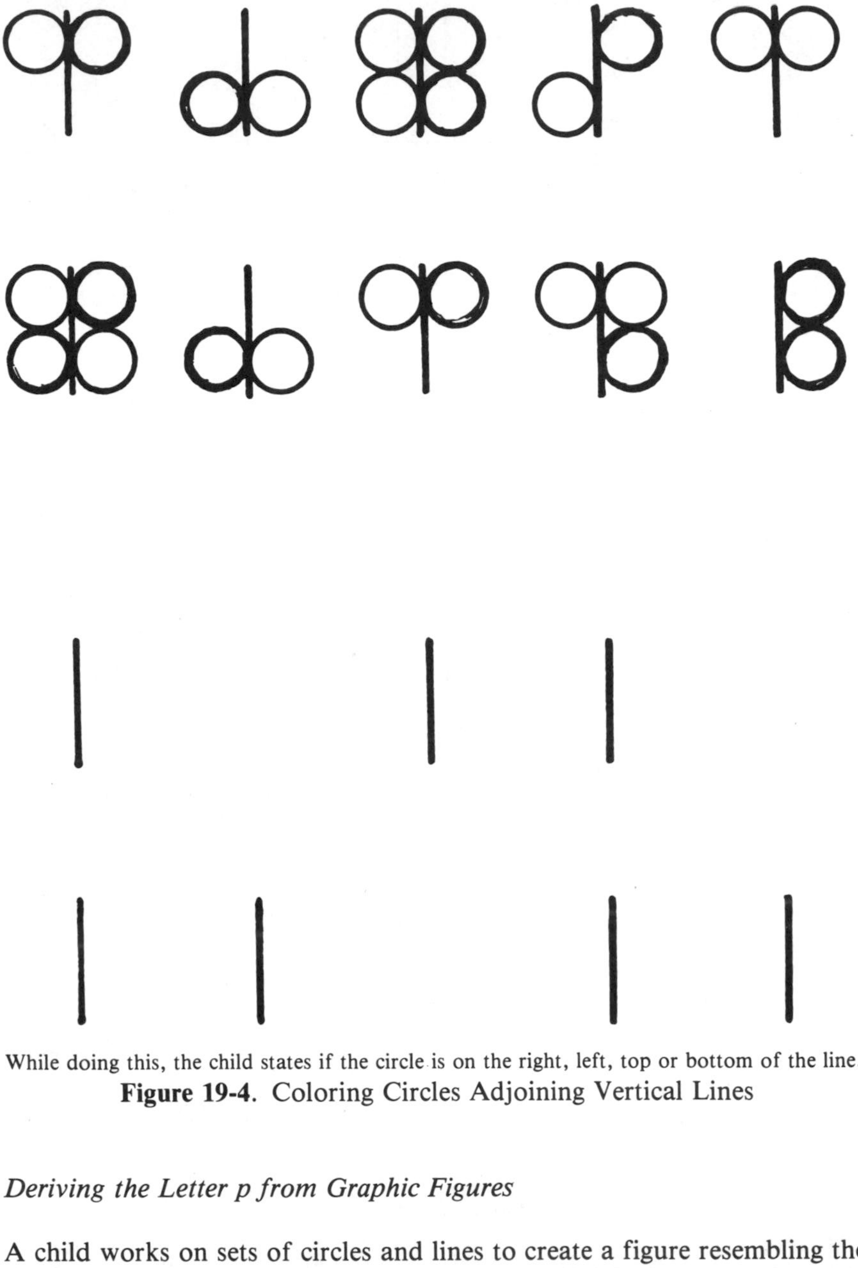

While doing this, the child states if the circle is on the right, left, top or bottom of the line.

Figure 19-4. Coloring Circles Adjoining Vertical Lines

Deriving the Letter p from Graphic Figures

A child works on sets of circles and lines to create a figure resembling the letter *p*, using the following operations: taking off unnecessary circles; adding extra circles in the right places; and coloring the entire surface of the correct circle (see figure 19-5). Similar sets of circles and lines should be prepared for *d*, *g*, and *b*.

Figure 19-5. Deriving the Letter *p* from Graphic Figures

*Constructing the Letter a from Square
and Triangular Elements*

Each of four cards contains, respectively, examples of small handwritten *a*,
capital handwritten *A*, capital printed *A*, and small printed *a*. All letters are
alike in size and shape and are repeated three times. In each group, one set

of *a*'s is cut into four squares and another into four triangles. One card in each group is left untouched as a model.

A child is presented with a card containing the complete handwritten small *a* and two other cards with the same *a* cut into squares and triangles. Looking at the model, the child works with squares and triangles to compose the complete letter. At the more advanced stage, the elements of different variants of the letter are placed in front of the child. The child picks up elements needed to compose a certain *a* as indicated by the teacher. He arranges the elements to derive as many *a* letters as possible. The same procedure is repeated in relation to every other *a* variant. The exercise may be adapted for other letters that create problems of differentiation.

Identifying Correct Forms of the Letter a

In optional places on a sheet, in four perpendicular positions, the following variants of *a* are written four times each: small and capital handwritten *a* in the correct positions; small and capital printed *a* in the correct positions; small and capital handwritten *a* in the reverse positions (reflection in a mirror); and small and capital printed *a* in the reverse position (reflection in a mirror).

Before the child begins, the fact that not all *a* variants are correct should be made quite clear. The child is presented with a sheet on which different correct variants of the letter *a* are shown, to be used as the model for further differentiation among other *a*-like forms. The child is instructed to turn the sheet around in order to make things easier. The child picks the *a* letters in the correct positions according to precedence: small handwritten *a* (outlining it in orange), capital handwritten *A* (outlining it in red), capital printed *A* (outlining it in blue), small printed *a* (outlining it in black). The child is told to reproduce the four correct types of *a* in modeling clay or soft wire. One can proceed similarly with other letters.

Other Exercises to Develop Total or Directional Visual Perception

Other exercises include copying two- and three-letter combinations and recognizing similar and different letters in a word. Exercises in the visual-spatial analysis of letters *b* and *d* are performed on paper and using building blocks. Only one group of letter combinations should be worked on in each session. Children should be watched for strain, in which case the exercises should be reduced to suit the child's ability to work.

Another form of practice is to have the child supply the missing elements of a text. The details to be found and supplied include dots, strokes, diacritical marks, and punctuation marks. If necessary, the child may consult the full original text. Finally, he reads the complete piece aloud. This exercise is followed by one involving supplying the missing parts of a vowel; six vowels are used.

New words are constructed by the child using blocks containing letters. The words are dictated, beginning with short words and proceeding to the longer ones. After making the word with blocks, the child writes the word and says it.

Another exercise involves supplying letters to fit into different positions in words having easy letter combinations (see figure 19-6). Looking at each

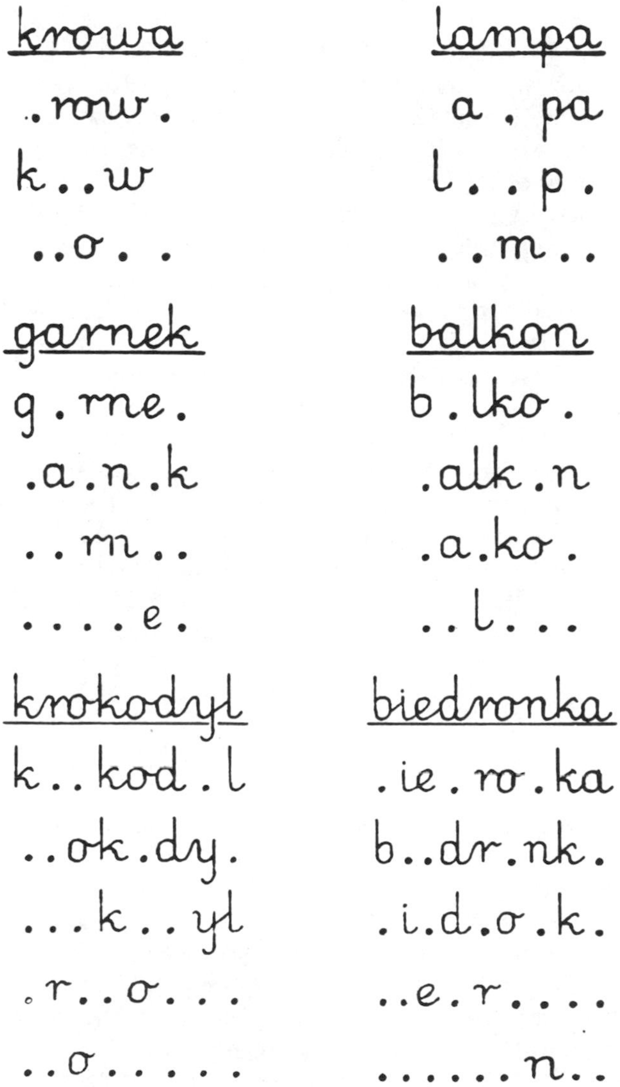

krowa

.. row .

k .. w

.. o . .

garnek

g . me .

. a . n . k

. . m ..

. . . . e .

krokodyl

k .. kod . l

.. ok . dy .

... k .. yl

. r .. o . . .

.. o . . . . .

lampa

a . pa

l . . p .

.. m ..

balkon

b . lko .

. alk . n

. a . ko .

.. l . . .

biedronka

. ie . ro . ka

b .. dr . nk .

. i . d . o . k .

.. e . r . . . .

. . . . . . n ..

Figure 19-6. Supplying the Missing Letters

model word, the child completes the blanks with one letter each. Each letter is written in red and pronounced loudly, then the child reads the complete word aloud. While completing the letters, he states its position in the word. Finally, without looking at the model, the child writes on the blackboard some letters selected from different positions in the words, as instructed by the teacher. A similar exercise with syllables may be performed next.

The next exercise involves recognizing words composed of the letters *a*, *k*, *t*, and *r*. The child writes the words he has memorized, consulting the model if necessary, and makes up his own words using these letters. The child may then be given a new set of letters and the procedure is repeated.

In the following exercise, the child supplies the letters, syllables and words that are missing in the text (see figure 19-7). Missing letters are marked by yellow dots, missing syllables are replaced by red dashes, and words left out are indicated by blue lines. The child writes the missing elements above the text, using the appropriate coloring. He may consult the text at the bottom of the page if necessary.

The next activity is to build shorter words from a base word such as *kontrola* or *komunikacja* (see figure 19-8). The child pronounces all the other words that can be made up through letter rearrangement. While working on the words, the child should be aware that to do really well he has to derive as many new words as possible. It is obvious, however, that some derivatives may have no meaning to the child and should therefore be explained.

At this point, the model sheet is taken away, and the child is given a plain sheet of paper with the same model word written on it. The child proceeds with the same problem, making up new words. The new words that the child either has memorized or created by himself are arranged into a column, so that each letter of the new word is located under the corresponding letter of the model word. This system gives the child a very clear idea of the position of each single letter in relation to the others. Finally, the child works on some additional selected words.

Case Study

K.W., a boy aged eight years, eight months, is in grade three of elementary school. His father is an engineer; his mother is a journalist.

Neither psychological nor physical hereditary taints are noticeable in the family. The home atmosphere appears peaceful and agreeable. The parents are on good terms with one another, wishing for a complete psychophysical development of their son. The boy is the only child in the family. No disorders were observed during pregnancy; however, the mother had her tonsils removed, with anesthesia, during pregnancy. Premature delivery was very fast, and blood-type conflict was found between the parents.

• litera

— sylaba

—— wyraz

K·zyś był li—nos·em Har·er-skiej ——. Je— o—wią·kiem —lo dorę—nie ——, —sanych przez ·udzi zagu—nych i —szukujących — w —bardowany· mieście.

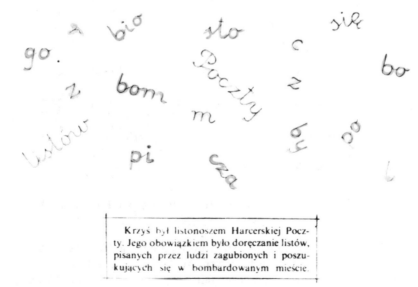

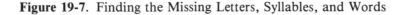

Krzyś był listonoszem Harcerskiej Poczty. Jego obowiązkiem było doręczanie listów, pisanych przez ludzi zagubionych i poszukujących się w bombardowanym mieście.

Figure 19-7. Finding the Missing Letters, Syllables, and Words

<u>kontrola</u>	<u>komunikacja</u>
kontr a	komuni a
kont o	komun a
ko t	kom ik
k t o	ko nik
ko r a	ko c
on	k un a
on o	k i j
on a	o n
o t o	o ni
n a	o n a
t ola	o j
t o	m ika
t a	m a j
rola	unik
ola	uni a

Figure 19-8. Finding as Many Short Words as Possible in Each Long Word

In K.W.'s early infancy, slow speech development was noticeable, but it disappeared entirely before the boy went to school. In addition to the speech problem, he showed a strong tendency toward left-handedness, which the parents never considered to be a serious problem.

He attended kindergarten for three years and seemed quite happy there, never showing any signs of homesickness. He adapted easily to the new environment. Neither at home nor in the kindergarten did he demonstrate anything but a happy, easygoing attitude, with no symptoms of nervousness.

He started attending school before the age of seven. He went there very unwillingly, because he had been strongly attached to his kindergarten teacher. From the start he encountered serious reading problems, accompanied by such symptoms as restlessness, impatience, inclination to tears, and body itching.

He read very slowly, with great difficulty, spelling out the words and confusing such pairs of letters as *b-d*, *y-u*, *a-o*, and *s-c*. He also dropped final letters and mangled the text, producing completely meaningless words. For example, instead of *domu* he would say *dojamu*; instead of *Mania*, *minianie*; and instead of *sadzawska*, *sanewka*.

However, he found writing from dictation relatively simple, or the least difficult. Seeing that the boy was having trouble, his mother made an effort to help him but with no positive results. She found a tutor, but traditional teaching methods proved entirely ineffective.

The boy's mental development seemed very uneven. On the Wechsler Intelligence Scale for Children he got 133 IQ on the Verbal scale and 101 IQ on the Performance scale. He was fairly good, however, in general knowledge and vocabulary. His special interests were biology and geography.

Visual perception was about four years behind his age-level; aural perception was much above his age-level. General motor and physical development were within his age standards. Tests dealing with coordination and precision of hand movements gave poor results. Ambidexterity, with right-handedness dominating, was observed.

Introductory Activities

In the initial stage of therapy, special emphasis was placed on increasing his feeling of satisfaction through successful experiences during each session. Compensation for school failures for a boy with a very high degree of intelligence was of paramount importance. Calming activities were centered on easy operations such as tracing and coloring, which are relaxing. We developed his manual skills together with his visual-motor coordination and directional functions through various activities such as tracing, technique, and materials (sticks and wires). The boy's special interests in biology and geography were put to good use through games, jigsaw puzzles, and albums of his own invention.

Proper Therapeutic Activities

Because of the isolated retardation of visual-perception functions, special emphasis in the course of reeducation was placed on the development of these functions in relation to the others, which were considered of secondary importance. The following means and methods were used in the reeducation process:

1. Booklets were created to deal with special problems (vowels, misspelled letters) and to take advantage of the boy's inventiveness.
2. Exercises included supplying in color the missing letters and syllables that the boy used interchangeably.
3. Visual total differentiation of words similar in structure (*boba, baba, bada*) was organized.
4. Visual differentiation with emphasis on directional function (words with the letters *b, d, g, p*) was practiced.
5. Various forms of selective reading and writing were encouraged.
6. Sets of words were organized to develop directional-spatial orientation in relation to words composed of letters used interchangeably or entirely misspelled.

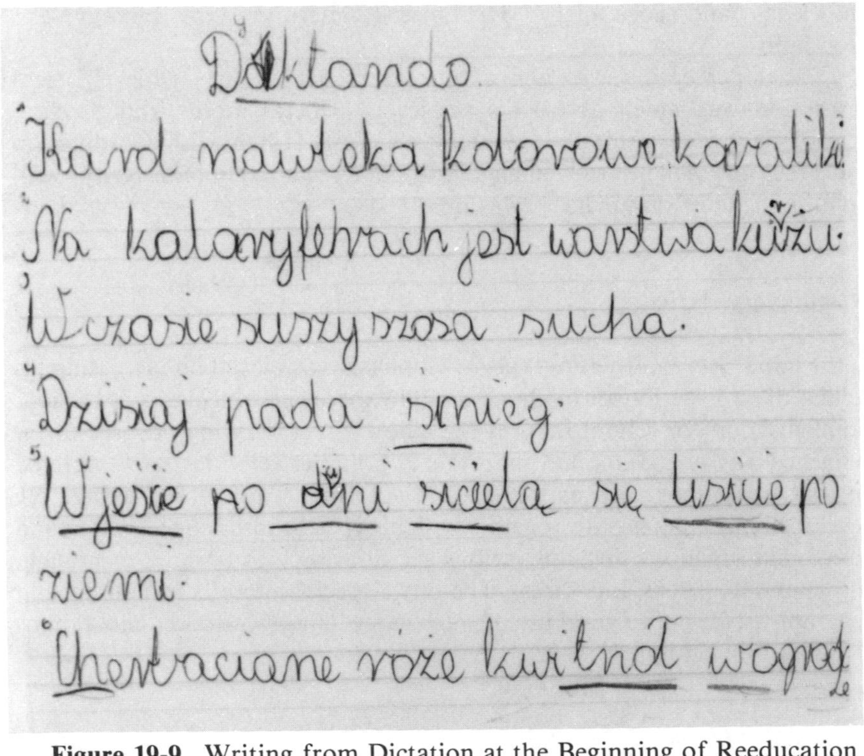

Figure 19-9. Writing from Dictation at the Beginning of Reeducation

Samples of writing from dictation at the beginning and after six months of reeducation are given in figures 19-9 and 19-10. An improvement is seen in both spelling and handwriting.

Conclusion

The exercises dealing with the operation of visual perception and memory—very important functions in the development of reading and writing skills—represent only a fragment of the complex reeducation process. What is most essential in the process may be characterized as

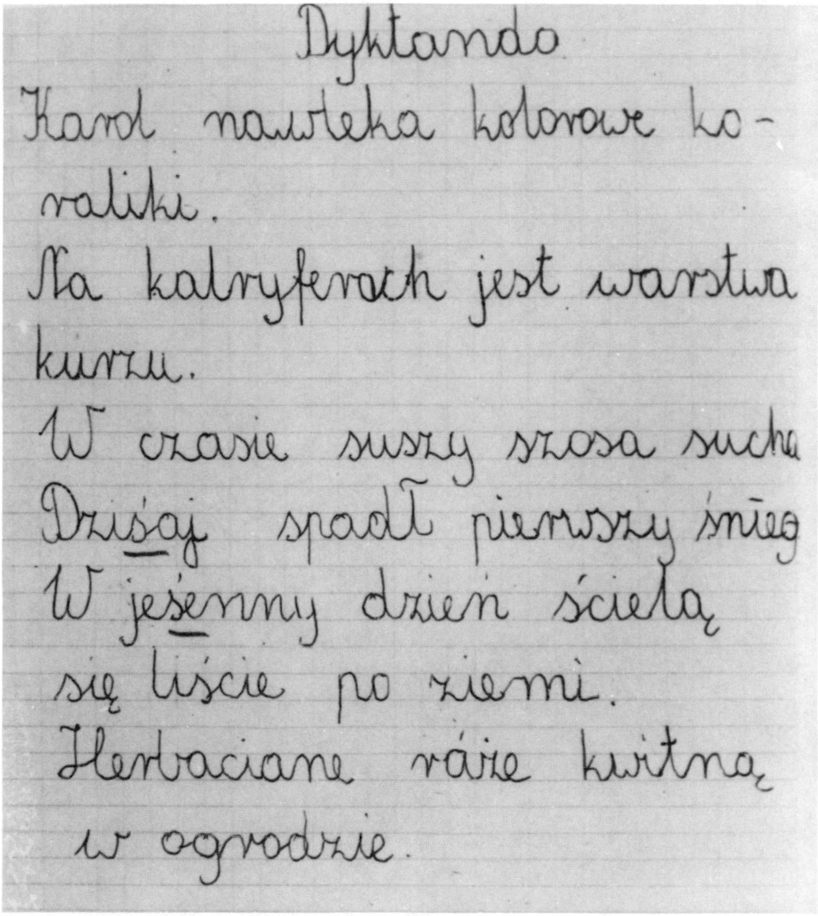
Dyktando
Karol nawleka kolorowe ko-
raliki.
Na kalryferach jest warstwa
kurzu.
W czasie suszy szosa sucha
Dziśaj spadł pierwszy śnieg
W jeśenny dzień ścielą
się liście po ziemi.
Herbaciane róże kwitną
w ogrodzie.

The improvement in both spelling and handwriting is apparent. Note the use of graph paper to help control the writing.

Figure 19-10. Writing from Dictation after Six Months of Reeducation

multifunctional, simultaneous development of perceptual-motor functions, with emphasis on certain individual functions depending on the specific needs of every dyslexic child.

Segregating exercises into groups (one of which has been presented in this chapter) helps to apply them practically during reeducational sessions. If necessary, the same material that has been recommended for the development of visual perception may be used analogically for developing aural perception and other functions fundamental to reading and writing skills.

References

A list of references will be supplied by the author upon request. All are in Polish.

20 Reading Disabilities in Swedish Children

Eve Malmquist

The development of a child's reading ability should be regarded not as an isolated technical problem of instruction but as a phase, an aspect of the child's total development, and as such it should be intimately integrated with this growth. This view is becoming widely accepted by Swedish reading specialists. There is, as we see it, a dynamic interaction between a pupil's physical, intellectual, emotional, and social development and the development of his reading ability.

Learning to read therefore becomes a very important factor in the individual's adjustment to life. Success or lack of success in the acquisition of elementary reading skills affects the whole behavior of a child and his attitude toward his environment. Failure to learn to read may negatively affect the development of the child's entire personality.

During his first days in school the child should not have cause for anxiety and ill-feeling because of tasks that are beyond his ability. On the contrary, he should be given confidence that he has the resources to benefit from what the school can offer. Every child should be given the opportunity to feel the great satisfaction and motivation for continued work that is connected with success. And that means that the teacher has to fulfill, both in the beginning situation and later on in school, the hard but essential task of establishing proper relationships between the child's capacities and the tasks he is expected to perform.

Preparatory Period before Formal Instruction

For the reasons mentioned, schooling in Sweden is started very cautiously, with the aim of making the child's transfer of activities from home to school easy and endurable. The teacher does her best to create positive attitudes in the children toward school and the working life there. To assist this process, during the first two or three weeks the child is at school only two hours a day.

Many children need preparatory teaching of various kinds before real reading instruction is started. Teachers at the primary stage spend time during the first weeks of school doing exercises and playing games to develop the children's speaking and listening abilities and their visual and auditory

453

perception. The teachers also try to enrich the children's vocabularies and to introduce general concepts and expressions that the children will need in order to understand more formal reading instruction later on.

Individual Differences and a Diagnostic Approach

During this preparatory period the children become accustomed to the classroom situation, and the teacher has opportunities to observe the children to get an idea of their maturity and capacity in different aspects of their development. A knowledge of the resources of an individual pupil in different areas is one of the fundamentals of planning the teaching in an appropriate and effective manner, and the primary teacher of today in Sweden is well aware of this.

One of the main regulations of the Swedish Education Acts of 1962 and 1969 is that the personal resources of the individual child not only must be respected but should be the starting point for the planning of education and teaching. According to the objectives stated in the school law, the school should stimulate each child's personal growth toward a free, self-activating, self-confident, and harmonious human being. The school must provide individualized education.

When maximum consideration is given to the interests and capacities of the individual pupil, children's performances within a class must vary. Therefore, the use of whole-class teaching as the only procedure in the primary grades, with the same learning requirements for all children as to speed, difficulty of material, and length of practice periods, interferes with sound reading development and contributes to reading disabilities. Children of the same chronological age differ widely in their capacity to learn, their intelligence, their background experiences, and their personality traits. The need to organize instruction to provide for these differences is therefore evident and urgent.

My own investigations of first-grade children in Sweden uncovered a range of from four years, eleven months, to eleven years, eight months in mental age, while differences between the children's chronological ages were very small (Malmquist 1977). A great range of ability in other variables at school entrance was also noted in another study. Several children in the population studied had very little knowledge of the letters in their own names. Some 2 to 3 percent knew all the lowercase letters; 80 percent could not read a single word in an easy prose test standardized for the end of the spring term; and 1 to 2 percent reached the beginning third-grade reading level (Malmquist 1969).

Under such circumstances, one cannot justify teaching children with the assumption that all need the same kind of instruction. Most teachers recognize these great differences between children and within children. Nevertheless, at least in Sweden, they often seem to strive to bring all the pupils in the class up to established norms. This main goal of teachers gives little satisfaction and stimulation to the bright pupils and is frustrating and unrealistic for the slow children. Teachers therefore have children of about the same reading-level form separate groups during part of the time assigned to reading. The need to organize instruction to provide adequately for individual differences is evident and urgent, although much still remains to be done in terms of practical application.

To a greater extent now than previously, a diagnostic approach and individualization in teaching are being stressed. In Sweden, steps to further this have included the following, among others:

1. The class size has been reduced to a maximum of twenty-five in the first three years and thirty in the remaining six years of compulsory schooling. (At present the mean size, for the country as a whole, lies between seventeen and eighteen children per class.)
2. The practice of having the child start school at the age of seven has continued, but flexibility as to beginning age is allowed.
3. Better opportunities than before exist for individual tutoring, small-group teaching, teaching in clinics, and the provision of special classes of various kinds.
4. The class may be divided in half for a certain number of hourly sessions per week for teaching reading, writing, and mathematics in the first three grades; and for biology, chemistry, physics, foreign languages, and Swedish, in the higher grades.

Early diagnosis is the keynote. With the new smaller class size and the additional time available for individual tutoring, the teacher has better opportunities than before to use a diagnostic approach and to provide learning steps, methods, and procedures suited to the individual learner. Furthermore, the concept of reading-readiness is applied not only to the beginning stages of reading but—in accordance with the new curriculum—to all reading-levels in all subjects. The teacher is expected to ask himself whether the individual is ready (maturationally) to gain both an understanding from the reading and the ability to put this understanding to use. This approach is also applied to the teacher's guidance of the student's development and to the student's interests and tastes in recreational reading in or out of school.

These ideas are accepted by nearly everyone. They may even sound so trite and obvious that they are not worth restating. To put them into practice, however, is another matter. It will take time to get all Swedish teachers to accept these views completely and to be able to apply them in their classes.

Factors Related to Reading Disabilities

Reading is now so intimately integrated with life, both within and outside the school, that a child's failure in learning to read may negatively affect the development of his personality. If this basic view of reading and writing disabilities is accepted—and its validity has been confirmed by the experiences of teachers and the results of Swedish research during recent decades—it must be considered necessary to advance on the broadest possible front when seeking factors that can affect success and failure in learning to read.

The complex nature of the process of reading makes a survey of the causes of reading disability very difficult. We are faced with many unsolved problems in this respect. Often we have had to be satisfied with the knowledge that certain symptoms coincide with reading disabilities. It has been found that certain factors or groups of factors seem to be related in some way to reading disabilities, but it has not always been possible to ascertain the relationship between cause and effect.

The following is a list of some of the factors that have been found in different studies to cause reading disabilities:

1. Lack of reading readiness.
2. General intellectual retardation.
3. Physical handicaps: impaired vision and hearing, neurological defects, hormonal disturbances, low stamina.
4. General retardation in linguistic development: impaired speech, other speech defects, limited vocabulary, limited background experience because of social and cultural handicaps.
5. Personality factors: emotional difficulties, and general problems of adjustment.
6. Social factors, environmental factors, irregular school-attendance, frequent changes of school or teachers, unsatisfactory home environment.
7. Shortcomings in instructional methods and school organization: teacher's inability to adapt instruction to the ability and maturity of the individual child, a too-rapid rate of learning at the elementary level, too little reading material of sufficient variety to satisfy different pupils' needs and interests, too many pupils in the class.

In recent years specialists in reading have stressed that it is very rare for reading disabilities to be attributed to only one cause. My investigations of factors related to reading disabilities in the first grade of the comprehensive school, made some years ago, included comparisons between different groups of readers taking into account one variable at a time and studies in which each factor was considered separately in relation to reading ability.

Several variables were studied, both separately and in interaction with other variables, using analysis of variance techniques of a higher order, that is, multifactorial design (Malmquist 1958, 1969, 1977).

Attention was paid to the children's preschool development (birth, state of health, development of speech, and the like), home environment, social and economic situation, parent's level of formal education, and other environmental variables. Tests of vision, hearing, reading ability, visual perception, ability to spell, and intelligence were also done. In addition, some teacher and school variables were included in the studies.

Studies of more than forty variables showed that the following factors were most closely related to reading disabilities in the first grade and also most distinctly differentiated the poor readers from the good readers:

1. Intelligence, ability to concentrate, stamina, self-confidence, and emotional stability.
2. Ability to spell and visual perception.
3. Socioeconomic group, parent's level of education, and interest in reading in the home.
4. Experience of child's teacher, measured by number of years in the profession.

On the basis of detailed case studies it was found that children with special reading disabilities (IQ above 90 on the Terman-Merrill Intelligence Scale) deviated markedly from the mean of the total population studied in several variables in addition to reading ability. Judging by the results of these investigations, reading disability in the first grade is never an isolated deficiency. In all the pupils studied, reading disabilities existed together with deficiencies, maladjustments, or unfavorable conditions in many other areas.

Delimitation of Cases of Reading Disabilities

The relation between the function of the brain and the development of reading ability has not yet been satisfactorily elucidated. It seems clear, however, that some especially grave cases of reading disabilities are caused by deviations from normal neurological development, for example, brain damage at birth, head injuries of various kinds, or such diseases as encephalitis. Some of these children function normally, while others are seriously impaired. It is also assumed that different parts of the brain develop at different rates. In some children the differences in rate of development of the different parts of the brain are accentuated. Some parts of the brain develop normally, while in other regions there is marked retardation. According to the medical view, such delayed and irregular development of the brain is a factor behind the rise of reading disability, together with the rather rare types of brain damage mentioned.

It is feasible to assume that, at some time in the future, improved diagnostic aids may verify the hypotheses still generally accepted by medical scientists in this area—that congenital neurological defects and maturational retardation in certain brain centers are specific causes of even the more common types of reading disabilities. For the time being, however, we have to regard these hypotheses as generaly unverified. The great majority of cases of reading disabilities show no tangible signs of neurological defects when the research instruments now available are used. Whatever their causes, most cases respond to a special teaching program and to medical and psychological attention. This fact has been demonstrated both by research and by educational practice.

From my point of view, it is extremely difficult to clearly differentiate a special group of poor readers who can be classified as dyslexic. The results of reading tests, qualitative evaluations of errors, and informal observations of reading achievement cannot identify certain readers designated as word-blind or dyslexic. The simple explanation is that such a specific group of poor readers does not exist as far as psychologists and educators are aware. It can only be determined that some children read much more poorly than others and, furthermore, that the gradation from poor readers to average readers, on the distribution curve for the reading tests used, is not so sharp that one can determine where the best of the poor readers end and the worst of the average readers begin.

I have found nothing to support the idea that the qualitative character of the reading errors made by poor readers differs from group to group or differs from the types of errors made by normal readers. All conceivable types of reading errors occur among normal readers, though with less frequency than among poor readers. Quantitative rather than qualitative differences distinguish different cases of reading disability. There are differences in degree of error-making rather than in kind (Malmquist and Valtin 1974; Malmquist 1977). I and many of my colleagues hold that a reading disability should be regarded as a phenomenon that falls within the framework of normal variation. From this point of view, it is not possible to differentiate a particular group of poor readers who can be classified as suffering from congenital word-blindness or specific dyslexia, as medical research presumes can be done. Since it is not possible to detect any qualitative differences in reading ability or reading errors between groups of poor readers and normal readers, we prefer to use quantitative terms—for example, *children with reading disabilities* or *poor readers*—to describe the degree of variation among readers.

Our preference for quantitative terms does not mean that we make no qualitative evaluations. A qualitative inspection of reading achievement should invariably precede remedial treatment. As an introductory phase of a differential diagnosis, it would tell us what kinds of reading and writing errors an individual is most troubled by. In determining whether or not reading disabilities are present, however, we should consider only quantitative scores.

Terms such as *children with reading disabilities* and *poor readers* may be criticized as vague and indefinite. The use of such comprehensive concepts hampers scientific discussion, practical educational work, and school administration. A more precise definition might provide better guidelines for scientific work and for the selection of children for special instruction. I propose, however, that these comprehensive terms be retained, since they are firmly established in psychology and education. It would be of great value if psychologists and educators could agree on the scope of these terms.

The quantitative terms are appropriate only under the following conditions: that we limit ourselves to stating that the pupils' reading abilities are conspicuously below the minimum standards required for their age and class, and that reading ability is measured by standardized reading tests. The delimitation of the poor readers can then be made at the point of distribution curve that is most suitable for the purposes of practical education and school administration. The way in which this delimitation is carried out should be stated, and the measuring instruments should be identified. For example, we believe that a child in the first grade has reading disabilities of such a nature that special teaching of some kind is required if his test results on a standardized reading test fall below -1 sigma (lowest 16 percent) on the distribution curve for his grade.

A term such as *children with special reading disabilities* is appropriate under the following conditions: when the children have poor reading ability (for example, below -1 sigma on an approved standardized reading test for the age in question) but have normal or above normal intelligence as measured by a conventional intelligence test (for example, Terman-Merrill), and when reading ability as measured by an approved standardized reading test for the age in question deviates significantly from expectancy based on intelligence testing. Retardation in the development of reading ability is commonly defined as a significant discrepancy between actual reading ability and the level that could be expected from the potential learning capability of the individual, judged primarily by conventional intelligence tests. The concept of reading disability is considered to be relative, not absolute, and is defined in an operational way, that is, by indicating the measuring instruments and the procedures of delimitation.

Frequency of Special Reading
Disabilities in Sweden

There is considerable difference of opinion over where to draw the line between children with and without reading disabilities. Often the demarcation must be somewhat arbitrary, depending on the purpose it is intended to serve, the resources a school has for special teaching, and variations in the definition of the term *disabilities*. Variations in reported frequency of reading disabilities in different countries may also be caused by differences in such factors as socioeconomic and cultural background, teaching methods and materials, the age of the pupils when beginning school, degree of phonetic complexity of the language in question, teacher competence, and so forth (Malmquist 1969, 1977).

Using an operational definition of the concept of children with special reading disabilities, I have calculated the percentage of the whole population of children in Sweden with such disabilities. It was found that children with special reading disabilities (below − 1 sigma on the distribution curve for the reading tests employed) but with normal or above normal intelligence made up 4.8 percent of the sample (normal intelligence was 100 IQ on the Terman-Merrill Intelligence Scale) (Malmquist 1977).

Methods of Testing and Diagnosis

Research studies carried out in Sweden indicate that it is most unusual for an investigator to pin down one single factor that causes reading and writing disabilities. Almost always there are entire clusters of factors. Therefore, when searching for causes of success or failure in reading and writing, one should proceed on as broad a front as possible. General intelligence, linguistic ability, acuteness of vision and hearing, general health, attitudes and interests, emotional balance, power of concentration, endurance, attentiveness, and many other factors play a role. This applies to all levels of development, from the first lesson in elementary school to more advanced reading by adults. Should there be any serious defect or deficiency in any one or several of these factors, the individual's success in reading and writing may be adversely affected.

An effective teacher must know each of his pupils quite well. Standardized tests are very useful in this regard, but informal observation of behavior and achievement are necessary for planning individualized programs. It is therefore recommended that teachers who are engaged in remedial instruction keep detailed notes on each student. These notes should contain general data such as age, home conditions, development during school, information from medical files, and results of diagnostic psychometric and educational tests and tests of vision, hearing, and so forth.

If the child is attending a reading clinic, there should be a record of his absences from school, the number of visits he has paid to the reading clinic, and the difficulties that have been dealt with on each visit. Without notes of this kind it is not possible to organize the instructional program systematically to obtain good results. The higher a child scores on a conventional intelligence test, the higher the probability that he will learn to read without difficulty. However, there are instances in which a child with fairly low intelligence is able to learn the basic concepts of reading without any particular difficulty, whereas some children with average or above-average intelligence fail. Intelligence-test scores for children with reading and writing disabilities should be interpreted with great care, because the reliability of some tests of older children depends on the child's ability to read. Tests of this kind tend to underestimate the IQ of children with reading disabilities. Standardized tests are available in Sweden in such areas as reading-readiness, school maturity, intelligence, reading ability, spelling, perception, and handwriting. We recommend that the teachers construct interest inventories and maintain individual records for each pupil. Such informal observations are considered to be important supplements to the more-formal evaluations supplied by standardized tests.

Special Teaching

Special teaching in Sweden is an important aspect of the school's effort to create a teaching method and course of studies suited to the needs of each pupil. Such teaching is arranged either for individual pupils or for small groups and is coordinated with other teaching in an ordinary class (coordinated special teaching) or for pupils in a special class. Pupils encountering complex difficulties can receive more than one kind of special teaching. The main difficulties that may warrant complementary, auxiliary, or substitute teaching of a special nature are intellectual retardation; behavioral disturbances; difficulties in starting school; learning difficulties in Swedish and mathematics; impediments of vision, hearing, and speech; and impaired movement.

According to the school law in Sweden, special teaching by specifically trained teachers shall be provided individual pupils, small groups, and classes after comparatively large-scale analysis and follow-up. Work will be carried out with the help of specially trained methods, techniques, and aids. This gives circumstances favorable to proper mental hygiene and individualized teaching suited to the needs of each pupil.

*Coordinated Special Training and Teaching
a Special Class*

A general policy in teaching pupils who encounter difficulties is that they attend ordinary classes as much as possible. The need for individualized assistance is met by complementary and auxiliary teaching coordinated with activities in the class where the pupil receives the greater part of his instruction. Coordinated special teaching is arranged in the form of assistance teaching; observation teaching; school-maturity teaching (for pupils encountering difficulty when they first start school); teaching for those with special learning difficulties in Swedish and mathematics; and teaching for those with visual, auditory, and speech impediments or motor difficulties. Other types of coordinated special teaching may also be arranged, with the permission of the National Board of Education.

According to their needs, pupils may receive coordinated special teaching of one or several types. Coordinated special teaching can be arranged in such a way that the special teacher supervises the work of one or more pupils, while the class teacher takes the rest of the class. Complementary and auxiliary teaching are provided either in the relevant classroom or in an adjoining room. Such teaching can also be assigned to special premises (school clinics). In many cases, a pupil working in an ordinary class will require special arrangements and measures by reason of his handicap, for example, technical aids, personal assistance, and medical and psychotherapeutic treatment.

Close collaboration between class teachers, special teachers, and pupil-welfare staff (school psychologists, medical doctors, guidance personnel) is considered necessary by the school authorities for an overall approach to a pupil's difficulties. In this cooperation, the special teacher concentrates mainly in making diagnostic examinations, providing individualized teaching on the basis of diagnoses, and working out teaching and training programs for the future work of the pupils in a regular class. The nature and scope of the measures required will be decided by an analysis and assessment of how the pupil's handicap affects his total performance at school.

In the case of pupils with difficulties that markedly affect total performance, it may prove necessary to broaden the impact of such supportive measures. The pupil may need both special training and modification and adjustment of his social environment in the school. Various groups of the following kinds can be organized: classes for slow learners, remedial reading classes, school maturity classes, observation classes, sight classes, hearing classes, and classes for pupils with motor handicaps (National Swedish Board of Education 1969).

Remedial Reading and Writing

Individual treatment or group treatment in reading clinics or remedial-reading classes in Sweden does not differ substantially from effective teaching in normal classes. The remedial teaching is based on a more carefully elaborated plan and is more intensive and more systematically arranged, but there are no essential differences in principles or methods. More and more today's teachers accept the principles that are basic to programs of special teaching and apply them as much as possible to the normal classroom. I consider seven of the most important principles of effective teaching to be as follows:

1. Give all possible consideration to the individual differences of each student within a class.
2. Learn as much as possible about the needs and the potential resources of every child and adjust the teaching to the child's level of development and attainment.
3. Begin teaching at the child's present level, regardless of his chronological age and grade-placement.
4. Use materials that are adapted to the child's ability and interests.
5. Motivate the child to learn; arouse his interest and try to maintain it.
6. Treat every child in such a way that he feels accepted, that he gets something out of his work, and that he is aware of his progress.
7. Evaluate the results of one's teaching continuously; determine whether goals are being met; try to discover deficiencies in the teaching design when planning for the future.

In practice, special remedial teaching and treatment and good normal teaching within the framework of the regular class are very much alike if both employ these basic methodological principles. The differences between the two is a matter of degree.

Diagnostic Methods in Teaching and Treatment

Efficient remedial teaching should follow a pattern. First, the teacher should try to find out what kinds of deficiencies the student has. Using the results of a careful investigation, he then designs a plan of supportive and therapeutic activities. The teacher starts by thoroughly reviewing the cause of the malfunctioning. He administers appropriate tests, evaluates the results, and reaches a diagnosis. Only then is he ready to begin treatment. Sound procedures follow a specific sequence:

1. Diagnostic testing.
2. Teaching and treatment on the basis of the test results.
3. New diagnostic testing.
4. Continued teaching and treatment, modified according to the results of follow-up tests, and so on.

It is generally accepted that we should start teaching at the pupil's current level of achievement or somewhat lower. Within reasonable limits, the teacher will also determine the pupil's status with regard to intellectual, emotional, social, and motor development, and the like. But the diagnosis must not be regarded as finished once it has been made at the beginning of a teaching period. It should be reviewed day by day, week by week, throughout the school year.

Prevention of Reading and Writing Disabilities

Ideally, we should like to prevent the occurrence of reading and writing disabilities. One of the conditions for a preventive program is the effective identification of potential cases of disability before the child begins school. A second condition is that classroom instruction, from the child's first day at school, should be individualized or adapted to each child's particular needs.

Six-Year Longitudinal Study

I conducted a six-year longitudinal study of children from grades one to three in which one of the chief aims was to analyze the possibility of preventing the development of reading problems (Malmquist 1969). The pilot study included twenty classes with a total of 386 pupils; and the field experiments comprised seventy-two classes with a total of 1,653 pupils from twelve cities in various parts of Sweden.

The aims of the investigation were:

1. To determine if it is possible to prevent special reading disabilities among children in grades one to three.
2. To study the prognostic value of the readiness test used in Sweden prior to first grade.
3. To construct and standardize additional measuring instruments for the diagnosis of reading- and writing-readiness and for the prediction of reading and writing ability at the end of the first, second, and third grades.

The following main hypothesis was advanced: After a careful diagnosis of children's reading-readiness and general school-readiness at the beginning of school, followed by continuous diagnosis through grades one to three, it is possible to reduce considerably the frequency of reading disabilities by providing suitable remedial treatment for children who, if given ordinary instruction only, would be expected to experience reading and writing disabilities.

Pilot Study

The twenty classes included in the pilot study were divided into a control group and an experimental group, made as equivalent as possible in number of pupils in a class, sex distribution, general intelligence, reading-readiness, parent's social and economic status, teacher competence, and so forth.

Before they entered school at age seven, school-readiness tests of a conventional type were administered to all children participating in the investigation. This was done to obtain an initial basis for predicting reading and writing achievement during the first three school years. But since the results of the school-readiness tests alone could be expected to have only moderate prognostic value, specially constructed reading- and writing-readiness tests were also administered. These tests measured visual perception, auditory perception, phonetic analysis, sound synthesis, vocabulary, speech, memory-span, motor-manipulation ability, vision, and hearing. Interviews with parents, based on special rating scales and forms, provided information about the behavior and development of the children from birth to school-start. Most of this information was not quantifiable, but it was assumed to have some predictive value. It was of great help in planning methods of instruction that would take account of the different potential resources of individual pupils (Malmquist 1977).

From the results of these diagnostic instruments, we predicted that certain children would develop reading disabilities if no special auxiliary measures were taken. From the very beginning of school, children who fell into this category were given special help if they were part of the experimental group, but not if they belonged to the control group. The remedial teaching was given by a reading-clinic teacher, in cooperation with the regular classroom teachers. Altogether the reading clinic teacher took care of pupils from twelve elementary classes. Of her weekly service time, she devoted eight hours to experimental-group children in grade one, six hours to children in grade two, and five hours to children in grade three. The study was continued until the children had completed the third grade.

From the results of tests given at the end of the first, second, and third grades, we found that the experimental group attained significantly better results on reading tests than did the control group. The number of cases of reading disabilities, based on our operational definition of the term, was much lower in the experimental group than in the control group. The results of the experiment were very promising. Judging from the experiences of the pilot study, we concluded that this kind of approach might effectively contribute to the prevention of special reading and writing disabilities.

The Main Study

In order to confirm the results of the pilot study, we began a new study of the same character, with about the same design but on a larger scale, using seventy-two classes. Each class included in the study was divided into two groups, as equivalent as possible in age, number of pupils, sex, intelligence, socioeconomic status of parents, and so forth. The two groups in each class had the same teacher. In this way we controlled the teacher variable. Remedial instruction by a reading-clinic teacher was given to those pupils in the half of the class that was randomly designated the experimental group but not to pupils in the other half—the control group.

The differences between the experimental group and the control group were tested by analysis of covariance. The effect of possible initial differences between the two matched groups would be eliminated statistically. We also used a special method of covariance analysis not dependent on the assumption of common slope for group-regression lines, the "matched regression estimates" method described by Walker and Lev (1953). A series of multiple-regression and correlation analyses was made to investigate the prognostic value of several predictors of the level of reading and writing ability in grades one to three. These analyses demonstrated that the number of predictive instruments could be considerably reduced with only a negligible reduction in prognostic value.

Three variables were isolated, each of which could be expected to contribute significantly to a good prognosis: first, the battery of reading-readiness tests; second, one of the five visual-perception tests (visual letter perception); and third, the battery of school-readiness tests (see figures 20-1, 20-2, and 20-3). Of thirty criterion variables registered (ten variables at the end of each of the three grades), we calculated composite indexes for three major groups of variables: reading-accuracy, reading-comprehension, and spelling. Of the different predictors studied, the reading-readiness variable had the highest prognostic value throughout (between 58 percent and 86 percent of the combined predictive power of the three predictors), regardless of which criterion variable was examined (see table 20-1).

Source: Malmquist, E. 1971. *Lasmognadstest for Nyborjare*. Linköping: Malmquist.

Figure 20-1. An Example from Reading Readiness Test: Test 5, Phonetic Analysis

mc	nc	mc	nn	cm
py	pj	yp	py	fj
nl	ml	nt	nl	ln
xuc	xau	xuc	uxa	xuz
pga	bga	pag	pga	gpa
nmk	mnk	nkm	mmk	nmk
pbcx	bpcx	pbex	pdcs	pbcx
etrz	etrs	tenz	etrz	efrz
hmln	hmln	kmln	hmen	hnln

Source: Engwall, J. and Malmquist, E. 1975. *Visuell Perception 1-5*. Linköping: Kristianstads Länstryker.

Figure 20-2. Examples from the Visual Letter Perception Test

Accuracy of Predictions

For all types of criteria, the accuracy of prediction decreased with increasing grade-level. The decrease was rather small between grades two and three (see table 20-2). Reading accuracy was obviously the most stable of the three groups of criterion variables, with a correlation of 0.774 between the grade one and grade three measures. Reading-comprehension and spelling were measured with different tests at different grade-levels, which may partly explain their lower stability. The correlation between grades one and three measures was 0.645 for spelling and 0.502 for reading-comprehension. The rather low stability in reading-comprehension may also be due to the increasing complexity of the factors influencing comprehension.

The grade-to-grade decrease in correlation between reading-accuracy and reading-comprehension—0.848 in grade one, 0.797 in grade two, and 0.523 in grade three—seems also to suggest that these abilities become more and more differentiated. The correlation between reading-comprehension and spelling at different grade-levels shows the same tendency—0.661 in grade one, 0.576 in grade two, and 0.442 in grade three. It appears

Source: Malmquist, E. 1975. *Skolmognadsprov för Nybörjare*. Linköping: Östgöta Correspondenten.

Figure 20-3. An Example from the School Readiness Test: Absurdities

Table 20-1

Reading-Readiness, School-Readiness, and Visual Perception of Letters at the Beginning of Grade 1 as Predictors of Reading-Accuracy, Reading-Comprehension, and Spelling in Grades 1, 2, and 3

| | | | | R^2 Component | | |
Grade	Criterion	R	R^2	Reading-Readiness	School-Readiness	Visual Perception
1	Reading-accuracy	0.507	0.257	0.183	0.043	0.031
1	Reading-comprehension	0.622	0.387	0.226	0.076	0.085
1	Spelling	0.553	0.306	0.251	0.023	0.032
2	Reading-accuracy	0.421	0.177	0.148	0.007	0.027
2	Reading-comprehension	0.457	0.209	0.124	0.042	0.043
2	Spelling	0.529	0.280	0.223	0.013	0.044
3	Reading-accuracy	0.400	0.160	0.130	0.006	0.023
3	Reading-comprehension	0.433	0.186	0.121	0.062	0.003
3	Spelling	0.527	0.277	0.237	0.002	0.038

R = multiple correlation coefficient; R^2 = variance. The R^2 components are a measure of the extent to which each of the predictors contributes to the variance in R. Reading-readiness is composed of the combined results of five subtests: digit-span, sentence-span, auditory perception 1 and 2, and phonetic analysis of initial consonants. School-readiness is composed of seven subtests: criticism of absurdities, memory, arithmetic, drawing, similarities, picture-comparisons, and classification.

reasonable to assume, therefore, that from grades one to three reading-comprehension becomes differentiated from reading-accuracy and spelling, while the two latter abilities remain intimately correlated throughout the whole period.

The purpose of the remedial instruction was to prevent reading and writing disabilities among pupils in the experimental group. The reading-accuracy and spelling criteria seem to be most suited to indicate reading and writing disability at this stage. The fact that the analysis of these two variables gave significant group mean differences in favor of the experimental group in five cases out of six gives strong support to the hypothesis that the remedial instruction had the anticipated effect.

The data also lent support to the hypothesis that there is an increase in this effect from grade to grade, particularly with respect to reading-accuracy. The following group mean differences were noted: +0.191 in grade one, +0.236 in grade two, and +0.255 in grade three. The group mean differences in the three criteria of the investigation were studied by analysis of covariance; the reading-readiness scores and school-readiness scores were used as covariates.

Table 20-2

Correlation Matrix for Criterion Variables of Reading-Accuracy, Reading-Comprehension, and Spelling in Grades 1, 2, and 3

Criterion Variable and Grade	RA1	RA2	RA3	RC1	RC2	RC3	S1	S2	S3
RA1		0.829	0.774	0.848	0.734	0.471	0.659	0.682	0.637
RA2	0.829		0.922	0.720	0.797	0.492	0.592	0.701	0.712
RA3	0.774	0.922		0.654	0.768	0.523	0.554	0.667	0.716
RC1	0.848	0.720	0.654		0.745	0.502	0.661	0.626	0.555
RC2	0.734	0.797	0.768	0.745		0.551	0.541	0.576	0.618
RC3	0.471	0.492	0.523	0.502	0.551		0.462	0.449	0.442
S1	0.659	0.592	0.554	0.661	0.541	0.551		0.700	0.645
S2	0.682	0.701	0.667	0.626	0.576	0.449	0.700		0.785
S3	0.637	0.712	0.716	0.555	0.613	0.442	0.645	0.785	

Based on 230 controls. RA = reading accuracy; RC = reading comprehension; S = spelling.

The analyses of covariance yielded significant F-values for group mean differences in seven of the nine criteria, as against only five significant values without adjustment for regression of covariates. The grade three criteria may be regarded as the final criteria of reading and writing achievement in the present study. The analysis of covariance yielded clearly significant F-values for group mean differences, favoring the experimental group in reading-accuracy ($F = 9.84$) and spelling ($F = 7.52$). The F-value for reading-comprehension ($F = 3.00$) was not significant, but the difference was in favor of the experimental group (see table 20-3).

Since in some cases the analyses of correlation and regression gave lower coefficients of regression within groups for the experimental group than for the control group, the method called matched-regression estimates

Table 20-3

Analysis of Covariance

Grade	Criterion	Experimental Group	Control Group	F	p
1	Reading-accuracy	0.110	−0.106	7.42	.01
1	Reading-comprehension	0.093	−0.090	6.11	.05
1	Spelling	0.080	−0.077	4.35	.05
2	Reading-accuracy	0.130	−0.126	9.04	.01
2	Reading-comprehension	0.077	−0.075	3.32	NS
2	Spelling	0.118	−0.112	8.02	.01
3	Reading-accuracy	0.138	−0.135	9.84	.01
3	Reading-comprehension	0.072	−0.070	3.00	NS
3	Spelling	0.113	−0.112	7.52	.01

Based on 454 pupils. Comparisons of Z-score differences between the experimental group ($N = 224$) and the control group ($N = 230$). The predictors used were reading-readiness and school-readiness scores. p = probability level; F = covariance F ratio; NS = not significant. Z-scores = standard scores.

was also used to study reading-accuracy and spelling in grade three, with reading-readiness as a single covariate. Reading-accuracy did not yield any significance region in the predictor, that is, the superiority of the experimental group in this criterion is about the same at all reading-readiness levels. In the analysis of spelling in grade three, however, a region of significance (experimental group pupils were better than control group pupils at reading-readiness levels below $+0.4$ sigma) and a region of non-significance (no significant difference between groups at reading-readiness levels above $+0.4$ sigma) were found. (Sigma represents one standard deviation from the mean.)

Therefore, the superiority of the experimental group in spelling ability is due mainly to the superiority of the experimental-group pupils with a low or moderate level of reading-readiness at the beginning of the investigation. Since seventy-two of the seventy-eight pupils in the clinics belonged to this category, it seems reasonable to conclude that the results support the hypothesis that remedial instruction increases spelling ability significantly.

Results of Remedial Instruction

Starting with the operational definition of special reading disabilities employed in the study, it may be said that more than four-fifths of the potential cases of reading disability identified were prevented from occurring. In a subpopulation composed of pupils from the two groups that scored low on certain tests in the first term of grade one, a number of criterion variables were subjected to analysis of variance, using different multifactorial designs. The results of these analyses are also interpreted as supporting the main hypothesis that early remedial instruction has a positive effect on the development of reading and spelling ability. The frequency of pupils with both reading and spelling disabilities was consistently lower in the experimental groups than in the control groups. In the experimental groups less than 1 percent of the population, as against the expected frequency of approximately 5 percent, had such disabilities.

The results also showed that the reading clinics established in conjunction with the experiments contributed to a reduction in the variances among the pupils in the experimental group in comparison with the variances of samples used in reading- and spelling-test standardization procedures.

Reliability of Selection Based on Test Data

The study showed that the efficiency of the different groups of predictors declines considerably as the duration of the prediction period increases (Malmquist 1969, 1973). If these predictors are to be used to select pupils for remedial instruction, it would be best to restrict the first prediction, at the beginning of school, to a relatively brief period—in this case one term—and later to check and correct the selection at different points during the first three school years. Suitable times for predictions may be at the beginning of first grade, the end of the first semester, the end of first grade, and the end of second grade.

The prediction of reading-accuracy in the first grade was best made by combining the scores from the reading-readiness, school-readiness, and visual-perception tests. In grades two and three, reading-accuracy scores made in the preceding grade were the best predictors. Similarly, reading-comprehension scores in the first grade were best predicted by combining reading-readiness, school-readiness, and visual-perception scores. In grades two and three, the reading-comprehension scores from the previous grade were the most efficient predictors. And finally, the spelling scores at the end of grade one were best predicted by reading-readiness, school-readiness, and visual-perception scores combined. In grades two and three, the spelling scores from the previous years were the best predictors.

The Risk of Error in Selection

To throw more light on the predictive efficiency of the different periods, we analyzed the risk of error in selecting pupils for remedial instruction on the basis of the measurements employed in the study. Since remedial instruction in clinics has been shown to have the greatest effect on pupils' reading-accuracy, and since reading-accuracy must also be regarded as the most important area of the work in clinics during the early school years, reading-accuracy was used as the criterion in calculating the risk of error. The potential error of greatest interest is that a pupil would not be selected for remedial instruction although, according to accepted criteria, he needs such instruction.

At a given critical value in the criterion variable (expressed conveniently in z-scores), the extent of the risk of error at different percentages of a group assigned to reading clinics can be calculated. Values for size of the group selected (20 percent, 15 percent, and 10 percent) were chosen by what seemed reasonable in view of the amount of work in clinics in the first three years of school and by the necessity for a "surplus selection" at the beginning of school in order to include as many as possible of the potentially weak readers in the clinic instruction. Pupils were distributed among the grades so that 20 percent of the grade-one pupils would be assigned to the clinic, 10 to 15 percent of the grade-two pupils, and 5 to 10 percent of the grade-three pupils. The surplus selection in the lower grades does not imply that all those selected will attend the reading clinic for a long period. Minimization of the risk of error implies an increase in the risk that pupils will be assigned to reading clinics who do not really need such instruction. Selection errors of this kind can easily be corrected by simply removing the pupils from the clinic.

The risks of error are consistently greater for the first period (school start) than for the other periods. With an assignment to clinics of 20 percent of the pupils at start of school, the risk of error is never greater than 18 percent. For very poor readers the maximum risk of error is never greater than 10 percent in this selection. It should be observed that the choice of criterion in this analysis—measure of reading-accuracy—implies that the selection will include pupils with potential reading disability independent of level of general intelligence. No special analysis of risks of error in the selection of pupils with specific reading disability (as we defined this term) was considered necessary. There were two main reasons for this: (1) the pupils with specific reading disability were included in the group of poor readers, and (2) the analysis of the effects of reading-clinic instruction showed that there were no strong reasons why instruction in reading clinics should be given only—or even preferably—to pupils with specific reading disability.

In summary, it may be said that the risk that a pupil needing instruction in a reading clinic will not be assigned to such a clinic can be kept at a low level if selection of pupils is checked and corrected at regular intervals during the first three years of school with the help of instruments of the kind used here, and if available places in clinics include a surplus selection at the beginning of first grade.

Diagnosis During Grades One to Three

To be sure that cases of special reading and writing disabilities are discovered early and are given expert remedial treatment, many school districts administer standardized group tests in reading and spelling to all pupils at the end of the first grade. On the basis of the test results and the classroom teacher's recommendations, children are selected for individual examination by a school psychologist. If the classroom teacher suspects that a child is having reading or writing difficulties—even though he performed well on the group test—this child, too, may be selected for individual examination by experts of various kinds. On the basis of these tests, recommendations are made as to the need for remedial instruction and treatment.

The advantages of such a system are obvious. By having all children, without exception, tested at the end of the first school year and then again in grades two and three, the chances are rather small that children with reading and writing disabilities will miss the opportunity to receive the remedial instruction and treatment they need.

Influence of Inappropriate Techniques on Learning and Personality

As has been emphasized, it is important to provide remedial treatment as early as possible for children who have difficulty in learning to read and write. This rule applies to all forms of learning. Findings in pedagogical psychology indicate, among other things, that good habits are crucial in the acquisition of any new skill. Such statements as "practice makes perfect" cannot be unqualifiedly accepted. Repetition is good only if what is being repeated is appropriate and desirable; otherwise, it can be very harmful. Inappropriate attitudes, as well as inappropriate techniques, can be extremely difficult to unlearn. Therefore, the first stages of learning are crucial for the whole learning process; they constitute the basis for all subsequent work.

Sometimes it is easy to acquire a new skill by means of trial and error. At times this may be done in a single step. However, it may require weeks, months, and on occasion even a lifetime to correct inappropriate habits, attitudes, and subconscious prejudices. Therefore, the planning of first-year reading instruction must be done with care and with due consideration to the specific needs of each pupil. Failure to acquire the basic skills of reading and writing can have severe repercussions on later achievement, not only in reading and writing but also in other school subjects. And what may be even worse, failure in learning to read is likely to have a negative influence on the child's personality and attitudes. The condition becomes more serious the older the child becomes and the longer he is permitted to go without any special assistance or remedial support. Negative attitudes toward reading and writing and failure in other subjects because of lack of reading and writing skills lead to feelings of defeat and a rejection of school and schoolwork.

Consequently, if remedial instruction is introduced only on the intermediate or upper level, it will take far more time and will run into many more difficulties than if it had been initiated earlier. This does not mean, however, that we should ignore the reading and writing disabilities of older students. On the contrary, we should offer them assistance as soon as their difficulties are discovered. Today it is generally recognized that practically all children with special reading and writing disabilities can acquire acceptable skills in these subjects provided they receive professional assistance. It is comforting for parents whose children might once have been "incurable and hopeless cases" to see the good results achieved in remedial-reading classes, in reading clinics, and in corrective instruction by the regular classroom teacher.

References

Malmquist, E. 1958. *Factors Related to Reading Disabilities in the First Grade of Elementary School.* Stockholm: Almqvist and Wiksell.

———. 1969. *Reading Disabilities in the Lower Grades of the Comprehensive School: Experimental Studies.* Falköping: Svenska Utbildningsförlaget Liber AB. (In Swedish with an English summary.)

———. 1973. *Les Difficultés d'Apprendre à Lire.* Translated and adapted by A. Inizan. Paris: Librairie Armand Colin.

———. 1977. *Läs-och Skrivsvårigheter hos Barn.* Lund: Liber Läromedel.

Malmquist, E., and Valtin, R. 1974. *Förderung Legasthenisher Kinder in der Schule.* Weinheim and Basel: Beltz Verlag.

National Swedish Board of Education. 1969. Curriculum for the Comprehensive School.

Walker, H.M., and Lev, J. 1953. *Statistical Inference.* New York: Henry Holt.

21

U.S. and California Legislation for Handicapped Children

Leonard Levine

Historical Development

The education of handicapped children has progressed considerably over many years. The growth of research, development, and legislation has accelerated during the past twenty years so that programs that began in a few isolated school districts now have reached almost all districts throughout the nation.

This same growth and development can also be followed in California. In 1963 legislation was signed into law that marked the beginning of significant growth in programs for handicapped children. This legislation addressed itself to one disability, educationally handicapped children, defined as "minors other than physically handicapped . . . or mentally retarded minors who, by reason of marked learning or behavioral problems or a combination thereof cannot receive the reasonable benefit of ordinary education and facility." (Levine 1969). Federal law was later to define it in more detail and call it "specific learning disability," which meant a disorder in one or more of the basic psychological processes involved in understanding or using language, spoken or written, and manifesting itself in an imperfect ability to listen, think, speak, read, write, spell, or do mathematical calculations.

What began as a program for children with learning disabilities developed into California's pilot master plan for special education in 1974. This plan authorized ten responsible local education agencies to set up pilot programs for handicapped children, which ultimately served more than 140 school districts throughout California. By 1979 there were 250 districts under the master plan, and more than 113,000 special-education students were receiving assistance through its services. In July 1980 the master-plan concept was extended to all school districts under Senate Bill 1870. By 1982 more than 400,000 handicapped youngsters in California (about 10 percent of the total student population) will be receiving the benefits of special education through the Master Plan for Special Education. This plan was designed to incorporate the elements of the federal legislation—Public Law 94-142, the Education for All Handicapped Children Act of 1975.

California has been in the forefront of the nation in providing special education over the years. When new legislation from the Federal government was enacted in 1975, it was looked upon as a boost to the existing programs that are currently dealing with students who are designated as educationally handicapped, retarded, dysphasic, deaf, blind, orthopedically, visually, or hearing-impaired, and speech-handicapped.

Court Decisions and Due Process

Federal legislation came about through court decisions that held that the educational needs of many handicapped children were not being met. The most frequently involved legal issues appeared to be based on the Fifth and Fourteenth Amendments to the Constitution of the United States. The Fifth Amendment is a constraint on the federal government, which provides that "No person shall be deprived of life, liberty, or property, without due process of law." The Fourteenth Amendment refers to the same due-process rights in the form of the equal-protection clause, but it is applicable to the individual states.

Due process as a term in education, and particularly in special education, has been clearly articulated only in the last several years. The momentum of court cases involving due-process issues in special education appears to have increased in the 1970s. A case in point is *Pennsylvania Association for Retarded Children* v. *Commonwealth of Pennsylvania*, heard in 1971, which some experts hold to be the foundation for the Education for All Handicapped Children Act of 1975 (Public Law 94-142). This landmark decision was the result of a case in which thirteen mentally retarded children brought a class-action suit against the Commonwealth of Pennsylvania for that state's failure to provide access to free public education for all retarded children. The court ordered that Pennsylvania could not apply any law that would postpone, terminate, or deny mentally retarded children access to a publicly supported education, including a public-school program, tuition, and homebound instruction. Other noteworthy federal special-education legislation that reinforces the due-process concept can be found in Public Laws 93-112 and 93-380.

Rehabilitation Act of 1973 (Public Law 93-112, Section 504)

It took four years for the regulations that affected the handicapped to be approved after Public Law 93-112 was enacted in 1973. It was reported that the delay was caused by lack of the money that would be required to implement the law as it related to access to public buildings, transportation, and places of employment. Section 504 of the act provides that "no otherwise qualified handicapped individual . . . shall, solely by reason of his handicap, be excluded from the participation in, be denied the benefits of, or be subjected to discrimination under any program or activity receiving federal financial assistance.'' It establishes a mandate to end discrimination and to bring handicapped persons into the mainstream of American life, which means not only employment and physical accessibility to transportation, buildings, and so forth, but also education. When Public Law 94-142 was written two years later, it was noted that many of the concepts in Section 504 were included in that legislation.

Education of the Handicapped Amendments of 1974
(Public Law 93-380)

Public Law 93-380 required all states to develop a plan for educating handicapped children that included due-process commitments, if the states were to continue receiving or be eligible for federal special-education funds. It mandates that the states provide procedures for insuring that handicapped children and their parents are guaranteed procedural safeguards in decisions regarding identification, evaluation, and educational placement of handicapped children, including prior notice to parents when the educational agency wants to change the child's placement (see figure 21-1). It further provides an opportunity for the parents to obtain an impartial due-process hearing and to examine all relevant records. It allows the parent to obtain an independent educational evaluation of the child, the cost of which is borne by the educational agency (Saunders and Sultana 1979).

California law is similar on this point. The Education Code reiterates this right of the parents to obtain their own assessment of the child if they disagree with the educational agency's assessment. However, this has caused concern among local school districts because of the unknown and often great expense for such independent assessments. They feel that their own professional staffs are capable of giving an objective evaluation of the children. Thus, the local education agency is placed in the awkward position of requesting a due-process hearing to establish its evaluation process as objective and unbiased. However, it should be noted that Public Law 94-142 reinforced this parental right to an independent assessment a year later.

Education for all Handicapped Children Act of 1975
(Public Law 94-142)

Public Law 94-142 further confirmed due-process procedures. It detailed them through the elements of informed consent, notice, evaluation, placement, record-examination, hearing, and the appeal process.

DUE PROCESS

APPEAL REQUEST

- IDENTIFICATION
- ASSESSMENT
- IEP
- PLACEMENT

INITIATED BY:

- PARENT
- PUBLIC EDUCATION AGENCY

APPEAL REQUEST:
- FILED WITH STATE SUPERINTENDENT

- FREE OR LOW COST LEGAL SERVICES
  (3 DAYS)

VLBN: August, 1980

Reproduced with permission of San Mateo County Office of Education.

Figure 21-1. The Elements of Due Process

Consent by Parents

When the parent gives "informed consent," this means that the parents must have been fully informed in his or her native language of all information relevant to the activity for which consent is being sought. Consent further means that the parent agrees in writing to the stipulated activity, including lists of the records to be released and to whom. Moreover, consent may be revoked at any time by parents. In an average-sized school district in California, such as the South San Francisco Unified School District, a great number of different languages are spoken by parents. In chapter 4, it was noted that fifteen different languages were spoken at home by the parents of the children in one elementary school, including Arabic, Chinese, German, Hindi, Hungarian, Ilocano, Italian, Japanese, Pampango, Portuguese, Samoan, Slovenian, Spanish, Tagalog, and Thai. The language spread clearly creates great difficulty for many school districts.

If the school district feels that the child needs special education or related services and the parent refuses, the district could provide the education or services or not provide them in accordance with its own state law. If the state law requires parental consent, then these procedures govern. If there is no state law requiring consent, the public agency can proceed to a hearing to obtain a determination of whether the child may be evaluated or given special education or related services without the parents' consent.

The California Education Code further states: "If the final decision resulting from the due process hearing is that the assessment is appropriate, the parent still has the right for an independent educational assessment, but not at public expense" (see figure 21-2).

The usual practice is for the parent to initiate the hearing. Fortunately, most of the disputes that could lead to hearings are settled to the parents' satisfaction through an informal conference with the local superintendent. However, many are not, and these must proceed to a formal hearing. The reasons for these hearings seem to focus on disputes regarding eligibility, placement, related services, transportation, private-school placement, or private-school costs. The expense of these hearings in terms of school personnel time and other costs has been tremendous, but a new, advanced concept of children's and parents' rights is emerging.

Notice to Parents

"Notice" refers to written notice given to the parent within a reasonable time, and it covers identification, evaluation, or placement of the child or refusal thereof by the educational agency. It must be written in an understandable manner, in the native language of the parent unless it is not feasible to do so.

REFERRAL PROCESS FOR
SPECIAL EDUCATION

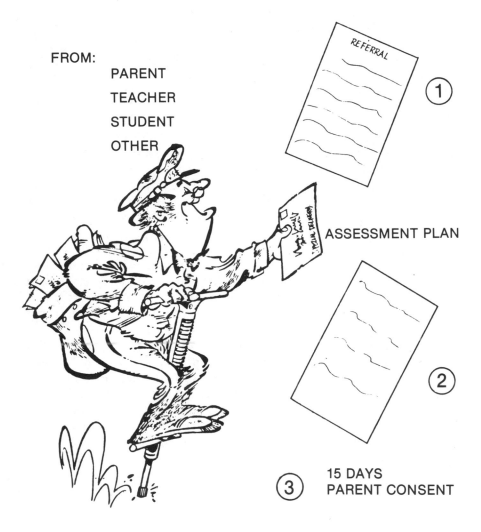

FROM:

PARENT
TEACHER
STUDENT
OTHER

ASSESSMENT PLAN

15 DAYS
PARENT CONSENT

VLBN: August, 1980

Reproduced with permission of San Mateo County Office of Education.

Figure 21-2. The Referral Process for Special Education

The notice is required to include a full explanation of all the safeguards available to the parents. A description must be given of the action or refusal thereof by the education agency, plus an explanation of the agency's reasons for the proposal or refusal, as well as the options that were considered and why they were rejected. Each evaluation, procedure, test, record, or report used or refused by the agency must be included in the notice.

Pupil Evaluation

"Evaluation" refers to the assessment of the child to determine his needs. This evaluation must be conducted in accordance with several requirements. State and local education agencies are required to insure that tests and other evaluation materials are given in the child's native language and are validated for the specific purpose for which they are used. They are to be administered by trained personnel and to be tailored to specific areas of educational need and not merely to provide a single intelligence quotient. No single procedure may be used as a sole criterion for determining the appropriate program for the child. A multidisciplinary team develops the evaluation, and a specialist in the area of the suspected disability must be included on the team. The child is to be assessed in all areas related to the suspected disability.

With limited or non-English-speaking children, the assessment plan must include materials that are in the primary language of the child and are nondiscriminatory. The evaluation requirements for foreign-language-speaking children are, strictly speaking, impossible to meet, since there are no assessment-test batteries available in many languages; those that exist may not have been properly validated; and psychologists who can function adequately in the many different languages are not easily found. Moreover, after a child has been in the United States for a few years, he tends not to progress in his native language as his English develops. Often the children enter a stage when they are underdeveloped (or even illiterate) in both languages. This condition precludes competent assessment, at least, of the child's verbal abilities, and promotes reliance on nonverbal testing. Under the circumstances, it may be most difficult to acquire an adequate assessment of the pupil for special education.

Pupil Placement

When making placement decisions concerning a child, the local school district is required to use a variety of sources of information, such as tests, teacher input, physical condition, cultural background, and adaptive behavior. It must further determine that the information is documented and that the actual placement is the result of a group decision, taking into account the concept of "least-restrictive environment." One of the most important aspects of the placement of a child in a special-education program is that, "to the maximum extent appropriate, the handicapped child is to be educated with children who are not handicapped." This is the definition of the least-restrictive environment.

Furthermore, each school district is required to insure that the child's placement is reconsidered annually, is based on the individual educational program, and is as close to the child's home as possible (see figure 21-3).

Examination of Pupil Records

Another element in the federal law concerns examination of records. Public Law 94-142 requires school districts to permit parents or their representative to inspect and review any educational records relating to their children. It goes a step further in that the local district must provide the parent with copies of the records. A fee requirement may be made for this service except where the cost may prevent the parent from getting the information.

If the parent believes that the records are misleading or inaccurate, a request can be made to amend the record. If the district refuses the request, the parent has the right to a hearing on the matter.

Hearing

The due-process hearing is referred to in the federal law as "impartial," whereas the California law refers to "procedural safeguards." The essential elements of the former are found in the latter, but the California due-process procedures are more detailed. It should be noted that the parent is not the only party who can take advantage of the hearing process. The local school district is also allowed to initiate a hearing if the parent refuses to allow assessment or placement of the child. This is rarely undertaken, however, because, among other considerations, school districts believe that without the parents' cooperation academic progress will be minimal.

Under the California Education Code, all requests for a due-process hearing are to be filed in writing with the state superintendent of public instruction. Within three days the public-education agency has to advise the parent of free or low-cost services. If the initiating party so chooses, an informal, nonadversarial meeting will be arranged among the participants and con-

PLACEMENT   (6)

• 20 SCHOOL DAYS

(7) ANNUAL REVIEW

• IEP REVIEW
• PARENT PARTICIPATION

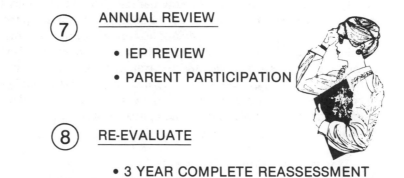

(8) RE-EVALUATE

• 3 YEAR COMPLETE REASSESSMENT

VLBN: August, 1980

Reproduced with permission of San Mateo County Office of Education.

Figure 21-3. The Time Lines for Placement, Annual Review, and Reevaluation of a Child

ducted by a state mediator on any of the issues of identification, assessment, placement, education, or the no-cost provision thereof. If the initiating party is satisfied with the outcome, the need to continue with the hearing is terminated.

Public Law 94-142 describes much of the foregoing in similar language. If the issue involves an application for initial admission to public school, the child is to be placed in school pending the completion of the proceedings. Parental consent is required, however. It should be noted that the child's status during the proceedings is to remain in his or her educational placement unless the parent and agency agree otherwise.

If at this point the issue is not resolved, the superintendent of the school district is required to ensure that a mediation hearing is begun and completed within forty-five days from the date of the original request for the hearing.

Appeal

If the mediation conference fails, a state-level hearing is arranged. This hearing is conducted by a person knowledgeable in administrative hearings at a time and place convenient to the parents. The parents may be accompanied by counsel and others with knowledge of handicapped children. Although these proceedings are not a formal legal trial, many of the elements have a judicial emphasis, such as the compelling of witnesses to testify and be cross-examined and the transcribing of the hearing.

Under Public Law 94-142, a hearing decision by a public-education agency or a mediation conference may be appealed to the state education agency, which is required to have an impartial review of the proceedings, including

1. Examination of the entire record.
2. Insuring that the procedures permitted due process to the parties.
3. Seeking additional evidence, if necessary.
4. Permitting, at the reviewing official's discretion, an opportunity for the parties to present oral and written arguments.
5. Making a decision no later than 30 days after request for the review.
6. Giving a copy of the findings and decision to the parties.

California's appeal process, which follows the federal guidelines, commences when the mediation conference fails to resolve the issues to the satisfaction of both parties. It is these unresolved issues that form the basis of the appeal and review at the state level. Finally, either party has the right to bring a civil action in a court of competent jurisdiction (see figure 21-4).

HEARING RIGHTS

- 5 DAY DISCLOSURE
- EXAMINE WITNESSES
- PROCEDURAL SAFE-GUARDS

HEARING HELD

- 45 DAYS TOTAL TIMELINE
- 30 DAYS FROM MEDIATION CONFERENCE
- DECISION RENDERED

COURT OF COMPETENT JURISDICTION

Figure 21-4. The Hearing Rights of Parents and School Districts

Individualized Educational Programs

One of the unique features of special education under both federal and California laws is the individual education program (IEP). The IEP is a statement written by a team in a meeting. It includes a number of elements:

1. Present levels of the pupil's educational performance.
2. Annual goals and short-term instructional objectives.
3. Specific educational instruction and services required by the pupil.
4. Extent to which the pupil will be able to participate in regular educational programs.
5. Projected date for initiation and anticipated duration of such programs and services.
6. Appropriate objective criteria, evaluation procedures, and schedules for determining, on at least an annual basis, whether the short-term instructional objectives are being achieved.
7. For individuals whose primary language is other than English, linguistically appropriate goals, objectives, programs, and services.
8. Extended school-year services (summer school) when needed and as determined by IEP.
9. Provision for transition into the regular class program if the pupil is to be transferred from special education.

At all grade-levels an IEP has to be developed within fifty days, excluding July and August, from the date of receipt of the parents' written consent for assessment. The parents can give an extension in writing, however. After the beginning of the next school year, the local district has thirty days to develop the IEP for the student who was referred for assessment twenty days or less prior to the end of the regular school year.

If the pupil is at the secondary level, it is necessary to specially design vocational and career-development programs, with emphasis on vocational training. It is also necessary to include for secondary-school students any alternative means and modes necessary for the pupil to complete the local district's prescribed course of study and to meet or exceed proficiency standards for graduation.

Meetings

The Federal Rules and Regulations related to meetings state, as does the California Education Code, that each school district is required to initiate and conduct meetings to develop, review, or revise the individualized education program. These meetings are conducted by an IEP team.

The California Education Code further requires that the IEP team meet whenever any of the following occur:

1. A pupil has received a formal assessment.
2. The pupil's placement, instruction, and services, as specified in the IEP, are initiated, changed, or terminated.
3. The pupil demonstrates a lack of anticipated progress.
4. The parents request a meeting to develop, review, or revise the IEP.
5. Annually, to review pupil's progress, IEP, and appropriateness of placement, and to make necessary revisions. Federal regulations on review also require an annual meeting.

Participants in Meetings

Public Law 94-142 has a brief description of who is an IEP team member:

1. The public agency's representative, other than the child's teacher, who is qualified to provide or supervise the special-education service.
2. The child's teacher.
3. One or both parents.
4. The child, when appropriate.
5. Others at the discretion of the parents or school district.
6. When the child is evaluated for the first time, a member of the evaluation team, the child's teacher, or some other person knowledgeable about the evaluation procedures used with the child and familiar with the results of the evaluation.

The California Education Code states that the IEP team shall include all but not be limited to the following:

1. A representative, other than the child's teacher, designated by the local school district, who may be an administrator, program specialist, or other specialist who is knowledgeable about the pupil's program options and who is qualified to provide or supervise the special education.
2. The pupil's present teacher; if the pupil has no teacher, the regular class teacher who made the referral or a qualified special-education teacher.
3. One or both parents or their representative.
4. When appropriate, the pupil.
5. Others at the parents' or district's discretion.
6. When the team is developing, reviewing, or revising the IEP, a person who has conducted an assessment of the pupil or who is knowledgeable about and familiar with the results of the assessment.

7.   For pupils with suspected learning disabilities or behavior disorders, at least one member of the IEP team, other than the regular teacher, who has observed the child in an appropriate class.

In the case of secondary-school students, many of whom will have several regular teachers, the school counselor has been used by districts in an effort to comply with the teacher requirement.

The development of the IEP, with its time limit and participant requirements, is probably the one element in the education of handicapped students that is proving the most difficult problem to solve. The fifty-day time limit seems on its face to be an ample period in which to assess, conduct meetings, and place the child in an appropriate educational setting (see figure 21-5). In practice, the fifty-day requirement is generally not enough time. When the parent signs and returns the consent form to assess the child, which starts the fifty-day period, the person responsible for following the case may not be able to organize the assessment team immediately because of a case load that is already on-going. This team member may be a psychologist or other staff person who is dealing with several referrals simultaneously, all of which have their own fifty-day time limits. In some instances information is requested from a child's physician, therapist, or other professional. These data may take several days or even weeks to arrive. Another delaying factor is the scheduling of the IEP meeting. It is difficult to get all the participants together at a specific time. Because of team members' previous commitments, the meeting dates are usually scheduled several weeks in advance. All of this frequently results in the IEP being developed after the fifty-day time limit.

Least-Restrictive Environment

A goal in California's Master Plan for Special Education states that public education must offer special assistance to exceptional individuals in a setting that promotes maximum interaction with the general school population and that is appropriate to the needs of both.

Weintraub and Abeson (1974) have expressed this goal as follows. Educational placement may be considered to be a continuum. Those placements that are normal go to regular classrooms and are at one end. Those that are most abnormal, as an institution, are at the other end. Since the courts require schools to use the "least restrictive placements, this mandates that the settings in which educational programs are provided to handicapped children be as close to normal as possible."

It is believed that children's similarities are more important than their differences and thus that it is necessary to educate the handicapped youngster in a setting that is closest to normal. Abeson (1974) calls this "educational normalization."

TEAM MEETING

- DETERMINE ELIGIBILITY
- DEVELOP INDIVIDUAL EDUCATION PROGRAM   ④

50 DAYS

PARENT CONSENT

⑤

- PLACEMENT
- IEP

VLBN: August, 1980

Reproduced with permission of San Mateo County Office of Education.

Figure 21-5.   Team Meeting to Determine Eligibility and to Develop the Individual Program with Parental Consent

Public Law 94-142 recognized this concept and has mandated that, to the maximum extent appropriate, handicapped children will be educated with children who are not handicapped. It further states that handicapped children are to be removed from regular classes and placed in special classes or schools only when their handicap is so severe that regular education, even with supplementary aids and services, cannot be satisfactorily achieved. The overriding rule is that placement decisions are to be made on an individual basis. This requires the local school district to have various alternatives available when considering placement of the child. One of the facts to be considered when choosing alternatives is the need to place the child as near to home as possible. This becomes a problem when the only educational program meeting the child's needs is outside the local school district's boundaries.

The Federal Rules and Regulations require local school districts to provide a continuum of placements. These cover instruction in regular classes; in special classes; in special schools; and in home, hospital, and institutional instruction. The requirement extends to making provision for supplementary services and itinerant instruction in conjunction with regular class placement.

Mainstreaming

The term *mainstreaming* has often been used to describe the least-restrictive environment. However, nowhere in either federal or California legislation can the word *mainstreaming* be found. It is generally accepted that this term refers to the placement of handicapped children into regular education classes, whereas the least-restrictive environment is broader and relates to handicapped children being placed either into regular classes or into other settings, such as special classes, schools, or centers, and nonpublic or residential schools.

Related Services

Many kinds of auxiliary or related services are necessary to the proper functioning of the child in special education. These services refer mostly to support of the handicapped child who is already in an appropriate educational setting. However, a related service that in and of itself is considered special education is speech therapy. Here, the child is in the regular class except for a brief time daily or weekly when he is being instructed by the speech specialist.

Related services include transportation, developmental, corrective, and other support services. More specifically they include psychological services, physical and occupational therapy, speech therapy, recreation, counseling, medical services for diagnostic or evaluation purposes, school health services, social-work services, and parent counseling and training.

Some of these related services have proved difficult to provide because of lack of funds or qualified personnel. The inability of a local district to pay does not appear to be an acceptable excuse for not providing the service. There has been a tendency among school districts not to include any related service in the IEP unless it could pay for and provide it. Authorities in the U.S. Department of Education have indicated that lack of money does not constitute a waiver of service. If the child needs the service, it must be written into the IEP and implemented with due haste.

Nonpublic Schools

Despite the traditional ban on spending public funds for private purposes, recent legal interpretation permits local school districts to contract with approved private educational institutions for the purpose of educating handicapped children. This is based on the theory that, since handicapped children must be provided with a free appropriate public education, a private school can be selected as that setting if the local district has no appropriate program.

Federal regulations require that each annual program plan include policies and procedures that insure that the regulations on private schools are met, and that an IEP must be developed before a handicapped child can be placed in a private school. Regulations also require providing for special education and related services at no cost to the parent for those handicapped children placed by a public agency as well as for those handicapped pupils in a private school but not placed by a public agency. California's Education Code supports the federal mandate for nonpublic schools. However, it requires that every effort be made to provide a public-school setting before seeking an appropriate private school. It also spells out the details for tuition, education, and services. There is also a provision that allows for partial attendance at the private school. The assumption is that the student may be served in both the public and nonpublic sectors at the same time.

Special-Education Funding

When Public Law 94-142 was passed in 1975, many states thought that the increasing costs of programs for the handicapped would be alleviated by federal appropriations. A formula was established, based on an increasing percentage of the average national expenditure per public-school student, times the number of handicapped children in the nation's schools, plus an inflation factor. This was to increase each year until 1982, when it would level off and remain at 40 percent, as follows:

1977-1978	(5 percent)
1978-1979	(10 percent)
1979-1980	(20 percent)
1980-1981	(30 percent)
1981-1982	(40 percent)

Congress figured the national per-pupil expenditure in 1975 as $1,250 and based on that amount computed the estimates as follows:

1977-1978	$378 million (5 percent)
1978-1979	$775 million (10 percent)
1979-1980	$1.2 billion (20 percent)
1980-1981	$2.32 billion (30 percent)
1981-1982	$3.16 billion (40 percent)

When the states were requested to search for and count their handicapped students, they originally came up with approximately seven million children. Congress had been told there were about twelve million handicapped children in need of special education in the fifty states and was dismayed at the difference.

It should be noted that, unlike many legislative bodies that appropriate money within the law itself, the U.S. Congress passes the law first and then in a separate piece of legislation acts on the appropriation bill that funds the original law. When the word reached Congress that the number of handicapped children was significantly lower than expected, it appropriated less money than had originally been intended.

Meanwhile, the laws and their mandates have been promulgated, and the states are finding that the amounts they expected to receive for each child are considerably less than was originally estimated. This has caused serious problems. Local school districts are finding that they have to dip into general-fund budgets and reserves in order to comply with the mandate of the laws that require all handicapped children to be given free, appropriate education.

In California, the new master-plan law, Senate Bill 1870, has attempted to deal with this dilemma by increasing the state's contribution to local special-education programs to 109 percent over the 1979-1980 school-year expenditures for handicapped students. Those districts that are considered to be operating in the state's plan have the option to take either the 109 percent (available for one year only) or the income derived from a complicated formula, whichever is the highest. However, if the formula method is selected, the state is allowed to deduct the amount of federal money local districts receive under Public Law 94-142. Furthermore, California has set a cap of 10 percent of the local school district's total enrollment as the basis for state reimbursement. Any amount over that cap is to be paid out of the district's general funds.

Although the U.S. Congress appropriated funds for the education of handicapped children based on the national average expenditure of $1,250 per pupil in 1975 plus an inflation factor, many states, including California, spend much more than this amount per student. Moreover, a number of students have been placed in local, private special-education facilities at a cost of about $6,000 per year for tuition; and in some cases of multiply handicapped children, individual placements have cost over $40,000 per year. These costs, plus the expenses involved in the assessment of these children and, in many cases, the hearings required to settle the questions concerning appropriate placement, have added materially to the financial burdens of school districts.

The result of the mandates of the laws, and the increasing cost of programs required to comply with the mandates, has caused a backlash from those in regular education who see continued encroachments on their programs to educate the overwhelming number of pupils. This, in turn, has created a morale problem among special educators, who feel attacked on all sides—from the parents for not providing programs, from the federal and state authorities for failing to comply with the mandates, and from their own associates, who accuse them of draining already dwindling financial resources.

It would appear that only a substantial increase in federal money will be able to solve this serious problem. Any attempt to change the laws themselves will undoubtedly be met with stiffening resistance on the part of the parents through the various advocacy groups, which will lean heavily upon the Constitution of the United States to support their cause.

References

Abeson, A. 1974. Movement and momentum: government and the education of handicapped children. *Exceptional Children.* (October).

California State Department of Education. 1974, 1977, 1980. Master Plan for Special Education. Sacramento.

California State Legislature. 1963. Assembly Bill 464.

Levine, L. 1969. Administration of a program. In L. Tarnopol (ed.), *Learning Disabilities: Introduction to Educational and Medical Management.* Springfield, Ill.: Thomas.

Pennsylvania Association for Retarded Children v. Commonwealth of Pennsylvania. 1971. 334 F Supplement 1257.

Saunders, M., and Sultana, Q. 1979. Due process rights of the handicapped: familiarity of professionals. *Education Unlimited* 1:5.

U.S. Congress. 1973. Rehabilitation Act of 1973. Public Law 93-112, Section 504. 1977.

_____ . 1974. Education of the Handicapped Amendments of 1974, Public Law 93-380.

_____ . 1975. The Education for All Handicapped Children Act of 1975, Public Law 94-142.

_____ . 1975. Title 45, Code of Federal Regulations.

Weintraub, F.J. 1980. Personal communication.

Weintraub, F.J., and Abeson, A. 1974. New education policies for the handicapped: the quiet revolution. *Phi Delta Kappan* 55:8.

22 Reading and Learning Disabilities in Venezuela

Nusia Feldman and
Moisés Feldman

In Venezuela the study of children with learning disabilities has had an evolution similar to that of other countries. Beginning in 1935, tests were used in schools to differentiate children according to their intelligence. As retarded children were distinguished from normal ones, an interest developed in students of normal or superior intelligence who had low scholastic achievement.

In the middle 1960s the study of children with learning disabilities began in Venezuela. We most frequently use the terms *learning disabilities* and *specific learning disabilities,* following the criteria issued in 1970 by the U.S. Office of Education, with only a few minor modifications. The term *specific learning disabilites* is used mostly by psychologists, special teachers, and other members of the behavioral professions. However, physicians tend to use the terms *dyslexia* and *minimal cerebral dysfunction.* The etiology is considered to be varied, the most accepted causes being related to neurological and genetic dysfunctions, with secondary emotional problems.

We still lack a statistical survey for the incidence of specific learning disabilities at the national level. However, the Foundation for the Development of Special Education estimated that 10 percent of the population at the elementary-education level have learning disabilities (Ministerió de Education 1978).

Many culturally deprived children attend our public schools, and it is often difficult to establish a differential diagnosis of these children for specific learning disabilities (Feldman and Feldman 1974). In many cases it is through the progress made by the child during his or her psychoeducational training program that we are able to make the diagnosis. The pure cases of specific learning disabilities are usually found in children who come from an intermediate or upper socioeconomic level.

Education

Venezuela has an estimated population of about 13.9 million. Fifty-two percent of the population is under age nineteen. Accelerated movement of people to the cities has created a 75 percent urban and 25 percent rural population distribution. This situation produces serious social maladjustments.

In accordance with the report of the Ministry of Education for 1979, the student population at various educational levels corresponding to the school year 1978-1979 was 4,173,380 students and 165,988 teachers. The preschool and elementary-school enrollments were 2,707,528 children, and the day high schools had registration levels of 787,032 students. Only 11.1 percent of elementary education is private. It   noteworthy that a large percentage of the Venezuelan population has the ⁄pportunity of receiving free education from preschool through college.

In comparison with preceding years, there has been a remarkable increase in attendance of preschoolers. In 1969-1970, 44,463 students attended preschool and in 1978-1979, 328,827. Nevertheless, many children in marginal areas still do not go to kindergarten.

Regarding repetition of the same grade in elementary school, 8.6 percent repeat overall. In the first grade, with the highest percentage, 12.7 percent are repeaters, while in the sixth grade only 2.5 percent are retained.

Our elementary schools are made up of six grades. The normal ages for school range from seven through thirteen years. During the 1978-1979 school term, 20.3 percent of the students had ages beyond normal. This reduces the physical capacity of the schools to take care of pupils of proper age, so many are absent from the schools. These children usually come from homes with cultural deprivation, and some have specific learning disabilities. The percentages of students in Venezuela who leave school prior to the end of the school year are 8.8 percent for elementary school and 15.9 percent for high school. There is very little assistance for adolescents with learning disabilities, which together with their social and economic needs may account for some of the reasons for leaving school. The other problem that we must face is where these youths shall go, since technical education is still not sufficiently developed in our country. Also, there is the danger that these young individuals lacking suitable assistance may end up unemployed, delinquent, and possibly addicted to drugs.

Of those children entering the first grade in 1973, 64 percent were able to complete the sixth grade. Of those who started their first year of high school during 1974, 38 percent finished all five years of high school. Only 21 percent of students enter college, and of these only 3 percent are able to graduate.

Special Programs

The Children's Foundation (Fundación del Niño), directed by the wife of the president of the republic, being sensitive to the problems of the working mother from marginal areas with respect to the care of her children, is sponsoring a Program of Daily Care Homes as well as Centers of Preschool Education. The Program of Daily Care Homes is intended for children of working mothers ranging from birth to age five. These homes try to cover the nutritional, sanitary, affective, and educational needs of the children by means of a well-structured plan. A team that has been previously trained is responsible for providing training to the mothers, who act as "caregivers." This program brings physical and emotional protection to the children and it permits the detection of any insufficiencies in motor, intellectual, emotional, and social development of children.

Project ME-VAL, which cares for preschoolers from marginal areas of the metropolitan zone, is sponsored by the Ministry of Education and the B. Van Leer Foundation. It provides help to children of preschool age using paraprofessional staff, duly trained and chosen from within the same marginal areas. The project is investigating the possibility of educating children in that age group at less cost than by conventional methods. It consists of a program providing both prevention and assistance to children who come from marginal areas and cannot attain proper education.

In March 1979 Doctor Luis Alberto Machado was appointed as state minister for the development of intelligence. It is probably the first time in the world that intelligence has been granted a political dimension at ministerial level. This caused a great deal of discussion, but soon the evolving projects were able to secure the support of the scientific community. Among these projects, it is very important to mention Proyecto Familia ("family project"), which has as its objective to train the mothers and the other adults surrounding children with the necessary motivation and knowledge to achieve the complete development of children from the prenatal stage until age six. One project of the new Ministry is to apply early stimulation techniques in a pilot study held at the Concepción Palacios Maternity Hospital of Caracas.

Project Aprender a Pensar ("learning how to think") is under development with the assistance of Dr. De Bono, director of the Center for the Study of Thinking Skills of Cambridge, England. There is also an agreement with Harvard University to make available the latest discoveries in teaching methods and materials favoring the development of thinking skills. Project Enriquecimiento Integral ("integral enrichment") is being carried out based upon a system development by Doctor Reuven Feurstein. The purpose of this project is to increase the levels of cognitive development and consequently the ability to learn, and to help children who come from culturally deprived social groups to become capable of good school achievement.

Historical Evolution of Special Education

Since the turn of the century, Venezuela has shown keen interest in special education. The 1912 Education Code emphasizes the need to create special types of schools to provide care for the blind, the deaf-mute, and the abnormal, as these children were called at that time. The Public Education Law of 1948 authorized the establishment of special-education classrooms and provision for the examination of children to be included in these classes.

The Organic Law of Education (Ley Orgánica), also enacted in 1948, in referring to special schools, provides that they be dedicated to children who are physically and mentally deficient, maladjusted, or in an abnormal social situation. Thus, according to the needs felt at that time, the Ministry of Education began to create its first special schools, acting more as warehouses for children with handicaps than as institutes providing special technical types of education. However, these children received the attention and the love that were absent in their own homes.

In addition to the work being carried out by the Ministry of Education, the National Institute of Minors serves a most valuable function. Also, there is the Venezuelan League for Mental Health and Child-Mother Centers (Centros Materno Infantiles,) developed by the Ministry of Health and Social Welfare; the Institute of Child Psychiatry (INAPSI); the Venezuelan Institute for Hearing and Language (IVAL); and the Venezuelan Association of Parents and Friends of Exceptional Children (AVEPANE), with its main offices in Caracas. AVEPANE has established contact with twelve to fourteen parent associations in the interior of the country that have become federated, forming a central agency called FEVEPANE, which maintains relationships with national associations of different countries and with international organizations.

In 1960 the first class of psychologists of the country graduated from the School of Psychology of Central University of Venezuela, and the following year the first graduation of psychologists from Andrés Bello Catholic University occurred. A group of psychologists have devoted themselves to clinical and school psychology, creating psychological services in the schools and institutions in which the first child-care centers for children with learning disabilities are being created.

The practice centers of the school psychology departments, in those public schools where they operate, have converted to giving services to students, and some of them have become a part of psychoeducational units of the special education office. These units are made up of interdisciplinary teams. Many theses written by students majoring in school psychology deal with learning disabilities and training programs for children with specific learning disabilities.

In 1966 the Special Education Service of the Ministry of Education was created, and the following year it was restructured as a department attached to the Division of Preschool and Elementary School Education. At the end of 1967 the first special classroom in a public school was organized for children with learning disabilities. The team was made up of a psychologist, a psychiatrist, a special teacher, a regular teacher, and students of school psychology from Central University of Venezuela who came to practice at this school.

In 1968 a group of professionals who were conscious of the need that existed in the country for a child-care center for children with learning disabilities, together with a group of parents, created the Venezuelan Association for Children with Learning Disabilities (AVENDA). At the same time, Caracas College was created as a pilot center for AVENDA.

Toward the end of 1969 the Venezuelan Society of School Psyhology was established, the members of which have largely contributed to the development of school psychology in Venezuela. The society has, as one of its fields, assistance to children with learning disabilities as well as participation in teaching specialized staff.

Other private institutions were created later, such as the Harmonic Training Institute for Exceptional Children (ICANE), followed by the Advanced School for Special Teachers and the Jean Piaget Institute. All three institutes provide care in educational centers for children with general learning disabilities and give courses for special teachers at the college level.

Some years ago, the Venezuelan Institute for Integral Development of Children (INVEDIN) was created, providing assistance for trainable and educable retarded children, with diagnostic teams and multidisciplinary care. This group also gave an early stimulation service, a maternal program, and behavior-modification training.

The Federation of Private Institutions for Assistance to Children (FIPAN) was organized primarily for gathering all private institutions into common or joint actions; it is a nonprofit organization catering to the care of minors, youths, and families, and is currently made up of thirty-four institutions.

A Permanent Commission for the Care of the Mentally Retarded was created by decree of the president of the republic. It is presided over by Dr. Gustavo Leal and is composed of representatives from the various ministries. This commission is in charge of the publication of books and handouts written by Venezuelan authors that are of interest to professionals in the behavioral sciences, especially those working in special education.

In 1977, also by presidential decree, the Foundation for the Development of Special Education in Venezuela was established. Its objective is the planning, coordination, supervision, and evaluation of educational programs for children and adolescents with exceptional needs requiring guidance and special care, through institutes, special classes, and workshops. It also provides for their integration into society and for assistance in helping them become a part of the work force according to their potential. It is in charge of carrying out educational actions tending to stimulate and sponsor the development of superior intellectual potential in children and adolescents with special abilities and talent, and it takes care of scheduling both human resources and research activities.

Areas of Concern in Special Education

The areas of concern in special education in Venezuela are mental retardation, learning disabilities, hearing deficiencies and speech problems, visual deficiencies, motor handicaps, multiple handicaps, and superior talent.

Daza de Gamboa (1978) stated that the total population that received care at special education services during 1977-1978 amounted to 15,012 children from 355 services, of which 148 operate in the metropolitan area of Caracas and 207 in the interior of Venezuela. During the last two years, the number of services as well as the population receiving care has increased throughout the country.

Services of the Special Education Office

The Special Education Office provides the following services: mental-retardation institutes, institutes for hearing deficiencies and speech problems, institutes for visual deficiencies, institutes for motor handicaps, psychoeducational units, special classrooms, centers for psychoeducational evaluation, child-care development centers, centers for early intervention, speech-rehabilitation centers, centers for the rescue of talent, centers for learning disabilities, protected workshops, vocational-exploration workshops, and labor-skills workshops.

The policy of special education is aimed at prevention through the Early Detection Unit at the Concepción Palacios Maternity Hospital, and by Development Centers devoted to early identification and early education of high-risk children from the biological viewpoint. Through early-intervention methods, children's difficulties are to be cared for from their onset by a team of physicians, psychologists, social workers, and special teachers, with parental involvement to enable them to become better therapists to their own children. This task is performed by two ministries, the Ministry of Education and the Ministry of Health and Social Welfare.

In Venezuela in 1978, 46.7 percent of the staff working in special education at government levels was dedicated to mental retardation; however, during the past two years, staff dedicated to children with learning disabilities has increased. Also in 1978, the First National Congress for Special Education took place, a most important event in the development of this field. In 1980 the Special Education Office of the Ministry of Education and the Foundation for the Development of Special Education began publication of the journal *Special Education*.

In Venezuela the care of children with special needs has taken place in the same manner as in many other countries; that is, first they were placed in special institutions, but now the trend is to try to place the children into the regular classroom by means of individual educational progams, which are usually carried out in attached special classes. Their return to the regular classroom must be gradual and cautious, depending on the opportunities that education as a whole may offer them, both in curriculum and in special methods and techniques. The regular classroom teacher who receives children with learning disabilities must be informed of the psychoeducational strategies for these children, and the special teacher must know the official program pertaining to the grade of the child with whom she is working.

Formation of Human Resources for Special Education

Human resources for special education in Venezuela have been created at the same time that the staff was being trained. According to Mateo Alonso (1974) the Venezuelan League for Mental Health was one of the first institutions concerned with providing education for specialized teachers. In 1958 the first mental-hygiene course for teachers was given in Caracas, sponsored by the Mental Health League and by the Pedagogical Institute. Courses were continued in succeeding years and were also given at the National Institute of Puericulture. Later the Venezuelan League for Mental Health, together with the School of Psychology of Central University of Venezuela, organized an Introductory Course to Teaching (1960-1961) and developed two-year courses for special teachers. The teachers who graduated from these courses were the first special teachers trained in Venezuela.

The Ministry of Education, upon assuming responsibility for special education, promoted training courses for teachers and developed programs with specific goals, including both short courses providing systematic education and professional courses of longer duration. Through its Elementary and Teaching Office, jointly with the Ministry of Health and with the Institute for Professional Improvement of the Ministry of Education, an extension program for special education in Venezuela was sponsored in 1962, giving attention to areas of hearing deficiencies and speech problems. This program included the education of personnel; the creation of special schools for deaf children; and the implementation of programs in the area of mental retardation.

In 1965 the government created the first institute for educating special teachers at the Institute of Child Psychiatry (INAPSI), under the Ministry of Health and Social Welfare, with which other institutes became incorporated in the years that followed. In 1968 the first course for systematic education at the graduate level for teachers in special education was given for teaching deaf children and those with speech problems. Teachers were also sent to other countries, especially to Uruguay, where they took one-year courses in the specialty of mental retardation.

In 1977 the education of special teachers acquired more-advanced status. The six university colleges in Venezuela are now responsible for training teachers in special education, offering the following majors: mental retardation, learning disabilities, and emotional disturbance. These are three-year courses, open to those who are either high school graduates or teachers. Psychologists, especially from the area of school psychology, together with teachers and other professionals in the behavioral sciences, play an active role in the education of specialized teachers.

In Venezuela psychologists may obtain undergraduate education at the Department of School Psychology of Central University of Venezuela and at the Chair of School Psychology of Andrés Bello Catholic University. In 1976 the first learning-disabilities courses for psychologists at the graduate level were sponsored by the Faculty of Medicine and the Faculty of Humanities and Education of Central University of Venezuela.

Research

Sardi de Selle and Leal (1961) discussed learning disabilities, with a brief reference to the literature on hyperkinetic syndrome. Of the 300 clinical histories taken at random from among the children in the files of the Central Mental Health Clinic, 101 cases had behavioral disturbances, 53 were hyperkinetic, and 40 had normal intellectual quotients.

Santana de Salazar (1969) reported on the diagnosis and reeducation of twenty children from the first grade of a public school in Caracas who had serious disabilities in learning to read and who had repeated the same grade for several years and had problems in their conduct plus signs of malnutrition. Among the conclusions, she pointed out that intelligence factors and perceptual age were meaningfully related to learning to read. Also, the better readers came from higher socioeconomic levels. Each child was given an individualized program according to his need. The reeducational programs generally consisted of visual-motor training, orientation, visual and aural memory, and a language-improvement program. Phonetic methods and visual-auditory-kinesthetic-tactile (VAKT) teaching were used. Training was provided for one school year, after which eighteen of the children passed to the second grade.

Sardi de Selle, Feldman, and Eskenazi (1971) summarized the findings on forty-two children with scholastic retardation attending a public school in Caracas, of whom 47 percent were in the second grade and 53 percent the third grade. The students came from lower socioeconomic classes and showed signs of malnutrition, chronic diseases, and hearing and visual deficiencies. Six percent were reported to have had pathological perinatal histories related to perceptual-motor immaturity found in the psychological tests and low school achievement, which gave rise to suspicions of cerebral dysfunction. A high percentage of these pupils had emotional problems. The families of these children were disorganized, and in half of them there was no responsible father. In practically all of them, the mothers worked outside the home and left the children without any adult to protect and educate them and act as a role model. It was concluded that the basic causes for the school retardation were the late initiation of schooling in 76 percent of the children, repetition of the first grade because of learning disabilities in reading, and cultural deprivation.

Cadenas (1971) applied Piaget's theory to the study of the elementary spatial and geometrical notions of children with learning disabilities. She observed that these children acquire the notions of conservation of continuous and discontinuous amounts very late in comparison with a group of normal children.

Sardi de Salle and Feldman (1971) conducted a study of the self-image of a group of children with learning disabilities who had attended special classes in a public school in Caracas. The sample consisted of fifty-five students, of whom 40 percent were in first grade and 60 percent were in second grade; 58 percent were male and 42 percent were female. The great majority of the children came from the working class, where the number of children per family was large. The children were individually interviewed and were asked to make a drawing of themselves, with the following instructions: "Paint yourself the way you feel now," and "paint yourself as you will feel once you have learned" (see figures 22-1, 22-2, 22-3). The drawings were analyzed using the Goodenough-Harris technique. It was concluded that all the children had a poor self-image, and a large portion of them devaluated themselves and felt small, inefficient, and rejected. They appeared insecure and dependent, with great emotional needs and with affective ambivalence toward the mother, the teachers, and their peers. The majority of the group reacted to these feelings with depression, a passive attitude, and isolation, accompanied by guilt, shame, and fear. As defense mechanisms, they used compensating fantasies. They thought of their failures as being inherent in themselves. A minority responded with aggression directed at the environment, accompanied by a substratum of anger and fear, and negation was the defense mechanism used by this group. For them, their failures were brought about by agents that were external to themselves.

Platone (1973) conducted a study of the characteristics of human-figure drawings using the Koppitz technique. She compared a group of children attending special classes in several public schools of the metropolitan area with a group of children diagnosed as educable mentally retarded who attended special schools. The results indicated that the drawings of the

The drawing on the left shows his present feeling of rage because of his learning problems. On the right is a happier representation of himself once he has learned.

Figure 22-1. Drawings of Himself by a Second-Grade Boy

children with mental retardation showed a higher frequency of emotional indicators and little capacity to control impulses, while the drawings of children with learning disabilities presented the characteristics of withdrawal, insecurity, and self-devaluation.

In 1973 Sardi de Selle, Feldman, Eskenazi, and Ponce (1980) with a multidisciplinary team, studied a sample of thirty-one children from a special class in a public school of Caracas. The ages ranged from seven years, five months, to twelve years, four months, with an average age of nine years, six months; 61.3 percent were male and 38.7 percent were female. The children studied were first- to fourth-grade pupils, the majority from the second and third grades. Intellectual functions ranged between normal and low-normal on the various tests used (Goodenough, Wise, Benton). Their deficits were related to attention span, concentration, recognition of retained verbal learning, visuomotor speed, auditory and visual sequential memory, and poor development of psycholinguistic abilities (ITPA). These students also presented noticeable perceptual-motor immaturity (Bender-Koppitz), and obtained an average age for visual-motor integration of seven years, eleven months (Beery). Regarding visual perception, their most important difficulties were in form-constancy, figure-ground, position in space, and spatial relationships (Frostig). They showed good gross-motor development on the Kephart Scale and in the psychoeducational inventory of basic abilities for learning (Valett). Also, many deficiencies were found in the development of orientation and in conceptual abilities.

She drew herself crying in the lower picture because of her learning problem. Later, when she can read, she will be happy, as depicted in the upper drawing.

Figure 22-2. Drawings of Herself by a First-Grade Girl

Their abilities to face situations of daily life, as well as their associative thought processes, were in agreement with their chronological age. Only 27 percent of the group mastered syllabic reading. In writing 84 percent omitted letters, 63 percent had letter-substitutions, and 33 percent showed reversals of letters. In arithmetic they had noticeable difficulties in grouping, in adding and subtracting digits, and in problem-solving; and reversals of numbers were seen in 26.6 percent of the cases. Fifty-five percent of the sample had pathological histories at birth, 34 percent showed psychophysiological alterations, and 10 percent were hyperkinetic. One of these cases summed up his problems: "Why don't you give me classes when it's recess time, and let me have recess when I am in class?"—an excellent suggestion for planning educational programs for hyperkinetic children who have brief attention spans.

The pupils showed a background of depression, possibly as a consequence of the sum of their failures, including feelings of incapability, fear of grow-

In the upper drawing, she represents herself as ashamed of her reading problem by covering her face. After she can read, she will be happy and will face the world, as depicted in the lower drawing.

Figure 22-3. Drawings of Herself by a Second-Grade Girl

ing up, and a negative self-image. Regarding interpersonal relationships, parental figures were seen with conflicting feelings, and fathers appeared to be more rejected than mothers. Also, their attitudes toward peers and school were ambivalent. Among the defense mechanisms of the ego, negativism, compensating fantasies, and maniac defenses prevailed. Twenty-four percent evidenced malnutrition, but only 3 percent presented current pathology capable of influencing their school achievement. The neurological study revealed that 50 percent of the EEGs were clearly abnormal, and the ophthalmological examination revealed that 10 percent of the cases had visual handicaps considered to be capable of creating retardation in learning. From the sociocultural viewpoint, they revealed conditions of cultural deprivation. The authors called attention to the necessity of providing systematic assistance in school to such children.

Fierro de Ascanio (1974) analyzed the vocabulary of fifty-five children from a sample with scholastic retardation. The words making up this vocabulary were selected from those constituting part of the Wechsler Preschool and Primary Scale of Intelligence (WPPSI). The majority of these children came from an environment of social disadvantage, which did not enable them to acquire an elaborate linguistic code. The language of these children was concrete, with a tendency to use definitions "according to usage." The children seemed to possess the concepts, but were unable to transmit them in an adequate way. The author posed the question of how this vocabulary was going to interfere with the learning processes in school. She pointed out the importance of having educational programs that provide experiences that stimulate the child's development.

Brazón (1976) made a study of thirty children with scholastic disabilities exhibiting characteristics of social disadvantage, who were referred to the school psychology services of a public school in the metropolitan area. She concluded that because intelligence has such a complex, multidimensional construction, the use of the intelligence quotient as a criterion for diagnosis is simplistic and highly inadequate for the study of individuals deemed to be unadapted. She also pointed out that the children had serious disabilities when facing psychological tests geared to the cultural level of the middle class, since these children probably lacked experiences to help them handle such tasks. Thus, she emphasized the need to act very cautiously when trying to set forth a differential diagnosis with this type of children.

Noguera (1976) indicated the importance of the use of Piaget-type tests for examining children with minimal cerebral dysfunctions, both to complete profiles and to plan treatment strategies. The study consisted of evaluating two groups of thirty children each. The experimental group was taken from an institution specializing in the care of children with learning disabilities, and the control group was taken from a school for normal children. The curriculum for both groups ranged from first to fourth grades. The achievement shown by the experimental group was significantly below that of the control group in all tests with respect to the notion of space. Noguera concluded that there was a link between minimal cerebral dysfunction and disabilities in the understanding of space.

Granell de Aldaz (1976) described how she applied techniques of behavior modification for the control of hyperactivity in the natural environment. The main objective was to demonstrate that hyperactive behavior may be controlled and replaced by more adequate behavioral patterns by reinforcing contingencies in the natural environment. The results obtained support the hypothesis that the disruptive or inadequate responses of a hyperactive child may be diminished by changing the environmental contingencies, based upon a program for the reinforcement of appropriate responses.

Feldman (1978) made a psychohistorical study of some outstanding people in the arts, sciences, and politics who appeared to have had learning disabilities during their childhood. He especially studied Simón Bolívar, the Latin American hero and liberator of Venezuela, Colombia, Ecuador, Perú, and Bolivia. Churchill, Edison, Einstein, and Bolívar, were slow or late in learning to read and write. Bolívar, an orphan from early childhood, was ambidextrous, and according to several descriptions was always restless and hyperactive. At age twelve he ran away from his tutor and his uncle's house. The positive aspect of this interference in Bolívar's education, and also in the lives of other historically important persons, is believed to be that it prevented an authoritarian education from absorbing their minds as children, which might have made them less creative and unruly. Escaping from the severity of an eduation in accordance with his aristocratic rank, Bolívar used to walk and ride horseback with boys who did not come from his class. In this manner, at a very early age he was able to become acquainted with the lives of slaves and artisans and to learn the language of the people in the village. This contributed to his ability to become a popular leader.

At age fifteen, in Bolívar's first known longhand letter, there are omissions and confusions of letters, short words joined, and long words separated. Later, when he had become a liberator of South America, his habit of dictating several letters at the same time became known. He did this with three secretaries at the same time. This was interpreted as an eccentricity; however, it was more likely a creative adaptation of his style of attention and his constant mobility.

Sardi de Selle, Granadillo de Anciano, and Mata (1979) presented a three-year evaluation of treatment of children with learning disabilities in a psychoeducational unit at Vargas Hospital. They described the treatment of forty students carried out by a multidisciplinary team. The research methods used with the children were both psychotherapeutical and pharmacological. The types of psychotherapy most often used were orientation therapies improving self-esteem, emotional symptoms, and psychosomatic manifestations, which were present in 52 percent of the cases. Expression therapy was also used, as well as group therapy. With respect to pharmacological treatment, they used methylphenidate hydrochloride (Ritalin) in three cases during three years, suspending the drug during the children's vacations. Two children were treated with diphenylhydantoin. In both cases, the results were good, but the sample was quite small. The family was treated by means of family therapy, and the mothers entered guidance groups.

In the psychoeducational treatment, progress was slow; the group attended for at least two years, and the results for those who improved were modest for visual memory, visual perception, fine-motor coordination, and arithmetical operations. Improvement ranged from little to moderate in auditory memory and perception, equilibrium, temporal orientation, and numerical relationships.

Chaberman (1979) discussed the use of behavior modification in the treatment of children, applying it to children with learning and behavior disabilities in school with good results.

Segal and Pereira and colleagues (1980) reviewed 100 cases of children diagnosed as having minimal cerebral dysfunction, who were examined by neurologists, psychologists, psychiatrists, audiologists, and special teachers. They found that males exceeded females for insufficiencies in school achievement, behavioral disturbances, and hyperactivity. Intellectual level was generally found to be normal, with a high rate of sensory-motor immaturity and abnormal Bender tests. Soft neurological signs were outstanding, including speech defects, hypotony, posture disturbances, hyperkinesia, and crossed laterality. An important finding was the alteration of family dynamics combined with inadequate handling of the emotional problems of these children in the school environment. The biological factors that may have caused these problems were pathological pregnancies and deliveries, central nervous system traumas, and Rh incompatibilities.

Muñoz and Gorodeckis (1980) examined the influence of the systematic reading of children's fairy tales on some of the dimensions of children's language. She studied fifty-eight preschool children ranging in age from three years to seven years, four months, including thirty-five males and twenty-three females from every socioeconomic level. An experimental design of three groups was used: two experimental groups and one control group, with pretests and posttests. The conclusion was that the reading of fairy tales is an effective means to increase comprehension of vocabulary, to learn grammatical structure, and to increase the ability to retain specific information. The particular situation under which the reading was performed did not seem to influence the findings, so it may be carried out with equally positive results at home and in school.

Méndez Castellano and López (1979) presented some preliminary results in a research study called *Proyecto Venezuela* (Venezuelan Project). The purpose of this survey was to establish a reliable statistical basis for the characteristics of growth and development. In the preliminary psychological evaluation it was found that children under age two had psychomotor development generally coinciding with chronological age without any differences in relation to sex or socioeconomic status. Thereafter, when verbal development gains importance, girls ranked better than boys, and socioeconomic-stratum-5 rankings on the verbal scale diminished with increasing age, except on the information subtest. In other strata the rankings increased progressively with age.

In 1978 a team of professionals participated in the development of the Test For Learning, which measures psychomotricity, visual-motor integration, language perception, memory, and association. This research project is being performed by the Foundation for the Development of Special Education, and the test is currently in process of being standardized. This instrument is of use both for diagnosis and for the planning of corrective methods.

Early Stimulation

In Venezuela interest in detection and early stimulation of high-risk children started in the 1970s. At the same time, compensatory educational programs appeared at preschool level to prevent the effects of environmental disadvantages in school for children from the lower classes relative to middle-class children. For the study of these high-risk children, there are two projects: Project Aryet and one from the Early Detection Unit (UDP) operating at the Concepción Palacios Maternity Hospital of Caracas. Currently these projects are carrying out early-stimulation programs for these children in which the mothers and other family members play very important roles. Their evaluation will be of utmost importance for future investigations in this field.

Recagno (1979) investigated child-raising habits, guided stimulation, and mental development of six-year-old marginal children. One of the objectives was to determine whether it is possible to make changes in certain patterns of behavior by helping the mothers through behavior-modification programs and consequent short-term changes in the intellectual achievement of their children. Many difficulties were encountered by these mothers in raising and socializing 317 children when there were only 37 stable spouses cooperating. Although they were illiterate the mothers acquired a great number of guiding principles for stimulating learning. The children achieved up to 68 percent of the behavior taught by their mothers. There was no increase in intellectual quotients in the group of children, who ranged from one to six years of age. It was considered that the time elapsed may have been too short.

Since 1976, in the Department of School Psychology of Central University of Venezuela, studies have been done applying the PORTAGE Guide to Early Education (Bluma et al. 1976). Groups of students have used it for their theses, and each group has taken a set area from the program. The training program was applied at home by the mother under the guidance of a psychology student. Small samples were taken from among culturally deprived children. Although training only had an approximate duration of six weeks, important differences were obtained between experimental and control groups (Arias and Jiménez 1976).

Diagnostic Procedures

In general, the child with specific learning disabilities who is referred to a psychoeducational unit operating in a public school is evaluated by an interdisciplinary team formed by the teacher, a psychologist, a special teacher, and a social worker. The psychological tests used most frequently are: the Wechsler Intelligence Scale for Children, the Stanford-Binet Intelligence Scale, the Bender Visual Motor Gestalt Test with Koppitz scoring, Human-Figure Drawing with Goodenough and Koppitz scoring, the Frostig Developmental Test of Visual Perception, the Illinois Test of Psycholinguistic Abilities, and the Wepman Auditory Discrimination Test. In some cases we also use the Developmental Test of Visual Motor Integration by Beery, the Visual Retention Test by Benton, the Kephart Scale of Psychomotricity, the Frostig Movement Skills Test Battery, the Piaget Tests, and the Detroit Tests of Learning Aptitude. Sometimes we include projective tests and tests for emotional and social adjustment.

We still lack standardized tests for reading, writing, and calculation. In general, for the evaluation of reading we use passages of the text corresponding to the grade that the child is in. For writing, we perform the evaluation through a paragraph of dictation and a composition. We usually ask the child to write a letter, which enables us to analyze its content.

In 1976 Raúl Chamorro prepared a psychoeducational test battery for the evaluation of motor, perceptual, psycholinguistic, and academic abilities that is used frequently by special teachers who also use the orientation and relationship tests by the same author (Chamorro 1980).

The regular teacher fills out the referral application blank for the student, which contains an evaluation providing us with the first information about the behavior of the student, his auditory comprehension, spoken language, spatial and temporal orientation, motor coordination, and school achievement in each subject. This information is extremely useful to us and serves as a guide in the study of each case. Also, the psychologist interviews the mother, the teacher, and the child and makes observations on his or her behavior in the classroom. The analysis of the school material, based on the child's textbooks, notebooks, and school supplies, is further important information to be taken into account. In those services where there are social workers, they interview these children, providing us with information on the family and social environment of the child and on the community resources that are available.

After the evaluation is made by each member, the team meets and discusses the case and the psychoeducational strategies are planned for the special class and the regular class. Some of these cases also require psychological help for their emotional problems. Others are referred to the neurologist, psychiatrist, or speech therapist, in accordance with the needs of each child, to complete the diagnosis and treatment.

Therapeutic Procedures

From the psychoeducational viewpoint, the child with specific learning disabilities requires an individualized educational program that is based on studies performed by an interdisciplinary team, specifically from the results of the clinical analysis of the profile obtained from the test battery used for the diagnosis, as has been discussed (Tarnopol 1976, Tarnopol and Tarnopol 1976). This program is carried out by the special teacher and rein- forced by the regular teacher. Here lies the need for both teachers to remain in constant communication. We also try to incorporate the family in the ac- tivities that we carry out with these children. When the child starts attending a special class, we first try to perform activities in which he or she will be successful, along with some group sessions. According to the specific learn- ing disabilities of the child, he or she will attend a special class for two hours, either daily or several times per week, to receive either individual or small-group attention.

The training most frequently used, depending on the problems pre- sented, includes:

1. Developmental programs of gross and fine coordination.
2. Relaxation techniques for some children who have specific learning disabilities in writing.
3. Programs of development of auditory perception and discrimination at the receptive level, and developmental programs for visual perception and visual discrimination.
4. Programs to develop memory, especially sequencing in auditory and visual memory.
5. Programs in the area of association at the auditory and visual levels.
6. Programs for the enrichment of vocabulary.
7. Programs for the stimulation of psycholinguistic abilities.

With children from the more advanced grades, we work with grammatical constructions, reading-comprehension, left-right body-orientation exercises, spatial and temporal training, and precalculation and calculation programs.

Since we often find children with low self-esteem, frustration, and inadequate handling of their aggressiveness, in some centers there are groups for emotional development; in others the program Developing Understanding of Self and Others (Dinkmeyer 1973) is beginning to be used. It is a program designed to help children to better understand social and emotional behavior. We also have parent groups for children who attend special classes. As for the teaching methods, we most frequently use the multisensory approach of Fernald. The phonetic method has had good results with children who have reading disabilities, and the current trend is to use simplified cursive writing with these children. The progress being made by the child depends not only on the programs and methods being used but also on the feedback received by the child for the efforts he or she is making. Thus, the criterion used by the regular teacher to grade the children with specific learning disabilities mainstreamed into his class is important, since these children require constant social reinforcement.

Pharmacological Treatments

The use of medications appears effective for hyperkinetic children with learning disabilities, and they have been prescribed in Venezuela just as in other countries. Methylphenidate hydrochloride (Ritalin) has been especially used to control hyperkinesia and to improve attention and concentration. It is used primarily during the school period and suspended during vacations. Ritalin requires special prescriptions, and some physicians prefer antidepressive drugs such as imipramine or tranquilizers such as chlordiazepoxide.

For irritable, impulsive children with epileptiform alterations, diphenylhydantoin has been used, as has carbamazepine, especially when the EEG reveals abnormalities in the temporal lobe. Pharmacological therapy is only one aspect of the integrated therapeutical approach to learning disabilities.

Conclusion

In Venezuela the field of learning disabilities has had wide development, and several investigations have been performed by professionals from the fields of psychology, medicine, and education. There is a clear awareness of these problems, and work is being done to try to improve the diagnostic techniques and the treatments. Research began in a rather diverse fashion, but in 1977 the Foundation for the Development of Special Education was created, with one of its objectives the integration of these activities in the country.

References

Arias, G., and Jiménez, T., 1976. Aplicación de la Guía PORTAGE para la Educación Temprana en una mestra de niños de 3 a 5 años. Thesis, Central University of Venezuela.

Beery, K., and Buktenica, N. 1967. *Developmental Test of Visual-Motor Integration.* Chicago: Follett.

Bluma, S., Shearer, M., y col. 1976. *PORTAGE Guide to Early Education.* Cooperative Educational Service.

Brazón, M. 1976. Consideraciones en torno al diagnóstico y prob-. lemática educativa de niños en situación de desventaja social. Thesis, Central University of Venezuela.

Cadenas, J. 1971. Nociones de conservación en un grupo de niños con dificultades de aprendizaje. Thesis, Central University of Venezuela.

Chaberman, L. 1979. El uso de la técnica de modificación de conducta en el tratamiento con niños. *Boletín* XVIII, *3 y 4.*

Chamorro, R. 1980. Aportes del psicólogo escolar en la evaluación psicopedagógica. Primeras Jornadas de Psicología Escolar. Caracas.

Daza de Gamboa, E. 1978. Supervisión en educación especial. *Memorias del Primer Congreso Nacional de Educación Especial.*

Dinkmeyer, D. 1973. *Developing Understanding of Self and Others.* Circle Pines, Minn.: American Guidance Service.

Feldman, M. 1978. *Las Crisis Psicológicas de Simón Bolívar.* Caracas: Nueva Psiquiatría.

Feldman, M., and Feldman, N. 1974. Síndrome de privación cultural. *Archivos Venezolanos de Psiquiatría* 20.

Fierro de Ascanio, J. 1974. Aporta al estudio del vocabulario en niños retardos escolares. *Revista Psicología* 1:1.

Frostig, M. 1972. *The Developmental Program in Visual Perception.* Chicago: Follett.

Grannell de Aldaz, E. 1976. Aplicación de téchnicas de modificación de conducta para el control de la hiperactividad en el ambiente natural. Thesis, University Simón Bolívar.

Mateo Alonso, A. 1974. *Evolución de la Higiene Mental en Venezuela.* Ediciones del Rectorado. Caracas: Central University of Venezuela.

Méndez Castellano, C., and López, M. 1979. Análisis descriptivo de algunas variables estudiadas en el preescolar en la prueba piloto Carabobo, Proyecto Venezuela. Fundación Centro de Estudioa Biológicos sobre crecimiento y desarrollo de la población venezolana.

Ministerio de Educación. 1978. Guiá para la organización y funcionamiento de las aulas especiales anexas a grupos escolares. Fundación para el desarrollo de la educación especial.

Muñoz, E., and Gorodeckis, M. 1980. Influencia de la lectura sistemática de cuentos infantiles sobre algunas dimensiones de lenguage del niño. Primeras Jornadas Nacionales de Psicología Escolar. Abril.

Noguera, C. 1976. La construcción del espacio según Piaget en el niño con disfunctión cerebral mínima. Thesis, Central University of Venezuela.

Platone, M. 1973. Estudio comparativo del dibujo de la figura humana de un grupo de niños con retardo mental educable y con problemas de aprendizaje. Tranajo presentado en las II Journadas de Avepane. Caracas.

Recagno, V. 1979. *Hábitos de Crianza, Estimulación Dirigida y Desarrollo Mental en Niños Marginados de 1 a 6 Años.* Caracas: Central University of Venzuela.

Santana de Salazar, H. 1969. Analysis y tratamiento de un grupo de niños con dificultades para la lectura. Thesis, Central University of Venezuela.

Sardi de Selle, M., and Feldman, N. 1971. Le imagen de sí mismo en el niño con dificultades de aprendizaje y su proyección en el medio escolar. *Rivista Niños* 4:14-15.

Sardi de Selle, M., Feldman, N., and Eskenzai, S. 1971. Consideraciones generales acerca del estudio de un grupo de niños con retardo pedagógico. República de Venezuela, Ministerio de Educación, Primaria y Normal.

Sardi de Selle, M., Feldman, N., Eskenazi, S., and Ponce, C. 1980. Dificultades de aprendizaje. Estudio multidisciplinario. Ediciones de la Comisión Permanente para la Atención del Retardo Mental. Caracas.

Sardi de Selle, M., Granadillo de Anciano, L., and Mata, T. 1979. Tratamiento de dificultades de aprendizaje. Tres años de experiencia. Hospital Vargas. Caracas.

Sardi de Selle, M., and Leal, G., 1961. El síndrome hiperquinético de conducta, Folleto mimeografiado. Primer Congreso Venezolano de Psiquiatría. Caracas.

Segal, J., Pereira, F., y col. 1980. Enfoque interdisciplinario de la disfunción cerebral mínima. Primeras Jornadas de Psicología Escolar. Abril.

Tarnopol, L. (ed.). 1976. *Dificultades para el Aprendizaje.* Mexico City: Médica Mexicana.

Tarnopol, L., and Tarnopol, M. (eds.) 1976. *Reading Disabilities: An International Perspective.* Baltimore: University Park Press.

Valett, R. 1969. *Programming Learning Disabilities.* Belmont, Calif.: Fearon.

23 Dyslexia and Dysgraphia in Yugoslavia

Vladimir Stančić, Ruža Sabol,
Gojke Zovko, and *Nada Zovko*

The Socialist Federal Republic of Yugoslavia consists of six socialist republics, Bosnia and Hercegovina, Croatia, Macedonia, Montenegro, Serbia, and Slovenia, and two autonomous provinces, Vojvodina and Kosovo. Yugoslavia covers an area of 255,804 square kilometers and has a population of 20.5 million according to the census of 1971.

Special Education

After World War II education in general and special education in particular developed rapidly in Yugoslavia. Obligatory free education lasting eight years for all children of school age was instituted. Elementary schooling is mandatory for all children from seven to fifteen years of age, and the extended system of secondary schools makes it possible for the majority of students to continue their education. All nationalities and national groups have the right and opportunity to pursue their education in their native languages.

The sudden expansion of elementary education and the almost total inclusion of all school-age children brought about numerous difficulties. Although the declared pedagogical principle that educational treatment should be adapted to the individual differences and capabilities of the pupils was always accentuated in theory, practice very often showed a tendency to homogenize the populations of classes. This tendency came from several sources, which may be assembled into two groups. First, there was insufficient direction of teaching and school psychology aimed at qualifying the teachers to handle individual differences and, as a consequence, frequent lack of teacher competence to individualize instruction. Second, in a number of cases, inordinately large classes, overburdened curricula, insufficient equipment in many schools, and sometimes inadequate educational and instructional methods reduced the individualization of teaching to a minimum (Stančic 1977).

These difficulties were often manifested by the retarded learning of a number of pupils. A proportion of pupils did not finish elementary school on time or didn't finish at all, which brought about serious problems in

519

their vocational orientations, qualifications, and employment. In order to remove or palliate these difficulties, developmental classes were instituted. Their task was to extend assistance to those pupils who were not able to follow the tempo and rhythm of the schoolwork done by their peers. Such developmental classes are now extinct, but efforts have been made and are still being made, with specially organized supplementary schoolwork done in groups or individually, to compensate for students' retardation.

Some of these children, however, did not show satisfactory progress in their learning in spite of the extra tutoring. These were children with mild to extreme deficiencies of cognitive functions, serious disabilities of hearing and sight, emotional disturbance, and so forth. They were therefore sent to special schools, which already included a considerable number of pupils. Because of the tendency to homogenize the population of each class in regular schools, many children with learning and behavior deviations who created problems for teachers were sent to special schools without real justification.

Legislative measures have been taken to ensure that needy children receive certain benefits. The Regulations on the Categorization and Evidence of Children Hindered in Psychological and Physical Development were issued in 1960. According to these regulations, a child can only be enrolled in a special school on the basis of an examination and the professional opinion of a special commission. The commission members include a pediatrician, a psychologist, a social worker, a specialist (audiologist, ophthalmologist, or other), and a suitable defectologist. This commission must establish the kind and degree of impairment and recommend a suitable program for the education, instruction, and rehabilitation of the child. The regulations refer to children and adolescents with deficient sight, hearing, or speech, mental retardation, and physical disabilities. The Regulation of 1973 includes, in addition, children with behavioral disorders of organic etiology.

The education, instruction, and rehabilitation of children who according to the regulations are handicapped is carried on in various institutions. Traditional institutions for the education of such children have boarding facilities and social and health facilities for the children. In addition to this, there are special day schools, special classes in regular schools, and special departments at hospitals and health resorts. Individual work is also carried out in the homes of the children, particularly in Slovenia. There are schools for children with impaired sight (boarding schools for the blind and both day schools and classes in regular schools for the partially sighted); for children with impaired hearing (for the deaf and hard-of-hearing); and for physically disabled children and children with chronic diseases. Also, there are schools for educable mentally retarded children, institutions for moderately and seriously retarded children, and both educational institutions and schools for children and adolescents with disorders of behavior and personality. Some special elementary schools contain departments for children with multiple disorders. There are no special schools for children with speech and voice disorders. Speech correction is carried out in regular schools, in health institutions, or in special speech therapy institutions.

After World War II the system of special schools and other institutions for the rehabilitation of handicapped children and adolescents developed rapidly in Yugoslavia. Before the war there were only 18 such schools and institutions, but now there are more than 350, for the most part new and modern establishments. Although this development allows most of the handicapped children and adolescents to receive adequate treatment, it has also led to the development of the special-schools system, which has an unfortunate tendency to segregate such children and youths.

In Yugoslavia, as in other countries, more and more researchers have pointed out the difficulties that may result from the segregated education in special schools and institutions. Warnings regarding the need for the integrated education of children and youths with disabilities have been sounded for over fifteen years. It is feared that special schools might lead to difficulties in integrating handicapped children and adolescents into normal social life because of the separation of these children from the broader social environment, as well as the reduced possibility for others to get acquainted with the problems and abilities of these children (Stančić 1964; Budak 1965).

However, both in the past and today, a number of handicapped children have always been included in normal classes in regular schools. This also holds true for children with impaired speech (if this is their only disorder), for over 90 percent of children and adolescents with behavior disorders (borderline cases in the field of cognitive functions), for a number of blind and deaf children, and so forth. Such an integrated education for these children can only be possible when there are suitable objective conditions in the regular school and suitable subjective conditions on the part of the handicapped children and their parents. Although the acceptance and education of handicapped children has been well organized and implemented in some regular schools, most of the regular schools in our country still are not able to cope with these students.

Today a radical reform of the whole school system is in full swing—from preschool institutions through universities. This reform did not bypass special education, which, because of inherent segregational tendencies, is subject to social and professional criticism. There is a demand for more comprehensive school integration of handicapped children and adolescents, which should also create the conditions for later professional and more extensive social integration. The demand for integrated education was expressed in the concept of general elementary education and instruction, which was developed by the Educational Council of Croatia. This reform states:

> The education and instruction of persons with disorders in psychophysical development is a constituent part of the educational system, and consequently, of elementary instruction and education. According to the concept of elementary learning and education, these persons should be ensured specialized teaching methods within the framework of the regular school system with the maximum possibility of individual treatment, and when absolutely necessary, in special classes or groups, if available. In exceptional cases, the education of these persons will be carried out in separate distinct institutions.

Similar reforms have been legislated in the other republics and autonomous provinces. For instance, the Elementary Education Law of the Socialist Republic of Serbia requests every elementary school to organize special education for those pupils who need specific help.

The reform of special education makes two demands: (1) where conditions permit, handicapped children and adolescents should be included in regular schools as much as possible; and (2) regular schools should be made capable of accepting these children and adolescents. The extent and pace at which this integration of handicapped students into regular schools will be realized will depend on the development of the school system in general as well as the development of each individual school.

An education is to be available to every child, even those who have minimal subjective prerequisites. The new ways of identifying and diagnosing handicapped children should be within the framework of normal, not exceptional, treatment in order to avoid stigmatization.

Children with Learning Disabilities

The problems of instruction and education of children with serious sight and hearing disorders, as well as those who are mentally retarded and physically disabled, were evident long ago, and solutions were sought to meet the educational needs of these children. There is also an organized system of services to help children with speech disorders. However, the situation is different with respect to children of approximately normal intelligence who have learning disabilities. The regular scholastic system does not devote sufficient attention to these children. Since their disorders are more moderate, these children are not included in the special schools. Special education for these children means a unique approach based on the recognition of the child's individual characteristics and the causes of his learning difficulties and on finding and applying treatment adequate to his abilities, needs, and interests.

The term *children with learning disabilities* is relatively new. It refers to that category of children who, in spite of average or above-average intellectual abilities, are not successful in school or, to be more precise, are not up to the particular tasks that the school sets for them.

There had been attempts to solve the problems of children with learning disabilities by organizing developmental classes, and later by providing supplementary and extended instruction. These forms of assistance were not fully satisfactory because the method of eliminating these disabilities, based on an accurate diagnosis that could indicate the proper treatment, was not specified.

Learning disabilities may arise from many causes (Eisenberg 1966). Although it was once thought that they are mainly caused by retardation in the development of visual-perceptual and visuomotor abilities, today we believe that these are only a few of the factors within the complex etiology of learning disabilities. Minor disorders of the sensory apparatus and all those conditions that lower the general vitality of the organism, such as anemia, minimal cerebral dysfunctions, emotional disturbances, and even the conditions of psychic infantilism, can be connected with learning disabilities. Infantile children are motorically restless. This is the result of retardation in the development of the cortical mechanisms that regulate motor activity such that the extrapyramidal system outweighs the pyramidal. We often note that these children have difficulty solving more-complicated problems because of an inability to discern the problem and to concentrate on it. This is caused by the instability of their attention and their hastiness (Pevzner 1972).

We generally accept the viewpoint that children with learning disabilities are for the most part of average or above-average intelligence. In some cases there is a deficiency predominantly in the field of visual perception, which lowers their IQs on the performance scales of intelligence tests, such as the Wechsler Intelligence Scale for Children (WISC). For this reason, diagnosis must differentiate between children who fail in school because of intellectual subnormality and those whose failure is caused by learning disabilities (Tyson 1970). Learning disabilities are mostly evident in reading and arithmetic, but they may also appear in the whole range of children's reactions to all kinds of situations that offer important experiences for learning (Tyson 1970).

The terminology in reference to children with learning disabilities is not standardized in Yugoslovia. The terms most used include *dyslexia, dysgraphia, difficulties in perception, difficulties in arithmetic, emotional disturbances,* and *behavioral disorders.* Also, medical experts differentiate the cerebral-palsy defects of a lesser degree and mark them with special terms as syndromes of various forms of cerebral damage, accenting visual, hearing, motor, and perceptual deficits. The etiological term *minimal cerebral dysfunction,* proposed by Bax and McKeith in 1963 (Hajnšek 1976) is coming more and more into use. The nonconformity in terminology results from the fact that some terms refer to various manifestations of behavior and some terms describe certain brain deficits (Sabol 1963).

By differential diagnosis and research into etiology, it has been found that not all children with learning disabilities have minimal cerebral dysfunction, but that the etiology of these disabilities is much broader and may be partially caused by socioeconomic variables. Consequently, our understanding of the term *learning disabilities* does not fully correspond either to the term *general learning disabilities,* which embraces mental retardation as well, or to the term *specific learning disabilities,* which is defined as "a disorder in one or more of the basic psychological processes involved in understanding or in using language" (Tarnopol and Tarnopol 1976). Our definition of learning disabilities is both more restrictive, since it excludes mental retardation and other serious handicaps, and more extensive, since it includes not only disabilities in connection with linguistic functions but also those that are related to a considerably wider phenomenology and etiology.

In Yugoslavia there are no reliable data regarding the proportion of children with learning disabilities. However, we know that this proportion is not negligible, based on the numerous tests carried out to establish the extent of some conditions which could have an etiological meaning in relation to learning disabilities.

The proportion of children with sight disorders in the school population in Croatia ranges from 9.93 to 24 percent, depending on chronological age and type of school. The proportion of children with abnormal but corrected vision increases with chronological age, while the proportion with abnormal uncorrected vision decreases (Zovko 1976).

The frequency of bodily deformities and bad posture among the schoolchildren in Serbia in the school year 1968-1969 amounted to 18.56 percent boys and 16.61 percent girls (Stefanović et al. 1972). Testing of the child population in Zagreb has shown that 4 to 5 percent of the children have had rheumatic fever and recovered. However, a weak residual heart murmur was found in only one-third of this group (Vukadinović et al. 1972). Anemia is also found relatively frequently among children of elementary-school age, ranging from 6.9 to 11 percent (Popović 1972; Donadini 1972).

At the Congress of Physicians of Croatia in 1974, data obtained on the basis of systematic examination of preschool children for a period of five years was presented. In some Zagreb districts, of 10,000 school children 4.7 percent were dyslalic, 1.2 percent were dysarthric, 5.6 percent had minimal cerebral dysfunction, 8.6 percent were neurotic, 0.8 percent were epileptic, and 2.6 percent were educationally neglected children (Vukadinović et al.

1975). We should approach these findings with some caution because of possibly differing data-gathering methods, investigators, locations, and so on.

These findings and others are relevant to the etiology of learning disabilities, although not all are necessarily connected with them, and they indirectly point to the magnitude of the problem.

> Experience shows that children with minor disorders are confronted in schoolwork and everyday life with difficulties that are larger than and unlike those that normal children meet. To this we must add the fact that they are treated somewhat differently from others by their schoolfellows, teachers and parents. In practice, this unusual treatment tends to create a different relationship towards them, which may act as a supplemental factor on the school achievements of these children and on their personal and social adaptation (Zovko 1976).

In 1973 Zovko studied a sample of 1,049 pupils attending the seventh and eighth grades of regular schools in Hercegovina to investigate some sociopsychoeducational implications of minor disorders in elementary-school pupils. In this sample it was found that 13.32 percent of the pupils had minor disorders of sight, speech, or body or a chronic disease. It was further found that those pupils with minor disorders of sight, speech, and body had greater difficulty in reading and writing than normal children; that all groups except the pupils with body disorders made poorer grades in school than normal children; and that all groups achieved poorer grades in conduct and participated less in broader school obligations and activities organized by the school than did normal children. According to their teachers, children with minor disorders are at a disadvantage under a methodical teaching approach compared with children without any disorder; and they are more often the subject of discussion as problem cases at teachers' meetings. Children with minor disorders say that they experience a less-positive relationship with and treatment from their parents, teachers, and other pupils. It was found that "minor disorders do not only result in functional disorders within the sphere of the disabled organs or abilities, but they also result in more extensive social-psychological and pedagogical consequences" and that "when comparing children with minor disorders with children without disorders, it has been found that children with impaired sight come closest to normal children, and that chronically diseased children come at the bottom of the list" (Zovko 1976).

This research leads to the following four conclusions relevant to learning disabilities:

1. Pupils with minor sight, speech, and body disorders have greater difficulty in reading and writing.

2. Chronically ill pupils and pupils with speech disorders achieve less in school, on the average, than pupils without disorders.
3. Chronically ill pupils and those with speech and body disorders participate less in broader school obligations and activities.
4. According to their teachers, pupils with minor disorders are taught under less-favorable conditions.

It is this last conclusion that should convince us that learning disabilities are mainly determined by the relationship between the pupil and the instructional program. The pupil possesses the inherent attributes of a pupil as well as the attributes of the social microenvironment in which he develops and lives, while the program includes both the educational content and certain patterns of behavior. If we accept the maxim that every child should be found a place in the educational continuum and that the allocation of the child in this continuum depends upon his abilities, needs, and interests, and if suitable and efficient educational methods and programs are provided, then the term *learning disabilities* loses both its absoluteness and its weight.

Dyslexia and Dysgraphia

Definition and Terminological Questions

Within the population of children with learning disabilities in Yugoslavia there is a special group in which the learning disabilities are confined predominantly or completely to failure in reading and writing. Various terms are used concerning this group of children: retardation in reading, shortcomings and difficulties in reading and writing, disorders in reading and writing, legasthenia, dyslexia, and dysgraphia. In Yugoslavia the terms *dyslexia* and *dysgraphia* are becoming more and more predominant.

Trenc (1973) proposed a series of definitions concerning dyslexic and dysgraphic children that supplement each other. We reproduce them here in condensed form:

1. Such children have difficulty in mastering reading and writing, although there are sufficient and suitable opportunities for learning these skills for most of the children of the same age and intelligence.

2. These children do not progress by the application of customary and otherwise suitable forms of instruction in reading and writing.

3. These children can have average or above-average intelligence, with the proviso that dyslexia, if we assume that it is caused by hereditary factors or by an impairment of the central nervous system, can also be manifested in persons whose intelligence is below the contemporary conception of accepted normalcy.

4. These children can show differences in success in school subjects, such as their accomplishment in their native language or mathematics. Failure in mathematics can also result when dyslexics are solving problems that call for written expression or reading comprehension.

5. To some extent, these children have accompanying or primary neurotic signs.

6. These children need help and should be identified as soon as possible; more suitable forms of reducing their difficulties must be found.

Theoretical Work

The problems of dyslexic and dysgraphic children in Yugoslavia have been relatively neglected for a number of years. Although some medical institutions have been concerned with serious cases of dyslexia and dysgraphia, and although there were also institutions engaged in research and practical work in the field of reading and writing disabilities, there were no extensive national programs for the early detection (even in preschool age), diagnosis, and treatment of dyslexic and dysgraphic children until recently. During the past ten years, the interest of experts dealing with this problem has increased, there has been an increase in research and published works, and the first textbooks for work with these children have been written.

At the Second Congress of Defectologists of Yugoslavia, held in 1965, only two papers dealt with dyslexia and dysgraphia. Blagojević (1966) pointed to the difference between primary and secondary dyslexia. In 1972 she introduced the concept of developmental dyslexia (Blagojević 1973). According to this classification, primary or specific dyslexia is congenital or hereditary and is connected with dysfunctions in the occipital lobe. Secondary dyslexia appears as a result of disorders in the visual, auditory, or motor spheres and disorders in spatial orientation, due to hypofunction of the dominant hemisphere, and is often connected with lateralization disorders. Developmental dyslexia, from the point of view of symptomatology, does not differ much from primary and secondary dyslexia, but its duration is temporary and it is connected with immaturity and beginning reading and writing. Therefore, the teaching methods, the emotional attitude of the child to learning in general and to reading in particular, the preliminary knowledge with which the child enters school, and the like, are important factors.

Reading and Writing Difficulties in School by Ribić and Matanović (1966) is used as a guide for teachers in the lower grades of elementary school. The book is divided into two parts. The first part deals with the maturation of the child, the physiological elements of reading and writing, and problems of dyslexia and dysgraphia in school. The second part tells of the experiences gained in working with dyslexic and dysgraphic children in Yugoslavia and the diagnosis of these difficulties. Data are given on the analysis of cases at the Advisory Institute for Children with Learning Disabilities at the school dispensary of the health center in one of the Zagreb districts. This part of the book also presents methods of work for correcting reading and writing disabilities. One of the main purposes of the book was to arouse interest in the problems of dyslexia and dysgraphia in elementary schools, and at the same time to help the teachers approach these problems.

Vladisavljević (1971) analyzed the errors that appeared in reading and writing and stated that she found a small number of cases with distinct dyslexia and dysgraphia and that these disorders accompanied cluttered and undeveloped speech. She assumed that dyslexia in connection with cluttering has its origin in the dysfunction of the speech mechanism and its coordination as shown in expression; however, dyslexia caused by disorderly articulation and undeveloped speech may be treated as a linguistic problem connected to the development of language. The problems of reading and writing disabilities were seen as problems of visual perception, auditory perception, spatial orientation, ability to analyze and synthesize the received and emitted signals during reading and writing, and their memorization and association. It became more and more clear that what we call dyslexia and dysgraphia represent a group of various disorders that, apart from leading to failure in reading and writing, need not have anything in common either in their origin or in their typology.

Practical Work

A symposium on dyslexia and dysgraphia was held in Zagreb in 1972, at which defectologists, speech therapists, pedagogues, psychologists, and physicians took part. The symposium had the purpose of bringing into focus the "existence of dyslexia, drawing attention to the existence of such disorders among children and even among adults, and stimulating work on diagnosis and systematic treatment of the disorders." The conference recommended early diagnosis and treatment (preferably at preschool age, the latest at school enrollment), which as a rule should be implemented in the regular schools. It was further recommended that educational programs to include dyslexia and dysgraphia be established at teachers' colleges and the departments of pedagogy, psychology, and medicine at the universities. Refresher courses for teachers of the lower grades should inform them of the main principles of treating dyslexia and dysgraphia.

In Yugoslavia there are a number of institutions that are concerned with theoretical and practical problems of dyslexia and dysgraphia within the framework of more extensive problems, usually auditory and speech disorders. In the Institute for Experimental Phonetics and Speech Pathology in Belgrade, the Department for Speech Pathology has been involved with dyslexia for years, either as a separate disorder or within the complex of a general speech-pathological clinical concept, on the level of detection, diagnosis, and correction (Blagojević 1973). In the Center for the Rehabilitation of Hearing and Speech (SUVAG) in Zagreb, speech-rehabilitation includes reading and writing disabilities. The Center for Hearing and Speech Rehabilitation in Ljubljana and the Center for the Correction of Hearing and Speech in Portorož are also concerned with dyslexia.

Epidemiological Research

There has been no systematic research aimed at determining the proportion of pupils with reading and writing defects. It has been said that the proportion of such pupils in Yugoslavia, considering the phonetic spelling, is probably smaller than in countries where etymological orthography is prevalent. However, two alphabets are taught in Yugoslav schools—the Latin and Cyrillic alphabets—which differ considerably and which can bring about difficulties, particularly because some Latin and Cyrillic letters are identical in writing but are different in pronunciation (*B* in Cyrillic reads like *V* in the Latin alphabet; similarly *H* and *N*). Therefore, it might not be expected that the percentage of children with reading and writing disabilities would be lower than in other countries, and some tests confirm this. A test of third-grade pupils showed that 12.7 percent of them had reading and writing disorders. In another school, it was found that, of 425 pupils from the second to fifth grades, 9.7 percent had difficulties with printed texts and writing (Rabić and Matanović 1966). Another test in Zagreb elementary schools found an identical percentage of pupils with specific dyslexia, 9.7 percent of 421 tested pupils (Plavec 1973). Another test of 578 pupils in an elementary school found 8.7 percent of the pupils with reading and writing disabilities (Vuletić 1973). In Varaždin, of 579 third-grade pupils, there were 16 percent with reading and writing disabilities and of 572 fourth-grade pupils there were 13 percent (Metz 1973). These data are similar to much that has been obtained in other countries, although useful comparisons are hardly possible when differences in definition, methods of diagnosing, and criteria are taken into account.

A series of tests were carried out on special populations and with diverse aims, of which we will mention only a few. Stančić tested the reading of cerebral-palsied children in both regular and special classes of an elementary school for such children in Zagreb using the One Minute Test of Reading Aloud, Form A (Furlan 1965). Several criteria of reading retardation were employed: the percentage of errors made, the reading speed, and a combination of both. On the basis of these criteria it was found that 68 percent of cerebral-palsied children with an IQ above 80 were retarded in reading, while all the mentally retarded children were also retarded in reading. It is necessary to stress that only children with more severe forms of cerebral palsy attend this school; less-affected cases attend regular schools (Stančić 1968).

The reading disabilities of children and adolescents with behavioral disorders were analyzed (Leljak 1973). It was found that, of 137 cases, all but 7 were of normal intelligence. Of these children and adolescents who were brought to the diagnostic departments of institutions for resocialization in Croatia, 40.6 percent read slowly, 22.5 percent made errors in reading, 12.1 percent swallowed sounds, 9.5 percent read too fast, and 2.2 percent swallowed words.

Diagnostic Procedure

Identification of potential dyslexics and dysgraphics should be carried out at preschool age. It is possible, on the basis of an anamnesis (examination of past history) and other current examinations, to identify children who mature slowly, have cerebral disorders or speech difficulties, are motorically inept, have perceptual difficulties, and so forth. Identification is possible during the systematic examinations of all children that take place before they begin school or during their last year in kindergarten. Although initial steps are being taken in Yugoslavia, this system of identification is limited because of the relatively small proportion of children who attend kindergarten. However, it is planned to include a greater number of children in preschool institutions in the near future, so that it will be possible to identify potential dyslexics and dysgraphics. Therefore, when these children enter school, the teachers will be prepared for children who need special help.

In an elementary school the first diagnosticians should be the teacher, the school pedagogue, the school psychologist, and the school physician. It is quite simple for the teacher, if he is informed about the problem, to detect the children who show disabilities in reading or writing. By introducing an educational-psychological service into our schools, particularly the larger ones, the diagnosis and treatment of such children may be carried out within the school.

At present the teachers draw the attention of the educational service to children with reading and writing difficulties in the second grade. However, they also draw attention in the first grade to extreme cases where there is no progress at all in reading and writing (Gašparović and Grdenić 1973). All pupils whose tests point to the possibility of dyslexia or dysgraphia are directed to a specialized diagnostic institution. When a final diagnosis is obtained from such an institution, the pedagogue or psychologist informs the teacher and parents of the results and proposes suitable treatment. Less-severe cases are given supplementary tutoring, with exercises in oral and written expression; more-severe cases are sent to institutions with corresponding specialists. It should be mentioned that such treatment is not organized in all schools, and in some schools there is no treatment at all.

To illustrate the approach toward diagnosis in a specialized institution we will give as an example the work in the Institute for Experimental Phonetics and Speech Pathology in Belgrade:

> In the Department for Speech Pathology we approach dyslexia as a multidimensional disturbance. . . . The etiology of dyslexia is elucidated by a neurologist, otolaryngologist, psychologist and speech therapist. The speech therapist determines the symptoms of dyslexia, by analyzing the types of errors of each case; he also gives directions for further examination. . . . If a substitution of voiced consonants for voiceless consonants appears as a typical error, or any other substitution in speech, it indicates the need for a stricter control of hearing and phonematic discrimination. If we establish as a typical error an inversion of direction up-down, right-left (d-p, d-b), metathesis (inversion of syllables in words), a general confusion in the direction of reading, or difficulties in following the sequence of letters—it is a sign that the defect perhaps lies in the sphere of visual perception, in a hypofunction of the dominant hemisphere, in poor spatial orientation, and so forth. The mechanical reading of texts, without sufficient comprehension, points to a need to examine the general state of intelligence, agnostic or aphasic defects. Finally, if letters and words are not perceived as symbols, further testing should be undertaken by an ophthalmologist and a neurologist. Experience with aphasics taught us that it is also necessary to check silent reading (Blagojević 1973).

In the Center for the Rehabilitation of Hearing and Speech (SUVAG) in Zagreb, the specialist diagnostic team consists of a speech therapist, a psychologist, an audiologist, a neurologist, and if necessary a psychiatrist and an ophthalmologist. There is a similar team of specialists in the other institutions in our country occupied with these problems.

With certain variations, the diagnostic procedures in specialized institutions and in schools for a developed pedagogic-psychological service include the following phases of work, all of which may not be necessary in any given child.

1. Anamnestic information is received by interviewing parents and teachers. It is desirable to obtain data on the somatic, motor, and psychic development of the child; on illnesses, traumas, interfamily relations, and the attitude of the parents toward the education and upbringing of their child; and on possible reading and writing disabilities of the parents or other

relations. The educator and teacher give information on the behavior of the child in his group, on school achievement, and on the attitude toward learning, particularly reading and writing.

2. The somatic status of the child, testing sight and hearing, a neuropsychiatric report, and an EEG may be required.

3. Testing is done on the condition of speech, articulation, phonemic discrimination, and so forth.

4. Testing of reading and writing includes speed and accuracy of reading, writing from dictation, and composition.

5. Testing is done on the cognitive functions of the development of perceptual abilities (eye-hand coordination, distinguishing image from background, perception of spatial position, and so on), visual memorizing, lateralization, and the like.

Different institutions and schools may not use identical measuring instruments or methods of diagnosis. This tends to result in lack of correspondence of criteria in testing and assessment. The differences in individual republics in Yugoslavia are significant. In Serbia the Institute for Experimental Phonetics and Speech Pathology began to standardize tests and methodology a few years ago in order to improve diagnostic work.

Therapeutic Approaches

Because scientific research and therapeutic practice in relation to reading and writing disabilities do not have a long tradition in Yugoslavia, it is understandable that there is no generally accepted pattern of therapy as yet. The analysis and presentation of therapeutic procedures is difficult because of differences in the terminology used by specialists in our country. Although some authors are of the opinion that in setting up a final diagnosis of dyslexia it is necessary to exclude neglect in upbringing, mental retardation, emotional disturbances, or any other somatic affliction (Krznarić 1973), others speak of an emotionally conditioned dyslexia, which is assumed in cases of a failure in therapy carried out according to some of the special methods of learning to read, and they suggest that psychotherapy should be applied (Beck-Dvoržak, 1973).

The therapy of reading and writing disorders is the concern of speech therapists, psychologists, teachers, and physicians. They supplement each other working as a team and, in some places, by overlapping functions. In some institutions the psychologist carries out the therapeutic treatments; in other institutions the speech therapist does this. We are of the opinion that in some mild cases the teacher can do much in extending aid to a dyslectic child, and, when necessary, he can perform this work with the assistance of a specialist (speech therapist, psychologist, and the like). In such cases priority is given to cooperation among the teacher, the parents, and every person treating the child.

It has recently been suggested that teachers should introduce individualized supplementary classwork of twenty to thirty minutes for such children. Furthermore, the teacher should give special treatment during regular classwork (individualize their approaches, giving less-difficult tasks, more-frequent commendations, and so forth), make regular reports regarding the progress of the child, and give the class group work in order to remove possible harmful attitudes toward a dyslexic pupil. In the course of treatment, the teacher should make use of various devices, such as pictures, drawings, illustrated spelling books, recorded tapes, and phonograph records with correct articulation. The teacher may use preliminary exercises with these children, such as orientation in space, recognizing individual letters with which they encounter difficulties, and copying words and sentences saturated with these letters (Blagojević 1973). The tasks that face the teacher reflect the growing demand that the therapy for reading and writing disorders should be implemented as much as possible in regular schools.

Serious and less-serious cases of dyslexia and dysgraphia, and even mild cases for which the teacher is not able to offer help, are treated in special institutions. Each therapeutic program is preceded by determining the intensity of the disorder and deciding on the etiology. Vladisavljević (1971) said that the way to correct these defects consists of strengthening and integrating all the mechanisms that participate in the functions of reading and writing, particularly those that in each case represent the major causes of the disorders. The speech therapist must distinguish between an unmastered reading technique and an actual disorder. The development of concentrated attention is the only common prerequisite for correcting these disorders. She recommends special procedures for children with disordered spatial orientation, for those with problems of articulation connected with difficulties in discriminating sounds, for children with sight-related problems, with undeveloped fine-motor coordination of the fist and fingers, and so on. When those factors that we assume to be the cause of the disorder are removed, it is necessary to apply further treatment, such as leading the child's hand in writing letters of large size, pronouncing the sounds at the beginning of writing, accustoming the child to connecting two time-distant sounds with the interval becoming gradually smaller, dictating to the child and pronouncing each letter while he is writing so that he will gradually learn how to spell the words, developing the child's self-control, teaching the child to visualize what he pronounces and what he writes, and teaching the child to remember a sequence.

In cases of personality problems, particularly emotional disturbances, which are either the cause or consequence of reading and writing disabilities, psychotherapy should be applied (Bojanin 1973). For children with reading and writing difficulties that are linked with minimal cerebral dysfunctions and a psychomotor disorder, medications serving as sedatives are applied (Plavec 1973).

Diagnosis

Reading and writing integrate complex functions because they are multisensory. They include many psycholinguistic abilities, such as visual and auditory perception, visual and auditory memory, psychomotor coordination, orientation in space, and gnostic abilities (speech-comprehension and expression). If one or more of these functions is deficient, disorders may appear in reading and writing. When treating dyslexia and dysgraphia, we have found in many of the diagnosed cases a syndrome that most frequently includes disorders of visual and auditory perception, disorders of psychomotor and sensory integration, and speech disorders. We have also found that the emotional problems of these children are for the most part a superstructure on the existing dysfunctions.

After a medical (audiological, neurological, ophthalmological) examination of children with reading and writing disorders, there is a detailed psychological and speech and language examination. The psychological tests examine the following:

1. Intellectual level.
2. Visual-motor perception.
3. Auditory perception.
4. Visual and auditory memory.
5. Lateralization.
6. Right-left orientation.
7. Reading and writing skills.

In examining the intellectual development of a child, we always use the Wechsler Intelligence Scale for Children (WISC), along with other intelligence tests, in order to obtain a comprehensive view of the development of both the nonverbal and the verbal mental abilities of the child. To investigate visual-motor perception, we use the Bender Visual Motor Gestalt Test and the Frostig Developmental Test of Visual Perception. To investigate the development of auditory perception, we use nonstandardized tests of our own construction wherein the child makes a phonemic analysis and phonemic synthesis of speech sounds in words. These tests consist of a list of words (twenty-three to twenty-five) arranged from simple one-syllable words to words of two, or more syllables, and from familiar words to less frequently used words. To investigate the development of visual memory, we use the Benton Visual Retention Test. We obtain information about auditory memory by analyzing the Digit Span subtest of the WISC.

To investigate lateralization, we use nonstandardized tests of our own construction. We examine the dominance of the hand and leg through dynamic coordination, in which voluntary control and imitation are excluded. Then we examine eye dominance (gazing through a kaleidoscope and a keyhole) and ear dominance (telephoning and listening to the ticking of a watch or clock). We investigate the child's perception of his body scheme, his right-left orientation, and his grasp of the orientation of objects in space. Tests are performed according to the Benton-Kemble standard tests.

Reading is tested by various methods and techniques, among which are the Furlan Test and Šali's Test. We primarily employ a nonstandardized test that applies to all grades from the second to the eighth. The pupil reads a story three times in succession. His reading is recorded on tape. Then the reading is analyzed to determine the number and nature of the errors as well as the duration of the first, second, and third readings.

Writing is tested based on the text that has been read. After the third reading, the child writes the story in his own words. We check the time spent, the number and kinds of errors, the quality of the composition, and the handwriting. Dictation is also used to test writing.

Logopedic testing defines the speech status of the child. From the psychological and logopedic examinations, a program of treatment is constructed of each child.

Our experience in dealing with cases of dyslexia and dysgraphia leads us to conclude that the problem is primarily on the level of hearing and speech, that is, poorly developed auditory perception, especially the processes of phonemic analysis and synthesis together with speech disorders, such as dyslalia, stuttering, and dysphasia. These children are often unable to analyze and synthesize auditorily, even with two-syllable words. For example, a child beyond the age of seven may analyze the word *skola* as *s-k-l-a* or *s-k-l-o-a,* or *dobar* as *t-o-p-a-r* or *d-b-a-r.* In the case of multisyllable words, it is sometimes impossible to recognize the structure of the analyzed word. For instance, the word *osposobljavanje* may become *o-s-p-o-t-n-j-t-o,* and so on. In the case of aural phonemic synthesis, they encounter similar difficulties. The child may identify *v-e-l-i-k* as *vike* or *vera.*

The processes of phonemic analysis and synthesis are fundamental and to some extent automatic, so that every successive linguistic integration that occurs on higher cortical levels (reading, writing, speech) is dependent on them. A deficiency in one area is likely to affect performance in another area. Therefore, it is not accidental that children with disorders in auditory perception also have disorders in reading and writing and in speech.

It has often been said, concerning English-speaking children, that the main problem of dyslexia and dysgraphia is on the visual level. However, the difficulties facing a child who is learning to read and write in Serbo-Croatian are different from those of a child learning to read and write in English. For example, in English, the sound /i/ can be written as *ee* (as in *see*), as *e* (as in *we*), as *ea* (as in *read*), and so on. In Serbo-Croatian, a language that is written as it is spoken, the sound /i/ is always written as *i*. Therefore, whereas in English it is necessary to have a visual picture of the word, in Serbo-Croatian it is necessary to have a clear auditory "picture" of the word and an ability to discriminate and analyze phonemes in correct sequence.

Guberina's Verbotonal Method (VTM) for the rehabilitation of speech disorders stimulates the development of auditory perception with the Suvag Lingua. This is an electronic device that consists of two series of octaval acoustic filters and several low and high permeable filters. In addition, the apparatus transmits unfiltered speech through the direct channel. The apparatus covers a sound frequency spectrum from 20 Hz (cycles per second) to 2,000 Hz and from 3,000 Hz to 20,000 Hz. It has a microphone and tape-recorder input, and earphones or a loudspeaker may be used at the output.

The incorrect auditory images of words are broken down and replaced by correct ones with the Suvag Lingua. This leads to better speech habits. These exercises help dyslexic and dysgraphic children because they accelerate the development of their auditory perception and speech expression.

Since multisensory integration is essential for the development of reading and writing skills, we stimulate not only the development of auditory-vocal abilities but the development of all relevant functions.

Since a dyslexic child is not capable of grasping the structure of a word as a whole, either aurally or visually, in the first phase of reading and writing, we help him to observe minor structures, that is, syllables of words. The therapist leads the child to aurally analyze the speech sounds in each syllable; then the child writes the syllables, reads the word containing these syllables, and covers the syllables with his hand and writes the whole word again from memory. By comparing the written word with the syllables, the child sees whether the word is correctly written or not. If the word is not written correctly, the child repeats the syllable analysis. The incorrectly written syllable or syllables are then circled for emphasis, and he again writes the whole word from memory. The whole procedure is repeated until the child succeeds in writing and reading the word correctly.

In figure 23-1, the left-hand column contains the syllables that the child wrote with the help of a therapist when he was analyzing words; the right-hand column contains the attempts of the child to reconstruct (write) the words from memory.

Thus, through a multisensory approach, the child masters the structure of each individual word. He analyzes and synthesizes the parts into a whole,

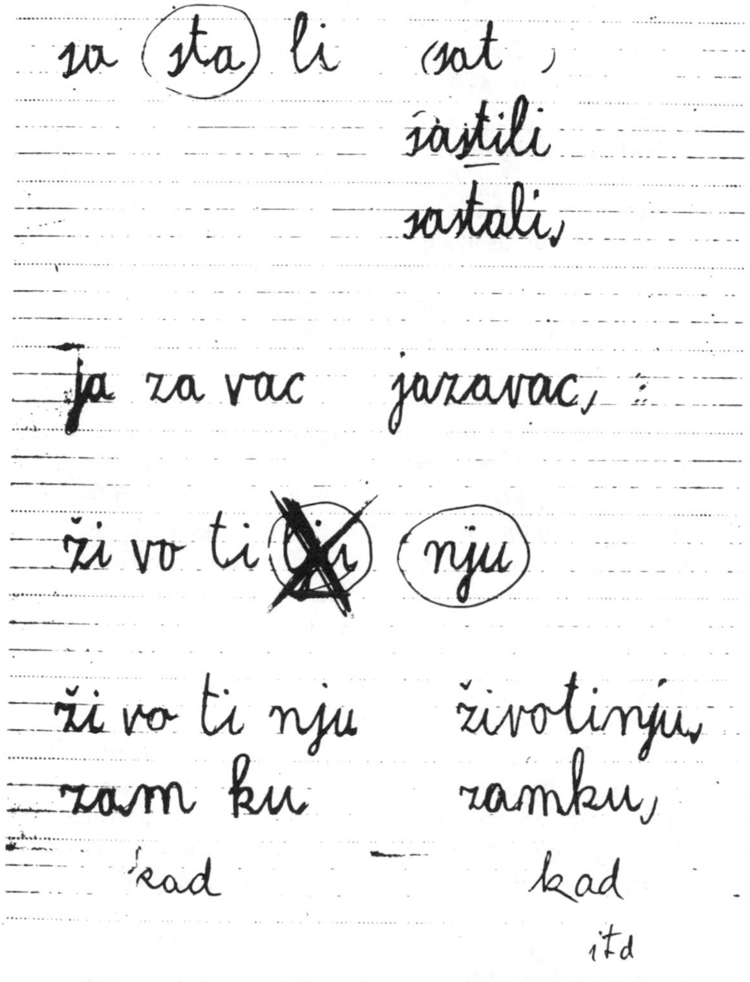

The left-hand column contains the syllables written by a child with the help of a therapist. The right-hand column has the same words written by the child from memory.

Figure 23-1. Illustration of the First Remedial Phase of Reading and Writing

both aurally and visually, then articulates the word clearly and memorizes the gestalt. In consequence, aural perception, visual-motor perception, speech and mnemonic functions, and auditory and visual memory are activated simultaneously. It is important to note that by this method the child gives up his habit of learning reading and writing by the method of trial and error (spelling and guessing), because he realizes the correlation between speaking, writing, and reading, which helps him to check his errors by himself. This clearly becomes an important incentive to building self-confidence in the child. He begins to experience achievement, and the emotional problems that arose as a result of his frustrations in school gradually disappear.

In many cases of stuttering and dyslexia, these exercises for reading and writing had a positive effect on the children's speech as well as on their self-confidence and socialization at school. We found that some children, in the course of treatment for dyslexia and dysgraphia, completely altered their personalities when they realized that they were solving this acute problem.

Naturally, our treatment follows basic pedagogical principles. We move on from elementary material to more complex, from subjects with which students are more familiar to those that are less familiar, and we take the children's interests into account. We begin the exercises with one-syllable words; then we move on to simple two-syllable words and gradually to multi-syllable words. Particular attention is paid to consonant-vowel groups (*ska, stra, pre, kle,* and so on), which the children have difficulty grasping. In the beginning we also make efforts to work on words taken from school texts with which the child is familiar but which present difficulties. The children show particular interest in the picture books of the "My First Book" series, which have been translated into Croatian, because they are richly illustrated, the text is interesting and instructive, and the large type facilitates learning. In normal speech the children use about 90 percent of the words in these booklets.

In the second phase of therapy, when the children are able to join syllables but are not yet sure in their reading, we instruct them when blending syllables to trace arches above the syllables with their fingers, because the motor activity helps them concentrate better. Later it is not necessary for them to trace the arches, but we tell them, "Take a good look at the first letter and the first syllable," to ensure a proper reading sequence from left to right. This imprint of the first syllable is necessary because most of the dyslexics have disorders of left-right orientation, have difficulties in grasping the sequence of words and syllables, skip lines, or fail to distinguish similar letters (*b, d; a, e; p, b, d*).

During the second phase of learning to write, the children write from simple dictations (enigmas, putting mixed words in proper order, and so on) and are instructed to write slowly. Thus they are given the chance to analyze the syllables by themselves and blend them into words. The inaccurately written words are corrected as we described in the first phase (see figure 23-2).

When the child has mastered the elementary technique of reading and writing, we start working on the development of the gnostic functions, that is, comprehensive reading, answering questions from texts that have been read, and finally writing free compositions. In this phase we urge faster reading and writing.

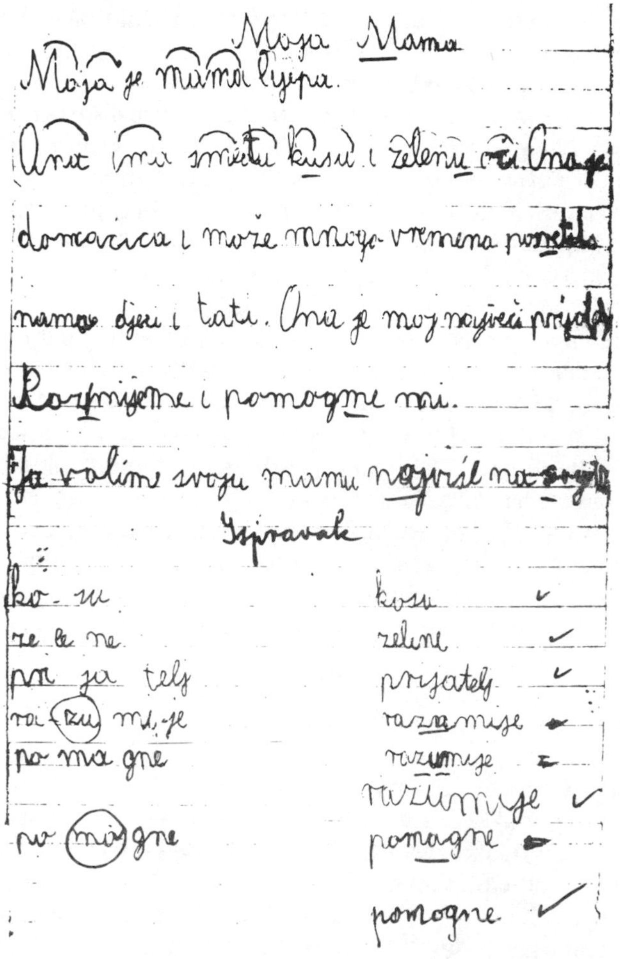

The child writes from dictation. The therapist marks the arches above the syllables to assist the child in reading them. As the child reads this material, he traces the arches with his finger.

Figure 23-2. Illustration of the Second Phase of Therapy

Case Study 1

H.S., a boy aged eight years, four months, was brought by his parents to the SUVAG Center when he was in the second grade. The parents sought the aid of specialists because of the child's failure in school and his disorders in behavior.

During the diagnostic process, it was established that the pupil was of high normal intelligence (WISC IQ 117). He was normally developed physically, and his speech was adequate. He was the child of educated parents who were divorced, and he lived with his mother. In school he had particular difficulties in language studies, which caused emotional suffering.

It was also established that the pupil had specific disorders (dyslexia and dysgraphia). These difficulties were manifested by poor analysis and synthesis, particularly in phonemic analysis and synthesis of polysyllabic words. He hadn't mastered left-right orientation. In comparison with pupils without similar difficulties, in reading a given text he took three times as long, and the ratio of errors in reading was sixteen to three, to the disadvantage of H.S. In writing, he made similar errors.

On the basis of this diagnosis, a program of individual exercises, with particular regard to remedying the emotional disturbance, was worked out for the pupil. This program was carried out at the center over a period of three months, with two hours of exercises each week. In composing and carrying out the program, a neuropsychiatrist, a psychologist, a speech therapist, a teacher, and the parents took part.

As a result of the implementation of this program, the pupil gained self-confidence and developed motivation for reading and writing, and now, in the third grade, he is advancing at a satisfactory pace, assisted and understood by the classmaster and the teachers.

Case Study 2

Pupil D.B., a boy aged ten years, six months, attends the fifth grade of elementary school. Because of his constant failure in school, his parents began to express doubts regarding the intellectual capacity of their child and brought him to the SUVAG Center.

During the first interview the boy showed insecurity, saying, "I can't do this," "I don't know this." On that occasion he displayed a certain fear of individual teachers and said, "When the teacher asks me, my hands begin to tremble and I don't know anything." A diagnosis of the case at the center showed a WISC IQ of 115. He had disorders in visual-motor perception and he needed considerable time to carry out an analysis and synthesis of information when reading and writing. No aberrations were found in other psycholinguistic abilities.

He read the text slowly and made a great many errors, particularly in compound words. In reading, he often used guesswork and did not rely on reading as an analytic-synthetic process. He was not able to comprehensively narrate the text that had been read, and when he did succeed, he did it confusedly. In writing, he made a large number of mistakes of the dysgraphic type.

According to his parents, expressive difficulties started in the fifth grade, when he passed from class teaching to subject instruction. In the lower grades his class teacher showed some understanding, and the pupil passed relatively successfully and was promoted to higher grades. In the fifth grade, however, instruction is given by different teachers for each subject, and there was no such understanding any more. The pupil encountered unsurmountable difficulties and began to earn negative marks, especially in the mother tongue, which brought about emotional pain. He became a problem and his case was discussed in the class and the teachers' councils. Perceiving that the boy gave good answers, the classmaster suggested an examination by psychiatrists at the SUVAG Center.

On the basis of a diagnosis, the center worked out a program of exercises, which are now in course, and in which relevant members of a team of specialists, parents, and classmaster cooperate. The first results are encouraging, because the pupil has abandoned guesswork as a reading method and it is to be expected that he will succeed in surmounting his difficulties and return to the grade and school that he attends.

Conclusion

In summary, Yugoslavian education has begun to incorporate programs for diagnostic and remedial efforts in learning disabilities of children of average or above-average intelligence. Diagnosis is multidisciplinary and is being offered at preschool levels. This is possible because a systematic examination of all children takes place before they begin kindergarten or during their kindergarten years. Remediation is individualized, multisensory, and based on positive reinforcement or frequent teacher commendation. There is a growing demand that the therapy for reading and writing disorders be implemented as much as possible in the regular schools to avoid the stigmatization that has occurred when special children are placed in separate schools.

References

References in Yugoslavian have not been listed here. For a complete list, write to the senior author.

Eisenberg, L. 1966. The epidemiology of reading retardation and program for preventive intervention. In J. Money (ed.), *The Disabled Reader.* Baltimore: Johns Hopkins University Press.

My First Book series. 1971. London: Macdonald.

Sabol, R. 1969. Remediation of Learning Difficulties. *Proceedings of the Eleventh World Congress of Rehabilitation International,* Dublin. pp. 289–292.

Tarnopol, L., and Tarnopol, M. (eds.). 1976. *Reading Disabilities: An International Perspective.* Baltimore: University Park Press.

Tyson, M. 1970. The design of remedial programs. In P. Mittler (ed.), *The Psychological Assessment of Mental and Physical Handicaps.* London: Methuen.

Index

List of Contributors

L. R. Aratangy, B.A., M.S., Professor of Psychobiology and Genetics, Pontifícia Universidade Católica de São Paulo, São Paulo, Brazil.

C. Bastos, B.A., Professor of Language Evaluation, Pontifícia Universidade Católica de São Paulo, São Paulo, Brazil.

Luis Bravo-Valdivieso, Ph.D., Professor of Special Education, Pontifícia Universidad Católica de Chile, Santiago, Chile.

George Fargo, Ph.D., Associate Director, Hawaii UAF Satellite Program, Honolulu, Hawaii.

Moisés Feldman, Ph.D. in medical science. Professor of Medicine and Psychology, Central University of Venezuela, Caracas, Venezuela.

Nusia Feldman, M.A., Assistant Professor of School Psychology, Central University of Venezuela; President, Venezuelan Association of School Psychologists, Caracas, Venezuela.

David A. Gauntlett, B.A., B.Sc., Research Psychologist, Open University, Milton Keynes, England.

M. Goulart, B.A. Psychologist, Group for Studies in Neuropsychology, São Paulo, Brazil.

Wei-fan Kuo, Ed.D., President, National Taiwan Normal University, Taipei, Taiwan, Republic of China.

Janice E. Laine, Ed.D., Superintendent, Diagnostic School for Neurologically Handicapped Children, Fresno, California.

Betti R. Lerner, B.S., Professor of Physiology, Pontifícia Universidade Católica de São Paulo, São Paulo, Brazil.

Leonard Levine, Ed.D., Director, Pupil Personnel Services, South San Francisco Unified School District, South San Francisco, California.

Eve Malmquist, Ph.D., Professor of Education, Linköping University, Linköping, Sweden.

Badrig Mélékian, M.D., Foundation de Recherche sur la Dyslexie, Paris.

David R. Mitchell, Ph.D., Senior Lecturer in Education, University of Waikato, Hamilton, New Zealand.

Rajalakshmi Muralidharan, Ph.D., Head, Child Study Unit, National Council of Educational Research and Training, New Delhi.

Yoshitatsu Nakano, Ed.D., Professor of Special Education, University of Hiroshima.

Thomas W. Nicholson, Ph.D., Senior Lecturer in Education, University of Waikato, Hamilton, New Zealand.

Margarita E. Nieto Herrera, Catedrática de la Escuela Normal de Especialización; Fundadora del Centro para Niños Disléxicos en México No. 1.

M. Paulino, B.A., Psychologist, Group for Studies in Neuropsychology, São Paulo, Brazil.

L. Rosenberg, B.A., Research Assistant, Educational Division, Fundação Carlos Chagas, São Paulo, Brazil.

Ruža Sabol, M.D., Dr. Sc., Professor, Institute of Defectology, University of Zagreb, Zagreb, Yugoslavia.

J.S. Schwartzman, M.D., Professor of Psychophysiology, Pontifícia Universidade Católica de São Paulo, São Paulo, Brazil.

Vladimir Stančić, Dr.Sc., Professor and Chief, Institute of Defectology, University of Zagreb, Zagreb, Yugoslavia.

Dartha F. Starr, Ph.D., Director, The Reading Center; Associate Professor, Department of Elementary and Early Childhood Education, Southern Illinois University at Edwardsville, Edwardsville, Illinois.

Fay H. Starr, Ph.D., Professor, Department of Psychology, Southern Illinois University, Edwardsville, Illinois.

Masaki Suzuki, M.D. (deceased), Department of Medicine, Tokyo University.

Lester Tarnopol, Sc.D., Consulting Psychologist and Engineer, San Mateo, California.

Muriel Tarnopol, M.A., Assistant Professor, Departments of Counseling and Special Education, San Francisco State University, San Francisco, California.

Bent Wenstrup, Principal, School for Deaf and Hearing Impaired Children, Aalborg, Denmark.

Barbara Zakrzewska, Ph.D., Polish Academy of Sciences, Center of Experimental and Clinical Medicine, Research Group of School Psychohygiene, Warsaw.

Gojke Zovko, Dr.Sc., Professor of Special Education, Institute of Defectology, University of Zagreb, Zagreb, Yugoslavia.

Nada Zovko, Psychologist, Center for Rehabilitation of Speech and Hearing, Zagreb, Yugoslavia.

About the Editors

Lester Tarnopol received the B.S. and M.S. in physics from the Massachusetts Institute of Technology in 1934 and 1935. He was research associate in geophysics at Harvard University in 1936-1937 and received the Sc.D. in metallurgy there in 1938 following which he was associate professor at the University of Kentucky. Subsequent teaching positions included professor of mathematics at Loyola University in Los Angeles, and lectureships at the University of Southern California. In 1949, he attended the National Training Laboratory in group dynamics at Bethel, Maine, and took courses in psychology at several universities while teaching at the City College of San Francisco in the departments of engineering, mathematics, and psychology. He also headed several federally funded research teams studying delinquency and learning disabilities, and was a visiting lecturer in education at the University of San Francisco and the College of Notre Dame. Since 1963 Dr. Tarnopol has lectured at many universities and international conferences on learning disabilities and has been president of the California Association for Neurologically Handicapped Children. He has published 70 journal articles and books in the fields of physics, engineering, industrial psychology, and learning disabilities. His other books on reading and learning difficulties include *Learning Disabilities: Introduction to Educational and Medical Management* (also in Spanish and Japanese); *Learning Disorders in Children: Diagnosis, Medication, Education* (also in Italian, Russian, Portuguese, and German); *Reading Disabilities: An International Perspective* (with Muriel Tarnopol); and *Brain Function and Reading Disabilities* (with Muriel Tarnopol).

Muriel Tarnopol has been a consultant in special education to public and private schools for fifteen years. Prior experience as a teacher at the kindergarten through secondary levels and as a specialist working with mentally retarded adolescents and inner-city delinquents was followed by a directorship in Inservice Projects for Classroom Teachers of Educationally Handicapped Minors, a federally funded Title VI Elementary and Secondary Education Act project. She has been employed as a curriculum consultant to firms specializing in the development of materials for teaching the reading and learning disabled. She has produced several television shows for California school districts, as well as audio-visual modules for teacher training.

She was a cofounder (with Lester Tarnopol) of the San Francisco Chapter of the California Association for Neurologically Handicapped Children (now CANHC-ACLD) and coeditor of a number of articles and books dealing with learning problems. She organized and directed four international symposia on learning disorders.

Professor Tarnopol is a member of the advisory boards to two private schools specializing in the education of the learning disabled and is serving as special-education commissioner for the California State Parent Teachers Association. Current activities include working in a number of organizations to improve curriculum and the quality of schools.

She has received the B.M. from the University of Miami and M.A. from San Francisco State University and has been a visiting lecturer in special education at California State University at Hayward, College of Notre Dame, and University of the Pacific. She is assistant professor in the Department of Counseling at San Francisco State University.